Caribbean
POLITICAL THOUGHT

D1567108

Caribbean
POLITICAL THOUGHT

The Colonial State to
Caribbean Internationalisms

Edited by
Aaron Kamugisha

IAN RANDLE PUBLISHERS
Kingston • Miami

First published in Jamaica, 2013 by
Ian Randle Publishers
11 Cunningham Avenue
Box 686
Kingston 6
www.ianrandlepublishers.com

Introduction and Editorial material
© 2013 Aaron Kamugisha

NATIONAL LIBRARY OF JAMAICA CATALOGUING-IN-PUBLICATION DATA

Caribbean political thought : the colonial state to Caribbean internationalisms
   / edited by Aaron Kamugisha

   p. ; cm.
ISBN 978-976-637-618-5 (pbk)

1   Political science – Caribbean Area   2. Internationalism
3. Post- colonialism – Caribbean Area   4. Decolonization
5. Anti-imperialistic movements
I. Kamugisha, Aaron

320   - dc 23

Cover Artwork: 'Negus' by Ras Akyem
Cover and book design by Ian Randle Publishers

Printed and bound in the United States of America

To the People of Haiti
Kenbe La

Table of Contents

The Colonial State

Anti-Colonial Thought

Caribbean Internationalisms

Afterword:

Acknowledgements

This collection would be impossible without the anti-colonial warriors, intellectuals, activists and scholars who have fought for Caribbean freedom over the last five centuries. They often paid for their courage and vision with their lives, and no words can express the debt that we owe to them. So first, to the ancestors.

The creative process of writing, compiling and editing is never a singular exercise, and I have incurred many debts. First, I would like to thank Paget Henry, with whom I had the first discussion about this work. Paget's immediate enthusiasm left me in no doubt that this collection would be timely and worthwhile, and his ready agreement to write two perceptive afterwords has enriched it in ways I could not have initially imagined. My colleague and co-editor in an allied project, *Caribbean Cultural Thought: From Plantation to Diaspora*, Yanique Hume, made many valuable suggestions, for which I am very thankful. I am also grateful to the wonderful scholars and friends who gave me perceptive critiques of early drafts of the table of contents, particularly Peter Hudson, Melanie Newton, Matthew Quest, Greg Thomas and Alissa Trotz. A superb artist, Ras Akyem, graciously allowed me to use the incredible image on the cover, for which I am very grateful.

The creation of this volume in Caribbean Political Thought would have been impossible without generous support from the Faculty of Social Sciences, the Principal's Office and the School for Graduate Study and Research at the University of the West Indies, Cave Hill Campus, and the University of the West Indies Office of Research. For these grants, I would like to especially thank Professor Sir Hilary Beckles, Dr Justin Robinson, and Professor Wayne Hunte. I would also like to extend my gratitude to the Dean of the Faculty of Humanities and Education, Professor Pedro Welch, for his enthusiastic support for this project from its inception. Thanks also to Bernadette Farquhar for her translation of Dantès Bellegarde, Jacques Roumain and Frantz Fanon's articles. To the many living scholars who kindly consented to have their work reproduced in these pages, thank you! Further afield, I would like to express my appreciation to Vanessa Spence, for proofreading the text, and Code Mantra, for rendering it ready for submission. Managing Director at Ian Randle Publishers, Christine Randle's immediate enthusiasm about the project, and dedication to producing work on Caribbean intellectuals, well seen in the *Caribbean Reasonings* series, has been a great inspiration. Thanks to the entire Ian Randle Publishers team, but especially Christine Randle, and Susan Callum for her professionalism and thoroughness in tracking down the rights and permissions for this volume.

Over the years, on my journeys through Barbados, Berkeley, Toronto and Chicago, I have benefitted from the wisdom of so many intellectuals, activists and friends that one scarcely knows how to list them all, or present a true acknowledgment of the value of their counsel. I'd like to thank my many friends at York University and University of Toronto in Toronto, in the Department of African American Studies of Northwestern University in Chicago, and at all the campuses of the University of the West Indies. Above all, though, thanks to two persons – Percy Hintzen and Patrick Taylor, for their inspiration and enrichment of my thinking for over a decade. To all my many wonderful friends throughout the world, thank you for the fun, laughter and solidarity you have given me, which makes life worth living.

My family is where my greatest debts lie. For a lifetime of caring work, and for instilling an appreciation of the wonder and excitement of seeking knowledge in the quest for the meaning of life, I wish to thank my sister, mother, aunt, and grandmother (now among the ancestors), respectively Kemi, Stephanie, Arlette and Dorin: my love always.

Publisher's Acknowledgements

The editor and publisher would like to thank the following for permission to reproduce the material in this volume:

The Haitian Constitution 1805:
From *Slave Revolution in the Caribbean 1789–1804: A Brief History with Documents*, by Laurent DuBois and John D. Garrigus. Copyright © 2006 by Bedford/St Martin's. Reprinted by permission of the publisher.

The Platt Amendment:
Treaty Between the United States and the Republic of Cuba Embodying the Provisions Defining Their Future Relations as Contained in the Act of Congress Approved March 2, 1901, signed 05/22/1903; General Records of the United States Government, 1778–2006, RG 11, National Archives.

Trevor Munroe:
Trevor Munroe, 'The Imperial Origins of the 1944 Constitution' from *The Politics of Constitutional Decolonization: Jamaica, 1944–62* (Mona, Jamaica: Sir Arthur Lewis Institute of Social and Economic Research, 1972). Reprinted by permission of the publisher.

Jean-Jacques Dessalines:
Jean-Jacques Dessalines, 'Liberty or Death, Proclamation' from *The Balance and Columbian Repository Vol. III* (Hudson, New York: Harry Croswell, 1804).

Political Program of the Independent Party of Color:
'Political Program of the Independent Party of Color' from *The Cuba Reader*, edited by Aviva Chomsky, Barry Carr and Pamela Maria Smorkaloff (Durham and London: Duke University Press).

Declaration of Rights of the Negro Peoples of the World:
'Declaration of the Rights of the Negro Peoples of the World' from *The Philosophy and Opinions of Marcus Garvey, or Africa for the Africans*, Vol. 1&2, edited by Amy Jacques Garvey (Massachusettes: Majority Press, 1986).

Dantès Bellegarde:
Dantès Bellegarde, 'The USA and Latin America at the Bar of the League of Nations' from *Revue de l'Amerique Latine* 20, no. 107 (November 1930)

Jacques Roumain:
Jacques Roumain, *Analyse Schématique 1932–1934* (S.I.: Editions Idées Nouvelles, Idées Prolétariennes, 1999).

Appeal to the United Nations Conference on International Organization on Behalf of the Caribbean Peoples:
Richard B. Moore, Caribbean Militant in Harlem 1920–1972, Joyce Moore Turner and W. Burghart Turner, Copyright © 1998, Joyce Moore Turner and W. Burghart Turner, Reprinted with permission of Indiana University Press.

Fidel Castro:
Fidel Castro, 'History Will Absolve Me' from *The Cuba Reader*, edited by Aviva Chomsky, Barry Carr and Pamela Maria Smorkaloff (Durham and London: Duke University Press, 2004).

Walter Rodney:
Walter Rodney, 'Black Power – Its Relevance in the West Indies' from *The Groundings with My Brothers* (London: Bogle-L'ouverture Publications, 1990).

Maurice Bishop:
Maurice Bishop, 'In Nobody's Backyard' from *In Nobody's Backyard: Maurice Bishop's Speeches, 1979–1983: A Memorial Volume*, edited by Chris Searle (London: Zed Books, 1984). Reprinted by permission of the publisher.

Sylvia Wynter:
Sylvia Wynter, 'New Seville and the Conversion Experience of Bartolomé de las Casas PT. I' *Jamaica Journal* 17, no. 2 (May 1984); and PT.II' from *Jamaica Journal* 17, no. 3 (August/October 1984). Reprinted by permission of the author.

Gordon Lewis:
Lewis, Gordon K. *Main Currents in Caribbean Thought: The Historical Evolution of Caribbean Society in its Ideological Aspects, 1492–1900*. pp. 94–109; 161–70. 1983 The Johns Hopkins University Press. Reprinted with permission of The Johns Hopkins University Press.

Anthony Bogues:
Black Heretics, Black Prophets: Radical Political Intellectuals by Anthony Bogues. Copyright 2003 by Taylor & Francis Books, Inc. Reproduced with permission of Taylor & Francis Books, Inc. via Copyright Clearance Center.

Hilary Beckles:
Hilary Beckles, 'Caribbean Anti-Slavery: the Self-Liberation Ethos of Enslaved Blacks' from *Journal of Caribbean History* vol. 22, nos. 1&2 (1988). Reprinted by permission of the author.

Bechu:
Bechu, 'Memorandum by Bechu to the West India Royal Commission, 1897' from *Bechu: 'bound coolie' Radical in British Guaina 1894–1901*, edited by Clem Seecharan (Kingston: UWI Press, 1999).

Roy Augier:

Roy Augier, 'Before and After 1865' from *Caribbean Freedom: Economy and Society from Emancipation to the Present*, edited by Hilary Beckles and Verene Shepherd (Ian Randle Publishers, 1993). Reprinted by permission of the author.

David Scott:

Scott, David; *Refashioning Futures*. © 1999 Princeton University Press, Reprinted by permission of Princeton University Press.

Anténor Firmin

Anténor Firmin, 'The Role of the Black Race in the History of Civilization' from *The Equality of the Human Races*, translated by Asselin Charles (Urbana and Chicago: University of Illinois Press, 2000).

José Martí:

'Our America,' from *José Martí: Selected Writings* by José Martí, introduction by Roberto Gonzalez Echevarria, edited by Esther Allen, translated by Esther Allen, copyright © 2002 by Esther Allen. Used by permission of Viking Penguin, a division of Penguin Group (USA) Inc.

J.J. Thomas:

J.J. Thomas, *Froudacity: West Indian Fables by James Anthony Froude* (London: New Beacon Books, 1969).

Hubert Harrison:

Hubert Harrison, *A Hubert Harrison Reader* © 2001 by Hubert Harrison. Reprinted by permission of Wesleyan University Press.

Marcus Garvey:

Marcus Garvey, 'Africa for the Africans' from *The Philosophy and Opinions of Marcus Garvey, or Africa for the Africans*, Vol. 1&2 (Massachusettes: Majority Press, 1986).

Rhoda Reddock:

Rhoda Reddock, 'Feminism, Nationalism and the Early Women's Movement in the English-Speaking Caribbean' from *Caribbean Women Writers: Essays from the First International Conference*, edited by Selwyn Cudjoe (Massachusetts: Calaloux Publications, 1990).

Pedro Albizu Campos:

Pedro Albizu Campos, 'Puerto Rican Nationalism' from *Boricuas: Influential Puerto Rican Writings – An Anthology* (New York: Ballantine, 1995).

George Padmore:

George Padmore, 'Fascism in the Colonies' from *Controversy* 2, 17 (February 1938).

Suzanne Césaire:

Negritude Women, edited by T. Denean Sharpely-Whiting, the University of Minnesota Press. Copyright © 2002 by the Regents of the University of Minnesota.

Aimé Césaire:
Discourse on Colonialism by Aimé Césaire. Copyright 2000 by Monthly Review Press. Reproduced with permission of Monthly Review Press via Copyright Clearance Center.

Claudia Jones:
Claudia Jones, 'American Imperialism and the British West Indies' from *Political Affairs* 37 (1958). Reprinted with permission of the publisher.

Cheddi Jagan:
Cheddi Jagan, 'Fascism or Freedom' from *The West on Trial: My Fight for Guyana's Freedom* (St John's: Hansib Caribbean, 1997). Reprinted with permission of Nadira Jagan-Brancier.

Lloyd Best:
Lloyd Best, 'Independent Thought and Caribbean Freedom' from *New world Quarterly* 3, no. 4 Cropover 1967. Reprinted with permission of Carmel, Kamla and Ayiti Best.

Frantz Fanon:
Frantz Fanon, 'The Pitfalls of National Consciousness' from *The Wretched of the Earth*, translated by Constance Farrington (London: Penguin Books).

C.L.R. James:
C.L.R. James, 'Dialectical Materialism and the Fate of Humanity' from *The C.L.R. James Reader* (Oxford, UK and Cambridge, Massachusettes: Blackwell, 1992). Reprinted by permission of Curtis Brown Group Ltd.

Ernesto Che Guevara:
Che Guevara, *Notes on Man and Socialism in Cuba* (New York: Merit Publishers, 1968).

George Padmore:
'Introduction' by Azinna Nwafor, copyright © 1971 by Doubleday, a division of Random House, Inc., from *Pan-Africanism or Communism* by George Padmore. Used by permission of Doubleday, a division of Random House, Inc. Any third party use of this material, outside of this publication, is prohibited. Interested parties must apply directly to Random House, Inc. for permission.

Claudia Jones:
Claudia Jones, 'An End to the Neglect of the Problems of Negro Women!' from *Political Affairs* (June 1949). Reprinted by permission of *Political Affairs*.

Lewis R. Gordon:
Lewis R. Gordon, 'Problematic People and Epistemic Decolonization: Towards the Postcolonial in Africana Political Thought' from *Postcolonial and Political Theory*, edited by Nalini Persram (Lexington Books, 2007). Reprinted by permission of Lexington Books.

Introduction: The Responsibility of Caribbean Intellectuals

> Each generation must, out of relative obscurity, discover its mission, fulfil it, or betray it.
>
> Frantz Fanon, *The Wretched of the Earth* (1961)[1]

> People of the West Indies, you do not know your own power. No one dares to tell you. You are a strange, a unique combination of the greatest driving force in the world today, the underdeveloped formerly colonial coloured peoples... Know that at this stage of world history and your own history there can never be any progress in the West Indies unless it begins with you and grows as you grow.
>
> C.L.R. James, *Party Politics in the West Indies* (1961)[2]

In 1961, a hemisphere apart, two Caribbean intellectuals made powerful statements about the historical conjuncture their communities inhabited, statements filled with a desperate urgency for the future of the anti-colonial revolution to which they had dedicated their lives. These were indeed heady times. A year previously, 17 African countries had gained their independence, while the Caribbean had been shaken by Cuba's revolution of 1959. Despite the collapse of the West Indian Federation, independence for the Anglophone Caribbean was on the horizon, with Jamaica and Trinidad and Tobago gaining theirs in 1962, followed by Guyana and Barbados in 1966 and associated state status for much of the rest of the Anglophone Caribbean in 1967. Yet simultaneously the tragedy of neo-colonialism was never far from the surface. The Republic of the Congo's first prime minister, Patrice Lumumba, had been deposed and murdered in a coup staged by Western imperialism, while the nature of the demise of the West Indian Federation, and the temper of its elites, left no reason to believe that the quality of the Anglophone Caribbean's independence would be much else but neo-colonial.

That C.L.R. James and Frantz Fanon are perhaps the exemplary political thinkers of the Caribbean's twentieth century is scarcely in doubt. Of their many fine contributions, I am drawn to the urgency of 1961, the year in which both men came to a reckoning with their vision of a post-colonial order – its promise and potential despite the spectre of a creeping failure. Frantz Fanon wrote *The Wretched of the Earth* between April and July 1961, an almost unbelievable pace fuelled by the need to complete it before leukemia ended his life – as indeed it did, two weeks after *The Wretched of the Earth*'s publication in Paris.[3] C.L.R. James's *Party Politics in the West Indies*, an account of his break with Eric Williams's People's National Movement in his native Trinidad and Tobago was largely written in 1961 but published with the defiant introduction, excerpted above, in 1962. Fanon would not live to see the culmination of the

Algerian revolution with which he had thrown his lot, dying mere months before Algerian independence. While in Trinidad and Tobago, James, who in three decades of writing and activism had done so much to usher in the Anglophone Caribbean's independence, would slip away from Trinidad and Tobago, a few days before its independence was celebrated.[4]

Both James and Fanon, in the epigraphs above, Fanon's famous, James's less well known, speak about nothing less than the responsibilities of the third world for itself and for humanity. Neither spoke to a third world intelligentsia that Fanon had dismissed in *The Wretched of the Earth* as 'spoilt children of yesterday's colonialism', a position that James would come to later at the 1969 Tricontinental Congress in Cuba at which he would declare the necessity for 'the abolition of the intellectuals as embodiment of culture.'[5] While Fanon's critique of the middle classes who 'discovers its historic mission: that of intermediary' between metropolitan power and the continued exploitation of the third world is more devastating than James's at this moment in their writings. It is in James's solitary critical engagement with Fanon that the weight of both men's perspective on the third world's colossal importance becomes clear.[6] In a January 1967 speech in Detroit, James would say the following of Fanon's *The Wretched of the Earth*:

> Fanon was swept away by a certain conception, the necessity to finish off what is bound to corrupt and pervert the development of a colonial population. And the value of the book is not only what it says to colonials. It is recognized more and more by Europeans that something of this spirit is needed to rid from Western Civilization the problems and burdens that are pressing down humanity as a whole!

> Now I think that this is the final stage which we have reached so far. I don't know where we will reach tomorrow...Fanon calls his book *Les Damnes de la Terre*; it is translated as "The Wretched of the Earth," but I prefer "The Condemned of the World." I want to end by saying this: the work done by Black Intellectuals, stimulated by the needs of the Black people, had better be understood by the condemned of the earth whether they're in Africa, the United States or Europe. Because if the condemned of the earth do not understand their pasts and known the responsibilities that lie upon them in the future, *all on the earth will be condemned*. That is the kind of world we live in.[7]

This knowledge that the fate of the modern world lies with those who have been condemned by it – people who as Sylvia Wynter once put it, have paid the 'most total psycho-existential price' for the contemporary Euro-American West's dominance – resonates as clearly today as it did half a century ago.[8] We live in a world in which the sovereignty of third world states is being constantly annulled by Western imperial aggression – from Iraq to Libya, and most profoundly, in Palestine. A world in which neoliberal globalization's attempt to reduce the globe to the logic of the market, or, as Pierre Bourdieu puts it, 'the utopia … of unlimited exploitation' has engineered one of the most spectacular economic collapses in a century, with no clear end in sight.[9] We inhabit a time in which it is impossible to walk without being haunted by the loss of 300,000 souls as a result of the January 2010 earthquake in Haiti, the greatest tragedy a Caribbean people have had to bear since slavery.

The demand for ideas, movement, and activism for alternative futures beyond our present at times seems overwhelmingly intense. This work, *Caribbean Political Thought: The Colonial*

State to Caribbean Internationalisms takes its inspiration from Walter Rodney's observation that 'the major and first responsibility of the intellectual is to struggle over ideas.'[10] It offers two centuries of political thought from a region whose people have been inseparable with the creation of the modern world for the last 500 years, the Caribbean. Its political purpose is to contribute to the critical elaboration of a Caribbean intellectual tradition that is increasingly the labour of many scholars, sustain and remind us of a radical tradition not past, and most fundamentally, to disenchant the condemnation of human beings – the culmination, result, and sign of the coloniality of power in the region.

The Caribbean Political Thought Collections

Caribbean Political Thought: The Colonial State to Caribbean Internationalisms is the first of two discrete, but linked collections. The second is titled *Caribbean Political Thought: Theories of the Post-Colonial State*. These collections uncover, collect and reflect on the wealth of political thought produced in the Caribbean region. They hope to fill a lacuna in the intellectual work of the region, which though rich in its presentation of ideas that we may consider fall to under the ambit of the political, has not been systematized and collected them for another generation of scholars, students and a larger Caribbean intelligentsia. This is attempted for the first time in these volumes, which spans the region, though with a focus on the Anglophone Caribbean. The ideas of revolutionaries and intellectuals are counterposed with manifestos, constitutional excerpts and speeches to give a view of the range of political options, questions, and choices that have faced the region's people over the last 500 years.

The choice of articles for the *Caribbean Political Thought* volumes has been burdened somewhat by the incredible range of sources that had to be considered, ranging from little known gems to classics in the Caribbean intellectual tradition. In making my selections, I have been anxious to show a fidelity to the territorial, linguistic and cultural complexity of the region, while constructing a narrative that illustrates my reading of the main trends of the political thought of the region, and acknowledges new directions perhaps not yet quite recognized as intrinsic to its traditions. Despite this interest, the collections focus on the Anglophone Caribbean due to incredible costs and problems associated with gaining access to, and principally, translating many of the remarkable political documents existing in the Caribbean, and this debt is felt most greatly in the offerings available from the Hispanophone part of the region.[11] The difficulties posed by questions of the correct balance between primary documents and secondary commentaries, easily available classics which demand inclusion and hard to find material which deserves a wider audience has been immense. I have sided with rare or out-of-print articles that are now quite difficult to access, and work that has been non-country specific, conceptual and daring in its scope and range as representative of the best work in Caribbean political thought.

Caribbean Political Thought: The Colonial State to Caribbean Internationalisms consists of five sections – constitutions, manifestos and speeches, the colonial state, anti-colonial thought and Caribbean internationalisms. It traces Caribbean political thought from its inception to the mid-twentieth century, when the conditions of possibility for the survival of formerly colonial states had changed in the aftermath of the Second World War. The brief opening section on constitutions comprises three documents all of which speak to the tremendously difficult conditions that Caribbean states have laboured under over the last 200 years. It commences with the Haitian Constitution of 1805, the first independent constitution in the Caribbean, followed by the Platt Amendment that curtailed Cuba's sovereignty a century later, and an insightful dissection of the process of constitution formation in the Anglophone Caribbean by Trevor Munroe.

'Manifestos and Speeches' incorporates famous addresses by Jean-Jacques Dessalines, Fidel Castro, Walter Rodney and Maurice Bishop. It also contains crucial manifestos by the Independent Party of Color in Cuba, the Garveyites' 'Declaration of Rights of the Negro Peoples of the World', an appeal to the United Nations' inaugural conference on behalf of Caribbean people, and English translations of Dantès Bellegarde's 1930 speech to the League of Nations, and Jacques Roumain's analysis of the Haitian Communist Party.

The third section, titled 'The Colonial State', presents work largely by contemporary critics who have sought to theorize the nature of the Caribbean colonial state. It opens with a dazzling retelling of the story of Bartolomé de las Casas and his debate at Valladolid in 1550 with Ginés de Sepúlveda by Sylvia Wynter, a debate which is absent from the canon of Western political thought, but is of overwhelming significance for tracing the invention of the category of man as a rational being and his stigmatized colonial others in the Western world. The question of the broad trends in pro-slavery from above and anti-slavery liberation thought from enslaved persons are discussed by Gordon Lewis and Hilary Beckles, while Anthony Bogues provides a reading of the political thought of Quobna Cugoano. Cugoano, a seminal figure of anti-slavery thought, belongs to a long tradition of Africana thinkers who in their anti-colonial dissent radicalized the political thought of their age beyond the complacent liberal gaze of Western political thought. A nineteenth century radical, Bechu, gives us a rare glimpse of the resistance to the colonial state by an indentured worker from India, in his memorandum to the 1897 West India Royal Commission. Roy Augier and David Scott give analyses which, respectively, describe the consolidation of colonial power a generation after slavery, and a re-reading of Thomas Holt's landmark text *The Problem of Freedom: Race, Labor and Politics in Jamaica and Britain, 1832–1938* through the lens of Michel Foucault's theory of governmentality – the latter raising larger questions about the writing of power, freedom and colonialism in Caribbean historiography and political thought.

Anti-colonial thought constitutes the largest section in this collection of essays. The range, power and scope of the work that could be included under the banner of Caribbean anti-colonial thought defies any simple summary, and more here than anywhere else this editor is acutely aware of the privilege and burden of choice in making these selections. The articles included here represent a range of thought that begins in the late nineteenth century and ends in the mid-twentieth century. They commence with the work of three late nineteenth century figures – Anténor Firmin (Haiti), José Martí (Cuba) and J.J. Thomas (Trinidad and Tobago). Their contributions in this volume were all written within a decade 1880–1891, from widely divergent locations – Firmin, a scholar and statesman in an independent Haiti, Martí, a martyr of the Cuban war of independence from Spain, Thomas, a schoolteacher and public intellectual in Trinidad and Tobago. Yet, they all in their denunciations of the late nineteenth century's overwhelming theories of race and empire, and in Martí's case, armed insurrection against the colonial state, articulated what would become a tradition of anti-colonial thought that, though constantly refashioned, would remain unbroken through the twentieth century.

The power of the colonial state and its laws against sedition, techniques of surveillance and claustrophobic levels of social control contributed to the production of much Caribbean anti-colonial thought in the first half of the twentieth century outside of the region. The metropolitan cities of New York, London and Paris, particularly provided places in which Caribbean dissidents could meet, exchange ideas, and practice radical activity outside the very restricted spaces of Caribbean territories. Pan-Africanism and négritude as political and cultural movements, and journals of the black world, most famously *Presénce Africaine*, provided solidarity and space for the production of ideas about politics, culture and a future beyond colonialism, and the Caribbean radicals Hubert Harrison, Marcus Garvey, George Padmore, Aimé and Suzanne Césaire and Claudia Jones were all part of this milieu. However, this is not to deny the reality of anti-colonial resistance in many forms in the colonies and on nations at the cusp of independence ranging from a developing national consciousness, the fight for emergent nations' freedom, and the quest for a distinctively Caribbean social and political thought. Frantz Fanon's 'The Pitfalls of National Consciousness' closes this section, as it remains unsurpassed as a warning against the euphoria nationalism promotes, which for Fanon must not ignore the neo-colonialism so sedulously facilitated by the post-colonial elites in the aftermath of constitutional decolonization.

'Caribbean Internationalisms' may well seem a misnomer, given the international dimension of Caribbean thought clearly seen in its anti-colonial thought, and throughout the body of scholarship produced by Caribbean intellectuals. Yet I conclude with this section, as inseparable and overlapping as it may be with others, to highlight the internationalist scope and vision of so many Caribbean political thinkers, whose work sustained a radical quest that sought to embrace all of humanity. The inspiration for this quest was frequently guided by an international socialism, seen here in the work of C.L.R. James and Ernesto Che Guevara. For George Padmore and Claudia Jones, it meant theorizing the autonomy and coherence of black struggle, beyond the limits of their original communist affiliations. In all these thinkers we see a radical cosmopolitanism, internationalist in its scope and vision, one of the gifts of Caribbean social and political thought to humanity. This section and volume closes with Lewis Gordon's contemporary essay on epistemic decolonization and Africana thought, a major essay with international dimensions by a contemporary Caribbean thinker, and one which guides us towards the companion collection to this work, *Caribbean Political Thought: Theories of the Post-Colonial State*.

****

Fanon and James's urgent epigraphs that began this collection yearn for Caribbean people to recognize the weight of their history and the gravity of their contemporary conjuncture. This collection responds to that call with a reminder of the power of the ideas created by

Caribbean people in their agonistic journeys through the last five centuries. It alone is never enough, but it is the hope that this knowledge of the past will *compel* more just Caribbean futures. I dedicate it to the people of Haiti, in recognition of their past sacrifice for a different world, and in memory of the souls who perished in the earthquake of January 2010 – the greatest disaster to afflict the Caribbean since slavery. *Kenbe La.*

Bathsheba, Barbados

October 2011

Notes

1. Frantz Fanon, *The Wretched of the Earth*, trans. Constance Farrington (London: Penguin Books, 1990).
2. C.L.R. James, *Party Politics in the West Indies* (San Juan: Vedic Enterprises, 1962), 4.
3. Alice Cherki, *Frantz Fanon: A Portrait*, trans. Nadia Benabid (Ithaca, NY: Cornell University Press, 2006), 160–61.
4. Kent Worcester, *C.L.R. James: A Political Biography* (Albany, NY: State University of New York Press, 1996), 148.
5. Frantz Fanon, *The Wretched of the Earth*, 122; C.L.R. James, 'The Responsibility of Intellectuals.' Paper delivered at the First Cultural Congress of Havana, 4–11 January 1969.
6. James also commented on Fanon's life as part of an international tribute to him, see C.L.R. James, 'Fanon and the Caribbean,' in *International Tribute to Frantz Fanon* (New York: United Nations Centre Against Apartheid, 1978), 43–46, and in his article 'Presence of Blacks in the Caribbean and its Impact on Culture,' in *At the Rendezvous of Victory* (London: Allison & Busby, 1984), 218–35.
7. C.L.R. James, 'C.L.R. James on the Origins,' *Radical America* II, no. 4 (July/August 1968): 20–29, my italics. This document is an excerpt from a speech given in Detroit in January 1967.
8. Sylvia Wynter, 'Unsettling the Coloniality of Being/Power/Truth/Freedom: Towards the Human, After Man, Its Overrepresentation – An Argument,' *The New Centennial Review* 3, no. 3 (2003): 306.
9. Pierre Bourdieu, 'The Essence of Neoliberalism,' *Le Monde Diplomatique*, December 1998. http://mondediplo.com/1998/12/08bourdieu.
10. Walter Rodney, *Walter Rodney Speaks: The Making of an African Intellectual* (Trenton, NJ: Africa World Press, 1990), 113.
11. I wished to include an excerpt from Oliver Cox's book *Capitalism and Slavery*, but the fee to reproduce a chapter was well beyond the budget of the collection.

CONSTITUTIONS AND LAWS

The Haitian Constitution 1805

We, Henri Christophe, Clervaux, Vernet, Gabart, Pétion, Capoix, Magny, Cangé, Daut, Magloire Ambroise, Yayou, Jean-Louis François, Gérin, Moreau, Férou, Bazelais, Martial Besse;

As individuals and in the name of the Haitian people who have legally constituted us the faithful voices and interpreters of their will;

In the presence of the Supreme Being before whom all mortals are equal, and who has spread so many different creatures over the surface of the globe only in order to demonstrate his glory and power by the diversity of his works;

Before all of nature, we who have been for so long and so unfairly considered to be its unworthy children, declare that the terms of this constitution are the free, voluntary, and unchanging expression of our hearts and of our constituents' general will;

We submit it to the approval of his Majesty the Emperor Jacques Dessalines, our liberator, for prompt and complete execution.

Preliminary Declaration

Article 1. By this document the people living on the island formerly called Saint-Domingue agree to form a free and sovereign state, independent of all the other powers of the universe, under the name of the Haitian Empire.

Article 2. Slavery is abolished forever.

Article 3. Brotherhood unites Haiti's citizens; equality before the law is irrefutably established; and no other titles, advantages, or privileges can exist, other than those which necessarily result from respect and compensation for services rendered to liberty and independence.

Article 4. There is one law for everyone, whether it punishes or protects.

Article 5. The law cannot be retroactive.

Article 6. Property rights are sacred; violations will be vigorously pursued.

Article 7. Persons who emigrate and become citizens in a foreign country forfeit their Haitian citizenship, as do those convicted of corporal or disgraceful crimes. The former instance is punishable by death and confiscation of property.

Article 8. In cases of bankruptcy or business failure, Haitian citizenship is suspended.

Article 9. No one is worthy of being a Haitian if he is not a good father, a good husband, and, above all, a good soldier.

Article 10. Fathers and mothers may not disinherit their children.

Article 11. Every citizen must know a mechanical trade.

Article 12.   No white man, regardless of his nationality, may set foot in this territory as a master or landowner, nor will he ever be able to acquire any property.

Article 13.   The preceding article does not apply to white women who the government has naturalized as Haitian citizens or to their children, existing or future. Also included in this are the Germans and Poles naturalized by the government.

Article 14.   Because all distinctions of color among children of the same family must necessarily stop, Haitians will henceforth only be known generically as Blacks.

About the Empire

Article 15.   The Haitian Empire is one and indivisible; its territory is divided into six military districts.

Article 16.   A major general will command each military district.

Article 17.   Each of these major generals will be independent of the others and will report directly to the emperor or the general-in-chief named by His Majesty.

Article 18.   The following islands are an integral part of the empire: Samana, Tortuga, Gonaïves, Cayemittes, Île à Vache, la Saône, and other neighboring islands.

Article 19.   Haiti is governed by a first magistrate who will take the title of Emperor and Supreme Chief of the Army.

Article 20.   The people recognize Jacques Dessalines, the avenger and liberator of his fellow citizens, as the Emperor and Supreme Chief of the Army. He is addressed as Majesty, as is his distinguished spouse, the Empress.

Article 21.   The persons of Their Majesties are sacred and inviolable.

Article 22.   The state will pay a fixed stipend to Her Majesty the Empress as dowager princess.

Article 23.   The crown is elective and nonhereditary.

Article 24.   The state will allocate an annual stipend to the recognized children of His Majesty the Emperor.

Article 25.   Like other citizens, the emperor's recognized male children will be required to work their way up from rank to rank, successively, with the single difference that their military service in the fourth demi-brigade will be counted from the day of their birth.

Article 26.   The emperor will designate his successor in the manner he judges most appropriate, either before or after his death.

Article 27.   The state will set an appropriate pension for this successor at the moment he comes to the throne.

Article 28.   Neither the emperor nor any of his successors will have the right in any situation or for any reason to surround himself with a privileged group under the name of honor guard or any other title.

Article 29.   Any successor who strays from either the provisions of the preceding article, or from the course laid out for him by the reigning emperor, will be considered a threat to society and declared as such. In this event, the counselors of state will meet to proclaim his removal and choose their worthiest member to replace him; and if it happens that the said successor tries to oppose this legally authorized measure, the council of state, comprised of the generals, will appeal to the people and the army, which will lend a hand and assist in maintaining liberty.

Article 30. The emperor makes, seals, and promulgates the laws; as he sees fit, he names and dismisses the ministers, the army's general-in-chief, the counselors of state, the generals and other officers of the empire, the officers of the army and navy, the members of local government administrations, the government commissioners in the courts, the judges, and other public functionaries.

Article 31. The emperor directs the collection of state funds and their expenditure and oversees the manufacture of currency. He alone orders coins to be put into circulation and sets their weight and kind.

Article 32. He alone has the power to make peace or war, to maintain political relations and establish contracts with foreign powers.

Article 33. He provides for the state's internal security and defense, and decides on the territorial distribution of the army and navy.

Article 34. In the event of some conspiracy against public security, the constitution, or his person, the emperor will immediately arrest its leaders or accomplices, who will be judged by a special council.

Article 35. Only His Majesty will have the right to pardon a guilty person or to commute his sentence.

Article 36. The emperor will never undertake any project with the idea of conquest or to disturb the peace and the internal regime of foreign colonies.

Article 37. All public deeds will be made in these terms: *The First Emperor of Haiti and the Supreme Chief of the Army by the grace of God and the constitutional law of the state....*

On Religion

Article 50. The law does not recognize any dominant religion.

Article 51. Freedom of worship is allowed.

Article 52. The state does not provide for the expenses of any form of religion or ministry.

General Measures

Article 1. The emperor and the empress will choose the persons who make up the court and set their stipend and support.

Article 2. After the death of the reigning emperor, when it is decided that the constitution needs to be revised, the council of state will meet for this purpose under the leadership of the member with the greatest seniority.

Article 3. Crimes of high treason and the crimes committed by the ministers and the generals will be judged by a special council named and led by the emperor.

Article 4. The army's fundamental duty being to obey, no armed body can make political decisions.

Article 5. No one can be judged without having been heard by legal authorities.

Article 6. Every citizen's house is inviolable.

Article 7. One may enter in case of fire, flood, or a legal complaint from the ministry of the interior or by virtue of an order from the emperor or any other legal authority.

Article 8.   He who kills his fellow man deserves to die

Article 9.   No capital punishment or death penalty can be legally carried out unless it has been confirmed by the emperor.

Article 10.   Theft will be punished according to the situation preceding and accompanying the crime.

Article 11.   All foreigners residing in Haitian territory, as well as all Haitians, are subject to the criminal laws and penalties of the country.

Article 12.   All property formerly belonging to a white Frenchman is confiscated for the profit of the state, without appeal.

Article 13.   All Haitians who acquired the property of a white Frenchman, but who paid only part of the price specified in the deed of sale, must pay the remaining sum to the state.

Article 14.   Marriage is a purely civil deed that is authorized by the government.

Article 15.   The law authorizes divorce in certain specific cases.

Article 16.   A special law will be passed regarding children born outside of marriage.

Article 17.   Respect for leaders, subordination, and discipline are absolutely necessary.

Article 18.   A penal code will be published and strictly enforced.

Article 19.   In each military district, a public school will be established to educate the youth.

Article 20.   The national colors will be black and red.

Article 21.   Agriculture, the first, most noble, and most useful of the arts, will be honored and protected.

Article 22.   Trade, the second source of a state's wealth, seeks to be free of obstacles. It must be favored and specially protected.

Article 23.   In each military district, the emperor will name the members of a commercial court, chosen from the merchant class.

Article 24.   Honesty and fairness in commerce will be religiously observed.

Article 25.   The government guarantees safety and protection to neutral and friendly nations that establish commercial relations with this island, on the condition that they obey the regulations, laws, and customs of this country.

Article 26.   Foreign trading posts and merchandise will be under the protection and guarantee of the state.

Article 27.   There will be national holidays to celebrate independence, the birthday of the emperor and of his august wife, as well as agriculture and the constitution.

Article 28.   At the first sound of the alarm cannon, the towns will disappear and the nation will rise to its feet.

We, the undersigned representatives, place this explicit and solemn pact of the sacred rights of man and the duties of the citizen under the protection of the officials, of the fathers and mothers of families, of the citizens and the army.

We recommend it to our descendants and recommend it to the friends of liberty, to those who love mankind in every country as remarkable proof of divine goodness, whose immortal decrees have given us the opportunity to break our chains and form a free people, civilized and independent.

The Platt Amendment

Treaty between the United States and Cuba Embodying the Provisions Defining the Future Relations of the United States with Cuba Contained in the Act of Congress

56th Congress, Session II, Ch. 803

Signed at Habana, May 22, 1903
Ratification advised by the Senate, March 22, 1904
Ratified by the President, June 25, 1904
Ratified by Cuba, June 20, 1904
Ratifications exchanged at Washington, July 1, 1904
Proclaimed, July 2, 1904

I.   Treaties with foreign powers.
II.   Public depts.
III.   Intervention to maintain independence.
IV.   Acts during military occupation.
V.   Sanitation of cities.
VI.   Island of Pines.
VII.   Coaling stations.
VIII. Ratification.

BY THE PRESIDENT OF THE UNITED STATES OF AMERICA, A PROCLAMATION

Whereas a Treaty between the United States of America and the Republic of Cuba embodying the provisions defining the future relations of United States with Cuba contained in the act of Congress approved March 2, 1901, was concluded and signed by their respective Plenipotentiaries at Habana on the twenty-second day of May, one thousand nine hundred and three, the original of which Treaty, being in the English and Spanish languages is word for word as follows:

Whereas the Congress of the United States of America, by an Act approved March 2, 1901, provided as follows:

Provided further, That in fulfillment of the declaration contained in the joint resolution approved April twentieth, eighteen hundred and ninety-eight, entitled, "For the recognition of the independence of the people of Cuba, demanding that the Government of Spain relinquish its authority and government in the island of Cuba, and to withdraw its land and naval forces from Cuba and Cuban waters, and directing the President of the United States to use the land and naval forces of the United States to carry these resolutions into effect," the President is hereby authorized to "leave the government and control the island of Cuba to its people" so soon as a government shall have been established in said island under a constitution which, either as a part thereof or in an ordinance appended thereto, shall define the future relations of the United States with Cuba, substantially as follows:

"I.   That the government of Cuba Shall never enter into any treaty or other compact with any foreign power or powers which will impair or tend to impair the independence of Cuba, nor in any manner authorize or permit any foreign power or powers to obtain by colonization or for military or naval purposes or otherwise, lodgement in or control over any portion of said island."

"II.   That said government shall not assume or contract any public debt, to pay the interest upon which, and to make reasonable sinking fund provision for the ultimate discharge of which, the ordinary revenues of the island, after defraying the current expenses of government shall be inadequate."

"III.   That the government of Cuba consents that the United States may exercise the right to intervene for the preservation of Cuban independence, the maintenance of a government adequate for the protection of life, property, and individual liberty, and for discharging the obligations with respect to Cuba imposed by the treaty of Paris on the United States, now to be assumed and undertaken by the government of Cuba."

"IV.   That all Acts of the United States in Cuba during its military occupancy thereof are ratified and validated, and all lawful rights acquired thereunder shall be maintained and protected."

"V.   That the government of Cuba will execute, and as far as necessary extend, the plans already devised or other plans to be mutually agreed upon, for the sanitation of the cities of the island, to the end that a recurrence of epidemic and infectious diseases may be prevented thereby assuring protection to the people and commerce of Cuba, as well as to the commerce of the southern ports of the United States and the people residing therein."

"VI.   That the Isle of Pies shall be omitted from the proposed constitutional boundaries of Cuba, the title thereto being left to future adjustment by treaty."

"VII.   That to enable the United States to maintain the independence of Cuba, and to protect the people thereof, as well as for its own defense, the government of Cuba will sell of lease to the United States lands necessary for coaling or naval stations at certain specified points to be agreed upon with the President of the United States."

"VIII. That by way of further assurance the government of Cuba will embody the foregoing provisions in a permanent treaty with the United States."

Whereas the Constitutional Convention of Cuba, on June twelfth, 1901, adopted a Resolution adding to the Constitution of the Republic of Cuba which was adopted on the twenty-first of February 1901, an appendix in the words and letters of the eighth enumerated articles of the above cited act of the Congress of the United States;

And whereas, by the establishment of the independent and sovereign government of the Republic of Cuba, under the constitution promulgated on the 20th of May, 1902, which embraced the foregoing condition, and by the withdrawal of the Government of the United States as an intervening power, on the same date, it become necessary to embody the above cited provisions in a permanent treaty between the United States of America and the Republic of Cuba;

The United States of America and the Republic of Cuba, being desirous to carry out the foregoing conditions, have for that purpose appointed as their plenipotentiaries to conclude a treaty to that end,

The President of the United States of America, Herbert G. Squires, Envoy Extraordinary and Minister Plenipotentiary at Havana,

And the President of the Republic of Cuba, Carlos de Zaldo y Beurmann, Secretary of State and Justice, - who after communicating to each other their full powers found in good and due form, have agreed upon the following articles:

ARTICLE I.

The Government of Cuba shall never enter into any treaty or other compact with any foreign power or powers which will impair or tend to impair the independence of Cuba, nor in any manner authorize or permit any foreign power of powers to obtain by colonization or for military or naval purposes, or otherwise, lodgment in or control over any portion of said island.

ARTICLE II.

The Government of Cuba shall not assume or contract any public debt to pay the interest upon which, and to make reasonable sinking-fund provision for the ultimate discharge of which, the ordinary revenues of the Island of Cuba, after defraying the current expenses of the Government, shall be inadequate.

ARTICLE III.

The Government of Cuba consents that the United States may exercise the right to intervene for the preservation of Cuban independence, the maintenance of a government adequate for the protection of life, property, and individual liberty, and for discharging the obligations with respect to Cuba imposed by the Treaty of Paris on the United States, now to be assumed and undertaken by the Government of Cuba.

ARTICLE IV.

All acts of the United States in Cuba during its military occupancy thereof are ratified and validated, and all lawful rights acquired thereunder shall be maintained and protected.

ARTICLE V.

The Government of Cuba will execute, and as far as necessary, extend the plans already devised, or other plans to be mutually agreed upon, for the sanitation of the cities the island, to the end that a recurrence of epidemic and infectious diseases may be prevented, thereby assuring protection to the people and commerce of Cuba, as well as to the commerce of the Southern ports of the United States and the people residing therein.

ARTICLE VI.

The Island of Pines shall be omitted from the boundaries of Cuba specified in the Constitution, the title thereto being left to future adjustment by treaty.

ARTICLE VII.

To enable the United States to maintain the independence of Cuba, and to protect the people thereof, as well as for its own defense, the Government of Cuba will sell or lease to the United States lands necessary for coaling or naval stations, at certain specified points, to be agreed upon with the President of the United States.

ARTICLE VIII.

The present Convention shall be ratified by each party in conformity with the respective Constitutions of the two countries, and the ratifications shall be exchanged in the City of Washington within eight months from this date.

In witness whereof, we the respective Plenipotentiaries, have signed the same in duplicate, in English and Spanish, and have affixed our respective seals at Havana, Cuba, this twenty-second day of May, in the year nineteen hundred and three.

H.G. SQUIERS [SEAL.]
CARLOS DE ZALDO [SEAL.]

BY THE PRESIDENT OF THE UNITED STATES OF AMERICA, A PROCLAMATION

Whereas, it is provided by section 13 of the act of Congress of March 3, 1891, entitled "An act to amend title sixty, chapter three of the Revised Statues of the United States, relating to copyrights", that said act "shall only apply to a citizen or subject of a foreign state or nation when such foreign state or nation permits to citizens of the United States of America the benefit of copyright on substantially the same basis as its own citizens; or when such foreign state or nation is party to an international agreement which provides for reciprocity in the granting of copyright, by the terms of which agreement the United States of America may, at its pleasure, become a party to such agreement";

And Whereas it is also provided by said section that "the existence of either of the conditions aforesaid shall be determined by the President of the United States by proclamation made from time to time as the purposes of this act may require";

And Whereas satisfactory official assurance have been given that in Cuba the law permits to citizens of the United States the benefit of copyright on substantially the same basis as to the citizens of Cuba:

And Whereas the said Treaty has been duly ratified on both parts, and the ratifications of the two governments were exchanged in the City of Washington, on the first day of July, one thousand nine hundred and four:

Now, therefore, be it known that I, Theodore Roosevelt, President of the United States of America, have caused the said Treaty to be made public, to the end that the same and every article and clause thereof may be observed and fulfilled with good faith by the United States and the citizens thereof.

In testimony whereof, I have hereunto set my hand and caused the seal of the United States of America to be affixed.

Done at the City of Washington, this second day of July, in the year of our Lord one thousand nine hundred and four, and of the Independence of the United States of America the one hundred and twenty-eighth.

THEODORE ROOSEVELT

By the President:

ALVEY A. ADEE

Acting Secretary of State.

SUPPLEMENTARY CONVENTION BETWEEN THE UNITED STATES AND CUBA EXTENDING THE PERIOD WITHIN WHICH MAY BE EXCHANGED THE RATIFICATIONS OF THE TREATY OF MAY 22, 1903, BETWEEN THE UNITED STATES AND CUBA, EMBODYING THE PROVISIONS DEFINING THEIR FUTURE RELATIONS.

Signed at Washington, January 29, 1904.
Ratification advised by the Senate, January 27, 1904.
Ratified by the President, June 25, 1904
Ratified by Cuba, June 20, 1904
Ratifications exchanged at Washington, July 1, 1904
Proclaimed, July 2, 1904.

BY THE PRESIDENT OF THE UNITED STATES OF AMERICA, A PROCLAMATION

Whereas a Supplementary Convention between the United States of America and the Republic of Cuba, extending the time within which may be exchanged the ratifications of the treaty signed May 22, 1903, embodying the provisions defining the future relations of the United States with Cuba, contained in the Act of Congress of the United States approved

March 2, 1901, was concluded and signed by their respective Plenipotentiaries at Washington, on the twentieth day of January one thousand nine hundred and four, the original of which Supplementary Conventions, being in the English and Spanish languages, is word for word as follows:

The United States of America and the Republic of Cuba, considering it expedient to prolong the period in which, by Article VIII of the treaty signed by their respective plenipotentiaries on May 22, 1903, embodying the provisions defining the future relations of the United States with Cuba, contained in the act of Congress of the United States approved March 2, 1901, the exchange of ratifications of the said treaty shall take place, have for that purpose appointed their respective Plenipotentiaries, namely:

The President of the United States of America, John Hay, Secretary of State of the United States; and

The President of Cuba, Gonzalo de Quesada, Envoy Extraordinary and Minister Plenipotentiary of Cuba at Washington;

who, after having communicated to each other their respective full powers, found in good and due form, have agreed upon the following additional article to be taken as part of the said treaty.

The respective ratifications of the said treaty shall be exchanged as soon as possible, and within six months from January 21, 1904.

Done in duplicate at Washington, in the English and Spanish languages, this 20th day of January A.D. 1904.

JOHN HAY [SEAL.]

GONZALO DE QUESADA [SEAL.]

And whereas the said Supplementary Convention has been duly ratified on both parts, and the ratifications of the two governments were exchanged in the City of Washington, on the first day of July, one thousand nine hundred and four;

Now, therefore, be it known that I, Theodore Roosevelt, President of the United States of America, have caused the said Supplementary Convention to be made public to the end that the same may be observed and fulfilled with good faith by the United States and the citizens thereof.

In testimony whereof I have hereunto set my hand and caused the seal of the United States of America to be affixed.

Done at the City of Washington, this second day of July, in the year of our Lord one thousand nine hundred and four, and one thousand nine hundred and four, and of the Independence of the United States of America the one hundred and twenty eighth.

THEODORE ROOSEVELT

By the President:

ALVEY A. ADEE

Acting Secretary of State.

The Imperial Origins of the 1944 Constitution

Trevor Munroe

The new Constitution was the result not only of specific Jamaican agitation but also of general change in colonial policy. Before about 1940 "trusteeship" sought to end the abuses of colonialism; after the war "partnership" contemplated termination of colonialism itself. In economic terms, this meant the provision by the Imperial Power of material assistance to the colonies in the ostensible interest of modifying the colonial economy and improving colonial social welfare. The Colonial Development and Welfare Act (1940) and its subsequent extensions embodied this resolve. In the political sphere, the granting of constitutions acknowledged as "transitional" to self-government marked the new approach. In 1945 alone, for example, Nigeria, Kenya and Ceylon experienced constitutional changes which to greater or lesser degree hastened the termination of the Imperial constitutional presence.

To a significant extent therefore the origins of the 1944 constitution are to be found in the origins of the new approach. This latter grew out of a gradual movement in Colonial Office opinion during the inter-war years which World War II brought to a climax. For example the idea that colonial government had "a direct part to play" in economic development and social welfare though mooted ever since Chamberlain's August 1895 speech[1], expressed itself in effective legislation only after the 1930 economic crisis had clinched the argument for state planning in the metropolis and the African—West Indian labour riots of the thirties had demonstrated the failure of *laissez-faire* trusteeship in the colonies. Roosevelt insisted in the face of Churchill's disagreement on the universal applicability of the Atlantic Charter. On the economic front the state planning endorsed by the Colonial Office after 1940 represented by and large a "principle, acquired in Britain through British experience...in process of extension to the colonial empire".[2] On the other hand the appearance of phased constitutional withdrawal on the Colonial Office was much more closely related to the war.

In fact on the eve of the conflagration, official action gave little inkling of the general reorientation of which the Jamaica constitution was one symptom. In Africa, certainly the Colonial Office subscribed to what one of its governors has called "the belief in indefinite time ahead".[3] 1938 saw a Secretary of State for the Colonies assuring the Commons that "it may take generations or even centuries for the peoples in some parts of the Colonial Empire to achieve self-government".[4] The constitutional question was not even mentioned in the terms of reference of the Moyne Commission, appointed in the wake of the "shock and revelation"[5] of the West Indian riots. The Commissioners themselves having been forced to consider constitutional reform could not agree even on the readiness of the West Indies for adult suffrage. This was the conclusive evidence that official thought had not yet accepted the programme of rapid constitutional decolonization.

Thus though "cracks in the British colonial system were clearly visible"[6] in September 1939, the war was decisive in opening these fractures beyond the point of mending. Pressure on the colonial system became irresistible. Firstly, the strength, indeed the very survival, of the British war effort rested on two props both of which were anti-colonialist—the United States Government and the argument against Hitler. In the four years after the Battle of Britain, the President, the Vice-President and the Secretary of State of the United States had all at various times made clear the support of the United States for colonial freedom. Even after the new approach signalled by the Colonial Development and Welfare Act of 1940, Creech-Jones brought back from his United States tour impressions of considerable suspicion felt for the British Empire by American officialdom.[7] Not only this but the colonial nationalist saw the allied war effort against the fascist axis as in a sense identical with his own fight against the colonial system. The Imperial power's struggle for freedom and equality in Europe could seem such a contradiction of its relations with the colonies that something had to give. The constitutional front represented the line of least resistance. Finally, the course of the war itself exploded a number of ideological myths which had helped hold together the old imperial structure. In particular, the fall of Singapore meant the crash of the illusions of British military invincibility in the face of 'native' arms and of colonial loyalty to the empire in hours of crisis.[8]

The implications of all this for colonial policy were drawn together and pressed by various groups in the metropolis. Foremost among these was the Fabian Colonial Bureau, one of whose main achievements was the bridging of the gap between colonial agitation and imperial decision-making. Pressure from the Bureau was largely responsible for the clause in the C.D.& W. Act which required that the colonial administrations modernise their labour legislation in order to become eligible for imperial assistance. On the more directly political front, interestingly enough, an historian of the Bureau recorded that "one of the biggest struggles was over the Jamaican constitution … The Bureau strongly supported these (the Jamaicans', particularly the PNP's) claims … The matter was constantly raised in the British Parliament; many representations were made to the Colonial Office".[9] With these pressures and with the sustained activity of persons like Creech-Jones in the Commons and Olivier in the Lords, the change in the language of colonial policy was hardly surprising nor the fact that the first concrete constitutional development expressed itself in Jamaica.

The perspectives which accompanied and to some extent justified the general break with the past are worth noting for their direct influence on Jamaican Government. The official writing on the wall came in 1943 when Oliver Stanley, the liberal Conservative Secretary of State told the House of Commons that "the word 'trustee' is rather too static". He then went on to make it quite clear that though it was no part of Government's policy "to confer political advances which are not justified by circumstances … if we really mean as soon as practicable to develop self-government … it is up to us … as soon as possible … to ensure that as quickly as possible people are trained and equipped for eventual self-government."[10] Both the idea of training and the note of urgency are important—the latter being a quality which most statements of colonial policy had hitherto lacked. The first notion of course accorded with a timeless feature of empire which may well have had particularly clear expression in some of the assumptions of Victorian colonialism and certainly was implied by trusteeship. What made the idea new was its understanding that the period of training would end in the foreseeable future. When Hailey spoke of the relationship between the Imperial Power and the colonial peoples as one of senior to junior partner[11] and when Harlow defined the "principle of partnership" as one of "collaboration for mutual benefit",[12] they both envisaged a time-horizon by which the partners or collaborators would become constitutional equals.

More important, however, the notion of training necessarily implied a frame of reference accepted by both trainer and trainee. If the colonial politician accepted the right of the Imperial Power to grade his political performance on certain criteria, and if he saw further constitutional advance as a prime objective it was natural for him to try his best to excel on imperial standards. Consequently there was a direct relationship between the understood criteria for awarding marks in the imperial constitutional examination and the way in which colonial politicians attempted to perform.

Before the war, official thought had resisted the idea that "native" politicians ought necessarily to emulate Westminster behaviour or Westminster institutions.[13] This followed of course from the fact that self-government in the black colonies was not a foreseeable objective: consequently institutions and behaviour which assumed autonomy had to be discouraged. Even within the framework of the "transitional" constitutions behaviour which crudely copied Westminster might be disruptive. After all it was in July 1946 that Sir Allan Burns cautioned the unofficial members of the Gold Coast Legislative Council against seeing themselves as "a permanent Parliamentary opposition. That is not your function. There is no more certain way of making the Constitution a failure than by taking up an attitude of uncompromising opposition to all government measures".[14] But there had been reasons other than the desire to discourage premature colonial autonomy or constitutional stalemate which informed the metropolitan reluctance to spawn a "brood of Westminsters".[15] These, set out in the classic treatises of the Simon and Donoughmore reports, related to the desirability of governmental institutions and practice evolving in accordance with local usage and the need to avoid reproduction of Westminster forms in circumstances "where the conditions and mental habit of the people are very different".[16] Both the content and logic of the stated intention to decolonize however meant the effective abandonment of the traditional inclination toward autochthony and away from assimilation.

Clearly once it was laid down that the "central purpose" of policy would be "to guide the colonial territories to responsible government within the Commonwealth",[17] the local politicians would feel compelled to argue for further advance toward this goal in terms of their ability to display expertise in the constitutional forms and procedures common to the older dominions of the Commonwealth. Furthermore the local guide in the joint enterprise of partnership would certainly know little and care less for governmental models other than Westminster. In addition, the Governor and his departmental heads would be quite ill-equipped to devise jointly institutions appropriate to local contexts, especially where the junior partners often considered any deviation from the British Parliamentary model as "derogatory to their status as fellow citizens of the British Commonwealth of Nations and as conceding something less than...is their due".[18] Increasingly of course any disposition to innovate lost ground, in the early and late 1950's, to the need for assurances of stability arising out of the cold war situation. Thus both the Colonial Office and the colonial politician came to see the elaboration of the Westminster constitution as at once a symbol of ideological purity and an insulation against communist incursions. Thus increasingly there was agreement that constitutional advance had to be argued or denied on the basis of ability to act, talk and behave in line with the traditions of Westminster.[19] In Jamaica this meant that the social/ psychological imprint of colonialism on the nationalist "heir-apparent" was reinforced by the imperatives for legitimate succession to the colonial estate.

The supreme paradox of course was that the cause of constitutional change was not its justification. To put this another way, "preparation theory"[20] does not explain the attitude of the Colonial Office to colonial constitutional demands, so much as administrative expediency. Certainly the former cannot explain the timing and character of Jamaican constitutional change in 1883, 1895 and 1944 so much as the necessity to preserve administrative order. This need to guarantee trouble free adminstration was the priority which accounted for the constitutional concessions of the 19th century to the local plantocratic and professional *élites*. This was a need the fulfillment of which the Colonial Office invariably saw as more important than living up to its self-imposed moral responsibility for the black masses. Though accompanied by some soul-searching, the straight choice between protection of the disenfranchised and concessions to the enfranchised invariably favoured the latter. This sensitivity of British colonialism to threats either to social peace or administrative order is crucial to an understanding of Moyne's recommendations and, more broadly, of the fact that advance to self-government had very little to do with the actual growth of nationalism.

Wood's 1922 report was significant in this regard. First of all he detected the asymmetry between the loudness of Jamaican constitutional demands and the narrowness of real support for these. He observed that:

> with an ignorant and uneducated population it is comparatively simple for good
> organisers to arrange effective mass meetings to advance a cause, with regard to which
> not one person in twenty, if cross-examined as to what it was all about, would be able
> to give an intelligent reply.[21]

Nevertheless despite the acknowledged hollowness of the existing demand for constitutional change Wood concluded that "it would be an act of grave unwisdom to allow this consideration to lead to the refusal of the privileges now claimed".[22] This concession was therefore explicitly pressed as a preemptive tactic[23]—if some constitutional change was not granted the "irritating minority of today would grow into the threatening majority of tomorrow". The implications of this approach are clear. For one it makes preparation theory little more than an ideological rationalisation though one which had real effects on the political style of the colonial *elite*. But secondly, and most important, judicious constitutional retreat at the first sign of trouble, but before it was necessary, meant that mass nationalism was invariably unnecessary for the creation of the new state out of the former dependency.

The Jamaican struggles of 1938 served as the flashpoint for this cycle of "riot-agitation-concession-peace". As we have already pointed out the Commissioners did not come to the West Indies to consider constitutional reform; they only did so when it appeared that not to have done so would have alienated educated West Indian opinion from cooperating in the implementation of socio-economic reform.[24] Secondly, the extent of the constitutional democracy recommended was not justified in terms of the level of "readiness" of West Indian politicians; rather it was based on an estimate, incorrect as the PNP's continued agitation indicated, of how much change was needed to contain local protest while at the same time retaining decisive constitutional authority in the hands of the Crown. Moyne felt that "the initiative in formulating policy should remain with the Governor in Executive Council but the representatives of popular opinion can be given more opportunity to influence policy, and *some of them may perhaps be converted from criticism to cooperation*".[25] The Commissioners felt the point worth repetition—"careful consideration", they urged, must be given to the appointment of electives to the Executive since "we are impressed with the desirability of thus securing the co-operation of the elected element in the work of the executive ..." [26] These reforms were precipitated by spontaneous rioting and its aftermath of nationalist agitation, though obviously enlightened intentions played a significant role. Equally certainly however, reform had its basis in realpolitik not in some idealistic assessment that the 'colonials' were nearly sufficiently advanced to have their freedom.

The fact is the constitutional recommendations were designed in part to deflect nationalist agitation into governmental cooperation and thus remove any vested interest in—indeed create a counter interest against—any mass rebellion. To the extent that systematic political education in socialistic nationalism had inherent in it the probability of mass action, to that extent those who insisted on that course would be subverting the process of orderly change.[27] Furthermore to the extent that these elements were neutralized, mass nationalism would hardly be effectively promoted. Not only was nationalism unnecessary to trigger off the highly sensitive constitutional-concession mechanism of the Colonial Office, but it could become a positive liability, threatening the agreed programmes of the joint partnership. These factors in the origins and character of the 1944 Constitution certainly go a long way to explaining the inattention to political education in socialistic nationalism which became increasingly apparent in Jamaican politics after 1944.

Conceptions of administrative expediency were at the basis of constitutional change. The course of its development however also related to the enterprise of West Indian Federation. In this regard the war was again, an important factor. It encouraged the Imperial Power to take decisive action toward regional organization. Equally the need for rational administration of the West Indies meant the establishment of central coordination. The Anglo-American Caribbean Commission and the Office of the Comptroller of Development and Welfare[28] were the respective institutional consequences of the twin need to execute the war and plan the peace. They also provided a concrete framework which would facilitate any regional designs on the part of the Colonial Office. This was especially important since the commitment to decolonize meant some grouping of the islands together. In the post-war Colonial Office, Jamaica and the other British Caribbean territories were seen as viable autonomous constitutional entities only in Federal formation.[29] Official thought held that a colony had to be able to attain a certain level of economic development, probably beyond the capacity of any single territory, in order to qualify for self-government. The interest in decolonization therefore encouraged the Colonial Office to promote Federation. It certainly felt that "since the war the most important issue raised in this area has been that of regional association of the British dependencies in and adjoining the Caribbean Sea".[30] The Colonial Office could hardly disguise this perspective and the Jamaican politicians could not fail to suspect it. This was one important reason why the latter very often[31] took umbrage at the British Government's advocacy of Federation but nevertheless went along with the idea.

To conclude this survey of the historical background it is necessary to bring together the main features which influenced Jamaican constitutional development and political change after 1944.

Firstly the pronounced differentiation in the social order would provide initial points of reference for political organization. Furthermore certain characteristics of each social section had direct political significance. For example, the traditional political attitudes of the blacks - moving, often rapidly, from apathy towards established politics to riotousness-would continue despite constitutional change unless politics showed itself more able to meet the needs of the poorer classes. Their "anti-brown" consciousness would also affect the initial response to nationalist ideology. At another level, the "white bias" to which the middle section was particularly susceptible reinforced the normal tendency of the successor political class to copy the political culture of the Imperial Power.

Cutting across these class-colour divisions was the cleavage between town and country. In this context the rapid growth of the urban area would, among other things, provide support for competing political organizations, less purely based than on cultural sections.

The economic systems bequeathed a host of problems to the new legislators. Foremost among these was chronic unemployment which before 1940 was held in check primarily by emigration outlets and the provision of casual work. The choice after 1944 was at least theoretically, between radical reorganization of the economy and the certainty of growing unemployment.

From the constitutional point of view, the modern period followed on a historical past of subordination of the governmental order to the interests of small propertied and professional groups. To that extent the significance of constitutional change had always been dependent on the distribution of socio-economic power. How far the formal democratization of the polity modified this relationship will be considered below.

In terms of the specific traditions of Crown Colony politics two deserve special notice: first the authoritarian assumptions of the system and secondly the normalcy of opposition-government division in the Legislative Council. When democratic politics displayed similar tendencies, it was so much the easier to excuse or sanction the familiar.

Finally, the Imperial Power's approach to colonial administration would exert significant influences. For one, the stated commitment to constitutional decolonization reinforced the effect of the traditional tendency to yield to threats to colonial order. Both removed any immediate political point from the systematic building of nationalist sentiment. Especially after 1944, the door against which the nationalists might have pushed was not only rarely bolted but was also to their knowledge being gradually opened. On the other hand, the ideology of "preparation" moved the local political class even further away from creative activity and toward emulative behaviour. Lastly the Colonial Office's known interest in Federation was very much responsible for both the presence, treatment and future of that particular issue in Jamaican politics.

In these and other ways, this setting, moulded from the cumulative experiences of chattel slavery, plantation peonage and Crown Colonialism, produced a politics which combined both the commonplace and developments peculiar to Jamaica.

Notes

1. In that speech Chamberlain told the Commons that he regarded 'our colonies as being in the condition of undeveloped estates, and Estates which can never be developed without Imperial Assistance' cf E.R. Wicker 'Colonial Development and Welfare, 1929–1957: The Evolution of a Policy' *Social and Economic Studies* Vol. 7, No. 4, Dec. 1958, pp. 170–191.
2. *The London Times* (leader article) January 10, 1945.
3. Sir Andrew Cohen *British Policy in Changing Africa*, London, 1959, 25.
4. *Parliamentary Debates* Fifth Series, Volume 342, 1938-1939, 1246.
5. *C-J Papers*. Box 25, No. 7: 1.
6. Cf. e.g. the statement by the United States Secretary of State, Cordell Hull in 1942: 'We have always believed ... that all people without distinction of race, color or religion, who are prepared and willing to accept the responsibilities of liberty are entitled to this enjoyment.' Cited in Kenneth Robinson, 'World Opinion and Colonial Status' *International Organisation* Vol. 8. 1954, 471.
7. Cf. 'A Note on Opinion in America on British Colonial Policy,' *C-J papers*, 12 1: 27, 28.
8. Cf. e.g., Parkinson's opinion, 'to them [i.e., the Colonial Office] the worst moment of the war' was the fall of Singapore, Sir C. Parkinson *The Colonial Office from Within 1909-1945* (London, 1947), 87.
9. Rita Hinden *Socialists and the Empire* London 1946, p. 14–15.
10. *Parliamentary Debates* Fifth Series, Vol. 391 pp. 48–49. For an illuminating discussion of the changes in Colonial Office thinking during this period and subsequently cf. J.M. Lee *Colonial Development and good Government: a study of the ideas expressed by the British official classes in planning decolonization 1939–1964* . Oxford 1967.
11. Cited in Lee *op. at.*, p. 18.
12. V. Harlow *The British Colonial Empire and the British Public* London. 1945, p. 13.
13. Cf. egs. The two classic expositions on the need for colonial constitutional autochthony, *viz.*, Great Britain *Report of the Indian Statutory Commission Volume II-Surrey* Cmnd. 3560 London 1930 (especially pp. 17 et. sq.); Great Britain *Ceylon: Report of The Special Commission on the Constitution* Cmnd. 3131 London 1928 (especially p. 45).
14. G.E. Metcalfe *Great Britain and Ghana: Documents of Ghana History 1807–1957*, London 1964, 682.
15. The phrase is that of A. F. Madden in *The Commonwealth and the Westminster Model.* Unpublished paper for discussion, November 1964, Postgraduate Seminar, Institute of Commonwealth Studies, London University.
16. *Simon Report*, 7.
17. Rt. Hon. Arthur Creech-Jones, report to Parliament 1948. Cited in Sir Charles Jeffries *Transfer of Power*, London 1960, p. 15.
18. Great Britain. *Ceylon: Report of Committee on Constitutional Reform* Cmnd., 6677, Sept. 1945, p. 110.
19. E.g. one of the reasons for suspending the British Guiana constitution in 1953 was the failure of the PPP to behave as if it understood that "democratic values require that a government elected by the majority of the people should nevertheless consult the interests of all and respect the rights of minorities". Great Britain *Report of the British Guiana Constitutional Commission* Cmnd. 9274, London 1954, p. 68. (Herinafter referred to as *the Robertson Commission Report.)*
20. This phrase of B.B. Schafer's is used to indicate the body of opinion which argues that colonial

constitutional advance took place in accordance with Colonial Office plan to "prepare" the colonies for higher and higher levels of constitutional democracy. Cf. B.B. Schafer "The Concept of Preparation: Some Questions about the Transfer of Systems of Government". *SOAS and IDS (Sussex) Joint Reprint Series No. 4.* (From *World Politics* Vol. XVIII, No. 1, Oct. 1965, 42–67.)

21.   *Wood Report,* 6.

22.   Ibid.

23.   Cf. the ex-colonial governors who have written about the period of decolonization as well as the careers of Sir Allan Burns and Sir Arthur Richards in particular. Sir Andrew Cohen most explicitly records the tactic of preemption as "keeping one step in front of public opinion". Sir A. Cohen. *British Policy in a Changing Africa* London 1959; pp 37–38.

24.   *Moyne Report,* 373.

25.   Ibid., 374. Emphasis mine.

26.   Ibid., 375.

27.   This was one of the underlying reasons why the P.N.P.'s left wing would constitute a permanent potential embarrassment to the Party's decision to cooperate with phased decolonization. Cf. Chap. 2, 79 *el seq.*

28.   The second was established in 1940, the first in 1942.

29.   The time-table for colonial constitutional advance set by the Attlee Government toward the end of the 40's remains a Cabinet secret. It is known however that Jamaica was considered among the category of colonies "whose contiguity of resource meagreness suggested that constitutional advance depended on some kind of regional grouping. *C-J Papers.*

30.   *Notes on Colonial Constitutional Changes 1940–1951.* Colonial Office Information Department. Memo. No. 4 April 1951, 18.

31.   Cf. e.g. Chap. 4, 119 below.

MANIFESTOS AND SPEECHES

Liberty or Death, Proclamation

Jean-Jacques Dessalines

JEAN JAQUES DESSALINES Governor General to to the inhabitants of Hayti.

CRIMES, the most atrocious, such as were until then unheard of, and would cause nature to shudder, have been perpetrated. The measure was over-heaped. At length the hour of vengeance has arrived, and the implacable enemies of the rights of man have suffered the punishment due to their crimes.

My arm, raised over their heads, has too long delayed to strike. At that signal, which the justice of God has urged, your hands righteously armed, have brought the axe upon the ancient tree of slavery and prejudices. In vain had time, and more especially the internal politics of Europeans, surrounded it with triple brass; you have stripped it of its armour; you have placed it upon your heart, that you may become (like your natural enemies) cruel and merciless. Like an overflowing mighty torrent that tears down all opposition, your vengeful fury *has* carried away every thing in its impetuous course. Thus perish all tyrants over innocence, all oppressors of mankind!

What then? bent for many ages under an iron yoke: the sport of the passions of men, or their injustice, and of the caprices of fortune; mutilated victims of the cupidity of white French men; after having fattened with our toils these insatiate blood suckers, with a patience and resignation unexampled, we should again have seen that sacrilegious horde make an attempt upon our destruction, without any distinction of sex or age; and we, men without energy, of no virtue, of no delicate sensibility, should not we have plunged in their breast the dagger of desperation? Where is that vile Haytian, so unworthy of his regeneration, who thinks he has not accomplished the decrees of the Eternal, by exterminating these blood-thirsty tygers? If there is one, let him fly; indignant nature discards him from our bosom; let him hide his shame far from hence: the air we breath is not suited to his gross organs; it is the pure air of Liberty, august and triumphant.

Yes, we have rendered to these true cannibals war for war, crime for crime, outrage for outrage; Yes, I have saved my country; I have avenged America. The avowal I make of it in the face of earth and heaven, constitutes my pride and my glory. Of what consequence to me is the opinion which contemporary and future generations will pronounce upon my conduct? I have performed my duty; I enjoy my own approbation; for me that is sufficient. But what do I say? The preservation of my unfortunate brothers, the testimony of my own conscience, are not my only recompence: I have seen two classes of men, born to cherish, assist and succour one another—mixed, in a word, and blended together—crying for vengeance, and disputing the honor of the first blow.

Blacks and Yellows, whom the refined duplicity of Europeans has for a long time endeavored to divide; you, who are now consolidated, and make but one family; without doubt it was necessary that our perfect reconciliation should be sealed with the blood of your butchers. Similar calamities have hung over your proscribed heads: a similar ardour to strike your enemies has signalized you: the like fate it reserved for you: and the like interests must therefore render you for ever one, indivisible, and inseparable. Maintain that precious concord, that happy harmony amongst yourselves: it is the pledge of your happiness. Your salvation, and your success: it is the secret of being invincible.

Is it necessary, in order to strengthen, these ties to recall to your remembrance the catalogue of atrocities committed against our species: the massacre of the entire population of this Island meditated in the silence and sangfroid of the Cabinet: the execution of that abominable project to me unblushingly proposed and already begun by the French with the calmness and serenity of a countenance accustomed to similar crimes. Guadaloupe, pillaged and destroyed: its ruins still reeking, with the blood of the children, women and old men put to the sword, PELAGE (himself the victim of their craftiness) after having basely betrayed his country and his brothers: The brave and immortal DELGRESSE, blown into the air with the fort which he defended, rather than accept their offered chains. Magnanimous warrior! that noble death, far from enfeebling our courage, serves only to rouse within us the determination of avenging or of following thee. Shall I again recall to your memory the plots lately framed at Jeremie? The terrible explosion which was to be the result, nothwithstanding the generous pardon granted to these incorrigible beings at the expulsion of the French army? The deplorable fate of our departed brothers in Europe? and (dread harbinger of death) the frightful despotism exercised at Martinique? Unfortunate people of Martinique, could I but fly to your assistance, and break your fetters! Alas! an insurmountable barrier separates us. Perhaps a spark from the same fire which inflames us, will alight into your bosoms: perhaps at the sound of this commotion, suddenly awakened from your lethargy, with arms in your hands, you will reclaim your sacred and inprescriptable rights.

After the terrible example which I have just given, that sooner or later Divine Justice will unchain on earth some mighty minds, above the weakness of the vulgar, for the destruction and terror of the wicked; tremble, tyrants, usurpers, scourges of the new world! Our daggers are sharpened; your punishment is ready! Sixty thousand men, equipped, inured to war, obedient to my orders, burn to offer a new sacrifice to the names of their assassinated brothers. Let that nation come who may be mad and daring enough to attack me. Already at its approach, the irritated genius of Hayti, rising out of the bosom of the ocean appears; his menacing aspect throws the waves into commotion, excites tempests, and with his mighty hand disperses ships, or dashes them in pieces; to his formidable voice the laws of nature pay obedience; diseases, plague, famine, conflagration, poison, are his constant attendants. But why calculate on the assistance of the climate and of the elements? Have I forgot that I command a people of no common cast, brought up in adversity, whose audacious daring frowns at obstacles and increases by dangers? Let them come, then, these homicidal Cohort? I wait for them with firmness and with a steady eye. I abandon to them freely the sea-shore, and the places, where cities have existed; but woe to those who may approach too near the mountains! It were better for them that the sea received them into its profound abyss, than to be devoured by the anger of the children of Hayti.

"War to Death to Tyrants!" this is my motto; *"Liberty! Independence!"* this is our rallying cry.

Generals, officers, soldiers, a little unlike him who has preceded me, the ex-general Toussaint Loverture, I have been faithful to the promise which I made to you when I took up arms against tyranny, and whilst *the last s*park of life remains in me I shall keep my oath. *Never again shall a Colonist or an European set his foot upon this territory with the title of master or proprietor.* This resolution shall henceforward form the fundamental basis of our constitution.

Should other chiefs, after me, by pursuing a conduct diametrically opposite to mine, dig their own graves and those of their species, you will have to accuse only the law of destiny which shall have taken me away from the happiness and welfare of my fellow-citizens. May my successors follow the path I shall have traced out for them! It is the system best adapted for consolidating their power; it is the highest homage they can render to my memory.

As it is derogatory to my character and my dignity to punish the innocent for the crimes of the guilty, a handful of whites, commendable by the religion they have always professed, and who have besides taken the oath to live with us in the woods, have experienced my clemency. I order that the sword respect them, and that they be unmolested.

I recommend anew and order to all the generals of department &c. to grant succours, encouragement, and protection, to all neutral and friendly nations who may wish to establish commercial relations in this Island.

Head Quarters at the Cape, 28th April, 1804, first year of independence.

The Governor General, (Signed)

DESSALINES.

A true Copy. The Secretary-General, Juste Chanlatte.

Political Program of the Independent Party of Color

The Independent Party of Color

El Partido Independiente de Color

POLITICAL PROGRAM OF THE INDEPENDENT PARTY OF COLOR

The "Independent Association of Color" hereby constitutes itself as a national organization in the entire territory of the Republic. We seek to maintain a balance among all Cuban interests, spread love for the Fatherland, develop cordial relations, and interest everybody in the conservation of Cuban nationality, allowing everybody born in this land to participate equally in public administration.

Our motto is an egalitarian, sovereign, and independent republic, without racial divisions or social antagonisms. All Cubans who are worthy should be able to be named to the diplomatic corps, and, as a matter of important and urgent necessity, citizens of the race of color should be named, so that the republic can be represented in all of its hues.

We believe that all court trials that take place in the Republic should be trials by jury, and that the duty of serving on the jury should be mandatory and free.

We call for
- The abolition of the death penalty, and for the creation of penitentiaries that fulfill the needs of modern civilization.
- The creation of correctional School-ships [*Barcos-escuelas*] for youthful offenders who, according to the law, cannot suffer greater penalties.
- Free and compulsory education for children from ages six to fourteen.
- The creation of polytechnic [vocational] schools in each of the six provinces, free and compulsory for adults, to be considered as the second stage of compulsory education, and consisting of Arts and Trades.
- Official, national, and free university education available to all.
- The regulation of private and official education, under the auspices of the state, so that the education of all Cubans will be uniform.
- The creation of a Naval and Military Academy.
- Free and faithful [*leal*] admission into military, administrative, government, and judicial services of citizens of color, so that all of the races can be represented in the service of the state.

- Immigration should be free for all races, without giving preference to any. The free entrance of all individuals who, within sanitary prescriptions, come in good faith to contribute to the development of the public good.
- The repatriation, at public expense, of all Cubans from foreign shores who want to return to their native land but lack the necessary resources.
- The creation of a Law to guarantee that in employment in all public enterprises, in Cuba and abroad, Cubans will be given preference to foreigners, until the latter are naturalized, and preventing new enterprises from being established in other countries.
- We will work to make the eight-hour day the norm in all of the territory of the republic.
- The creation of a Labor Tribunal to regulate any differences that arise between capital and labor.
- The promulgation of a law prohibiting the immigration of minors, and of women, except when they are accompanied by their families.
- The distribution of plots of land from State reserves, or from lands acquired by the state for this purpose, among veterans of the War of Independence who lack resources and who wish to devote themselves to agriculture, giving preference to those who are not suited for public office.

CONSTITUTIONAL ACT OF THE AGRUPACIÓN INDEPENDIENTE DE COLOR

In the city of Havana, in the residence of General Evaristo Estenoz, 63 Amargura Street, on the night of 7 August 1908, after a long and well-thought out discussion, those who have signed below unanimously approved the following:

That in light of the results of the elections of 1 August throughout the Republic to fill the positions of provincial governors, provincial councilors, municipal mayors, and municipal councilors, in which the candidates of color were excluded, with preconceived intent, from the candidate lists of the different political parties that participated in the election;

This being a self evident demonstration that the black race cannot rely on the political parties for the betterment which it deserves for the services that it has lent and continues to lend to the national interest;

We solemnly agree, with our sights set on universal cordiality, on love for the progress of humanity, on the collective good of all of the inhabitants who make up the territory of the homeland, and above all, on the mutual respect and consideration that in accordance with human law, and with political and civil law should exist so that all who enjoy the light of the sun in this land can love each other and understand each other, and;

collecting the general sentiment of all of the elements of the race of color in the whole island, who have consulted us daily, showing their dissatisfaction with the current state of things;

We believe that in order to bring about an era of moral peace for all Cubans; we resolve to present a candidate list made up of men of color, covering all of the elective positions.

This proposal is not based on hatred, nor animosity toward anybody, for all Cubans have the right to support us or to combat us. We simply say that we, inspired by a high and generous goal, have the duty to maintain the balance among all Cuban interests, and that the black race has the right to participate in the government of its country not with the objective of governing anybody, but rather with the aim that we should be well governed.

President Evaristo Estenoz
Secretary Gregorio Surin

Declaration of Rights of the Negro Peoples of the World

Drafted and adopted at Convention held in New York, 1920, over which Marcus Garvey presided as Chairman, and at which he was elected Provisional President of Africa.

(Preamble)

"Be it Resolved, That the Negro people of the world, through their chosen representatives in convention, assembled in Liberty Hall, in the City of New York and United States of America, from August 1 to August 31, in the year of our Lord, one thousand nine hundred and twenty, protest against the wrongs and injustices they are suffering at the hands of their white brethren, and state what they deem their fair and just rights, as well as the treatment they propose to demand of all men in the future."

We complain:

I. "That nowhere in the world, with few exceptions, are black men accorded equal treatment with white men, although in the same situation and circumstances, but, on the contrary, are discriminated against and denied the common rights due to human beings for no other reason than their race and color."

"We are not willingly accepted as guests in the public hotels and inns of the world for no other reason than our race and color."

II. "In certain parts of the United States of America our race is denied the right of public trial accorded to other races when accused of crime, but are lynched and burned by mobs, and such brutal and inhuman treatment is even practised upon our women."

III. "That European nations have parcelled out among themselves and taken possession of nearly all of the continent of Africa, and the natives are compelled to surrender their lands to aliens and are treated in most instances like slaves."

IV. "In the southern portion of the United States of America, although citizens under the Federal Constitution, and in some states almost equal to the whites in population and are qualified land owners and taxpayers, we are, nevertheless, denied all voice in the making and administration of the laws and are taxed without representation by the state governments, and at the same time compelled to do military service in defense of the country."

V. "On the public conveyances and common carriers in the Southern portion of the United States we are jim-crowed and compelled to accept separate and inferior accommodations and made to pay the same fare charged for first-class accommodations, and our families are often humiliated and insulted by drunken white men who habitually pass through the jim-crow cars going to the smoking car."

VI. "The physicians of our race are denied the right to attend their patients while in the public hospitals of the cities and states where they reside in certain parts of the United States."

"Our children are forced to attend inferior separate schools for shorter terms than white children, and the public school funds are unequally divided between the white and colored schools."

VII. "We are discriminated against and denied an equal chance to earn wages for the support of our families, and in many instances are refused admission into labor unions, and nearly everywhere are paid smaller wages than white men."

VIII. "In Civil Service and departmental offices we are everywhere discriminated against and made to feel that to be a black man in Europe, America and the West Indies is equivalent to being an outcast and a leper among the races of men, no matter what the character and attainments of the black man may be."

IX. "In the British and other West Indian Islands and colonies, Negroes are secretly and cunningly discriminated against, and denied those fuller rights in government to which white citizens are appointed, nominated and elected."

X. "That our people in those parts are forced to work for lower wages than the average standard of white men and are kept in conditions repugnant to good civilized tastes and customs."

XI. "That the many acts of injustice against members of our race before the courts of law in the respective islands and colonies are of such nature as to create disgust and disrespect for the white man's sense of justice."

XII. "Against all such inhuman, unchristian and uncivilized treatment we here and now emphatically protest, and invoke the condemnation of all mankind."

"In order to encourage our race all over the world and to stimulate it to a higher and grander destiny, we demand and insist on the following Declaration of Rights:

1. "Be it known to all men that whereas, all men are created equal and entitled to the rights of life, liberty and the pursuit of happiness, and because of this we, the duly elected representatives of the Negro peoples of the world, invoking the aid of the just and Almighty God do declare all men women and children of our blood throughout the world free citizens, and do claim them as free citizens of Africa, the Motherland of all Negroes."

2. "That we believe in the supreme authority of our race in all things racial; that all things are created and given to man as a common possession; that there should be an equitable distribution and apportionment of all such things, and in consideration of the fact that as a race we are now deprived of those things that are morally and

legally ours, we believe it right that all such things should be acquired and held by whatsoever means possible.

3. "That we believe the Negro, like any other race, should be governed by the ethics of civilization, and, therefore, should not be deprived of any of those rights or privileges common to other human beings."

4. "We declare that Negroes, wheresoever they form a community among themselves, should be given the right to elect their own representatives to represent them in legislatures, courts of law, or such institutions as may exercise control over that particular community."

5. "We assert that the Negro is entitled to even-handed justice before all courts of law and equity in whatever country he may be found, and when this is denied him on account of his race or color such denial is an insult to the race as a whole and should be resented by the entire body of Negroes."

6. "We declare it unfair and prejudicial to the rights of Negroes in communities where they exist in considerable numbers to be tried by a judge and jury composed entirely of an alien race, but in all such cases members of our race are entitled to representation on the jury."

7. "We believe that any law or practice that tends to deprive any African of his land or the privileges of free citizenship within his country is unjust and immoral, and no native should respect any such law or practice."

8. "We declare taxation without representation unjust and tyrannous, and there should be no obligation on the part of the Negro to obey the levy of a tax by any law-making body from which he is excluded and denied representation on account of his race and color."

9. "We believe that any law especially directed against the Negro to his detriment and singling him out because of his race or color is unfair and immoral, and should not be respected."

10. "We believe all men entitled to common human respect, and that our race should in no way tolerate any insults that may be interpreted to mean disrespect to our color."

11. "We deprecate the use of the term 'nigger' as applied to Negroes, and demand that the word 'Negro' be written with a capital 'N.' "

12. "We believe that the Negro should adopt every means to protect himself against barbarous practices inflicted upon him because of color."

13. "We believe in the freedom of Africa for the Negro people of the world, and by the principle of Europe for the Europeans and Asia for the Asiatics; we also demand Africa for the Africans at home and abroad."

14. "We believe in the inherent right of the Negro to possess himself of Africa, and that his possession of same shall not be regarded as an infringement on any claim or purchase made by any race or nation."

15. "We strongly condemn the cupidity of those nations of the world who, by open aggression or secret schemes, have seized the territories and inexhaustible natural wealth of Africa, and we place on record our most solemn determination to reclaim the treasures and possession of the vast continent of our forefathers."

16. "We believe all men should live in peace one with the other, but when races and nations provoke the ire of other races and nations by attempting to infringe upon their rights, war becomes inevitable, and the attempt in any way to free one's self or protect one's rights or heritage becomes justifiable.

17. "Whereas, the lynching, by burning, hanging or any other means, of human beings is a barbarous practice, and a shame and disgrace to civilization, we therefore declare any country guilty of such atrocities outside the pale of civilization."

18. "We protest against the atrocious crime of whipping, flogging and overworking of the native tribes of Africa and Negroes everywhere. These are methods that should be abolished, and all means should be taken to prevent a continuance of such brutal practices."

19. "We protest against the atrocious practice of shaving the heads of Africans, especially of African women or individuals of Negro blood, when placed in prison as a punishment for crime by an alien race."

20. "We protest against segregated districts, separate public conveyances, industrial discrimination, lynchings and limitations of political privileges of any Negro citizen in any part of the world on account of race, color or creed, and will exert our full influence and power against all such."

21. "We protest against any punishment inflicted upon a Negro with severity, as against lighter punishment inflicted upon another of an alien race for like offense, as an act of prejudice and injustice, and should be resented by the entire race."

22. "We protest against the system of education in any country where Negroes are denied the same privileges and advantages as other races."

23. "We declare it inhuman and unfair to boycott Negroes from industries and labor in any part of the world."

24. "We believe in the doctrine of the freedom of the press, and we therefore emphatically protest against the suppression of Negro newspapers and periodicals in various parts of the world, and call upon Negroes everywhere to employ all available means to prevent such suppression."

25. "We further demand free speech universally for all men."

26. "We hereby protest against the publication of scandalous and inflammatory articles by an alien press tending to create racial strife and the exhibition of picture films showing the Negro as a cannibal."

27. "We believe in the self-determination of all peoples."

28. "We declare for the freedom of religious worship."

29. "With the help of Almighty God, we declare ourselves the sworn protectors of the honor and virtue of our women and children, and pledge our lives for their protection and defense everywhere, and under all circumstances from wrongs and outrages."

30. "We demand the right of unlimited and unprejudiced education for ourselves and our posterity forever."

31. "We declare that the teaching in any school by alien teachers to our boys and girls, that the alien race is superior to the Negro race, is an insult to the Negro people of the world."

32. "Where Negroes form a part of the citizenry of any country, and pass the civil service examination of such country, we declare them entitled to the same consideration as other citizens as to appointments in such civil service."

33. "We vigorously protest against the increasingly unfair and unjust treatment accorded Negro travelers on land and sea by the agents and employees of railroad and steamship companies and insist that for equal fare we receive equal privileges with travelers of other races."

34. "We declare it unjust for any country, State or nation to enact laws tending to hinder and obstruct the free immigration of Negroes on account of their race and color."

35. "That the right of the Negro to travel unmolested throughout the world be not abridged by any person or persons, and all Negroes are called upon to give aid to a fellow Negro when thus molested."

36. "We declare that all Negroes are entitled to the same right to travel over the world as other men."

37. "We hereby demand that the governments of the world recognize our leader and his representatives chosen by the race to look after the welfare of our people under such governments."

38. "We demand complete control of our social institutions without interference by any alien race or races."

39. "That the colors, Red, Black and Green, be the colors of the Negro race."

40. "Resolved, That the anthem 'Ethiopia, Thou Land of Our Fathers,' etc., shall be the anthem of the Negro race."

The Universal Ethiopian Anthem
(Poem by Burrell and Ford)

I

Ethiopia, thou land of our fathers,
Thou land where the gods loved to be,
As storm cloud at night suddenly gathers
Our armies come rushing to thee.
We must in the fight be victorious
When swords are thrust outward to gleam;
For us will the vict'ry be glorious
When led by the red, black and green.

Chorus

Advance, advance to victory,
Let Africa be free;
Advance to meet the foe
With the might
Of the red, the black and the green.

II

Ethiopia, the tyrant's falling,
Who smote thee upon thy knees,
And thy children are lustily calling
From over the distant seas.
Jehovah, the Great One has heard us,
Has noted our sighs and our tears,
With His spirit of Love he has stirred us
To be One through the coming years.

CHORUS—Advance, advance, etc.

III

O Jehovah, thou God of the ages
Grant unto our sons that lead
The wisdom Thou gave to Thy sages
When Israel was sore in need.
Thy voice thro' the dim past has spoken,
Ethiopia shall stretch forth her hand,
By Thee shall all fetters be broken,
And Heav'n bless our dear fatherland.

CHORUS—Advance, advance, etc.

41. "We believe that any limited liberty which deprives one of the complete rights and prerogatives of full citizenship is but a modified form of slavery."

42. "We declare it an injustice to our people and a serious impediment to the health of the race to deny to competent licensed Negro physicians the right to practise in the public hospitals of the communities in which they reside, for no other reason than their race and color."

43. "We call upon the various governments of the world to accept and acknowledge Negro representatives who shall be sent to the said governments to represent the general welfare of the Negro peoples of the world."

44. "We deplore and protest against the practice of confining juvenile prisoners in prisons with adults, and we recommend that such youthful prisoners be taught gainful trades under humane supervision."

45. "Be it further resolved, that we as a race of people declare the League of Nations null and void as far as the Negro is concerned, in that it seeks to deprive Negroes of their liberty."

46. "We demand of all men to do unto us as we would do unto them, in the name of justice; and we cheerfully accord to all men all the rights we claim herein for ourselves."

47. "We declare that no Negro shall engage himself in battle for an alien race without first obtaining the consent of the leader of the Negro people of the world, except in a matter of national self-defense."

48. "We protest against the practice of drafting Negroes and sending them to war with alien forces without proper training, and demand in all cases that Negro soldiers be given the same training as the aliens."

49. "We demand that instructions given Negro children in schools include the subject of 'Negro History,' to their benefit."

50. "We demand a free and unfettered commercial intercourse with all the Negro people of the world."

51. "We declare for the absolute freedom of the seas for all peoples."

52. "We demand that our duly accredited representatives be given proper recognition in all leagues, conferences, conventions or courts of international arbitration wherever human rights are discussed."

53. "We proclaim the 31st day of August of each year to be an international holiday to be observed by all Negroes."

54. "We want all men to know we shall maintain and contend for the freedom and equality of every man, woman and child of our race, with our lives, our fortunes and our sacred honor."

These rights we believe to be justly ours and proper for the protection of the Negro race at large, and because of this belief we, on behalf of the four hundred million Negroes of the world, do pledge herein the sacred blood of the race in defense, and we hereby subscribe our names as a guarantee of the truthfulness and faithfulness hereof in the presence of Almighty God, on the 13th day of August, in the year of our Lord one thousand nine hundred and twenty.

Marcus Garvey, James D. Brooks, James W. H. Eason, Henrietta Vinton Davis, Lionel Winston Greenidge, Adrion Fitzroy Johnson, Rudolph Ethelbert Brissaac Smith, Charles Augustus Petioni, Thomas H. N. Simon, Richard Hilton Tobitt, George Alexander McGuire, Peter Edward Baston, Reynold R. Felix, Harry Walters Kirby, Sarah Branch, Marie Barrier Houston, George L. O'Brien, F. O. Ogilvie, Arden A. Bryan, Benjamin Dyett, Marie Duchaterlier, John Phillip Hodge, Theophilus H. Saunders, Wilford H. Smith, Gabriel E. Stewart, Arnold Josiah Ford, Lee Crawford, William McCartney, Adina Clem. James, William Musgrave La Motte, John Sydney de Bourg, Arnold S. Cunning, Vernal J. Williams, Frances Wilcome Ellegor, J. Frederick Selkridge, Innis Abel Horsford, Cyril A. Crichlow, Samuel McIntyre, John Thomas Wilkins, Mary Thurston, John G. Befue, William Ware, J. A. Lewis, O. C. Kelly, Venture R. Hamilton, R. H. Hodge, Edward Alfred Taylor, Ellen Wilson, G. W. Wilson, Richard Edward Riley, Nellie Grant Whiting, G. W. Washington, Maldena Miller, Gertrude Davis, James D. Williams, Emily Christmas Kinch, D. D. Lewis, Nettie Clayton, Partheria Hills, Janie Jenkins, John C. Simons, Alphonso A. Jones, Allen Hobbs, Reynold Fitzgerald Austin, James Benjamin Yearwood, Frank O. Raines, Shedrick Williams, John Edward Ivey, Frederick Augustus Toote, Philip Hemmings, F. F. Smith, E. J. Jones, Joseph Josiah Cranston, Frederick Samuel Ricketts, Dugald Augustus Wade, E. E. Nelom, Florida Jenkins, Napoleon J. Francis, Joseph D. Gibson, J. P. Jasper, J. W. Montgomery, David Benjamin, J. Gordon, Harry E. Ford, Carrie M. Ashford, Andrew N. Willis, Lucy Sands, Louise Woodson, George D. Creese, W. A. Wallace, Thomas E. Bagley, James Young, Prince Alfred McConney, John E. Hudson, William Ines, Harry R. Watkins, C. L. Halton, J. T. Bailey, Ira Joseph Touissant Wright, T. H. Golden, Abraham Benjamin Thomas, Richard C. Noble, Walter Green, C. S. Bourne, G. F. Bennett, B. D. Levy, Mary E. Johnson, Lionel Antonio Francis, Carl Roper, E. R. Donawa, Philip Van Putten, I. Brathwaite, Jesse W. Luck, Oliver Kaye, J. W. Hudspeth, C. B. Lovell, William C. Matthews, A. Williams, Ratford E. M. Jack, H. Vinton Plummer, Randolph Phillips, A. I. Bailey, duly elected representatives of the Negro people of the world.

Sworn before me this 15th day of August, 1920.
[Legal Seal]

JOHN G. BAYNE.
Notary Public, New York County.
New York County Clerk's No. 378;
New York County Register's No. 12102.
Commission expires March 30, 1922.

Latin America to the League of Nations

Dantès Bellgarde
Translated by Bernadette Farquhar

Mr. Chairman, Ladies and Gentlemen, my first task is a very painful one: my Latin American friends have asked me to convey a message of sympathy to the people and Government of the Dominican Republic. You are aware that the Dominican Republic has been struck by a disaster. The newspapers provide us daily with increasingly alarming reports of the distress and misery suffered by the population of that country. It is good that the eleventh Assembly of the League of Nations is declaring its solidarity in the face of this distress by expressing its sympathy.

But words are not enough. We should also provide material aid. Unfortunately, the budget of the League of Nations makes such generosity impossible. We can, nevertheless, consider some practical means of relieving the country of its distress. First of all, we could perhaps grant it a waiver of its annual subscription at least for the current exercise. Secondly, we could ask the Assembly chairman to launch an appeal to all the member states of the League, asking them to provide the unfortunate victims of the disaster with the necessary aid.

On behalf of all the Latin American delegations, I would also like to direct a very urgent appeal to the journalists present. We are asking them to start a fund among their readers. This act of solidarity will do honour to the press and will certainly be considered as one of its kindest actions.

That duty done, I have a second one, more difficult, to complete. After the Honourable Sir Robert Borden, former Prime Minister of Canada, after Mr. Aristide Briand, the French Foreign Affairs Minister, after Mr. Henderson, the British Minister of Foreign Affairs, I can imagine your surprise at seeing at the podium the representative of a very small distant state that is not well known, is misunderstood, disparaged, whose very suffering seems not to move anyone anywhere. But in this assembly there are no small or large nations and therein lie the beauty and the strength of this institution in Geneva. Any voice raised on this platform is sure to be well received as long as it is sincere. I can assure you that the voice you are hearing today is sincere and that it will say what it believes to be the truth. Mr. Briand said this morning: "Open the windows so that the air from outside can pervade the League of Nations." I should like to open a window so that an acceptable air quality can pervade this room, because truth is always acceptable.

Diplomats are usually accused of being in the clouds, of making pronouncements that everyone interprets as he sees fit. The criticism is sometimes justified but not always true. For my part, I will not speak to you in diplomatic language. I will tell you exactly what I think in all candour and honesty. However, I don't claim to represent Latin America. I speak, rather, in a personal capacity.

The great idea of a European union that Mr. Briand presented with such distinction is global in nature, although seemingly purely continental. In fact, solidarity cannot be strictly continental. The interests of nations are so interwoven that no economic or political measure of significance can be instituted without immediate global repercussion. That is the idea that I will try to demonstrate in this speech, with particular reference to Latin America. I will describe Latin America's situation in relation to the United States and Europe. I will do, as I said, in all candour and honesty.

Ladies and gentlemen, there is a world economy, which Professor Elemer Hantos of the University of Budapest defines as: "the sum total of national economic activities which are interdependent and interconnected."

There is no doubt that this world economy is a reality, founded on the inter-dependence of nations and on international economic solidarity. That economic crises in different countries surface at the same time is cogent testimony to that idea. A concrete demonstration that no country, however big and prosperous, can be completely inward looking and isolate itself from the rest of the world, is seen in the 1929 depression in the United States, whose deep causes can be traced to an excess wealth that the national economy could not sustain..

But it is not enough to note the existence of this world economy. We must also try to organize it according to the natural laws in each State that govern the organization of national economies through the collaboration of private enterprise and the public sector.

Such organization of the world economy is necessary, because it is undoubtedly the essential foundation of world peace. The International Economic Conference clearly sought to emphasize this point in its meeting in Geneva in 1927 when it wrote in the preamble to its general resolutions that: "the maintenance of world peace depends largely on the principles governing the design and application of national economic policies."

What principles govern the design and application of the policy of each of the countries of the world? A landmark publication of the League of Nations entitled *Memorandum on International Trade and the Balances of Payments* gives us some idea of them by providing statistical data pertaining to 64 countries. I will not attempt to analyze the publication in this presentation. I must, however, mention its very important lesson, which is that very wide disparities in working conditions and production from country to country are used to justify protectionist tendencies and have created and now maintain a competition which is an obstacle to the free movement of goods and to a perfect balance between productivity and consumption. This competition, which has given rise to a race for uncontrolled tariff increases as dangerous as an arms race, must be replaced by a system of collaboration which, above all, provides more rational and equitable bases for the free movement of goods internationally.

The League of Nations fully appreciates that this task of reorganization is principally its own and therefore is increasing initiatives for the establishment of economic harmony among nations. It behoves me to classify among those initiatives, which are under the aegis of the League of Nations, the proposal of the French Minister of Foreign Affairs for a political and economic assembly in the manner of the Locarno meeting of 1925, involving all the nations of Europe.

Whether currently feasible or not, Mr. Briand's proposal represents a very serious attempt at organization of the world economy, an attempt undertaken in one of the most divided parts of the world and where such division is the main weakness faced.

In his memorandum and today in his very eloquent speech, the author of this ambitious proposal was very careful to assert that the dream of a European union is not directed against anyone. We do believe him. Nevertheless, it cannot be denied that one of the desired goals, if not one of the stated goals, is to free Europe from the financial and economic imperialism of the United States.

Does such imperialism exist? It does, indubitably. Whatever name we give to the economic and financial might of the United States, we must agree that it controls world affairs. The American writer, Mr. Hiram Motherwell, was quite right in giving the title *The Imperial Dollar* to a book in which he discusses this advantageous position of the United States in world economy ...

The United States owe their economic and financial dominance to the wonderful resources of their soil and subsoil, as well as to the remarkable energy of a people who have been able to push human effort to the limit as they transformed these natural resources into vast and varied wealth.

However, we would not be belittling American worth if we recognized that their present prosperity is largely the result of the last war. It can be said that they more than others were the greatest profiteers of that war, taking the word profiteer in its best sense. But such prosperity has dangers and the crisis of the end of 1929 seems to be a serious warning for the United States.

In his message to Congress on the 3rd of December last, President Hoover attributed the stock market panic to "excessive optimism manifested in reckless market speculation."[1] We need to go further, perhaps, and see in the stock market collapse of the past year, a result of the situation created in the United States by credit inflation and overproduction, taking place against the background of domestic consumption which seems to have reached saturation point. The financial and economic policy practised in the United States has led to a staggering accumulation of capital which cannot be expended in that country, as well as to massive production exceeding domestic consumer needs, a production sustained through the fear of unemployment. *The United States is therefore constrained to find outlets for its capital and production ...*

It can therefore be easily understood why Europe, whose economic life is particularly threatened by North-American expansion and the increasing industrialization of the British Commonwealth countries, is attempting to resist American dominance by marshalling its strengths through a continental economic plan that it is trying to define feverishly. Its success in this area spells the definite restriction of its North-American imports. Furthermore, as Europe's productivity resumes after the war, the United States cannot hope to increase its exports to the continent. Latin America is therefore becoming its greatest hope. The possibilities are limitless in Latin America: a territory of 8 million square miles, double that of Europe; a population of 85 million that is increasing steadily; 20 young, enthusiastic republics fired by the idea of liberty and progress and aspiring to wealth and well-being.

What economic relations exist presently between the United States and Latin America? What policy should the United States pursue with Latin America for the future development and strengthening of those relations?

In an excellent World Peace Foundation publication entitled *Investments of United States capital in Latin America*, Dr. Max Winkler showed the extent of these relations up to 1928. The following figures are from that publication: In 1913, Latin American total foreign trade stood at 3 billion dollars; in 1927 5 billion dollars, an increase of 71%. In 1913, American foreign trade with Latin America was 816 million dollars. This rose to 1,782 million dollars in 1927, an increase of 118%. American capital investments in Latin America stood at approximately 1,242 million dollars. Today, they are more than 5 billion dollars.

Inter-American solidarity is therefore not merely an expression, but rather a concrete reality supported by a colossal mass of primary resources and wealth of all kinds.

So Latin America needs the United States as much as the United States needs Latin America. Indeed, the United States gets a good portion of the raw materials and agricultural products necessary for its industry and for its food supply from Latin America. Furthermore, as I have said, their industrial output, stimulated by the war, already exceeds the rate of domestic consumption by 15% and this excess is becoming more and more pronounced.

The only solution to this dangerous overproduction is the extension of the American market. But the term "extension" is not to be taken to mean *territorial expansion*. Market extension means the acquisition of a clientele with high purchasing power and an absorption capacity capable of increasing in proportion to industrial production. The most immediate priority of the United States is therefore to increase the purchasing power of its Latin American clientele, a region which is a source of raw material and a consumer of manufactured products.

How can Latin America's purchasing power be increased? Through the development of its production capacity. Where will most of the capital necessary for that development, for the exploitation of its vast natural resources, come from? From the Americans who, debtors before the war, are today the greatest creditors and lenders worldwide.

But here the most delicate issue arises, one which dominates the whole future of international relations. Credit, in its etymological sense, is synonymous with trust. When you lend money to someone, you have confidence in his morality, his solvency, in the worth of the guarantees that he can offer. *But the borrower must also have confidence in the lender*: the confidence that the lender isn't harbouring any notion of monopoly as an ulterior motive, any notion of conquest, of violent seizure of his assets, denial of his liberty, his rights. He must have confidence that the money loaned isn't a trap in which he could lose his shirt and his very life.

Now it must be admitted that there is a lack of trust on both sides. American lenders – those who are only after economic gain – are afraid of investing their money in struggling companies or in companies that are not really aiming for an increase in wealth. For their part, Latin-American borrowers, in a kind of fleeting image, see the American army and navy or the formidable silhouette of giant American battleships, behind every Yankee capitalist.

This reciprocal mistrust must be eliminated by a policy of candour and honesty as well as close collaboration between all businessmen of the American continent.

Pan-American conferences and international conferences of major international associations based in the United States regularly bring together in an atmosphere of conviviality and good will, those persons who are highly interested in the strengthening of the bonds of trust and peace between the countries of the Americas. Such persons can therefore suggest the most appropriate ways of infusing the economy of that continent with a moral base and a solid policy, that policy being *the strict application of the principle of the legal equality of the 21 sovereign states of the Americas and the absolute respect of their independence.*

The question of investment of capital overseas is one of the most difficult to resolve. This is because armed or diplomatic intervention can occur as a result of financial breaches, a phenomenon dubbed "financial aggression" by a Latin-American writer.

The recommended policy in this regard was brilliantly outlined by Mr. Hoover in his speech to the third Pan-American Trade Conference. Then American Secretary of Trade, Mr. Hoover asked governments to pledge not to approve loans to countries for military purposes, for arms, for wasteful projects or for useless spending. His comments were so categorical that the next day, the Department of State issued a release in which the United States seemed to disassociate itself from them. Now that Mr. Hoover occupies the presidency of the United States, *it is highly desirable that his very wise comments take the form of an international agreement.*

On the occasion of the anniversary of the Armistice, the 11th of November, 1929, President Hoover spoke in a particularly eloquent style about peace and freedom of the seas, stating that fear is the most dangerous of national emotions. There is a pervasive fear of the United States in Latin America, and that fear will continue as long as United States' policy in Latin America is not formulated in a manner that leaves no room for abusive interpretation or abusive application.

The Monroe Doctrine, originally designed to protect the American continent from European designs, has in the course of time been given interpretations that make it a threat for those it claims to protect. Touted by the American government as an instrument of exclusive national policy, it has become, according to an English writer, "a blank cheque on which the State Department writes the amount that it wishes." And so we have Theodore Roosevelt's interpretation, which accords to the United States the power of international policeman never given to any other country or sovereign state by international law.

Mr. J. Reuben Clark, former Assistant Secretary of State, restored the original interpretation of the doctrine and it is generally believed that this interpretation conforms to the present views of the government in Washington as well as to the personal sentiments of Mr. Hoover and Mr. Stimson. *But for how long?* It is that uncertainty that must be dispelled in order to re-establish lost trust, which can only be done through the adoption of a policy of non-intervention which leaves no room for misinterpretation and which becomes a positive rule of American international law, or rather, of international law pure and simple. I can't imagine an international law that is only continental. In this regard, it is regrettable that the formula adopted by the Conference of American Lawyers held in Rio de Janeiro in April 1927 was not accepted by the 6th Pan-American Conference in Havana.

But lovely declarations are nothing compared with deeds. *As long as the military occupation of the Haitian Republic continues – legally unjustifiable and relying on a treaty imposed on the Haitian people by force – fear and mistrust will continue among the peoples of the Americas.*

As we have seen, this fear and mistrust is a barrier to commerce and a threat to peace. Mr. Victor M. Cutter told the Third Pan-American Trade Conference: "*We business men know that from an economic point of view imperialism is a failure.*" The case of Haiti is a cogent illustration of this.

Haiti wants to be rich. All of Latin America wants to be rich. But those countries will not accept wealth with dishonour. We know what can be expected from having science and technology. All of us aspire to comfort and well-being. But we place certain realities above material wealth. These are individual freedom, national independence and racial dignity. We are willing to labour, but we will do so "hitching our wagon to a star", to use a phrase by Ralph Waldo Emerson.

Strengthening the links between the members of the pan-American community in a union founded on friendship, trust and mutual respect doesn't mean positing that community as a war machine opposing legitimate political and economic interest groups which may exist in other parts of the world. We need only examine the foreign trade statistics of Latin American countries to be convinced of the close solidarity which links us, for example, to Europe, a region whose economic recovery is essential to the stability of our affairs. It was for this reason that I considered it a privilege to lay the following resolution before the 3rd Pan-American Trade Conference, which received unanimous approval:

"Recognizing the economic solidarity of all the nations of the world, the Third Pan-American Trade Conference presents its warmest wishes to the International Economic Conference convened in Geneva under the auspices of the League of Nations, and expresses the hope that the deliberations of the conference will bring about favourable conditions for European reconstruction and for the improvement of living conditions in countries everywhere."

That resolution is the best conclusion that I can give to my presentation. What we want is peace and happiness for all, guaranteed by the collaboration of all; collaboration between the citizens of given country, collaboration between social classes, between nations, between races. And we are here pledging our enthusiastic support for Mr. Briand, who has tried to ensure that this collaboration exists between the countries of Europe.

The desire for international peace is considered an impossible dream, a utopia, as madness. Those who dare speak of universal peace are called mad. On the contrary, the mad people are those who speak of war. The real criminals are those who pit nation against nation so that they will continue slaughtering each other. Mad people are put away. A way should be found to make it impossible for criminals to hurt. I hope that a day will come when all civilized states will consider the act of inciting to war a premeditated crime punishable by law.

What Mr. Briand is trying to do is also done by the scientist in his laboratory. What is a scientific hypothesis but an anticipation of the future, the coordination of phenomena not yet well known? The scientist leaves the *terra firma* of reality to aspire to the creation of a new order which must be tested. Scientific hypothesis is a provisional explanation which will eventually die. Its death takes two forms. The hypothesis may be contradicted by data and therefore disappears, or may be supported by data, in which case it also disappears, becoming a truth, a scientific law.

Mr. Briand has left the *terra firma* of historical experiment and has designed a new order, a European order. His idea can die in two ways: it can come up against insurmountable opposition, becoming inoperable, or with the support of all, can become one of the greatest achievements of our time.

Whether the proposal for a European federation becomes a shining reality depends on you, the people and Governments of Europe.

Dantès Bellegarde

Note

Editor's Note: Hoover's exact words were actually "The long upward trend of fundamental progress, however, gave rise to over-optimism as to profits, which translated itself into a wave of uncontrolled speculation in securities, resulting in the diversion of capital from business to the stock market and the inevitable crash." Herbert Hoover, "State of the Union address", 3 December 1929 [http://www.infoplease.com/t/hist/state-of-the-union/141.html]

A Preliminary Analysis of the Years 1932–1934

Jacques Roumain
Translated by Bernadette Farquhar

THE COLLAPSE OF THE NATIONALIST MYTH

The most significant development and the most instructive, was the collapse of the Haitian nationalist myth between 1932 and 1934. So, what is Haitian nationalism?

Haitian nationalism is certainly born of the American occupation of that country. But it would be a mistake to see it merely as a sentimental reaction. Haitian nationalism sprang from the forced labour re-established on our soil by the invading troops, from the massacre of over 3,000 proletarian Haitian peasants and from the dispossession of Haitian peasants by large American companies.

Haitian nationalism therefore has its roots in the suffering of the masses, in their economic deprivation made more acute by American imperialism and their struggle against forced labour and dispossession. Whatever the sentimental surface manifestation of these struggles, they are probably a relic history, but are nevertheless a profound and conscious anti-imperialism having as its tenet the formulation of economic demands. They are very much a mass movement.

During the massacre of peasants in the north of the country and in Artibonite and the Central Plateau, the Haitian bourgeoisie happily played hosts to the leaders of the assassins in the drawing rooms of Haiti's fashionable circles and at home. It was a willing accomplice of the Occupation, working for it, crawling at the feet of the masters, looking for favours such as the presidency or posts in the civil service. Some received favours, others did not. That dissatisfaction was the beginning of bourgeois opposition.

The parallel between Saint-Domingue and the present-day Haitian Republic is striking in terms of the relationship between the social classes: the American imperialists are the French colonists of yesterday, today's bourgeoisie the freed slaves and today's proletariat the slaves.

This thesis will be analyzed in detail in a subsequent publication. At the moment, we will concentrate on the following ideas. Since they lived by the exploitation of the enslaved population, the freed slaves could not contemplate its freedom. They sought only their own rights. In 1915, the Haitian bourgeoisie lived from the oppression of the masses and could therefore not make their cause its own. A natural and historical accomplice of imperialism, it merely demanded the continuation of its own privileges and the granting of new emoluments under the Occupation. The satisfied faction collaborated "**honestly and faithfully**" while the other faction revolted.

Let me say once again that I am speaking in terms of class and not in terms of persons. There were traitors and sincere combatants in all camps. However, considered as a whole or, better, in terms of class, the bourgeoisie betrayed and the proletariat resisted.

What informed this opposition on the part of the frustrated bourgeoisie? The masses had serious economic grievances. The right to plunder was the economic grievance of the bourgeoisie. But of course, it could not own up to this. Initially, its nationalism was verbal. Its newspapers raised vehement laments and churned out millions of well known jingoistic clichés such as "**Our ancestors, sublime beggars of 1804**", etc, etc.

A few fines and some imprisonments discouraged that to a certain degree, so that the bourgeoisie then turned its attention to the anti-imperialist masses, pretending to defend their rights, to support their protest against taxes. It spoke solemnly about the destiny of our race, the same race that it despises and is ashamed of. The masses listened and followed and Haitian nationalism was born. The bourgeoisie as the avant-garde of the proletariat. Unbelievable!

Let's define this nationalism. It is the shameless exploitation by a politically scheming bourgeoisie of the anti-imperialist masses, for private motives.

From 1915 to 1930, an incessant battle against the Occupation and its Haitian underlings continued despite massacres, beatings and incarcerations. It reached its high point in 1930 when President Borno, honest and faithful collaborator, left the government. The masses, a powerful lever, then brought the nationalists to power.

With the arrival of the nationalists to power, the disintegration of nationalism began, a phenomenon easy to explain: at its base, this nationalism was anti-imperialist and therefore anti-capitalist, while its upper echelon was made up of the bourgeoisie and petite bourgeoisie. The movement therefore contained internal contradictions doomed to destroy it. The nationalist movement could not keep its promises, since the promises of the bourgeois nationalists, upon their ascension to power, conflicted with their class interests, proving to be electoral deception.

As a result, the law on retail trade was promptly buried, because the class interests of the exploiting minority and therefore of the Haitian State, are linked to those of international capitalism. The Jolibois-Cauvin bill suffered the same fate. Small alcohol producers continued to close their distilleries, agricultural labourers continued working 10 to 12 hours per day for one and a half piastres. The crippling taxes on goods continued, as did the merciless exploitation of workers. Furthermore, no consideration was given at all to reinstating the peasants dispossessed of their land by large American companies. Hence the collapse of Haitian nationalism. Most of the working class now understands the lie of bourgeois nationalism. Increasingly, that class links the idea of the anti-imperialist struggle to the idea of class struggle. More and more, it realizes that to fight against imperialism is to fight against foreign or domestic capitalism, is to fight tooth and nail against the Haitian bourgeoisie and bourgeois politicians, lackeys of imperialism, cruel exploiters of workers and peasants.

COLOUR AND CLASS PREJUDICE[1]

Colour prejudice is an unavoidable reality. It would be clever but fallacious argument to consider it as a moral problem. Colour prejudice is the sentimental expression of class conflict, of the class struggle, the psychological reaction of an economic and historical phenomenon, the unbridled exploitation of the Haitian masses by the bourgeoisie. As the misery of the workers and peasants reaches its height and the proletarianization of the petite bourgeoisie continues at a furious pace, it is important to note that the resurgence of this age-old question. For the Haitian Communist Party, the question of colour prejudice is of primordial importance, that prejudice being the mask behind which black and mulatto politicians try to hide class struggle. The issue has been raised in various manifestos circulating lately under cover. These manifestos reveal in a sentimental way certain truths which are really economic and therefore social and political and also reveal the impoverishment of the middle class, the causes of which are examined below in a critique of the manifesto of the group "La Réaction Démocraique." For the moment we will simply point out that the social, economic and political degradation of blacks is not merely the result of colour prejudice. The simple truth is that a black proletariat and a largely black petite bourgeoisie are mercilessly oppressed by a crippled minority, which is the largely mulatto bourgeoisie proletarianized by a huge international industry.

As we have seen, we are dealing with economic oppression which manifests itself socially and politically. The real root of the problem is therefore the class struggle. The Haitian Communist Party (HCP) addresses the problem scientifically, fully aware, nevertheless, of the validity of the psychological reactions of the black population, wounded in its dignity by the foolish contempt of the mulattos, an attitude which is merely the social expression of economic oppression perpetrated by the bourgeoisie.

But the duty of the HCP, a party which by the way is 98% black, being a workers party in which the colour question is stripped systematically of any consideration of pigmentation and placed in the context of the class struggle, is to warn the proletariat, the poor sections of the petite bourgeoisie as well as the black intellectual workers against black bourgeois politicians who would exploit their justified anger to their own advantage. They must be imbued with the reality of the class struggle, which colour prejudice tends to efface. A black bourgeois is not better than a mulatto or a white bourgeois and a black bourgeois politician is as vile as his white or mulatto counterpart. The motto of the HCP is:

AGAINST BLACK, MULATTO AND WHITE BOURGEOIS CAPITALIST SOLIDARITY: ONE UNITED PROLETARIAN FRONT INDIFFERENT TO COLOUR DISTINCTION

The petite-bourgeoisie should ally itself with the proletariat, because it is being proletarianized more and more by bourgeois and imperialist exploitation.

The HCP, applying its watch word "Colour is nothing, class is everything", calls on the masses to join the class struggle under its banner. By itself, a merciless battle against a capitalist Haitian bourgeoisie that is mostly mulato with a black minority, a battle free of any consideration of pigmentation and placed in the context of the class struggle, can eliminate privileges which are the fruit of oppression and exploitation, eradicating not only colour prejudice, but also the social, economic and political degradation which it entails

The belief that a new society can be built with State assistance as easily as a railroad can be built is quite typical of the presumptuous thinking of Lassalle.

Karl Marx, *Critique of the Gotha Programme*

MANIFESTO OF THE GROUP *LA RÉACTION DÉMOCRATIQUE*

Some time ago, a small booklet appeared in Port-au-Prince under the title *Manifeste de la Réaction Démocratique* (the RD). Of twenty or so pages, it presents the point of view of its authors – a few young people – and their disciples, on the Haitian problem. The booklet is characterized by a general muddled thinking and a dangerous tendency towards political idealism that must be ruthlessly exposed. This will be done here very succinctly under the following headings:

    a.   The *Réaction Démocratique* and the organization of a Rational National Economy.
    b.   The *Réaction Démocratique* and its Concept of the State.
    c.   The *Réaction Démocratique* and the Class Struggle.
    d.   The *Réaction Démocratique* and the Race question.
    e.   The *RéactionDémocratique* and the Question of Imperialism
    f.   The General Tendencies of the *Réaction Démocratique*.
    g.   The *Réaction Démocratique* and the Labour Question..

A. The *Réaction Démocratique* and the Organization of a Rational National Economy

As is to be expected, economics occupies the major part of the manifesto: the *Réaction Démocratique* is obviously interventionist. And of course, the group isn't afraid of collectivization. On page 7 of the booklet we read: "The treasury will invest the necessary funds in large plantations for the cultivation of export crops **FOR IDENTIFIED MARKETS.** It will provide those plantations with the equipment necessary for export packaging, for the benefit of the entire region." It also talks about tractors to pull the poor peasant struggling on a small plot of land, out of a deadly routine. Even a rural centre of civilization was planned: "Next to each plantation, the State will build a hamlet comprising a school, a store, a dispensary, a church and a cinema."

You have to admire the boldness of the *Réaction Démocratique*. However, a detailed examination of these ideas soon reveals that a <u>fundamental</u> question, one which determines the worth of these fancy plans, has been avoided. That question is the relationship between these state farms and the strictly private large companies. Conflict is inevitable between these two forms of enterprise. They are naturally conflicting and in the final analysis private capitalist enterprise will always take a dim view of state interference in the economy, unless such interference takes place with its approval and ultimately to its advantage. This fundamental question was evaded, and deliberately so, because this little fragment of a sentence says volumes about the *Réaction Démocratique*: "Small businesses allied to the State will be aided and protected by the State, <u>because in a country of such limited resources it would be criminal to stifle private enterprise</u>. The emphasis on the latter part of the sentence is ours. The sentence is like a slip of the tongue, occurring where it was least expected. Not surprising! At least, it allows us to identify the position of the *Réaction Démocratique* on the fundamental, decisive question of the private ownership of the means of production and trade, such as land, mines and equipment. The *Réaction Démocratique* sticks to its position and that makes it a party of the right. But it doesn't do so outright, of course, nor does it tackle the problem head on. The editor of the manifesto is clever and counts on the political naiveté of the public. So it is done very subtly and delicately as if unintentionally, in a seemingly innocent sentence fragment surrounded by very pleasant words, appearing under the guise of the protection of "the small businesses allied to the State."

But the *Réaction Démocratique* is careful to inform that "it would be criminal to stifle private enterprise." It does so without further elucidation, an indication that it is putting in the same enclosure the hound and hare, the Haitian American Sugar Company (HASCO)and the small Haitian distillery that is being proletarianized; the Haitian American Sugar Company, Alfred Vieux[2] and the small landowner of the plains who has been dispossessed of his lands. So under the trappings and the suits of private enterprise, the *Réaction Démocratique* is trying to pass off a very cumbersome package, which is the capitalist private ownership of the means of production and trade.

And that trick, although done in the name of the "small businesses allied to the State," is in reality completely against them. The successes of HASCO, of Pettigrew and of the Pineapple Company at the detriment of the peasant masses are maintained purely and simply "because it would be criminal to stifle private enterprise", even when this private enterprise translates into the right of the strongest to gobble up the weakest or even to make a meal of them very quietly, as in the case of HASCO and Pettigrew. In reality, the *Réaction Démocratique* radically suppresses the creative initiative of the "small businesses allied to the State" and of the peasant class in general, by endorsing their legal dispossession through the rewards granted to uncontrolled private enterprise, the result of which is that they become social outcasts. But this problem can be solved radically, through the socialization and use of land for the good of all, in reference to those state farms identified by the *Réalité Démocratique*. This must be done in a systematic way, however, and with the reduction of the size of the uncontrolled private sector, a long and arduous task probably not to the liking of the *Réaction Démocratique*. To quote Max Hudicourt, you have to be in power to make things happen.

We will now examine two of the significant results of capitalist private ownership, and we do mean capitalist.

a.   The technical aspect of management of the economy

Any State intervention to rationalize the economy is an unattainable goal because of private ownership of the means of production and trade. This is because the only behaviour acceptable to capitalist private enterprise is the mad race for profit, profit at all costs, even at the expense of a rational production programme. Politically speaking, the mixed economy advocated by the *République Démocratique* can only lead to fascism and to a chaotic production plan coupled with its logical result, regular crises and unemployment.

b.   The social aspect

The maintenance of capitalist ownership results in a monopoly of national economic resources to the benefit of the international bourgeoisie and the Haitians in its service. The vast majority of the country's assets will therefore be in the hands of a monopoly comprising HASCO, Pettigrew and a handful of Haitian families who are large property owners. This private control of the country's resources nullifies any serious programme of social regeneration, because of the lack of funds. To cite one example of our major problems, no serious reform of the education system to make education truly free <u>by guaranteeing the supply of food and drink and the usual personal school supplies</u> is possible without the prerequisite socialization of the economy so that resources can be used for the benefit of all instead of being monopolized by a minority.

B. The *Réaction Démocratique* and its Concept of the State

There was a time when one concept of the State was predominant. It held that all power comes from God. Except Soviet power, the parish priest is careful to add even today. That is the concept of power by divine right. But this very convenient theory has been smashed to smithereens by the development of scientific thinking and so another idea of the State had to be found. Bourgeois intellectuals are never short of ideas. But all these ideas saw the State as some ethereal entity having no basis in reality.

Karl Marx easily dismantled all these idealist theories, to show that the State refers to a relationship between real and objective social forces and that in a class society, the State represents, <u>in real terms</u>, the mandatory regulation of the dominant class.

As is to be expected, the *Réaction Démocratique* didn't consider it necessary to explain what the State is, the State that must participate in the country's production. It probably considered that unnecessary. We will now demonstrate to them the primordial importance of such an explanation, taking as our point of departure an important aspect of their programme, which is the position they take on the relationship between capital and labour.

On page 19 the Manifesto states:

> **"The State must therefore intervene in this area as well to protect the working classes against harsh labour laws, whether instituted by the individual or by the State. The worker cannot be expected to work in dangerous conditions, etc."**

In other words, the *Réaction Démocratique* seems to be making the following proposals to management: 1) adoption of the regular work day; 2) adoption of legislation governing accidents at work, etc. This is another way of saying that they are going to ask for huge sacrifices and for the surrender of a very wide profit margin. But has the *Réaction Démocratique* considered the inevitable reaction of management when faced with these measures, which threaten their sacrosanct profit margins?

The goodly gentlemen will probably reply that the State will keep HASCO, Pettigrew, the National Bank, Brandt and others in check. But suppose the State is in collusion with HASCO, Pettigrew, the National Bank, Brandt, etc? These gentlemen of the *Réaction Démocratique* are nationalists fiercely ensconced in things strictly Haitian, but were they to forget their petit-bourgeois prejudice and cast an eye back on the history of the triumphs of the working class internationally in relation to labour legislation, they would observe that the proletariat had to engage in fierce struggles in order to gain recognition of its rights that they now propose to summon miraculously from the sky. Furthermore, they would notice that the working class has had to struggle hard and continues to struggle hard to retain the gains it has made. Whenever the bourgeois State has taken part in a struggle it has always been through fear of working class pressure. The *Réaction Démocratique* is interested only in things specifically Haitian. We are therefore not surprised in the least that, like the unspeakable Mr. Alix Mathon, it dismisses the idea of the class struggle, presumably because, to quote Mathon the influence peddler, "The economy doesn't exist." We can assure the *Réaction Démocratique* nevertheless that it is wrong, dead wrong.

One of two things is possible. Perhaps the *Réaction Démocratique* will pursue its demands for workers rights to the end, in which case it will come up against an irreparably hostile bourgeois front determined to do its utmost to get revenge on this upstart, namely, the *Réaction Démocratique*. This bourgeois front will be all the more dangerous as the minority Haitian ownership class will be at its command. Furthermore, HASCO, the National Bank, Petttigrew and Reimbold will call the tune, with all the effects of competition and foreign imperialism that that entails. Indeed, Wall Street will call the tune: we musn't ever forget that our economy is three fourths colonial in nature. Ostensibly a movement to defend its demands and those of the Haitian masses (We insist on the term the Haitian masses), the programme of the *Réaction Démicratique* will turn out to be a movement of a national proletariat uneducated about the class struggle, which as far as we are concerned is being confused with the anti-imperialist struggle. The movement will therefore be easily circumvented by local politicians looking for handouts and will be willingly exploited by foreigners. A dirty trick will be played spelling the end of the *Réaction Démocratique*. The repression could even be a bloody one in the name of law and order, meant to serve as an example once and for all.

The second possibility is that the *Réaction Démocratique* will retract its proletarian demands and instead trot out some piece of paper full of good intentions that are sentimental to the hilt, in which it will explain what we have always stated. What we stated when the Labour Bill by Jolibois and Cauvin and all the other parliamentarians sleeping in the archives of our two Houses of Parliament, a bill that was rather incomplete and idealistic, had to be shot down. We demonstrated that the profit margins reported by the goodly gentlemen of the so called national industries (HASCO, Pettigrew, and Brandt) are too small and that the national proletariat has the right to expect better.

It goes without saying that the section of the Haitian proletariat which might be won over by the *Réaction Démocratique* will soon acknowledge the existence of the class struggle, so that when the next political crisis arises, that section will assume a real class position and send that old bourgeois political machine, the *Réaction Démocratique,* to the rubbish heap.

The preceding illustrates that the main criticism to be made of the *Réaction Démocratique* is that in preparing its political programme, it failed to take account of the class struggle. The class struggle is a given based on capitalist ownership of the means of production by a minority, rather than on an arbitrary concept formulated by those damned Marxists! Because of the nature of its programme, the *Réaction Démocratique* is forced to reconcile on paper ideas that are irreconcilable in reality. It finds itself adrift in a sea of political illusionism, preparing rude awakenings for the national proletariat, should the proletariat become its recruits. Given the primordial importance of the class struggle, we shall now examine that question more closely.

C. The *Réaction Démocratique* and the Class Struggle

On the question of the class struggle, which is a most vital issue and the corner stone of any political programme, the *Réaction Démocratique* took a position, a timid one to be sure, in one of its little delightful literary sentences attesting to years of mental paralysis:

> "No social class has the privilege of virtue or of moral decay for that matter. Alas, social barriers have nothing to do with corrupt nature. Despite the caste inequalities caste observable on the surface, the entire human race is characterized by a deep-seated layer of selfishness and ferocity."

So, what's the conclusion of this bit of lyricism? It is, quite simply, let's leave things as they are, because it would be dangerous to "develop a class philosophy." Dangerous for "democratic balance", says the *Réaction Démocratique*. The term is incomprehensible. We interpret it here in the only way possible: dangerous for the tightrope walkers of bourgeois democracy and their juggling act, who will be mercilessly swept away by the proletariat of tomorrow, that will be more informed, swept away along with their ideological claptrap! Note, by the way, the harmony between the *Réaction Démocratique* and the group *La Relève* in the denial of the existence of the class struggle and therefore of the reality of class in Haiti. In that harmony, the attention-seeking quarrel between young and old disappears, as do the little tea-party differences between the goodly gentlemen of the leadership of *La Relève*.

That point made, it would be useful to give these gentlemen a little lesson in Marxist sociology. On the question of social class, the *Réaction Démocratique* makes blunders worthy of Leroy-Beaulieu, arguing in terms of the individual whereas Marxism argues in terms of class. It goes without saying that in any social class there are honest people as well as crooks. Even the bourgeoisie has members who are not only honest but also heroic, among them Marx and Engels, to name the greatest. This dual makeup of the social classes might suggest, incidentally, that those members of the Haitian bourgeoisie who have taken up the cause of the proletariat should be accused of insincerity. Far from it. Something entirely different is at issue here.

At any period of the history of a class society – and a capitalist society is a class society whether developed or not – there exists a class whose interests coincide with the general welfare of the society, a class which can espouse any clearly progressive programme which has something to offer it. We refer to the exploited class, the class which has to demand justice and which by nature espouses any evolutionary trend which aims to change the status quo. On the other hand, the dominant class, precisely because of its dominance, rejects as a class any major change, simply because any major change would affect its privileges as a class, because the status quo is the status quo in its favour. By considering this general law on the development of class societies in historical terms, particularly in terms of the history of Haiti, we hope to at least to destroy the pitiful ideological structure of the goodly gentlemen of the *Réaction Démocratique*, a structure worthy of Leroy-Beaulieu himself, if not convert them.[3]

On the eve of the Haitian war of independence, there were three classes in *Saint-Domingue*: the colonists, the freed slaves and the slaves. From a bourgeois point of view, the colonists were most certainly the "civilized" class. It had the privilege of birth, good breeding, "good manners" and all the rest. Its class interests represented nevertheless the most horrible combination of obscurantism in the direct enslavement of man by man and the retention of the slave trade.

As for the class of freed slaves, it had something to ask of history, which was the satisfaction of its political and economic demands. However, its class interests were very much circumscribed, because it, too, practised slavery, was rich and had no intention of shouldering the demands of mankind in general. It was indeed a rather reactionary class, somewhat progressive only in terms of its own interests. In fact, it called first of all for equality for itself and itself alone, as in the case of the Ogé and Chavanne uprising and the Suisse massacre.[4]

It was the large proletarian masses, victims of slavery, that had everything to ask of history. They did so and supported the most radical movement possible during that period of history, which was the independence movement. The large slave population waged war because its class interests were at stake. The freemen joined the slave revolt as a way of choosing the lesser of two evils. The choice was between maintaining a system giving them the right to own slaves and the maintenance of a system which denied them all the rights of a citizen.

And now as we examine contemporary Haitian society to determine which class is unreservedly progressive, it can easily be seen that it is the organized national proletariat alone that can pursue to the end a radical reform of immense proportion, because its interests are at stake and because presently, those interests merge with the general interest of all concerned.

Since we live in a country suffering from intellectual paralysis, it would be useful to describe the characteristics of the national proletariat. Now a given social class is identified not by its colour but by the position it occupies economically. The real bourgeois possesses certain considerable means of production with which he can hire the proletarian workforce. With this point of view -- the only scientific one -- and taking into account the status of the large majority of the black and mulatto families of Haiti, it can easily be seen that this country is fundamentally proletarian. This isn't surprising, given that the economy of the country is three fourths colonial. Haiti is nothing but a fief of Great International Capitalism, more precisely of American capitalism, with or without a repurchase agreement from the so-called Haitian National Bank.

Born proletarian but suddenly become through force masters of a country of infinite riches, an authentic national bourgeoisie with its roots firmly entrenched in the economy was able to take shape, but with a very serious handicap from the beginning: a very costly independence obtained to deter any criminal undertaking on the part of the former masters; the arrival of a ruling class which, because of the nature of its formation, was not at all up to the task of governing; the inevitable development of the economic imperialism practised in the 19th century by the capitalist superpowers . It meant that the ruling class surrendered its arms without fighting! With independence, it became the country's large landowner, engaging in systematic absenteeism and playing politics. International capitalism was able to establish itself as a result, so that as we write, the only Haitian agricultural companies worthy of the name are American companies such as HASCO, Pettigrew, the Pineapple Company, the only industrial companies worthy of the name are foreign companies such as those that make ghee, the major coffee factories, the Electric Company, the Wharf Company, the ice factory. The major foreign firms are Reimbold, Siegel, Silvera and Altieri, among others. Our so-called bourgeoisie is nothing but a class of small retailers and civil servants. In other words, it is not, technically, a bourgeoisie, but rather a privileged stratum of a class that is rapidly becoming proletarian. And it shall evermore be thus.

Indeed, the proletarianization process continues at a deadly pace. In terms of the acceleration of the proletarianization movement in Haiti, the period of American occupation is quite a record. During that period, local small industries, particularly shoe making, all died out, to be replaced by technologically produced assembly line goods from the United States or elsewhere. Talk of a Haitian distillery is now only a subject of insincere electoral promises. Proletarianization was particularly striking among the peasant population. The peasant of the country's northern plain in particular has been violently separated from his means of production, to the point where he had to sell the shirt off his back, his labour mercilessly exploited.

Any attempt at economic autonomy on the part of the local population will be met with systematic opposition from our guardians. Recently, a Haitian textile group tried to organize and was brought to heel by some American advisor/financier or other.

Does that mean that the proletariat is a homogenous entity? Far from it! How could it be, when nobody took the trouble to tell it the truth, or at least to help it examine truth scientifically? The Haitian proletariat is a heterogeneous entity. Like any other proletariat, it includes certain social strata more privileged than others. The junior Bank of Canada typist is obviously more privileged when compared with the HASCO worker but their interests are the same, nevertheless. The HASCO worker and the soft, refined typist will both have to continue making their contribution to the country's capital in the form of hours of excessive work, unless a large labour front comes into being representing both of them, imposing a legal limit to the number of working hours. This difference in circumstances corresponds to a difference in the ways of seeing things, a psychological difference, which is that the non-unionized junior typist will shed tears when told that she is part of the proletariat. It is a psychological reaction typical of the petite bourgeoisie but which does not negate objective reality in any way.

The Haitian Communist Party therefore has the task of making these various social strata of the national proletariat aware that their class interests are identical and of creating a common front so that exploitative, avaricious imperialism and its accomplice, the Haitian plutocracy, are forced to surrender their ill-gotten gains. We wish to stress that this collective movement must first take place among the poorest of the proletariat, the class which, once educated, is most worthy of taking the struggle to its very end, which is emancipation. Emancipation from avaricious imperialism and its Haitian lackeys.

D. The *Réaction Démocratique* and the Question of Imperialism

The *Réaction Démocratique* hasn't considered the imperialism question worthy of special attention. Of course, here and there in their manifesto, we can identify any number of little sentences that are seemingly anti-imperialist, at best nationalist! Even these goodly gentlemen speak of economic self sufficiency. But they neglect to tell us if they will take their provisional point of view to its full, logical conclusion. We have already pointed out the attitude, ambiguous at least, of the *Réaction Démocratique* towards the large capitalist firms operating in Haiti. These gentlemen seem not to have understood that such firms are the outposts of Wall Street and that any action against imperialism will inevitably target the said firms.

We note in this regard the inexcusable muddled thinking of the *Réaction Démocratique*, whose goodly members didn't take the trouble to carry out a serious, scientific analysis of the imperialist question. Presumably, they subscribe to the nationalist, petite bourgeoisie view of imperialism as primarily a sentimental offshoot of nationalism. These fine gentlemen are nationalists who secretly admire the Dominican Republic and dream of their glorious entry into that country. Uncle Sam is in Haiti? Oh well! That's a reaction resulting from the insurmountable pressure of the purest nationalist sentiments. Sorry, but we have no intention whatsoever of following their example, however attractive it seems.

Clearly, because of their confused assessment of imperialism, these gentlemen have been singing the praises of the concept of private enterprise with a big "E" while failing to indicate if they are talking about enterprise as exemplified by Pettigrew and HASCO, companies that have dispossessed peasants and ruined small brewers.

It is impossible to address the imperialism question without a scientific study of its economic basis. Imperialism is above all a requirement of large capitalist economies. Large capitalist economies have carved the world into private zones, their zones of influence. North Africa is the preserve of France, India the preserve of England and the West Indies the preserve of the United States. On the world's capitalist chessboard, we are countries in a dead end position, colonial countries subject to the laws of the Grand Master King Capital. Any serious anti-imperialist attitude must of necessity be ruthlessly anti-capitalist. But presumably, for these gentlemen of the *Réaction Démocratique*, the small Haitian who through countless sacrifices manages to set aside a few hundred cents, is a capitalist!

Whatever the case, on a question of such capital importance, the position of the *Réaction Démocratique* is solidly defeatist. In spite of its statements, which by the way are the same in any "programme" set out by our "great leaders" in 1930 and at any other time, the *Réaction Démocratique* is always keeping time to someone else's music. We, on the other hand, have insisted on keeping our own time.

E. The *Réaction Démocratique* and the Race Question

Their manifesto declares: "The Black race has its history, its civilization, its own spirit, its superiority. Haiti must take its place at the head of black civilization." When we examine closely this seemingly friendly declaration, we can easily show it to be a vacuous statement inappropriate to the Haitian situation and to international reality.

1.   Inappropriateness of race to explain the Haitian situation

In terms of race, the Haitian population is a virtual mosaic of all racial types ranging from mahogany black to white. And they are all Haitian, if you please. Talk of racial consciousness in Haiti is therefore sure to be met with a little smile, even with a laugh up one's sleeve depending on the political climate. And no wonder. The consciousness of which race? Asking the mulatto to forget that his ancestry is part white is as unscientific as asking the black man to forget his African ancestry. This racial consciousness generally accepted as creole in nature is therefore certain to increase our traditional colour prejudice.

There's more to it than that and this racist fashion of analyzing the colour prejudice problem in Haiti leads to a catastrophic confusion in which reality is disregarded and predator and prey, that is to say the ruling class and the ruled class, are invited to unite under the banner of consciousness. Of course, colour prejudice is not without consideration of the epidermis and furthermore, the old concept of colour prejudice persists. Thus, the exploitative black politician will exploit those of his own colour, just as the exploitative mulatto politician will. We are back to the good old days. But the *Réaction Démocratique* lacked the courage to admit that colour prejudice will only end in Haiti with the end of the shameless exploitation of the working masses by the economically and politically dominant class, mulatto in the majority with a black minority, which inevitably implies the political, economic and social destruction of the oppressive bourgeois class, which is both mulatto and black.

2.   Inappropriateness of any racist formula to explain the international situation

One need only look at the map of the world, particularly of regions near to us, to realize the threat that would be posed to a small population of 3 million if it tried to oppose all these white countries that surround us, especially America, even black America, which is certainly well intentioned towards us, but which would refuse to be considered inferior by us.

Furthermore, every national community comprises great political parties that are clearly anti-racist (communist parties) and which are in fact the only anti-imperialist parties. Up to this point, our political administration has failed to capitalize on this fact through its lack of knowledge. Any Haitian racism will be met with the marked hostility of these anti-imperialist parties. We doubt that Haitian racism will fare any better than German racism.

Can we conclude from all the preceding comments that the problem which the *Réaction Démocratique* has tried to solve does not exist, that we shouldn't be concerned about it? Not at all! Our environment is certainly afflicted by a dreadful racial inferiority complex that is colonial in original. The mulatto kowtows before any white man arriving like a thief on our shores, just because the latter's skin is white. Certain black people, especially those that are a part of the bourgeoisie because of their economic power, behave in the same manner in relation to the mulatto and the white man. This racial inferiority complex must be destroyed. We must **TEACH** the black and the mulatto to be themselves. We must teach them to respect their worth as human beings and to have that worth respected. That is all that is required. There is no need for a ridiculous racism that would create external animosity and which, internally, would lead to the continuation of political exploitation, to bourgeois political exploitation that is both black and mulatto, practised by all colours.

F. General Tendencies of the *Réaction Démocratique*

The *Réaction Démocratique* has its little prejudices, one of which it adheres to tenaciously: it likes to think that it has a very good grasp of reality, despising those who, instead of sharing its illusion of living in an ivory tower, affirm the predominance of great economic laws over national characteristics.

Given this peculiarity of the *Réaction Démocratique*, it is quite tempting to expose it for what it is, to trace its pedigree on an international level. The *Réaction Démocratique* is throwing a nice little tantrum, but it's the usual attempt to avoid objective reality by denying the existence of the class struggle, the same recourse to abstractions which pacify simply because they have no foundation in reality and in the final analysis require no commitment whatsoever, being nothing more than racial awareness, a utopian nationalism that exists in word only, and so forth. We see here the same attempt at a partial application of Marxist economics, as with the talk of starting State farms; the same attempt typical of fascist schemes, whether in the style of Hitler, Mussolini or Cil Robles, to reconcile the irreconcilable: management with workers, the bourgeoisie with the proletariat. We are dealing here with a latent fascism that has no exponent of significant stature but which must be denounced, nevertheless. The Haitian Communist Party has denounced it ruthlessly.

G. The *Réaction Démocratique* and the Labour Question

The fascinating nature of the *Réaction Démocratique* is particularly evident on the matter of trade unions. It doesn't credit Haitian workers with enough intellectual maturity to understand trade unionism, and yet it dares speak of racial pride. As a matter of fact, it denies the Haitian proletariat the right to oppose exploitation by management, to protest against starvation wages and in favour of better working conditions. Presumably, it thinks its sentimental arguments and its proposal for worker participation in profit sharing will persuade managers to soften their hearts and pry their coffers wide open to the benefit of the worker. We all know about the so-called "good-hearted "nature of management ...

> For the Central Committee of the Haitian Communist Party
> Jacques Roumain
> Member of the Central Committee

EMERGENCE OF THE HAITIAN COMMUNIST MOVEMENT M.C.H.

1934   <u>P.C.H. (*Haiti Communist Party*) The party is illegal</u>

Jacques Roumain, Secretary General 1934 – 1936
General membership: Étienne Charlier
Anthony Lepès
Chrisitan Beaulieu. Also Secretary General from 1936 and others

1945   P.S.P. (People's Socialist Party

    Declared illegal in 1948 and then dissolves.
    Etienne Charlier
    Anthony Lespès
    Christian Beaulieu
    Max Hudicourt
    Pierre L. Hudicourt
    Roger Cauvin
    Antonio Vieux
    Jules Saint-Anne
    Rossini Pierre-Louis and others

    Party newspaper: *La Nation*

1945   P.C.H. (Haitian Communist Party)

    Dissolves voluntarily in April, 1947
    Félix d'Orléans Juste Constant
      (Episcopal priest in charge of
      the parish of l'Archahaie;
      Secetary General of the party)
    Edris St. Amand
    Max Ménard
    Jacques Stéphen Alexis
    René Dépestre
    Théodore Baker
    Roger Mercier
    Francis Vulcain
    Roger Gaillard and others
    Party newspaper: *Combat*

1947   P.D.P.J.H. (*Haitian Young People's
               PopularDemocratic Party)*
    Jacques Stephen Alexis
    as Secretary General

1954   P.D.P. (People's Democratic Party)
    Founded by former members of the People's
    Socialist Party, including the traitor Roger Gaillard

1956-57   L.J.P. People's Youth League

1959   P.E.P. People's Alliance Party
    Newspapers: *La Voix du Peuple*,
    launched 27 May 1963
    Le Cerf-volant

1961   P.P.L.N. People's National Liberation Party
    Student demonstrations, Nov 1960 – March 1961
    Death of Jacques Stéphen Alexis, 1961

1963   F.D.U.L.N. United Democratic Front of the National Liberation Movement

1964 *Francs-Tireurs* (a resistance movement)   F.N.R. National Resistance Front

"Piétonville incident", July 1965

1965   <u>P.U.D.A. Haiti United Democratic Party</u> *
Party newspaper: *Demokrasi**
TRANSLATOR'S NOTE : Unlike the other party names, these are in Haitian Creole

<u>July 1966 P.T.H. Haitian Workers' Party</u>
Party newspaper: *Le Courrier Rouge*

18th January 1969   <u>P.U.C.H. Haitian United Communist Party</u>
Party newspapers: *Le Boucan*, #2   1st March 1969
Le Lambi

Notes

1. Title of a subsequent work by Comrade Roumain in which the question of colour prejudice and class struggle will be examined in detail.
2. Translator's note: *Le Nouvelliste*, a Haitian newspaper available online, carries the death announcement of a Mr. Raymond Louis Roy (15/2/1915 – 9/5/2010), who at age 23 married Fernande Vieux, "fille de l'industriel Alfred Vieux, lequel aura été un de ses mentors". Alfred Vieux, father of Fernande Vieux, was therefore a businessman, and quite an influential one: a school and other landmarks in Haiti bear his name.
3. Translator's note: Possibly Pierre Paul Leroy-Beaulieu, 1843-1916, a French economist, or his brother Henri Jean Baptiste Anatole Leroy-Beaulieu, 1842-1912.
4. Translator's note: In August, 1791, a group of freemen and slaves calling themselves *les Suisses* set fire to a cane field in Port-au-Prince, killing or wounding hundreds of whites.

Appeal to the United Nations Conference on International Organization on Behalf of the Caribbean Peoples

Richard B. Moore

West Indies National Council. Submitted to the United Nations Conference at its founding, San Francisco, May 25, 1945. Richard B. Moore Papers.

To this historic Assembly of Delegates of the United Nations met to lay the foundations of World Security and Peace, the Caribbean Peoples which are still held as colonial dependencies now look with eager hope and confident expectation. In this Conference these peoples see the great opportunity never before afforded by history for the adoption at last of those democratic principles and the establishment of effective means of enforcement which will enable them to realize their long sought goal and inalienable human rights to freedom, security, and self-government along with all the liberty-loving nations of the world.

Events preceding and during this war have shown that security and peace depend upon organization which will ensure justice, equal rights and protection to all peoples, to small and weak nations as well as to great and strong, and which will provide guarantees for the effective exercise of genuine democratic rights by all people who cherish and defend democracy.

It is therefore essential that the voice of dominated peoples, seeking justice and the exercise of those democratic rights for which they fought and bled, should be heard and accorded due consideration by this World Conference upon which the solemn responsibility rests to rescue mankind from the ravages of war, insecurity, and slavery.

Colonial Status Renders Appeal Necessary

Because the very status of colonial dependency imposes onerous restrictions which render it extremely difficult if not impossible for these peoples to make direct representation, it is necessary for the West Indies National Council to present this Appeal on behalf of the peoples of the British, French, and Dutch West Indies, the Guianas and British Honduras. This Council, organized by natives of these areas, and supported by liberty-loving individuals and organizations irrespective of nationality, creed, or race, reflects the fundamental aspirations of these peoples based upon original ties, constant contact and knowledge, and the statements of responsible democratic representatives of the peoples of these areas.

This Appeal is therefore respectfully and earnestly presented together with seven proposals, adopted by this Council and endorsed by a public meeting assembled on April 16, 1945, at the Renaissance Casino in New York City and further endorsed by the Paragon Progressive Community Association, Inc., the Congress of Dominated Nations, and other organizations and prominent individuals. The Council requests that this Appeal be duly considered and urges this World Conference to adopt its recommendations and proposals in the form appropriate to secure their enforcement. The Council further desires to assure this World Conference that the peoples of these Caribbean areas may be depended upon wholeheartedly to support every measure necessary to the establishment of security, peace, and democracy, as their record amply demonstrates, and also to assume and discharge all duties and responsibilities in furtherance thereof.

Declaration of Rights—Act of Havana

The Declaration of Rights of the Caribbean Peoples to Self-Determination and Self-Government was presented by the West Indies National Emergency Committee to the Pan-American Foreign Ministers' Conference at Havana in July 1940. As a result, the Act of Havana while providing for concerted action by American Powers, recognized certain democratic rights of the Caribbean peoples.

Nevertheless, the Act of Havana was never invoked, though the French and Dutch Empires failed to provide protection and ceased in fact to exist as effective governing heads for these colonies. For a period indeed the people of the French West Indies and Guiana found themselves subject to the control of the fascist Vichy regime against their will and profound democratic conviction.

Vital Support Rendered by Caribbean Peoples

Despite the debilitating hindrances and galling yoke of colonial domination, the Caribbean peoples have loyally and unstintingly supported the United Nations in the present war against Nazi barbarism and fascist domination. In proportion to their size and numbers and the meager actual resources left to them after centuries of colonial retardation and impoverishment, they have made notable contributions to the armed forces and in labor power, finance, and essential materials such as oil, bauxite, etc.

Situated around the approaches to the Panama Canal, which was built mainly by their labor, at the strategic center of the defenses of the Americas, the peoples of the West Indies have suffered and withstood savage attacks by German submarines. Sites for vital bases and labor for their construction have been willingly furnished for the defense of the Americas and the United Nations, even though the rights of these peoples to consultation were not considered.

The Anglo-American Caribbean Commission has conducted broadcasts, made studies, and held conferences, but has done nothing practically to implement the rights of these peoples to self-government and self-determination. These fundamental rights are contravened by the very composition of this Commission which does not include a single direct representative of the Caribbean peoples or any one allied with them by ties of origin, feeling, and contact, in spite of repeated requests for such representation.

Colonial Conditions Menace World Security

The economic and social conditions prevailing in these areas are inhuman, tragic, and unbearable. The overwhelming majority of the population must labor when employment is available at wages far below the level of human subsistence. Housing and health conditions are among the worst in the world; illegitimacy, illiteracy, and the death rates are appallingly high. These dire conditions, resulting directly from centuries of slavery and colonial rule, have been intensified by the war to the point of "almost famine conditions in some places," as acknowledged in a recent bulletin of the British Information Services. Yet the Secretary of State for the Colonies of Great Britain in a recent statement publicly laments that the British taxpayer will be called upon to contribute to a small proposed fund for social development in the colonies.

The West Indies National Council respectfully but firmly submits to the United Nations' Conference that such colonial conditions constitute a major menace to World Security and Peace. The resolute liquidation of these menacing economic conditions should therefore be begun immediately. For this is imperative to raise the level of living standards and purchasing power of the Caribbean peoples, as of all peoples still subjected to colonial rule, in order to transform them into free and valuable participants in that increased production and exchange of goods and services which is no less essential to the security and peace of the people of the industrially advanced nations than it is to the welfare and progress of these now retarded colonial peoples.

Abolition of Imperialism Essential to World Peace

The Council also submits that such economic rehabilitation and progress, so essential to World Security and Peace, can be achieved only by breaking the fetters of imperialist domination and colonial dependency. For in no other way can the free political relations of mutually co-operating, self-governing peoples, fully respecting the democratic rights of each and all, be realized as the indispensable condition for social development and for the full release and stimulation of the energies of all in that increased production and exchange so vital to the security and peace of all mankind.

The Council further submits that the abolition of imperialist domination and colonial dependency will at the same time eliminate those conflicts over colonies which constitute the major source of war in the modern world. The logic of history now demands that imperialist control and colonial subjugation must cease that men may live and attain security and peace. A definite time in the immediate future should therefore be set in agreement with these peoples for the realization of full self-government and democratic rights for the Caribbean peoples and for all other colonial peoples.

Recommendations for Economic Rehabilitation

In accordance with the foregoing, the West Indies National Council earnestly recommends that a Fund adequate for the economic rehabilitation and social development of the Caribbean areas should be established under international supervision through the proposed International Bank for Reconstruction and Development or some similar agency. This Fund should be open to private and government subscription and substantial contributions to this Fund should be made by the British, French, and Dutch Empires. Since a large share of the vast fortunes and immense wealth of these Empires has been derived from the forced labor of the Caribbean peoples, these contributions would not only be in accord with justice but would also materially spur the increase in production and exchange which is recognized to be necessary to world prosperity, security, and peace.

Oppose Any Change without Self-determination

In respect to their readiness for self-government, it is undeniable that the Caribbean peoples possess all the characteristics of nationality and have many times proclaimed their demand for self-government. To settle this question it is necessary only to point to the numerous West Indians who have occupied and now hold administrative posts in every branch of government and to the late Governor General of Free French Africa, Felix Eboué, a native of the West Indies, whose administrative genius and timely action saved the greater part of Africa, and perhaps all Africa, from falling into the barbarous hands of the Vichy regime and the Nazi hordes in the darkest hours of the present war for the United Nations.

Present discussion and renewed proposals affecting the sovereignty of the West Indian peoples render it our duty to call attention to the following statements affirmed in the Declaration of Rights presented to the Havana Conference and to the supporting evidence adduced therein.

Reflecting and expressing the profound sentiments of the peoples of the Caribbean areas, this Committee declares that it is firmly opposed to any sale, transfer, mandate, trusteeship, or change of sovereignty of these peoples without the exercise of their inalienable human and democratic right of self-determination.

Trusteeship Thoroughly Discredited

In view of the urgency with which various proposals for mandates and trusteeship are being pressed upon this World Security Conference, it is imperative to affirm with renewed emphasis the following protest contained in the Statement of the West Indies National Emergency Committee on the Address delivered by Secretary Hull at the Havana Conference:

For, however well intentioned such a proposed collective trusteeship might appear, it cannot be forgotten that this device of trusteeship or mandate has been used and is now being used by imperial governments of the Old World as a means of maintaining control over various peoples and subjecting them to tyrannous oppression and unbridled exploitation.

It cannot be conceded for a moment that this discredited formula of trusteeship could be successfully employed in connection with the Caribbean peoples, when it is well known that it has signally failed either to ensure the democratic rights or to preserve the vital interests and welfare of the many down-trodden peoples to whom it has been applied.

International Commission Acceptable

In the opinion of this Council however, no truly representative objection might be expected from the Caribbean peoples to an International Commission specifically established to supervise the transition from colonial dependency to full self-government, provided their rights to self-government and self-determination were unequivocally recognized and a definite time mutually agreed upon for the realization of such complete self-government, and provided also that adequate and effective representation on such an International Commission were accorded to bona fide natives of these areas truly representative of the majority of these peoples.

Action Requisite against Prejudice and Terror

This Council would fail in its sacred duty if it did not urge this World Security Conference to give serious consideration to the grave menace to world security and peace which stems from racial, national, and religious prejudices. This venomous ideology was developed to its monstrous height in the "master race" mania with which the Nazi imperialist butchers, the Italian fascist slaughterers, and the Japanese military war mongers incited their followers to plunge the world into the present holocaust of slaughter and terror. Full cognizance must therefore be taken of the existence of racial, national, and religious prejudices and of the fact that such poisonous prejudices have already reached alarming proportions within most of the democratic nations themselves, with dire results to minorities therein and to colonial peoples controlled by these states.

Moreover, it is imperative to be aware of the fact that these vicious prejudices are inherent in the system of imperialism in which they are rooted and from which they inevitably develop. It is likewise salutary to mark that the horrible atrocities perpetrated at Belsen, Buchenwald, Dachau and elsewhere, at which mankind is now properly aghast, differ only in detail and degree from similar atrocities perpetrated upon colonial and semi-colonial peoples. The security and peace of mankind require that the lesson of history be now practically drawn that terror and torture developed first in colonial areas inevitably reach back to the dominating peoples and menace all mankind.

The resolution adopted at the Chapultepec Conference, recognizing the existence of racial, national, and religious prejudices within the frontiers of any country to be a matter of international concern, is an important step forward. This Council earnestly recommends that this World Conference adopt such a resolution, as a vital principle for the organization of world security and peace, requiring that all nations shall enact and enforce laws with adequate penalties against any and all overt manifestations of such racial, national, and religious prejudices, and shall undertake a vigorous campaign of education for the extirpation of such prejudices and animosities.

Urges Adoption of Seven Point Proposals

The West Indies National Council earnestly and finally urges this World Security Conference to consider and to adopt the following seven proposals in the interests of the Caribbean peoples and of World Security and Peace.

a. Forthright recognition of the inalienable right of the Caribbean peoples to self-government and self-determination.

b. Practical recognition of the age-long objective of the West Indian peoples for voluntary federation.

c. Integration, on the basis of equality, of the Caribbean peoples into the regional organization of the American nations and for their representation in the making of all plans for the political, military, economic and social security of all the peoples of the Americas.

d. Specific inclusion of the Caribbean peoples in the plans of the Conference for post-war rehabilitation and social security in view of the dire economic conditions of these peoples, resulting from colonial rule, which have been intensified by the war and which have reached almost famine conditions.

e. Recognition of the right of the Caribbean peoples to representation at the United Nations' Conference by delegates of their own choosing, as a matter of democracy and justice and by virtue of the vital contribution which the Caribbean peoples have made to the war effort and to democracy in this hemisphere and to the world.

f. Guarantees for the abolition of all discriminatory laws and practices based on race, religion, color or previous condition of servitude or oppression, and for the assurance of full protection of life and liberty for the Caribbean peoples, for the African peoples, and for all peoples without regard to race, creed, or color.

g. Genuine equality of rights both in fact and in law for all peoples everywhere and full democratic citizenship rights, including universal adult suffrage, for all people.

The West Indies National Council sincerely hopes for the success of this World Security Council and for the adoption of these measures which will enable the Caribbean peoples to take their rightful place among the nations of the world in a new era of freedom, security, peace and prosperity.

WEST INDIES NATIONAL COUNCIL

RICHARD B. MOORE
Vice-President and Chairman Conference Committee

LEONARD LOWE
Secretary

CHARLES A. PETIONI, M. D.
President

History Will Absolve Me

Fidel Castro

In terms of struggle, when we talk about people we're talking about the *six hundred thousand* Cubans without work, who want to earn their daily bread honestly without having to emigrate from their homeland in search of a livelihood; the *five hundred thousand* farm laborers who live in miserable shacks, who work four months of the year and starve the rest, sharing their misery with their children, who don't have an inch of land to till, and whose existence would move any heart not made of stone; the *four hundred thousand* industrial workers and laborers whose retirement funds have been embezzled, whose benefits are being taken away, whose homes are wretched quarters, whose salaries pass from the hands of the boss to those of the moneylender, whose future is a pay reduction and dismissal, whose life is endless work, and whose only rest is the tomb; the *one hundred thousand* small farmers who live and die working land that is not theirs, looking at it with the sadness of Moses gazing at the promised land, to die without ever owning it, who like feudal serfs have to pay for the use of their parcel of land by giving up a portion of its produce, who cannot love it, improve it, beautify it, nor plant a cedar or an orange tree on it because they never know when a sheriff will come with the rural guard to evict them from it; the *thirty thousand* teachers and professors who are so devoted, dedicated, and so necessary to the better destiny of future generations and who are so badly treated and paid; the *twenty thousand* small businessmen weighed down by debts, ruined by the crisis, and harangued by a plague of grafting and venal officials; the *ten thousand* young professional people: doctors, engineers, lawyers, veterinarians, schoolteachers, dentists, pharmacists, newspapermen, painters, sculptors, etc., who finish school with their degrees, anxious to work and full of hope, only to find themselves at a dead end, all doors closed to them, and where no ear hears their clamor or supplication. These are the people, the ones who know misfortune and, therefore, are capable of fighting with limitless courage! To these people whose desperate roads through life have been paved with the bricks of betrayal and false promises, we were not going to say: "We will give you … " but rather: "Here it is, now fight for it with everything you have, so that liberty and happiness may be yours!"

The five revolutionary laws that would have been proclaimed immediately after the capture of the Moncada Garrison and would have been broadcast to the nation by radio must be included in the indictment. It is possible that Colonel Chaviano may have deliberately destroyed these documents, but even if he has I remember them.

The first revolutionary law would have returned the power to the people and proclaimed the 1940 Constitution the supreme law of the state until such time as the people should decide to modify or change it. And in order to effect its implementation and punish those who violated it—there being no electoral organization to carry this out—the revolutionary movement, as the circumstantial incarnation of this sovereignty, the only source of legitimate power, would have assumed all the faculties inherent therein, except that of modifying the constitution itself: in other words, it would have assumed the legislative, executive, and judicial powers.

This attitude could not be clearer nor more free of vacillation and sterile charlatanry. A government acclaimed by the mass of rebel people would be vested with every power, everything necessary in order to proceed with the effective implementation of popular will and real justice. From that moment, the judicial power—which since 10 March had placed itself against and outside the constitution—would cease to exist, and we would proceed to its immediate and total reform before it would once again assume the power granted it by the supreme law of the republic. Without these previous measures, a return to legality by putting its custody back into the hands that have crippled the system so dishonorably would constitute a fraud, a deceit, one more betrayal.

The second revolutionary law would give nonmortgageable and nontransferable ownership of the land to all tenant and subtenant farmers, lessees, sharecroppers, and squatters who hold parcels of five *caballerías* of land or less, and the state would indemnify the former owners on the basis of the rental which they would have received for these parcels over a period of ten years.

The third revolutionary law would have granted workers and employees the right to share 30 percent of the profits of all large industrial, mercantile, and mining enterprises, including the sugar mills. The strictly agricultural enterprises would be exempt in consideration of other agrarian laws which would be put into effect.

The fourth revolutionary law would have granted all sugar planters the right to share 55 percent of the sugar production and a minimum quota of forty thousand *arrobas* for all small tenant farmers who have been established for three years or more.

The fifth revolutionary law would have ordered the confiscation of all holdings and ill-gotten gains of those who had committed fraud during previous regimes, as well as the holdings and ill-gotten gains of all their legates and heirs. To implement this, special courts with full powers would gain access to all records of all corporations registered or operating in this country, in order to investigate concealed funds of illegal origin and to request that foreign governments extradite persons and attach holdings rightfully belonging to the Cuban people. Half of the property recovered would be used to subsidize retirement funds for workers and the other half would be used for hospitals, asylums, and charitable organizations.

Furthermore, it was to be declared that the Cuban policy in the Americas would be one of close solidarity with the democratic peoples of this continent, and that all those politically persecuted by bloody tyrannies oppressing our sister nations would find generous asylum, brotherhood, and bread in the land of Martí; not the persecution, hunger, and treason they find today. Cuba should be the bulwark of liberty and not a shameful link in the chain of despotism.

These laws would have been proclaimed immediately. As soon as the upheaval ended and prior to a detailed and far-reaching study, they would have been followed by another series of laws and fundamental measures, such as the agrarian reform, the integral educational reform, nationalization of the electric power trust and the telephone trust, refund to the people of the illegal excessive rates these companies have charged, and payment to the treasury of all taxes brazenly evaded in the past.

All these laws and others would be based on exact compliance with two essential articles of our constitution: one of them orders the outlawing of large estates, indicating the maximum area of land any one person or entity may own for each type of agricultural enterprise, by adopting measures which would tend to revert the land to the Cubans. The other categorically orders the state to use all means at its disposal to provide employment for all those who lack it and to insure a decent livelihood to each manual or intellectual laborer. None of these laws can be called unconstitutional. The first popularly elected government would have to respect them, not only because of moral obligations to the nation, but because when people achieve something they have yearned for throughout generations, no force in the world is capable of taking it away again.

The problem of the land, the problem of industrialization, the problem of housing, the problem of unemployment, the problem of education, and the problem of the people's health: these are the six problems we would take immediate steps to solve, along with restoration of civil liberties and political democracy.

This exposition may seem cold and theoretical if one does not know the shocking and tragic conditions of the country with regard to these six problems, along with the most humiliating political oppression.

Eighty-five percent of the small farmers in Cuba pay rent and live under the constant threat of being evicted from the land they till. More than half of our most productive land is in the hands of foreigners. In Oriente, the largest province, the lands of the United Fruit Company link the northern and southern coasts. There are *two hundred thousand peasant families* who do not have a single acre of land to till to provide food for their starving children. On the other hand, nearly *three hundred thousand caballerías* of cultivable land owned by powerful interests remain uncultivated. If Cuba is above all an agricultural state, if its population is largely rural, if the city depends on these rural areas, if the people from our countryside won our war of independence, if our nation's greatness and prosperity depend on a healthy and vigorous rural population that loves the land and knows how to work it, if this population depends on a state that protects and guides it, then how can the present state of affairs be allowed to continue?

Except for a few food, lumber, and textile industries, Cuba continues to be primarily a producer of raw materials. We export sugar to import candy, we export hides to import shoes, we export iron to import plows. Everyone agrees with the urgent need to industrialize the nation, that we need steel industries, paper and chemical industries, that we must improve our cattle and grain production, the technique and the processing in our food industry in order to defend ourselves against the ruinous competition of the Europeans in cheese products, condensed milk, liquors, and edible oils, and of the United States in canned goods; that we need cargo ships; that tourism should be an enormous source of revenue. But the capitalists insist that the workers remain under the yoke. The state sits back with its arms crossed and industrialization can wait forever.

Just as serious or even worse is the housing problem. There are *two hundred thousand* huts and hovels in Cuba; *four hundred thousand* families in the countryside and in the cities live cramped in huts and tenements without even the minimum sanitary requirements; *2.2 million* of our urban population pay rents which absorb between one-fifth and one-third of their incomes; and *2.8 million* of our rural and suburban population lack electricity. We have the same situation here: if the state proposes the lowering of rents, landlords threaten to freeze all construction; if the state does not interfere, construction goes on so long as the landlords get high rents; otherwise they would not lay a single brick, even though the rest of the population had to live totally exposed to the elements. The utilities monopoly is no better; they extend lines as far as it is profitable, and beyond that point they don't care if people have to live in darkness for the rest of their lives. The state sits back with its arms crossed, and the people have neither homes nor electricity.

Our educational system is perfectly compatible with everything I've just mentioned. Where the peasant doesn't own the land, what need is there for agricultural schools? Where there is no industry, what need is there for technological or vocational schools? Everything follows the same absurd logic; if we don't have one thing we can't have the other. In any small European country there are more than two hundred technological and vocational schools; in Cuba only six such schools exist, and the graduates have no jobs for their skills. The little rural schoolhouses are attended by a mere half of the school-age children—barefooted, half-naked, and undernourished—and frequently the teacher must buy necessary school materials from his own salary. Is this the way to make a nation great?

Only death can liberate one from so much misery. In this respect, however, the state is most helpful—in providing early death for the people. *Ninety percent* of the children in the countryside are consumed by parasites that filter through their bare feet from the ground they walk on. Society is moved to compassion when it hears of the kidnapping or murder of one child, but it is criminally indifferent to the mass murder of so many thousands of children who die every year from lack of facilities, agonizing with pain. Their innocent eyes, death already shining in them, seem to look into some vague infinity as if entreating forgiveness for human selfishness, as if asking God to stay wrath. And when the head of a family works only four months a year, with what can he purchase clothing and medicine for his children? They will grow up with rickets, with not a single good tooth in their mouths by the time they reach thirty; they will have heard ten million speeches and will finally die of misery and deception. Public hospitals, which are always full, accept only patients recommended by some powerful politician who, in turn, demands the electoral votes of the unfortunate one and his family so that Cuba may continue forever in the same or worse condition.

With this background, is it not understandable that from May to December over a million persons are jobless and that Cuba, with a population of five and a half million, has a greater number of unemployed than France or Italy with a population of forty million each?

When you try a defendant for robbery, Honorable Judges, do you ask him how long he has been unemployed? Do you ask him how many children he has, which days of the week he ate and which he didn't; do you investigate his social context at all? You just send him to jail without further thought. But those who burn warehouses and stores to collect insurance do not go to jail, even though a few human beings may have gone up in flames. The insured have money to hire lawyers and bribe judges. You imprison the poor wretch who steals because he is hungry; but none of the hundreds who steal millions from the government has ever spent a night in jail. You dine with them at the end of the year in some elegant club and they enjoy your respect. In Cuba, when a government official becomes a millionaire overnight and enters the fraternity of the rich, he could very well be greeted with the words of that opulent character out of Balzac—Taillerfer—who in his toast to the young heir to an enormous fortune said: "Gentlemen, let us drink to the power of gold! Mr. Valentine, a millionaire six times over, has just ascended the throne. He is king, can do everything, is above everyone, as all the rich are. Henceforth, equality before the law, established by the constitution, will be a myth for him; for he will not be subject to laws: the laws will be subject to him. There are no courts nor are there sentences for millionaires."

The nation's future, the solutions to its problems, cannot continue to depend on the selfish interests of a dozen big businessmen nor on the cold calculations of profits that ten or twelve magnates draw up in their air-conditioned offices. The country cannot continue begging on its knees for miracles from a few golden calves, like the biblical one destroyed by the prophet's fury. Golden calves cannot perform miracles of any kind. The problems of the republic can be solved only if we dedicate ourselves to fight for it with the same energy, honesty, and patriotism our liberators had when they founded it. Statesmen like Carlos Saladrigas, whose statesmanship consists of preserving the status quo and mouthing phrases like "absolute freedom of enterprise," "guarantees to investment capital," and "the law of supply and demand," will not solve these problems. Those ministers can chat away in a Fifth Avenue mansion until not even the dust of the bones of those whose problems require immediate solution remains. In this present-day world, social problems are not solved by spontaneous generation.

A revolutionary government backed by the people and with the respect of the nation, after cleansing the different institutions of all venal and corrupt officials, would proceed immediately to the country's industrialization, mobilizing all inactive capital, currently estimated at about 1.5 billion pesos, through the National Bank and the Agricultural and Industrial Development Bank, and submitting this mammoth task to experts and men of absolute competence totally removed from all political machines, for study, direction, planning, and realization.

After settling the one hundred thousand small farmers as owners on the land which they previously rented, a revolutionary government would immediately proceed to settle the land problem. First, as set forth in the constitution, it would establish the maximum amount of land to be held by each type of agricultural enterprise and would acquire the excess acreage by expropriation, recovery of the lands stolen from the state, improvement of swampland, planting of large nurseries, and reserving of zones for reforestation. Second, it would distribute the remaining land among peasant families with priority given to the larger ones and would promote agricultural cooperatives for communal use of expensive equipment, freezing plants, and single technical, professional guidelines in farming and cattle raising. Finally, it would provide resources, equipment, protection, and useful guidance to the peasants.

A revolutionary government would solve the housing problem by cutting all rents in half, by providing tax exemptions on homes inhabited by the owners; by tripling taxes on rented homes; by tearing down hovels and replacing them with modern apartment buildings; and by financing housing all over the island on a scale heretofore unheard of, with the criterion that, just as each rural family should possess its own tract of land, each city family should own its own home or apartment. There is plenty of building material and more than enough manpower to make a decent home for every Cuban. But if we continue to wait for the golden calf, a thousand years will have gone by and the problem will remain the same. On the other hand, today possibilities of taking electricity to the most isolated areas on the island are greater than ever. The use of nuclear energy in this field is now a reality and will greatly reduce the cost of producing electricity.

With these three projects and reforms, the problem of unemployment would automatically disappear and the task of improving public health and fighting against disease would become much less difficult.

Finally, a revolutionary government would undertake the integral reform of the educational system, bringing it into line with the projects just mentioned with the idea of educating those generations which will have the privilege of living in a happier land. Do not forget the words of the Apostle: "A grave mistake is being made in Latin America: in countries that live almost completely from the produce of the land, men are being educated exclusively for urban life and are not trained for farm life." "The happiest country is the one which has best educated its sons, both in the instruction of thought and the direction of their feelings." "An educated country will always be strong and free."

The soul of education, however, is the teacher, and in Cuba the teaching profession is miserably underpaid. Despite this, no one is more dedicated than the Cuban teacher. Who among us has not learned his ABCs in the little public schoolhouse? It is time we stopped paying pittances to these young men and women who are entrusted with the sacred task of teaching our youth. No teacher should earn less than two hundred pesos; no secondary teacher should make less than 350 pesos if they are to devote themselves exclusively to their high calling without suffering want. What is more, all rural teachers should have free use of the various systems of transportation; and, at least once every five years, all teachers should enjoy a sabbatical leave of six months with pay so they may attend special refresher courses at home or abroad to keep abreast of the latest developments in their field. In this way, the curriculum and the teaching system can be constantly improved. Where will the money be found for all this? When there is an end to the embezzlement of government funds, when public officials stop taking graft from the large companies that owe taxes to the state, when the enormous resources of the country are brought into full use, when we no longer buy tanks, bombers, and guns for this country (which has no frontiers to defend and where these instruments of war, now being purchased, are used against the people), when there is more interest in educating the people than in killing them, there will be more than enough money.

Cuba could easily provide for a population three times as great as it has now, so there is no excuse for the abject poverty of a single one of its present inhabitants. The markets should be overflowing with produce, pantries should be full, all hands should be working. This is not an inconceivable thought. What is inconceivable is that anyone should go to bed hungry while there is a single inch of unproductive land, that children should die for lack of medical attention. What is inconceivable is that 30 percent of our farm people cannot write their names and that 99 percent of them know nothing of Cuba's history. What is inconceivable is that the majority of our rural people are now living in worse circumstances than the Indians Columbus discovered in the fairest land that human eyes had ever seen.

To those who would call me a dreamer, I quote the words of Martí: "A true man does not seek the path where advantage lies, but rather the path where duty lies, and this is the only practical man, whose dream of today will be the law of tomorrow, because he who has looked back on the essential course of history and has seen flaming and bleeding peoples seethe in the cauldron of the ages knows that, without a single exception, the future lies on the side of duty."

I know that imprisonment will be harder for me than it has ever been for anyone, filled with cowardly threats and hideous cruelty. But I do not fear prison, as I do not fear the fury of the miserable tyrant who took the lives of seventy of my comrades. Condemn me. It does not matter. History will absolve me.

Black Power — Its Relevance to the West Indies

Walter Rodney

About a fortnight ago I had the opportunity of speaking on Black Power to an audience on this campus.[1] At that time, the consciousness among students as far as the racial question is concerned had been heightened by several incidents on the world scene — notably, the hangings in Rhodesia and the murder of Dr. Martin Luther King. Indeed, it has been heightened to such an extent that some individuals have started to organise a Black Power movement. My presence here attests to my full sympathy with their objectives.

The topic on this occasion is no longer just 'Black Power' but 'Black Power and You'. Black Power can be seen as a movement and an ideology springing from the reality of oppression of black peoples by whites within the imperialist world as a whole. Now we need to be specific in defining the West Indian scene and our own particular roles in the society. You and I have to decide whether we want to think black or to *remain* as a dirty version of white. (I shall indicate the full significance of this later.)

Recently there was a public statement in *Scope* where Black Power was referred to as 'Black supremacy '. This may have been a genuine error or a deliberate falsification. Black Power is a call to black peoples to throw off white domination and resume the handling of their own destinies. It means that blacks would enjoy power commensurate with their numbers in the world and in particular localities. Whenever an oppressed black man shouts for equality he is called a racist. This was said of Marcus Garvey in his day. Imagine that ! We are so inferior that if we demand equality of opportunity and power that is outrageously racist ! Black people who speak up for their rights must beware of this device of false accusations. It is intended to place you on the defensive and if possible embarrass you into silence. How can we be both oppressed and embarrassed? Is it that our major concern is not to hurt the feelings of the oppressor? Black People must now take the offensive — if it is anyone who should suffer embarrassment it is the whites. Did black people roast six million Jews? Who exterminated millions of indigenous inhabitants in the Americas and Australia? Who enslaved countless millions of Africans? The white capitalist cannibal has always fed on the world's black peoples. White capitalist imperialist society is profoundly and unmistakably racist.

The West Indies have always been a part of white capitalist society. We have been the most oppressed section because we were a slave society and the legacy of slavery still rests heavily upon the West Indian black man. I will briefly point to five highlights of our social development: (1) the development of racialism under slavery; (2) emancipation; (3) Indian indentured labour; (4) the year 1865 in Jamaica; (5) the year 1938 in the West Indies.

Slavery. As C.L.R. James, Eric Williams and other W.I. scholars have pointed out, slavery in the West Indies started as an economic phenomenon rather than a racial one. But it rapidly became racist as all white labour was withdrawn from the fields, leaving black to be identified with slave labour and white to be linked with property and domination. Out of this situation where blacks had an inferior status in practice, there grew social and scientific theories relating to the supposed inherent inferiority of the black man, who was considered as having been created to bring water and hew wood for the white man. This theory then served to rationalise white exploitation of blacks all over Africa and Asia. The West Indies and the American South share the dubious distinction of being the breeding ground for world racialism. Naturally, our own society provided the highest expressions of racialism. Even the blacks became convinced of their own inferiority, though fortunately we are capable of the most intense expressions when we recognise that we have been duped by the white men. Black Power recognises both the reality of black oppression and self-negation as well as the potential for revolt.

Emancipation. By the end of the 18th century, Britain had got most of what it wanted from black labour in the West Indies. Slavery and the slave trade had made Britain strong and now stood in the way of new developments, so it was time to abandon those systems. The Slave Trade and Slavery were thus ended; but Britain had to consider how to squeeze what little remained in the territories and *how to maintain the local whites in power. They* therefore decided to give the planters £20 million compensation and to guarantee their black labour supplies for the next six years through a system called apprenticeship. In that period, white society consolidated its position to ensure that slave relations should persist in our society. The Rastafari Brethren have always insisted that the black people were promised £20 million at emancipation. In reality, by any normal standards of justice, we black people should have got the £20 million compensation money. We were the ones who had been abused and wronged, hunted in Africa and brutalised on the plantations. In Europe, when serfdom was abolished, the serfs usually inherited the land as compensation and by right. In the West Indies, the exploiters were compensated because they could no longer exploit us in the same way as before. White property was of greater value than black humanity. It still is — white property is of greater value than black humanity in the British West Indies today, especially here in Jamaica.

Indian Indentured Labour. Britain and the white West Indians had to maintain the plantation system in order to keep white supreme. When Africans started leaving the plantations to set up as independent peasants they threatened the plantation structure and therefore Indians were imported under the indenture arrangements. That was possible because white power controlled most of the world and could move non-white peoples around as they wished. It was from British-controlled India that the indentured labour was obtained. It was the impact of British commercial, military and political policies that was destroying the life and culture of 19th century India and forcing people to flee to other parts of the world to earn bread. Look where Indians fled — to the West Indies! The West Indies is a place black people want to leave not to come to. One must therefore appreciate the pressure of white power on India which gave rise to migration to the West Indies. Indians were brought here solely in the interest of white society — at the expense of Africans already in the West Indies and often against their own best interests, for Indians perceived indentured labour to be a form of slavery and it was eventually terminated through the pressure of Indian opinion in the homeland. The West Indies has made a unique contribution to the history of suffering in the world, and Indians have provided part of that contribution since indentures were first introduced. This is another aspect of the historical situation which is still with us.

1865. In that year Britain found a way of perpetuating White Power in the West Indies after ruthlessly crushing the revolt of our black brothers led by Paul Bogle. The British Government took away the Constitution of Jamaica and placed the island under the complete control of the Colonial Office, a manoeuvre that was racially motivated. The Jamaican legislature was then largely in the hands of the local whites with a mulatto minority, but if the gradual changes continued the mulattoes would have taken control — and the blacks were next in line. Consequently, the British Government put a stop to the process of the gradual takeover of political power by blacks. When we look at the British Empire in the 19th century, we see a clear difference between white colonies and black colonies. In the white colonies like Canada and Australia the British were giving white people their freedom and self-rule. In the black colonies of the West Indies, Africa and Asia the British were busy taking away the political freedom of the inhabitants. Actually, on the constitutional level, Britain had already displayed its racialism in the West Indies in the early 19th century when it refused to give mulattoes the power of Government in Trinidad, although they were the majority of free citizens. In 1865 in Jamaica it was not the first nor the last time on which Britain made it clear that its white 'kith and kin' would be supported to hold dominion over blacks.

1938. Slavery ended in various islands of the West Indies between 1834 and 1838. Exactly 100 years later (between 1934-38) the black people in the West Indies revolted against the hypocritical freedom of the society. The British were very surprised — they had long forgotten all about the blacks in the British West Indies and they sent a Royal Commission to find out what it was all about. The report of the conditions was so shocking that the British government did not release it until after the war, because they wanted black colonials to fight the white man's battles. By the time the war ended it was clear in the West Indies and throughout Asia and Africa that some concessions would have to be made to black peoples. In general, the problem as seen by white imperialists was to give enough power to certain groups in colonial society to keep the whole society from exploding and to maintain the essentials of the imperialist structure. In the British West Indies, they had to take into account the question of military strategy because we lie under the belly of the world's imperialist giant, the U.S.A. Besides, there was the new and vital mineral bauxite, which had to be protected. The British solution was to pull out wherever possible and leave the imperial government in the hands of the U.S.A., while the local government was given to a white, brown and black petty-bourgeoisie who were culturally the creations of white capitalist society and who therefore support the white imperialist system because they gain personally and because they have been brainwashed into aiding the oppression of black people.

Black Power in the West Indies means three closely related things: (i) the break with imperialism which is historically white racist; (ii) the assumption of power by the black masses in the islands; (iii) the cultural reconstruction of the society in the image of the blacks.

I shall anticipate certain questions on who are the blacks in the West Indies since they are in fact questions which have been posed to me elsewhere. I maintain that it is the white world which has defined who are blacks — if you are not white then you are black. However, it is obvious that the West Indian situation is complicated by factors such as the variety of racial types and racial mixtures and by the process of class formation. We have, therefore, to note not simply what the white world says but also how individuals perceive each other. Nevertheless, we can talk of the mass of the West Indian population as being black — either African or Indian. There seems to have been some doubts on the last point, and some fear that Black Power is aimed against the Indian. This would be a flagrant denial of both the historical experience of the West Indies and the reality of the contemporary scene.

When the Indian was brought to the West Indies, he met the same racial contempt which whites applied to Africans. The Indian, too, was reduced to a single stereotype — the coolie or labourer. He too was a hewer of wood and a bringer of water. I spoke earlier of the revolt of the blacks in the West Indies in 1938. That revolt involved Africans in Jamaica, Africans and Indians in Trinidad and Guyana. The uprisings in Guyana were actually led by Indian sugar workers. Today, some Indians (like some Africans) have joined the white power structure in terms of economic activity and culture; but the underlying reality is that poverty resides among Africans and Indians in the West Indies and that power is denied them. Black Power in the West Indies, therefore, refers primarily to people who are recognisably African or Indian.

The Chinese, on the other hand, are a former labouring group who have now become bastions of white West Indian social structure. The Chinese of the People's Republic of China have long broken with and are fighting against white imperialism, but *our* Chinese have nothing to do with that movement. They are to be identified with Chiang-Kai-Shek and not Chairman Mao Tse-tung. They are to be put in the same bracket as the lackeys of capitalism and imperialism who are to be found in Hong Kong and Taiwan. Whatever the circumstances in which the Chinese came to the West Indies, they soon became (as a group) members of the exploiting class. They will have either to relinquish or be deprived of that function before they can be re-integrated into a West Indian society where the black man walks in dignity.

The same applies to the mulattoes, another group about whom I have been questioned. The West Indian brown man is characterised by ambiguity and ambivalence. He has in the past identified with the black masses when it suited his interests, and at the present time some browns are in the forefront of the movement towards black consciousness; but the vast majority have fallen to the bribes of white imperialism, often outdoing the whites in their hatred and oppression of blacks. Garvey wrote of the Jamaican mulattoes — 'I was openly hated and persecuted by some of these coloured men of the island who did not want to be classified as Negroes but as white'. Naturally, conscious West Indian blacks like Garvey have in turn expressed their dislike for the browns, but there is nothing in the West Indian experience which suggests that browns are unacceptable when they choose to identify with blacks. The post-1938 developments in fact showed exactly the opposite. It seems to me, therefore, that it is not for the Black Power movement to determine the position of the browns, reds and so-called West Indian whites — the movement can only keep the door open and leave it to those groups to make their choice.

Black Power is not racially intolerant. It is the hope of the black man that he should have power over his own destinies. This is not incompatible with a multi-racial society where each individual counts equally. Because the moment that power is equitably distributed among several ethnic groups then the very relevance of making the distinction between groups will be lost. What we must object to is the current image of a multi-racial society living in harmony — that is a myth designed to justify the exploitation suffered by the blackest of our population, at the hands of the lighter-skinned groups. Let us look at the figures for the racial composition of the Jamaican population. Of every 100 Jamaicans,

> 76.8% are visibly African
> 0.8% European
> 1.1% Indian
> 0.6% Chinese
> 0.1% Syrian
> 91% have African blood
> 14.6% Afro-European
> 5.4% other mixtures

This is a black society where Africans preponderate. Apart from the mulatto mixture all other groups are numerically insignificant and yet the society seeks to give them equal weight and indeed more weight than the Africans. If we went to Britain we could easily find non-white groups in the above proportions[2] — Africans and West Indians, Indians and Pakistanis, Turks, Arabs and other Easterners — but Britain is not called a multi-racial society. When we go to Britain we don't expect to take over all of the British real estate business, all their cinemas and most of their commerce as the European, Chinese and Syrian have done here. All we ask for there is some work and shelter, and we can't even get that. Black Power must proclaim that Jamaica is a black society — we should fly Garvey's Black Star banner and we will treat all other groups in the society on that understanding — they can have *the basic right of all individuals* but *no privileges to exploit Africans* as has been the pattern during slavery and ever since.

The present government knows that Jamaica is a black man's country. That is why Garvey has been made a national hero, for they are trying to deceive black people into thinking that the government is with them. The government of Jamaica recognises black power — it is afraid of the potential wrath of Jamaica's black and largely African population. It is that same fear which forced them to declare mourning when black men are murdered in Rhodesia, and when Martin Luther King was murdered in the U.S.A. But the black people don't need to be told that Garvey is a national hero — they know that. Nor do they need to be told to mourn when blacks are murdered by White Power, because they mourn everyday right here in Jamaica where white power keeps them ignorant, unemployed, ill-clothed and ill-fed. They will stop mourning when things change — and that means a revolution, for the first essential is to break the chains which bind us to white imperialists, and that is a very revolutionary step, Cuba is the only country in the West Indies and in this hemisphere which has broken with white power. That is why Stokely Carmichael can visit Cuba but he can't visit Trinidad or Jamaica. That is why Stokely can call Fidel 'one of the blackest men in the Americas' and that is why our leaders in contrast qualify as 'white'.

Here I'm not just playing with words — I'm extending the definition of Black Power by indicating the nature of its opposite, 'White Power', and I'm providing a practical illustration of what Black Power means in one particular West Indian community where it had already occurred. White Power is the power of whites over blacks without any participation of the blacks. White Power rules the imperialist world as a whole. In Cuba the blacks and mulattoes numbered 1,585,073 out of a population of 5,829,029 in 1953 — i.e. about one quarter of the population. Like Jamaica's black people today, they were the poorest and most depressed people on the island. Lighter-skinned Cubans held local power, while real power was in the hands of the U.S. imperialists. Black Cubans fought alongside white Cuban workers and peasants because they were all oppressed. Major Juan Almeida, one of the outstanding leaders of Cuba today, was one of the original guerrillas in the Sierra Maestra, and he is black. Black Cubans today enjoy political, economic and social rights and opportunities of exactly the same kind as white Cubans. They too bear arms in the Cuban Militia as an expression of their basic rights. In other words, White Power in Cuba is ended. The majority of the white population naturally predominates numerically in most spheres of activity but they do not hold dominion over blacks without regard to the latter's interests. The blacks have achieved power commensurate with their own numbers by their heroic self-efforts during the days of slavery, in fighting against the Spanish and in fighting against imperialism. Having achieved their rights they can in fact afford to forget the category 'black' and think simply as Cuban citizens, as Socialist equals and as men. In Jamaica, where blacks are far greater in numbers and have no whites alongside them as oppressed workers and peasants, it will be the black people who alone can bear the brunt of revolutionary fighting.

Trotsky once wrote that Revolution is the carnival of the masses. When we have that carnival in the West Indies, are people like us here at the university going to join the bacchanal?

Let us have a look at our present position. Most of us who have studied at the U.W.I. are discernibly black, and yet we are undeniably part of the white imperialist system. A few are actively pro-imperialist. They have no confidence in anything that is not white — they talk nonsense about black people being lazy — the same nonsense which was said about the Jamaican black man after emancipation, although he went to Panama and performed the giant task of building the Panama Canal — the same nonsense which is said about W.I. unemployed today, and yet they proceed to England to run the whole transport system. Most of us do not go to quite the same extremes in denigrating ourselves and our black brothers, but we say nothing against the system, and that means that we are acquiescing in the exploitation of our brethren. One of the ways that the situation has persisted especially in recent times is that it has given a few individuals like you and I a vision of personal progress measured in terms of front lawn and of the latest model of a huge American car. This has recruited us into their ranks and deprived the black masses of articulate leadership. That is why at the outset I stressed that our choice was to *remain* as part of the white system or to break with it. There is no other alternative.

Black Power in the W.I. must aim at transforming the Black intelligensia into the servants of the black masses. Black Power, within the university and without must aim at overcoming white cultural imperialism. Whites have dominated us both physically and mentally. This fact is brought out in virtually any serious sociological study of the region — the brainwashing process has been so stupendous that it has convinced so many black men of their inferiority. I will simply draw a few illustrations to remind you of this fact which blacks like us at Mona prefer to forget.

The adult black in our West Indian society is fully conditioned to thinking white, because that is the training we are given from childhood. The little black girl plays with a white doll, identifying with it as she combs its flaxen hair. Asked to sketch the figure of a man or woman, the black schoolboy instinctively produces a white man or a white woman. This is not surprising, *since* until recently the illustrations in our text books were all figures of Europeans. The few changes which have taken place have barely scratched the surface of the problem. West Indians of every colour still aspire to European standards of dress and beauty. The language which is used by black people in describing ourselves shows how we despise our African appearance. 'Good hair' means European hair, 'good nose' means a straight nose, 'good complexion' means a light complexion. Everybody recognises how incongruous and ridiculous such terms are, but we continue to use them and to express our support of the assumption that white Europeans have the monopoly of beauty, and that black is the incarnation of ugliness. That is why Black Power advocates find it necessary to assert that BLACK IS BEAUTIFUL.

The most profound revelation of the sickness of our society on the question of race is our respect for all the white symbols of the Christian religion. God the Father is white, God the Son is white, and presumably God the Holy Ghost is white also. The disciples and saints are white, all the Cherubim, Seraphim and angels are white — except Lucifer, of course, who was black, being the embodiment of evil. When one calls upon black people to reject these things, this is not an attack on the teachings of Christ or the ideals of Christianity. What we have to ask is 'Why should Christianity come to us all wrapped up in white?' The white race constitute about 20 per cent of the world's population, and yet non-white peoples are supposed to accept that all who inhabit the heavens are white. There are 650 million Chinese, so why shouldn't God and most of the angels be Chinese? The truth is that there is absolutely no reason why different racial groups should not provide themselves with their own religious symbols. A picture of Christ could be red, white or black, depending upon the people who are involved. When Africans adopt the European concept that purity and goodness must be painted white and all that is evil and dammed is to be painted black then we are flagrantly self-insulting.

Through the manipulation of this media of education and communication, white people have produced black people who administer the system and perpetuate the white values — 'white-hearted black men', as they are called by conscious elements. This is as true of the Indians as it is true of the Africans in our West Indian society. Indeed, the basic explanation of the tragedy of African/Indian confrontation in Guyana and Trinidad is the fact that both groups are held captive by the European way of seeing things. When an African abuses an Indian he repeats all that the white men said about Indian indentured 'coolies'; and in turn the Indian has borrowed from the whites the stereotype of the 'lazy nigger' to apply to the African beside him. It is as though no black man can see another black man except by looking through a white person. It is time we started seeing through our own eyes. The road to Black Power here in the West Indies and everywhere else must begin with a revaluation of ourselves as blacks and with a redefinition of the world from our own standpoint.

Notes
1.   The U.W.I, campus.
2.   As the non-blacks in Jamaica. Editor's note.

In Nobody's Backyard

Maurice Bishop

National Broadcast on RFG, 13 April 1979

Today, one month after our historic People's Revolution, there is peace, calm and quiet in our country. Indeed, there has been a tremendous drop in the crime rate since our Revolution. Foreign residents in the Levera/Bathway are feeling so comfortable and safe nowadays that they have advised the Commissioner of Police that he could close down the sub-Police Station in that area. An unusually high number of tourists for an off-season period are presently enjoying the beauty of our land and the warmth of our people, and this is so in spite of the fact that we have just had a Revolution and that a real and present threat of mercenary invasion is faced by our country. In fact, it is almost impossible to rent a vehicle or to find an empty cottage at this point.

Tourists and visitors to our country have all been greatly impressed by the discipline of our troops, and the respect that has been shown for the lives and property of local and foreign residents and visitors. From all over the island the same report have come to us that the tourists are commenting on the warmth, friendliness and discipline of our people and the People's Revolutionary Army. The same comments are being daily made by the hundreds of medical students studying in Grenada.

The annual boat race from Trinidad to Grenada took place as usual last night with a bigger than ever participation. The great sense of relief and happiness of our people are obvious to all. In fact, it is clear that there is no sense of panic here or hesitation by the tourists who daily continue to stream into Grenada.

Big Stick and Carrots

For this reason we want the people of Grenada and the Caribbean to realize that if all of a sudden tourists start panicking and leaving the country, or stop coming to our country, then they should note that this came after veiled threats by the United States Ambassador with respect to our tourist industry. The Ambassador, Mr Frank Ortiz, on his last visit to Grenada some days ago, went out of his way to emphasise the obvious importance of tourism to our country. He argued that as Grenada imported some $32 million a year in goods but exported only $13 million, we had a massive trade deficit of some $19 million, which earnings from the tourist industry could substantially lessen. His point was, and we accept that point, that tourism was and is critical to the survival of our economy. The Ambassador went on to advise us that if we continue to speak about what he called 'mercenary invasions by phantom armies' that we could lose all our tourists. He also reminded us of the experience which Jamaica had had in this regard a few years ago.

As some of you will undoubtedly recall, Jamaica at that time had gone through a period of intense destabilisation. Under this process the people of Jamaica were encouraged to lose faith and confidence in themselves, their government and their country and in the ability of their government to solve the pressing problems facing the country and meeting the expectations of their people. This was done through damaging news stories being spread in the local, regional and international media, particularly newspapers, aimed at discrediting the achievements of the Jamaican government. It was also done through violence and sabotage and by wicked and pernicious attempts at wrecking the economy through stopping the flow of tourist visitors, and hence much needed foreign exchange earnings of the country. The experience of Jamaica must therefore remind us that the economies of small, poor Third World countries which depend on tourism can be wrecked by those who have the ability and the desire to wreck them. In his official meetings with Minister of Finance Brother Bernard Coard, and then with me on Tuesday of this week, and in his unofficial discussions with a leading comrade of the People's Revolutionary Army at Pearls Airport on Wednesday, the Ambassador stressed the fact that his government will view with great displeasure the development of any relations between our country and Cuba. The Ambassador pointed out that his country was the richest, freest and most generous country in the world, but, as he put it, 'We have two sides'. We understood that to mean that the other side he was referring to was the side which stamped on freedom and democracy when the American government felt that their interests were being threatened. 'People are panicky and I will have to report that fact to my government', he advised us. However, the only evidence of panic given by the Ambassador was the incident which took place last Monday when the People's Revolutionary Army, as a result of not having been warned beforehand, shot at a plane which flew very low, more than once over Camp Butler. He calls that panic. The people of Grenada call it alertness.

At the end of our discussion on Tuesday the Ambassador handed me a typed statement of his instructions from his government, to be given to us. The relevant section of that statement reads, and I quote:

> Although my Government recognises your concerns over allegations of a possible counter-coup, it also believes that it would not be in Grenada's best interests to seek assistance from a country such as Cuba to forestall such an attack. We would view with displeasure any tendency on the part of Grenada to develop closer ties with Cuba.

We Are No One's Lackey

It is well established internationally that all independent countries have a full, free and unhampered right to conduct their own internal affairs. We do not, therefore, recognise any right of the United States of America to instruct us on who we may develop relations with and who we may not.

From day one of the Revolution we have always striven to have and develop the closest and friendliest relations with the United States, as well as Canada, Britain and all our Caribbean neighbours — English, French, Dutch and Spanish speaking, and we intend to continue to strive for these relations. But no one must misunderstand our friendliness as an excuse for rudeness and meddling in our affairs, and no one, no matter now mighty and powerful they are, will be permitted to dictate to the government and people of Grenada who we can have friendly relations with and what kind of relations we must have with other countries. We haven't gone through 28 years of fighting Gairyism, and especially the last six years of terror, to gain our freedom, only to throw it away and become a slave or lackey to *any* other country, no matter how big and powerful.

Every day we fought Gairy we put our lives on the line. On the day of the Revolution we started out with almost no arms and in so doing we again put our lives on the line.

We have demonstrated beyond any doubt that we were prepared to *die* to win our freedom. We are even more prepared to die to maintain that freedom now that we have tasted it.

We feel that people of Grenada have the right to know precisely what steps we have taken in our attempts to establish relations at various levels with the United States, and the response which we have so far received.

From the second day of our Revolution, during our first meeting with American government representatives in Grenada, we were at pains to emphasise the deplorable and ravished state in which the Gairy dictatorship had left our economy and our country. We pointed out then that massive assistance, technical and financial, would be required in order to begin the process of rebuilding the economy. The American Consul-General told us that he was not surprised to hear this, and assured us that he would encourage his government to give us the necessary assistance, particularly as he had been so impressed by the bloodless character and the self-evident humanity of our prompt assurances in the first hours of the Revolution that the safety, lives and property of American and other foreign residents were guaranteed. Indeed, he freely admitted that his American residents had all reported to him that they were happy, comfortable and felt secure. However, one month later, no such aid has arrived. It is true that the Ambassador did point out — and correctly so — that his Government generally grants aid on a multilateral basis through the Caribbean Development Bank. It is also true that he said his government would prefer to maintain that approach rather than help directly, despite his admission that red tape and bureaucracy could cause delays of up to one year in receiving such multilateral aid.

It is also true that he advised us that his Government is monitoring movements and that it is against United States law for Gairy to recruit mercenaries in the United States of America. This we appreciate.

US $5,000 is Not the Price of Our Dignity

However, we must point out that the fact is, that in place of the massive economic aid and assistance that seemed forthcoming, the only aid the American Ambassador has been able to guarantee that he could get to Grenada in a reasonably short time would be $5,000.00 (US) for each of a few small projects.

Sisters and brothers, what can a few $5,000.00 (US) do? Our hospitals are without medicines, sheets, pillowcases and proper equipment. Our schools are falling down. Most of our rural villages are in urgent need of water, electricity, health clinics and decent housing. Half of the people in the country who are able to and would like to work are unable to find jobs. Four out of every five women are forced to stay at home or scrunt for a meagre existence. $5,000.00 cannot build a house, or a health clinic. We feel forced to ask whether the paltry sum of a few $5,000.00 is all that the wealthiest country in the world can offer to a poor but proud people who are fighting for democracy, dignity and self-respect based on real and independent economic development.

Let us contrast this with the immediate response of our Caribbean brothers. We will take two examples: Guyana and Jamaica, countries thousands of times poorer than the United States of America; countries, indeed, like ourselves, poor, over-exploited and struggling to develop. These two countries have given us technical assistance, cheaper goods, and are actively considering our request for arms and military training. This assistance has included a shipment of rice which arrived two days ago, a six-man team of economic and other experts from Guyana presently in our country, and the imminent arrival of Mr Roy Jones, Deputy Governor of the Bank of Jamaica and Professor George Eaton, a leading authority on public service structures. And notwithstanding these concrete and much appreciated acts of assistance and solidarity they have never once attempted to instruct us as to the manner in which we should conduct our own internal affairs or as to which countries we should choose to develop relations with.

The American Ambassador is taking very lightly what we genuinely believe to be a real danger facing our country. Contrary to what anyone else may think we know that the dictator Gairy is organising mercenaries to attack Grenada in order to restore him to his throne. We know the man Gairy. Nobody knows him better than we the people of Grenada and we recognise the meaning and implications of the evidence which has come before us.

We say that when Frank Mabri Jr. and Mustaphos Hammarabl, Gairy's underworld friends, write to him indicating how much and what kind of arms are available, and when Gairy says on radio broadcasts and in newspaper interviews that he will never give up and that he intends to return to Grenada as prime minister, that he can only mean that he will use force in order to achieve these ends. And because our Revolution is a popular one, supported by the vast majority of our population, and because many of our patriots are armed, force here can only mean getting another country to intervene on his behalf, or hiring mercenaries to do his dirty work for him. And this in turn could only mean the mass killing of thousands of innocent Grenadians, regardless of which political party they support. It is in these circumstances, and because we have an undoubted freedom that we called on the Americans, Canadians, British, our fellow-countries in CARICOM, like Guyana and Jamaica, Venezuela and Cuba, to assist us with arms.

And we reject *entirely* the argument of the American Ambassador that we would only be entitled to call upon the Cubans to come to our assistance *after* mercenaries have landed and commenced the attack. Quite frankly, and with the greatest respect, a more ridiculous argument can hardly be imagined. It is like asking a man to wait until his house is burning down before he leaves to buy a fire extinguisher. No, we intend if possible to provide ourselves with the fire extinguisher before the fire starts! And if the government of Cuba is willing to offer us assistance, we would be more than happy to receive it.

We Are Not in Anybody's Backyard And We Are Definitely Not For Sale

Sisters and brothers, what we led was an *independent process*. Our Revolution was definitely a popular revolution, not a *coup d'etat*, and was and is in no way a minority movement. We intend to continue along an independent and non-aligned path. We have stayed in the Commonwealth, we have stayed in the Organization of American States and in CARICOM; despite pressures we have stayed in the Eastern Caribbean Common Market and in the expanded West Indies Associated States Organization (WISA). We have applied to join the Non-Aligned Movement. We will be applying to join the International Labour Organization — the ILO.

We are a small country, we are a poor country, with a population of largely African descent, we are a part of the exploited Third World, and we definitely have a stake in seeking the creation of a New International Economic Order which would assist in ensuring economic justice for the oppressed and exploited peoples of the world, and in ensuring that the resources of the sea are used for the benefit of all the people of the world and not for a tiny minority of profiteers. Our aim, therefore, is to join all organisations and work with all countries that will help us to become more independent and more in control of our own resources. In this regard, nobody who understands present-day realities can seriously challenge our right to develop working relations with a variety of countries.

Grenada is a sovereign and independent country, although a tiny speck on the world map, and we expect all countries to strictly respect our independence, just as we will respect theirs. No country has the right to tell us what to do or how to run our country, or who to be friendly with. We certainly would not attempt to tell any other country what to do. We are not in anybody's backyard, and we are definitely not for sale. Anybody who thinks they can bully us or threaten us, clearly has no understanding idea or clue as to what material we are made of. They clearly have no idea of the tremendous struggles which our people have fought over the past seven years. Though small and poor, we are proud and determined. We would sooner give up our lives before we compromise, sell out, or betray our sovereignty, our independence, our integrity, our manhood and the right of our people to national self-determination and social progress.

LONG LIVE THE REVOLUTION!

LONG LIVE GRENADA!

THE COLONIAL STATE

New Seville and the Conversion Experience of Bartolomé de Las Casas

Sylvia Wynter

PART ONE

This article is abstracted from a book **The Rise and Fall of New Seville 1509-1536** *being written for the New Seville Restoration Project by the author.*

The priest Casas having at the time no knowledge of the unjust methods which the Portuguese used to obtain slaves, advised that permission should be given for the Import of slaves into the islands, an advice which, once he became informed about these methods, he would not have given for the world ...

The remedy which he proposed to import Black slaves in order to liberate the Indians was not a good one, even though he thought the Black slaves, at the time to have been enslaved with a just title; and it is not at all certain that his ignorance at the time or even the purity of his motive will sufficiently absolve him when he finds himself before the Divine Judge (Las Casas, History of the Indies, Bk 3).

> Clearly one cannot prove in a short time or with a few words to infidels that to sacrifice men to God is contrary to nature. Consequently neither anthropopagy nor human sacrifice constitutes just cause for making war on certain kingdoms ... For the rest, to sacrifice innocents for the salvation of the Commonwealth is not opposed to natural reason, is not something abominable and contrary to nature, but is an error that has its origin in natural reason itself.
>
> Las Casas' reply to Ginés de Sepúlveda on the occasion of the 1550-1 debate at Valladolid, Spain, as to whether or not the new world Indians were equally 'men' (Las Casas) or 'slaves-by-nature' (Sepúlveda).

In June, 1514, a certain Pablo De La Rentería who was on a business trip to Jamaica stayed for a while at the Franciscan monastery in New Seville.[1] Whilst there, he underwent a conversion experience. This experience took place almost at the same time as a conversion experience undergone by his partner on their jointly owned estate near the recently settled town of Espiritu Santo, Cuba.

Pablo De La Rentería remains a somewhat obscure figure. What we know of him we know from his partner's account of their parallel experiences. And there was to be no one, after Columbus himself, who was to be more historically significant in the new era of human affairs that opened with Columbus' first arrival in the Caribbean in 1492, than De La Rentería's partner, Bartolomé de Las Casas.

Nor was there to be an event of more crucial significance to this era of history that had opened, than the conversion experience of Las Casas which, like St. Paul's vision on the road to Damascus, shifted Las Casas' way of seeing out of the normative reference frame and uniform perception of his fellow Spanish settlers. This religio-conceptual leap led to the transformation of Las Casas from an *encomendero* – i.e. an owner of an allotted number of Arawaks incorporated as a labour force (an *encomienda*) under a traditional Spanish system which, however, took on new and harsher aspects in the frontier context of the new world — to the most determined antagonist of the entire system of Indian forced labour, whether in the form of the *encomienda* or in the form of outright Indian slave-labour.

Two consequences of this transformation were to be of special significance to contemporary Jamaica. The first was that as a result of his conversion-inspired mission to secure the abolition of all forms of Indian forced labour, Las Casas was to propose the importation of a limited quantity of African slaves both to recompense the settlers for their Indian labour supply; and as an incentive to Spanish peasant migration. This limited scheme proposed to the Emperor Charles V and his royal bureaucracy was the initial occasion for the subsequent sale by the Crown in 1518 of a licence to one of the Flemish courtiers at the court of the half-Burgundian King of Spain, one Gouvenot – who later sold it to some Genoese merchants – to import 4,000 slaves from West Africa into the Caribbean islands and the mainland. This *asiento* was to be the charter, at one and the same time, of the transatlantic slave trade, and, at a terrible human cost, of the African presence as a constitutive unit of the post-Columbian civilization of the Caribbean and the Americas.

Once he was informed of the *unjust methods* used in the enslavement of the Africans, Las Casas, who had worked on the assumption that he was submitting men and women who had been *justly* enslaved according to the moral-legal system of Latin Christianity, for Indian men and women whom he knew from *personal experience* to be *unjustly enslaved within the* context of these same moral-legal doctrines, was to bitterly repent of his original proposal.[2]

The second consequence of his conversion experience was to lead to a daring conceptual leap made by Las Casas. This was during the course of his theoretical dispute with the theologian-humanist scholar and official royal historian, Ginés de Sepúlveda in the context of the formal debate held at Valladolid, Spain, before a conclave of theologians, jurists, scholars, royal bureaucrats and councillors in 1550-1.

Sepúlveda in order to provide a legitimatizing basis for the Spanish conquest of the Indies, to represent it as 'just' and 'holy' and to derive the *encomienda* system as therefore just and lawful, used a Neo-Aristotelian formulation to argue that the Indians were 'slaves-by-nature'; that there is a difference of 'natural capacity' between peoples, and that this differential gave those of a higher 'natural capacity' (the more perfect) the right to rule and govern those of a lower 'natural capacity' (the less perfect).

Las Casas, in the course of countering Sepúlveda's thesis of a predetermined *natural* difference of rational capacity between peoples, and the servile-by-nature Neo-Aristotelian formulation of his antagonist, made a conceptual leap to propose – almost heretically, given the context of his time – that the human sacrifices made by peoples like the Aztecs and their ritual eating of human flesh was not, as his antagonist Sepúlveda took it to be evidence and proof of a *lack* of natural reason but rather was an *error* of natural reason.

In other words the practice of human sacrifice for the Aztecs did not constitute a *mode of irrationality* but rather a *form of rationality*, an error made by natural reason itself. And in this form of natural reason, practices seen as vices by the Spaniards 'in truth were not thought of as vices by the Indians but virtues answering to a life view much closer to natural reason than that of the Spaniards'.

Within the frame of this reason, assuming their false gods to be the true God, those Indians who sacrificed humans to their gods offered as they did so, 'what seemed most valuable to them', 'sacrificing innocents for the good of the Commonwealth', only because it seemed to them supremely rational to do so.

With this formulation Las Casas anticipated by some four and a half centuries what anthropologists, post-Einstein, and post-Levi-Strauss, are only now beginning to make us see, in the reference frame of an on-going Copernican and decentring revolution, as the *relativity of all human systems of perception including our own;* as the reality, not of a single absolute reason, but of culturally determined modes of reason, as the reality of the cultural-historical relativity of our own.

There are two paradoxical implications here. The first lies in the fact that as the terms of Las Casas' repentance with respect to his first proposal reveals, in proposing the importation of African slaves as a means of ensuring the abolition of the *encomienda* system and the Indian slave trade, he too had been trapped by an 'error' of natural reason, i.e. not only by the fact that he had not known of the *unjust methods* and therefore of the *unjust titles* by which the Africans were enslaved both by the Portuguese and their 'African' partners[3] but also by the logic of a specific mode of cultural reason, that of the 15th and 16th century Catholic Christianity. For, as J.F. Maxwell points out, it was not to be until 1965, that the common teaching of the Catholic Church handed down by its 'fallible ordinary magisterium' a teaching which had approved of the institution of slavery, on condition that the slaves were held by specifically defined 'just titles' for some 1400 years, was finally to be corrected by the second Vatican Council [Maxwell 1974].

The second paradox lies in the fact that it was by his daring, if necessarily limited given the time and circumstances, and religio-monarchical frame of his thought, implication of the existence of *culturally relative forms of rationality*, that Las Casas not only laid the basis for the theoretical delegitimization of all forms of inter-human domination and subordination,[4] but also laid the conceptual basis, some four and a half centuries before it was to become an empirically urgent necessity, for that 'higher-order of synthesis' now vital to the survival of the post-atomic human subject.

> Indeed mankind is already unified in a material sense. It is this very fact that renders higher orders of synthesis necessary if mankind is to survive. The race has always existed, but its unity was in earlier times mostly a dream, a distant image. Now, almost suddenly, mankind has become an inter-communicating and inter-dependent whole in which every part is vulnerable to destruction by other parts. For the first time our planet is living a single history. The material unity which already and irrevocably exists must be reinforced by legal, moral and spiritual unity, which sadly – despite all of our good intentions – still does not exist. [Hirschfeld 1971].

We shall attempt in this two-part article to glance at the background and implications of both paradoxes. To do so it will be necessary to look briefly at the *before* and *after* of the conversion experience; the before of Las Casas' life in Española and Cuba, the conversion experience itself, and the *after* which was to climax in the formal Valladolid dispute against his humanist/theologian antagonist, Ginés de Sepúlveda.

Before the Conversion

Las Casas as Settler/Priest and Encomendero

Bartholomew (Bartolomé) de Las Casas was born in Seville, Spain in 1474. When he was 20 years old, his father, one Pedro de Las Casas, and a merchant, sailed with Columbus on the second voyage of settlement, the expedition with which Spain was to, lay the basis for the emergence of what Hirschfeld calls the 'single history' that all mankind is living today. (It is often forgotten that this basis was first laid by Spain, even more forgotten that it was in four Caribbean Islands, i.e. Española (today's Santo Domingo and Haiti), Puerto Rico, Jamaica and Cuba.)

When Bartolomé's father returned to Seville in 1495 he brought back an Arawak whom he had enslaved – and gave him to his son as his personal attendant. Neither father nor son saw anything wrong with this, in the climate of belief and practice in which a non-racial and non-credal slavery (i.e. slaves were both white/European, black/African, Berber and Arab, Christian, Pagan and Muslim) essentially domestic and artisan, was traditional and widespread.

When Las Casas' father returned to Española to settle there, Bartolomé de Las Casas soon joined him, sailing in the retinue of the newly appointed governor of the Indies, Nicolás de Ovando.

From the time of his arrival in 1502 until the time of his conversion in June 1514, Las Casas, even though he was to be ordained as a priest in 1510 and was always to treat the Arawak peoples more considerately than most, behaved more or less like any other Spanish settler, even as a 'conquistador'. From the scanty indications that we have of his early life in Española, i.e. that he took part in the pacification campaign on the east end of the island, as well as 'in several Indian-hunting expeditions', that although 'he does not seem to have engaged in gold mining at this period', he owned food production estates and had allotted to him numbers of Arawaks within the *encomienda* serf-labour that had been set up to secure a steady labour supply, that he supervised the Indians in the growing of cassava and the making of cassava bread, and that he made considerable sums of money from this [Wagner and Parish 1967] Las Casas fully shared in what might be called the 'land/gold/and *hidalgo* complex', of the average conquistador/poblador; in the psychic complex that underlay the expansionist drive of the first world empire, that of Catholic-Christian Spain's.

The First World Empire and the Complex of Limpieza De Sangre

Spain's year for destiny had been 1492. After eight centuries of having been occupied and invaded by the expanding forces of Islam, the Spanish Christian troops laid siege to, and finally conquered, the last outpost of the Islamic faith in Spain – the city and province of Granada.

The contract that the Spanish sovereigns signed with Columbus was signed in the town of Santa Fé from where the siege of Granada was being directed. Spain's conquest and her expansion into the new world following on Columbus' windfall find, at once shifted both the balance of power and the dynamic of expansion decisively away from Islam to the Latin-Christian European peoples and their dazzling rise to world domination spearheaded by Spain.

The latter's expulsion of all Jews who refused Christian conversion in the high year of 1492 was an act related to her growing sense of national destiny, as well as to the rise of a new system of centralized monarchy based on the unifying cement of a single faith – the Christian.

With her capture of Granada in 1492, Spain now gave the descendants of the former Islamic invaders the same ultimatum that she had given her Jews – convert or leave. Many converted both Jews and Muslims, and were to become known as the 'New Christians' or *conversos*. Purity of faith, *limpieza de fé*, became linked with purity of old Spanish Christian blood, i.e. *limpieza de sangre*, and both were increasingly linked to loyalty to the rising new monarchical state. To be a morisco (a converted Muslim) or a marrano (a converted Jew) was to be suspected, before the fact, of un-Spanish activities.

The concept of *limpieza de sangre*, cleanliness of blood, was a centralizing concept deployed by the monarchical revolution to cut across the rigid caste hierarchy of the feudal nobility. All Christians of genetically Spanish birth of whatever rank, were now incorporable as 'we' and the *limpios* (of *clean* descent and faith), as opposed to the *non-limpios* i.e. the Spaniards of Jewish or Moorish descent. For the monarchical revolution did not abolish the feudal status-prestige system of *nobleza de sangre* (nobility of blood) but rather drew it into a new symbolic machinery of monarchical rationalism, one in which the *hidalgo complex* (the aspiration to noble status, and to the title of Don), and the *limpieza complex* (the aspiration to 'clean' status, to being the Spanish Christian socio-symbolic norm) cross cut, balanced and reinforced each other in a dynamic equilibrium.

J.H. Elliot in his perceptive book on Imperial Spain, points out that the concept of *limpieza* was used as a class weapon by a new stratum, i.e. the sons of lowly born peasants and artisans who through 'natural' ability and education were able to aspire to the higher levels of the Church and state bureaucracy. Finding their way to these posts blocked by powerful members of the aristocracy who reserved them for their own highly-born caste, the new *letrado* class (the lettered class, the literati) consisting of jurists, theologians, scholars, pushed the introduction of new statutes which reserved these higher posts, especially those in the Church, for those who could prove their 'purity of blood' during several generations [J.H. Elliott, 1960].

In medieval Spain there had been considerable intermingling between the aristocracy and powerful members of the Jewish community, many of whom controlled the higher reaches of finance and of the learned professions. In addition, in 1492, many Jews had accepted conversion rather than endure expulsion, and they now formed a powerful stratum, officially Christian, able to rival the Spanish *letrado* class in learning and to outrank them, backed as they were by highly-placed aristocratic connections.

With the rise of a theocratic monarchical state, the new *letrado* class, making social use of the theological stigma placed on Jews as a people who had 'rejected' Christ and refused 'His Word', had constructed a concept of orthodoxy in which the heresy of this original act of rejection was represented as being carried in the blood, generating in all their *non-limpio* descendants a 'natural inclination' to heresy.

Men risen from lowly origins, from the villages, where there had been no intermarriage, were therefore represented as bearers of the socio-theological orthodoxy of *limpieza de sangre/ limpieza de fê,* as the nobility – including the powerful *converso* Jews – were the bearers of the socio-symbolic orthodoxy of *hidalguía* and noble blood. Each group, the nobility and new *letrado* class, vied to play off their orthodoxies against each other.

Recent scholarship has raised the possibility that Las Casas was of *converso,* New Christian Jewish descent, i.e. a *marrano.* Las Casas himself was to insist that he was of 'good old stock', i.e. an old Christian. He could genuinely have believed this. Once converted, families went to great lengths to 'pass', to repress all traces of their Jewish or Moorish origins, since these origins barred many avenues to preferment in Church and state. Indeed, New Christians, whether of Jewish or Moorish descent were officially banned from entering the new world even though their de facto widespread clandestine and unofficial presence is now being documented by scholarly research (several documents, for example, indicate the presence of both *marranos* and *moriscos* in New Seville).

But even had he known it, Las Casas would never have admitted to it. The lesser evil, he insisted in another context, was always to be preferred to a greater. Superb strategist that he was, he would have known that the struggle that he fought to abolish the *encomienda* would have been lost even before the start had he admitted to such a 'taint'. Nevertheless, his struggle for a universally applicable, rather than for a 'nationalist', Christianity, might have not been unconnected to the creative ambivalence of his own origins.

Landedness/Landlessness
The Reconquest and the Hidalguía Complex

Both complexes, that of *limpieza* and that of *nobleza de sangre,* can only be understood in the context of the centuries long crusade waged to reconquer Spanish territory from the Moors. This crusade, called the Reconquest was essentially a long 'anti-colonial' struggle against the religious imperialism of Islam. For in a wave of expansion, after the death of their prophet Mohammed, the followers of Islam had entered Spain in AD 711, advancing into Europe as far as Tours until stopped by Charles Martel (AD 732) in a battle which saved Christendom.

Christian Spain, however, from the eighth century onwards, was corralled in, and confined to, the small northern-enclaves, whilst Islam occupied the rest of Spain, developing a dazzling civilization which reached its high point in a 10th century apogee of commercial development and learning. This civilization was based on the co-existence of the three Semitic-derived monotheistic faiths, Judaism, Christianity and Mohammedanism, with the latter of course, hegemonic, but relatively tolerant.

Although an interracial faith, Islam was primarily borne by the Arabs. Latin-Christendom, as it fought against Islam, and as it was cut off from its original Mediterranean range of differing peoples, gradually 'ethnicized' itself, becoming a Carolingian, Frankish/Gothic type of Euro-Christianity. It was this particularistic Euro-Christianity which provided the ideological basis for the Reconquest.

Both the *hidalgo* and the *limpieza* complexes carried by the settlers to the new world were therefore generated from a *religious racism* dynamically forged in the struggle against an Arab-dominated Islam, during which the aristocracy had come to play a central role. For the imperative of retaking the lands occupied and ruled by the Spanish Moors had placed a premium on the religio-military machine consisting of the great nobles, the military orders and the higher dignitaries of the Church. The additional fact that the Reconquest was sanctified as a Holy War and was quite clearly a 'just war', i.e. an offensive/defensive war legitimatized the Spanish nobility's amassing of vast political and economic power. Even more crucially the model of the noble – the *hijo d'algo* or 'son of someone', i.e. the hidalgo, whose fighting qualities were ascribed to the genetic superiority of his caste and lineage – became the normative model of identity of the society.

The complex of *hidalguía* generated from the 'deep rooted crusading spirit ... linked to a modernized medieval warrior/complex' [Moya Pons 1984], was expressed in a two caste system in which the socio-symbolic norm, those of predominantly noble and fighting lineage, looked down upon the agriculturalists *(labradores* and *campesinos,* i.e. peasants) as well as on the free artisan urban class. Manual labour or any connection with non-military or non-religious activities tended to be deeply stigmatized. To be lowly born – of peasant or of artisan origin – carried a stigma as powerful as that of Blackness in the pre-1938 Caribbean.

The symbolic material apparatus of valorization/stigmatization logically coded the normative desire. All Spanish skins wore *Don* masks (cf. Fanon's Black Skins/White Masks). However lowly-born, every Spaniard, like Cervantes' plain Alonso Quijana, aspired to reinvent himself as Don Quixote; aspired to be a Don.

The dominance of the aristocracy – through its control of what might be called the psychic desire/aversion apparatus of the order as a whole, was expressed at the economic level by its control of a new system – the latifundium system. For whilst the long centuries of the Reconquest had helped to undermine the feudal order by creating a more open and mobile frontier situation, it had also led to a situation in which vast expanses of the lands recaptured from the Moors had become concentrated in the exclusive ownership of the great nobles, the high clergy and the military orders. The latifundium complex was reinforced by the poverty of the soil, and the high prices paid in Northern Europe for Spanish wool, with both factors leading to the expansion of a nomadic pastoral system of sheep-rearing [Moya Pons 1984].

This in turn led to a de facto form of enclosure system in which *landlessness* for a growing stratum of the dispossessed *in the context of a demographic explosion* became a fact of life. And since the ownership of land was the basis of wealth and the symbol of power in the *hidalguía* complex, the opening up of *new world lands* to Spanish settlers and the opportunity to become *landed* in the context of a new frontier provided a powerful psychoeconomic motivation to emigration and settlement.

Unhearing of the Voice in the Wilderness

Are They not Men?

The Las Casas of before his conversion shared in this psychoeconomic motivation. And since New World land without a steady labour supply was valueless, the Las Casas of the *before*, saw nothing wrong in intra-Caribbean slave-raiding and trading nor in the *encomienda* system. In other words his mode of perception was determined by this always already societally-coded motivation.

As a result, Las Casas found himself on the side of the settlers in December 1511, when the Dominicans in a famous sermon openly attacked and denounced both Indian slaving and the *encomienda* systems.

The attack was delivered in a Christian sermon by Fray Antonio Montesinos, a member of the Dominican order, but the position put forward was that of the Dominicans as a whole. Members of the order had only that year arrived in the island of Española and they were horrified at the disastrous effects on the Arawaks of the regimes of forced labour, slave and *encomienda*.

His voice, Montesinos said, was the voice of one crying in the wilderness. By what right, he asked, or justice do you keep these Indians in such horrible servitude?… Are these not men? Have they not rational souls? Are you not bound to love them as you love yourselves? All Spanish-Christians who were holders of *encomienda* Indian labour were in mortal sin, he warned; had condemned their immortal souls to hell. The settlers, led by Diego Columbus, were furious. For a while the lives of the Dominicans were in danger.

The Dominicans who had based their arguments on a consensually arrived at theological-juridical position based both on their concepts of what were the just titles under which people could be enslaved, and on the conditions under which the Spanish sovereigns had a *just title* to the Indies, refused to retract.

The Santo Domingo settlers sent (in 1512) a Franciscan, Alonso del Espinal, to argue against the Dominican's position. The Dominicans for their part sent Fray Alonso de Montesinos to defend their position. The crucial debates that were to determine the future mode of relations between the Spanish settlers and the new world peoples had begun.

Las Casas was, at that time, unhearing of the voice in the wilderness; unheeding too, when, not long after, he was refused absolution on the grounds that he was both a priest and an *encomendero*. At the time he saw nothing wrong in the *encomienda* since the setting up of an estate in the frontier conditions needed a steady and continuous supply of labour. And his position was at that time not only that of the majority but the state position. For the institutions of *encomienda* and of Indian-slaving provided the basis not only for settler-aspirations, but at the macro-level, for the commercial network called by the historians Pierre and Huguette Chaunu 'Seville's Atlantic'; a network which in turn provided the economic basis for the expansion of Spain as a world empire.

Spain, Seville's Atlantic, and the Modern World System

The new Spanish state based on the juridical political system of absolute monarchy, was headed by the Catholic sovereigns Isabel of Castile and Ferdinand of Aragón. The earlier marriage of these two sovereigns had laid the basis for the monarchical revolution in Spain, against the decentralized semi-feudal system which they inherited. With the help of a new cadre of jurists (letrados) learned in Roman law, they began to weld together a powerful modern state out of two separate entities, Castile and Aragón; and after 1492 to initiate the world's first global empire.

Between 1494 and 1560, Spain came to gain control of over half of the population in the western hemisphere. Between 1494 and 1670 when the Treaty of Madrid confirmed Spain's loss of Jamaica to the English, the land-mass area under European control 'went from about 3 million kilometres to about 7'. This led to an unprecedented shift in the land-labour ratio. This shift was to provide the empirical conditions for the development of the mercantile system that the Chaunus call Seville's Atlantic; as well as for the historical rationale of the intra-Caribbean slave/trading and encomienda system.

The Chaunus have documented the putting in place of the new commercial network with its centre in Seville, Spain, 'where the world's heart beats' [Braudel]; the putting in place of its mercantile, political and juridical structures, all of which, transported from the Mediterranean, were to be reinvented by Spain, leading to new and original structures which were to evolve 'during the long passage of a century and a half' [Chaunu 1959].

These new and original structures were to be at the same time the founding structures of what Immanuel Wallerstein has recently defined as the first economic world system in history. The structures of this emerging world system were integrated, in its first phase, by the formula of mercantilism, a politico-economic doctrine which although invented by the Spaniards, was soon to become the 'fundamental law of all Europe' [Eric Williams 1964]. And the central tenet of this doctrine – that a trade balance based on the excess of exports over imports was the goal of national policy – led to the implementation of policies which could ensure the autarchic self-sufficiency of the network.

The Role of New Seville and the Visit of Pablo de la Rentería

The town of New Seville after its founding by Juan de Esquivel in 1509 came to constitute one of the chain of settlements of the mercantile network of Atlantic 1. Its role was therefore determined by the overall logic of the system.

As the Chaunus point out, until about 1518 when some gold deposits were discovered on the island, Jamaica occupied a bottom-of-the-ladder role in the context of the gold cycle as contrasted with the gold-producing islands of Santo Domingo, Puerto Rico and Cuba. Because of its relative backwardness with respect to the gold cycle, Jamaica got off to a bad start under its founder Esquivel. Arawak Indians were at first exported as slave labour to the other islands to work in gold-mining and 'washing' there; this export of Indian labour then led to the emigration of some of the original Spanish settlers.

It was soon to flower, however, once the Crown ordered a shift in its role and the governor and other officials were instructed to develop the island as a food supply and provision base. Esquivel, in pursuance of this instruction had established two royal estates at Pimienta and Melilla on the basis both of the encomienda labour of the Arawaks and of their already cultivated lands (conucos). And what the Chaunus call New Seville's 'brilliant beginning' was to be largely due to the rapid development of livestock rearing and food growing in its hinterland. Already in 1514, it had become the food provision supplier of the Caribbean.

Pablo De La Rentería's visit to Jamaica and to New Seville was caused by his and his partner's need for live-stock and food supplies. For in 1512 Las Casas had gone with the expedition sent from Española under Velasquez to conquer and settle Cuba. However, as a friend of the governor Velasquez, Las Casas after taking part in the settlement of the town of Espiritu Santo, was assigned, together with his friend De La Rentería, a 'good big' *encomienda* (land and labour of the Indians who lived in the vicinity) in 'the nearby Ariamo River the richest in gold yet'. [Wagner and Parrish 1967].

In 1514 Las Casas' partner went off to Jamaica – his goal was to arrange to purchase and bring back a shipload of livestock and other foodstuffs both to feed their *encomienda* Indians who were now engaged in washing the sands for gold, and to begin livestock rearing on their Cuban estate.

Stained is the Offering: The Conversion Experience of Las Casas

Whilst preparing a sermon to preach to the Spaniards of Espiritu Santo, Cuba during the absence of his partner in New Seville, Jamaica, Las Casas was struck by the verse from Ecclesiastes that read 'stained is the offering of him that sacrificeth from a thing wrongfully gotten… .' The verse led to a train of reflection in which he remembered the hard certainty with which he had rejected the Dominicans' position, and the logical sequence of his own behaviour which had been generated by the complex of *a priori* settler-assumptions.

These Deadly Allotments Against the Purpose of Jesus Christ

At this moment, as Las Casas would later relate, he saw that no king nor indeed any earthly power whatsoever, could 'justify our tyrannical entrance into the New World, nor these deadly allotments as is clear in Española, in San Juan and Jamaica, and in the Bahamas'. The actions of the Spanish settlers, and therefore of his before-conversion-settler-self, had brought a great evil on the Indians precisely because these actions were in explicit contradiction to the teachings of the Catholic Christian faith.

All that we did and do, he concluded sombrely, 'go against the purpose of Jesus Christ and against the charity commanded in the Scriptures'. Above all, the 'deadly system of allotments' the *encomienda* system, was, in the context of Catholic Christian doctrines, *'unjust* and *tyrannical'*.

Following on his conversion Las Casas went to see the governor, his friend, Velasquez, and stunned the latter by his decision to renounce the generous *encomienda* which had been allotted to him. In August 1514, he went public with his decision. Taking up the cry of Montesinos, Las Casas preached a sermon in which he told of his own conversion and set forth to the settlers of Espiritu Santo what he now saw as the mortal sin in which those Spaniards who held *encomiendas* were living. He announced his own giving up of the *encomienda* allotted to him, and urged on his fellow settlers the restitution they would have to make if they were not to lose their immortal souls.

Men Become Insensible, Blind and Inhumane

Las Casas in the meanwhile had written his partner asking him to speed up his return. The latter concluded his arrangements in New Seville – a later document reveals that a shipload of provisions taken from the King's estates at Melilla and Pimienta had been handed over to one Salvador De La Rentería, De La Rentería's brother – and sailed from New Seville.

In his account of his conversion and its sequence, Las Casas records that as the caravel arrived off Cuba, he went out in a canoe to meet his partner at ship-side. As they went back to the shore and then on to their estate on the Ariamo River, they recounted their experiences to each other. They both saw the parallelism of their conversions, their common turning away from the normative settler-mode of perception, almost at the same time, as a sign that the mission on which they were to embark had been divinely appointed.

Las Casas told his partner of the mission that he now saw before him, of the need that he would have to wage a struggle on two fronts. On the one front his aim would be to save the Arawaks from the physical extinction which he saw taking place, because of the *encomienda* system which harnessed them to a regime of intensive labour undreamt of and unimaginable in the context of their former mode of life.

On the other front, he told De La Rentería his mission was to save the Spanish settlers from the eternal *damnation of their souls.* For Las Casas had an existential knowledge of how his former settler colleagues thought and felt, of how spurred on by the wide open frontier of possibility which promised rapid enrichment and social ascension, the Spanish settlers like his before-conversion-self, had become hardened and callous, trapped by the demands of a settler-psyche – (insensibles, *hechos como hombres ciegos e inhumanos, i.e.* become insensible, transformed into blind and inhumane men). And Las Casas knew that the conversion experience for him had been an awakening from this spiritual and perceptual 'blindness'.

Those We Hold in Contempt Will Sit At the Right Hand of God: Predestination and Renterías Conversion

De La Rentería's conversion had followed similar lines. The latter, Las Casas tells us, had 'always been a servant of God and very compassionate with respect to the calamitous state of the Indians'. Spending the 'Lenten season in a Franciscan monastery which at that time existed in the island' (of Jamaica). De La Rentería too experienced a process of reflection in which the thought of the 'oppression of these people and of the miserable life they endured' brought to his mind the idea 'that he ought to ask the king to grant him a licence and authority to establish a number of schools, in which all Indian children could be assembled and instructed *(doctrinarios)* so that the children at least could be freed from perdition and extermination *(mortandad) and that those whom God had elected to be saved could be saved'.* With this aim in view, he was determined, after his return to Cuba, to go to Castile and to ask the King to give him leave to set up such a school.

De La Rentería's conversion centred about the theological concept of predestination, a concept central to the great disputes of the age. For the conflict between the Augustinian/Pelagian attitudes to human salvation, with St. Augustine insisting on God's grace as the true means to salvation, and on the predestining by God of some to be saved, others to be damned, and Pelagius to the contrary positing a strong role for human free will in the attaining of salvation, could almost be called *the* structuring controversy of Catholic Christianity. But both currents of this controversy had been maintained in a kind of dynamic equilibrium before first Luther, then Calvin – and the new historical forces in whose name and from whose perspectives they spoke, – split the church on the basis of a now absolute either/or between Predestination/Faith/Grace on the one hand and Free Will/Good Works on the other.

Both De La Rentería and Las Casas tended towards the predestination wing of the orthodox Catholic Christian continuum. And the spiritual universal egalitarianism generated by this attitude to predestination was to provide the key point of difference between Las Casas and Sepúlveda in the Valladolid dispute of 1550. However, even before the dispute with Sepúlveda, against a Dominican antagonist Fray Domingo de Belanzos who declared to the Council of the Indies that the Indians were 'bestial', that God had prepared a specific reprobation for them, condemning them to extermination for their sins, Las Casas had insisted on a divine election and reprobation, specific to all men, universally applicable to all peoples.

All men, he warned his fellow Spaniards, were God's people and 'it may be that once God has exterminated these people [the Indians] through our cruel hands, He will spill his anger over us all, … inspiring other nations to do unto us what we have done unto them, destroying us as we destroyed them *and it may be that more of those whom we hold in contempt will sit at* the right hand of God than there will be of us, and this consideration ought to keep us in fear day and night'.

With this new way of seeing, the partners now agreed together that Las Casas should go to Castile to petition the King in both their names so that they attain the goals, now become the driving force in their lives, after the 'joy and wonder' *(alegría y admiración:* Las Casas) of their dual conversion experiences, one in Espiritu Santo, Cuba, the other in New Seville, Jamaica.

(Bibliographical References will be given at the end of Part 2).

Notes

1. The first town founded by the Spaniards in Jamaica 1509 was originally and officially called Seville. In 1518 the site of the town was moved and as was customary, the name New Seville seems to have been used to differentiate the new site from the old. We have used the latter name since this seems to have been customary in everyday usage.
2. See quotation at the beginning of this article.
3. One uses 'African' here only in a geographical sense since the African system of identification was tribal-lineage and it was therefore as metaphysically 'just' for the Christian to enslave the Muslim and vice versa.
4. The Latin American historian Juan Freide has recently documented his claim that Las Casas was both the political and theoretical forerunner of all later anti-colonial struggles [Juan Freide 1976].

PART TWO

I put forward and proved many propositions that no one before me had touched upon nor written about, and one of them was that it was not against law and natural reason to offer men as a sacrifice to God, assuming their false god to be the true one.

(*Las Casas, commenting upon the Valladolid Dispute*)

In another treatise — written in Latin — Las Casas declared that all men and things are free 'if the contrary is not shown'. The liberty of man is a natural attribute. It could only be lost per accidents, *by circumstantial causes, and not by Nature as Sepúlveda sustained.*

(*Juan Freide*)

The first part of this article told of the parallel conversion experiences of Bartolomé de Las Casas, and of his friend and partner, Pablo De La Rentería . Both of these experiences had taken place in mid-1514, that of Las Casas at their newly acquired estate near the town of Espiritu Santo, Cuba, that of his partner at the Franciscan monastery in the town of New Seville, Jamaica. De La Rentería had gone to New Seville from Cuba, on a business trip to bring back livestock for their estate, and a shipload of provisions to feed themselves and the group of Arawak Indians who had been allotted to them in the context of a compulsory work system known as the encomienda system. The shipload of provisions, and the livestock, was intended to tide them over whilst they laid the basis for the rapid development of domestic food production on their own estate.

Their conversion experiences were to entirely divert them from this goal. Las Casas, after his own experience which had been triggered off by a verse from Ecclesiastes – Stained is the offering which is wrongfully gotten – was to devote the rest of his life (from 1514 to 1566); after first giving up his own encomienda group of Indians, in a prolonged struggle not only to secure the abolition of the encomienda system as well as of the outright slave-trading in Indians which had also sprung up, but also to get the Spanish settlers to make direct financial restitution to the Indians for all that (from his post-conversion new way of seeing) they had 'wrongfully gotten' as Christians from the original new world peoples.

With De La Rentería now in Cuba, the two friends translated their transformed mode of perception into practical action. They agreed that Las Casas should travel to Castile to petition the King in both their names, the one for the abolition of the *encomienda* and the Indian slave trade, the other for permission to set up a school in Cuba for the children of the Indians. In order to find sufficient money to pay the expenses of Las Casas' passage, as well as to 'enable him to remain at Court all the time necessary to find a remedy for the plight of these peoples' (Las Casas), the two men also agreed that they would pool the money that they had available and add to this whatever sums they could get from the sale of the shipload of livestock and provisions that De La Rentería had brought from New Seville.

Amongst these provisions. Las Casas tells us, were many pigs and much cassava bread and maize and other things, all of which were worth a great deal. For it was a seller's market in Cuba where the settlers' gold fever had drawn the majority of the Indians away from the food production which was their forte – and which had become central to the daily life of the goldless Jamaica – to the search for and washing and extraction of gold.

Las Casas was therefore able to finance the first two years of his lifelong mission in a great part with the proceeds from the sale of the livestock and provisions from New Seville. And, as a later letter from Pedro de Mazuelo who had arrived in New Seville towards the end of 1514, newly appointed as treasurer and royal business manager suggests with a fine historical irony, the shipload of livestock and provisions, taken on credit from the royal estates at Pimienta and Melilla by one Salvador De La Rentería, Pablo's brother who had later died in Santo Domingo, had not been repaid.

Yet from the perspective of contemporary Jamaica, and of our 'individual national' history, the episode of the ship-load of provisions from Seville, linked to the dual conversion experiences of the two friends, was to be involved in greater and more far-reaching historical paradox. As the historian Peter Jones points out, the history of all post-Columbian new world societies can no longer be grasped as a 'mere extension of European culture' but rather as part of a complex process in which whilst 'European armies, European technologies and ideas and European diseases disrupted and sometimes destroyed traditional cultures ... [and] ... almost annihilated native populations' as they attempted to impose 'a European way of life', after the conquest was over and settlement began, something else occurred:

> Once settlement was stabilized, it was not always clear who had conquered whom, and culture assimilated to each other in areas **where the numerical advantage** was not too heavily in favour of the invaders. Out of this cauldron of change, a variety of independent nations eventually emerged ... as distinct from each other as Haiti is from Uruguay, the United States from Bolivia, or Canada from Brazil ... . [Their] individual national histories ... have been moulded by particular geographic, climatic, and locational differences, by whatever existing native cultures were already there, and by the particular type, source and timing of the European invasion [Peter Jones].

Labour Supply

Arriving in Spain in 1515 Las Casas had managed to secure an audience with the King in December. He had persuasively put the entire matter of the abuses inflicted on the Indians and of their rapidly increasing death rate and possible extinction, to King Ferdinand in the context of a matter which needed to be dealt with if the royal conscience were to be absolved. After hearing the case put forward by Las Casas, the King arranged to see him again so that the issue could be dealt with in depth. However, the King, already ill at the time of the December meeting, died on 25 January 1516 before the second meeting could take place. He was succeeded by his grandson Charles, the son of Isabel and Ferdinand's daughter Juana and her husband Prince Philip of Burgundy. Charles remained for a while still in the Low Countries and during his absence Spain was ruled by two co-regents, one, the cardinal of Spain, Ximenez de Cisneros, the other, sent by Charles from the Low Countries, a Flemish councillor of his, Adrian, the dean of the University of Louvain.

Las Casas obtained an interview with the co-regents. Both men, deeply shocked at what they had heard, asked him to prepare a written proposal, putting forward his ideas on what measures could be taken so as to remedy the situation and to stop the rapid rate of extinction of the Arawaks.

Las Casas presented his first memorial to the co-regents in 1516. The plan proposed measures by which to convert the Indians from their status as *encomienda* serfs and slave labour into that of free tribute-paying vassals, eventually the co-equal subjects, with the Spanish settlers, of the Crown. The basic problem that had to be solved by the project was the provision of alternative mechanisms by which the following three key functions played by the *encomienda* system could continue to be implemented.

1. The ensuring of a steady labour supply for the Spanish Christian settlers.
2. The ensuring that the Indies venture yield rapid and regular revenues for the Spanish monarchy already embarked on a policy of imperial expansion in Europe.
3. The ensuring of a regular extraction of gold, the regular provision of food supply products, in the context of the trading network of Seville's Atlantic 1.

To lay the basis for the abolition of the *encomienda* as the chief source of labour, Las Casas proposed in his 1516 plan that White and Black slaves be brought from Castile 'to keep herds and build sugar mills, wash gold, and engage in other things which they know about and in which they can be occupied'.

Two key points need to be noted here. The first is that slavery as it was then practised in Spain, and in the rest of the Mediterranean world was credally rather than racially defined, i.e. based on a religious system of categorization. Slaves in Spain were of all races. And this credal system was at the basis of another crucial concept, that of slaves won in a just war, or bought with 'just title' as contrasted with those who were not.

The second point to be noted is therefore linked to the first: Las Casas is not here proposing, the substitution of White and Black slaves for Indian slaves per se, but instead the substitution of enslaved men and women who can be categorized as 'justly enslaved' within the system of classification legitimated by Catholic Christian doctrine, for a group of enslaved men and women who cannot be so classified.

Las Casas proposed that 'communities' consisting of a Spanish town and a group of annexed Indian villages be set up. The Indians, freed from the *encomienda* system should first be allowed to 'rest and replenish their energies'; then they were to be organized into a common pool with the Spaniards being assigned a certain number of Indians but no particular ones (Wagner and Parish 1967].

In this transitional arrangement, the Indians were to live in large new settlements of a thousand souls each, near the mines and the Spanish town. Whilst they would still provide a labour pool for both, strict rules and regulations limited the hours to be worked, with ample leisure and vacation times enabling a work rhythm far closer to that to which the Arawak was culturally accustomed. The settlers were to be shareholders in the overall 'company' and to receive a share in the profits. In exchange for this they would surrender to the community company 'suitable lands, livestock and farming tools' [Wagner and Parish 1967].

A single administrator was to oversee 'a complete staff of Spanish officials and artisans' all of whom were to be employed in the enskilling and the instruction of the Indians. Among this group of teachers and trainers were to be included 'priests, to minister to their religious requirement, and even a bachelor of letters (bachiller de gramática) to teach reading and writing and Spanish' [Wagner and Parish 1967]. Both the priests and the bachelor, one supposes, from a memorial that Las Casas wrote to the Pope in 1565, a year before his death would, in order to teach the Indians, have to learn the letter's languages (the Pope, Las Casas would write then, should order all Bishops to learn the language of the Indians, and not to display the contempt for these languages that they so often did).

Wagner suggests that Las Casas had most likely seen the post of administrator as one for which he would have been more than suitable. And there is little reason to doubt that the proposed bachelor of letters for the first community school would have been De La Rentería; or at least that his idea of a school for the Indians, born out of his conversion experience, was here being incorporated into the overall plan.

The radical nature of Las Casas' proposal to provide large scale training in new agricultural and artisan skills as well as the making literate of large sectors of the Indian population along with their conversion to Christianity, in order to socialize them as free subjects, can be grasped if we observe the parallel 'native' model that had been put in place in Granada, Spain. After the Spanish Christians reconquered the last holdout of the Spanish Moors, whose Islamic ancestors had conquered and occupied Spain from the eighth century onwards, Spanish Muslims were forced to convert to Christianity, and were subjected to a deliberate policy of what might be called 'nativization'.

Las Casas' counter-native model failed. The memorial was submitted to a junta, but the advice of the junta was for reform rather than for the radical organization that Las Casas had proposed. The regents decided to send out a group of Heironymite friars as commissioners-at-large to oversee the government of the islands, and to reform conditions on the spot. Las Casas was also appointed as protector of the Indians, and sent out as a special witness to give the commissioners suitable aid and counsel. But the fine title could not hide the fact that the first memorial that had arisen directly out of the vividness of his and De La Rentería's transformed perceptions, had been rejected in favour of a 'common sense' reform approach.

The Gouvenot Asiento, New Seville

The Sugar-Mill and the 'Negro'

The common sense reform approach failed to stop the increasing mortality rate of the Indians and the abuse to which they were subjected by the settlers in the frontier situation. Las Casas came into sharp conflict with the commissioners who had begun to listen to the settlers' angry diatribes against him, and had begun to compromise with their powerful vested interests. By 1518 he was back in Spain to press for the abolition of the *encomienda* on the basis of a new scheme, which being of a more pragmatic nature, might find greater support in court circles.

The new scheme proposed that the type of settlers in the new world be changed. Spanish peasants and day labourers, accustomed to a degree of steady disciplined labour, and having no social aspirations which caused them to reject manual labour as did the bulk of the settlers already there, should be strongly encouraged to emigrate. The *encomienda* system should be abolished and the new type of settler should set the model for the Indians, teaching them the new skills and techniques of the Spanish system of agriculture.

To compensate the settlers who were already there for the loss of their *encomiendas*, each settler should be allowed a licence to import from Spain two Christianized Black Ladino, slaves each, to help them with their urgent needs. Incentives should be offered to the peasant settler both to get him to settle in the Indies and to stimulate him to grow crops for food and export. One incentive was that any peasant who built a sugar mill should be allowed a licence to import 20 Black slaves directly from Africa as the labour complement of the mill.

This plan for the peasant migration was adopted and a royal decree issued. For various reasons, the plan as a plan was to fail. Three of its components, however, i.e. the idea of incentives for the growing of sugar and building of sugar mills, the idea of the importation of Black slaves directly from Africa into the Indies, and the justifying rationale that Black slaves should be imported in order to liberate the Indians, took on a historical dynamic of their own, going far beyond and in quite other directions to what Las Casas had intended.

Thus in 1518, as a direct result of his proposals, the Spanish Crown granted a licence to a Flemish courtier, Gouvenot, which gave him permission to import 4000 African slaves (trade names *negros* and *negras*) into the Indies. Since this licence was also a form of negotiable currency, Gouvenot at once sold off a part of it to some Genoese merchants in Seville who were linked to the slave-trading houses in the Cape Verde islands off the Guinea coast.

Whilst the Flemish faction at court who strongly backed Las Casas had no vested interest in the new world *encomienda* and intra-Caribbean slave trading system as did the Spanish councillors, Flemish capital had just begun to be invested in the slave trade out of Guinea, with the Portuguese supplying manpower and ships. In other words, at wider levels, historical processes were already at work in whose context, instead of the strictly regulated individual licences to be awarded to those peasant settlers who built sugar mills, the large scale importation of *negros bozales* directly from Africa had been set in motion.[1] Las Casas' protest at this distortion of his original intention was unavailing:

> I asked for and got permission from his Majesty [for the importation of African slaves into the New World] but I did not do so for them to be sold to the Genoese or to court favourites, but in order that they could be allotted to the new settlers.

Opponents of Las Casas have attacked him for, among other charges, having been responsible for the introduction of African chattel slavery into the Americas, with the implication that he saw the Africans as 'lesser beings' than the Indians.

Other historians, not so much defending Las Casas as setting the record straight, have pointed to the historical conjuncture by which, just as the source of White slaves was drying up from the Black Sea, with the Turkish capture of Constantinople, the source of Black slaves from the Guinea coast was opening up in the context of a general European expansion in which Black slavery and the agro-industry of the sugar cane were to be irrevocably connected from early in the 15th century.

The Portuguese arrived off the Guinea coast in 1441 and in 1470 had discovered the uninhabited island of São Torné off the African coast. The island, rapidly settled by Portuguese traders and exiled Jews, soon developed a sugar plantation system based on African slave labour, much of it drawn from the Congo. São Tomé was an instant success, due not only to its soil and climate but also to the rapidly increasing European demand for sugar and the wholesale intensive use of slave labour. As Mellafe [1975] points out, in São Tomé sugar production increased 30 - fold in 20 years (1530-1550) from 62.5 to 1,875 short tons a year.

The sugar cane plant had been taken to the Caribbean islands on the second voyage of settlement (1494). The first sugar mill was built in Española (Cuba) in 1506. In 1510, the rising price of sugar on the emerging world market led to two others being built. By 1516, Francisco de Garay had built a sugar mill in New Seville, Jamaica, and would soon start another.[2] By 1520 some six mills had been built in Española and by 1521 sugar had begun to be exported in small quantities.

Indian slaves had at first been used for sugar production. For instance, in New Seville Francisco de Garay, in partnership with King Ferdinand, had from 1515 exported food provisions to the settlers on the mainland in exchange for the Indian slaves that these settlers raided and captured. When these Indian slaves were sent to New Seville, Garay used some for his mill, but reshipped the majority for sale in Santo Domingo.

From 1518, with the arrival of the first batch of African slaves resulting from the Gouvenot *asiento*, the settlers began to turn more and more to sugar and to clamour for permission to import more and more *negros bozales*. And since some of the slaves from the Gouvenot *asiento* fell to the lot of Jamaica, the two mills of Garay in New Seville would most probably have used some African slave labour after 1518.

As the dynamic of sugar production began to displace the gold-washing complex in the islands, the compulsory work system based on African slavery began to gradually displace the slave trade in Indians, obeying increasingly a purely mercantile and commercial logic that from the 15th century (with the breakdown of the Catholic Church's prohibition against usury — that is against what an English contemporary of Las Casas called 'making the loan of money a merchandise,') had begun to displace the Catholic Christian ethic as the organizing principle of secular life.

By another stroke of historical irony, New Seville as a capital town indeed even as a town had come to an end, partly due to the dynamic of the new commercial logic which linked the destiny of the Caribbean islands to sugar and African new world slavery, and partly due to those aspects of Las Casas' proposals which could be placed at the service of the new mercantile dynamic.

For in 1534, the treasurer Pedro de Mazuelo obtained royal permission to shift the capital town from the north to the south coast. And the main reason for this granting of royal permission was Mazuelo's plan to build the new town about the site of a sugar mill which he had already built there, and his plans to develop the new town around the sugar industry, To do this he also asked for and got permission for the incentive proposed by Las Casas, i.e. a licence to import 25 *negros bozales* as the labour complement for a sugar mill which he had begun to build on the south coast near to his estate at Maymona. Mazuelo had also been granted permission to arrange for the emigration of 30 Portuguese peasants from the Azores who were knowledgable in the making of sugar. But they were not to be the yeomen farmers of Las Casas' proposal. Rather they were part of an agro-business complex owned and organized by Mazuelo; part then of a settler economy rather than of the peasant model of development (Spanish and Indian) dreamt of by Las Casas.

The town was shifted in 1534. New Seville would disappear from history, and with it the memory of the Franciscan monastery and of De La Rentería's experience there, of his plans for a school to instruct the Indians in Christian doctrine, making them literate in order to do so. The Arawak Indians too began to disappear from memory. For whilst sugar and the slave trade out of Africa would gradually displace the slave trade in Indians (by 1542 the Indians had been declared free men de jure) it did not secure the abolition of the *encomienda* (the latter was to be simply, in time, shifted to the *hacienda* system) nor stop the extinction — the rationale of all Las Casas' proposals — of the Arawaks as a cultural-biological entity.

The Paradox of the Just Title

Las Casas had retired to the Dominican monastery at Puerto Plata in Santo Domingo after the defeat of his third scheme, i.e. his project for the peaceful conversion of the mainland Indians on the Paria coast. The intensive slave raiding and slave trading carried out on the coast by the settlers had so enraged the Indians that they had risen up and wiped out the settlement, killing all the friars during the brief absence of Las Casas. He had remained silent in the monastery until 1531 when the accelerated rate of Arawak mortality led to another memorial that year in which he urgently asked that the Arawaks be withdrawn from all forms of labour and that they be allowed to 'rest and replenish themselves'. Except this were done the islands would be depopulated of their presence. To replace their labour he again proposed that some 500 or 600 slaves imported from Africa should be allotted to the settlers in the different islands.

But the importation of Black slaves had already begun to respond to the economic dynamic of the expansion both of the slave trade itself and of the sugar industry rather than to what Las Casas saw as the categorical imperative of the Spanish presence in the Indies, i.e. that of the peaceful conversion mission on the model of the original Apostles. For Las Casas the importation of African slaves was intended to facilitate that Christian mission — doing all that I ought to as a Christian — as he had pledged to the head of the Dominicans before he left for Spain. However, the dynamic of a secular commercial-economic rationale that had begun to use spiritual ends only as a means to the securing of temporal interests was becoming increasingly determinant. And Las Casas had begun to sense this when he charged in his *History of the Indies* that the settlers and their ideologues had 'inverted the spiritual end of this whole affair by making it the means; and the means — that is to say, temporal and profane things ... have come to constitute the end of this Christian exercise'.

This inversion of the spiritual for purely temporal ends was linked to the fact that increasingly Charles V came to depend on the revenues from the Indies and the slave trade — the royal treasury received so many ducats a head for each *pieza* imported as well as the purchase prices of the *asiento* — to repay the exorbitant rates of interest of moneylending groups like the Fuggers with which he had financed both his election as Holy Roman Emperor (1519) and his policy of imperial expansion in Europe. This was to underlie the first documented appearance of the major African (in its cultural/biological definition) component in the contemporary Jamaican ethos.

By 1520 the audiencia of Santo Domingo had seized on the rationale provided both by the Heironymite commission and by Las Casas that African slaves should be imported to replace the Indians and had asked for a licence to introduce more *negros bozales* into the island. They argued that 'they would not be able to give full freedom to the Indians, nor to establish them in towns (as free tribute paying vassals)' without African slaves as a substitute source of labour. By 1536 the documented presence in Jamaica of some 38 Africans listed as *piezas* (23 men and 15 women, some with infant children) attest to the rapidity with which the Christian theological rationale of the substitution of slaves-with-a-just-title for those unjustly enslaved, had taken on a purely secular dynamic.

Of the 38 men and women listed by their Catholic Christian names as having been tallied at Pedro de Mazuelo's south coast estate at Maymona, some 11 were auctioned off at the first documented auction which took place in the new south coast town that was transitionally called Seville on the River Caguaya. The prices were high. One African, the settlers wrote the Crown, was worth the labour of four Indians. The genetically tough and culturally flexible and adaptable rice farmers from the relatively harsher low lying swamplands, i.e. the cultural-agricultural bulom complex of the Upper Guinea coast [Walter Rodney 1970] would, as a group, survive the rigorous intensive labour of a commercial mode of mass production, where the Arawaks would not. The Arawak mode of the human developed on the basis of the domestication of cassava (manioc) whose higher yield of starch per acre, higher than maize and potatoes, even wheat and barley, as well as its easy propagation, gave the opportunity for the creation of a leisure civilization whose relative grace, gentleness and conviviality struck the more perceptive of their conquerors. It would disappear under the pressures of their abrupt acculturation to the cultural system of the highly aggressive mode of the human which had evolved in the geohistorical trajectory of the Mediterranean clash and conflict of multiple civilizations, empires, and of fiercely exclusive monotheistic creeds.[3]

It was not until 10 years after the auction in Seville on the River Caguaya, that is, about 1546 at a conference on slavery held in Mexico, that Las Casas began to question his own position as he began to receive verified information that the assumptions on which he had based the justifying rationale for his proposal, i.e. that the African slaves had been justly captured in war — those who had become Muslims — and justly bought and traded, was a false assumption.

What one might call a second conversion experience of Las Casas begins after 1546 with this realization. For once he knows of the 'unjust methods by which the majority of the Africans too have been enslaved', his entire rationale for the substitution of one people by another falls to the ground. Las Casas now 'sees' his former position as a result of his own blindness, and he implores God's forgiveness, since he considers that he himself has been guilty of complicity in 'all the sins committed by the Portuguese on the Africans, not to mention our own sin of buying the slaves'. For 'the reduction of the Africans to slavery', he would write at this moment of awareness, 'was as unjust and as tyrannical as the reduction to slavery of the Indians'. He had now to confront the possibility that in the face of the consequences of his proposal, not even the original purity of his motive nor his ignorance of the 'unjust methods used' would sufficiently absolve him on that day of judgement when he found himself before the divine judge. Without such absolution, he would find himself excluded from the body of the spiritual elect, and would have failed to 'have done all that he ought to as a Christian'.

Yet the paradox here was that the 'error' in which Las Casas had been involved went beyond his ignorance of the unjust methods used by the Portuguese to a more far reaching 'error' central to the symbolic logic of Catholic Christianity itself, and to the paradoxical nature of the just/unjust title distinction. For as J.W. Maxwell has pointed out, the institution of slavery was approved doctrinally by the Catholic Church for some 1400 years until 1965 when it was officially corrected by the Second Vatican Council.

And in the 16th century, with the shift from a traditional Mediterranean system of slavery — in whose geohistorical environment the just/unjust title distinction had been meaningful to the new purely secular mode of the mass-commercial slavery of the transatlantic trade, the paradox had become a truly tragic one.

For the just/unjust distinction in the context of a now utterly changed geo-historical environment would gradually come to serve as the enabling rationalization of the transatlantic slave trade; and the Catholic Church thus become the non-conscious yet tacitly very real accomplice for some three and a half centuries, of the new world system of plantation slavery. And the paradox of the just/unjust title distinction and its consequences in history were only to be explained and absolved by the daring conceptual leap – 'I put forward propositions no one had touched upon' – made by Las Casas with respect to errors which had their origins in natural reason, in his historic dispute with Juan Gines de Sepulveda, at Valladolid.

The Valladolid Debate: Sepúlveda vs Las Casas

Juan Ginés de Sepulveda, a humanist scholar and a translator of Aristotle as well as official royal historian wrote a treatise in the form of a Latin dialogue in 1545, putting forward a closely reasoned defence of what he saw as the 'just causes' which the Spaniards had for making war on the American Indians; and for the Spanish Crown to establish its sovereignty over the new world peoples by forcible conquest.

Las Casas, on hearing of the treatise which was then circulating in manuscript form, promptly made moves to have its publication blocked on his return from the Indies. A struggle then began between the two men which came to a climax in a special junta called officially by the Crown to hear their opposing arguments with respect to the legality or illegality of all Spanish conquests in the new world.

The formal debate was held in Valladolid between 1550 and 1551. It dealt with the debating topic in the context of a more far reaching question: what kind of relation — hierarchical or reciprocal — was to be established between the two modes of the human, one agro-artefactual, the other neolithic, that now confronted each other on the Caribbean islands and mainland territories.

Logically linked to this question was another. Now that Columbus' discovery that the western antipodes hitherto classified as non-inhabitable in the medieval Euro-Christian episteme, were in fact *inhabited*, and by a people that quite clearly had never been reached by the original Christian gospel, what new system of classification was to be adopted for these people whose existence now placed in question the very universality of the Euro-Christian figural scheme. Following upon Spain's incorporation of these new peoples and of their lands into a new Euro-American entity, was the system of classification to be that of an Empire [Sepulveda] ? Or was it to shift from that of a particularistic Euro-Christianity to that of a universal-Christian civilization [Las Casas].

Summary of Major Implications

At Valladolid, Sepúlveda used a long established doctrinal teaching of the Church which laid down that those who were 'incapable' should be ruled for their own good, to give a general ideological validity to a new thesis which went far beyond the original intention of the original thesis and to legitimate the Euro-Mediterranean mode of the human over, eventually, all other modes of the human. This new (in scale and intention) essentially secular system of classification based on a represented essential difference between modes of the human, displaced the concept of the papal donation and the traditional just/unjust distinction with what may be called a *natural law charter*.

Not long after, Sepúlveda was to use this same natural law representation to legitimate the Portuguese Christians' capture and enslavement of Black Africans. The latter, he would write, were 'disobedient by nature' and had as a consequence to be subjected to paternal rulership [Maxwell 1975].

At Valladolid therefore, Sepúlveda made use of the very real *geohistorically evolved differences between the neolithic mode of the human* as embodied in the American Indians and the *agro-artefactual/mode of the human* as embodied in the Spaniards, to represent an inherent and a natural system of difference between the two peoples.

Since, as Stephen J. Gould [1983] argues, 'historical changes in classification are the fossilized indicators of conceptual revolutions', the debate at Valladolid can be seen as the official occasion of the conceptual revolution that formally ushered in the modern world. It was a debate which Sepúlveda as the Spanish nationalist won (as O'Gorman argues, according to Phelan) precisely because his mode of reasoning corresponded to the great changes that were taking place in Europe, ushered in by the commercial revolution both before and after 1492. These changes were to lead to the organization of human life on secular rather than on religious terms. Sepúlveda, in spite of his still hybrid use of religious terminology and concepts, can be said to have provided the first secular operational self-definition of the human subject, one whose universally applicable verbal symbol was that of natural law rather than that of the Christian God, even where still couched in terms of the latter. In doing this he spoke to the reality of his times and to the rise of the nation-state and its reasons-of-state rather than the Christian Church as the regulatory system of an emerging world system at the level of everyday existence.

Las Casas, on the other hand, lost that debate because he was at once behind his time and ahead of his time. Yet the conceptual leap that he made from the very contradiction of his position, is a leap now resonantly in tune with our own, also transitional, times. For in providing a conceptual challenge to the new system of classification being put in place by Sepúlveda, the system that still provides the epistemic laws for our contemporary human system in its global dimension, Las Casas opened the way towards the evolution of a genuine science of human systems, in very much the same way as a science of natural systems followed in the wake of Columbus' challenge to the Mediterranean-centric classification of the earth's geography, and of Copernicus to the geocentric system of classification of the universe.

Columbus with his empirical voyage made possible a science of geography based on a purely encyclopaedic knowledge of the earth. Las Casas at Valladolid made the same leap (not to be followable up until our own century) *with respect to the possibility of a science of human systems based on the encyclopaedic knowledge of their laws of functioning.*

He did this in the context of what O'Gorman [1951] calls the 'providential design'. In this he refused to accept Columbus' discovery - that the new world and all the earth was habitable and that therefore there were peoples in the world still unreached by the gospel — as a contradiction to the universality of the Christian figural schema. He saw it, rather, as a providential design of God which had appointed Spain and her clergy to fulfill now, that as yet unfulfilled universality by evangelizing the new peoples; to make the Christian model of identity the unifying model for all the peoples of the earth, from whom in time, God would select the body of his spiritual elect.

Over against Sepúlveda's natural law thesis with its new, secular concept of the Spaniards as constituting a natural body of the elect, Las Casas, both at Valladolid and in his *Apologética Historia* defined the human as being the same *(per esse)* everywhere *even and because of the fact that they were geohistorically different (per accidens).*

Las Casas, as Phelan notes, was the first person to write comparative world history. Using the Christian schema of a single origin for humans, then tracing their separation and later isolation from each other, he argued that in this isolation, all groups of men — and there were never anywhere any race of monstrously deformed men — had lived according to what they held to be a system of virtues and vices. The practice of human sacrifice was only carried out because it seemed to some a virtue, because this was the offering to God that seemed to them an offering of the very best that they possessed — in other words because to them human sacrifice appeared *positively* as a rational act. As such, therefore, it was an error of natural reason and not its lack, since, as he later developed more fully in the Ciceronian definition of his book the *Apologetica Historia* all the peoples of the world are men: and all men are rational. It was their rationality which defined them.

From the 'Unseen Planets' to the Representation Which Have Woven Us

Las Casas at Valladolid, in putting forward propositions that no one had put forward before, by introducing the novel conception that there was no inherent difference of rational substance between the Spaniards and the Indians since the practices such as human sacrifice seen as rational by the Indians were an 'error which had its origin in natural reason', made possible a science of human systems, as Columbus made possible a science of geography (by positing and proving that there was no difference of zonal substance, that the earth was the same everywhere, habitable in all five zones and in the western antipodes as well as in Jerusalem); and as Copernicus, Galileo then Newton made possible a science of natural systems. For if Copernicus, as Hans Jonas [1979] points out, made thinkable the quite novel conception that since the earth was a star and the planets 'earths' there was no difference between *celestial* and *terrestrial substance* as had been laid down in the geocentric Greek-Christian Ptolemaic view of the universe, then it meant that nature was the same *everywhere and homogenous in substance.*

This novel conception and its implication had then made possible Newton's new way of seeing or *theoria* [Bohm 1980] in which both earth and planets could be seen in the context of a universally *applicable law of gravitation.*

In this new way of seeing, Newton was now able to conceive of the planets no longer in the Greek-Christian terms of their orbital circular (formal/spiritual) perfection, but rather in new terms — in that of 'the rates of fall of all matter towards various centres'. This new way of seeing then enabled prediction and conscious human control of natural forces, that would lead eventually to the splitting of the atom, ushering in a new era of human history. For when in this new way of seeing, Bohm points out, 'something was seen not to be accounted for in this way, one looked for and then discovered new and as yet unseen planets towards which celestial objects were falling'.

Las Casas at Valladolid, given his *a priori* conviction of a universal and potentially realizable system of human co-identification, in other words, the universal-Christian, and thereby refusing to accept 'human sacrifice' or even cannibalistic rites as proof of a naturally determined difference in human *rational substance*, by a great conceptual leap made thinkable the possibility of a universally applicable law of human identification, in whose context the 'errors' of specific forms of reason and of behaviours are *lawlike and rule-governed.*

For if, in doing 'all that he ought to as a Christian' Las Casas continued to see as 'rational', not the call for the abolition of slavery *per se* (that would be for another episteme, in another time, 150 years ago) but rather that slaves acquired with a 'just title' should be substituted for slaves not so acquired, so, quite clearly, did the Aztec mode of the human see human sacrifice as supremely rational, *doing all that he ought to as an Aztec.*

And since in order to re-present itself each mode of the human must *conceive* itself in that specific mode — and this is the moment of human freedom, its *discontinuity* with the other natural species, its unique function as the medium through which consciousness enters the life of the planet — then the form of reason or episteme must as its primary function ensure the incorporation of the group as this specific group entity, by stabilizing and disseminating this shared self-conception.

For we think in the mode of the symbolical self-representation. As we act upon the world in the mode of our hands. And both the insights and the oversights - Las Casas' errors — are always governed by our *historically relative* systems of self-representation.

The decoding of the 'errors' of natural reason — of Las Casas, of the Portuguese, of their African partners, of the Catholic Church, of the Protestant sects and others — which made the 'time on the cross' of our 'unique individual history' the dually tragic/creative origins of our history possible, would seem to make our putting in place of a science of human systems, by which we would make ourselves the paradoxical heirs to Las Casas' great argument at Valladolid, the fitting conclusion to a historical process that began with two conversion experiences and a shipload of provisions from New Seville.

It is not man, to paraphrase Ricoeur, but his systems of representations that should be accused. We truly absolve Las Casas then, when putting an end to the pre-history of the human we take as the object of our metadisciplinary inquiry (because the present separation between the natural and the social sciences is itself a culture specific representation) the thousand representations out of which the Human has woven itself — and its Others.

References

A Note on Documents

The references to the early history of New Seville are taken mainly from a series of documents relating to early Spanish Jamaica. They were transcribed by the historian Irene Wright who was commissioned by the Institute of Jamaica to do so and are now in the National Library of Jamaica.

The greatest insights into the daily life of New Seville during the period are given by a hitherto unpublished document, located by the Government's Research Mission to Spain in the summer of 1982. The document found bound in with same others relating to the early history of Cuba is labelled as Accounts for the island of Santiago from it was settled until the year 1536, Contaduria section No. 1174, Archives of Seville, Spain.

Balandier, George S. 1966. *Daily Life in the Kingdom of the Kongo from the Sixteenth to the Eighteenth Century* (Trans. H. Weaver). New York: Pantheon Books.

Bohm, David. 1980. *Wholeness and the Implicate Order*. London: Routledge and Kegan Paul.

Braudel, Ferdinand. 1972. *The Mediterranean and the Mediterranean World in the Age of Philip II*. Vol. 1. NY: Harper and Row.

Chaunu, Huguette and Pierre, 1955–59. *Seville et l' Atlantique, 1504–1560*. 8 vols, in 12. Paris: A Coling, S.E.V.P.E.N.

Elliott, J.H.1963. *Imperial Spain: 1469–1716*. London: Edward Arnold.

Freide, Juan, n.d. *Bartolomé de las Casas: Precurso de le Anti-Colonialismo Su Lucha y Derrota*. Mexico: Siglo Ventiuno.

————. and Keen, Benjamin, (eds.) 1971. *Bartolomé de las Casas in History: Towards an Understanding of the Man and His Work*. Illinois: Northern Illinois University Press.

Gould, Stephen J. 1983. *Hen's Teeth and Horse's Toes*. New York: Norton and Company.

Hirschfeld, Gerald. 1971. "Introduction" to *History and the Idea of Mankind, The Council for the Study of Mankind*. Edited by Warren Wagar. Albuquerque, N.M.: University of New Mexico Press.

Hanke, Lewis. 1974. *All Mankind is One: A Study of the Disputation between Bartolomé de Las Casas and Juan Ginés de Sepúlveda in 1550 on the Intellectual and Religious Capacity of the American Indians*. Northern Illinois University Press.

Jonas, Hans. 1979. *The Phenomenon of Life: Towards a Philosophical Biology, Greenwood*.

Landstrom, Bjorn. 1967. *Columbus: The Story of Don Cristobal Colon*. New York: Macmillan.

Las Casas, Bartolomé de. 1971. *The History of the Indies*. Translated by Andree M. Collard. Harper and Row.

———, Obras Escogidas de Bartolomé de las Casas. 1957. *Historia de las Indias I*. Madrid: B.A.E. XCV.

———. 1979. *Brevissima Relación de la Destrucción de las Indias*. Barcelona: Edicion Fontanmara.

———. 1974. *La Larga Marcha de las Casas: Selección y Presentación de Textos*. Lima: Centro de Estudios y Publicaciones.

Maxwell, J.F. 1975. *Slavery and the Catholic Church: The History of Catholic Teaching Concerning the Moral Legitimacy of the Institution of Slavery*. Chichester and London: Barry Rose Publishers.

Moya Pons. 1984. *Manual de Historia Dominicana*. Republica Dominicana: U.C., M.M.

Mellafe, Rolando. 1975. *Negro Slavery in Latin America*. Translated by J. Judge. Berkeley: University of California Press.

O'Gorman, Edmundo. 1951. *La Idea del Descubrimiento de America: Historia de esa Interpretación*. Mexico: Centro de Estudios Filosóficos.

Rodney, Walter. 1970. *A History of the Upper Guinea Coast 1545–1800*. Oxford: Clarendon Press.

Taviani, Paolo Emilio. 1974. *Cristobal Colon: Genesis dal Gran Descubrimiento*. Vols. 1 and II. Barcelona: Editorial Tiede.

Wagner, H.R. with parish, H. 1967. *The Life and Writings of Bartolome de las Casas*. Albuquerque: The University of New Mexico Press.

Wllliams, Eric. 1961. *Capitalism and Slavery*. Kent: Russell & Russell.

Notes

1. Bozales: the term for the lineage-cultural African slaves imported directly from Africa as distinct from the Christian-cultural Black slaves (Ladinos) born in Spain.
2. The remains of one of these mills have been excavated at the New Seville site.
3. Colin Turnbull [1978] notes the interrelation between the cultural systems or modes of the human and the physical environment in the case of Africa. Where the environment is abundant and the climate moderate, he notes it has never been necessary for a complex industrial technology to develop. Rather the African physical environment had demanded an 'economic adequacy' which everywhere 'depends upon a sympathetic, adaptive response from the human population that must under these conditions function with the totality of fauna and flora as part of a natural world … . Whereas other cultures for various reasons have had to develop an industrial technology and have sought increasingly to dominate the environment and control it, the African throughout the continent sees himself a part of the natural world, and adapts himself and his culture … to its varied demands. This leads to … as many cultural types as there are environmental types … . The same correlation is highly significant also in any consideration of physical.

The Eighteenth and Nineteenth Centuries: The Proslavery Ideology

Gordon Lewis

THE GENERAL CHARACTER OF THE IDEOLOGY

The heyday of the slave-based sugar plantation economy was the period of the eighteenth and nineteenth centuries, only ending as late as the second half of the nineteenth century: 1834 in the British islands, 1848 in the French islands, 1873 in Spanish Puerto Rico, and 1886 in Spanish Cuba. Its very longevity is astonishing: The slave trade, with its various permutations, lasted for more than four hundred years. It was at once an economic institution and a political system; and it left its indelible mark, in varying degree, on the collective social psychology of all the Caribbean peoples. It reached its apogee at different times in different sugar islands: in Jamaica and Saint Domingue in the eighteenth century, in Cuba in the nineteenth century. Geographically, it extended in one vast district from the southern states of the American Union to northern Brazil, out of which developed the black under-class of the Americas. There was an enormous variety, of course, in the etiology of the slave plantation, from small estate to mammoth park. But the institutive principle of the slave regime was constant throughout: that (as Marx put it, quoting from the English economist Cairnes) in slave-importing countries the most effective economy is that which takes out of the human chattel in the shortest space of time the utmost amount of exertion it is capable of putting forth.[1] It constituted an integral part of the emerging Atlantic capitalist system; its main purpose, therefore, was the maximization of profit. That this has not always been fully appreciated is due to the fact that much of the vast literature on the institution, motivated by the philanthropic drive to abolish it, has been more concerned with its moral evil than with its economic function.

Slavery, this is to say, was originally an economic category rather than a racial category. That is evident enough, as the Dutch scholar Herman J. Niebohr showed in his early volume of ethnographical studies on slavery of 1900, from the fact that slavery is, historically, a worldwide phenomenon that has characterized most societies where there has been present a pattern of dominance and subordination between ruling and ruled groups, ranging from the Ottoman Empire to the pastoral tribes of the Pacific coast. Since, too, the classic definition of slavery is that, with variations, it constitutes a system of compulsory labor in perpetuity, in which the owner possesses not only the right of property in the person of the slave but also complete and arbitrary power over the will of the slave, the Roman *potestas dominica*, it follows that racial differentiation between owner and subject is not central or even necessary to the functional operation of the system. The social and political consequences of the system, correspondingly, are not of necessity racially oriented: as Niebohr points out, for example, a slave regime with many domestic slaves guarantees the freedom of women, since free women are no longer overtaxed with work, and slavery accelerates the social differentiation between rich and poor, since the poor man cannot purchase slaves as easily as the wealthy man. Slavery is thus functionally related to the growth of class society; although Niebohr, in a curious digression, hastens to assure his readers that this must not be taken as a supporting argument for the Socialist ideas of his own time, which he sees as a dangerous romanticism that underestimates the social function of the great manufacturer.[2]

Marx, as always, saw this clearly. "Direct slavery," he wrote in his important letter of 1846 to P. V. Annenkov, "is as much the pivot of our industrialism today as machinery, credit, etc. Without slavery no cotton; without cotton no modern industry. Slavery has given their value to the colonies; the colonies have created world trade; world trade is the necessary condition of large-scale machine industry."[3] Marx was referring to North American cotton-based slavery. But his observation applies equally, if not more so, to Caribbean sugar-based slavery. For the Caribbean was the perfected expression of the total Atlantic slave economy, with the cotton plantations of the American South being little more than a pale echo of the sophisticated sugar plantations of Jamaica, Saint Domingue, and Cuba. It was, then, only an accident of literature that the most famous of all popular novels on the system should have been Mrs. Stowe's *Uncle Tom's Cabin,* a crude and sanctimonious exposé that in no way matches the earlier works of the French eighteenth century novelists and playwrights of the *littérature négrophile.* The main function of the system, as Eric Williams has shown in his classic study *Capitalism and Slavery,* was to provide the accumulated capital for European capitalist expansion; and it is testimony to the essential correctness of that thesis that the attempt of later scholarship to impugn it has succeeded no more than the effort of subsequent investigators to disprove the thesis of the remarkable books of the Hammonds that the price the English village laborer had to pay for his forced transformation into the English town worker between 1760 and 1850 was a massive deterioration in the total quality of his life-style.[4]

These general principles, along with Niebohr's discussion of the land-population relationship in the development of comparative slavery systems, clearly apply to the Caribbean situation. The major problem of the Caribbean settler and planter, from the beginning, was a labor problem: it was essential to have at immediate command a large, regular, and plentiful supply of obedient labor. The problem was solved in the early period with, first, Indian labor and, second, white indentured servant labor. But it was only a temporary solution. The enslaved Indian was at once too physically weak and too psychologically negative to accept the hard labor of mine and *encomienda,* while the indentured servant was too expensive: as the governor of Barbados reported in 1676, the planters of that island had already discovered that the labor of three blacks was equal, in financial costs, to the labor of one white man.[5] The Indian labor force died out, without possibility of self-replacement; the white labor force, fleeing from the meshes of manorial serfdom in Europe, reemigrated north to the New England colonies, where land was plentiful and where they could more easily work for themselves. In the face of those difficulties, the Caribbean planter oligarchy turned to the African labor supply, not because it was black, but because it was cheaper. It possessed enormous economic advantages: as Cairnes pointed out, it admitted of the most complete organization; it could be combined on an extensive scale and directed by a controlling mind to a single end; and, notwithstanding its defects, its cost never rose above that which was necessary to maintain the slave in health and strength.[6] To all that was added the special considerations of tropical agriculture: in the northern temperate zone of cereal crops, the small proprietor could manage, whereas in the semitropical zone, to which tobacco, rice, cotton, and sugar were more adaptable, the advantage was with the large estate. Negro slavery was thus the end result of an economic revolution in the Caribbean economy, not the outcome of a race-based preference for black labor. As Eric Williams has succinctly put it, slavery was not born of racism, but racism was instead the consequence of slavery.

All this had important consequences for the general character of the Caribbean settler-planter ideology. It has been seen, too simplistically, as merely Negrophobic. On the contrary, there is much evidence to suggest that, in the beginnings, it was color-blind. The fact that the aboriginal Indian stock were fair-skinned, and perceived to be so by the discoverers, did not prevent the rapid emergence on the part of the Spanish settlers of a deep contempt for their Indian subjects; as early as 1517 the Hieronymite commissioners found in response to their enquiries that the Spanish settlers in Cuba vigorously upheld the doctrine of Indian depravity, denying that the Indians possessed any capacity for living in civilized fashion and even sustaining the curious thesis that their depravity and inconstancy were due to lunar influence on islanders. In similar fashion, a typically European class hatred developed between the planter magnates of the early Barbadian colonial Assembly and the dispossessed lower-class whites, reflected in the contemptuous epithets conferred upon the latter group: *poor whites, mean whites, redlegs*. It was a hatred compounded by old ancestral hatreds, that of the English for the Irish, for example; and even a colonial gentleman as humane as Codrington could express his contempt for the Irish in terms so crude that Père Labat was driven to ponder on the vanity of the English. The Barbadian "poor white," in fact, was the equivalent of the "white trash" of the later American South; and merely to read the history of their attempts throughout the eighteenth century to be enrolled into the colonial militia is to understand how even the possession of a white complexion did not in any way guarantee them a role in island government.[7]

Racial prejudice, then, was mixed up with class prejudice in the planter mentality. It was also mixed up with religious prejudice. The religious toleration enjoyed by the Jewish communities in the English and Dutch colonies has already been noted. Yet the medieval temper of anti-Semitism still prevailed sufficiently to impose upon them civil disabilities that were not finally removed until the nineteenth century. That is evident enough, to take only one example, from the revealing *Essai historique sur la colonie de Surinam* that was published in 1788 by the *Regenten*, the governing body of the communal leaders of the Sephardic group in Dutch Guiana. Inspired by the earlier publication of the plea for Jewish emancipation made by the eminent German liberal publicist Von Dohm, which they had read with excitement, it was at once an expression of gratitude to the Dutch republic for the religious freedom enjoyed by the Jewish community in the colony—which, the authors say, would certainly form the happiness of the Jews of France and Germany—and a vigorous protest against a continuing tendency on the part of the Christian element to blame the Jews for everything that went wrong.[8] The irony of the document lies in the fact that although its authors were urban businessmen and estate owners who fully accepted without criticism the institution of slavery, even to the point of cataloging with immense pride the record of Jewish militia captains in hunting down runaway slaves in innumerable expeditions into the bush,[9] they nonetheless expressed a real bitterness about the failure of the Dutch Company, the colonial governors, and the local Christian governing group to fully appreciate that loyalist spirit. They pointed with pride to the social quality of the early Jewish settlers: "It was certainly not with vagabonds and with wretches drawn from the dungeons of England that the colony was founded, as several others in America were."[10] Yet the complaints of prejudice and ill-regard throughout the book indicate clearly that being of European lineage, white, and well-to-do did not in and of itself buy full acceptance even in a slave colony.

It was only in the eighteenth century that the plantation economy became wholly and exclusively identified with the Negro slave and that there took place the growth of a systematic racist ideology that identified the slave, in turn, with nonhuman and antinatural attributes. The system only needed an ideological rationalization once it had become fully established as an economic structure; and also, suggestively, when it came under attack from its religious and humanitarian critics sometime after the 1770s. Until then, slavery was not axiomatically identified with the white master-black servant axis. According to Rochefort, it existed among the Caribs, who believed that their bravest warriors after death would live in happy islands with their enemies, the Arawaks, as their slaves; Negro slaves captured as prisoners in the wars with the Spanish were kept as such; and captive women became slaves, their children given liberty if the mothers were taken as wives.[11] Up until the end of the seventeenth century, the French state recruited the bulk of its galley slaves in the royal navy from Moslem prisoners sold in the European slave marts and even compromised its Christian principles to enslave such nonconformist Christians as Russians and Greeks—so much so that the Marseilles merchants and shippers who effectively monopolized that trade openly opposed Colbert's plan to change to Negro slaves on the ground that they could not expect to break into an African trade already dominated by other companies.[12] It was not, all this is to say, until all of the earlier and alternative sources of labor supply—native Indian, indentured servant, peasant emigrant, transshipped prisoner and convict—had either dried up or proved unsatisfactory that the planter class moved to acceptance of the African trade. Like capitalism everywhere, Caribbean sugar capitalism was no respecter of persons.

It is only at that point, then—when the demand for labor coincided with the African supply—that the racist component began to emerge as the main property of the planter ideology. Or, rather, that the prejudices of social caste and of religious belief finally were joined together with the physiological prejudice to compose a more or less coherent view concerning black and white, which the planter class and its defenders promulgated in a growing literature after 1700. In that view the black person was condemned, and his slave status justified, from three different angles, now fused with each other: from the angle of social position because he was identified with menial labor; from the angle of religious belief because he was seen as pagan or heathen, beyond the reach of Christian compassion; from the angle, finally, of blackness itself, identified with evil bestiality. Irrevocably, after much loose terminology, the institution of slavery became equated with the Afro-American person in the imagination of Western society, and thereafter operated as a fixed article of faith.

The planter ideology has thus to be seen as the ideological superstructure of the revival of slavery as a mode of production in the post-Reformation period. It had its antecedents, as scholars like Winthrop Jordan have shown, in theological and pseudoscientific concepts that went back to the foundations of Judeo-Christian thought: the curse of Ham in popular biblical anthropology, the distinction between the children of light and the children of darkness, the Puritan obsession with sexuality so easily transferred to blacks, the concept of the non-Christian stranger.[13] But a theory of antecedents is ultimately unsatisfactory as an explanation for the rise of modern slavery and its accompanying theology. First, because it is tempted to exaggerate color prejudice to the exclusion of other, equally potent, prejudices. It is at least arguable that the medieval mind was more preoccupied with anti-Semitism than with Negrophobia. In the English literary tradition alone, the anti-Jewish note is strident from Chaucer to Shakespeare; and the marked difference between Shakespeare's portrayal of Shylock as the capitalist Jew (notwithstanding Portia's famous plea) and of Othello as the honorable Moor, is symptomatic. Second, although it is true that the racist creed goes back some two thousand years (the attribution of feelings of guilt and shame to color is at least as old as the Song of Solomon), the theory of antecedents still leaves unexplained why it lay dormant for so long, only to be revived in the eighteenth century—fomenting, among other things, new problems of legal definition of the status of the slave for the English common law. The answer lies in the sociology of ideas. Ideas realize themselves in the form of social institutions only when forms of production make it possible. Therefore, just as Plato's idea of sexual equality became capable of realization only when the nineteenth-century factory system replaced mere physical strength with manual dexterity—thus facilitating the entry of women into factory work—so the racist creed only became of practical utility once the system of modern Caribbean slavery created a new master class of slave owners who needed it for ideological justification.

The heart of the Caribbean planter ideology is, it goes without saying, the search for a rationalizing justification of Negro slavery. As such, it goes back to the very beginning of Caribbean history in its European phase. The motives were varied. In quantitative terms, the slave regime was of such enormous proportions that it could not be hidden from sight, like the longstanding Arab trade of North and East Africa; as such, it had to be defended from the beginning against its critics. Qualitatively, it violated at once Spanish medieval precepts and the English common law, both of which viewed slavery as a *status contra naturam*, only to be justified on the narrow ground of captivity in war; thus, it constituted a gross moral affront to all the principles on which Western Christianity, at its best, was founded.

The challenge of that contradiction between slavery and Christianity could not be avoided. No apologist for the system could adopt the attitude of Machiavellian amoralism that the Renaissance mind for a period made fashionable, summed up in Pope Leo X's remark, "now that we have the Papacy let us enjoy it." The early conquistadores, admittedly, shared much of that cynical outlook, as is evident from Fray Bernardino de Minaya's scandalized account of how, finally meeting with Pizarro in Peru and informing that soldier of fortune of the Emperor's instructions concerning humane treatment of the Indians, he was met with the Machiavellian retort that Pizarro had come from Mexico to take their gold away from the Indians and would do nothing else.[14] But no apologist for the slavery regime, European or Creole, putting pen to paper, could dismiss the problem in that contemptuous fashion. Being immersed in the value system of Western Christianity, he was forced to meet it more responsibly. That, as much as anything else, explains the sheer magnitude of the literature on the subject, which did not die until the slave system itself had died.

The debate on slavery, then, like the debate between feudalism and capitalism, or the debate between science and religion, became one of the great debates of the age and engaged the learned of both the old European societies and the new American societies. Its very longevity testifies to its importance, for it raged as incessantly in nineteenth-century Cuba as it had done in eighteenth-century Jamaica. Like other seminal issues—imperialism, for example, or women's rights—it was the sort of issue that cut across traditional ideological loyalties. Voltaire's attitude to the issue was equivocal; an aristocrat like Mirabeau was outspokenly antislavery. The socially conservative Methodist John Wesley fiercely attacked the system in his savage *Thoughts upon Slavery* of 1744; Gibbon, the great sceptic, could denounce it in the ancient world but could see nothing wrong about it in its modern form. Wilberforce, a reactionary in domestic politics, spearheaded the abolitionist drive; by comparison, Cobbett (the most famous of all Radicals), in his well-known letter to Wilberforce, properly condemned him for his indifference to the cause of the poor, yet went on to assert that Wilberforce's charges against the West Indian planter were completely false and misrepresentative of the true facts. Finally, Dr. Johnson, as a religious Tory of the old school, could propose a toast to "the next insurrection of the Negroes in the West Indies," which Bryan Edwards reported in tones of scandalized horror, while Jefferson, as a freethinking deist, could compose in his *Notes on Virginia* one of the most offensive passages in the literature of racial animosity.

THE DISCUSSION ON INDIAN AND NEGRO

The planter ideology starts, in effect, with the early movement to replace Indian labor with imported African labor. The continuous campaign of the Dominicans and Franciscans in defense of the Indians; the increasing requests from the settlers for Negro slaves; the profit to the Crown to be reaped from the slave trade: all of these factors facilitated the change. Even Oviedo, anti-Indian as he was, could argue that the rapid decimation of the Indians was due to their maltreatment at the hands of Spanish factors and overseers, acting on behalf of powerful court favorites who never visited the islands.[15] The enslavement of the African thus, through a cruel paradox, was justified in terms of the salvation of the Indian; the argument can be seen as the first expression of the general proslavery apologetic that African slavery, as an institution, worked for beneficent results. Even Las Casas petitioned the Crown in support of the trade. [16] But it would be historically inaccurate to accept the thesis, advanced by his enemies, that Las Casas was responsible for the change of policy. The thesis rested for a long time on the assumed veracity of Herrera's original accusation, on the basis of which eighteenth century writers as different as Robertson, Raynal, and Corneille de Pau repeated the charge. But the extracts of documents on the Negro trade put together in the great collection of Juan Bautista Muñoz, during the late eighteenth century, and on which Quintana in part based his corrective monograph on Las Casas of 1833, prove conclusively that the trade was already flourishing even before Las Casas's suggestion of 1518.[17] Las Casas's Sevillian background may have been responsible for his initial acceptance of Negro slavery. But the institution had its roots in collective interests and vague ideas present in the mental climate of the sixteenth century that could have had little to do with the outlook of one man, even although that man was as influential as Las Casas.

The theme of Indian emancipation thus became recruited into the slavery apologetic. The arguments were varied. The new African trade would bring profit to the Crown. Negroes were better than Indians since, as Judge Zuazo of Hispaniola told the regent of Spain in 1518, it was very rarely that a Negro died in the islands.[18] Negro slaves, as the bishop of San Juan advised in 1579, would revive the former prosperity of the Puerto Rican colony, since they could be made to work in the gold mines.[19] Or there was the argument that if the Spanish did not enter the slave trade, it would remain in the hands of the Portuguese, to the detriment of Spanish wealth and security. There was even the curious argument that slaves brought from overseas were much less likely to attempt escape than Indians enslaved locally; yet the argument had little ground in fact, for as early as 1574 the Havana *audiencia* was obliged to reprimand in stern tones those persons who helped runaway slaves—already by that time, obviously, a serious problem.[20] Underpinning all of these arguments there rested the general European ethnocentric tendency to place all non-European peoples in a sort of color continuum, with those more closely approximating white appearance being regarded as the more pleasing. Not even Las Casas himself was exempt from that prejudice; and in those chapters of the *Historia* in which he denounced the Portuguese slave raids in Africa, he innocently described the various gradations of the captives, "those who were reasonably white, handsome and elegant, others less white, who seemed to be *pardos* (gray or dusky), and others as black as Ethiopians, so malformed in their faces and bodies that they appeared to those who looked at them to be the image of another and lower hemisphere."[21] The prejudice helps to explain why African slavery failed to generate in the Spanish theologians and jurists of the time anything comparable to the great controversy on the Indian question.

The anti-African feeling finally matured, of course, into the proslavery ideology. Yet it is worth emphasizing the truth that it was neither an easy nor a rapid victory. The European mind was still dominated by the virtually universal assumption, dictated by both church and scripture, that all mankind stemmed from a single source and therefore enjoyed a common brotherhood. Notwithstanding their religious hatred of each other, the sentiment was voiced by both Spanish Catholic and English Protestant. As early as 1573 Bartolomé de Albornoz, in his *Arte de los Contratos*, answered the specious argument that slavery was justified because it saved men from an African paganism with the assertion that it would be better for an African to be king in his own country than a slave in Spanish America; in any case, the argument about the welfare of the slave did not justify, but rather aggravated, the reason for holding him in servitude. "I do not believe," added Albornoz finally, "those persons who will tell me that there is anything in Christ's law to the effect that freedom of the soul must be paid for by slavery of the body."[22] Fray Tomás Mercado described in grim detail the horrors of the Middle Passage in his *Suma de Tratos y Contratos* of 1587; his account makes it clear how the theory of the just war—half-plausible enough when used against Arab, Moor, and

Mohammedan—had become dishonestly twisted into an excuse for the forcible capture of innocent African women and children.[23] Finally, Fray Alonso de Sandoval, in his treatise of 1627, invoked the authority of Plato, Philo Judaeus, and Euripides to deliver an impassioned condemnation of the slavery institution. "For if," he exclaimed, "the civil laws classify exile as a form of civil death, with how much more reason may we call abject slavery death? For it involves not only exile but also subjugation, and hunger, gloom, nakedness, outrage, imprisonment, perpetual persecution, and is, finally, a combination of all evils."[24] English writers echoed similar sentiments. The Reverend Samuel Purchas, who completed Hakluyt's work of compilation, expressed it in his elegantly worded declaration that "the tawney Moore, black Negro, duskie Libyan, ash-coloured Indian, olive-coloured American, should with the whiter European become one sheep-fold, under one great sheep-heard, till this mortalitie being swallowed up of Life, we may all be one...without any more distinction of Colour, Nation, Language, Sexe, Condition."[25]

Attitudes such as these, undoubtedly, were important. They came, especially in the Spanish case, from priests and officials who were often colonial residents, so that it could not be said of them that they were armchair critics who had never set foot in the islands (a frequent charge of the proslavery writers against their opponents). At the same time, they were clearly not much more than ideological survivals of the older medieval teachings. They lasted longer in Spain, where the influence of the priest maintained itself more effectively than in England or Holland. But outside of Spain the new forces of the age—mercantilism, capitalist acquisitiveness, the victory of the commercial bourgeoisie over the landed aristocracy, and the general secularizing tendency—combined to discredit the moralistic viewpoint. Slavery, when discussed at all, was seen in economic and not in religious terms, as is evident enough, in the English case, in the economic writings of men like Locke and Sir Josiah Child. By 1700, possibly even before, slavery had not only become an integral part of the new Atlantic industrial system but had also been accepted by the European mind, at all social levels, as a part of the natural order of things.

There is yet another sense in which the European-Indian confrontation constituted, as it were, a dress rehearsal for the later chattel-slavery regime. It gave a new impetus, in a new environment, to the values of the European master class. Those values, essentially, were two: that Europe possessed a natural right to arbitrary rule over non-European peoples, and that it was the obligation of the new subject-peoples, again by natural law, to work for their new masters. They are evident, from the very beginning, in the literature of the Conquest. After the first enraptured impressions, it is the common complaint of Columbus and his successors that the Indians do not like to work. Even Las Casas was not prepared to give the Indians complete liberty; his reform schemes envisaged that they would be organized in new communities along more rational lines in a regime of humanely controlled communal work. The Indians, it is charged against them, show no real appreciation of the value of gold and silver, which they use only for ornamental purposes (in a similar fashion, it was held against the Aztec and Inca Indians that they hoarded their wealth in palace treasure rooms instead of putting it to productive use). This is clearly the genesis of the later argument of the proslavery apologetic that if the slave is not forced to work, he will lie under a tree and live on mangoes and bananas. There is present here, first, the old Christian-medieval conviction that man must work by the sweat of his brow and, second, the new capitalist belief that natural resources must not be allowed to lie idle, but must be rationally exploited for the purpose of accumulating wealth.

THE SETTLER HISTORIANS

This general sense of Europe as a superior civilization with a manifest destiny to develop the New World was shared by all the colonizing powers. In the English case, it makes its appearance in the eighteenth century with the writings of the settler-historians and their like such as Atwood in Dominica, Poyer in Barbados, Dallas in Jamaica, and Sir William Young in St. Vincent. As early "local" historians, they wrote openly as apologists, mainly addressing British public opinion in defense of the West Indian social order. Their essentially paternalistic and favorable view of the planter society was complemented by their tendency to regard the stability of the slave system as a vital element in the continued viability of the political and social structure of the British colonial empire in the region as a whole. For Atwood, Dominica is an island healthier than St. Lucia and more capable of planned economic improvement than Trinidad. A combination of English immigration and free grants of the unappropriated Crown lands would soon put it ahead, in terms of commercial prosperity, of the old and exhausted sugar islands. In addition, the island's strategic position, situated between the two main French colonies, was inestimable. Atwood, again, writes almost as a tourist agent as he describes, in classic Arcadian style, the beauties of the island, not to mention its importance as a watering spa for invalids; he even manages to claim that lovers of astronomy would find in the island new opportunity to advance their science. The only urgent problem that threatens the island's development is the existence of the runaway-slave settlements. They must be crushed, if only because the cost involved in pacification—which Atwood describes in detail—places a tax burden so onerous on the planters that it threatens to put them out of business. The note of jealous island particularism, so much a part of the planter creed, is clearly struck in Atwood's book: Dominica is healthy virgin territory awaiting the energetic settler, while St. Lucia is only the burying place of thousands of brave Englishmen.[26] The insularism was only overcome when planters needed help from other islands to repress a slave revolt, for rebellion in one island encouraged rebellion in another. A sense of regional identity was fragile at best, essentially narrow and selfish in its motives.

The Young book on St. Vincent was even more expansionist in its tone. It is the voice of the white settler on the frontier, righteously indignant at the continued existence of an aboriginal group—in this case, the Black Caribs of St. Vincent—which by its endemic hostility to the settler presence places the whole white European "civilizing" process in jeopardy. Young obviously felt it necessary to construct some plausible thesis to justify the group's deportation since, unlike the Negro slaves, its members were keepers of an original aboriginal heritage that rested on prior occupancy. He found the thesis in the doctrine of the right by conquest. The English had conquered them, and therefore, they possessed no rights beyond those granted by the Crown; correspondingly, those rights were forfeited by their rebellion and by their partiality for the French. The thesis was completed by the typical method of defamation of character: the Caribs were a barbarous and cruel set of savages beyond reason or persuasion and must therefore be eliminated.[27] It is worth noting, comparing Atwood and Young, how the planter ideology singled out for that defamatory process the group or groups that posed the greatest danger to the planter interest. In Dominica, the real danger came from the runaway slaves, not from the Caribs, who formed no more than twenty or thirty families; in St. Vincent, by contrast, the Carib himself was the danger, constituting as he did a strong and militant tribal enclave. So, Atwood saw the Carib, in benign terms, as a "native Indian," while Young saw him as a predominantly Negro person, with all of the Negro's negative traits. So again, Atwood wanted to organize a political union with the Caribs, so that they could become hunters of escaped slaves, following the Jamaica policy; Young saw deportation as the only solution. Both apologists, with an unerring instinct based on the sentiment of English moral paramountcy, identified their main enemy and then proceeded to vilify him, which in turn justified his extinction.

This theme of the white settler battling against a hostile internal enemy reached its fullest expression, however, in the Dallas account of the Jamaican Maroon wars. As an ex-liberal, Dallas felt compelled to embellish his defense of slavery as a civilizing force with pseudolearned observations. Like a lesser Burke, he saw the root cause of the Maroon revolt in the "mischievous effect" of the Enlightenment philosophy, although he provides no evidence that any Maroon leader had ever even heard about it. He also saw that philosophy as influencing planters to more humane treatment of their slave charges, again without supporting evidence. He even managed to defend the Maroons against the shrill invective of Bryan Edwards's portrait of them as a lawless banditti of cruel animals; their marriage customs, he acutely argues, ought not to be judged by alien European standards, and far from being animals they possessed most, if not all, of the senses in a superior degree.[28] He even gives the benefit of the doubt to the Maroons concerning the original cause of the war in his admission of the Maroon argument that they had been forced into hostilities out of self-preservation, being persuaded that the whites planned their destruction. He goes yet further, and admits that the technical violation of the treaty on the part of the whites—against which only General Walpole, to his credit, earnestly protested—and which was made the pretext by the local Assembly for their deportation, was probably due to the Maroons' suspicions of bad faith on the part of the colonial authorities.[29] Despite making all these concessions, Dallas arrived at substantially the same conclusions as the more reactionary Edwards. The Maroons had committed "horrid atrocities." They had rebelled against the legitimate authority of the Jamaica Assembly. Enslavement, after all, was not only God's will but also necessary in the light of the fact that the Negro "character" could never itself operate the sugar economy without the guidance of the whites.[30]

Three leading themes, characteristic of the planter outlook, infuse these writings of the settler-historians. First, there is the theme of the absolute monopoly of the slave-worked plantation system. It cannot tolerate any alternative system, nor indeed coexist with any alternative system. It must, therefore, crush any attempt at creating such an alternative, such as the elementary Maroon food-crop economy or the Carib self-sufficient economy; or such alternatives, as with the Carib regime, must at least be safely isolated by a policy of controlled reservations. Nor, of course, could any such alternative be allowed to become the economic basis for organized resistance to the plantation regime. "A cordial reconciliation between them [the Maroons] and the white people," Dallas concluded, "was hardly to be expected."[31] The white settler has taken that intransigent view of native peoples who stand in his way everywhere; and the treatment of the Maroons and Caribs in the West Indies anticipated the later treatment of the Maori tribes in Australasia and of the Plains Indians in the American West—with the same perfidious record of military repression, governmental treachery, broken treaties, and forced evacuation from lands coveted by the whites.

Second, there is the theme of the "divide and rule" strategy, devised to prevent the emergence of a united front against the whites, pitting one set of native interests against another. Dallas saw that clearly. "Had the Maroons," he wrote, "shown that their rebellion was not a temporary struggle but a permanent and successful opposition to the government, it is highly probable that the example might in time have united all the turbulent spirits among the slaves in a similar experiment; if not in the same interest; or indeed such a decided triumph might have tempted numbers of the plantation negroes, unwilling before to change a state of peace for warfare, to join the Maroons. At all events, they would have been a rallying point for every discontented slave, and for all who dreading punishment were incited by their fears to escape." Such an event, he adds, would have meant total economic ruin for the island.[32] The danger was avoided by the policy of tolerating the Maroons so long as they faithfully served as hunters of runaway slaves and, indeed, of making that role a condition of their final surrender. Had there been such a body at Santo Domingo, General Walpole wrote to Lord Balcarres at the end of the war, the brigands would never have risen. The remark sums up a whole policy.

Third, there is the theme of Negro incapacity for freedom. For Atwood, there was, he wrote, "something so very unaccountable in the genius of all negroes, so very different from that of white people in general, that there is not to be produced an instance in the West Indies, of any of them ever arriving to any degree of perfection in the liberal arts or sciences, notwithstanding the greatest pains taken with them"; although, illogically, he conceded, as against that theme of natural inferiority, that second-generation Negroes, under the proper social influence, were capable of losing some of their "stupidity," thus allowing, inferentially, that their state was related to environment and not to inherent deficiency. For Dallas, as he put it in turn," the notion of a free, active, negro republic, does not seem to have any reasonable foundation."[33] Such a republic, if it came to pass, would simply reveal a people without direction, union, or energy; he seems not to have realized that his own description of the Maroon social organization and fighting strategy belied the accusation. It was left to Edwards, in that section of his book that was originally written as an introduction to the published proceedings of the Jamaica Assembly on the Maroon affair, to develop the theme into an argument against slavery abolition. The "calm and unprejudiced reader," he wrote hopefully, will agree with him that the "wild and lawless freedom" of the Maroons proves that abolition would be nothing more than a state of things without control or restraint, neither benefiting society at large nor promoting the happiness of the slaves themselves.[34] The particular circumstance of a beleaguered racial minority engaged in a death struggle with a more complex and ruthless exploiting civilization was thus arbitrarily identified with the general circumstance of Negro freedom understood in its larger context.

These settler-historians, notably Atwood, Young, and Dallas, may properly be seen, as it were, as the Robinson Crusoe apologists of the slave regime; that is to say, they were all concerned with a crucial period when the colonial society was threatened, in Robinson Crusoe fashion, by a hostile force—runaway slaves in Dominica, Caribs in St. Vincent, the Maroons in Jamaica. The analogy is an apt one. For far from being the epic of primitive life, an idyll of tropical island life away from it all, that it has been popularly supposed to be, Defoe's famous book is better seen as a celebration of the heroic exploits of the *homo faber europeanus* in the New World, utilizing his European technology, in the form of goods and tools salvaged from his wrecked ship, to cultivate his island, once he had at hand a subordinate labor supply in the person of Man Friday; undertaking, that is to say, an economy of primitive capital accumulation. Along with that there went a sort of neo-evolutionary view in which the bands of *mauvais sauvages* (evil savages), the rescued native Friday, and Crusoe himself embodied perceived different stages, from lower to higher, in the growth of "civilization." Only the tropical setting of the story, facilely invoking the European dream of the idyllic island paradise, made it seem to the European reader to be something else, so that it was ironic that the book should have been seen by Rousseau's Emile as a picture of the ideal state of nature. It is closer to the truth to say that in its portraiture of Crusoe, incessantly working each day to build up his little empire against the threat of dark and unknown enemies, the book describes the European settler struggling to maintain his supremacy in the colonial world, just like the white groups of settler-historians. Nor was it incidental that Defoe should have made the foundation of Crusoe's success his earlier venture as a slave owner in Brazil, for it was from Brazil that many of the early Caribbean planters emigrated in order to establish the slave-based sugar economy in the islands.

The proslavery ideology reached its zenith in the period between the mid-eighteenth century and the latter part of the nineteenth century, when the slave economy entered into its golden age. It was centered primarily in English Jamaica, French Saint Domingue, and Spanish Cuba, with a distinct and recognizable literature of books and pamphlets written by the various schools of historians and publicists that developed in those three leading societies: the Jamaican planter historians; the publicists, both white colonist and "free coloreds," of Saint Domingue; the Cuban Creole writers and political leaders. To those sources must be added others, of course: colonial assembly debates, metropolitan state papers, the correspondence of governors, the vast literature of travelers' reports, not least of all the growing local press— all of which enable the student to catch glimpses of the self-image of the plantocracy and the images that class entertained of the other actors in the dramatis personae of the colonial scene. For the essence of ideology is perceived self-image, how any societal group sees its function within the general matrix of the social structure, how it sees other groups, and what particular arguments it produces as a means of self-justification.

PARTICULAR CONSIDERATIONS

Concerning the proslavery ideology, certain particular considerations present themselves to the reader of the vast literature. In the first place, it is a defensive literature. Historically, every ruling class has been mainly concerned with power and the uses of power and has only attempted some sort of philosophic rationalization of its position when challenged by hostile forces. The Caribbean plantocracy was no exception. Its English echelon was responding to the abolitionist campaign mounted after the 1770s; its French echelon was reacting to the attack of the philosophes of the Enlightenment, given practical impetus by the assault on its position unleashed by the revolution of 1789; while its Cuban echelon, after the abolition of the slave trade in 1807, had to meet the hostile public opinion of nineteenth-century liberal Europe. It is enough to glance through the exhaustive compilation of the literature spawned by the English abolitionist campaign put together by the historian Lowell Joseph Ragatz—*A Guide for the Study of British Caribbean History, 1763–1834, Including the Abolition and Emancipation Movements*—to realize how the majority of pro-West Indian titles were improvised answers to the abolitionist writers.[35]

Second, it is noteworthy that, almost in the nature of things, the defensive literature was usually written not by planters themselves but by publicists who, sympathetic to the planter cause, were marginally placed in relationship to the slave institution. Although they were planters themselves, both of the Jamaican planter-historians, Long and Edwards, were educated Englishmen who had become creolized; men like Moreau de Saint-Méry in Saint Domingue were moderates distrusted by the *colon;* and the most ardent defender of Cuban slavery, for a while, was José Antonio Saco, not so much a planter as a leading member of the Cuban Creole intelligentsia. It is not surprising then that the proslavery movement in the Caribbean did not produce a Calhoun—who, in the North American case, fashioned a formidable and persuasive case for the Southern cause that was at once a brilliant defense of the plantation economy, an astute critique of the economic principle of the rival Northern industrial capitalist organization, and a presentation of the slave South as a civilization nobler and of finer texture than the coarse materialism of the North. Those particular arguments were also present in the Caribbean literature, of course, but they were never presented with the learning of a Calhoun. And that, probably, is due to the fact that the Caribbean plantocracy constituted the most crudely philistine of all dominant classes in the history of Western slavery. Even Labat, worldly realist that he was, lamented that everything had been imported into the Indies except books. One whole minor theme of Caribbean literature—Luffman's account of the Antigua planter class; Schomburgk's description of Guianese planter society with its ceremonial stiffness and affection; or the description of a decadent Cuban creole society penned by nineteenth century visitors such as Atkins, Turnbull, Hazard, and others[36]—is almost unanimous in its general portrait of a planter way of life that is at once crassly materialist and spiritually empty. Anything even remotely approaching the intellectual was unlikely to make its appearance in such a milieu. Mental excitement, indeed, was provided by the outsider; reading Labat's diary or Lady Nugent's journal, for example, one is struck by the fact that in both cases intelligent conversation was provided by the resident and visiting-officer class present in the islands as a consequence of a wartime situation—the War of the Spanish Succession in Labat's case, the Napoleonic Wars in Lady Nugent's case. *Le luxe est grand dans les Isles* (Luxury is rampant in the islands), wrote Du Tertre early on. As much as anything else, the remark explains the intellectual paucity of the planter mind. It explains, equally, why the planter ideology cannot be seen in any way as constituting a serious philosophical system. It was, rather, little more than a series of rationalized prejudices and unexamined assumptions, trying to justify the vested interests of the dominant Caribbean groups.

[...]

GENERAL CONCLUSION

What then, by way of conclusion, must be said about the proslavery ideology in its special New World locale of the Caribbean plantocratic order? Modern research in the disciplines of social and cultural anthropology has shown that it is possible to posit the existence of clearly defined structural-functional regularities in the plantation system of the region, as well as the existence of territorial diversities traceable to the differences among the socioeconomic-cultural mores brought in by the different European colonizing powers. A similar distinction between overall regularities and subtypical differentiations can be made in the analysis of the ideological superstructure that grew up, over the prolonged slavery period, between the English, Dutch, French, and Spanish Antillean systems.

The differentiae of the superstructure are readily identifiable. All of the colonizers brought with them the general values of Europe shaped by Renaissance, Reformation, and Counter-Reformation. But each motherland gave its particular impress to the general pattern: Catholic or Protestant, monarchical or republican. Linguistic colonialism, again, was a general feature, for all of the colonizer-planter groups conducted a process whereby the slave, forced to yield up his own language forms, was compelled to learn some vulgar variant of the master language in order to survive: it would have been unheard of for a planter to learn, say, Ibo or Ashanti, while for the middle "free colored" groups it became a symbol of respectability to speak the metropolitan language perfectly. Language thus became a value-symbol, a cultural mechanism to reinforce the general ideology of white superiority and black inferiority. It thus shaped, permanently, the linguistic map of the Caribbean. But again, each separate European power gave particular expression to the general practice. So, in the English Caribbean, it was the juxtaposition of "good" English and "bad" English; in the French islands, the rivalry between Parisian French and local patois; in the Dutch territories, the contest between Lowland Dutch and papiamento; and in the Hispanic Antilles the animosity between classical Spanish and the folk idioms of Boricuan Spanish and Afro-Cuban Spanish.

Or, yet again, there were the variations played on the general theme of the ideology of technology. All of the sugar islands joined in the adulation of the creoledom of King Sugar. As Ortiz has shown magisterially, sugar was not only a mode of economic production in the tropical capital-labor regime; it was also, in the imaginary world that the plantocracy constructed, a sort of divine, mystical cult.[37] But even here, at the very material base of the planter ideology, there were wheels within wheels. The attitude of the Jamaican planter of the 1760s was in many ways different from the attitude of the Cuban planter of the 1860s. Ragatz has described in a chapter of his classic study the ingrained technological conservatism of the English Caribbean planters and their opposition to innovations such as the plow and the steam engine in their tropical agriculture.[38] By contrast, Fraginals's classic work describes how successive generations of Cuban planters, including the self-made Spanish immigrant entrepreneurs and the plantation corporate managers who came to dominate the industry after the middle of the century, used every technological innovation to direct the transition from the old *trapiche* (traditional grinding machine), with its more patriarchial form of slavery, to the more modern *ingenio* (sugar mill), based on a more systematic exploitation of a landless labor force.[39] The difference, of course, went back to the nature of the market system within which each group operated; for whereas the Jamaicans operated within a closed and protective British market that only encouraged their mercantilist prejudices, the Cubans, almost from the beginning, had to learn to survive in a world free-trade capitalist market far more competitive in its character. That difference, obviously, did not mean that Cuba, any more than Jamaica, could escape the basic contradiction of the slave productive regime, so that even in Cuba the modernization process never ran its full course, simply because too many planters preferred to rely on the twin factors of unparalleled soil fertility and a ready supply of cheap, unskilled slave labor rather than to risk capital in innovative methods that required skilled wage-labor. Even so, the difference was noticeable; and a work like Reynoso's classic manual of 1862, *Ensayo sobre el cultivo de la caña de azúcar* —which stands out, like the earlier work of Achard and Deresne, as a leading item in the exhaustive bibliography on sugar put out by Ling Roth in 1890[40]—was received with enthusiasm in Havana, while, by contrast, the few individual planters in Jamaica who tried new experimental methods got practically nowhere in the face of entrenched custom.

Yet in the last resort, the structural-functional regularities constituted the more important properties of the slave system. It was—from Cuba to the Guianas—a regional economic system, notwithstanding the fact that it never developed a regional political thought. Whatever the very real variations from sugar island to sugar island—in size of estate, white-mulatto-black population ratios, residency versus absenteeism in the planter group, conditions of work and the relative degrees of harshness, and so on—the system everywhere was based on, as it were, a series of common propositions. (1) In spirit, it was a system geared exclusively to capital investment for continuing capital accumulation; (2) in form, it was an industrial-type discipline of African gang slavery, so that capitalist-type class distinctions became assimilated into non-capitalist-type racial caste lines; (3) its successful operation, therefore, depended upon the development, on the part of the master groups, of methods of control and coercion aimed not only at productive work discipline and maximum productivity on the part of the subject groups but also at habits of respect and obedience in a total master-slave relationship in which the usual distinctions of class were compounded by the more volatile distinctions of race and color.

Ideally, no doubt, the European and Creole master groups hoped to bring together all of those purposes into a single, harmonious whole. Their institutional ideal was probably of some such kind. "Though rarely voiced in any explicit detail," Mintz and Price opine, "it is clear that the European colonists hoped for the 'acculturation' of slave populations to a total acceptance of slave status—and surely many of them believed that proper methods, unrelenting discipline, and enough time would bring this about."[41] To some extent, it was the vision of the colonial gentleman class to become, so to speak, an European territorial baronage overseas: summed up in Bolingbroke's lyrical invitation to young British farmers, in his account of Guiana at the turn of the eighteenth century, *A Voyage to the Demerary, 1799–1806,* to emigrate to a society "where the superintendence of an agricultural concern, confers not merely the rank of a country gentleman, but that baron-like authority over the growing population of the vassals, which the ancestors of the country gentleman enjoyed in England during the feudal ages."[42] To some extent, it was the deluded belief, perhaps at times sincerely accepted by its protagonists, that the West Indian slaves were genuinely a happy and contented crowd: summed up in the ease with which "Monk" Lewis, in his *Journal* recording his visits to his Jamaican estates in the period after Waterloo, could persuade himself, in a spirit of Sternian whimsy, that his slaves were really black rustics enjoying a simple life of singing, dancing, and general jollity.[43] Or yet again, there was the religious gloss on all of this presented by the clerical apologists of the system: So, the cleric-historian Bridges advanced in his *Annals* the pleasing picture of a new multiracial community moving, under the wise guidance of the slaveowners, to a fuller civilization, while a little later Gardner's *History of Jamaica* treated the theme of a West Indian society becoming, once the distorting element of slavery had been removed, a sort of overseas English Victorian society tempered by the civilizing influence of Christianity.[44]

But this was little more, as it were, than the Utopian element of the planter belief-system. That things were different, and known to be different, is evident from the nonutopian elements of the system. There were the slave laws revised regularly by the island assemblies and councils, with their mass of harsh and detailed punishment for every sort of slave misbehavior, from independent economic activity to traveling without a pass, on to attempted escape, insubordinate behavior to whites, and, of course, rebellion—and all of them resting on the planter recognition of the truth, that as Sir William Young (himself a West Indian) put it, "the authority of the few over the many rests everywhere on the resources for sustaining and enforcing it."[45] Goveia's study of the slave legislation in the case of the later eighteenth century British Leeward Islands is significant in this respect, for it shows that despite a noticeable relaxation of statutory punishments (the enactments of Antigua and St. Kitts prohibiting mutilation of slaves, for example) and furthermore, despite evidence of growing leniency in the administration of slave offenses (as in the case of the Montserrat Council), the underlying principle of all of the legislation was the strict subordination of the slave population. Even more than that: the subordination was seen not merely as a necessary device to maintain the sugar economy but as an indispensable mechanism for maintaining a whole social and moral order that, in the planter mentality, became almost an end in itself, even when its economic raison d'être had disappeared. "The slave system," concludes Goveia, "had become more than an economic enterprise which could be abandoned when it became unprofitable. It had become the very basis of organized society throughout the British West Indies, and therefore it was believed to be an indispensable element in maintaining the existing social structure and in preserving law and order in the community. The idea of a society in which Negroes were released from their subordination and allowed legal equality with whites was so antithetical to the principles on which the slave society rested that it seemed to threaten complete social dissolution and chaos."[46]

That general attitude—in which racial hostility superseded even economic self-interest—was, in turn, in itself part cause and part result of the overall climate of opinion that invested every New World plantation. For it was, in general, an isolated world of an island of whites surrounded by an ocean of blacks. In Goveia's words, the source of the whites' strength—their exclusive, oligarchical control over the blacks—was also the source of their weakness. The mental atmosphere of the white world was therefore dominated by the ever-present fear of black servile revolt, even when objective conditions made it highly unlikely. Miss Janet Schaw noted the fear among the Antiguan planters of the 1770s, especially during the dangerous Christmas holiday season.[47] Periods of war made the fear even more endemic, for it was yet another paranoic conviction of the planter mind that the planters of a rival island would even stoop to fomenting slave unrest in the general struggle of interisland economic competition. "I am sure," wrote Lady Nugent in Jamaica in 1805, "that the blacks are to be as much dreaded as the French."[48]

Granted this overriding fear, it was only natural that the Caribbean ruling class, like ruling classes everywhere, should construct, as one defense mechanism, a code of behavior every member was required to observe. The literature is full of anxious admonitions on that score. Not only was the massa-planter the symbol of white authority; he also lived, as Lewis noted, an open life in tropical housing conditions that allowed little room for privacy. The behavioral code, then, demanded of him that he not compromise his authority, and thereby the collective prestige of the white race, by behavior that could call it into question. The message ran from one extreme to the other. On the one hand, it admonished masters against barbaric treatment that could only be counterproductive; and the Huggins case of 1810 in Nevis and the Hodge case in the Virgin Islands a little later showed that even local-planter-controlled assemblies would at times move swiftly against individual masters who exercised needless brutality against their charges.[49] On the other hand, and far more frequently, it brought planter public opinion to bear against those, and especially newcomers, who "spoiled" the blacks by inconsiderate kindness: Lady Nugent was gently reprimanded by her Jamaican lady friends and told that dancing with Negroes at a plantation house party, as if it were nothing more than a servants' hall affair in England, could only have the effect of putting them on an equal footing with whites and might even produce a rebellion in the island;[50] while "Monk" Lewis found, to his astonishment, that the local magistracy considered him a threat to public order merely because he had advocated the "dangerous doctrine" that the evidence of Negroes should be permitted in court proceedings against whites.[51] In other slave colonies reprimand moved on to persecution. The missionary John Smith faced martyrdom in British Guiana; d'Auberteuil met imprisonment in Saint Domingue; and the antislavery voices in Cuba, like Varela and

Martí, found it safer to live most of their lives in exile. In all of these cases the cardinal tenet of the planter creed was at stake, summed up in the protest of the West Indian planters and merchants in London to the British government that "opinion governs the world, and the moment the Negroes shall lose their opinion of the Superiority of White Men, the authority of the White Men will become precarious."[52]

The planter creed, in fact, was caught on the horns of a terrible dilemma. It needed slavery. At the same time, it feared slavery. If only, it seemed at times to be saying, we could have slavery without the slave, the institution without the person. It could not solve the problem with a policy of expulsion—following the original Spanish policy of the expulsion of the Jews and the Moors in the fifteenth and sixteenth centuries—nor with a policy of extermination—following the original English and French policy of the extermination of the Caribs in the seventeenth century—for its very existence depended upon the extracted surplus value of slave labor. Prudence itself dictated considerate treatment; after all, to kill or seriously maim a slave was to destroy a principal source of production, to risk a reduction of fixed capital. Conservation, therefore, became an important maxim of the planter's manual of estate management. Rochefort laid down the general rule early on in his book of the 1650s. "It is therefore requisite," he wrote, "that in the conduct of them (the slaves) there should be a mean observed between extreme severity and too much indulgence, by those who would keep them in awe, and make the best advantage of them."[53] The day's work, after all, had to be done. The estate had to show a profit at the end of the financial year or go into bankruptcy, to be taken over by a rapacious merchant or lawyer (and, indeed, the hatred of the town merchant-lawyer class was always a very real subsidiary element in the total planter ideology). Many a planter or overseer, then, must have found it more productive, in the long run, to cajole the slave-workman than to coerce him—making them amateur psychologists, as it were, of the slave character. That explains yet another note in the planter ideology, its indignation, not always insincere, at the temptation of its abolitionist critics to portray the plantation as a scenario of daily conflict between cruel masters and suffering slaves. To the degree that this was so, the proslavery maxim that the interest of the master guaranteed the welfare of the slave was an important half-truth: "Be assured, you philanthropists who are so alarmed by this institution," declared Dubuisson in the Saint Domingue case, "that the lives of our slaves are too costly to us for us to deal with them unreasonably."[54]

But it was a half-truth only, for a combination of other considerations— the fear of "spoiling" the slave, the savage pressure to produce as rapidly as possible with a high cost in lives, the planter's cherished belief that it was better to rely on a steady stream of new imported labor than to nurture the existing labor force and supplement it by planned natural increase—placed a real and serious limit on the policy of prudence. The appalling work regime of the plantation—and it is the defect of a document like Lewis's *Journal* that it shows us the slave at play rather than at work—meant that the slave, literally, was worked to death. No human material would tolerate such a regime except under the stimulus of steady and systematic pressure, mercilessly executed. It followed logically, as the planter mind saw it, that the only sure control lay, not in the policy of prudence, but in a policy of terror. The attitude was summed up in the defiant defense of the Saint Domingue planter Lejeune in his celebrated trial of 1788. He declared:

> My cause in this matter becomes the cause of every *colon*. … The unhappy condition
> of the negro leads him naturally to detest us. It is only force and violence that restrains
> him; he is bound to harbor an implacable hatred in his heart, and if he does not visit
> upon us all the hurt of which he is capable it is only because his readiness to do so is
> chained down by terror; so, if we do not make his chains as heavy as, proportionately,
> to the dangers that we run with him, if we let loose his hatred from the present state in
> which it is stifled, what can prevent him from attempting to break the chains? The bird
> trapped in its cage will take advantage of the slightest negligence to make its escape. I
> dare to assert that there is only wanting in the negroes sufficient courage and resolution
> to purchase their liberty by means of the blood of their masters. Just one single step is
> necessary to make them aware of what it is they have in their power to accomplish…
> it is only fear and the equity of the law that holds back the negro from stabbing his
> master in the back, only the sensation of the absolute power that we hold over his
> person. Take away that rein, and he will try everything.[55]

Grim, uncompromising, realistic, this is the language of naked power, stripped of any
pretense at apology or moralizing justification. It is the language of Hobbes, not of Rousseau.
Consent yields to fear. There is no room for the social contract; everything is in the state of
nature.

To read that kind of defense is to recognize the fundamental character of the slavery
institution: the difference between its essences and its accidents. The policy of terror was its
essence; the policy of prudence, only one of its accidents. As a modern Guyanese scholar has
put it, placing the matter in the context of a general principle:

> The fundamental element of the terror process is the specific act or threat of
> violence which induces a general psychic state of extreme fear, which in turn produces
> typical patterns of reactive behavior. The system of violence may be a means of
> destruction, an instrument of punishment, or a method of control. One could construct
> a typology of power systems based on the use of violence. At one pole are systems that
> use violence as a last resort; at the other, those that use it as a first measure. Were we
> to fill out this skeleton with the flesh of historical experience, we could identify at one
> pole the systems blessed with concord, in which power is supported by minimal force,
> and in which violence is truly an *ultima ratio*. At the other extreme, we should find the
> terror systems, in which violence is *prima ratio potestatis*. Plantation despotism, which
> punished the smallest infractions with the severest violence, is to be placed nearer the
> latter pole.[56]

How empty was the policy of prudence, as distinct from the reality of that policy of
terror, is evident enough from the record of amelioration in the sugar colonies, based as it
was on the precepts of prudence. The record, as already noted, was almost wholly negative.
No doubt there was a real spirit of pity for the lot of the nonwhites within the "moderate"
elements; even a planter-historian as obdurate as Long could write a sympathetic account
of the social tragedy of the light-skinned illegitimate sons and daughters of Jamaican white
fathers who, educated as young ladies at finishing schools in Chelsea or as young men at Eton
itself, returned to the island only to find themselves in a no-man's-land, accepted neither

by the white parental society nor by the black slave society.[57] Yet that spirit of pity could never bring even the moderate voices—much more sympathetic than Long—to a wholesale denial of the system. That is why Edwards, in the Jamaican case, weighing his humanitarian spirit against what he termed the "absolute coercive necessity" of the system, came down finally in favor of the latter, and why even a plantocrat like Richard Barrett who, much more than Edwards, had so imbibed the Enlightenment spirit that he was generally regarded as an agnostic, perhaps even an atheist, could remain as a leader of his class in the 1820s and 1830s in its struggle to maintain slavery.[58] That is why, again, d'Auberteuil, in the Saint Domingue case, while readily conceding that liberty is what the slave wants most, deprived the concession of any real meaning by recommending that freedom should only be granted to those few slaves who in moments of crisis had demonstrated loyalty and respect to masters; for, he added, to give a slave freedom simply because he has cooked well for twenty years is as ridiculous as allowing membership in the Academy of Sciences to a man who can write the letters of the alphabet exactly.[59] That is why, finally, in the Cuban case, when Zarragoitia, as the voice of the nonsugar, cattle-raising economy of the eastern province, came to write his important report of 1805 to the *Real Consulado* (royal tribunal), he took issue on many counts with the sugar planters' viewpoint but could not bring himself, in the final instance, to impugn their sugar-obsessed capitalist ideology or to challenge its slave-labor base.[60] In all of these cases, certainly, there were "reformers" who did not accept the status quo in its entirety, for it would be idle to suppose that in the plantocratic membership, as in all ruling classes, there did not exist different factions espousing different views. Yet the differences were always about tactics, never about the leading principle of the slave system. The arguments of the reformers in favor of better treatment of the slaves—more protection, for example, in the courts—were in themselves proslavery, since better treatment was seen as weakening the case for early emancipation.

For all the accidents of the system—pity, prudence, amelioration, the nice legalistic distinctions between the various slave codes, the phenomenon of what Marvin Harris has called the "myth of the friendly master"[61]—were fragile plants bound to wither away under the gross pressures of the moral atmosphere that was at the heart of slavery and that constituted its essence. Any social order in which the exercise of authority by one group or class over another is not tempered by accountability to a neutral sovereignty or by internal moral constraint rapidly degenerates into unbridled absolutism. The ultimate moral criticism of New World slavery, then, was not that it produced individual cruel planter-masters but, rather, that it was governed, to its innermost recesses, by a general spirit of amoral caprice in which all human sentiment was eroded by the daily habit of irresponsible and untrammeled power. The Swiss traveler Girod-Chantrans acutely perceived how that general spirit was the result of the transition from Europe to America, illustrating, as it were, the Americanization of metropolitan European values. "Every day in this colony," he observed of Saint Domingue in 1782, "one sees young people newly arrived who show themselves to be at first human and sensible, and assert themselves with warmth against the tyranny (of the masters), and who end up by being almost as harsh as the oldest inhabitants. ... After a certain time, naturalized in some fashion in the New World, the European becomes a different man." Moreau de Saint-

Méry commented on the same spirit of callousness in the white Creole youth, contracted indeed in childhood itself. Dr. Pinckard also noted it in the womenfolk of the Dutch planters in the Guiana of the 1790s: "The corporal punishment of slaves is so common," he wrote, "that instead of exciting the repugnant sensations, felt by Europeans on first witnessing it, scarcely does it produce, in the breasts of those accustomed to the West Indies, even the slightest glow of compassion."[62]

There is implicit in observations such as these the final justificatory argument of the proslavery creed. America, the argument goes, is not Europe. The truths, whether religious or philosophical, that Europe regards as universalist relate only, in fact, to European particular customs and experience. In America, where customs and experience are radically different, those truths are irrelevant. America must only be judged by American standards. Thus, the earlier idea of America, developed in the earlier literature of the European Utopians, as a new world of paradisiacal innocence and an ideal poetic landscape against which the ills of European society could be critically measured, was cleverly perverted by the Caribbean slavocracy into a thesis placed at the service of the slavery system. The Europeans had used it, so to say, in order to speak for Caliban. The Caribbeans used it in order to speak for Prospero.

A final observation is in order on the proslavery ideology. It would be naïve to assume that, as slavery ended, it also ended. Ideological systems long survive the concrete economic conditions that originally give rise to them. In the Caribbean case a particular expression of that truth is to be found in the French Antilles. Slavery there was abolished finally in 1848. But the proslavery racism survived for the rest of the century and, indeed, into the twentieth-century proper. The white Creole descendants of the old sugarocracy never really surrendered the claim that by skin color alone they were the natural ruling class of the society. The claim received fresh impetus with the arrival, after 1870, of the Third Republic. For in the ideas of the new national status, the reactionary Antillean forces perceived all the evil and malignant forces hostile to their continuing hegemony: universal suffrage, secular schooling, republican egalitarianism, the primacy of the civil power, the rights of man as applied to the colonies, and anticlericalism. Like the colons of Saint Domingue in 1789, the Antillean ruling groups a century later proclaimed their loyalty to France. But the France they had in mind was the France of traditional yesterday, in which blacks and mulattoes knew their place as natural inferiors. It was an attitude, all in all, wholly reactionary; like their counterparts in Paris, these Antillean forces would substitute the Second Empire for the Third Republic at the slightest opportunity.

Nothing better illustrates the truth of all this than a study of the right-wing colonial press of the township of Saint Pierre in Martinique in the last two decades of the century before it was destroyed by the volcanic eruption of Mount Pelée in 1902. The contents of that press are full of all the vitriolic hatred of the Third Republic typical of the right-wing elements in France itself—the only difference being, of course, that the hatred is expressed in Antillean terms. It is an open and virulent racism, expressed in the most gross and vulgar terms. The anatomical characteristics of the Negro show him to be of small cranial size, with a brain so tiny that it explains why he is lazy, apathetic, untrustworthy, more given to idiocy than to mere folly. He has none of the sensibility or sensitivity of the European. He is an infant who has never grown up. The Koran of Muhammad tells us that all peoples have their prophets except the Negro. The present state of Haiti is proof that the Negro race is innately incapable of morality, self-government, and philosophy, thus proving at one and the same time its natural inferiority and the essential justice of slavery—a form natural to such inferior people. Slavery, indeed, is a natural state in which the Negro must accept the rule of the white master in the same way as the domesticated animal accepts the rule of his human owner. So, Toussaint L'Ouverture was a man certainly of high intelligence but mutilated by his antiwhite hatred, his crimes and his massacres—surely a lesson to all those misguided Antilleans who dream of separation from France. So, too, Schoelcher cannot be condemned too severely: He seeks to pollute the racial purity of his own race; he is indeed the vampire of his race; he dreams of a new mulatto domination in the Antilles while at the same time, as a Frenchman of Alsatian birth, he ignores the continuing subjection of Alsace and Lorraine to the German enemy. The Negro, to sum it all up, is more akin to the monkey than to other human races. That dictates all else. The mulatto politicians of the day, who are, in any case, only despicable renegade Africans, must be taught that lesson.[63] All in all, these journalistic extracts reveal an intractable white Creole racism of the crudest type. How it helped to destroy the happiness of all the groups involved in it in the Martiniquan society of the time comes out in the novel *Le Triomphe d'Eglantine*, published in the 1880s by the white Creole writer René Bonneville, in which everybody—the young white Creole scion, his colored mistress, his wife, and all the children, both legitimate and illegitimate, of the liaisons entered into—is made to suffer on the altar of color prejudice.[64]

Notes

1.   J.E. Cairnes, cited in Karl Marx, *Capital* (London: George Allen and Unwin, 1938). 1:251–52.
2.   Herman J. Niebohr, *Slavery as an Industrial System: Ethnological Researches*, B. Franklin Research and Source Works Series, no. 770 (London, 1971).
3.   Karl Marx, *Correspondence of Marx and Engels* (London: Marxist-Leninist Library, Lawrence and Wishart, 1941), 14.
4.   Eric Williams, *Capitalism and Slavery* (Chapel Hill: University of North Carolina Press, 1944). See also Roger Anstey, *The Atlantic Slave Trade and British Abolition, 1760–1810* (Atlantic Highlands, N.J.: Humanities Press, 1975).
5.   Cited in Williams, *Capitalism and Slavery*, 19.
6.   Cairnes cited in Niebohr, *Slavery as an Industrial System*, 303.
7.   Jill Sheppard, *The "Redlegs" of Barbados: Their Origins and History* (Millwood, N.Y.: KTO Press, 1977), Ch. 5.
8.   Preface to *Historical Essay on the Colony of Surinam. 1788*, ed. Jacob R. Marcus and Stanley F. Chyet (Cincinnati: American Jewish Archives, 1974).
9.   Ibid., 66–73.
10. Ibid., 36.
11. Charles de Rochefort, *Histoire naturelle et morale des Antilles de l'Amérique (Rotterdam, 1658)* – translated into English by John Davies as *History of the Caribby Islands* (London, 1666).
12. Henry Raup Wagner, *The Life and Writing of Bartolomé de Las Cases* (Albuquerque: University of New Mexico Press, 1967), 221.
13. Winthrop D. Jordan, *White over Black: American Attitudes Toward the Negro. 1550–1812* (Baltimore Books, 1969), chps. 1, 2.
14. Fray Bernardino de Minaya, *Memorial to Charles V* (n. d.), cited in Eric Williams, ed., *Documents of*

West Indian History, 1492–1655 (Port-of-Spain, Trinidad: People's National Movement Publishing Co., 1963), 136.

15. Fernando de Oviedo y Valdés, *Historia general y natural de las Indias* (Madrid, 1535–1556), cited ibid., 111–13.
16. Bartolomé de Las Casas, *Historia de las Indias* (Mexico City: Fondo de Cultura Económico, 1951), cited ibid., 141.
17. Cited in Wagner, *Life and Writings of Las Casas*, 11.
18. Alonzo Zuazo, Judge of Hispaniola, to Cardinal Ximenes, Regent of Spain, January 22, 1518, cited in Williams, *Documents of West Indian History*,144–45.
19. Diego de Salamanca, Bishop of San Juan, to Philip II, King of Spain, April 6, 1579, cited ibid., 144.
20. *Ordenanzas para el cabildo y regimiento de la villa de la Habana y las demás villas y lugares de esta isla que hizo y ordeno el ilustre Sr. Dr. Alonso de Caceres, oidor de la dicha Audiencia real de la ciudad ... ,* January 14, 1574, cited ibid., 153–54.
21. Quoted in Wagner, *The Life and Writings of Las Casas*, 247.
22. Bartolomé de Albornoz, *Arte de los Contratos* (Valencia, 1573), quoted in Williams, *Documents of West Indian History*, 161.
23. Fray Tomás Mercado, *Suma de Tratos y Contratos* (Seville, 1587), cited ibid., 158–60.
24. Fray Alonso de Sandoval, *De Instauranda Aethiopum Salute* (Seville, 1627), quoted ibid., 163.
25. Samuel Purchas, *Purchas his Pilgrimage, Or Relations of the World and the Religions Observed in all Ages and Places Discovered, from the Creation unto This present* (London, 1614), cited in Jordan, *White over Black*, 12–13.
26. Thomas Atwood, *The History of the Island of Dominica* (London, 1791, reprint ed., London: Frank Cass and Co., 1971).
27. Sir William Young, *An Account of the Black Charaibs in the Island of St Vincent's* (London, 1795).
28. R.C. Dallas, *History of the Maroons*, 2 vols. (London, 1803). 1. viii:87–95.
29. Ibid., 1:148.
30. Ibid., 1:45.
31. Ibid., 1:180–81.
32. Ibid., 2:2–3.
33. Atwood, *History of the Island*, 267; Dallas, *History of the Maroons*, 2:453–54.
34. Bryan Edwards, *The History, Civil and Commercial, of the British West Indies*, 5 vols. (London, 1819), 1:522–79.
35. Lowell Joseph Ragatz, *A Guide for the Study of British Caribbean History, 1763–1834. Including the Abolition and Emancipation Movements* (Washington, D.C.: U.S. Government Printing Office, 1932).
36. John Luffman, *A Brief Account of the Island of Antigua, 1786–1788* (London, 1789), reprinted in Vere Langford Oliver, *History of the Island of Antigua*, 3 vols. (London: Mitchell and Hughes, 1894), cxxviii–cxxxviii; Richard Schomburgk, *Travels in British Guiana, 1840–1844*, ed. Vincent Roth (Georgetown, British Guiana: Guiana edition, *Daily Chronicle*, 1953), 1:47; noted in Roland T. Ely, *Cuando reinaba su majestad el azúcar* (Buenos Aires: Editorial Sudamericana, 1963), ch. 28.
37. Fernando Ortiz, *Contrapunto Cubano*.
38. Ragatz, *A Guide*, ch. 2.
39. Manuel Moreno Fraginals, *El Ingenio*, pt. 4.
40. Note on Reynoso in H. Ling Roth, *Literature of Sugar*, 74.
41. Sidney W. Mintz and Richard Price, *An Anthropological Approach to the Afro-American Past: A Caribbean Perspective* (Philadelphia: Institute for the Study of Human Issues, 1976), 3.
42. *Henry Bolingbroke, A Voyage to the Demerary, 1799–1806* (Georgetown, British Guiana: *Daily Chronicle*, 1947), 150.
43. M.G. Lewis, *Journal of a West India Proprietor, 1815–1817* (London: George Routledge and Sons, 1929).
44. G.W. Bridges, *Annals of Jamaica*, 2 vols. (London: Frank Cass, 1968); W. J. Gardner, *A History of*

Jamaica from Its Discovery by Christopher Columbus to the Year 1872 (London: Frank Cass, 1971).

45. Sir William Young, *An Account of the Black Charaibs in the Island of St Vincent,* cited in Elsa Goveia, *Slave Society in the British Leeward Islands at the End of the Eighteenth Century,* Yale University Caribbean Series 8 (New Haven: Yale University Press 1965), 155.

46. Goveia, *Slave Society,* 329.

47. Evangeline and Charles M. Andrews, eds., *Journal of a Lady of Quality* (New Haven: Yale University Press, 1921), 108–9, 112.

48. *Lady Nugent's Journal* (Kingston: Institute of Jamaica, 1966), 237.

49. Richard Pares, *A West India Fortune* (London: Longmans, 1958), 150–58.

50. *Lady Nugent's Journal,* 156.

51. M.G. Lewis, *Journal,* 181–82.

52. Quoted in Goveia, *Slave Society,* 253.

53. John Davies, *History of the Caribby Islands* (London, 1666), 202.

54. Dubuisson, *Nouvelles considérations sur Saint-Domingue,* 1:83–84.

55. Cited in Gisler, *L'Esclavage aux Antilles Françaises,* 119–20.

56. Paul Singh, *Political Thought in Guyana: An Historical Sketch* (Georgetown: University of Guyana, 1972), 9.

57. Long, *History of Jamaica,* 2:328–29.

58. H.P. Jacobs, *Sixty Years of Change, 1806–1866* (Kingston: Institute of Jamaica, 1973), 46–47.

59. D'Auberteuil, *Considérations,* 1:86–97.

60. Fraginals, *The Sugar Mill,* 69.

61. Marvin Harris, *Patterns of Race in the Americas* (New York: W. W. Norton, 1974).

62. Girod-Chantrans, cited in Gisler, *L'Esclavage aux Antilles Françaises,* 70; Moreau de Saint-Méry, cited ibid., 70; Dr George Pinckard, *Letters from Guiana* (Georgetown, British Guiana: *Daily Chronicle,* 1942), 18–19.

63. René Acheen, "Les Blancs Créoles de Saint-Pierre au Debut de la Troisième République," *Colloque de Saint-Pierre* (Martinque: Centre Universitaire Antilles-Guyane, 1973), 57–67.

64. René Bonneville, "Vision de la Societe Pierrotine dans *Le Triomphe d'Eglantine,*" 71–75.

The Political Thought of Quobna Cugoano: Radicalized Natural Liberty

Anthony Bogues

I write what I like.
—Steve Biko

The slaves shall be free … [through a] … combination of ideas.
—Robert Wedderburn, former slave

Introduction

The 1969 publication of African-American poet Arna Bontemps's *Great Slave Narratives* consolidated the study of slave narratives as a genre of literature.[1] Bontemps made the case for the slave narrative as an "American genre" of popular autobiography. This classification has meant that subsequent studies on slave narratives have been primarily framed as memoirs, autobiography, and a genre of literature. To consider these frames as the *only* ones for the study of slave narratives is today problematic. First, it is well known that a common problem within the domain of knowledge production is the misconception that blacks produce experience and whites produce theory.[2] Therefore, when we study the written productions of black slaves *only* within the autobiographical or literary frame, we can miss their political ideas and purposes. The second difficulty is that the narrow autobiographical frame which focuses on life experiences often ignores the broad context of textual production. When this occurs, the complex relationships between the written testimony of the slave and the political language and context in which the testimony is embedded are elided or reduced to a secondary position. The autobiographical/literary frame of slave narratives confines the politics of many narratives to a form of "literary black vindicationism" similar in some respects to the "vindicationism" of black history.[3] The autobiographical frame also ignores the fact that the late eighteenth century and a good deal of the nineteenth century were periods in which black abolitionism was a significant radical plank on the world's political stage.[4] This essay challenges the dominant interpretive mode of the slave narratives as primarily literary and autobiographical. In doing so, it argues that Quobna Cugoano's *Thoughts and Sentiments on the Evil of Slavery* is a major late eighteenth-century text of political discourse on natural liberty and natural rights.

Henry Louis Gates, Jr.'s book *The Signifying Monkey* (1988) opened wider spaces for thinking about the location of slave narratives. However, it did so within the boundaries of the established literary canonization of the narratives. In this seminal work Gates argues that the slave narratives were an integral part of the African-American literary tradition. He further suggests that this tradition was a "double-voiced" one, and characterizes the slave narrative as "a talking book." Positing a theory of origins, Gates asserts that the "literature of the slave" at the level of meaning was an oxymoron, and that for the slave, the capacity to read and write was his or her ability to "transgress [a] nebulous realm of liminality."[5] He further observes that, "The slave wrote not primarily to demonstrate humane letters, but to demonstrate his or her membership in the human community."[6]

For Gates, blacks became subjects in the eyes of the world through the crafting of a written text. Probing this point, he demonstrates how the privileging of reason by the various European Enlightenments created writing as a badge and expression of Reason, and therefore of humanity. It is common knowledge that after Descartes proclaimed, "I think; therefore I am," thinking was transformed into Reason, and that "I am" became an epistemological question rather than one of being.[7] Over time, the written word became the signifier for Reason as rationality. As such, African slaves living in the "Age of the Enlightenment" did use writing as *one* means of human agency. Gates and others have suggested that slave narratives were also the early beginnings of a "Black Atlantic literary and cultural tradition ... [which shared] a common creolized cultural heritage that crossed national and ethnic boundaries ... defined political categories, social norms, and even literary genres."[8]

In one sense this is accurate, and acknowledges the fact that modern Atlantic slavery was a large system and that the trade yoked different societies into a set of relationships. However, in spite of the above, we are still left with working through the specific forms of political writings and criticism that the narratives were embedded within. One way to grapple with the issue of the precise nature of slave narratives is to suggest that they were not only literature, political criticism, or narrative history, but integrated all these modes of writing into a form of critical exposition. This form of writing had an ethical dimension, and its primary modes were both communicative and calls to action, thereby making the narratives moments of slave critique. This shift in interpretation means that the narratives were something else; they were *documents of freedom* that can be interpreted within the context of the language and political ideas of their times. Today the act of reading these texts confronts one with a peculiar task of interpretation—the relationship between the meaning of these texts, the structural world of slavery, and the general ideas of natural liberty in what the critic Roland Barthes calls a "narrative communication."

This essay will attempt to address some of these issues. Using Cugoano's narrative, I want to suggest that perhaps another way to read *some* of the slave narratives of the late eighteenth century is to grapple with them as discursive practices of slave criticism and critique that probed alternative meanings of racial slavery, natural liberty, and natural rights, and countered the dominant eighteenth-century ideas of racial plantation slavery. As documents of slave political criticism and critique, the narratives have a great deal to tell us about eighteenth-century social and political ideas, and form a central part of an Africana radical intellectual political tradition.

Writing as Political Criticism

Dena Goodman tells us that there were many modes of critical writing during the eighteenth century: epistolary, historical narrative, letters, memoirs, treatises, and dialogical.[9] The major objective of these forms of writing was to shape a society's thinking. According to Goodman, these modes of writing constituted "conscious acts carried out by leading figures as part of the Enlightenment's civic project."[10] Critical writing during this period involved a kind of dialectic. The production of a text was an engaged moment whereby the writer hoped that he or she would affect society's thinking. As a mode of critical action, writing had three aspects—there was an audience who would be persuaded, who would be changed, and who would, eventually, act. From this standpoint we can better appreciate the emphasis that the English abolitionist movement placed upon written textual productions during the late eighteenth century as an integral part of its campaign to abolish the slave trade.

Another dimension of the discursive practices of the period was the language and vocabulary of political discourse. In general, four main themes provided the grammar for political discourse: state of nature, natural law, natural rights, and natural liberty. In England these themes were complicated by an older political tradition that had emerged in Stuart England—the Bible as the divine word of God and the application of the principles of the New Testament as a catalyst for conceptions of a harmonious political order. This tradition of appropriating biblical texts for radical purposes and reworking the language of revolution through the prism of religious beliefs was consolidated in the revolution of the 1640s when the major radical groups, the Levellers and the Diggers, conducted much of their revolutionary propaganda and journalism in the language of religious discourse.[11] For many African ex-slaves and slaves, the Bible was also a central source for reading and gaining literacy skills. Slaves' biblical exegesis readapted the narrative and prophetic forms of biblical discourse to explain and understand their condition. What is interesting in many slave narratives is how these forms functioned alongside secular Enlightenment discourse as part of the complex intellectual labor of the eighteenth-century black writer. Thus one could get in the slave narratives of the period the language of natural rights mixed with prophecy.[12] At the heart of the themes (natural law, natural liberty, state of nature, natural rights, theories of human origins) was what Michel Foucault has described as the political rationality of governing men.[13]

The third feature of the eighteenth-century intellectual context that should draw our attention is the conception of the "Great Chain of Being." This hierarchical conception formulated an originary theory of the universe in which human beings and the social order replicated "the divine hierarchy of heaven." Basing itself on the natural history classification of Carolus Linnaeus, this system of classification led to a vigorous debate on polygenesis versus monogenesis as the theory of human origin. At the center of this debate was the location of Africans in a natural inferior position.[14] This debate about the origins of the human became critical in late eighteenth- and early nineteenth-century mainstream arguments about the humanity of the black slave, and a major point of contention between abolitionists of all races and advocates of slavery.

The late eighteenth-century was a period when the questions that animated Western thinkers were framed around what Edmund Burke called the "great ... unfolding map of mankind."[15] Part of this unfolding map was a preoccupation with the human and the development of a philosophical anthropology that postulated "natural" characteristics of the human. The evidence of this preoccupation can be discerned when we note the number of publications between George Berkeley's *Principles of Human Knowledge* (1710) and Mary Wollstonecraft's *Vindication of the Rights of Women* (1792), that had the human as a central focus. The following were some of the keys texts: Alexander Pope's *An Essay on Man* (1734), David Hume's *Enquiry Concerning Human Understanding* (1748), Gotthold Ephraim Lessing's *Education of the Human Race* (1780), and Johann von Herder's *Ideas for the Philosophy of the History of Mankind* (1784). The tragedy, of course, was that this *human subject* was narrowly defined, and excluded women, Africans, and other non-Europeans.[16] From within this exclusive paradigm the political grammar of natural liberty and natural rights was framed. However, because it was grounded in exclusions and silences, natural rights and natural liberty would morph over time to have narrow meanings.

Burke's "unfolding map" rested upon the notion of African inferiority, and was very dependent as well upon texts that reaffirmed Europe's "superiority" because many Western thinkers in this period drew heavily from the travel writings and literature of "explorers." Paul Kaufman's study of English reading habits of the period confirms the tremendous attraction of intellectuals and the literate public to travel literature and books.[17] Thus it is fair to say that there was during this period a general intellectual preoccupation in Europe with the nature of the New World and of colonialism. This preoccupation found its way into the writings and understandings of many early modern political thinkers, but via the musings and literate offerings of those who were conquering the New World. How these offerings infected political philosophy is detailed in Anthony Pagden's wonderful volume, *Lords of All the World* (1995).

Against the background of colonial conquest, and ideas of racial servitude and of African inferiority, Western political thinkers began their strivings for new forms of society that would replace crumbling European absolutism. In such a context, very few thinkers included the slave trade and racial slavery in their discussion of these questions, and when they did so, they were discussed within two main frameworks.

The first owed its foundational assumptions to Greek and Roman conceptions of slavery.[18] These conceptions stated that slavery was the result of war or of debt owed. John Locke's comments on slavery and natural liberty exemplify this current when he writes in *The Second Treatise of Government*:

> The *Natural Liberty* of Man is to be free from any Superior Power on Earth, and not to be under the Will or legislative Authority, but to have only the law of Nature for his Rule. ... This *Freedom* from Absolute, Arbitrary Power, is so necessary to and closely joined with a Man's Preservation. ... For a Man, not having the Power of his own life *cannot*, by Compact, or his own Consent, *enslave himself to* anyone ... the prefect condition of *Slavery*, which *is* nothing else, but *the State of War continued between a lawful conqueror, and the captive*. For, if once *Compact* enter between them, and make an

agreement for limited Power on the one side, and Obedience on the other, the State of War and *Slavery* ceases, as long as the Compact endures.[19]

An analysis of the above passage reveals not only that natural liberty was posed in terms of the relationship between government and citizens, what Isaiah Berlin has called "the central question in politics—the question of obedience and coercion"[20]—but also that Locke defined slavery as the result of conquest. For Locke, conquest meant that the conquered were outside the social contract, and since the compact was critical to the creation of conditions in which slavery as he defined it would cease, then wherever and among whomever slavery existed, such persons existed outside of the compact and had no rights.[21]

The second definition of slavery during this period was located within the ideas of what has been called "civic republicanism."[22] This "civic republicanism" some political theorists have argued meant that the conception of freedom and slavery was tied to ideas of citizenship that primarily focused on issues of how laws and the state shaped freedom as a form of political self-determination. Later on when this form of freedom is conceptualized as non-domination it is done so within the frame elaborated by Mill and Berlin, that of non-coercion and interference. I want to suggest that the elision of racial slavery and its meanings by the majority of the political thinkers of the period meant that over time, conceptions of natural liberty and natural rights narrowly folded into a set of political discourses about the state, government, and citizens' rights. This created a flawed space for a new discussion of rights, obligations, and notions of resistance for the male European citizen struggling against absolutism. At one level these new conceptions were perhaps best embodied in the 1789 French Declaration of Rights of Man and Citizen, and the American Constitution.

At another level there was a radical plebeian impulse that attempted to radicalize both the conception of rights and the notion of private property. This impulse drew its sources from Thomas Paine's defense of the French Revolution, *The Rights of Man*. In London it solidified around the formation of the London Correspondence Clubs, the writings and political activities of Thomas Spencer, and, by the 1820s, the preaching and chapels of persons like the former Jamaican slave Robert Wedderburn.[23]

Surveying the United States in this period, we can discern a preoccupation with natural liberty as a conception of republican civic freedom in the writings of Thomas Jefferson, John Adams, and James Madison. Mainstream American political thought in the late eighteenth century drew from two sources: republican political values of self-government and Lockean understandings of limited government and political liberty. Rogers Smith accurately sums up the early political goals of the American republic thus: "The goal remained a great but state-centric union of small agrarian republics, populated by self-supporting, educated white yeomen, joined and governed by the mutual consent of all those capable of being dedicated to free republican citizenship."[24] Within this political conception of republicanism, "slavery" was primarily identified as lack of self-government. Listen to Adams addressing the citizens of Massachusetts: "The people of Massachusetts uniformly think that the destruction of their Charter, making the council and judges wholly dependent upon the crown and the people subjected to the unlimited power of parliament as their supreme legislative is *slavery.*"[25]

Thus we can safely say that by the late eighteenth century, the language of natural liberty in America was the discourse of self-government as political liberty. This language was oblivious to the overshadowing presence of the system of human domination (racial slavery).[26] However, some political thinkers did pay some attention to racial slavery, and in doing so developed a radicalized version of natural liberty. One of the most outstanding cases in this regard was Thomas Paine. Paine's 1775 essay "African Slavery in America" refuted the arguments that slavery in America was the result of a state of war. He forcefully asserted that the slaves were "not prisoners of war, and redeemed from savage conquerors, as some plead."[27] Paine called slavery a "savage practice" and appealed for its abolition.

For the French philosophers the situation was only slightly different. Montesquieu's satirical arguments against African slavery in *The Spirit of Laws* are well known. Nevertheless, he continued to hold the view that Africans were uncivilized and not energetic, compared to Europeans of cooler climes.[28] Diderot's joint work with Abbé Raynal, *The History of the Indies,* was a "philosophical and political history of European trade and settlements in the Indies." It was also an antislavery text with profound consequences. However, the text was deeply ambiguous, and while being anticolonial as well as antislavery, it maintained the view that Africans were "primitive" beings. In describing the African and Africa, the *History* states "that they are more indolent, more weak, and unhappily more fit for slavery."[29] Diderot and Raynal further note, "Arts are unknown amongst them. All their labors are confined to certain rustic employments, scarce one hundredth part of their country is cultivated and that in a very wretched manner."[30]

There is one other important political thinker of the period to whom we should pay some attention: Mary Wollstonecraft. Wollstonecraft belongs to the group of political thinkers who advocated a radicalized version of natural rights in the late eighteenth century. However, she could not escape the enmeshment of the "Great Chain of Being." So even while she pressed the claims for the equality of women in her pathbreaking text, *Vindication of the Rights of Women,* she continued to hold the view of Africans as an "unmeditative people."[31] In her 1789 review of Olaudah Equiano's narrative, Wollstonecraft writes that although they are interesting, these "volumes do not exhibit extraordinary intellectual powers ... yet the activity and ingenuity, which conspicuously appear in the character of Gustavus, place him on par with the general mass of men who fill the subordinate stations in a more civilized society than that which he was thrown into at his birth."[32]

Diderot and Paine are comparable writers and thinkers, and their conceptions of natural liberty are closest to Cugoano's understanding of the relationship between natural liberty, natural rights, and the evil of racial slavery. However, there was a Rubicon that neither Paine nor Diderot seemed to be able to cross—the granting of *full human status* to Africans. In the end, many radical Enlightenment thinkers foundered on this point. The critical issue was that underneath the surface of modern political thought of this period lay a definition of the human that excluded African slaves.

Outside of these currents was another stream—the black abolitionist one. Cugoano belonged to this stream, and in many ways was for a short time one of its most radical exponents. From this frame we can now shift the focus to the study of Cugoano's narrative.

Cugoano's work may be treated as a treatise or an essay on racial slavery that speaks in the language of natural rights and natural liberty. Second, Cugoano's notion of justice and human equality, his adaptation of Christianity, his condemnation of colonialism and support for the rights of rebellion of the colonized; his call for a universal community based on common humanity, and his advocacy for the abolition of the African slave trade and racial slavery make him a radical political thinker of early modernity. His writing therefore not only should be compared with that of the major white abolitionists of the period—Thomas Clarkson, Granville Sharp, and James Ramsey—but also placed alongside the other radical natural rights thinkers of the period.

The Political Discourse of Cugoano

Quobna Ottobah Cugoano's *Thoughts and Sentiments on the Evil of Slavery* was published in two versions, the first in 1787,[33] the year that the British Anti-Slavery Association was formally constituted, and the second in 1791. In 1788 a French version of the text appeared in Paris. The 1787 and 1791 texts were published for two different audiences. The first was "humbly submitted to the inhabitants of Great Britain," and the second, to the "Sons of Africa." Commentators on Cugoano—Paul Edwards (1969), Vincent Carretta (1999), Henry Louis Gates, Jr. (1998)—all locate his writings as major pieces of black Atlantic writing. Gates writes that "Cugoano leans heavily towards the side of polemic" and that the text is "constructed as a response to the eighteenth century's major treatises on African enslavement."[34] Carretta notes that Cugoano "raised the most overt and extended challenge to slavery ever made by a person of African descent."[35] In an interesting essay, "The Master's Tools: Abolitionist Arguments of Equiano and Cugoano," June Ward argues that Cugoano's work should also be studied as an abolitionist text and that the categories of his political discourse were ones which developed "wholly new formulations of the anti-slavery argument."[36]

I want to take a different track—Cugoano's *Thoughts and Sentiments* was not only an important abolitionist text but also a carefully crafted piece of political discourse written by a political thinker who was preoccupied with the nature of natural liberty and natural rights as "common rights."[37] This preoccupation forms the political ground for his arguments against slavery. As an explicit political essay, Cugoano's text does not follow the typical structural conventions of the slave narrative with detailed recapitulations of the cruelties of slavery and the slave trade. Instead, it goes in the opposite direction: Cugoano is explicit about what he is *not* writing.

Early in the text Cugoano makes the point that he is refuting the system of slavery at the level of *logic, reason,* and *religion.* He writes:

> What I intend to advance against that evil and criminal and wicked traffic of enslaving men, are only some Thoughts and Sentiments which occur to me, as being obvious from the Scriptures of Divine Truth, or such arguments as are chiefly deduced from thence, with other such observations as I have been able to collect. Some of these observations may lead into a larger field of consideration, than that of the African slave trade.[38]

Three things are immediately clear. First, that one conceptual resource of his discourse will be Christian notions; second, that he will use empirical observations about society to make his arguments; and third, that his field of criticism will be all forms of what he considers evil, as long as it connected in some way to the slave trade. By making the third move, Cugoano centers the Atlantic slave trade as a focal point of eighteenth century European civilization. Both this fact and his condemnation of colonialism immediately take him outside the boundaries of the political ideas and practices of the English abolitionist movement and place him on a track different from that of the radical natural rights thinkers. The title and some ideas of Cugoano's text draw from two earlier abolitionists' texts: Thomas Clarkson's *An Essay on the Slavery and Commerce of the Human Species, Particularly the African* (1786) and James Ramsey's *An Essay on the Treatment and Conversion of the Slaves in the British Sugar Colonies* (1784). What is of interest is that while other slave writings called themselves narratives, memoirs, or the life and confession of, Cugoano's essay does not do this. It therefore announces early on that it is a different text. Sidestepping the typical slave narrative structures, Cugoano pays very little attention to his own condition. He does, however, make an obligatory gesture toward the slave narrative biographical structure and writes brief passages on how he became a slave. But, these passages are quickly dispensed with when he states:

> But it would be needless to give a description of all the horrible scenes which we saw, and the base treatment which we met with in its dreadful captive situation, as the similar cases of thousands which suffer by this infernal traffic. Let it suffice to say, that I was thus lost to my dear indulgent parents and relations, and they to me. All my help was cries and tears, and those could not avail … brought from a state of innocence and freedom, and, in a barbarous and cruel manner, conveyed to state of horror and slavery. This abandoned situation may be easier conceived than described.[39]

Is it not clear that what Cugoano is concerned with is a *conception* of what slavery meant, not a simply description of its brutalities? This is important because, as David Brion Davis points out in his magisterial studies of mainly white antislavery opinions and movements, there existed a current of antislavery thought that was generated by what he calls the "man of feeling."[40] Davis argues that this current began to show itself in England when, contrary to Thomas Hobbes, ideas began to be asserted that "men were not discrete particles of self-interest, requiring for harmonious union, a coercive external will."[41]

I wish to suggest that this sentiment, combined with the notion that there were depravities attendant to the slave trade, played a huge role in the English abolitionist movement and was one of the reasons why the slave narratives often pressed home the brutalities of the slave trade and slavery. Cugoano departed from this view and sought to take the grounds of reason and religion. After describing how he gained his freedom and literacy, Cugoano decides that any improvement in his condition should be used in the struggle against slavery. He writes: "Since, I have endeavored to improve my mind in reading, and have sought to get all the intelligence I could, in my situation of life, towards the state of my brethren and countrymen in complexion, and of the miserable situation of those who are barbarously sold into captivity, and unlawfully held in slavery."[42]

What are the main elements of Cugoano's political ideas that emerge from this text, and how are they similar to and different from the ideas and political language of late eighteenth-century radical political discourses on natural rights and natural liberty?

Natural Liberty as Political Horizon

I will proceed at two levels here. First, I will list what I consider to be the major tenets of Cugoano's political thought, then choose three for elaboration. The major political ideas of Cugoano can be distilled into the following themes and propositions:

1. Opposition to African slavery
2. A theory of history that conflates Enlightenment concerns surrounding geography and climate empiricism with a Christian notion of monogenesis
3. An overarching framework of natural liberty that is located in the emergence of civil society and not in a state of nature
4. That natural liberty is enriched rather than diminished by the growth of civil society
5. That natural liberty and monogenesis mean that all "men" (heathens, pagans, Christians) have property, civil, and political rights.
6. That racial slavery is evil and contrary to divine law, natural human law, and "common humanity"
7. That a consequence of racial slavery is restitutions to Africans who had suffered because of the trade
8. That colonialism and colonial conquest are contrary to civilization (civil society), natural law, and divine law
9. That society should be constructed as a common harmonious community which looks after its poor
10. A definition of natural liberty as self-ownership, and a critical attitude to the British crown and its involvement in the slave trade.
    This chapter will focus on Cugoano's antislavery ideas, his conceptions of evil, and his views on the relationship between natural liberty and natural rights.

Cugoano regards slavery as an activity that is rooted in stealing, kidnapping, and the selling of human beings, and as such is contrary to what he calls the "common rights of nature."[43] Declaring himself a liberal,[44] he announces that the enslavement of Africans is against the "common rights of nature," evil, and thus contrary to notions of justice, reason, and humanity. Here Cugoano is using the political language of radical eighteenth-century political thinkers. In his essay on slavery, Paine had declared:

> Our traders in MEN (*an unnatural commodity*) must know the wickedness of that SLAVE-TRADE ... . Such men may as well join with a band of robbers, buy their ill-got goods ... but none can lawfully buy without evidence that they are not concurring with menstealers ... so the slave who is the proper owner of his freedom, has a right to reclaim it, however often sold.[45]

The general conception of slavery posited by the radical natural rights thinkers was that slavery was the robbery of natural liberty. Cugoano puts the position plainly when he writes: "But the robbers of men, the kidnappers, ensnarers and slave-holders, who take away the common rights ... are ... pitiful and detestable wretches; for the ensnaring of others and taking away their liberty by slavery and oppression, is the worst kind of robbery."[46]

Cugoano's foundational assumption was that there existed a state of natural freedom which each person had. Slavery therefore was not just about brutality or inhumane conditions, but at root was the taking away of the freedom made possible by natural liberty. That robbery of natural liberty was therefore slavery's worst element. This was a view of natural liberty very different from that promulgated by the mainstream natural rights thinkers of the period. Cugoano sees natural rights as "common rights," and applies these rights to African slaves. In doing this he universalizes natural rights in ways others did not. The notion of "common rights" was a popular one in radical natural rights theory at the time. For example, in Paine's hands the notion was meant to convey *"the unity of man;* by which I mean, that men are all of *one degree,* and consequently that all men are born equal and with equal natural right."[47] Cugoano deploys the notion in a similar manner, but he uses slavery as his benchmark to characterize whether or not a country is really free and Christian.

Slavery as Evil

We now turn to Cugoano's characterization of slavery as evil. Cugoano argues that slavery is evil because it is contradictory to three elements: justice, humanity in a collective sense, and reason—that most celebrated dimension of the European Enlightenment. This is different from the descriptions of slavery as evil by both the radical natural right thinkers of the period and the white abolitionists. Thomas Paine calls slavery evil and a crime because it goes against natural rights. Many abolitionists felt that it was against divine law, and therefore a sin and evil. However, Cugoano links all these, and adds reason:

> By taking away the natural liberties of men, and compelling them to any involuntary slavery or compulsory service, is an injury and robbery contrary to all law, civilization, reason, justice, equity, and humanity: therefore when men break through the laws of God, and the rules of civilization among men, and go forth and steal, to rob, to plunder, to oppress and to enslave and to destroy their fellow creatures. ...[48]

For Cugoano the heart of this form of evil is that human beings are reduced from their human status. He writes that the "slaves, like animals, are bought and sold, and dealt with as their capricious owners may think fit."[49] Thinking about the meaning of evil has had a long history ranging from metaphysical and theological interpretations, to Manichaeanism (where good and evil are seen as binary opposites), to the psychology of evil, to Hannah Arendt's efforts to understand evil as banality.[50] In Arendt's thought there is a distinction between the "radical evil" of mid-twentieth-century totalitarianism and the "banality of evil" of Adolf Eichmann. In the latter, Arendt attempts to understand the quotidian nature of Eichmann's actions—what she calls its "normality." In describing "radical evil," Arendt wants to point to one way in which we might understand evil. She makes the point in a letter to Karl Jaspers:

Evil has proved to be more radical than expected. In objective terms, modern crimes are not provided for in the Ten Commandments. Or: the Western Tradition is suffering from the preconception that the most evil things human beings can do arise from the vice of selfishness. ... What radical evil really is I don't know but it seems to me it somehow has to do with the following phenomenon: making human beings as human beings superfluous.[51]

"Making human beings as human beings superfluous"—is this not what racial slavery did? Arendt also makes the point that one of the steps of domination which opens the pathways to evil is the process that kills "the juridical person in man."[52] In another letter to Jaspers, she argues that one dimension of evil "is the organized attempt ... to eradicate the concept of the human being."[53] In this regard evil is not simply about excessive selfishness or human wickedness, although both these traits can be involved. If, as Orlando Patterson has successfully argued, slavery was a system of "social death" in which human beings are a "subcategory of human proprietary objects," then this system that continued for hundred of years and marked early modernity was not only an inhumane system but an evil one as well.[54] It was particularly so because one context of the emergence of racial slavery was the great flowering of debates and revolutionary action that placed the "rights of man" on the political and social agendas, what Cugoano referred to as "civil society." This perspective suggests that Cugoano was very prescient when he argued that one evil of slavery was its turning of Africans into a subhuman category species. His deployment of the conception of evil therefore opens up vistas for moral philosophy to examine racial slavery and the slave trade as crimes against humanity.

A point that may startle the contemporary reader is how Cugoano argues about the nature of reason. For Cugoano, reason was the developed consciousness of the human being, and as such was contrary to racial slavery. Other writers, such as Paine, Diderot, and Montesquieu, would suggest that slavery was against natural liberty, but *reason*—none would venture there. For Cugoano, reason demanded a "common humanity" that could not tolerate slavery. The final point to make here is that by positing that the core of African slavery was the kidnapping and stealing of human flesh, Cugoano develops a conception of slavery different from that of other writers of the period except Thomas Paine and the founder of Methodism, John Wesley.

In developing his analysis of the nature of slavery, Cugoano distinguishes racial slavery from other forms of slavery and servitude in world history, and notes that African slavery and slave trade required robbery of natural rights in a context where society had evolved to a stage he calls "civilization." Cugoano posits a history of servitude with a narration that argues about the necessity of historical forms of servitude. Using biblical sources, he points out that although servitude existed under Mosaic law, it was in a state of equity and justice because such servitude was entered into by "a covenant with another man as a bond-servant."[55] His conceptions of the history of slavery and forms of servitude rely on the then accepted history that ancient slavery was the result of debt or war.

However, Cugoano makes three distinctions in drawing comparisons between ancient and racial slavery. First, he notes the conditions of racial slavery with specific reference to the West

Indian colonies. Second, he remarks on its racial element. Third, Cugoano argues that there is no evidence to suggest that the foundation of African slavery resided in the fact the African slaves were already prisoners of war. This was an important distinction at the time, because one of the major pro-slavery arguments was that Africans were already slaves or prisoners of war. The argument attempted to absolve Europeans' conduct of the Atlantic slave trade and plantation slavery from any culpability. The heart of the argument was that Africans were an inferior species already in slavery and were heathens; thus it was legitimate for Europeans to bring them to civilization and Christianity, even if it was done through the Atlantic slave trade. Cugoano rejects this and calls these arguments specious: "If the argument were true, it could afford no just and warrantable matter for any society of men to hold slaves. But the argument is false; there can be no ignorance, dispersion, or unsociableness so found among them, which can be made better by bringing them away to a state of degree equal to that of a cow or a horse."[56]

As for African slavery, Cugoano asserts that "The continent of Africa is of a vast extent, and the numerous inhabitants are divided into several kingdoms and principalities, which are governed by their kings and princes, and those are absolutely maintained by their free subjects. Very few nations make slaves of any of those under government; but such as are taken prisoners of war ... until they can be exchanged and dispose of them otherwise."[57] This process, Cugoano claims, creates a group of "slave-procurers" who are, he says, "a species of African villains, which are greatly corrupted, and even vitiated by their intercourse with the Europeans."[58] As an African who had been kidnapped by an African slave procurer, Cugoano does not shy away from condemning Africans who were European allies in the Atlantic slave trade. He wants to make the point, however, that there was no widespread slavery in Africa, and that where slavery existed, it was not based upon race. The majority of the slaves brought to the New World, Cugoano argues, were "born as free, and are brought up with as great a predilection for their own country, freedom and liberty, as the sons and daughters of fair Britain."[59] All these arguments laid the foundation for Cugoano to stake the profound claim that racial slavery was the robbery of human beings and resulted in the reduction of the status of the African human.

With regard to the racial element of slavery, Cugoano sets out in the text a series of arguments which demonstrates that Africans were not inferior to Europeans, and refutes the arguments about supposed African inferiority as a basis for slavery. He notes that ". . . we find that the difference of color among men is only incidental, and equally natural to all, and agreeable to the place of their habitation; and if nothing else be different or contrary among them, but that of features and complexion, in that they are all equally alike."[60] Engaging the common argument that the color black was a result of sin, Cugoano makes the following point:

> The external blackness of the Ethiopians, is as innocent and natural, as the spots in the leopards; and that the differences of colour and complexion, which it hath pleased God to appoint among men, are no more unbecoming unto either of them, than the different shades of the rainbow. ... It does not alter the nature and quality of a man, whether he wears a black or a white coat, whether he puts it on or strips it off, he is still the same man.[61]

Cugoano therefore was firmly within the camp which believed that the origin of the human was a monogenetic creation by God and that variety did not mean hierarchical differences which could then be transformed into justifications for racial slavery.

Thoughts and Sentiments moves seamlessly from the themes of racial slavery to natural liberty and colonialism. Cugoano notes that both colonialism and slavery were against divine law, and therefore those who participated in such ventures were not only un-Christian but also unhuman. *Thoughts and Sentiments* details a complex set of religious and historical refutations of the claims of those who favored slavery or the supposed inferiority of the African at the time. These included David Hume, Gordon Turnbull, James Tobin, and the infamous Edward Long. As could be expected, Cugoano is preoccupied with the notion of supposed African inferiority, and returns to it in different ways. In the text he flays the proponents of the then popular religious/historical arguments that the reason for African slavery could be found in the curse of Ham or the climatic conditions under which blacks lived.

The need for both secular and sacred refutations of racial arguments led Cugoano to a conception of history. He developed this conception by drawing from a providential cast of history, popular then in the plebeian radicalism of the times, as well as from eighteenth-century thinkers who framed the study of history and historical analysis in secular terms. Cugoano's conception of history mixed his radical Methodism and elements of secularism to form an interesting hybrid. The God of Cugoano was an interventionist one who watched over the evolution of civil society and civilization. However, his interventions were through humans (the prophets). Cugoano's historical analysis attempted to synthesize three things: biblical exegesis, an interpretation of divine law, and the affirmation of the secular in the growth of civilization. His assertion about the lawlike requirements for human equality amply demonstrates this point:

> ... there is but *one law and one manner* prescribed universally for all mankind, *for you and for the stranger that sojourneth with you,* and wherever they may be scattered throughout the face of the whole earth, the differences of superiority and inferiority which are found to be subsisting amongst them is in no way incompatible with the universal law of love, honor, righteousness, and equity.[62]

Here Cugoano is obviously referring to inequities in social status, not in what one might call foundational equality, and it is interesting that alongside what one would consider biblical injunctions, he places equity.

Historical analysis was an important element in Cugoano's writings, because the construction of racial oppression required a theory of human history and origins that justified the so-called inferiority of the African. Overturning racial conceptions of human history required an alternative historical discourse that could support alternative ideas of "natural liberty" and "common humanity."

Radicalized Liberty

I now wish to focus on Cugoano's conception of "natural liberty" and demonstrate how it was both different from and similar to conceptions of other political thinkers of the period.

Cugoano establishes in *Thoughts and Sentiments* that in human history there were different forms of human servitude, all of which violated natural liberty. However, he concedes that these different forms may have been necessary, given the different stages of the evolution of human society. Employing an evolutionary notion of history, very typical of Enlightenment historical discourse, Cugoano makes the point that the emergence of "civil society" negated all forms of servitude. This was a distinctive position. Cugoano's articulation of natural liberty is one in which natural liberty is enriched by the growth of a civil society (civilization). This conception of natural liberty is different from the way many political thinkers of the period perceived the relationship between civil society, the state of nature, and natural rights. The clearest example is of course that of Rousseau, who proclaimed, "Man is born free; and everywhere he is in chains." In *The Rights of Man,* Paine considered this problem in natural rights theory and argued that there was a distinction between natural rights and civil rights. Natural rights, Paine argued, are "those which appertain to man in the right of his existence … [while] civil rights are those which appertain to man in the right of his being a member of society."[63] Paine further argued that in civil society, humans give up some of those natural rights: "The natural rights which are not retained, are all those in which, though the right is perfect in the individual, the power to execute them is defective."[64]

The problem that then faced many natural rights thinkers of the late eighteenth century was how to construct a civil and political society which returned elements of natural liberty and natural rights that had been lost when civil society emerged. For Cugoano, on the other hand, *civil society developed natural rights and liberty* in two ways. In the first, Cugoano, unlike other radical natural rights thinkers of the period, claims that the laws of civilization are derived from divine laws, and therefore they enhance rather than diminish man's natural rights. In the second, he makes the point that civilization, and therefore civil society, had now removed any necessity for forms of slavery and servitude. This perspective, he argues, was confirmed by the emergence of Christianity: "In the establishment of Christianity there is nothing remaining in the law for a rule of practice to men, but the ever abiding obligations, and ever binding injunctions of moral rectitude, justice, equity and righteousness."[65] However, as regards civilization there is a contradiction in Cugoano's thought, because a few pages later he argues that "When [men] break … the laws of God, and the rules of civilization among men, and go forth to steal and rob, to plunder, to oppress and to enslave, and to destroy their fellow-creatures, the laws of God and man require that they should be suppressed, and deprived of their liberty, and perhaps their lives."[66]

Perhaps one answer to this apparent contradiction is that Cugoano was very aware of his audience, and felt that appeals to biblical injunctions did not necessarily carry enough weight to convince some of the slaveholders and their allies. In this regard he observes, "I am aware that some of these arguments will weigh nothing against such men as do not believe the scriptures themselves nor care to understand."[67] Another way to think about this apparent contradiction is to suggest that Cugoano, drawing on the two intellectual sources, secular and religious, was not able to satisfactorily resolve them. This is not unusual in the history of political thought, and certainly Paine in this period deployed notions of sacred history in some of his writings. However, the weight of Paine's gaze was on issues of political rule, whereas for Cugoano it was on racial slavery and colonialism.

Natural liberty, for Cugoano, was the foundation of human society. In such a condition human beings were distinct from property, and should be treated accordingly. They could neither be bought nor be sold, and any system based upon robbing human beings of this natural liberty was evil. Cugoano, while speaking the language of natural rights, extends those rights to the African slave. As a consequence, the basis of his political thought shifts from the traditional elements that then made up natural rights as political discourse. Natural liberty became the basis of all natural rights, including property rights. In Cugoano's political thought, nations, land, or properties could not be conquered with any justification. He observes: "The Spaniards began their settlements in the West Indies and America, by depredations of rapine, injustice, treachery and murder; and they have continued in the barbarous practice of devastation … ever since … and the maxims in planting colonies have been adopted in some measure in every other nation in Europe."[68] The remarkableness of this position should be obvious when we think of Locke's theory of property, which facilitated colonial conquest of lands in North America, and the general sentiment even of radical thinkers that although colonialism involved violence and domination, it brought "civilization."[69]

Cugoano's position is even more remarkable because he proudly embraced the Christian faith. However, for him Christianity was neither a marker of civilization nor an exclusive doctrine of humanness. For Cugoano the lands of the "pagans" and "heathens" could not be conquered even for missionary purposes. This was in direct opposition to the then official Catholic Church position instituted after the 1550 debate between Juan Ginas de Sepúlveda and Bartolomé de Las Cases. Colonialism for Cugoano was a "dreadfully perfidious method of forming settlements, and acquiring riches and territory."[70]

Cugoano's doctrines of natural rights and liberty were the foundations for his radical anticolonialism. He was also concerned about the poor, and argues that although they are free in a natural sense, poverty means the existence of problems of equity and justice.[71] He asked whether a London poor person would give up his condition of poverty to be a well-fed slave,[72] refuting the argument of James Tobin that the African slaves in the Caribbean were materially better off than the English poor.

The defining feature of Cugoano's conception of natural liberty is *self-ownership*, a radicalized version of natural liberty. The conception of self-ownership and its relationship to natural liberty were central to Diderot's and Paine's political ideas. Diderot writes in *History of the Indies*, "Natural liberty is the right which nature has given every man to dispose of himself as he wishes."[73] However, in his elaboration, Diderot makes a distinction between natural, civil, and political liberty. Cugoano, on the other hand, collapses all forms of liberty into "natural and common liberty." There is no separation in Cugoano's thought between different forms of liberty. For him, without political liberty there is no natural liberty, and certainly civil liberty is a function of the scope of natural liberty as well as the application of divine law. He consistently reinforces the point that slavery and servitude in any form are not compatible with civilized human society. While both Diderot and Cugoano concur that natural liberty was man's most marked feature second only to reason, Cugoano, while deploying the language of natural liberty, gave it a new set of meanings that focused on the nature of racial slavery during the late eighteenth century as a system of human domination.

This meaning of natural liberty later found resonance in the black plebeian radicalism of Robert Wedderburn.

As was stated before, in Western political thought, natural liberty emerges alongside the issues of popular sovereignty and the questions of political obligation. When John Locke inveighed against Robert Filmer, he asserted a counterposition to the conservative view that natural liberty was license.[74] However, Locke's description of natural liberty slid into civil liberty and instituted a historic practice of natural liberty as civil liberty. This practice became a formidable part of the political horizon in Enlightenment political thinking. It then worked to foreclose all other possible political languages about the meaning of natural liberty. Cugoano opens this closure by shifting the focus of natural liberty from issues of civil liberty, and sovereignty to racial slavery: "But the robbers of men, the kidnappers, ensnarers and slave-holders, who take away the common rights and privileges of others to support and enrich themselves ... for the ensnaring of others, and taking away their liberty by slavery and oppression, is the worst kind of robbery."[75] Natural liberty in this sense is for Cugoano not sovereignty over political self-determination but the absence of forms of human domination. He describes West Indian slave laws thus: "They do not take away a man's property like other robbers; but they take a *man himself* and subject him to their service and bondage, which is a greater robbery and a greater crime, than taking away property from men."[76]

This shift created by Cugoano's gaze places his perspective of natural liberty outside of the state of nature. The radical thinker with whom we have compared Cugoano, Thomas Paine, had a notion of a compact that was created and that distinguished the different stages of humanity's political evolution. Cugoano seems to operate with no such historical fiction, and his notion of civil society is one that emerged when sacred history and man's evolution began a unified development with the widespread emergence of Christianity. However Cugoano grants civil society to non-Christians and in Africa sees civil society as a form of government. He is not concerned with the practices of ruling, but rather with seeking to answer the question of the nature of racial slavery.

If for many of the political thinkers racial slavery was a side issue, subordinated to the issues of ruling and political obedience, for the slave it was the major issue. The European political thinkers who turned their attention to the role of colonialism and slavery in the building of empire, particularly after the American Revolution, did so, in the words of Edmund Burke, with a concern for "how to govern a Large Empire upon a plan of Liberty."[77] This liberty was a clear reference to the question of self-government and by the mid-nineteenth century it would become another marker for civilization.[78] Slavery and colonialism were not marginal to European and American life, and in the words of Daniel Defoe, "No African Trade, no Negroes, no Negroes, no Sugar; no Sugar, no Islands, no Islands no Continent, no Continent no Trade; that is to say farewell to your American Trade, your West Indian Trade."[79] Because slavery and colonialism were not marginal to the European experience of empire at the time, any questions of natural rights and natural liberty that did not take these two things into consideration would be unable to offer universal answers to the central problems of the human polity.

With his focus on modern racial slavery and colonialism, Cugoano developed a radical program for the period. It called for the total abolition of slavery and the slave trade, the ending of colonialism and colonial empires, and the dismantling of the Dutch Cape Colony (South Africa). It also advocated that the trade in human beings be replaced with agricultural trade, using some of the economic statements employed by Adam Smith in the *Wealth of Nations* (1776) to argue that free labor was cheaper than slave labor.

Conclusion

What are we to make of this extraordinary African ex-slave? First, the text on which I have based this essay clearly needs to be studied as part of modern political thought. It should be placed alongside Paine's *Rights of Man* and Wollstonecraft's *A Vindication of the Rights of Women* as representative of a different current of radical natural rights thinking in the late eighteenth century. In the history of political theory, natural rights discourse has been both connected to natural law (Locke) and disconnected from it (Thomas Hobbes). However, until Jeremy Bentham in the nineteenth century launched his attack upon natural rights as "nonsense upon stilts," the frame of natural rights and natural liberty was *the* frame of Western political thought. Cugoano's political discourse suggests the existence of a different stream that articulates notions about natural liberty and natural rights that do not fold into other conceptions of rights. For Cugoano, the fundamental natural right was the right of the individual to be free and equal, not in relationship to government but in relationship to other human beings.

This, I want to suggest was not only a radicalized version of natural rights but also, at the time, a heretic one. Keith A. Sandiford's comment in a fine critical essay on Cugoano states, "From the axiom that slavery was against sensibility, Cugoano moved ... to enunciate the axiom that slavery was against humanity."[80] This is an accurate interpretation, as any reading of some of the major abolitionist writings of the period will reveal. Then there is Cugoano's positive self-affirmation of blackness in an anti-black racist world.[81] Cugoano's dethronement of blackness as curse and badge of inferiority was astonishing for its time, given the normative weight of hegemonic whiteness naturalized as the universal self. Again this would separate him from many of the white abolitionists who argued against slavery but felt that Africans were uncivilized and could benefit from freedom only if they were subjected to a process of tutelage by civilized persons. When we add these things together, we cannot escape the conclusion that there existed in Cugoano's slave narrative a political counternarrative that moved in a different direction than the political horizons of the Enlightenment.

So we come to the final point, the subtext of this essay. What, precisely, was the discursive practice of Cugoano? An early critic of Cugoano, Henri Gregoire, opines that Cugoano's work is not "very methodical. There are repetitions, because grief is verbose. An individual deeply affected, is always afraid of not having said enough. ... We see talents without cultivation, and to which a good education would have given great progress."[82] One consequence of this is that *Thoughts and Sentiments* has been reviewed as a form of jeremiad. There is no doubt that the text does have elements of this form of denunciation and prophecy. However, I wish to suggest that *Thoughts and Sentiments* should not be confined to the limits of prophetic denunciation, but that in this instance the jeremiad typical of eighteenth-century English polemics was crafted onto a form of political writing, the treatise/essay, which emphasizes historical explanations and appeals to reason. Quobna Cugoano worked through many traditions, plucking from available intellectual resources, but his labor transformed his choices into a political language and discourse that had a meaning different from those which constituted the major traditions of political thought. The discursive practice in which he engaged forms a central part of a radical black intellectual tradition that circles around freedom. In the genealogy of this discursive practice he stands as a figure who raised the fundamental question that engaged all Enlightenment thinkers: What does it mean to be truly human? His heretical answers opened up spaces where none dared to go.

Notes

1.   Arna Bontemps, ed., *Great Slave Narratives* (Boston: Beacon Press, 1969).
2.   For a discussion of how autobiographical forms limit black writers and thinkers to experience, see Lewis Gordon, *Existentia Africana* (New York: Routledge 2000), chap. 4.
3.   "Vindicationism" is the term of St Clair Drake. He makes the point that the process of writing black history which validates the humanity of people of African descent can be called "vindicationism." See his *The Redemption of Africa and Black Religion* (Chicago: Third World Press, 1977). However, while "vindicationism" establishes humanness, it often does so on the terms of the dominant conceptions of the society. In the case of the slave narratives, because in early modernity writing was a sign of reason, many saw the written slave narratives as a sign that the slaves, too, had the capacity to be part of the human species. It is one reason why the frontispiece of many narratives proclaimed that the slave wrote the text. In this instance there was the need for double authenticity. First, the content of the text was accurate because it was written by someone who experienced slavery. This authenticity was required in the propaganda struggles against slavery because such descriptions were necessary to show how inhumane slavery was Second, by writing, the slave-author had arrived at the status where he or she could be considered human. The operation of these two processes can be called "literary vindicationism."
4.   See C. Peter Ripley, ed., *The Black Abolitionist Papers*, vols, i–iv (Chapel Hill: University of North Carolina Press, 1985–1991), for the documents of the period. A reading of these volumes will reveal the dimensions of the international nature of the black abolitionist movement of the time and its independent political import in nineteenth-century world politics. This is a story waiting to be written.
5.   Henry Louis Gates, Jr., *The Signifying Monkey* (Oxford: Oxford University Press, 1988), 128.
6.   Ibid.
7.   For a discussion of this, see Paul Ricoeur, "Heidegger and the Question of the Subject," in his *The Conflict of Interpretations* (Evanston, Ill: Northwestern University Press, 1974), 223–35.
8.   Henry Louis Gates, Jr., and William L. Andrews, *Pioneers of the Black Atlantic: Five Slave Narratives from the Enlightenment* 1772–1815. (Washington, D.C.: Civitas Counterpoint, 1998), vii.
9.   Dena Goodman, *Criticism in Action* (Ithaca, N.Y.: Cornell University Press, 1989), 4.
10.   Ibid., 3.
11.   See Christopher Hill, *The World Turned Upside Down* (London Penguin, 1991), and his *The English Bible and the Seventeenth-Century Revolution* (London: Penguin, 1994), for a discussion of this point.
12.   There is a noticeable phenomenon in late eighteenth-century and early nineteenth-century Western radicalism that is not often discussed in the standard historical accounts of radicalism. This silence is about the ways in which many radicals of the period wove religious discourse into their political thought. Thus this was not just a feature of slaves' radical political discourse. Later, on English plebeian radicalism in the nineteenth century, much of it influenced by Thomas

Paine's writings, developed a critique of bourgeois society that drew from both religious and secular sources. The most important individual here of course is Thomas Spencer. While English plebeian radicalism and black radical thought of this period drew from some of the same sources, they drew on different parts of the Bible.

13. Michel Foucault, "The Political Technology of Individuals, in *Technologies of the Self,* ed. by Luther Martin, Huck Gutman, and Patrick Hutton (Amherst: University of Massachusetts Press, 1998), 149.

14. For a discussion of the "Chain of Being" and its influence on racial thinking, see Winthrop D. Jordan, *White over Black: American Attitudes Toward the Negro. 1550–1812* (Chapel Hill: University of North Carolina Press, 1969), chap. 13.

15. Cited in P. J. Marshall and Glyndwr Williams, *The Great Map of Mankind* (Cambridge: Cambridge University Press, 1982), 1.

16. Some theories of the origins of human society located Asia as site of the origin of humankind, then argued that each race had a turn at being a dominant civilization. For example, Voltaire in his "Essay on the Manners and Spirit of Nations" makes the point of Asia being civilized and then becoming partly uncivilized. However, Africans were excluded from this paradigm, and it was concluded that Africa was never civilized. This view of the historical development of humanity continued well into the nineteenth century and can be found in the writings of Hegel, particularly his lectures on the philosophy of world history.

17. See Marshall and Williams, *Great Map of Mankind,* for a discussion of this, especially 56–57.

18. See for a discussion of the features of the system of western ancient slavery. Moses I. Finley, *Ancient Slavery and Modern Ideology,* ed. by Brent D. Shaw (Princeton, NJ: Markus Wiener Publishers, 1998).

19. John Locke, *Two Treatises of Government,* ed. by Peter Laslett (Cambridge: Cambridge University Press, 1988), 283–285. (Emphasis in the original.)

20. Isaiah Berlin, *Four Essays on Liberty* (Oxford: Oxford University Press, 1969), 121.

21. See Charles Mills, *The Racial Contract* (Ithaca, N.Y.: Cornell University Press, 1997), for an excellent discussion of how this social contract was really a racialized one that operated in the interest of whites.

22. The central figures who explicate this tradition are J. G. A. Pocock, *The Machiavellian Moment: Florentine Political Thought and the Atlantic Republican Tradition* (Princeton, N.J.: Princeton University Press, 1975), and Quentin Skinner, *Liberty Before Liberalism* (Cambridge: Cambridge University Press, 1998). For a recent attempt to develop the ideas of civic republicanism in the modern political context see, Philip Pettit, *Republicanism: A Theory of Freedom and Government* (Oxford: Oxford University Press, 1997).

23. For an early discussion of the Correspondence Clubs, see E. P. Thompson, *Making of the English Working Class* (New York: Vintage, 1966). For a first-class discussion of the plebeian radicalism of the period, see Peter Linebaugh and Marcus Rediker. *The Many Headed Hydra* (Boston: Beacon Press, 2000). Robert Wedderburn's writings are available in Ian McCalman, ed., *The Horrors of Slavery and Other Writings by Robert Wedderburn* (Kingston, Jamaica: Ian Randle Press, 1997).

24. Rogers Smith, *Civic Ideals* (New Haven, Conn.: Yale University Press, 1997), 165.

25. Cited in Robert H. Webking, *The American Revolution and the Politics of Liberty* (Baton Rouge: Louisiana State University Press, 1989), 116. (Emphasis added.)

26. For a discussion of political propaganda and anticolonial newspapers of the period that confirms this position, see Patricia Bradley, *Slavery, Propaganda and the American Revolution* (Jackson: University Press of Mississippi, 1998).

27. Thomas Paine, "African Slavery in America," in *The Thomas Paine Reader, ed.* Michael Foot and Isaac Kramnick (London: Penguin, 1987), 53.

28. Montesquieu, *The Spirit of the Laws, ed.* Anne Cohler, Basia Miller, and Harold Stone (Cambridge: Cambridge University Press, 1989).

29. Cited in Marshall and Williams, *Great Map of Mankind,* 248.

30. Ibid.

31. For a discussion of Mary Wollstonecraft's attitudes to slavery and African people, see Moira Ferguson, *Colonialism and Gender Relations: From Mary Wollstonecraft to Jamaica Kincaid* (New York: Columbia University Press, 1993).

32. Extract of review in Angelo Costanzo, ed., *The Interesting Narrative of the Life of Olaudah Equiano* (Peterborough Ontario: Broadview Press, 2001), 262.

33. This is the text I will use. The version cited throughout this essay is the one edited and introduced by Vincent Carretta, *Thoughts and Sentiments on the Evil of Slavery* (London: Penguin, 1999).

34. Gates, *Signifying Monkey*, 147.

35. *Thoughts and Sentiments*, xx.

36. June Ward, "The Master's Tools: Abolitionist Arguments of Equiano and Cugoano" in *Subjection and Bondage, ed.* Tommy Lott (New York: Rowman and Littlefield, 1998), 80.

37. *Thoughts and Sentiments*, 11.

38. Ibid.

39. Ibid., 15.

40. David Brion Davis, *The Problem of Slavery in Western Culture* (Oxford: Oxford University Press, 1966) and *The Problem of Slavery in the Age of Revolution 1770–1823* (Ithaca, N.Y.: Cornell University Press, 1975).

41. Davis, *The Problem of Slavery in Western Culture*, 355.

42. *Thoughts and Sentiments*, 17.

43. Ibid., 4.

44. I think that such a declaration was his way of saying that he was a radical.

45. Paine, "African Slavery in America," 52. (Emphasis in original.)

46. *Thoughts and Sentiments*, 11.

47. Thomas Paine, *The Rights of Man*, in *The Thomas Paine Reader*, 216. (Emphasis in original.)

48. *Thoughts and Sentiments*, 51.

49. Ibid., 20.

50. For a reader that attempts to include the major Western writings on the subject, see Amelie Oksenberg Rorty, *The Many Faces of Evil: Historical Perspectives* (New York: Routledge, 2001). For a sustained philosophical discussion on evil, see also Richard J. Bernstein, *Radical Evil: A Philosophical Interrogation* (Cambridge: Polity Press, 2002).

51. Cited in Dana R. Villa, *Politics, Philosophy, Terror: Essays on the Thought of Hannah Arendt* (Princeton, N.J.: Princeton University Press, 1999), 32.

52. Hannah Arendt, *Origins of Totalitarianism* (New York: Harcourt Brace Jovanovich, 1968), 447.

53. Lotte Kohler and Hans Saner, eds., *Hannah Arendt/Karl Jaspers: Correspondence 1926–1969* (New York: Harcourt Brace Jovanovich, 1992), 69.

54. See Orlando Patterson, *Slavery and Social Death: A Comparative Study* (Cambridge, Mass.: Harvard University Press, 1982).

55. *Thoughts and Sentiments*, 36.

56. Ibid., 23.

57. Ibid., 26.

58. Ibid.

59. Ibid., 27.

60. Ibid., 30.

61. Ibid., 41.

62. Ibid., 51.

63. *Thomas Paine Reader, 217.*

64. Ibid., 218.

65. *Thoughts and Sentiments*, 43.

66. Ibid., 51.

67. Ibid., 45.

68. Ibid., 72.
69. For a discussion of Locke, property rights, and the conquest of the New World see James Tully, *An Approach to Political Philosophy: Locke in Contexts* (Cambridge: Cambridge University Press, 1993), chaps. 2–5.
70. *Thoughts and Sentiments*, 65.
71. Cugoano worked among the free black poor in London. For a brief discussion of this and the organization, see James Walvin, *An African Life: The Life and 'Times, of Olaudah Equiano, 1745–1797* (London: Continuum, 1998), chap. 10. Walvin and others have argued that there was a small free black community, of which Cugoano was a part. This community was critical in the early stages of the abolitionist movement.
72. *Thoughts and Sentiments*, 19.
73. Denis Diderot, *Political Writings* (Cambridge: Cambridge University Press., 1992), 186.
74. Locke, *Two Treatises*.
75. *Thoughts and Sentiments*, 11.
76. Ibid., 71. (Emphasis added.)
77. Cited in Anthony Pagden, *Peoples and Empires* (New York: Modern Library. 2001), 92.
78. See John Stuart Mill, *On Liberty* (London: Penguin, 1974), for a clear enunciation of this point.
79. Cited in *Peoples and Empires*, 103.
80. Keith A. Sandiford, *Measuring the Moment: Strategies of Protest in Eighteenth Century Afro-English Writing* (London: Associated University Presses, 1988), 104. This text attempts to detail some of the intellectual influences that shaped Cugoano's thinking. However, it does not deal with the issues of the political languages of the period and sees Cugoano's work as primarily that of an abolitionist rather than of a political thinker who was primarily concerned with racial slavery and colonialism.
81. See Lewis R. Gordon, *Bad Faith and Anti-Black Racism* (Atlantic Highland, □ J Humanities Press, 1995), for a sustained elaboration of the workings of anti-black racism.
82. Henri Gregoire, *An Enquiry Concerning the Intellectual and Moral Faculties and Literature of Negroes*, trans. D.B. Warren (College Park, Md.: McGrath, 1967), 192.

Caribbean Anti-Slavery:
The Self-Liberation Ethos of Enslaved Blacks

Hilary Beckles

It is now commonly accepted by historians that in the British West Indies anti-slavery conflict was frequently of a revolutionary nature. In earlier articles, I have suggested that the many slave revolts and plots in these territories between 1638 and 1838 could be conceived of as the '200 Years' War' — one protracted struggle launched by Africans and their Afro-West Indian progeny against slave owners. Such endemic anti-slavery activity represented, furthermore, the most immediately striking characteristic of the West Indian world. Current anglophone historiography outlines in detail the empirical contours of this struggle — what amounts to an indigenous anti-slavery movement — though its philosophical and ideological aspects remain less researched.[1]

Anglophone literature on anti-slavery, however, has emphasized above other features, its trans-Atlantic dimension. This perspective has enriched significantly our general understanding of the diverse forces that succeeded ultimately in toppling the region's heterogeneous slave regimes. To some extent, this panoramic vision of the anti-slavery movement results from a more theoretical reading of slave resistance which suggests the need for closer investigation of slaves' political culture. Such an examination is necessary not only for an empirical understanding of resistance, but also for a fuller evaluation of slaves' consciousness and depth of political awareness. Such insights would make it possible for the historian to illustrate more precisely those linkages, real or imaginary, that existed between plantation-based politics and the international anti-slavery ethos.[2]

Many historians have responded to this challenge, and the theme of slave resistance or, more appropriately, the blacks' anti-slavery movement, has now become a leading growth area in Caribbean historiography. From the works of leading scholars, particularly Orlando Patterson, Michael Craton, Edward Brathwaite, Barry Gaspar, Mary Turner, Barbara Kopytoff and Monica Schuler, it is possible to demarcate some structural features in the development of Caribbean anti-slavery. Three basic stages have so far been identified. The first stage relates to early plantation construction, and corresponds approximately with the period 1500 to 1750. The second basic stage is characterised by mature plantation society and declining dependency on slave importation — 1750 to 1800. The third stage relates to the 'general crisis' in plantation slavery; it is linked with the impact of Haitian politics and serious anti-slavery discussions in the metropole — 1804 to 1838.

Within these three general phases, three types/levels of anti-slavery struggle have been described — though no systematic effort has been made to articulate them within the historical continuum. Firstly, a proliferation of acts of 'day-to-day' resistance are identified; these were generally designed not to overthrow the slave system, but to undermine its efficiency in order to hasten its eventual abandonment. Secondly, evidence is adduced of the large number of unsuccessful plots and revolts which were characterised by collective organisation with reformist and revolutionary objectives. Thirdly, there is the incidence, 'successful' rebellion, from long-term marronage to the St. Domingue revolution.[3]

Highly structured revolts, considered generally as the most advanced rebellious acts, have been given more research attention within the wide range of anti-slavery politics. Unfortunately, no attempt has been made to illustrate how, and under what conditions, non-violent day-to-day anti-slavery protest evolved into violent revolutionary designs.[4] According to Robert Dirks there are references within the literature to some seventy slave uprisings between 1649 and 1833, including large-scale insurrections that engulfed entire colonies and small-scale violence limited to single estates. Of this total, Dirks states that some thirty-two revolts did not materialise due to discovery, and some were undoubtedly the invented product of planters' paranoia. Craton's chronology of resistance between 1638 and 1837, however, lists some seventy-five aborted revolts and actual rebellions; in this computation some of these actions have been grouped together and appear as one event.[5] This record of resistance illustrates that there was hardly a generation of slaves in the English West Indies that did not confront their masters collectively with arms in pursuit of freedom. In this sense, therefore, the relations between slaves and masters in the West Indies can be shown as characterised by ongoing psychological warfare and intermittent bloody battles.

It is now a major concern of scholars interpreting this extensive record of resistance to assess the extent to which slaves' rebellious actions were informed by ideological choices in the context of maturing political consciousness. It has taken scholars many years of revising interpretations to arrive at this position in regard to slave politics, though it remains an influential argument that slaves wanted much less than what some recent historians now suggest. This interpretive inertia reflects, in part, a compulsive assumption within western historical science that the working classes rarely perceived effectively their group interest, an argument supported by what some refer to as irrationality and inhibiting conservatism in their collective responses to oppression.

Not surprisingly, recent revisionist literature produced by most Caribbean, European and American scholars, has centred upon the need to distinguish as clearly as possible the Caribbean and metropolitan anti-slavery movements, and to assess their relative potency. Technically, this is an important development because slave resistance had long been conceived of as a lower species of political behaviour, lacking in ideological cohesion, intellectual qualities and a philosophical direction. Generally considered as marginally more advanced than basic primitive responses to a crude and oppressive material and social world, it was not seen to be possessing any thing resembling theoretical significance. These perceptions have survived in spite of C.L.R. James' 1938 classic work, *The Black Jacobins*, which sought, perhaps with too much theoretical enthusiasm, to link rebel slaves in colonial St. Domingue with the philosophically progressive Jacobin equalitarianism of France that ultimately weakened the ideological hegemony of slave holders in that colony. The 'Black Jacobins' seized the colonial state and established an independent republic in 1804, — an achievement that cannot be divorced, according to James, from its European theoretic roots.[6]

At first glance the immediate goals of the Caribbean and European anti-slavery movements seem ideologically polarised and at variance. The metropolitan movement was essentially philosophical and respectably radical in character. It relied initially upon a strong moral perspective, though with an increasing reliance upon economic arguments in latter years. The Caribbean movement, on the other hand, spearheaded by enslaved blacks, with some Amerindian and free coloured support, was also generally non-violent, but occasionally erupted into revolutionary warfare. The metropolitan movement depended upon popular mobilisation and parliamentary lobbying in a legislative approach to emancipation. The slaves' approach, it may be implied, was more complex; they wanted freedom by all means necessary or possible, and engaged in activities which ranged from self-purchase to violent armed struggle for territory and political sovereignty.

There is some evidence, fragmented though it is, to suggest that more informed slaves saw their anti-slavery actions as articulated to those of metropolitan lobbyists, though they were not prepared to lose the initiative in terms of striking for freedom when circumstances, local or foreign, dictated autonomous actions. Some slaves, whether in revolutionary St. Domingue or rebellious Barbados and Jamaica in 1816 and 1831 respectively, had knowledge, considered crude and inaccurate by most historians, of developments in metropolitan anti-slavery ideas and strategies. This information base, it has been argued, assisted in shaping their costly movement for liberation (measured in human life) and thus illustrating, even if in a tamed manner, the internationalism of their political consciousness.[7]

Evaluating the relative potency of the two segments of the transatlantic anti-slavery movement cannot be an easy task for the historian. Contemporaneous writers on the English Caribbean did not attempt such analyses. Indeed, they generally saw the slaves' movement, most of the time, as having little more than nuisance value, and on those infrequent occasions when they recognised within it revolutionary proportions their analyses degenerated into negrophobic descriptions and commentaries.[8] Such outpourings were based, in varying degrees, upon the racist notion of angry and savage blacks in a vengeful and mindless lust for blood and white women.[9]

The most sophisticated pro-slavery writer, Jamaica's Edward Long, does not best illustrate this particular point, but he does demonstrate in the clearest manner slaveowners' reluctant recognition of slaves' maturing anti-slavery consciousness. Furthermore, he understood fully what it meant for the Caribbean world in particular and the politics of abolitionism in general.

Long was aware of the contradiction inherent in white colonists' claims for 'liberty' within the late eighteenth century Whig ideological framework, while at the same time denying black colonist any legitimate right to their own liberty. He admitted, moreover, that the 'spirit of liberty' was also a deep-rooted feature of the slave community, though for him this consciousness had its origins in the white community — the blacks being ideological victims of its 'contagious fever'.[10] The resolution of this contradiction within Long's thought was found in a head-long plunge into racial arguments, the structure of which had long been a feature of colonial elite social consciousness. He argued, for example, that the condition of colonial slavery for blacks was in itself an advancement in their claim to liberty. That is, blacks in general enjoyed more social and material rights on the West Indian plantations than they did in West Africa where their lot was generally one of abject poverty and submission to monarchical tyranny. Gordon Lewis suggests that social relations within eighteenth century planter ideology were based on the tenet that the slave required patronage in return for his labour. Long articulates this point by stating that the slave, once settled in his new home, enters into a limited freedom supervised by the master who is his 'friend and father'. This authority, Long adds,

> is like that of an ancient patriarch: conciliating affection by the mildness of its exertion, claiming respect by the justice and propriety of its decisions and discipline, it attracts the love of the honest and good; while it awes the worthless into reformation.[11]

This unrealistic view of stability in master-slave relations fell apart precisely at the stage where slaves rejected those reforms which meant the abandonment of their claim to liberty. The extensive record of rebellion and protest provides the empirical and theoretical evidence to support their stance on this question. It points, furthermore, to a refusal within the slave community to accept as legitimate any kind of slave-relation whatsoever, and the search for avenues to freedom was persistent.

Ideally, it could be said that rebel slaves and metropolitan anti-slavery lobbyists shared the same goals, and hence their respective movements ought to be considered as different levels of a general process. The attractiveness of this position is partly betrayed by its simplicity, and is easily abandoned when tested under the weight of empirical evidence. It may very well be suggested that slaves wanted more then legal freedom on many occasions: that they also wanted political power and economic autonomy. These were certainly objectives that most 'humanitarians' preferred blacks not to have. The records of slave rebellion also show, is it true, that in some instances slaves might well have wanted only the right to reasonable wages and conditions of work under their old masters. The 1831 Sam Sharpe rebellion of Jamaica has recently been so interpreted.[12] But rebellions in St. Domingue, 1791–1804, and Barbados in 1816 also suggest that blacks understood that meaningful freedom could be guaranteed only by means of seizing the organs of law and government and by imposing a revolutionary constitutionalism thereafter in order to enforce the reality of freedom.

Wilberforce, for instance, had no time for slaves' revolutionary approach to emancipation in the English colonies, and considered such actions, in spite of his friendship with King Henry of Haiti, as detrimental to the survival of English authority in America — not only in terms of economic and political leverage, but also in terms of the hegemony of western civilisation. The scenario of black revolution and the formation of Afro-Caribbean republics or monarchies, in addition to the subsequent freezing of 'things European', did not excite English anti-slavery lobbyists.[13] From this point of view, then, it may be suggested that the two segments of the transatlantic anti-slavery movement were heading in different directions most of the time. It was not simply a matter of the divergence of strategies and radically different levels of procedure, but also a matter of the kind of worlds that were to be created in the aftermath.

A simple statistical analysis might show that given some 400,000 blacks who gained revolutionary freedom in St. Domingue, together with the large numbers who freed themselves by means of marronage and otherwise, no concrete basis exists for the claim that European legislative emancipation should be given an obvious right to first consideration. Though the numbers analysis is not necessarily the best way to proceed on this question, it would perhaps impose some demographic constraints upon the ideological charge involved in the argument that, by and large, freedom was brought to the blacks, and that self-attained freedom was of marginal significance. In addition, it would illustrate more clearly the impressive record of achievement of slave communities as sponsors of the libertarian ideology.

Such an analysis is particularly relevant at this stage partly because one of the most striking features of the recent historiography has been the establishment of a dichotomous core/periphery structure within the trans-atlantic anti-slavery movement. Eric Williams was perhaps first to pose this dichotomous paradigm when he argued that, while metropolitan anti-slavery lobbyists intensified their campaign, during the early nineteenth century, the slaves had done likewise. By 1833, he said, 'the alternatives were clear', 'emancipation from above or emancipation from below, but Emancipation'.[14] Not surprisingly, only radical scholars seem perturbed by the assignment of the peripheral status to the slaves' movement and the core status to the metropolitan lobbyists. This has been the case in spite of a revisionist attempt to give greater value within the emancipation process to the autonomous anti-slavery actions of blacks. That is, whereas the traditional interpretations crudely negated the slaves' role, the modernist of subordination, the slaves' struggle within international abolitionism. The hands-on political movement of slaves, then, is yet to free itself conceptually of the hegemonic constraints imposed by a revised anti-slavery interpretation. Symbolically, the images of Wilberforce, Schoelcher, *et al.* still stalk the literature, transcending those of slave leaders such as Bussa, Kofi and Sam Sharpe.

It is not clear, however, why the slaves' struggle for freedom should be considered secondary or peripheral to the activities of European emancipationists. No coherent arguments have been given for this outside of the general statement that ultimately it was imperial law rather than colonial war which terminated the 'not very peculiar' institution of slavery. Michael Craton, for example, after evaluating the record of slave resistance in the English colonies, though in a rather technical and "eventist" manner, considered it necessary to add, by way of not distancing himself from what he perceived to be substantial empirical evidence, that white abolitionists won the day though black abolitionists helped in no small way. He has also treated us to other variations on this theme. There is the view, for example, that slaves created in part the ideological context for parliamentary legislation by rendering their societies irretrievably unstable. In this way they assisted in forcing the Imperial legislature into action in order to protect colonial life (white) and property (black and non-human). In addition, there is the argument that slave rebels had illustrated by 1832 that the colonial elite could rule in the long term only by means of extreme repression, and that Parliament was not prepared to pay the economic nor political cost implied, and acted to defuse an increasingly explosive situation.[15]

Whatever the perspectives, the perception that rebel slaves were featured in abolitionist debates by the imperial governments cannot be ignored. If these arguments have any weight then it becomes less clear what precisely was the overwhelming and more critical role of the 'humanitarians'. Unfortunately, analyses of these and related matters are hampered by insufficient data on specific ways in which the imperial government perceived the political action of slaves in relation to that of its own anti-slavery members.

The assignment of a peripheral status within anti-slavery thought to slaves is also to be found in the 'intellectual' work of David Brion Davis and more so in Roger Anstey's several accounts of British abolitionism. Following Davis, it could be argued that while the conceptual separation of Caribbean and European processes are perhaps inevitable, owing to different historiographic and philosophical traditions, the projection of an hierarchical order in the emergence of democratic ideology, and in the partial and full attainment of freedom, constitutes a major problem of anti-slavery in western culture.[16]

Two recent works on anti-slavery, the first by a longstanding anti-Marxist American scholar of British abolitionism, and the other by an English Marxist political historian, best illustrate this historiographical condition. First, in Seymour Drescher's 1986 work, *Capitalism and Anti-Slavery*, which represents a mild revision of Anstey's thesis, there are no references to Caribbean anti-slavery activities in the opening chapter entitled the 'Foundations of anti-slavery', Drescher, however, offered what can be interpreted as a dismissive aside in his summary where it is stated that 'the expansion of freedom was the central problem of abolitionists (including the slaves), ...[17] Second, Robin Blackburn in his recent impressively comprehensive study, *The Overthrow of Colonial Slavery*, argues in the opening chapter on the 'orgins of anti-slavery' that since the publication of Thomas Clarkson's seminal work on British slave trade abolition (1808), 'it has been common to identify the origins of anti-slavery within the works of the learned men who first published critiques of slavery or the slave trade.'[18]

Recognising the, persistence of this perspective in the study of anti-slavery, Marxist historians such as C.L.R. James, Richard Hart and Gordon Lewis, among others, have been suggesting for some time that slave politics be conceived of as the 'on the ground' (core) dimension of a general struggle to remove slavery from Caribbean and European political culture. James has long been concerned with illustrating how revolutionary ideology transcended the political barriers implicit in colonial slavery and racism. He insists that there should be no surprise in the fact that Caribbean slaves hammered out a political reality of anti-slavery with the assistance of European thought.

The equally vintage work of Hart on Jamaican slave resistance and rebellion now represents an historiographic core that illustrates as well as any other source the evolution of a hardened anti-slavery consciousness among blacks in that country. For him, the core of the anti-slavery movement resided undoubtedly within the Caribbean, and his personal political feel for contemporary consciousness gives a strong sense of continuity in his analysis.[19] Lewis, in addition, in his well known style, attempted to flesh out the theoretical and conceptual dimensions of international anti-slavery ideology, and gave full credit to the intellectual contribution of Caribbean slaves. He is not the kind of scholar who is limited by what has been said already. Furthermore, he had the courage to travel along unchartered areas in search of the 'hidden' ideological elements of the past world. What he found were the outer limits of a grand Caribbean anti-slavery tradition, whose actors were not only black and coloured, but also Amerindian and creole white. Conceptually, he does not detract from the achievements of Wilberforce, Clarkson, Buxton and Schoelcher, but he does suggest that the world created, even if temporarily, by the anti-slavery energies of Toussaint and Dessalines, Sam Sharpe, Tackey and other slave leaders, seemed comparatively more 'hell-bent' on destroying Caribbean slavery.[20]

English abolitionist leaders, of course, perceived themselves as constituting the vanguard of anti-slavery thought and practice, a vision which historians have continued to perpetuate. This perception, not surprisingly, has managed to survive long after the 1790s when blacks in St. Domingue overthrew the slave regime and established in 1804 the state of Haiti which boasted an aggressive anti-slavery constitution and foreign policy.[21] Haiti had emerged regionally and internationally as the real symbol and manifestation of anti-slavery. Toussaint having beforehand eclipsed Wilberforce in the watchful eyes of the western world as the prime anti-slavery leader. For the hard-working and determined English abolitionists, however, the presence of Haiti was, in general, more of a hindrance to their crusade than an asset, and they continued to see anti-slavery as being endangered by Caribbean slaves' impatient tendency to resort to arms. Eltis suggests that this is why abolitionists, in general, were in favour of the establishment of a strong police force, an independent magistracy, draconian vagrancy laws, and increased missionary activity.[22]

Historians have had little difficulty in endorsing the humanitarians' claim to possession of the philosophic 'mind' — and hence the core — of anti-slavery, and by extension in suggesting that slaves lived out at best the cruder socio-material aspects of the movement. According to David Geggus, no major figure appears to have openly approved of violent self-liberation by blacks. Wilberforce thought them still unready for freedom, however obtained, and he deplored the 'cruel' and 'dreadful' revolt in St. Domingue. Even Charles James Fox, the well known radical and abolitionist, uttered negrophobic statements which culminated in his call for an assurance by his government that the spirit of revolt would not find roots within English colonies. Thomas Clarkson, however, respected for his unemotional consistency on the question of anti-slavery, rejected the popular sentiments of abolitionists, and spoke of Haiti as representing, not the upsurge of brutish savagery, but the affirmation of the 'unalterable Rights of Men' to freedom. Clarkson had only few supporters within the abolitionists' camp, the most famous being the long standing abolitionist, Percival Stockdale, who saw in the St. Domingue experience a movement against tyranny, led by Africans 'acting like men', fulfilling the most honourable destiny of mankind as directed by 'Nature and by God.'[23]

It was the treacherous removal of Toussaint from St. Domingue, the scene of the greatest single anti-slavery triumph, that allowed the best in England's journalism and the finest in its philosophic and artistic tradition to address the real meaning of Caribbean anti-slavery. In 1802, for example, the *Annual Register* voted him the man of the year, while Samuel Coleridge rated him in terms of 'true dignity of character' the better of Napoleon, his captor.[24] William Wordsworth, perhaps, more so than any other thinker, concretized in 1802 the value of Toussaint to mankind's search for liberty in general and the anti-slavery cause specifically with his sonnet, 'To Toussaint L'Ouverture':[25]

> *Though fallen thyself, never to rise again,*
> *Live and take comfort. Thou has left behind*

Powers that will work for thee; air, earth, and skies;
There's not a breathing of the common wind
That will forget thee; thou hast great allies;
Thy friends are exultations, agonies,
And love, and man's unconquerable mind.

But Wordsworth, like Toussaint, did not breathe 'the common wind', as Geggus assures us in his treatment of British opinion on black self-liberation in the Caribbean. On the St. Domingue question, Geggus asserts: 'Among the abolitionists, with the exception of a few fringe figures, the black rebels found apologists rather than supporters; most avoided the question of the legitimacy of the use of violence, and none seem to have spoken out against Britain's brief, but traumatic attempt to restore slavery in the colony'. Geggus is not surprised that 'the response of the British Romantics' to this struggle for personal freedom and national self-liberation was surprisingly slight', since the evidence suggests that although 'the blacks' resistance won them respect, prejudice persisted...'[26]

Persistent anti-black prejudice within western thought, Eric Williams affirmed, has influenced considerably the development of British and European colonial historiography, which forces us to examine the extent to which it remains a feature of the theoretical claims of anti-slavery literature.[27] It can be argued, within the limits of reasonable deductions from the data available, that English abolitionists' rejection of the slaves' revolutionary approach to freedom suggests that they had conceived liberation strictly in legal and sociological terms. That is, they did not support slave politics which sought to undermine the hegemony of the planter elite and the supportive Christian missions. They wished slaves legally free and to some extent recognised as social and biological equals to whites. But they did argue, however, that the economic dependency and political subordination of blacks to whites were necessary and desirable for their own advancement as well as for the continued growth of the Caribbean. Blacks, they generally believed, had nothing of superior merit to offer the new world in advancing its civilisation, and therefore they were to play a submissive role in the expansion of Eurocentric culture via the white controlled plantation economic regime.[28]

The racism implied within this perception of black liberation was an entrenched feature of abolitionists' thought. Emancipation was not conceived in terms of liberation from Europeans' power, values, and domination. From this point of view, then, it was only when Toussaint showed himself, like King Christophe did at a later date, to be receptive of the European educational and religious mission and its cultural-language baggage, that he received some measure of ideological acceptance by English statesmen and humanitarians. Furthermore, the abolitionists' tendency to conceive of slaves as unfortunate children to be liberated from tyrannical parents, with the moral outrage which that implied for the reasonable mind, served to deepen the racist perception of their audience and enhance a fear among them that blacks seeking independence, economic autonomy, and political power, were irresponsible, rash, ungrateful, in addition to being naive.

With these ideological tenets so deeply embedded in abolitionist perceptions of blacks in struggle, it would have been a formidable, but necessary task for historians to transcend or penetrate them in order to observe as objectively as possible the intellectual features of the political culture of blacks. This remains a most necessary precondition for a proper evaluation of the Caribbean anti-slavery tradition as well as for an understanding of how it is related to the European movement.

Logically, then, a feature of anti-slavery that should have been addressed at the outset is the history of blacks' political consciousness in the general evolution of their conceptual understanding of their wants, needs and means. To do this, it would have been necessary to say something meaningful about the 'slave mind' — hence ideology. Gordon Lewis quite perceptively punctuated his fascinating treatment of Caribbean anti-slavery with this reference to the state of the 'slave mind' within the historiography:

> If, then, there was a planter mind, there was also a slave mind. This has not always been fully appreciated, even by authors sympathetic to the slave cause.[29]

Refusal to recongnise black rebels at this level of consciousness, more than any other factor, has held back the advance of the kind of conceptual analysis which is necessary for an incisive understanding of slave resistance, and the subject remains today a soft spot within the modern anti-slavery literature.

To conceive rebel slaves as intelligent political activists (in spite of their material and socio-legal oppression), who were capable of evaluating pro-slavery strengths and weaknesses, has not been an easy task for most historians. Occasionally, references are made to this inhibition in terms of it being rooted within a racist perception of blacks which, in part, relates to the abolitionist view of slaves as primitive, anti-intellectual beings in need simply of paternalistic and moral care. Take Michael Craton's conceptual development, for example. For many years he worked diligently on slave resistance in the English Caribbean. In 1974 he presented what he described as a typology, morphology and etiology of resistance — neatly packaged in what he also termed 'a sequential model.' Since then he has published several works on slave resistance, illustrating a praiseworthy need to revise and fine-tune his analysis. Indeed, he is generally considered to be a leading authority within this aspect of Caribbean historiography. It is interesting to note, however, what happened when he encountered the need to comment on the 'slave mind' — an encounter which resulted from a general recognition that structuralist models based squarely on demographic, topographic and economic forces were insufficient in explaining why the slaves rebelled and what their motivating ideas were. He ran into the minefield of his own [unconscious] race attitude and attempted to deal with it as follows:

> Because of my seduction by the neat model and simple causes, I went so far as to dismiss the influence upon the British West Indies slaves of the ideology of the Age of Revolution (1775–1815), even of the, slave rebellion in Haiti between 1791 and 1804…, finally, it seems to me now that to deprive the slaves of an ideology such as that normally ascribed to the rebellious Americans, the French Revolutionaries…is to be guilty once more of a racist denigration.[30]

Having cleared this hurdle, a major achievement within Euro-American historiography of black struggle, Craton goes on to assert what for him was the ideology of the rebel slaves throughout Caribbean history; it 'was that of all unfree men — that is the vast majority throughout history — freedom to make, or create, life of their own'.[31]

Craton's admission and subsequent assertion came some thirty years after C.L.R. James had illustrated quite remarkably in *The Black Jacobins* that a proliferation of conflicting ideas and socio-political visions existed within the Haitian revolutionary ranks on the issues of foreign policy, economic strategy, race relations, education and government. Indeed one could argue that, like Lenin, Stalin, and Trotsky, the Haitian leaders, Toussaint, Dessalines, and Christophe differed fundamentally from each other on ideology, and thus the revolution was characterised by deep-rooted conceptual heterogeneity.[32] The real tribute to slaves in Craton's point, then, is perhaps to be found more succinctly stated in Gordon Lewis' political theorem — 'without intelligence there can be no ideology.'[33]

Leading on from these conceptual developments, though not in a logical manner, is the belief, now generally associated with the work of Sidney Mintz and Douglas Hall, that rebel slaves wanted a limited measure of economic and social autonomy as represented by a peasant culture rather than formal political power.[34] It is not clearly stated whether this objective was that of rebel leaders or the generally non-violent majority of slaves. Neither is it clearly stated whether this 'peasanthood' was considered the end product of their politics — that is, after they had defeated their masters — or merely a base for a future revolutionary onslaught upon planter power. For Craton, "the black majority' wanted to be "free to work for planters or themselves as and when they wished', ambitions he considered to be 'comparatively moderate', but in 'consonance with what seems to have been the wishes of the mass following'.[35]

It is not difficult to recognise that these projections of rebel slaves' objectives represent the most conservative and restricted interpretation of their ascribed ideology — 'freedom to make a life of their own'. Is it not a little odd to state that rebel slaves would have used whatever means possible to win their freedom and then to suggest that this end could be realised by a 'moderate' peasanthood cocooned within a plantation/planter dominated world? Would slaves not have realised that this idea as an end itself was unattainable under plantation hegemony? If we look solely at the British West Indies where slaves failed, after 200 years, to wrestle political power from masters by means of arms, we also see that, in the period 1838 to 1870, landownership was used as a political tool with far-reaching constitutional implications, especially for Jamaica where the peasantry was numerically most advanced.

Where slaves succeeded in freeing themselves, whether in Haiti, in long lasting maroon communities, and in temporary slave regimes, the value of political power to their sense of freedom was considered critical. The labourers' and peasants' riots and voting practices in the mid-nineteenth century British West Indies clearly illustrate that blacks were aware that without political power their 'reconstituted' peasant culture could not deliver the quality of freedom envisaged. Historians, then, seemed to have taken one step forward in the recognition of a slave ideology of struggle, but have taken two backwards in implying that it was a depoliticised peasant world, dialectically opposed to plantation hegemony, which rebel slaves pursued.

More recently, this regressive trend within the historiography has received a significant boost from Dirks in what he describes as an analysis of 'conflict and its ritual expression' on British West Indian slave plantations. Dirks' thesis is that slaves possessed a 'proclivity to turn the holidays [especially Christmas] into a bloodbath and to try to topple their masters' regime'.[36] He computes that of the seventy slave revolts reported, aborted, imagined and actual, some thirty-seven occurred in the month of December, producing what he terms the 'darkside of Christmas'.[37] Dirks' analysis of this time-based phenomenon falls within the category identified by Craton as racist denigration — dark for whom! For him, the slaves were not driven by a political and military understanding, sophisticated or otherwise, of the impact of the Christmas festivities within the white community, but by forces of the belly rather than the brain. The month of December, he claims, without the presentation of adequate supportive data, was associated with a rather sudden increase in slave nutrition — preceding months being characterised by extensive hunger:

> The onset of dry weather in December brought immediate and dramatic relief. The energy-rich fields of cane started to ripen. At the same time yarns, sweet potatoes, maize, plantains, and bananas, as well as a great number of other fruits and vegetables, began to mature. Field-work slackened off for a brief interlude before the cane harvest. And the end of the hurricane season brought hundreds of vessels laden with provisions, much of it for holiday distribution. Together these events broke the pattern of hunger and lethargy and disease of the previous months and gave way to vigor and better health all around.

'This upsurge in available food energy', Dirks argues, 'is also related to tumultous celebrations' and aggressiveness among slaves in general. He asserts that 'the effect of this nutritional boost and the availability of other fresh sources of nourishment was nothing short of explosive'. Typically, some of this excessive energy went into 'jolly sport', but most went into 'extra-ordinary' aggressiveness'.[38]

One of Dirks' achievements is that he has managed to turn upside down the traditional analysis without attempting to remove it from nutritional or biological levels of conception. In 1974, for example, Richard Sheridan had argued that slaves 'tended to revolt when they were underfed, overworked, and maltreated'.[39] We are now told by Dirks that, on the contrary, they tended to revolt when overfed, underworked and well treated. The assumption underlying both arguments is that it was possible to produce in a general way an anti-rebellious consciousness by a sensitive, well planned manipulation of labour and nutritional factors. This suggests an objection to the notion that slaves practised 'politics' on a sophisticated and intellectually conscious level. Yet, the evidence illustrates fully that slaves made definite political analyses of the power structures they encountered, and used almost every force — natural and human — in their struggle. They rebelled when they could, and accommodated when they had to. The ebb and flow of rebellion and accommodation suggest that they understood 'time', including Christmas time, as a political factor in struggle. As a result, some planters were forced to appreciate the political skills and conscious determination of rebel slaves, in spite of the negrophobic nature of their social commentaries.

It can no longer be generally accepted, then, that slaves existed in an atheoretical world which was devoid of ideas, political concepts and an alternative socio-political vision. Their tradition of anti-slavery activity impacted upon the social culture and polity of the Caribbean world in more fundamental ways than anti-slavery lobbyists ever did in metropolitan societies. Indeed, the entire Caribbean reality was shaped and informed by the persistent forces of slavery and anti-slavery as long as the slave regimes lasted. From a Caribbean perspective, slaves' struggle for freedom should not be diminished when placed alongside the legislative interventions of European Parliaments. These metropolitan actions were part of the final episode in an epic struggle — initiated and propelled by its greatest sufferers — the slave population. Only in Haiti were blacks able to overthrow the slave regime and achieve their freedom. Yet, slaves throughout the region consistently rebelled in order to gain freedom, employing over time a wide range of political tools and methods in their struggle.

In terms of the Caribbean anti-slavery movement, no iron laws of slave resistance exist, and consequently most scholars have tended to emphasise the uniqueness of each colony's case. While recognising, at least philosophically, the temporal and spatial uniqueness of each historical moment, one can still illustrate that the fundamental ideological core of anti-slavery was almost identical: the slaves were saying to their masters, 'we want to be free, and we will pursue that freedom by all means necessary.' This was the essential stream of thought that ran through the region, from colony to colony, from plantation to plantation. Indeed, it was anti-slavery rather than sugar production which stamped the most prominent unifying marks upon the region. In this sense, then, black-led anti-slavery resided at the root of the Caribbean experience, and represented a critical element of the core of what was perhaps the first international political movement of the modern era — transatlantic abolitionism.

Notes

1. Hilary Beckles, 'The 200 Years War: Slave Resistance in the British West Indies: An Overview of the Historiography', *The Jamaican Historical Review*, 13 (1982): 1–10. Also, 'Slave Ideology and Self-Emancipation in the British West Indies', *Bulletin of Eastern Caribbean Affairs*, 10, 4, 1–8. See also Michael Craton, 'The Passion to Exist: Slave Rebellion in the British West Indies, 1650–1832', *Journal of Caribbean History*, 13, 1; Edward Long, *The History of Jamaica*. London, 1774, 1970 reprint, 348–355, 465–469; Bryan Edwards, *The History, Civil and Commercial of the British Colonies in the West Indies*, London, 1794, 1, 60–65.

2. See, for example, the following revisionist analyses of slave resistance: Barry Gaspar, *Bondsmen and Rebels: A Study of Master-Slave Relations in Antigua (with Implications for colonial British America)*. Baltimore, 1985 xiv–20. Michael Craton, *Testing the Chains: Resistance to Slavery in the British West Indies*. London, 1982, 19–51. Hilary Beckles, *Black Rebellion in Barbados: The Struggle Against Slavery, 1627–1838*. Bridgetown, 1984, 1–8.

3. See Orlando Patterson, "Slavery and Slave Revolts: A Socio-historical Analysis of the First Maroon War, Jamaica 1655–1740" *Social and Economic Studies*, 19:3 (1970): 289–325. Michael Craton, *Sinews of Empire: A Short History of British Slavery*. New York, 1974, 289–325. Edward Brathwaite, *Wars of Respect: Nanny, Sam Sharpe and the Struggle*. Kingston, 1977; also 'Caliban, Ariel and Unprospero in the Conflict of Creolisation: A Study of the Slave Revolt of Jamaica, 1831–32' in V. Rubin and A. Tuden (eds) *Comparative Perspectives on Slavery in New World Plantation Societies*. New York, 1977, 41–62. Barbara Kopytoff, 'The Early Political Development of Jamaican Maroon Societies', *William and Mary Quarterly*, 35:2, 1978, 287–307; The Development of Jamaican Maroon Ethnicity', *Caribbean Quarterly*, 22, 1976, 35–50. Monica Schuler, "Akan Slave Rebellion in the British Caribbean', *Savacou*, 1:1, 1970. also, 'Ethnic Slave Rebellions in the Caribbean and the Guianas', *Journal of Social History*, 3, 1970, 374–385. Barry Gaspar, 'The Antigua Slave Conspiracy of 1736: A Case Study of the Origins of Collective. Resistance'. *William and Mary Quarterly*, 35:2, 1978, 308–324: Mary Reckord-Turner, 'The Jamaican Slave Rebellion of 1831', *Past and Present*, July, 1968, No. 40, 108–125.

4.   See M. Schuler, 'Day-to-Day Resistance to Slavery in the Caribbean during the eighteenth Century', *African Studies Association of the West Indies*, Bulletin 6, Dec. 1973, 57–77. Also, Richard Sheridan, 'The Jamaican Slave Insurrection Scare of 1776 and the American Revolution', Journal of Negro History, 61:3, 1976, 290–308.

5.   Robert Dirks, *The Black Saturnalia: Conflict and its ritual expression on British West Indian Slave Plantations* Gainesville, 1987, 167; M. Craton, *Testing the Chains*, 335–339.

6.   C.L.R. James, *The Black Jacobins: Toussaint L'Ouverture and the San Domingo Revolution*. Reprint 1963. See also Gordon K. Lewis, *Main Currents in Caribbean Thought: The Historical Evolution of Caribbean Society in its Ideological Aspects, 1492–1900*. Baltimore, 1983, 171–239.

7.   For example, the Report of the House of Assembly's Select Committee which investigated the causes of the 1816 rebellion in Barbados concluded that the rebellion originated 'solely and entirely in consequence of the intelligence imparted to the slaves, which intelligence was obtained from the English newspapers, that their freedom had been granted them in England'; and that their hopes for emancipation were 'kept alive' by the information that 'party in England and particularly in Wilberforce…were exerting themselves to ameliorate their condition, and ultimately effect their emancipation'. (*Report from a Select Committee Appointed to Inquire into the Origins, Causes, and Progress of the Late Insurrection — April 1816.* Barbados, 1818.)

8.   For example, J. Oldmixon (*The British Empire in America*, London 1708) wrote of the rebels involved in the 1692 slave conspiracy in Barbados: 'Did they imagine that Christians would have suffered them to set up a Negro Monarchy, or Republick, in the midst of their Governments?…The English Dutch and French…would rather have leagued than suffer this unnatural and dangerous independence…They would have been looked upon as common enemies by all nations . . .' (p. 53). See Beckles, *Black Rebellion*, 48.

9.   See Craton, *Testing the Chains*, 109; Beckles, *Black Rebellion*, 110.

10.   Edward Long, *The History of Jamaica.* London, 1774, 1970. reprint, 1, 25.

11.   Lewis, *Main Currents*, 111; Long, 11, 270–271.

12.   See Mary Turner, *Slaves and Missionaries: The Disintegration of Jamaican Slave Society, 1787–1834.* Chicago, 1982, 153–154, 158; Craton, *Testing The Chains, 301.*

13.   See David Geggus, 'British Opinion and the Emergence of Haiti, 1791–1805' in James Walvin (ed.) *Slavery and British Society, 1776–1846*. London, 1982, 123–150; Michael Craton, 'Slave Culture, Resistance and the Achievement of Emancipation in the British West Indies, 1783–1838', 100–123. See also, Hilary Beckles, 'Emancipation by War or Law? Wilberforce and the 1816 Barbados Slave Rebellion', in David Richardson, (ed.), *Abolition and its Aftermath: The Historical Context, 1790–1916.* London, 1985, 80–105.

14.   Eric Williams, *Capitalism and Slavery.* (London, 1944) reprint 1964, 208.

15.   Craton, 'Slave Culture', 122; also, 'Proto-Peasant Revolts? The late Slave Rebellions in the British West Indies, 1816–1832', *Past and Present*, No. 85, 99–126; 'What and Who to Whom and What: The Significance of Slave Resistance', in Barbara Solow and Stanley Engerman, (eds) *British Capitalism and Caribbean Slavery: The Legacy of Eric Williams.* New York, 1987, 259–282.

16.   Davis, in *The Problem of Slavery in the Age of Revolution, 1770–1823* (Ithaca, 1975), marginalised the philosophical impact which persistent Slave rebellions in the Caribbean had upon English (European) anti-slavery thought, though conceptually this matter would have been critical to the thought of Locke and Hegel, both of whom he dealt with extensively. He attempted to address the matter in a rather peripheral manner by means of an epilogue entitled 'Toussaint L'Ouverture and the Phenomenology of mind', which does no justice to the historical and philosophical vision of either Toussaint or Hegel. See Roger Anstey's two most impressive works: *The Atlantic Slave Trade and British Abolition, 1769–1810.* London, 1975; 'Parliamentary Reform, Methodism, and Anti-Slavery Politics, 1829–1833', *Slavery and Abolition*, 2:3, 1981, 209–26.

17.   Seymour Drescher, *Capitalism and Anti-Slavery: British Mobilisation in Comparative Perspective.* London, 1986, 162.

18. Robin Blackburn, *The Overthrow of Colonial Slavery, 1776–1848*. London, 1988.35.

19. Richard Hart, 'The Formation of a Caribbean Working Class' *The Black Liberator*, 2:2, 1973/74, 131–148; *Slaves who Abolished Slavery: Vol. 1 Blacks in Bondage:* Kingston, 1980; *Blacks in Rebellion*. Kingston, 1985; *Black Jamaicans' Struggle Against Slavery.* London, 1977; 'Cudjoe and the First Maroon War in Jamaica', *Caribbean Historical Review*, 1, 1950, 46–79.

20. See G. Lewis, *Main Currents*, Chapter four, for an exciting analysis of Caribbean anti-slavery thought and actions.

21. For an interesting case of Haiti's anti-slavery foreign policy in action, see Richard Sheridan, 'From Jamaican Slavery to Haitian Freedom: The Case of the Black Crew of the Pilot Boat, Deep Nine', *Journal of Negro History*, 67:4, 1982, 328–339. See also David Geggus, 'The Enigma of Jamaica in the 1790s: New Light on the Causes of Slave Rebellions', *William and Mary Quarterly*. 44:2. 1987, 229–274.

22. D. Eltis, 'Abolitionist Perceptions of Society after Slavery? in James Walvin (ed), *Slavery and British Society*, 202–203.

23. Geggus, 'British Opinion', 127.

24. *Annual Register*, 1802, 210–20.

25. Published in the *Morning Post*, 9 November 1802.

26. Geggus, 'British Opinion', 149.

27. Eric Williams, *British Historians and the West Indies*. Trinidad, 1964, 1–13.

28. For an excellent analysis of this theme, see David Eltis, "Abolitionist Perceptions of Society after Slavery", 195–214. See also W.A. Green, 'Was British Emancipation a Success? The Abolitionist Perspective', in Richardson (ed.) *Abolition*, 183–203.

29. Lewis, *Main Currents, 182*.

30. Craton, 'The Passion to Exist', 2.

31. *Ibid.*, 18.

32. See Beckles, *Black Rebellion, 4*.

33. Lewis, *Main Currents, 180*.

34. See Sidney Mintz and Douglas Hall, 'The Origins of the Jamaican Internal Marketing System', *Yale University Publications in Anthropology*, 57 (1960): 1–26.

35. Craton, 'Slave Culture', 118. He further states: 'The chief of these aspirations was, naturally, to be free. Yet the form of that freedom seems to have become visualised as that of an independent peasantry, about which the slaves had quite clear notions and of which, in most cases, they already, had considerable experience.'

36. Dirks, *Black Saturnalia*, xvi–xvii.

37. *Ibid.*, 167.

38. *Ibid.*, 171.

39. Richard Sheridan, *Sugar and Slavery: An Economic History of the British West Indies, 1625–1775*. Bridgetown, 1974, 254.

Bechu and the Norman Commission, February 1897

Memorandum by Bechu to the
West India Royal Commission, 1897.

Wages

Although indentured coolies are, according to the letter of the law, entitled to one shilling *per diem*, and women and children to 8 and 4 pence respectively, for seven hours, without extra exertion, they do not as a matter of fact earn that wage unless they serve for nine or ten hours, and *not even then*. One witness is reported to have stated that, in consequence of the depression in the sugar trade the coolies 'in most cases accepted his reductions, realizing that estates were in difficulties on account of low prices'; but instead of saying, *'accepted the reductions'*, he ought to have said *tamely submitted* to the reductions from fear of being buckshotted, as some of their countrymen in Pln Non Pareil were because they claimed their rights. Again, the Hon the Immigration Agent-General is reported to have said that 'considering the large number of immigrants under indenture, he did not think there were many complaints about the amount of wages, but that there were more complaints against indentured immigrants for neglecting work'; but I know for a positive fact that from fear of their drivers, who keep indentured coolies so under subjection by abuses and threats, that *outspoken* complaints of that nature are rare. It is well known, however, that complaints against indentured immigrants are more numerous, and that is simply because drivers and overseers, to show off their *brief authority*, bring them up for the most trivial faults.

Tasks

Although it is *optional* for indentured immigrants to take *task work* they are *forced* to accept it, and the terms fixed by employers are so hard that it is often the case that a task cannot be completed in less than two days, thus making it *impossible* for an indentured coolie from earning a shilling *per diem*. I should feel deeply grateful if the *Order Book*, which is kept up in all estates, is referred to; it will only *then* be seen how during the past five years the rate, for the same nature of work, for which a man was paid one shilling when the Immigration Act of 1891 came into force, has now to be performed for 6 pence.

Under Section 18 of the Immigration Ordinance it is the duty of the Immigration Agent to give advice to coolies, conduct investigations, institute prosecutions, and to assist the Magistrate in the estimate of wages; but the officer in charge of the district to which I belong [H.J. Gladwin], beyond visiting the estate once a month for a little over an hour, taking down a few 'averages' of the earnings of the stronger men, and listening to a few family quarrels, does little else. Only a couple months back I had occasion to deny a statement which was made in *The Argosy*, to the effect that this officer most religiously explains to all newly arrived immigrants the terms of their contract, and that denial had the effect of bringing him to a sense of his duty when the last three shipments arrived. He seldom visits the hospital, and, as long as I have been on Pln Enmore has never on one occasion been to the 'nigger yards' or inspected any of the coolie dwellings. Besides taking no interest in the coolies, whose protector he is supposed to be, he is on such friendly terms with the Manager as to have succeeded in getting his daughter employment in his house as governess. How is it possible, under the circumstance, to receive justice at his hands?

Continuance of Immigration

Considering the accounts which have from time to time been sent to the English press, to the effect that social order in this colony will be at considerable peril unless a bounty is given to the planters, it is difficult to understand how more East Indian immigrants are wanted at the present time. There are now 100,000 coolies in this colony, and surely that number ought to more than suffice for the 64 estates under cultivation? 5,000 out of these immigrants will be eligible to return to India, but only 2,000 out of that number will, it is believed, be sent. Instead of retaining as many of them by offering them money in lieu of back passage, they are to be returned and a lot of half-starved unacclimatized men brought in their places. It is very doubtful if these time-expired men, even if they are offered a bounty as an inducement to remain will accept the offer, and even if they do so, the planters would be reluctant to have that class of re-indentured men, since they know the 'ropes' and will hardly allow themselves to be cheated out of their rights, whereas a newly arrived simpleton, in his blissful ignorance, will have to grin and take what is given him.

Immoral Relations of Overseers and Managers, in Some Cases, with Coolie Women

The Hon Darnell Davis, in the course of his evidence, pointed out that there is a paucity of women (East Indian) and suggested that the sexes be equalized, but is it possible that coolies will lawfully take unto themselves wives when such gross immorality exists in most of the estates, notwithstanding what the Royal Commissioners of 1871 had to say in the matter, and although the very same matter has on several occasions since been brought to the notice of all estate Managers by the Immigration Department, still it is an open secret that coolie women are in the keeping of overseers. I am in a position to state that a fellow shipmate of mine, a Punjabi, was at one time making overtures to a woman with a view to matrimony, but he was deterred from doing so, as he came to hear that she had got in tow with an overseer, who eventually gave her the money to purchase her freedom. I don't recollect the name of the overseer, but the name of the woman is Leloo, and she is at present residing at Pln Lusignan, East Coast. This is another ground for discontent and sometimes leads to riots, yet Immigration Agents close their eyes to the matter.

There is not the slightest doubt that if the suggestions made by the Hon Darnell Davis in his evidence, with regard to more women being brought to the colony to equalize the sexes, [were implemented] a great deal of both immorality and discontent among the emigrants would be avoided, and their people would be far more willing to settle in the country.

BECHU
Indentured Immigrant,
Pln Enmore, East Coast [Demerara]
***Report of the West India Royal Commission, 1897* [H.W. Norman, chairman],
(London: HMSO, 1897), Appendix C. – Part II, British Guiana, section 158.**

Before and After 1865

Roy Augier

A bare list of the events which followed the riots at Morant Bay provokes no argument. But whether these events are, or are not, the consequences of that affray, is a matter of debate. We offer the remarks which follow as a contribution to this debate.

If we interpret the events at Stony Gut and at the Court House in Morant Bay correctly as a statement, uttered in blood, about the unjust relations between men who belonged to different economic classes and also to different ethnic groups, then the direct effects of the riots must be sought in the subsequent attitudes of social groups towards one another. That is we have to answer such questions as, to what extent did the riots change the attitudes of blacks, browns and whites towards one another? Did such changes take place in St. Thomas alone, or over the whole island, or nowhere? Did the riots change the conception each ethnic group had of itself? Did it stiffen the spine of the one and make the other more accommodating? How did it affect the relations between planter and labourer? Did it alter the balance of political power between economic classes?

We cannot give satisfactory answers to most of these questions for three reasons. Firstly, we are limited in what we write here by the kind of historical documents we have used. The information we possess does not allow us to discuss the direct consequences of the riots on social attitudes. But we do have enough information to discuss the effect of the riots on politics.

Secondly, to answer questions of the kind which we have instanced, it is not enough to know what social attitudes were after the riots; it is also necessary to know with some precision what they were before that social disturbance. And this we do not know.

Thirdly, two events intervened between the riots and some of their possible consequences. The intrusion into the society of an alien military force which found no riot to suppress but remained to terrorize a part of that society. And following closely, the imposition of political authority from outside.

So although it is possible to sketch answers to some questions, such as the attitudes of employers to labourers, or the attitudes of ethnic groups to one another for the years before and after 1865, and although we know in general what the society was like before 1865, and what it was like afterwards, it remains difficult to assess the direct consequences of the riots on relationships within the society, because the British interposed themselves in ways which were bound to influence the relations of social groups one to another.

If this is so, it is not the riots which make 1865 a watershed in Jamaican history, but the abdication in that year of political authority by the Jamaicans who possessed it. Later, we shall discuss the relationship between the riots and the passing of responsibility for the society over to foreigners. Now we wish to notice that both the riots and the events which followed them were the working out of tendencies already existing in the society. Since the society survived the riots without alteration of its social and economic structures, the history of Jamaica after 1865 may be read as a record of the extent to which these tendencies were assisted or frustrated by crown colony government.

Notice first that crown colony government strengthened a relationship which already existed. This change in the intensity of the relationship between the society in Jamaica and the government of Great Britain had this effect, among others: it made the society as a whole more dependent, less responsible, less self-directing than it had been. But the society in Jamaica had always been a colonial society. That is to say it had always been dependent on a metropolitan society and its government.

To say that the society had always been dependent, is not to say that early in the life of the society, the white settlers wished it so. They appreciated the advantages, particularly the economic advantages, of independence; but they also understood its hazards. Nor, we may be allowed to guess, did the slaves wish it so. Rebellious slaves surely appreciated that the dependent status of the society was a disadvantage to them.

It was a relationship imposed by superior power, and one to which the white settlers accommodated themselves. Within the bounds set by this power, white property-holders made their lives and fortunes. Foreigners were kept at sea and slaves on the estates. The white community was dependent on the imperial power for its trade and its protection. This was the basis of the accommodation: the white community had an exclusive market for its produce and was protected from slaves and foreigners.

The accommodation of inferior to superior power was made palatable by a concession which the white community had risked much to achieve. In matters which concerned exclusively the ordering of their society, they were allowed to be their own masters. In general this meant that taxes were not imposed on them by the English Crown in order to pay its servants in the colony. The white settlers taxed themselves and so would keep the arrogance of the King's servants within some bounds by withholding public money from them. If meant also that they were left to police the slaves and repress the free black and brown inhabitants without English interference. Finally it meant that they could tax themselves for the few services such as roads, forts, harbours and public buildings which they required in common.

As if to make up for the realization that the important decisions governing the life of their society were taken outside of it, the white community vehemently defended the political jurisdiction they had gained, and even sought to encroach upon what the Crown had marked out for itself.

Fighting with governors, complaining to the Crown and Parliament about the condition of trade and repressing the lower orders is not high politics; but it left its mark on the society. It gave the community a political style which survived at least to the nineteen-thirties. Long after emancipation it was the chief substance of our politics. And it gave to succeeding generations the rhetoric of liberty which has in modern times been put to more substantial use. The seriousness with which the whites conducted their limited politics gave them a cohesion which justifies us in describing them as a community. It was of course the politics of a minority, male, white, propertied and Anglican.

For most of the eighteenth century this accommodation was, on balance, to the advantage of the white community. Gradually it became less so. But by then both the sugar economy based on an exclusive market and the social structure erected to support that economy, the slave society, had become to the white community the natural order of the universe. What had begun as a convenience had become a necessity. Sugar and slavery bound them to Great Britain.

But even in Great Britain the natural order changes. In that country critics of the old imperial economy and critics of the slave society that went with it, became sufficiently powerful to abolish both.

Emancipation did not shock the white community into a posture of independence. To adopt such a stance they would have had to embrace the doctrine of social equality of all men. What they chose to do, once they had stopped their trans-Atlantic debate with Great Britain about its invasion of their constitutional rights, was to use their political power to make of emancipation a mere word, without economic and social reality.

They were tempted to play this game because although emancipation had conferred civil rights on all ex-slaves, political rights accrued only to those who possessed property to the value required by the laws then in force. By the eighteen-forties their game had been stopped. But unfortunately for the society it had not been stopped by the ex-slaves swarming over the field. It had been whistled off by Great Britain in its role as referee. The white community had been stopped, the black community had been protected, by the British government using its imperial authority to declare null and void any colonial law which offended it.

The imperial power to review colonial legislation had in the past been used to regulate the relations between the two societies, Jamaica and England; now after emancipation it was being used to regulate the relations between two groups within the Jamaican society, ex-slaves and ex-masters. In the earlier period the superior power of England had been exercised to maintain an economic relationship between Jamaica and herself according to the principles of political economy then in vogue. Now British power was being used to establish social relations between ex-slaves and ex-masters according to such humanitarian principles as survived political expediency.

But although British power was now informed by different principles and used for different ends, its exercise served to reinforce the state of dependence of the society. Emancipation brought the blacks into a relationship with the British government which was analogous to the one which the whites had long had.

The society then was comprised of two communities living cheek by jowl; one white, rich and small in number; the other black, poor and numerous; dependent each in its way on an outside power for protection against the other. The whites were protected against the physical force derived from numbers and the blacks protected against the physical force derived from wealth and political power. This arrangement was on balance to the disadvantage of the black poor.

It is difficult for an outside power to protect the poor effectively, while the rich are allowed to exercise political power over them. Moreover, the presence of the alien power denies the poor their one advantage. For if they resort to force, it is unlikely that they will do so in the full strength of their numbers; and in the circumstances, inadequately armed, they can be speedily curbed. It needed more concern for the society, greater moral stamina than the British power was able to summon, to protect the poor effectively from the rich.

The machine of British imperial administration could, and for the most part after emancipation, did prevent the white community from using the law to fasten the blacks to the plantation; but that machine was ill-designed to promote the interest of the black community in more positive ways. Why did not the black community exert itself to correct this imbalance in the society?

We noticed earlier white accommodation to English superior power and its effect on that community and the whole society. Now we notice black accommodation to local white superior power. To discuss those who accommodated is not to deny the existence, or the importance, of the rebellious, the suicide and the saboteur. It is only to discuss the majority: and it is also to discuss less than extreme attitudes. We do not wish to make Uncle-Toms of the majority of the slaves, but wish to notice the existence of patterns of behaviour, simulated at first, but later becoming ingrained, becoming authentic elements in the personality.

The blacks lived in a society which was composed of a congeries of petty domains, the plantations and pens. But these were not merely forms of economic organization, not merely farms and mills for producing sugar. They were also to some extent isolated, self sufficient social and cultural systems. Within their confines the authority of the master was hardly trammelled by law. Beyond its gates all depended on the whim of the master and on the whim of those appointed to authority by his grace. The kick and the caress were equally arbitrary. This was the system of authority that a slave lived with, frequently imitated, and transmitted to his children.

It was on the plantation too that the slave was de-tribalized and slowly made into a creole. Into this creole culture his children were born. Later in the history of the society, if they lived on a plantation which permitted missionaries to instruct and baptize slaves, they could become Christians. But of necessity Christian instruction concentrated on redemption, love, obedience. It was the price missionaries paid for being allowed beyond the gates of the plantation.

It was not merely that the predominant values transmitted by the plantation to the slave reinforced the subordination to power inherent in his status. Men can and do reject some of the values of a social system not organized for their benefit. But, more important: conduct appropriate to a free society is a social habit, an art which can only be learned in a society which is engaged in the never ending process of helping all its members make themselves free men. There was hardly opportunity for black or white to learn so to conduct themselves before emancipation.

It is therefore no surprise that the black population did not seek power through political means to redress the imbalance in the society. It is more surprising that they did not attempt to do so by force. Riots there were; but when one considers the bitterness engendered during the period of apprenticeship, and the economic deprivation and injustice suffered afterwards, surprisingly few riots occurred. Explanations which refer to the geography of the island and to habits learnt during slavery do not seem adequate. Taken by themselves they are not. But add to them the freedom to starve guaranteed by the British government after the apprenticeship period, and we may have a clue to the absence of widespread violence and agitation. The blacks did not seek to change the political system because so many of them could ignore it. And of those who could not ignore it? Did they cling to some belief that the Missus Queen would protect them from the worst?

Emancipation was carried by votes, instead of being seized after bloodshed. The British thus had an opportunity to try to arrange its terms in ways which would have set the two communities to the learning to live as free men from the date of the establishment of a legally free society. This opportunity was neglected. The society was reconstituted by the will of the British. But for the work to be solidly founded, it needed close and sympathetic supervision. That the British could have done though they were not fit to do more than that. They were themselves only just beginning to learn how to run a free society. Their disgust with slavery had allowed the ground to be cleared. But although they appropriated the office of supervisor of the society in 1833, it was some time before they worked out what functions they were willing to perform.

The British policy of intervention in the domestic affairs of the society had been adopted reluctantly. It was the only way to end slavery peacefully. The policy was justified on the assumption that the slave masters would never themselves dismantle the slave society. But after the Act of Emancipation had been passed, the British government acted as if that assumption had been wrong. It seemed to believe that the masters would govern the society and manage their estates in harmony with the principles of the Act. Instead of co-operating, the masters sabotaged the Act again and again. They thus goaded the British government into accepting the argument that the only way to give substance to the Act of Emancipation was for it to take complete charge of the affairs of the society.

But the half-hearted effort made in 1839 to suspend the Jamaican Constitution for five years was carried the House of Commons by so small a majority that the government regarded it as a defeat. So within five years of emancipation the British government's resolve to function as the supervisor of the new society had been weakened by those Englishmen who had a sentiment for liberty as an abstraction. They were unwilling to disturb, the political privileges and the property rights of their kith and kin in Jamaica.

The British government now adopted the policy which would determine the way it exercised the role of supervisor between 1840 and 1865. The basis of the new policy was the conciliation of the white community. The old policy had been founded on mistrust of the masters. The hostility of the House of Assembly to the British government had been one result. The second was more grave than the first. For the old policy had served to exacerbate the painful social relations of slavery. To prolong that policy was to delay the beginning of new social and economic relations. It would be better for the blacks, better for the whole society, to change the policy. So argued the British administrators who recommended the new policy to the British government.

The attempt to make the white community accept responsibility for the whole society by force had failed. The attempt to assume full control of the affairs of the society had been abandoned. The attempt would now be made to persuade the white community of the wisdom of themselves conducting responsible politics.

The old policy assumed the absence of goodwill in the white community. The new policy assumed the absence of self-interest in the black community. This policy professed to have at heart the interest of all parties. In fact it suited the interest of two only, the white community and the British government. The essence of the new policy was that it put away a big stick which was never to be used anyway. To that extent it was more honest the old policy. But it was equally ineffective. It put away a stick, but dangled no carrots. The British government should have done in 1839 what it eventually did in 1944: enfranchised the whole population. Instead the British government coaxed the whites into lowering the voting qualifications they did, but only enough to enfranchise a minority.

It is true to say of the black that he was then unfit; but in all the senses in which this judgement is true and relevant, it is also true of the white. In both cases their disabilities were due to their being the creatures of a slave society. Therein lies whatever justification there was for allowing the British government a role in the affairs of the society. An effective role would have for a time, put both communities at an equal political disadvantage. The policy of conciliation buttressed the existing advantages of the white community and encouraged the blacks to be dependent on Missus Queen. We may judge the success of that policy both by the Appeal of the Poor People of St. Ann and by the reply to it, the Queen's Advice.

Some of the elected members did turn their energies to the constructive politics of establishing a free society. But they had to work within the old parliamentary system of the House of Assembly which had been perfected for opposing policies of the Executive. It was relatively easy for those who preferred to live in the past to use this machinery to wreck or frustrate efforts to grapple with the present. The result of such politics, the persistent neglect of the welfare of the society as a whole, was the riots which erupted in the middle years of the nineteenth century.

There is another reason why British intervention in the society did not take a more positive form. It was due to the eclipse of the humanitarians by the accountants, as a major force in British parliamentary politics. British colonial policy after 1830, so far as it was concerned with the protection of indigenous peoples against settlers in South Africa and New Zealand, and of ex-slaves in the West Indies, meant spending money on the soldiers and the administrators necessary for its execution. Between 1834 and 1845 the Negro Education Grant largely supported primary schools in the West Indies. But the accountants in the Imperial Parliament persistently questioned the philosophy behind these activities until the Colonial Office and the Treasury understood that it would be very difficult to get the House of Commons to vote the money necessary to sustain that policy. When in 1841 he signalled the approaching end of the Negro Education Grant, Lord John Russell justified the decision on the grounds that the Negroes were much better able to pay for the education of their children than could English labourers.

In equity the British government should have helped to pay for the building of a free society. Since it was unwilling to do so, it should have used its office of supervisor of the society to ensure an equitable incidence of taxation; that is to make those who benefitted most from the economic structure of the society contribute significantly to the public coffers.

The British government let the poor carry the public services for nearly a hundred years. Before 1865 it was content to lecture the House of Assembly. After 1865, although Governors reported on the tax structure from time to time, the Colonial Office did not go beyond the hand-wringing of the impotent. The British government reserved its largest gestures for propping up the plantation economy. When the policy of free trade had severely damaged that economy the government guaranteed in 1848 the interest on a large loan which the planters could use to import labourers to work on the sugar estates. Again when the inept financial management of the Assembly had made Jamaica practically bankrupt, the British government in 1854 guaranteed a loan of half a million pounds sterling to restore the country's public credit.

If one assumes that two communities, such as those in Jamaica after emancipation, whose lives and history are extensively intertwined, are better integrated, and if one also assumes that societies are the better for being self-governing and democratic, the years between 1838 and 1865 were largely wasted.

The British presence frustrated both processes. The whites did not accept political responsibility for the whole society and catered to their own interests. They resented the British for emancipating the slaves and for changing British commercial policy from imperial protection to free trade. They resented the blacks for refusing to work on the plantation at all, or for working there only when it suited them.

The services, notably education and health which the society needed after emancipation, were scarcely provided for out of local funds. The administration of justice particularly in the courts of petty sessions, was dominated by the white community and the property owners. Injustice flourished.

The blacks were for the most part excluded from the political system, and of those who qualified by virtue of property, many stayed outside. The black community also opted out of the plantation economy wherever possible. This process meant a search for land to buy or squat on, and the beginnings of the drift to the towns. Immediately after emancipation those who lived in the free villages shared a communal existence, even though it was one made rudimentary by poverty, and paternal close missionary supervision. But progressively the rejection of the life of an estate casual laborer meant living in isolation. And after about 1845 there was a falling away of that interest in church membership and school attendance which had marked the early years of emancipation. Some of the people had begun to opt out of the cultural system as well.

In the five years before the riots at Morant Bay the society was marked by a certain restlessness. The religious revival had involved its devotees in a long march around the island. Their provision grounds untilled, they poured out their energies, physical and emotional, in repeated acts of devotion. Their unrestrained fervour indicated how sick the society was. The American civil war had brought to all an economic depression, worsened by a succession of floods and droughts on provision grounds. To some it also brought the fear of invasion.

A section of the white community began to advocate the abolition of the representative constitution in its present state. The meetings held after Dr. Underhill's letter to the Secretary of State became public, criticized the House of Assembly for wasting taxes and demanded not its abolition but its reform. In 1859 there was prolonged rioting in Sav-la-Mar and in Falmouth. The rioters in both instances were tried with results which on the evidence seem equitable.

We may learn from these riots and from the Assembly's debates on the future of the constitution what dangers threatened the society. We can also see how they might have been averted. If one part of the society had not been able to look for help overseas, if it had no choice but to find its own solutions within the society, it would probably have responded, even at so late an hour, by providing political remedies. Indeed had a more balanced judgement presided over the Jamaican administration in 1865, would Ramsey and Hobbs and the Maroons have been let loose over seven hundred square miles of eastern Jamaica? As it was Eyre had his bad judgement reinforced by those who themselves sought the solution for the ills of the society overseas. Eyre unleashed an alien force at Morant Bay and two months later opened the door to alien political authority. Who remembers the Falmouth rioters? Who would have remembered the Morant Bay rioters? We remember them because as Eyre himself wrote, 'The retribution has been so prompt and so terrible that it is never likely to be forgotten'. Since so many were innocent the act of October 1865 was not retribution, it was murder. Ought we not to remember Morant Bay in greater measure for the many who suffered, rather than exaggerate the achievement of the few who rioted?

We wrote earlier that although the evidence with which we are familiar did not allow us to say in what ways social attitudes and social relations changed as a direct consequence of the riots, it did allow us to discuss whether the political changes after 1865 were directly due to the riots.

It may be said in support of the argument that the loss of the old constitution was a direct consequence of the riots that one of the accounts usually given of this event is that 'the English took it away'. And when it is so stated, it is implied that the English took the constitution away because the Morant Bay riots showed them that the society was unable to govern itself, that it was not fit for self-government.

About the British government's policy it need only be said that although the Colonial Office would have liked the constitution changed or abolished, the policy of waiting for Jamaicans to change their own constitution had been accepted by the Secretary of State in July 1865 as the only feasible policy. The constitution could not be touched in any way by the Minister simply acting in the name of the Crown, and exercising the Royal Prerogative. It could only be changed by the Imperial Parliament; and after the experience of 1839 no British government would lightly have gone to the House of Commons with a bill for suspending the Jamaican Constitution.

The decision not to use the Imperial Parliament meant that change could only come from the Jamaican Parliament itself. But even so the British government adopted the policy of keeping quiet and waiting hopefully for the deed to be done, because it feared that to give public encouragement to those who wished for change would cause such widespread resentment in the society that it would make it doubly difficult to get a majority for change in the House of Assembly.

Another explanation given for the change of constitution is that the white members of the House of Assembly panicked after the riots, fearing that they were about to be massacred by the blacks, and accepted Eyre's invitation 'to immolate the constitution on the altar of patriotism'. This explanation has the merit of looking for the reason for change *in* the local society, but it does not fit the information we have of the final session of the House of Assembly. It is true that the Assembly passed very quickly all the repressive laws which Eyre had prepared for them. But not the bill to change the constitution. That the members took of their leisure, trading concessions among themselves, and producing a hodge-podge of a law which changed the constitution but left political power in the hands of the white community.

The constitution was not changed by the British; it was changed by Jamaicans. They changed it after the riots, but not because of the riots. They did not intend to change representative government for crown colony government, they were tricked into this by Eyre.

We have already elaborated on the first two assertions, we now turn to the others. Was the constitution changed by the House of Assembly because of the riots? Notice first that the desire to change the constitution existed before the riots; also that this desire was felt and expressed by a variety of groups. The question then is why was the constitution not changed before? Is it because a majority did not exist in the Assembly for change before the riots, but was produced by the riots?

A majority existed for the abolition of the existing constitution, or as it was sometimes said, for the reform of the constitution but for how long before 1865 it is difficult to say. What did not exist was a majority for a constitution to replace the old one. For crown colony government there was hardly a vote. The 1865 Session of the Assembly ended without a majority for any definite form of government. It was Eyre's triumph that he got the second amending act through a much depleted House of Assembly. Before we elaborate on Eyre's role let us look at the attitudes expressed before Eyre took a hand.

We have to guess in the absence of precise information, but we guess that the largest group was the one moved by the desire to put the representative constitution out of reach of the black population. They argued that now was the time. The numbers of negroes qualified to vote had grown, was growing and would soon be such as to allow them to control the legislature by electing black members. There were other motives for changing the constitution; some thought that for its institutions to work well they had to be staffed by a greater number of able men than the island could supply. Others thought that as a device for making the old constitution more efficient the Executive Committee had failed; it had been the cause of faction and of party and it had been the source of corruption. Their remedy was to give the executive offices to Englishmen appointed by the Secretary of State. At the Underhill meetings yet another group expressed its opinions. The black propertied tax payers criticized the Assembly for waste and they warned it that if it persisted in its old habits it would be abolished.

Before 1865 the abolitionists were unable to agree on what was to replace the old constitution. This was not simply a division between those who wished to let the British have a bigger role in politics and administration and those who did not. It was also due to factions among the whites. The division was crudely between those who had, however timidly, worked for an integrated society, and those who were against them for this act of collaboration. Such men, angry both against the British and the blacks, wished to hoist the constitution above the reach of propertied negroes, abolish the Executive Committee and keep the British out of Jamaican politics.

What did the riots do to these attitudes? So far as one can tell, nothing. What it did do was to provide the abolitionists with a broker, or to use the metaphor of a contemporary, a midwife. It is of course possible to combine the explanation which adduces panic with the broker-midwife description of Eyre's role, though the description does modify the notion that the constitution was surrendered in a moment of intense panic out of fear of the blacks. But it is best for us to treat the two matters, the attitudes of the members of the Assembly and the role of Eyre in changing the constitution separately.

The attitude pre–1865 of those who wished to keep the blacks outside of politics was not to surrender power to Great Britain, but to raise the property qualification both for membership of the House of Assembly and for voting. The attitudes of those who thought the society could not produce forty-seven members of the House and seventeen members of the Legislative Council was manifest in their proposals to consolidate both houses into a single chamber legislature. There were a few voices raised before 1865 for 'strong government', by which was meant government by Englishmen. We do not know the evidence which shows panic because panic would have meant a wholesale conversion of the first two groups to the position of the third, government by Englishmen. This obviously did not happen.

What happened was that the various groups none of which before or after the riots was large enough to get its own way, were kept talking long enough to produce a law, the first act amending the constitution. This was the product of horsetrading; it was untidy, contained tidbits for everybody, and was certainly not what any of the parties wanted, least of all Eyre. Did the riots put the various groups in a mood for horsetrading which would have been absent without the riots? Almost certainly, but they would not have continued talking but for Eyre.

The riots gave Eyre the opportunity to propose a change of constitution which without them he would not have been able to do. That is, in the interval between the riots and the meeting of the legislature Eyre felt able to prepare a draft bill and introduce it to the House through the Executive Committee. An act which in normal times would have been difficult, since Westmoreland for instance, would not have introduced such a bill. Even so, Eyre understood from the start that although what he wished was crown colony government, if he drafted such a bill it would never pass the Assembly. So he drafted a bill to establish a single chamber, with half its members elected and half nominated, and the Crown in control through the casting vote of the governor. But even this bill the Assembly mauled according to its own prejudices and interests.

Whatever it was that kept them talking, the magnet, the force that held them together was spent by the time the deed was done. Badly mauled as was the first amending act, particularly where it sought to give control to the Crown, Eyre urged the Colonial Office to accept it rather than send it back to the floor of the House, for then it was sure to be entirely lost.

If this was the mood of the Assembly why was Eyre able to get the second act passed? Briefly he took advantage of two things; one was that the House had thinned towards the end of the session as the country members went home for Christmas. Secondly he made brilliant use of the general disagreement over what sort of constitution should replace the old. He had told the Secretary of State that there were almost as many opinions on that as there were members. Yet even in the reduced House Eyre could not have got a positive bill written. He was able to let each group feel that if they merely repealed the first amending act and left it to the Crown to enact a new constitution, they would get the constitution they wished for. Hence the consternation with which the crown colony government constitution was greeted in 1866.

Eyre was able to insert himself a second time into the legislative machine through his use of a despatch which the Colonial Secretary had written before he received the first amending act. This despatch he sent to the House in an abbreviated version, suppressing those passages which did not support his plans.

He explained to the House that since it passed the first amending act, a despatch had arrived from the Colonial Office which laid down the conditions on which the British government would accept responsibility for Jamaica, that is protect whites against blacks. He had informed them of these conditions by excerpts from the despatch because it was confidential, and so they could not see it all. In the process he made the Colonial Secretary say clearly, what in his despatch, could at most, be only doubtfully inferred. That is, he made it look as if the first amending act was certain to be rejected. This was enough to tempt those dissatisfied, for whatever reason with the first act. Here was the opportunity to get the form of constitution they preferred.

Eyre did not realize that what was clever politics was illegal. The English Attorney General informed the Secretary of State that the second amending act was *ultra vires*. The Assembly could amend the constitution but it could not abolish it and leave to the Crown the making of a new constitution. It matters here that the Secretary of State had decided before the riots that he would accept changes in the West Indian constitutions. The task of his staff was now only to find a way around the Attorney General's opinion. The only answer was an act of the Imperial Parliament. The Colonial Office staff was not sure that they could depend on House of Commons. But the choice was between the Commons and the Assembly. The Assembly was certain to reject a third amending act. The Colonial Office chose to use the House of Commons. There, the act to give the Crown authority to make a constitution for Jamaica passed quickly enough. Thus was the old constitution abolished.

We now discuss some of the consequences of crown colony government. What benefits did the society gain from passing political authority over to the British? And what price did it pay for the benefits? We may draw up a crude balance sheet by assessing how the British used the political authority they had acquired in 1866. They had claimed that their presence in the society was justified because only they would be able to do three things, all of which the society badly needed. First they would tidy the public service and administration and make them more efficient; secondly they would provide impartial government between conflicting classes; thirdly they would look after the interests of the blacks, protect them from the whites and from themselves. These statements of principles to guide the administrators who would *make*, in each case, their own political programme. The British said from time to time that crown colony government was temporary; that it worked towards its own death; that as soon as the society had learnt the arts of responsible politics, it would again govern itself.

The constitution of 1866 gave the British political authority in an autocratic form. The governor was sure of his majority and the society was represented only by his nominees. The Order-in-Council of 1884 set some limits to the extent that any governor could play the autocrat, by permitting the elected members when acting in concert to veto his bills and resolutions. But it did not modify the essentially autocratic character of the crown colony constitution. For the next sixty years this was the constitution of Jamaica.

We begin our assessment of the use the British made of their political authority in Jamaica by distinguishing between the constitution as written and politics as practised by the functionaries of the crown colony constitution. The theory of the constitution asserted autocracy. The practice of politics assumed an oligarchy.

The autocratic power was not in general use. It was conceived for a form of opposition which died with the old constitution. The Colonial Office likened the governor's permanent majority to a phalanx. If any group was unreasonable enough to block the road to progress, the governor had the powers with which to scatter them. But after 1865 the mercantile and planter classes had no need for such crude tactics. And so the autocratic power which originally was to have been the instrument for transforming the society, became merely the instrument for asserting the imperial interest, even when that was as crassly conceived as it was in the 'Florence' case; and later still the autocratic power was used principally to protect the salaries of civil servants from the attacks of the elected members. On such occasions it appeared only after the governor had uttered the formula 'of paramount importance to the public interest'.

To say that crown colony government was in practice an oligarchy, is to gloss over the differences in style and in substance which distinguished the administrations of different governors. But, with one exception, it is not to distort significantly. Grant was the exception. He was the only autocrat. He had the will, and he had the advantage of inaugurating the new constitution. The export economy was buoyant, and it was too soon after Morant Bay for the old politicians to engage in unrestrained protests. Towards the end of his regime, they did protest over his failure to consult them, but their voices were still muted. After he had retired, they attacked his policies in earnest, particularly the Rio Cobre irrigation works.

Grant's practice may have been true to the letter of the constitution, it was not true to the spirit in which the Colonial Office expected crown colony government to work. Sir Henry Taylor was against governor-autocrats on practical grounds. He feared that they would inflame the local populations and bring down crown colony government in a very short time. The nominated unofficial members of the Legislative Councils, were not for him mere window-dressing. He justified their nomination on two grounds. First they embodied the principle of no taxation without representation. As the owners of the largest properties, agricultural and commercial, Taylor presumed them the mainstay of the revenue, and so the most appropriate local voices. He was wrong; but the despatches on the incidence of taxation did not perceptibly shake his belief in this argument. Secondly he wished for an opposition to the governor, and through the protests of that opposition, for local criticism of schemes sent up by governors for his approval.

Yet Taylor did not expect the governors to become the creatures of the local oligarchies. He expected career officials to resist the influence of the larger commercial and agricultural interests. It was asking too much of them. By choosing the unofficial members to represent interests in the Council, by expecting them to be consulted, Taylor created within the system itself the opportunities for the large property holders to influence the decisions of the crown colony administrators. When one also takes into account that these men, for the most part, could be expected to share the general opinions which the local oligarchies had about the society, it is not surprising that crown colony government failed to live up to the large claims Taylor made on its behalf in 1865.

It was easier to establish a relatively efficient administration than to be both an impartial administrator and the protector of the blacks. It was impossible to prepare a people for responsible government and democratic politics by surrounding foreign administrators with propertied men, elected on a restricted franchise, and able to exercise a veto on expenditure. That was the way to teach sterile and irresponsible politics.

There is no doubt about the accomplishments of crown colony government. It came as close as was humanly possible to fulfilling the first of the three claims made on its behalf. Grant established the administrative apparatus of a modern state. Old departments were made more efficient, new ones were created. Rational procedures for the administration of the country's finances were introduced; detailed estimates of revenue were prepared, debts funded, taxes collected. New courts were established to dispense justice to the poor. Abandoned land was declared forfeited to the Crown, and squatters were given titles. The public system of elementary education was started. So too was the public medical service. Roads and bridges were built.

This list tells us that in seven years Grant did most of the things which the society needed since 1838, but had not done for itself. It is perhaps an exaggeration to say that emancipation created the state. But it may serve to emphasize the limited nature of public responsibilities before emancipation. The sessions of the House of Assembly during the period of slavery were the occasions when the slave-masters met to treat with the King and to settle a few matters of mutual concern. Whatever else was needed each master provided within his own domain. At emancipation one function was formally taken from him; that of judging and punishing the labourers on his estate. The Act of Emancipation specifically enjoined him to his other functions. He was to continue to provide the apprentices with the traditional services. He successfully flouted the act. He found ways to judge and to punish, and to withdraw the services he had provided.

The British at first paid for justice and education. In neither case was the service adequate, but that it was provided at all was a great boon to the newly emancipated population. When the British stopped paying, the masters, still in control of the public purse, left the services to volunteers; education to the churches and justice to themselves. The cholera epidemics forced them to spend large sums of money, but when it was over Jamaica was still without a public health service. So up to 1865 the state had barely acknowledged its responsibility to provide services for the whole society.

The British government lectured the Assembly on its duties to the society. The Assembly invariably replied that the economy ruined by emancipation and free trade could not afford public services. Is it then to the lack of means rather than to the absence of will that we must look for an explanation? The state of the economy may well have explained wide disparities in the public expenditure for services, between one year and the next. But what has to be explained is not uneven expenditure from year to year, for it was not the case, but the pittance spent on some things and the large sums spent on others, between 1838 and 1865. Compare for instance the total sum spent on education to that spent on immigration.

The explanation lies in the belief of the planters that widespread education was against their interest since it would quickly reduce the numbers of those willing to labour on estates. Moreover, they were convinced that the state had one responsibility above all others. And that was to keep the sugar estates in existence. The priority thus accorded sugar over welfare services was justified by equating the private interests of estate owners with the public interests of the state. Sugar was the revenue, and the revenue was sugar. No sugar, no revenue, no public services.

It is to Grant's credit that he challenged the assumptions which made this reasoning plausible. The failure of his successors in office and of their superiors in the Colonial Office to construct alternative bases for economic development was in great measure due to their acceptance of this reasoning as correct. The most important economic event of the last century, the export trade in bananas owed nothing to crown colony government. But the country was fortunate that the trade was so firmly established by the eighteen-nineties when sugar prices steeply declined.

However inadequate we judge the explanation that the Assembly gave for its neglect of the interests of the whole society before 1865, there is a connection between the export economy and the public welfare services. Where so much of the revenue came from import duties, the revenues were affected by the decline in imports which followed whenever the value of exports was reduced. When world market conditions for sugar and other products deteriorated, it was bananas and other fruit which prevented a disastrous decline in the revenue.

Eisner calculates that public expenditures between the end of the eighteen-sixties and the beginning of the nineteen-thirties rose seven-fold on health, eight-fold on public works and twenty-four times on education. It may also be appropriate to notice that from Eisner's calculations it does not seem that the expenditure on education or on health was ever steadily above 10% of the expenditure during the crown colony period up to 1930.

We have acknowledged what was done; we must now estimate its worth to the society. First we consider the machinery of administration; the claim that the system would be rationalized and made more efficient was fulfilled, but without wishing to deny what was accomplished, its limits are suggested by two comments. The efficiency of crown colony government, particularly during its first period when it shone by comparison with the inefficiency of representative government, need not overawe us. It was the inability of the Colonial Office to tell exactly where the finances of Jamaica stood in 1882 which led to the appointment of the Royal Commission of that year. Secondly, efficiency was attained by concentrating all power of making decisions in the hands of the Colonial Secretary.

So the price paid for the advance in administration, was centralization and paternalism. Almost certainly any reforming government would have centralized administration in the capital; but one *which* had its roots in the country would not have perpetuated the ascendancy of the Colonial Secretary and the Colonial Secretariat. As a device to bring order out of near chaos, the institution may have been necessary in the years after 1866 but if the functionaries of crown colony government had taken seriously their professed intention of working towards its death, authority would have been dispersed, at least after 1884.

Equally damaging to the society was the practice of appointing foreigners as heads of departments long after there had been time to train natives for these posts. In most cases it was simply alleged that natives with the qualities required were not available but for some posts, such as that of Chief Justice and that of Attorney General, it was argued that natives were not desirable in the interest of justice.

In general we may conclude that the price paid for administrative efficiency was high. In 1865 the high posts in the administration were no longer the preserve of white natives and during most of crown colony government such posts were reserved for white foreigners. Paternalism and the social importance of a white skin were still characteristic of the society in 1865 although these values were by then no longer sacrosanct. By restoring whiteness as a necessary quality for jobs at the top of the administration, crown colony government reinforced the racial prejudices inherent in the society.

Secondly, we consider the services provided through the administrative machinery. For most of the period the British adhered to the principle that a crown colony could have all the services its revenues could afford. Within these limits it was left to individual governors to divide the cake. The society benefitted from the public services in at least three ways; Jamaica became a more orderly and law abiding, a more healthy and less isolated society after 1865.

The administration of justice during crown colony government restored the confidence of the poor in the court as a place where they might expect a fair trial in a dispute between unequal contenders. They preferred to use the District Courts presided over by foreigners rather than go before the native justices in courts of petty sessions. However the weaknesses of crown colony government are apparent; there was not enough trained justices, those in offices were overworked and with the consequent delay in hearing cases and increased cost of seeking justice. Moreover there was no sustained examination of the substance of the law administered, nor of the extent of the punishment inflicted on the guilty. From time to time administrators in the Colonial Office had good intentions, but here as elsewhere these remained on paper. For instance against its better judgement the Colonial Office sanctioned flogging as part of the punishment for praedial larceny in response to local demand.

The building of roads and bridges gradually connected isolated communities. For a long time even the coastal towns had depended on communication by sea; the network of roads not only made it easier for some small settlers to market their crops, it also made possible the growth of that feeling of oneness which later served as the basis for nationalism. If less was done to open up the country than was possible, it was because peasant agriculture remained the unattended step-child of crown colony government, land settlements notwithstanding.

The impetus for much that was attempted came from the report of the Royal Commission of 1897. In urging the British government to establish a department of Economic Botany in the West Indies, they commented that 'the cultivator of one product is often quite ignorant of the best means of cultivating any other, and does not know whether his soil and climate might be better adapted for something else. These remarks have special reference to the small cultivators, but they are not wholly inapplicable to persons interested in the larger estates'. The Imperial Department of Agriculture was established and the local department of agriculture was enlarged, but the money spent on the crops of the small cultivator, the time and energy spent on his problems, were as nothing compared to what was lavished on estate agriculture.

Thirdly, we consider how far crown colony government achieved the other aims it set itself. The claim that it would provide impartial government and protect the interests of the poor and ignorant, can be stated as a promise to bring the society into equilibrium. Then when the contending classes were in equipoise crown colony government would come to an end. During the time when the poor were being developed and the rich restrained, the whole society would have learned the style of responsible politics appropriate to a free society.

The British failed to live up to claims made in a moment of hubris. British civil servants temporarily stationed in a foreign society, were supposed, without check, to adequately protect the interests of the poor and ignorant. They did not. This was not because they did not care, but because they should not have been expected to care so much. They were not subjected to pressure on behalf of the poor while the nominated and elected unofficial members effectively lobbied in their own interest. When the early vision had faded, the major concern of crown colony government became to avoid another riot. By rioting in 1938 the poor and ignorant wrote their own epitaph on the system. It did not bring two unequal social groups into equilibrium; it reinforced the dominance of the power of wealth and frustrated the thrust of the power of numbers.

Although the British failed in large measure to be impartial administrators and to protect the interest of the poor and to teach the society responsible politics, even here they achieved a measure of success. What the gain was to the society is difficult to assess, but bits of evidence suggest that some of the poor were persuaded of their impartiality between contending classes.

One bit of evidence comes from a memorandum submitted to the 1882 Royal Commission by a group who claimed to speak on behalf of the 'hundreds of the negro inhabitants of Kingston and its neighbourhood'. They said among other things that they were 'fully conscious that without the protection of the government our fellow colonists would not permit us to enjoy the breath we breathe'. The document is redolent of the belief that their enemy was the white and brown propertied class who controlled the island since slavery. The relevant question is how widespread were these opinions among the black population? The literary sources known to us do not say.

So we now only suggest that the opinions expressed in the document to the 1882 Royal Commission seem to make sense of the campaign and the results of the 1944 election. The party which made the immediate goal bread rather than independence, and which made the enemy the propertied class rather than the British, may have owed its victory in part to an appeal which was in harmony with the beliefs of a large portion of the electorate. The electorate may have been mistaken in identifying the party led by the professional men with the propertied class, but if so it was a natural mistake for them to make in the circumstances of the island's history. The slogan 'self-government is slavery', whatever it may have meant to those who used it, echoes the voice of 1883, 'without the protection of the government our fellow colonists would not permit us to enjoy the breath we breathe'. And it may well be that those to whom it was addressed took it to mean more than those who used it ever intended.

So at the end of 1944 the upward thrust of the power of numbers which had been stopped at the end of 1865, reasserted itself. It would please us to add that the thrust now took a form which showed the benefits that had accrued to the poor from eighty years of crown colony government. But of that there is no sign. They voted, as they might well have voted in 1866, in their own interest. How much had they learnt of democratic politics and of responsible government in the interval? One test is that they voted into power a party to whom the forms and nuances of parliamentary democracy were alien. The apprenticeship in responsible government may well have started for the society in 1838 or 1866 or 1884. It only began in 1945.

The Government of Freedom

David Scott

Time is still waiting in the heart of the oldest lands
in spite of a victory
of man over slavery that seems more legendary than true.
And in the desert of culture
the wind or earthquake comes and tumbles
the patience of history, the tribe or woman who is forgotten
but remembers her own bitter love like a far distant sail
in the darkening west.
(Wilson Harris, "Spirit of the Labyrinth")

THE DARKENING WEST

Reading and writing after Michel Foucault it is scarcely a controversial matter to assert that the investigation of the past ought to be connected to questions derived from the present. This, after all, is the now familiar idea of a history of the present. Such histories are concerned to destabilize the seeming naturalness or inevitability of the present, to show the ways in which the present is in fact assembled contingently and heterogeneously. They are concerned, in short, to historicize the present, in order to enable us to act—and act *differently*—upon it. But while this Foucauldian idea may now be more or less axiomatic, what is still not thought through often enough is that one implication of so understanding the theoretical project of historical (or genealogical) investigation is that alterations *in the present* we inhabit ought to urge us to alter the questions through which the past is made a resource for contemporary intellectual reflection. If, in other words, what we want the past to illuminate for us ought to be guided by the task of understanding the predicament in which we find ourselves, then as that predicament itself alters what we ask the past to yield up to us has also to alter. Surely the project of writing histories of the present, if they are not to be merely academic exercises, ought to hang on some such focus on a *changing present.*

Now, clearly, one of the conceptual-ideological fields in which the Foucauldian exercise of writing histories of the present has been pursued with much sophistication in recent years is the field of the recharacterization of colonialism. This exercise has indeed constituted an important strategy in postcolonial criticism. Part of the critical point of these exercises has been to demonstrate (against the claims of, say, liberal-rationalist historiographies, or Eurocentric ones) the hegemonic persistence into the post-colonial present of aspects of colonialist discourse and practice. I do not doubt the importance of these moves; indeed they have been enormously enabling in my own work.[1] However, the protagonists of these revisionist efforts (myself included) seem to have taken it for granted that we already *know* under (or in relation to) what general description *of the present* these recharacterizations of the colonial past are supposed to perform their labor of criticism. So that while the colonial past's supposed transparency is subjected to a searching skepticism, and meticulously scrutinized and deconstructed, the self-evidence of the postcolonial present is assumed and stands unexamined, indeed unproblematized. One consequence of this is that it always remains unclear exactly what demand in the present these historiographical strategies are being mobilized to meet, and therefore there is no way to judge whether in fact they are adequately doing so.

In the last decade or so, one of the questions that has acquired a new cognitive-political resonance and a new ideological salience for the present is the question of freedom. Indeed, "freedom" is one of the defining watchwords of the so-called New World Order which, supposedly, has come into being with the end of the cold war. Freedom, so we are told, has finally, after a long and difficult ordeal in the struggle with its totalitarian adversaries of the Left and Right, assumed its proper place as the supreme value, acknowledged and unchallenged, not only in the local history of Western culture, but in the History of Culture as such. The force of this story of our time is evident in the fact that the new discourse of freedom has reorganized the very context of cultural-historical and ethical-political debate, and in doing so has reorganized the old distinction between conservatives and radicals, between progressives and reactionaries. But even if we have to acknowledge the force of the historical claim that neo-liberalism's freedom has hegemonized contemporary global politics, and even if we cannot now *not* write from within a present marked by this transformation, do we need to embrace it *normatively?* This is the question. For those of us who are skeptical of the claims of the protagonists of the "liberal revolution" and of democracy's "third wave"[2] surely the present also exerts a counter-demand, namely the demand to problematize precisely the seeming transparency of these normalized claims to the self-evidence of freedom.

This is the challenge that Thomas Holt has taken up in his remarkable study of the problem of slave emancipation in colonial Jamaica. In the course of introducing this study, Holt reflects in the following way on the link between the historical matters that constitute the focal object of his investigation and the contemporary intellectual-political predicament that frames the conceptual problematic through which his questions emerge as visible questions of moment.

> This study grew out of, is connected with, and was partly formed by the concerns of my historical present—the decade of the 1980s. That amazing decade began with the election of Ronald Reagan to the American presidency; it ended with the collapse of communism in Eastern Europe and the threat of its collapse in the Soviet Union itself. Reagan's simple and forceful message was that the best policy was to let the market govern social relations and that those who did not make it in modern America had only themselves to blame. Thus, while in contemporary usage Democrats claimed the liberal label, Reagan and his modern conservative allies took up many of the essential elements of the original nineteenth-century liberalism, which differs from the so-called advanced liberalism of the late nineteenth-century.

Reagan's seemingly new and fresh approach had a powerful appeal, especially to people looking for respectable ways to evade the failure of American society to satisfy the basic needs of large sectors of its population. It is not irrelevant to the composition of this book that the 1980s were a period when the gap between rich and poor grew wider and racial tensions and despair grew worse. At the same time, self-determination and free enterprise were conflated in public discourse, and democracy and capitalism became synonyms.[3]

Holt's work is staged on this connection between slave emancipation and the *contemporary* predicament of freedom. It is the latter, in fact, that gives to the historical problem of the former its compelling significance.

As I understand him, Holt wants to make it impossible for us to buy the seeming transparency of contemporary liberalism's self-congratulatory story of freedom, particularly the claim that the "free market" is the neutral space of impartiality and equality, especially for those—like peoples of African descent in the New World—who have historically been objects of modern forms of systematic discrimination. He seeks to do this by exposing the contradiction—between freedom and constraint, autonomy and authority—that on his view is internal to, and constitutive of, liberalism as such. For Holt, liberalism is not what it takes itself to be in its autobiography—i.e., the unceasing extension of individual freedom. To the contrary, in his reading the story of liberalism is the story of the simultaneous extension/ containment and expansion/contraction of freedom. And what is illuminating for Holt about British slave emancipation is that in it, liberalism's constitutive contradiction stands out in sharp relief—and stands out, moreover, in the register of race.

In this chapter I will examine the story Holt tells about the problem of black freedom in post-emancipation Jamaica. I want to worry about the kind of historiographical project into which it is inserted—the politico-theoretical demand in the postcolonial present to which it takes itself to be responding—and to consider whether the conception of freedom that supports his argument is one with a continuing warrant, a continuing critical purchase in the postcolonial present. It is here that the whole question of what I will call the "government" of freedom is to be posed. I will employ this Foucauldian notion to rethink our assumptions about "freedom" and to urge a different conceptualization of "the problem of freedom" in post-emancipation Jamaica than the one urged by Holt. I should make it clear, however, that I do not intend in this exercise to offer even a partial rewriting of this post-emancipation history. The labor I offer is of another kind, one both more and less than such a history might purport to be. What I intend to offer is a reconsidered conceptual terrain upon which that history might be written. It is more in the sense that it seeks to be a critical inquiry into the assumptions through which the claims of history are made intelligible; it is less because it does not suppose itself to be a substitute for such a history, but only a recurrently necessary preface to it.

I shall begin elsewhere, however, with a different telling of the story of slavery and freedom than the one Holt offers, though arguably one as concerned as his is with the present from which he writes, and one that crosses many of the same intellectual debates. I am thinking of the work of Orlando Patterson.

FREEDOM IN THE AUTOBIOGRAPHY OF WESTERN CULTURE

It is not an exaggeration to say that Orlando Patterson has, over the course of an immensely productive career, been almost single-mindedly preoccupied with the problem—perhaps I should say, with the value—of freedom. One can trace, through all his major works (of both fiction and nonfiction), a relentless thematization of the value of freedom.[4] Recall, for example, the way he uses Albert Camus's *The Rebel* to stage the existential scenario with which he closes the otherwise academic prose of *The Sociology of Slavery.* Patterson is endeavoring to explain how it is that slaves who had been born into slavery and who therefore had never known freedom (i.e., creole slaves) could nevertheless have desired it so fervently as to give their lives for it. He has in mind, of course, the greatest of all slave rebellions in British colonial Jamaica, the so-called Christmas Rebellion of 1831/32 led by Sam Sharpe.

> What then, accounts for the presence of this need which seems to survive under conditions which in every way conspire to smother it? Every rebellion, Camus has written, "tacitly invokes a value". This value is something embedded deep in the human soul, a value discovered as soon as a subject begins to reflect on himself through which he inevitably comes to the conclusion that "I *must* become free—that is, that my freedom must be won". In the final analysis it is the discovery of this universal value which justifies and stimulates the most tractable of slaves to rebel.[5]

On my reading of Orlando Patterson, everything follows from this central paradox of the birth of the desire for freedom in the breast of the slave. All of his mature work has been an attempt to give an historical-sociological account—to form a theoretical understanding—of this animating paradox. I do not agree with the argument Patterson develops; in my view the story he ends up telling turns out to be an autobiographical account of Western culture's self-image of freedom. However, there is something of fundamental importance for us in the *itinerary* of Patterson's preoccupation, something that has to do with his pursuit of that question that animates him, the internal—dialectical—connection between slavery and freedom.

To get at his existentially defined question—How could a slave who had never known freedom nevertheless conjure up the desire for it, and formulate an idea of it?—Patterson feels constrained to pose and pursue a prior and more fundamental question, namely, what, in its essentials, is slavery? His second major book, *Slavery and Social Death,* is an attempt to give an answer to this question. Slavery, he says, is to be defined as "a permanent, violent domination of natally alienated and generally dishonored persons."[6] But even as he pursued that question of the fundamental definition of slavery, the original question of freedom forced itself into his preoccupations.

> It has been my objective to come to a definitive statement of the fundamental processes of slavery, to grasp its internal structure and the institutional patterns that support it. Throughout this work, however, the ghost of another concept has haunted my analysis....That is the problem of freedom. Beyond the socio-historical findings is the unsettling discovery that an ideal cherished in the West beyond all others emerged as a necessary consequence of the degradation of slavery and the effort to negate it.

The first men and women to struggle for freedom, the first to think of themselves as free in the only meaningful sense of the term, were freedmen. And without slavery there would have been no freedmen.

We arrive at a strange and bewildering enigma: are we to esteem slavery for what it has wrought, or must we challenge our conception of freedom and the value we place upon it?[7]

Or as he put it at the beginning of the book that followed this one, *Freedom in the Making of Western Culture:*

Originally, the problem I had set out to explore was the sociohistorical significance of that taken-for-granted tradition of slavery in the West. Armed with the weapons of the historical sociologist, I had gone in search of a man-killing wolf called slavery; to my dismay I kept finding the tracks of a lamb called freedom. A lamb that stared back at me, on our first furtive encounters in the foothills of the Western past, with strange, uninnocent eyes. Was I to believe that slavery was a lamb in wolf's clothing? Not with my past. And so I changed my quarry. Finding the sociohistorical roots of freedom, understanding its nature in time and context, became my goal.[8]

The project of this book, then, is an attempt to show the intimate interconnection between slavery and freedom as values, and the theoretical implications that follow from this. The basic argument is that the value of freedom was historically generated out of the experience of slavery. People, he says, came to value freedom, "to construct it as a powerful shared vision of life, as a result of their experience of, and response to, slavery or its recombinant form, serfdom, in their roles as masters, slaves, and nonslaves."[9]

Whether or not you are persuaded by the details of Patterson's argument there is a significant achievement here. Patterson has situated the institution and ideology of slavery in its widest possible sociohistorical context—not merely in the social history of capitalism, or of the West, but of humanity as such—and by so doing has helped to make the point that slavery anywhere cannot ever be taken as a merely marginal, local practice. So that those Jamaican slaves in Montpelier, St. James, with whom he begins his scholarly career can no longer be seen as isolated characters in a minor drama in a no-longer-consequential colony. For in his narrative they now take their place as central characters in the much larger story of the rediscovery—out of their own historical conditions— of a fundamental transhistorical human value: the value of freedom. This is the scope of Patterson's existential humanism.

There is, too, a compelling moral at work here, namely, that our most cherished and elevated ideals are often born out of our most debased institutions and practices. Patterson is an unremitting dialectician. His project has been to gift to Hegel the benefit of a professional historical sociology.

The history of freedom and its handmaiden, slavery, has bruited in the open what we cannot stand to hear, that inhering in the good we defend with our lives is often the very evil we most abhor. In becoming the central value of its secular and religious life, freedom constituted the tragic, generative core of Western culture, the germ of its genius and all its grandeur, and the source of much of its perfidy and its crimes against humanity. On both the secular and religious levels, its separate elements remained yoked in continuous, creative tension within themselves, and with each other, each at once good and evil, bearing the dread mark of its birth and the glow of its possibilities.[10]

But it is here that Patterson unfortunately joins the chorus of voices that take the West as a sort of historical plateau. "Individually liberating, socially energizing, and culturally generative, freedom is undeniably the source of Western intellectual mastery, the engine of its extraordinary creativity, and the open secret of the triumph of Western culture, in one form or another, over the other cultures of mankind."[11] But is this uncontroversially so? Whatever the virtues of Western culture—and no doubt there are such virtues—why are these to be taken uncritically as spelling out the best form of human flourishing? Leaving aside the large question of whether we buy Patterson's account of Western freedom, what of other virtues sheltered by other forms of life, in other traditions of human society—the virtues of courage, civic activism, social justice, or self-government? Part of the problem with Patterson's argument, in other words, is that while it claims to be an historical sociology what he is really doing is inscribing the story of slavery and freedom into a Universal History. This is why Thomas Holt's *The Problem of Freedom* provides a useful contrast.

LIBERALISM'S SLAVE EMANCIPATION

The Problem of Freedom is constructed as an intervention in the historiography of New World slave emancipation. It is, I think, an immensely important intervention. I want to say why I think this is so, and why also, in the end, I have a doubt about the *purchase* of the story he tells for the postcolonial conjuncture we inhabit.[12]

The question that has preoccupied modern historians concerned with the issue of slavery abolition in the British Caribbean is: What prompted the timing of its occurrence? Was slavery abolition the consequence of humanitarianism (the story of the rise, in the last decade and a half of the eighteenth century, of an organized abolitionism that captured the moral imagination of the British public and forced the hand of Parliament); of economics (the story that capitalism first encouraged slavery and then, when it began to impede further development, helped to destroy it); or of slave resistance (the story that were it not for the radical agency of the slaves themselves, especially the creole slave rebellions of the first decades of the nineteenth century—Barbados in 1816, Demerara in 1823, and Jamaica in 1831/32—the British Parliament would not have acted when it did)? Or what combination among these, or balance between them, is responsible for the timing of freedom? There is now a multi-volume archive of important historical work that addresses itself to the professional debate over these questions.[13] What interests me here, however, is not the empirical merit of one or another of these interpretive positions—how the historical evidence stacks up on one side as opposed to another—or whether (to use Collingwood's terms) the answers provided by one or another hermeneutic constitute logically appropriate answers to their underlying questions. Rather, what interests me is what I might call the political unconscious of the problem-space in which these interpretive apparatuses operate/operated. The question for me is not who got it right but what cognitive-political demand set the discursive conditions in which the interpretative questions as such were formulated, and whether this demand continues to exercise a legitimate claim on us. This is a *strategic* question. It is concerned with understanding the extent to which the questions in relation to which we have fashioned our practices of criticism continue to be questions worth having new answers to *in any given conjuncture*. When, for instance, in the 1930s and 1940s respectively, C.L.R. James and Eric Williams challenged the hitherto hegemonic Whig story that British colonial slavery was brought down by William Wilberforce, Thomas Clarkson, and the other "Saints" sensitizing the British conscience to the evils of plantation slavery, there was more at stake than the professional academic question of the proper weighing of the facts.[14] There was a crucial cultural-politics of the contemporary colonial present at stake. Both Williams and James were, in effect, writing nationalist, anticolonial histories: Williams, a liberal-nationalist history, and James a nationalist-liberationist one.[15]

In other words, the critical purchase of these antihumanitarianist versions of the story of slavery abolition has depended upon an anticolonial nationalist/liberationist demand to demonstrate the falseness of Europe's humanity (its hollow patronizing racism) and to set against that falseness the fullness and the legitimacy of the humanity of the colonized. The anti-colonial story's critical purchase has depended upon the nationalist/liberationist demand to secure the view that far from being the self-present agents of Universal History that they took themselves to be, Europe was obliged by the hitherto denied agency of the slaves themselves to accede to a new history. In short, that story of resistance and heroism— of slaves making their own history—has been crucial to the self-image of the emergent new nations, the legitimacy and dignity of whose sovereignty has not had the historical privilege of self-evidence. My own suspicion, though, is that there is not much more that this particular story of resistance and agency can yield because the postcolonial present does not offer a problem-space shaped by a nationalist/liberationist demand.

Holt wants to displace the centrality of these animating questions: What are the true causes of abolition? What is the appropriate weight to give to economics, humanitarianism, and slave resistance? While clearly sympathetic to the critique of Eurocentrism implied in Williams (and James, too, I imagine, though he is not named in this connection), Holt wants to redirect our attention to another issue.[16] What he wants to understand is this: What forces shaped the British government policymaker's perception of the alternatives to slavery and of how to achieve those alternatives?[17] Holt is interested, then, not so much in what the causes of abolition were, as in what went into the making of emancipation; not whether freedom was taken or given, but what the ideological materials were out of which freedom was constructed. With this shift the whole shape of the *kind* of social history of slave emancipation available to be written alters. Essentially it enables Holt to frame a story with a different set of preoccupations—one that examines the moral and political assumptions that underpinned the design and implementation of the project of emancipation. This, in turn, enables him to link the story of slave emancipation to the much larger story of liberalism, indeed to implicate deeply the project of the one in the conceptual-institutional claims of the other. So that the story of slave emancipation has now to be read as a central episode in the story of the social and political forms of modern power. Formulated in this way the story of race and freedom that shapes liberalism's slave emancipation can be connected to the story of race and freedom that shapes liberalism's present. I fully endorse this move. The question for me, however, is whether the *particular* story of liberalism Holt tells is the most adequate one for the present we inhabit. Or, to put it another way, in displacing the animating questions of an older radical-abolitionist problematic, does Holt manage to displace the nationalist/liberationist narrative in which they were posed?

The Problem of Freedom is the story of a slave emancipation conceived and delivered in liberalism's name. The "liberal awakening"[18] of the first decades of the nineteenth century and its political victory in the Reform Act of 1832 constitute the discursive space in which the formal "problem" of slave emancipation was given shape and articulated in colonialist discourse. Liberalism, in other words, provided the basic political and economic vocabulary—of rights, of individual autonomy, of interests, of the market, etc.—out of which the British colonial policymakers fashioned the Emancipation Act and imagined the transformation of a slave economy and society into a free one.

Holt's story of British slave emancipation is framed by Eric Hobsbawm's famous concept of the "dual revolutions"—economic and political, Industrial and French—that are the defining coordinates of the long European nineteenth century.[19] The "dual revolutions" constitute the defining coordinates of the new conception of "individual freedom" that emerged in this period. Holt's concern here is to highlight the social and historical character of liberal freedom in two important senses: first, to suggest the historical novelty of the liberal idea of the individual, of a disembodied, self-possessed individual whose social relations were essentially contractual and entered into voluntarily on the basis of a rationally deduced self-interest; and second, to elaborate the internal paradox of liberal freedom that consists in the impossibility of reconciling economic and political freedoms. As Holt argues, capitalist society required for its justification formal equality in rights yet inherently generated class differences in effective rights, powers, and possessions. Freedom defined by capitalist market relations "inevitably produces unequal class relations which undermines the substantive freedom of most members of the society. On the other hand, the freedom defined by civil and political institutions—to the extent that society is democratic and egalitarian—must threaten an economic system based on inequality."[20] Consequently, he goes on, though theoretically conjoined, "the dual revolutions rushed down two separate, mutually incompatible courses: the economic demanded greater scope for individual expression; the political required greater constraint."[21] Holt's point here is that this contradiction is constitutive of liberalism; and the history of liberalism, therefore, is the history of the unfolding of this internal contradiction.

For Holt, this contradiction internal to liberalism is crucial to an understanding of British slave emancipation inasmuch as the dual revolutions constituted the discursive frame within which the freedom of the slave was conceived. This is because the fundamental problem for British colonial policymakers and planters alike was how simultaneously to free the slaves and maintain the central features of the old social, economic and political order. The several proposed emancipation schemes—those of Henry Taylor, Henry Grey, Edward Stanley, and James Stephen—tilted on this dilemma. They all, to one degree or another, defended the right of the ex-slave to formal legal equality and rights. As Holt says:

All four rejected racist interpretations of slave behavior and insisted that blacks shared the basic, innate traits of other human beings, that is, that all human beings could be motivated by self-interest and the desire for self-improvement. This was the mainspring of social action in a rationally ordered society. They were committed to laissez faire, though to differing degrees. Artificial and arbitrary constraints on the free exercise of self-interested behavior must be removed to ensure an efficient and productive economy.[22]

At the same time, however, since a ready supply of cheap, continuous labor was the overriding concern of the plantation economy, it was understood that essential elements of the social order and its power structure were to be maintained. "They would be free, but only after being resocialized to accept the internal discipline that ensured the survival of the existing social order. They would be free to bargain in the marketplace but not free to ignore the market. They would be free to pursue their own self-interest but not free to reject the cultural conditioning that defined what that self-interest should be. They would have opportunities for social mobility, but only after they learned their proper place. This at least was the intent of the British policymakers who framed and implemented emancipation."[23]

Holt's point I think is clear. British slave emancipation was organized around a certain economy: the problem of the extension and containment of freedom. On this account, British colonial policy toward Jamaica between 1838 and 1938 constituted a series of departures, each of which sought simultaneously to extend and to contain freedom. Of the departures that came in the wake of the labor revolt of 1938 he writes:

But again, as in 1838, the policy and its ideological analogue sought to embed dependence within independence, to confine self-determination within vaguely defined, non-threatening limits. As in 1838, what was envisioned was a "freedom" drained of the power of genuine self-determination: materially, a freedom stripped of control over basic material resources; ideologically, a freedom that internalized its own antithesis. After a century-long struggle for freedom, Afro-Jamaicans confronted new forces on new terrain, yet the fundamental structure of the contest—the combatants, the ideological content and discourse—remained much the same.[24]

The success or failure of the liberal project of emancipation hangs on this tension. The problem of liberalism's freedom is that the freedoms it extends are invariably limited and are moreover "drained" or "stripped" of real content. And the moral point of the story is that slavery emancipation failed and this failure was not fortuitous. To the contrary, as Holt says, this failure "was not so simple a matter as a wish by the powerful not to see it succeed, or errors of judgment or policy. Something was amiss in the very project of emancipation, in the very premises on which it was founded. And those premises appeared to be linked to its outcomes and to the extreme racism that followed in its wake in the late nineteenth century."[25] The problem of race in post-emancipation Jamaica, in other words, constitutes something of a limit to the promise of liberal freedom. For Holt, in fact, it is on the horns of race that the liberal project collapses.

I have a doubt about this story. Whereas Holt has displaced the nationalist preoccupation with whether freedom was given or taken he nevertheless reproduces a story about the ultimate failure of the liberal emancipation project to confer substantive freedoms. His concern in effect is to demonstrate the failure of a liberalism that gives freedom with one hand only to take it back with the other. So that although his narrative eschews the liberal story of a steady unfolding of freedom it nevertheless treats freedom as a normative horizon. I suspect, in other words, that his narrative harbors a progressivist faith and a liberationist desire: an eschatology that envisages freedom as an overcoming, as the other side of domination, or as an end of constraining determinations.[26] I am not against normative horizons *per se,* but I doubt whether a story about slavery emancipation told in terms of success/failure and a story about freedom told in terms of extension/containment continues to offer the kind of critical purchase our postcolonial present demands. I wonder whether the anticolonial liberationist project of reading for the failure of liberalism (or indeed of the West, more generally) continues to be the reading of the colonial past most crucial to a present in which the Marxist and nationalist languages through which counter-horizons of freedom were defined and defended are no longer the options they used to be. These languages depended upon a *direction* of social emancipation and a conceptualization of sovereignty which are, at least, no longer clear. On my view the postcolonial present demands a different story, one concerned less with the *ideological* dispute between liberalism and its adversaries and more with the illumination, in a more considered and systematic way, of the conceptual-institutional space created by the reorganizing project of modern power.

This is why the Foucauldian story of "government" and its relation to modern power is useful. In his later work (as he turns his attention away from practices of modern sexuality to practices of modern politics), Foucault sketches in outline a form of power—government—that, he suggests, is intimately tied to the history of liberalism, or more properly, tied to a history of liberal political reason. The distinction is a crucial one because Foucault is not really interested in liberalism in the traditional sense of a political philosophy or a political ideology. As Graham Burchell has usefully summarized it, Foucault's approach to liberalism "consists in analyzing it from the point of view of governmental reason, that is from the point of view of the rationality of political government as an activity rather than as an institution. On this view, liberalism is not a theory, an ideology, a juridical philosophy of individual freedom, or any particular set of policies adopted by a government."[27] Rather, it is a form of political reason, a political rationality. Foucault, in other words, is concerned to illuminate something else about liberalism besides its ideological function, something about its modes of problematization and style of reasoning and about its distinctive targets, spaces, technologies, and modalities. And what is distinctive about the political reason of liberal government is that it constitutes a form of power that utilizes a range of strategies that support the civilizing project by shaping and governing the capacities, competencies, and wills of the governed. Government, in other words, is about "the conduct of conduct."

Like Holt I want to insist that freedom cannot be understood except in relation to power. But what interests me is not whether power negates freedom or empties it of real content. What interests me is how freedom is positively *shaped* by power—the shaping quality of the power that comes to reconstruct, or make over, the lives of the ex-slaves. Because Foucault is interested in how power shapes conduct, how it actively creates conditions that oblige behavior, freedom cannot appear as a desideratum, as what is left when restraint (i.e., negative power) is lifted. Rather what comes to be crucial is an understanding of the emergence of freedom as a central element in practices of rule—how, in effect, freedom has emerged as the condition and ground of political government, as well as an understanding of the conditions within which certain practices of freedom have been possible—those that have to do with the shaping and regulation of autonomy and free choice, with the emergence of a "responsibilized" liberty. As Nikolas Rose has put it, what is at stake in a Foucauldian understanding of liberal political reason is neither a matter of celebrating liberty (as a liberal might) nor of condemning it as an ideological fiction (as a Marxist might). What is at stake, rather, is understanding that "the freedom upon which liberal strategies of government depend, and which they instrumentalize in so many diverse ways, is no 'natural' property of political subjects, awaiting only the removal of constraints for it to flower forth in forms that will ensure the maximization of economic and social well-being. The practices of modern freedom have been constructed out of an arduous, haphazard and contingent concatenation of problematizations, strategies of government and techniques of regulation. This is not to say that our freedom is a sham. It is to say that the agonistic relation between liberty and government is an intrinsic part of what we have come to know as freedom."[28]

REFORM AND THE GOVERNMENT OF EX-SLAVES

How, then, do we sketch the story of liberalism in post-emancipation Jamaica from the point of view of governmentality? From the perspective of a liberalism understood not as an internally contradictory social and political philosophy or ideology but as a political rationality of rule, through what kinds of concepts would one think the history of the inscription of a liberal technology of government into the politico-institutional terrain of post-emancipation Jamaica? This is what interests me.

The moral-political question that confronted the construction of liberal mentalities of government consisted in this: How can a set of conditions be contrived such that the governed pursue ends that are only of value if pursued voluntarily? The liberal art of government depends, as Burchell suggests, upon the governed adopting "particular practical relations to themselves in the exercise of their freedom in appropriate ways." It thus depends upon an ensemble of governmental institutions that oblige or promote a *rational* and *responsible* self-conduct—"the promotion in the governed population of specific techniques of the self around such questions as, for example, saving and providentialism, the acquisition of ways of performing roles like father or mother, the development of habits of cleanliness, sobriety, fidelity, self-improvement, responsibility and so on"; in a word: reform.[29] Central to the political rationality (and political vocabulary) of nineteenth-century liberalism was the project of reform.

Now "reform" cannot be understood as merely the hoped-for end of liberal ideology and liberal policy, the naturalized horizon of a Universal History. It is important to detach the problem of reform from the normative liberal-progressivist narrative in which it is typically located. Reform has to be understood, rather, as central to modern power, to modern forms of political rationality. In this sense the problem of reform is connected to the construction of a certain kind of knowledge (a rationalist, universalist knowledge), a certain kind of division of social-institutional space (the secular/religious, state/civil society divisions), a certain kind of historical understanding (a teleological and progressivist history), and a certain kind of subject (a self-improving one). In other words, reform depends upon a "norm of civilization"; to put it another way, reform produces the fundamental link, internal to liberal political reason, between liberty (as individual autonomy) and social and moral progress. And in the nineteenth century, it did so in the register of "character." As Stefan Collini has suggested (and as Richard Bellamy has explored fruitfully in relation to J.S. Mill, T.H. Green, and L.T. Hobhouse), the problem of "character" played a crucial role in Victorian political discourse.[30]

Character was a central issue of liberal government. As a political rationality, what reform worked on was character. Individual liberty was crucial to the liberal project not so much because of its intrinsic value but because it was understood as a necessary condition for the reforming self-improvement of character. Understood in this way, it is not a matter of the constraints reform exercises on freedom or how much freedom is left over after reform, but what kind of freedom reform positively seeks to shape. On this view, it is not reform that is central to freedom but individual freedom that is an indispensable condition of reform, a condition of the improving project of liberal reason. Read this way, the liberal project was not so much about freedom but about reform; not so much about liberty but about improvement.

Maurice Cowling, the conservative critic of liberalism's self-image, has brought this out very nicely in his discussion of the work of J.S. Mill. As he says, the emphasis in Mill's justification of freedom "is neither on its intrinsic goodness nor on any belief man may have in its natural rightness, but on the fact that a free individual is more likely than an unfree one to contribute to the higher cultivation."[31] For Mill, in other words, contrary to normative readings of him (whether dismissive Marxist readings or congratulatory liberal ones), liberalism's claim on us is not derived from the intrinsic goodness of freedom, but from the part freedom plays in what Norbert Elias would call "the civilizing process."

> [Mill's] detailed delimitation of the power of society (and government) in relation to the individual is made, not in view of the natural right of individuals to be free, but from regard to the consequence to the general interest of imposing limitations on the exercise of social pressure to conform. For natural rights Mill had as much dislike as Bentham. Pursuit of individual liberty for Mill is not by itself and without regard to its consequences, a proper end of social action. Individuals must be left as free as possible from social pressure, not because they have a *right* to consideration of this sort, but because, if they are not left free, society may find it more difficult than otherwise to achieve the ends for which it exists.[32]

And what are these "ends"? They consist in the rational cultivation of secular truths. "The demand for liberty is not the assertion of a fundamentally binding end, but the designation of a means to the end—the end of allowing men to approach as close as possible to that highest of all pleasures which comes from mental cultivation of the closest approximation possible to knowledge of what is True."[33] Reform therefore depends upon a "norm of civilization" and a division between those who are ready for citizenship and those who have to be *made ready* for it (blacks, women, the colonized, the working class). This is why it is no contradiction for Mill to declare in *On Liberty* that liberal principles only applied to "human beings in the maturity of their faculties" and therefore naturally excluded "those backward states of society in which the race itself was in its nonage." A paternalistic despotism was appropriate for them "provided the end be their improvement, and the means justified by actually effecting that end."[34] The point here, though, is not simply to dismiss Mill as a racist liberal but to grasp the political rationality at play in his argument.

From the point of view of governmentality, then, the story of slave emancipation has to be the story of the putting into place the rationalities, institutions, and apparatuses of reform (in this expanded sense of the term). It ought to be the story of how the liberal project sought to alter the existing relations of power so that power would no longer operate (primarily) directly upon the body in the service of extraction, but would seek to operate upon character through the newly emerging space of the "social" in order to construct a "responsibilized" freedom or a rationalized self-conduct. This is not to denounce the freedom won by the slaves as a sham, insufficient, or contradictory. Rather it is to urge the writing of the history of the institutional spaces upon which that freedom depended and to write the history of the relations, conditions, discourses, and practices that have shaped modern colonial freedom. It is to write the history of an alteration in the conditions of the lives of the slaves such that they would be obliged to perform their freedom not merely in the ways they chose but in "appropriate" ways, such that they would be obliged (whether they liked it or not) to become modern, to exercise modern choices, and to acquire modern habits and tastes.

This project of colonial reform itself, however, has also to be understood historically. Colonial liberalism itself, as Holt rightly argues, alters across the nineteenth century. Recall that a central episode in the story he tells about the dilemma of freedom in post-emancipation Jamaica is that episode in which there is a shift in the ideological emphasis of colonial liberalism. This is a shift away from the Glenelg doctrine of the first decade of emancipation (a nonracist, civic egalitarian liberalism) to a more authoritarian, more paternalistic liberalism of the second half of the nineteenth century. On this account, the first decade of emancipation was governed by the optimistic liberal view that the freed people were to enjoy a substantive freedom: equal protection under the law, equal access to public institutions, the exercise of the franchise on the same property basis as whites. Moreover, references—implicit or explicit—to the race of the ex-slaves were to be expunged from colonial law. However, between the end of the first decade of emancipation and the middle decades of the second, there was a noticeable shift in colonial policy away from freedom and in the direction of constraint. And this constraint is articulated in terms of race. Colonial power is directed no longer at protecting the rights of freed people but at placing obstacles in the way of black political power. Over the course of these emancipation years freed people had demonstrated a desire to be their own freeholders and they had withdrawn their labor as far as possible from the control of the plantation. They were seeking, as Holt argues, not merely to be free laborers but to be a free people. For the colonial policymakers and for the planters, however, the refusal of the freed people to submit entirely to the plantation was interpreted as a regression to "African barbarism." As Holt writes:

> These years, 1844–54, constitute a transitional era in British politics, colonial policy and racial ideology; changes in all these areas stimulated new approaches to the problem of freedom. The political dimensions of that problem for British policymakers paralleled the economic: how to reconcile freedom with coercion, or more specifically, how to structure a political system in the colonies nominally consistent with liberal democratic principles, while maintaining ultimate control over black political expression.[35]

This shift is crucial to the overall story because it illustrates the claims Holt wishes to make about liberalism, namely the general claim about the constant tension between liberty and constraint, and the more specific claim that the racism that comes to define the later period was no anomaly but internal to liberalism's logic. For Holt, the crucial story about race is that black power was thwarted, blocked, constrained. Like David Goldberg in his discussion of the relation between racism and modernity, the problem of racism is framed largely in terms of power's practice of exclusion/inclusion.[36]

Without denying the importance of this story I want to suggest that there is another story about race in post-emancipation that is worth telling and that has a more critical purchase on our present. This is the story of the relation between race and the rationalities of reform. In this story it is necessary to understand the following: How does reform—the relations among power, self-interest, and character—come to depend upon a discourse of race? How was race inscribed into the social formation such that it came to be central to self-fashioning in everyday life? What we need to understand is how—through what conceptual apparatuses and through what grids of social division—we have been produced (and have produced ourselves) as the sorts of *raced subjects* we are, with the sorts of raced self-understandings we possess.

It is this story that needs to be told. This is important for our present because the contemporary postcolonial demand cannot simply be for inclusion into what colonialism has hitherto excluded us from (whether on the basis of race, class, or gender), nor can it be a matter of denouncing colonialism's (despotic, paternalistic, racist, etc.) attitude toward us. It must be a demand to understand in more profound ways than we do the cognitive-political game of power, the mentalities of rule, and the rationalities of government into which we have historically been inserted, or in which we ourselves have—however misguidedly—sought so far to play in the free exercise of our postcolonial self-conduct. From where we stand today, the problem of freedom cannot be a problem of the more or less of it, of the extension or limiting of it, or of the illusion or truth of it. If I agree with Holt that the problem of slave emancipation in Jamaica can teach us something about the problem of freedom in the modern world, that lesson is not that we have not really obtained freedom yet or that the promise of that August emancipation has been a false one. Rather it is simply that black freedom is a project, not a teleological movement in the direction of an already existing horizon. The issue today is not that we resisted colonialism or complied with it, but how the epistemological/institutional terrain on which resistance/compliance could appear as options as such was historically constructed. The issue today is not what attitudes of liberationist defiance we have struck up, but the senses in which the language through which those attitudes were constituted and its liberationist hopes embodied are governed by the normative assumptions of modernity.

To sum up, the question is, how do we think a history of the post-emancipation present, and with it the historical project of black freedom in the New World. I have not endeavored to rewrite such a history, but only to consider critically a particularly instructive telling of it—Thomas Holt's. What has interested me in large part has been the rhetorical economy of Holt's story of freedom, the conceptual protocols through which it is constructed—in a sense the politics of the kind of story he thinks ought to be told about post-emancipation Jamaica. What makes his story of special importance is not only its unsurpassed erudition and its deeply sympathetic narrative, but the connection he draws between the ideology of liberalism and the freedom of the ex-slaves. The importance of this connection hangs— as Holt himself well recognizes—on the relation between nineteenth-century classical liberalism and late twentieth-century neoliberalism; the connection hangs, in other words, on historicizing our present. The rhetorical thrust of Holt's story turns on the failure of liberal freedom, the inability of liberalism to overcome its constitutive contradiction, and in particular its giving rise to and sheltering racism. As Holt tells it, the story of liberal freedom in post-emancipation Jamaica is the story of the successive embattlement of freedom with its constituent un-freedoms.

I have offered the view that perhaps there is another story to be told about the problem of freedom in post-emancipation Jamaica, one about an alteration in the political rationality of colonial rule in which a new rationality comes to be inscribed into the cognitive-institutional terrain of social and political life, in which power seeks to operate through the shaping of conduct rather than the shaping of bodies. The central category of this rationality is reform. Liberal freedom does not exist outside of the project—and the constitutive apparatuses and technologies—of reform. Liberal freedom depends upon constructing a relation between government and governed that obliges individuals to become the "subjects of their lives," obliges them to exercise a responsible self-conduct, and this in turn depends precisely upon the "character" that an improving reform seeks to bring into being. On this reading the story of the relation between liberal reason and racism in mid to late nineteenth-century Jamaica is not (or not only) a story about the *exclusion* of blacks from access to political power on the basis of "race," but the story of the (re)organization of the rationalities, modalities, and instrumentalities through which raced subjects (and raced bodies) were constituted as such, and through which the conduct of conduct could come to articulate itself in the register of race.

Notes

1. See my *Formations of Ritual: Colonial and Anthropological Discourses on the Sinhala Yaktovil* (Minneapolis: University of Minnesota Press, 1994).
2. "Liberal revolution" is Bruce Ackerman's phrase. See his *The Future of Liberal Revolution* (New Haven: Yale University Press, 1992). The idea of a "third wave" of democracy is Samuel Huntington's. See his *The Third Wave: Democratization in the Late Twentieth Century* (Norman: University of Oklahoma Press, 1991).
3. Thomas Holt, *The Problem of Freedom: Race, Labor, and Politics in Jamaica and Britain, 1832–1938* (Baltimore: Johns Hopkins University Press, 1992), xviii–xix.

4. His three works of fiction, *The Children of Sisyphus* (Kingston: Bolivar, 1974 [1964]); *An Absence of Ruins* (London: Hutchinson, 1967); and *Die the Long Day* (New York: William Morrow and Co., 1972), center on the dialectical tension between forms of unfreedom and the desire for freedom.

5. Orlando Patterson, *The Sociology of Slavery* (Kingston: Sangster's, 1973), 282–83.

6. Orlando Patterson, *Slavery and Social Death* (Cambridge, Mass.: Harvard University Press, 1982), 13.

7. Ibid., 341–42.

8. Orlando Patterson, *Freedom in the Making of Western Culture* (London: I. B. Tauris, 1991), xiii.

9. Ibid.

10. Ibid., 402.

11. Ibid., 403.

12. For one critical appreciation of Holt's book that differs in some respects from mine, see Catherine Hall, review of *The Problem of Freedom*, by Thomas Holt, *Slavery and Abolition* 14 (April 1993): 229–32.

13. The literature is much too vast to list in full here. But see in particular the following: Roger Anstey, "Capitalism and Slavery: A Critique," *Economic History Review* 2d ser., 21 (1968): 307–20; Seymour Drescher, *Capitalism and Antislavery: British Mobilization in Comparative Perspective* (London: Macmillan, 1986); David Brion Davis, *The Problem of Slavery in Western Culture* (Ithaca: Cornell University Press, 1975); idem, *Slavery and Human Progress* (New York: Oxford University Press, 1984); Robin Blackburn, *The Overthrow of Colonial Slavery, 1776 to 1848* (New York: Verso, 1989); and James Walvin, *Questioning Slavery* (Kingston: Ian Randle Publishers, 1997).

14. I am referring to C.L.R. James, *The Black Jacobins* (New York: Vintage, 1963 [1938]); and Eric Williams, *Capitalism and Slavery* (Chapel Hill: University of North Carolina Press, 1944). For an overall view of the debate over Williams's work, see Barbara Solow and Stanley Engerman (eds.), *British Capitalism and Caribbean Slavery: The Legacy of Eric Williams* (New York: Cambridge University Press, 1987). On James's account, he was centrally involved in Williams's formulation of his argument. See "Interview with C.L.R. James," in *Kas Kas: Interviews with Three Caribbean Writers, ed.* Ian Munroe and Reinhard Sander (Austin: African and Afro-American Research Institute, 1972), 36–37.

15. This Jamesian theme of liberationist resistance would become more prominent from the late 1960s through to the 1980s. See Michael Craton, *Testing the Chains: Resistance to Slavery in the British West Indies* (Ithaca: Cornell University Press, 1982); and Richard Hart, *Slaves Who Abolished Slavery*, 2 vols. (Kingston: Institute of Social and Economic Research, 1980/85).

16. It is perhaps W.E.B. DuBois who is the nationalist/liberationist figure looming in the background of Holt's narrative.

17. Holt, *The Problem of Freedom*, 28.

18. The phrase is Elie Halévy's. See his useful history, *The Liberal Awakening (1815–1830)* (London: Ark Paperbacks, 1987 [1926]).

19. See Eric Hobsbawm, *The Age of Revolution, 1789–1848* (New York: Mentor, 1962).

20. Holt, *The Problem of Freedom*, 6.

21. Ibid.

22. Ibid., 50.

23. Ibid., 53.

24. Ibid., xxv.

25. Ibid., xix.

26. For some useful theoretical discussion, see Ernesto Laclau, "Beyond Emancipation," in his *Emancipation(s)* (New York: Verso, 1996).

27. Graham Burchell, "Liberal Government and Techniques of the Self," in Andrew Barry, Thomas Osborne, and Nikolas Rose (eds.), *Foucault and Political Reason: Liberalism, Neo-Liberalism and Rationalities of Government* (Chicago: University of Chicago Press, 1996), 21.

28. Nikolas Rose, "Governing 'Advanced' Liberal Democracies," in *Foucault and Political Reason*, 61–62.

29. Burchell, "Liberal Government," 26.
30. See Stefan Collini, "The Idea of 'Character' in Victorian Political Thought," *Transactions of the Royal Historical Society*, 5th ser., 35 (1985): 29–50; and Richard Bellamy, *Liberalism and Modern Society* (University Park: Pennsylvania State University Press, 1992).
31. Maurice Cowling, *Mill and Liberalism,* 2d ed. (New York: Cambridge University Press, 1990), 30.
32. Ibid., 41.
33. Ibid., 42.
34. J. S. Mill, *On Liberty* (Indianapolis: Hackett, 1978 [1859]), 9–10.
35. Holt, *The Problem of Freedom,* 217.
36. See David Goldberg, *Racist Culture: Philosophy and the Politics of Meaning* (Oxford: Blackwell, 1993).

ANTI-COLONIAL THOUGHT

The Role of the Black Race in the History of Civilization

Anténor Firmin

Et le génie m'indiquant du doigt les objets:
"Ces monceaux, me dit-il, que tu aperçois dans
l'aride et longue vallée que sillonne le Nil,
sont les squelettes des villes opulentes dont
s'enorgueillissait l'ancienne Éthiopie;
voilà cette Thèbes aux cent palais, métropole
première des sciences et des arts, berceau
mystérieux de tant d'opinions qui régissent encore
les peuples à leur insu."

Pointing at the objects, the genius said to me,
"This rubble, which litters the long and fertile
Nile valley, are the remains of the opulent cities
which were the pride of ancient Ethiopia.
Thereis Thebes, the city of one-hundred palaces,
pre-eminent center of the arts and sciences,
mysterious cradle of so many ideas which still rule
nations without their knowledge." **(Volney)**

1. ETHIOPIA, EGYPT, AND HAITI

In response to those who refuse to acknowledge that the Ethiopian race did play any active role at all in the historic development of our species, it suffices to evoke the existence of the ancient Egyptians. It has been possible to support the strange thesis of the original inferiority of the Black peoples as long as a willfully biased and guiltily complicit science persisted in the opinion that the *Retous* were a White race. Today, however, historical criticism has evolved to such a high degree that discerning and sincere minds are able to reestablish the truth about this extremely important point. It may no longer be possible, therefore, to close one's eyes to the light and to continue to propagate the same doctrine. In fact, the supporters of the theory of the inequality of the human races would find it very awkward to persist in their belief. It is now well known that the ancient inhabitants of the shores of the Nile were members of the Black race, and I have presented overabundant evidence in support of this fact. Let us now see what humanity owes to this race.

It is not necessary to draw up a long list of accomplishments. Students of Egyptian archeology and antiquities are aware of the pioneering and inventive role this industrious people have played in all sorts of fields. The basic technologies and manufacturing techniques that have been most useful for furthering the development of human societies were generally invented in Egypt or Ethiopia. There we find evidence for the practice of all the trades and all the professions. Never before or since has the genius for architecture reached such heights. Never before or since has a people created such magnificent art with such elementary means. The monuments of Egypt seem to challenge time in order to immortalise the memory of these Black peoples who distinguished themselves by their artistic genius. In the all-embracing light of Egypt, human imagination has created the most splendid, the most magnificent structures in the world. No sculptural tradition, no school of architecture, will ever match the boldness of the ancient Egyptian canon with its inimitable gigantic proportions and pure lines. Under the clear sky of Attica, one will find no doubt delicate and pure forms whose perfect execution imparts to the soul an ineffable impression of serenity. But this is not the majestic grandeur that both humbles the spirit and inspires a sentiment of invincible pride as one contemplates those colossal masses which the human will has shaped to its liking.

As regards the intellectual development of humanity, there is no doubt whatsoever that we owe to Egypt all the rudiments which contributed to the elaboration of modern science. The only thing that might seem foreign to Egyptian civilization is the moral evolution of the Western peoples which started with Greek philosophy and continues today, with successive crises of varying lengths and disruptive effects. But the more we understand the meaning of the ancient hieroglyphs preserved on the resilient Egyptian papyrus manuscripts or chiselled into the antique stelae and bas-reliefs, the more we become convinced of the high level of moral development achieved by the Nilotic populations of the era of the Pharaohs. We find that the same kind and humane morality, very restrained in terms of metaphysics and the supernatural, free of religious superstition, prevailed in a rudimentary form among the Black peoples of Sudanese Africa, until the invasion of Islam, a religion of which zeal is an essential and permanent characteristic.

The Greeks, who were, through the influence of Rome, Europe's educators, must have taken from Egypt the most practical principles of their philosophy, just as they have taken from her all the sciences which they cultivated and later improved with a marvelous intelligence. This can hardly be doubted, especially as we know that all the great Greek philosophers, the leading thinkers, those we might call the masters of Hellenic thought, from Thales to Plato, habitually dipped their cups into the Egyptian springs and that they all journeyed to Sesostris' homeland before setting out to propagate their doctrine. I shall not insist on the influence of Buddhism and on the impact of the thought of the Blacks of India on Oriental philosophical thought in general. This is because, on the one hand, the thesis of the historical importance of Blacks in the Hindu world has not been as clearly demonstrated as the thesis of the origin of the ancient Egyptians and, on the other hand, the civilization model of the Orient has never had a direct influence on the development of the occidental races. Whatever speculations an enthusiastic Europe did for a while weave around the Aryan myth, no scientist can insist on such an influence. It would suffice to remember the little success enjoyed by the gnostic doctrines among Westerners during the first centuries of Christianity.

Beside the ancient Ethiopian-Egyptian race, is it possible to identify another Black nation, great or small, that has directly influenced by its achievements the social evolution of the civilized peoples of Europe and America? Without succumbing to the temptation of chauvinism, I must once again return to the Black race of Haiti. It is interesting to note the extent to which this small nation made up of descendants of Africans has influenced world history since its independence. Barely a decade after 1804, Haiti played one of the most remarkable roles in modern history. The importance of Haiti's role may not be apparent to the less sophisticated minds of those who consider only the surface of phenomena and do not study the facts to elucidate their causes and consequences. Any imaginative thinker knows how small causes, or at least apparently small causes, bring about great consequences and affect the sequence of political and international events that determine the destiny of nations and their ruling institutions. An eloquent phrase or a generous and noble action sometimes has more bearing on the life of a nation than the greatest victory or the loss of the greatest battles. It is from this moral perspective that we must evaluate the great influence of the actions of the Haitian people on the events we are about to consider.

The great Simon Bolivar, the liberator and founder of five South American republics, had failed in the great project, in which he succeeded Miranda in 1811, aimed at shaking Spanish domination and making independent the huge territories that were the pride of the Catholic king of Spain. His resources and supplies having been depleted, Bolivar went to Jamaica to beg the help of England, whose representative was the governor of the island. His request for help was rejected. Desperate and without means, he decided to journey to Haiti and to appeal to the generosity of the Black Republic to solicit the help he needed to continue the liberation struggle which he had started with such remarkable vigor but which had lately stalled. That was a moment of the greatest import for a man who embodied the destiny of the whole continent of South America. Dared he hope to be successful? When the English, who had everything to gain from the fall of the colonial power of Spain, showed indifference, had he any reason to expect that an emerging nation, a weak state with a microscopic territory, still worried about its inadequately recognized independence, would join in such a perilous adventure as the one he was about to attempt? He came to Haiti perhaps with a sceptical mind. But Alexandre Pétion, the president of the western part of Haiti, welcomed him with great warmth.

With all the caution and legitimate prudence required at this delicate juncture in our national existence, the Haitian government made available to the hero of Boyaca and Carabobo all the resources he needed. Bolivar needed just about everything, and he was generously given men, weapons, and money. Pétion wished to act discretely in order to avoid upsetting the Spanish government. So the two men agreed that the men would sail stealthily as volunteers, and that no mention would ever be made of Haiti in any official statement of the government of Venezuela.

Bolivar left Haiti with the resources he needed, full of confidence in his genius and his great courage. The basic aspirations of his countrymen favored his undertaking; they were expecting, to manifest their support, only some bold move, some resolute action. So Bolivar orchestrated a heroic landing on the coast of Venezuela. After a victory over General

Morillo who tried to stop his progress, Bolivar advanced from triumph to triumph until all the Spanish troops were expelled and the independence of Venezuela was proclaimed and solemnly celebrated in Caracas.

But the great Venezuelan did not stop there. He continued his campaign with an indefatigable vigor and drive. With the celebrated victory of Boyaca, he conquered the independence of New Grenada and merged its territory with Venezuela to form the Republic of Colombia, honoring by this name the memory of the immortal Christopher Colombus. Unable to rest on his laurels, he knew no respite until he could bring the whole enterprise to its conclusion. He assisted the inhabitants of Upper Peru as they went on, with the help of the Colombians led by General Sucre, to defeat the Spanish in a decisive battle near Ayacucho. He then proclaimed the independence of the Republic of Bolivia. His victory at Junin over the Spanish troops consolidated the independence of Peru and ruined Spain's colonial power forever.

The impact of all these events on the political regime of the Iberian Peninsula is unarguable. As they fought with indomitable energy against the ascent of a French prince onto the Spanish throne and challenged Napoleon Bonaparte's pretensions to hegemony over the whole of Europe by replacing all the old dynasties with members of his own family, the *Cortés* showed that while resisting violence the Spanish people had understood the nobleness of the ideas which burst forth with the Revolution of 1789. The Constitution which they wrote in 1812 provides sufficient proof of such understanding. Then the Bourbons returned. After the imperial colossus had been overthrown by the coalition of monarchic Europe and disappeared from the scene, Ferdinand VII wished to sit on the ancestral throne, to which he was entitled by birth, without any loss of his royal privileges. Like the Bourbons of France, those of Spain took no account of the time that had gone by between the demise of their predecessors and the restoration of the monarchy. They had learned nothing; they had forgotten nothing.

Without the turmoil in the South American colonies, which liberated themselves from the Spanish yoke one after the other, the monarchy could have been powerful enough to repress all the demands for increased freedom. However, weakened by the efforts it had been forced to deploy in order to avoid the disintegration of the bleeding empire, it was powerless to do anything against an increasingly bold and demanding opposition. When the Spanish monarchy sought the help of France in 1823 to regain its privileges, the result was temporary and the repercussions superficial. This unintended consequence would later upset the very principle it was intended to safeguard by ruining totally the modicum of popularity the legitimist flag enjoyed in France.

When one follows carefully all these twists and turns of European history of that period, their cause-and-effect connections become astonishingly clear. The effects on Bolivar's heroic deeds in the shady gorges or on the burning plateaux of the Cordilleras ricocheted on the century-old institutions of Europe. The consequences of Bolivar's actions bolstered the torrent of revolutionary ideas which were then shaking with increasing force the decrepit foundations of the old regime. Throughout the Americas, it was the concept of the republic that prevailed. It was as if the New World had sensed that the ideas of liberty and equality would be the wave of the future. These ideas were believed to be indispensable to the progress of the younger generations. Thus, as the shrewd statesman prince Metternich makes clear in his *Memoirs,* one could not underestimate the significance of the successive crises experienced by all these South American countries which were opting for republican ideals. Still, with common sense and great insight, Metternich understood that there was nothing to be done and that the tide could not be turned back.

Undoubtedly there comes a specific moment when political events occur as if by destiny, regardless of our wishes. The human spirit progresses and often inspires some inner process which ultimately shakes nations and leads them to unavoidable commotions from which emerges a new era with institutions that are better suited to the times. But these events are the results of specific factors; they are produced by specific forces. We cannot neglect the least of these factors if we are to understand these events. Thus, when we consider the influence exercised by Bolivar directly on a considerable part of the New World and indirectly on European politics, we must admit that the original decision of the government of the Haitian republic to assist the great Venezuelan leader in his enterprise did morally and materially determine a whole sequence of remarkable events.

Beside this example, which is one the most beautiful actions for which the Black Republic deserves the whole world's esteem and admiration, we can say that the declaration of independence of Haiti has positively influenced the fate of the entire Ethiopian race living outside Africa. At the same time, Haiti's independence has affected the economic system and moral order of all the European powers that owned colonies. In addition, it had considerable bearing on the internal economy of all the American nations where slavery existed.

The end of the eighteenth century saw the emergence of a movement in favor of the abolition of slavery. Wilberforce, in England, and the Abbé Grégoire, in France, were two of those exemplary philanthropists who were inspired by a superior sentiment of justice and humanity in the face of the horrors of the slave trade. Raynal had predicted, in prophetic language, the end of this barbaric regime. He had foreseen the emergence of a Black genius who would destroy the colonial edifice and deliver his race from the opprobrium and debasement in which it was mired. But these were only eloquent words scattered to the four corners of the world. They moved the souls of high minded people but they could not convince those whose scepticism equalled their lack of a sense of justice, their contempt, and their greed. But when, using their own resources, the Blacks of Saint-Domingue made true these predictions which no one had wanted to believe, people started to think. Those whose faith only wanted the reassuring support of facts to become a strong conviction persevered in their principles. Those, on the other hand, whose lucidity and sense of justice were stifled by greed and pride, were shaken in their foolish complacency. Events strengthened the ones in their hopes and caused added anxiety in the others.

The actions of the Blacks of Haiti indeed offered the most complete refutation of the theory according to which the Negro was a being incapable of grand and noble actions, incapable especially of standing up to White men. The greatest military feats of the Haitian war of independence had proved the courage and energy of our ancestors. Still, the sceptics persisted in their incredulity. They conceded that these Ethiopian men, emboldened by the success of their first shots, could indeed have fought against and taken a perverse pleasure in kicking the Europeans out of the island. But these people were like children enjoying a new, and therefore attractive, game. Who could doubt that once the war was over, the former slaves, left to their own devices, would take fright at their own audacity and volunteer to be chained again by their former overseers? Could these inferior creatures maintain for two whole months an order of things in which the White man played no role and wielded no authority? The whole world scoffed at the idea that Jean-Jacques Dessalines and his comrades would want to create their own country and to rule themselves free of foreign control. These are not idly attributed opinions. Such thoughts were in fact printed in learned monographs and were widespread in Europe during the early years of Haiti's independence. Unsurprisingly then, the rulers of France, confident in the veracity of these absurd theories rooted in the belief in the inequality of the human races, kept hoping to recapture the old colony whose revenues had been such a reliable source of wealth for France. In 1814, under the provisional government of Louis XVIII, formal contacts were made with both King Henry Christophe in the North and President Alexandre Pétion in the West to propose that the island be placed again under French rule. Both Haitian leaders were offered a large sum of money and the highest possible military rank in the French king's army. Without ever losing their calm and dignity, the two leaders firmly and indignantly rejected those offers. The negotiations were conducted under the guidance of Malouet. All these facts can only considerably bolster the small republic's claim to universal respect.

In those difficult times, Haiti offered evidence of such common sense, of such intelligence in the management of its political affairs that all men of good will were impressed and had to reconsider the stupid prejudices that so many had harbored with respect to the moral and intellectual aptitudes of Black people. In just one of the Caribbean islands, Bory de Saint-Vincent writes alluding to Haiti, some of those men with a presumably inferior intellect gave more evidence of rationality than can be found in the entire Iberian Peninsula and Italy put together.[1]

Experience and observation led then to an irrefutable conclusion. The most intelligent statesmen, following the European philanthropists, came to understand that Black slavery was forever doomed. The very existence of the Black Republic was an overwhelming negation of the specious notion that served for so long to excuse slavery, namely, that Ethiopian man was congenitally incapable of behaving like a free man. Macaulay, in England, and the Duc de Broglie, in France, assumed the leadership of a new anti-slavery league. In 1831, Richard Hill, a socially prominent free man of color in Jamaica, was sent to Haiti on an observation mission and asked to report on his impressions about the country. He took note, with satisfaction but also with impartiality, of the rapid progress made by the descendants of Africans in Haiti. According to Malo, a few years earlier, in 1820, John Owen, a Protestant minister, had travelled to Haiti and observed the sudden development of the society and public administration.[2] Improved knowledge of the reality of Haiti eventually bore fruit. In 1833, England abolished slavery in all its colonies. In 1848, persuaded by the generous and courageous Victor Schoelcher, the provisional government of France decreed a similar measure and had it inserted in the country's Constitution.

As it is made convincingly clear in the excerpts from Wendell Phillips's speech [on Toussaint Louverture] quoted earlier, the example of Haiti was a determining argument in favor of the abolition of slavery in the United States. Appearances to the contrary, this big country is destined to strike the first blow against the theory of the inequality of the human races. Indeed, at this very moment, Blacks in the great federal republic have begun to play a prominent role in the politics of the various states of the American union. It seems quite possible that, in less than a century from now, a Black man might be called to head the government of Washington and manage the affairs of the most progressive country on earth, a country which will inevitably become, thanks to its agricultural and industrial production, the richest and most powerful in the world. These are not Utopian musings. We only have to to consider the increasing participation of Blacks in American society to cast aside our scepticism. Besides, we must remember that slavery in the United States was abolished only twenty years ago.

It is no exaggeration to maintain, regardless of arguments to the contrary, that the Black race has a history that is as positive and as important as the history of all the other races. Neglected and for a long time falsified by the lie that made of the ancient Egyptians a White race, that history is re-emerging at the beginning of this century. It is a history replete with facts and lessons, a history whose study is made absolutely fascinating by the significant achievements highlighted on every one of its pages.

2. THE HEART OF AFRICA

It should be evident that in the course of my demonstration I have avoided as much as possible references to known facts about the various peoples of central Africa, facts that considerably challenge whatever prejudices some people have long entertained about the supposed absolute savagery of Africans. In so doing, I have obeyed a scruple dictated by the science I love above everything. I wanted to limit myself to generally known fields where serious discussions can be conducted with evidence and verification. In this respect, even though the climate of Africa docs indeed impede in many ways the evolution of the Black populations who aspire to civilization, still it is clear that despite prevailing conditions these populations have achieved considerable progress. To evaluate their achievements fairly, it is necessary to consider their physical environment as well as the resources available to them.

Despite the debilitating heat of the tropical sun, the inhabitants of equatorial Africa are far from leading the kind of purely animal life that modern Europeans too often imagine. Their societies have not yet produced anything that would bring them glory or earn them the admiration of the civilized nations who are so difficult to impress. Still, the very nature of their societies gives reason to hope for the future. "From the heights of modern culture," writes Hartmann, "we imagine that life in the indolent land of Niger flows sterile and monotonous, like a muddy river in its muddy bed. In those highly civilized countries, where imprecise science and even ignorance are nevertheless still not uncommon, people cannot fathom that the inhabitants of the Sudan in fact live a distinct, it admittedly limited, life full of political, religious, and social activity. Psychologists must simply look into it."[3]

There is then much to challenge in all those half-learned expositions where Negroes are described as people who live only the material and vegetative lives of brutes. Indeed, the more enlightened and conscientious travellers journey in greater numbers into this Africa which remains as mysterious to us as the colossal Sphinx, the more we are gradually compelled to rectify those long accepted errors that are responsible for perpetuating the absurd theories against which I am fighting. Not only do the Negroes think and act like other human beings, in accordance with the education and training of the individual, it is also obvious that they do not live their lives in a total lack of the comfort which is indispensable to Europeans. "The towns inhabited by the Negroes," writes Louis Figuier, "could be mistaken sometimes for European towns. There is only a difference of degree between their civilization and industry and those of Europe. Towns as such are spaced out in the interior of Africa, but travellers discover new ones every day. The future perhaps will reveal to us barely suspected facts about central Africa."[4]

These words are no doubt inconsistent with Louis Figuier's earlier stated belief in the innate inferiority of the Black race. This seems to be the unassailable proof that those scientists who still lend the authority of their names to the theory of the inequality of the races do so without any reasoned conviction. There is, in these flagrant contradictions between the facts and the conclusion derived from them, the undeniable sign of a conspiracy or deep-rooted prejudice that keeps ethnographers and anthropologists from proclaiming the truth as their eyes can in fact behold it. Such is obviously the case. Those who maintain that Negroes are inferior to all the other human races know definitely that there are many Mongolian and even White nations that are a hundred times more backward than most of the peoples of central Africa. Still, to compare and contrast the races, they will persist in putting side by side the most savage among the Africans with the most cultured among the Europeans. They would pass judgment only on such false and artificial bases. It is as if the word was being spread around unchallenged, unexamined, as in a conspiracy.

But the truth is coming out, as it must. The future will show how useless would have been all those subterfuges intended to mask reality. The facts have asserted themselves with such irrefutability that it is impossible to overlook the Negro element in contemporary history. The impact of the Negro, whether positive or negative, ostensibly affects the political balance of Europe itself.

One must be patient, then, and strive to study better than before the important subject of the evolution of the human races. Consider the astonishment of travellers and explorers at finding deep inside the Black continent so many things that were thought to be the exclusive creations of European civilization. We know today that the most delicate industries, such as the manufacture of woven materials and metal works of the most exquisite and luxurious quality, are practiced there with superior taste and skill, despite the elementary tools and techniques in use. This ability to produce the most beautiful artefacts with rudimentary tools is precisely the African genius, which manifested itself with such distinction in ancient Egypt.

Most of the African languages, such as Hausa and Kanuri, are becoming increasingly supple, graceful, and grammatical idioms. It will soon be possible to create literary works in those languages, and thus to strike one final blow against some old prejudices. Meanwhile,

Arabic is used with great and admirable success by most of those peoples who are still labelled savages and given fantastical facial features, the most disgusting that could be imagined.

I will close this chapter by citing the conclusion of a study of the civilization of the Negro peoples authored by M. Guillien and presented at the International Convention of the Ethnographic Sciences (Congrés international des sciences ethnographiques) held in Paris in 1878. After analyzing all that has been written by the most qualified travellers, by such people as Caillé, Moore, Barthe, Raffenel and others, respecting public roads, industries, and trade in Africa, Guillien concludes thus:

> These data are very incomplete, and some of them have not even been proven. Nevertheless, they provide sufficient evidence that what Negroes lack is neither intelligence nor drive but, rather, culture and civilization. There is no doubt that the day is near when the ethnographers' motto, "Corpore diversi sed mentis lumine fratres," will be justified and when black-skinned men will be able to walk side by side with white-skinned men.[5]

I read such thoughts with a predictable sense of satisfaction. I am tempted to quote at length from the study to which they serve as conclusion. Meanwhile, I am particularly happy to find in Guillien's ideas a moral truth constantly overlooked by the partisans of the inequality of the races, the monogenists and religious dogmatists, namely, that one cannot proclaim the universal brotherhood of men without at the same time proclaiming their equality.

Yes, human beings can and do differ by their physical traits or the color of their skin. Yet, they are all brothers, that is to say, they are equal in intelligence and thought. Only a long process of perversion of the spirit and very powerful influences on the minds of White people could have made them overlook a truth that is so obvious and natural that it requires no scientific proof. Have such influences always existed? Are those we have already examined the only source of White people's prejudice respecting the inequality of the races? These are questions that need clear answers. We will have a chance of eradicating this prejudice from the minds of those who still harbor it only if we can show by what contrived means, through what false beliefs it has impregnated the intelligence of so many people. In the process, we will succeed in lowering the pretensions of an incomplete and ill-conceived science which continues unconsciously to validate the most hurtful errors through assertions that are as suspect as they are perverse.

Notes
1. Bory de Saint-Vincent, *Loco Citato*, vol. 2, 63.
2. Malo, *Histoire d'Haiti Depuis sa Découverte Jusqu'à, 1824*.
3. Hartmann, 'From the Heights of Modern Culture.'
4. Louis Figuier, *Les Races Humaines*.
5. Congrès international, 245.

Our America

José Martí

The prideful villager thinks his hometown contains the whole world, and as long as he can stay on as mayor or humiliate the rival who stole his sweetheart or watch his nest egg accumulating in its strongbox he believes the universe to be in good order, unaware of the giants in seven-league boots who can crush him underfoot or the battling comets in the heavens that go through the air devouring the sleeping worlds. Whatever is left of that sleepy hometown in America must awaken. These are not times for going to bed in a sleeping cap, but rather, like Juan de Castellano's men, with our weapons for a pillow, weapons of the mind, which vanquish all others. Trenches of ideas are worth more than trenches of stone.

A cloud of ideas is a thing no armored prow can smash through. A vital idea set ablaze before the world at the right moment can, like the mystic banner of the last judgment, stop a fleet of battleships. Hometowns that are still strangers to one another must hurry to become acquainted, like men who are about to do battle together. Those who shake their fists at each other like jealous brothers quarreling over a piece of land or the owner of a small house who envies the man with a better one must join hands and interlace them until their two hands are as one. Those who, shielded by a criminal tradition, mutilate, with swords smeared in the same blood that flows through their own veins, the land of a conquered brother whose punishment far exceeds his crimes, must return that land to their brother if they do not wish to be known as a nation of plunders. The honorable man does not collect his debts of honor in money, at so much per slap. We can no longer be a nation of fluttering leaves, spending our lives in the air, our treetop crowned in flowers, humming or creaking, caressed by the caprices of sunlight or thrashed and felled by tempests. The trees must form ranks to block the seven-league giant! It is the hour of reckoning and of marching in unison, and we must move in lines as compact as the veins of silver that lie at the roots of the Andes.

Only runts whose growth was stunted will lack the necessary valor, for those who have no faith in their land are like men born prematurely. Having no valor themselves, they deny that other men do. Their puny arms, with bracelets and painted nails, the arms of Madrid or of Paris cannot manage the lofty tree and so they say the tree cannot be climbed. We must load up the ships with these termites who gnaw away at the core of the patria that has nurtured them: if they are Parisians or Madrileños then let them stroll to the Prado by lamplight or go to Tortoni's for an ice. These sons of carpenters who are ashamed that their father was a carpenter! These men born in America who are ashamed of the mother that raised them because she wears an Indian apron, these delinquents who disown their sick mother and leave her alone in her sickbed! Which one is truly a man, he who stays with his mother to nurse her through her illness, or he who forces her to work somewhere out of sight, and lives off her sustenance in corrupted lands, with a worm for his insignia, cursing the bosom that bore him, sporting a sign that says 'traitor' on the back of his paper dress-coat? These sons of our America, which must save herself through her Indians, and which is going from less to more, who desert her and take up arms in the armies of North America, which drowns its own Indians in blood and is going from more to less! These delicate creatures who are men but do not want to do men's work! Did Washington, who made the land for them, go and live with the English during the years when he saw the English marching against his own land? These incroyables who drag their honor across foreign soil, like the incroyables of the French Revolution, dancing, smacking their lips, and deliberately slurring their words!

And in what patria can a man take greater pride than in our long-suffering republics of America, erected among mute masses of Indians upon the bloodied arms of no more than a hundred apostles, to the sound of the book doing battle against the monk's tall candle? Never before have such advanced and consolidated nations been created from such disparate factors in less historical time. The haughty man thinks that because he wields a quick pen or a vivid phrase the earth was made to be his pedestal, and accuses his native republic of irredeemable incompetence because its virgin jungles do not continually provide him with the means of going about the world a famous plutocrat, driving Persian ponies and spilling champagne. The incapacity lies not in the emerging country, which demands forms that are appropriate to it and a grandeur that is useful, but in the leaders who try to rule unique nations, of a singular and violent composition, with laws inherited from four centuries of free practice in the United States and nineteen centuries of monarchy in France. A guacho's pony cannot be stopped in midbolt by one of Alexander Hamilton's laws. To govern well, one must attend closely to the reality of the place that is governed. In America, the good ruler does not need to know how the German or Frenchman is governed, but what elements his country is composed of and how he can marshal them so as to reach, by means and institutions born from the country itself, the desirable state in which every man knows himself and is active, and all men enjoy the abundance that Nature, for the good of all, has bestowed on the country they make fruitful by their labor and defend with their lives. The government must be born from the country. The spirit of the government must be the spirit of the country. The form of the government must be in harmony with the country's natural constitution. The government is no more than an equilibrium among the country's natural elements.

In America the natural man has triumphed over the imported book. Natural men have triumphed over an artificial intelligentsia. The native mestizo has triumphed over the alien, pure-blooded criollo. The battle is not between civilization and barbarity, but between false erudition and nature. The natural man is good, and esteems and rewards a superior intelligence as long as that intelligence does not use his submission against him or offend him by ignoring him – for that the natural man deems unforgivable, and he is prepared to use force to regain the respect of anyone who wounds his sensibilities or harms his interests. The tyrants of America have come to power by acquiescing to these scorned natural elements and have fallen as soon as they betrayed them. The republics have purged the former tyrannies of their inability to know the true elements of the country, derive the form of government from them, and govern along with them. Governor, in a new country, means Creator.

In countries composed of educated and uneducated sectors, the uneducated will govern by their habit of attacking and resolving their doubts with their fists, unless the educated learn the art of governing. The uneducated masses are lazy and timid about matters of the intellect and want to be well-governed, but if the government injures them they shake it off and govern themselves. How can our governors emerge from the universities when there is not a university in America that teaches the most basic element of the art of governing, which is the analysis of all that is unique to the peoples of America? Our youth go out into the world wearing Yankee – or French – colored glasses and aspire to rule by guesswork a country they do not know. Those unacquainted with the rudiments of politics should not be allowed to embark on a career in politics. The literary prizes must not go to the best ode, but to the best study of the political factors in the student's country. In the newspaper, lecture hall, and academies, the study of the country's real factors must be carried forward. Simply knowing those factors without blindfolds or circumlocutions is enough – for anyone who deliberately or unknowingly sets aside a part of the truth will ultimately fail because of the truth he was lacking, which expands when neglected and brings down whatever is built without it. Solving the problem after knowing its elements is easier than solving it without knowing them. The natural man, strong and indignant, comes and overthrows the authority that is accumulated from books because it is not administered in keeping with the manifest needs of the country. To know is to solve. To know the country and govern it in accordance with that knowledge is the only way of freeing it from tyranny. The European university must yield to the American university. The history of America from the Incas to the present must be taught in its smallest detail, even if the Greek Archons go untaught. Our own Greece is preferable to the Greece that is not ours; we need it more. Statesmen who arise from the nation must replace statesmen who are alien to it. Let the world be granted onto our republics, but we must be the trunk. And let the vanquished pedant hold his tongue, for there is no patria in which a man can take greater pride than in our long-suffering American republics.

Our feet upon a rosary, our heads white, and our bodies a motley of Indian and criollo we boldly entered the community of nations. Bearing the standard of the Virgin, we went out to conquer our liberty. A priest, a few lieutenants, and a woman built a republic in Mexico upon the shoulders of the Indians. A Spanish cleric, under cover of his priestly cape, taught French liberty to a handful of magnificent students who chose a Spanish general to lead Central America against Spain. Still accustomed to monarchy, and with the sun on their chest, the Venezuelans in the north and the Argentines in the south set out to construct nations. When the two heroes clashed and the continent was about to be rocked, one of them, and not the lesser one, turned back. But heroism is less glorious in peacetime than in war, and thus rarer, and it is easier for a man to die with honor than to think in an orderly way. Exalted and unanimous sentiments are more readily governed than the diverging, arrogant, alien, and ambitious ideas that emerge when the battle is over. The powers that were swept in the epic struggle, along with the feline wariness of the species and the sheer weight of reality, undermined the edifice that had raised the flags of nations sustained by wise governance in the continual practice of reason and freedom over the crude and singular regions of our mestizo America with its towns of bare legs and Parisian dress-coats. The colonial hierarchy resisted the republic's democracy, and the capital city, wearing its elegant cravat, left the countryside, in its horsehide boots, waiting at the door; the redeemers born from books did not understand that a revolution that had triumphed when the soul of the earth was unleashed by a savior's voice had to govern with the soul of the earth and not against or without it. And for all these reasons, America began enduring and still endures the weary task of reconciling the discordant and hostile elements it inherited from its perverse, despotic colonizer with the imported forms and ideas that have, in their lack of local reality, delayed the advent of a logical form of government. The continent, deformed by three centuries of a rule that denied man the right to exercise his reason, embarked – overlooking or refusing to listen to the ignorant masses that had helped it redeem itself – upon a government based on reason, the reason of all directed toward the thing that are of concern to all, and not the university-taught reason of the few imposed upon the rustic reason of others. The problem of independence was not the change in form, but the change in spirit.

Common cause had to be made with the oppressed in order to consolidate a system that was opposed to the interests and governmental habits of the oppressors. The tiger, frightened away by the flash of gunfire, creeps back in the night to find his prey. He will die with flames shooting from his eyes, his claws unsheathed, but now his step is inaudible for he comes on velvet paws. When the prey awakens, the tiger is upon him. The colony lives on in the republic, but our America is saving itself from its grave blunders – the arrogance of the capital cities, the blind triumph of the scorned campesinos, the excessive importation of foreign ideas and formulas, the wicked and impolitic disdain for the native race – through the superior virtue, confirmed by necessary bloodshed, or the republic that struggles against the colony. The tiger waits behind every tree, crouches in every corner. He will die, his claws unsheathed, flames shooting from his eyes.

But 'these countries will be saved', in the words of Argentine Rivadavia, who erred on the side of urbanity during crude times; the machete is ill-suited to a silken scabbard, nor can the spear be abandoned in a country won by the spear, for it becomes enraged and stands in the doorway of Iturbide's Congress demanding that 'the fair-skinned man be made emperor.' These countries will be saved because, with the genius of moderation that now seems, by nature's serene harmony, to prevail in the continent of light, and the influence of the critical reading that has, in Europe, replaced the fumbling ideas about phalansteries in which the previous generation was steeped, the real man is being born to America, in these real times.

What a vision we were: the chest of an athlete, the hands of a dandy, and the forehead of a child. We were a whole fancy dress ball, in English trousers, a Parisian waistcoat, a North American overcoat, and a Spanish bullfighter's hat. The Indian circled about us, mute, and went to the mountaintop to christen his children. The black, pursued from afar, alone and unknown, sang his heart's music in the night, between waves and wild beasts. The campesinos, the men of the land, the creators, rose up in blind indignation against the disdainful city, their own creation. We wore epaulets and judge's robes, in countries that came into the world wearing rope sandals and Indian headbands. The wise thing would have been to pair, with charitable hearts and the audacity of our founders, the Indian headband and the judicial robe, to undam the Indian, make place for the able black, and tailor liberty to the bodies of those who rose up and triumphed in its name. What we had was the judge, the general, the man of letters, and the cleric. Our angelic youth, as if struggling from the arms of an octopus, cast their heads into the heavens and fell back with sterile glory, crowned with clouds. The natural people, driven by instinct, blind with triumph, overwhelmed their gilded rulers. No Yankee or European book could furnish the key to the Hispanoamerican enigma. So the people tried hatred instead, and our countries amounted to less and less each year. Weary of useless hatred, of the struggle of book against sword, reason against the monk's taper, city against the tempestuous or inert natural nation, we are beginning, almost unknowingly, to try love. The nations arise and salute one another. 'What are we like?' they ask, and begin telling each other what they are like. When a problem arises in Cojimar they no longer seek the solution in Danzig. The frock-coats are still French, but the thinking begins to be American. The young men of America are rolling up their sleeves and plunging their hands into the dough, and making it rise with the leavening of their sweat. They understand that there is too much imitation, and that salvation lies in creating. Create is this generation's password. Make wine from plantains: it may be sour, but it is our wine! It is now understood that a country's form of government must adapt to its natural elements, that absolute ideas, in order not to collapse over an error of form, must be expressed in relative forms: that liberty, in order to be viable, must be sincere and full, that if the republic does not open its arms to all and include all in its progress, it dies. The tiger inside came in through the gap, and so will the tiger outside. The general holds the cavalry's speed to the pace of the infantry, for if he leaves the infantry far behind, the enemy will surround the cavalry. Politics is strategy. Nations must continually criticize themselves, for criticism is health, but with a single heart and a single mind. Lower yourselves to the unfortunate and raise them up in you arms! Let the heart's fires unfreeze all that is motionless in America, and let the country's natural blood surge and throb through its veins! Standing tall, the workmen's eyes full of joy, the new men of America are saluting each other from one country to another. Natural statesmen are emerging from the direct study of nature; they read in order to apply what they read, not copy it. Economists are studying problems at their origins. Orators are becoming more temperate. Dramatists are putting native characters onstage. Academies are discussing practical subjects. Poetry is snipping off its wild, Zorilla-esque mane and hanging up its gaudy waistcoat on the glorious tree. Prose, polished and gleaming, is replete with ideas. The rulers of Indian republics are learning Indian languages.

America is saving herself from all her dangers. Over some republics the octopus sleeps still, but by the law of equilibrium, other republics are running into the sea to recover the lost centuries with mad and sublime swiftness. Others, forgetting that Juárez traveled in a coach drawn by mules, hitch their coach to the wind and take a soap bubble for coachman – and poisonous luxury, enemy of liberty, corrupts the frivolous and opens the door to foreigners. The virile character of others is being perfected by the epic spirit of a threatened independence. And others, in rapacious wars against their neighbors, are nurturing an unruly soldier caste that may devour them. But our America may also face another danger, which comes not from within but from differing origins, methods, and interests of the continent's two fractions. The hour is near when she will be approached by an enterprising and forceful nation that will demand intimate relations with her, though it does not know her and disdains her. And virile nations self-made by the rifle and the law love other virile nations, and love only them. The hour of unbridled passion and ambition from which North America may escape by the ascendency of the purest element in its blood – or into which its vengeful and sordid masses, its tradition of conquest, and the self-interest of a cunning leader could plunge it – is not yet so close, even to the most apprehensive eye, that there is no time for it to be confronted and averted by the manifestation of a discreet and unswerving pride, for its dignity as a republic, in the eyes of the watchful nations of the Universe, places upon North America a brake that our America must not remove by puerile provocation, ostentatious arrogance, or patricidal discord. Therefore the urgent duty of our America is to show herself as she us, one in soul and intent, rapidly overcoming the crushing weight of her past and stained only by the fertile blood shed by hands that do battle against ruins and by veins that were punctured by our former masters. The disdain of the formidable neighbor who does not know her is our America's greatest danger, and it is urgent – for the day of the visit is near – that her neighbor come to know her, and quickly, so that he will not disdain her, he will remove his hands from her in respect. One must have faith in the best in man and distrust the worst. One must give the best every opportunity, so that the worst will be laid bare and overcome. If not, the worst will prevail. Nations should have one special pillory for those who incite them to futile hatreds, and another for those who do not tell them the truth until it is too late.

There is no racial hatred, because there are no races. Sickly, lamp-lit minds string together and rewarm the library-shelf races that the honest traveler and the cordial observer seek in vain in the justice of nature, where the universal

identity of man leaps forth in victorious love and turbulent appetite. The soul, equal and eternal, emanates from bodies that are diverse in form and color. Anyone who promotes and disseminates opposition or hatred among races is committing a sin against humanity. But within that jumble of peoples which lives in close proximity to our peoples, certain peculiar and dynamic characteristics are condensed – ideas and habits of expansion, acquisition, vanity, and greed – that could, in a period of internal disorder or precipitation of a people's cumulative character, cease to be latent national preoccupations and become a serious threat to the neighboring, isolated and weak lands that the strong country declares to be perishable and inferior. To think is to serve. We must not, out of a villager's antipathy, impute some lethal congenital wickedness to the continent's light-skinned nation simply because it does not speak our language or share our view of what home life should be or resemble us in its political failings, which are different from ours, or because it does not think highly of quick-tempered, swarthy men or look with charity, from its still uncertain eminence, upon those less favored by history who, in heroic stages, are climbing the road that republics travel. But neither should we seek to conceal the obvious facts of the problem, which can, for the peace of the centuries, be resolved by timely study and the urgent, wordless union of the continental soul. For the unanimous hymn is already ringing forth, and the present generation is bearing industrious America along the road sanctioned by our sublime forefathers. From the Rio Bravo to the Straits of Magellan, the Great Cemi, seated on a condor's back, has scattered the seeds of the new America across the romantic nations of the continent and the suffering islands of the sea!

Froudacity: West Indian Fables by James Anthony Froude (excerpt)

J.J. Thomas

PREFACE

Last year had well advanced towards its middle — in fact it was already April, 1888 — before Mr Froude's book of travels in the West Indies became known and generally accessible to readers in those Colonies.

My perusal of it in Grenada about the period above mentioned disclosed, thinly draped with rhetorical flowers, the dark outlines of a scheme to thwart political aspiration in the Antilles. That project is sought to be realised by deterring the home authorities from granting an elective local legislature, however restricted in character, to any of the Colonies not yet enjoying such an advantage. An argument based on the composition of the inhabitants of those Colonies is confidently relied upon to confirm the inexorable mood of Downing Street. Over-large and ever-increasing — so runs the argument — the African element in the population of the West Indies is, from its past history and its actual tendencies, a standing menace to the continuance of civilisation and religion. An immediate catastrophe, social, political, and moral, would most assuredly be brought about by the granting of full elective rights to dependencies thus inhabited. Enlightened statesmanship should at once perceive the immense benefit that would ultimately result from such refusal of the franchise. The cardinal recommendation of that refusal is that it would avert definitively the political domination of the Blacks, which must inevitably be the outcome of any concession of the modicum of right so earnestly desired. The exclusion of the Negro vote being inexpedient, if not impossible, the exercise of electoral powers by the Blacks must lead to their returning candidates of their own race to the local legislatures, and that, too, in numbers preponderating according to the majority of the Negro electors. The Negro legislators thus supreme in the councils of the Colonies would straightway proceed to pass vindictive and retaliatory laws against their white fellow-colonists. For it is only fifty years since the White man and the Black man stood in the reciprocal relations of master and slave. Whilst those relations subsisted, the white masters inflicted, and the black slaves had to endure, the hideous atrocities that are inseparable from the system of slavery. Since Emancipation, the enormous strides made in self-advancement by the ex-slaves have only had the effect of provoking a resentful uneasiness in the bosoms of the ex-masters. The former bondsmen, on their side, and like their brethren of Hayti, are eaten up with implacable, blood-thirsty rancour against their former lords and owners. The annals of Hayti form quite a cabinet of political and social object-lessons which, in the eyes of British statesmen, should be invaluable in showing the true method of dealing with Ethiopic subjects of the Crown. The Negro race in Hayti, in order to obtain and to guard what it calls its freedom, has outraged every humane instinct and falsified every benevolent hope. The slave-owners there had not been a whit more cruel than slave-owners in the other islands. But, in spite of this, how ferocious, how sanguinary, how relentless against them has the vengeance of the Blacks been in their hour of mastery! A century has passed away since then, and, notwithstanding that, the hatred of Whites still rankles in their souls, and is cherished and yielded to as a national creed and guide of conduct. Colonial administrators of the mighty British Empire, the lesson which History has taught and yet continues to teach you in Hayti as to the best mode of dealing with your Ethiopic colonists lies patent, blood-stained and terrible before you, and should be taken definitively to heart. But if you are willing that Civilisation and Religion — in short, all the highest developments of individual and social life — should at once be swept away by a desolating vandalism of African birth; if you do not recoil from the blood-guiltiness that would stain your consciences through the massacre of our fellow-countrymen in the West Indies, on account of their race, complexion and enlightenment; finally, if you desire those modern Hesperides to revert into primeval jungle, horrent lairs wherein the Blacks, who, but a short while before, had been ostensibly civilised, shall be revellers, as high-priests and devotees, in orgies of devil-worship, cannibalism, and obeah — dare to give the franchise to those West Indian Colonies, and then rue the consequences of your infatuation! . . .

Alas, if the foregoing summary of the ghastly imaginings of Mr Froude were true, in what a fool's paradise had the wisest and best amongst us been living, moving, and having our being! Up to the date of the suggestion by him as above of the alleged facts and possibilities of West Indian life, we had believed (even granting the correctness of his gloomy account of the past and present positions of the two races) that to no well-thinking West Indian White, whose ancestors may have, innocently or culpably, participated in the gains as well as the guilt of slavery, would the remembrance of its palmy days be otherwise than one of regret. We Negroes, on the other hand, after a lapse of time extending over nearly two generations, could be indebted only to precarious tradition or scarcely accessible documents for any knowledge we might chance upon of the sufferings endured in these Islands of the West by those of our race who have gone before us. Death, with undiscriminating hand, had gathered in the human harvest of masters and slaves alike, according to or out of the normal laws of nature; while Time had been letting down on the stage of our existence drop-scene after drop-scene of years, to the number of something like fifty, which had been curtaining off the tragic incidents of the past from the peaceful activities of the present. Being thus circumstanced, thought we, what rational elements of mutual hatred should *now* continue to exist in the bosoms of the two races?

With regard to the perpetual reference to Hayti, because of our oneness with its inhabitants in origin and complexion, as a criterion for the exact forecast of our future conduct under given circumstances, this appeared to us, looking at actual facts, perversity gone wild in the manufacture of analogies. The founders of the Black Republic, we had all along understood, were not in any sense whatever equipped, as Mr Froude assures us they were, when starting on their self-governing career, with the civil and intellectual advantages that had been transplanted from Europe. On the contrary, we had been taught to regard them as most unfortunate in the circumstances under which they so gloriously conquered their merited freedom. We saw them free, but perfectly illiterate barbarians, impotent to use the intellectual resources of which their valour had made them possessors, in the shape of books on the spirit and technical details of a highly developed national existence. We had learnt also, until this new interpreter of history had contradicted the accepted record, that the continued failure of Hayti to realise the dreams of Toussaint was due to the fatal want of confidence subsisting between the fairer and darker sections of the inhabitants, which had its sinister and disastrous origin in the action of the Mulattoes in attempting to secure freedom for themselves, in conjunction with the Whites, at the sacrifice of their darker-hued kinsmen. Finally, it had been explained to us that the remembrance of this abnormal treason had been underlying and perniciously influencing the whole course of Haytian national history. All this established knowledge we are called upon to throw overboard, and accept the baseless assertions of this conjuror-up of inconceivable fables! He calls upon us to believe that, in spite of being free, educated, progressive, and at peace with all men, we West Indian Blacks, were we ever to become constitutionally dominant in our native islands, would emulate in savagery our Haytian fellow-Blacks who, at the time of retaliating upon their actual masters, were tortured slaves, bleeding and rendered desperate under the oppressors' lash — and all this simply and merely because of the sameness of our ancestry and the colour of our skin! One would have thought that Liberia would have been a fitter standard of comparison in respect of a coloured population starting a national life, really and truly equipped with the requisites and essentials of civilised existence. But such a reference would have been fatal to Mr Froude's object: the annals of Liberia being a persistent refutation of the old pro-slavery prophecies which our author so feelingly rehearses.

Let us revert, however, to Grenada and the newly-published *Bow of Ulysses*, which had come into my hands in April, 1888.

It seemed to me, on reading that book, and deducing therefrom the foregoing essential summary, that a critic would have little more to do, in order to effectually exorcise this negrophobic political hobgoblin, than to appeal to impartial history, as well as to common sense, in its application to human nature in general, and to the actual facts of West Indian life in particular.

History, as against the hard and fast White-master and Black-slave theory so recklessly invented and confidently built upon by Mr Froude, would show incontestably — (a) that for upwards of two hundred years before the Negro Emancipation in 1838, there had never existed in one of those then British Colonies, which had been originally discovered and settled for Spain by the great Columbus or by his successors, the *Conquistadores*, any prohibition whatsoever, on the ground of race or colour, against the owning of slaves by any free person possessing the necessary means, and desirous or doing so; (b) that, as a consequence of this non-restriction, and from causes notoriously historical, numbers of blacks, half-breeds, and other non-Europeans, besides such of them as had become possessed of their 'property' by inheritance, availed themselves of this virtual license, and in course of time constituted a very considerable proportion of the slave-holding section of those communities; (c) that these dusky plantation-owners enjoyed and used in every possible sense the identical rights and privileges which were enjoyed and used by their pure-blooded Caucasian brother-slave-owners. The above statements are attested by written documents, oral tradition, and, better still perhaps, by the living presence in those islands of numerous lineal representatives of those once opulent and flourishing non-European planter-families.

Common sense, here stepping in, must, from the above data, deduce some such conclusions as the following. First that, on the hypothesis that the slaves who were freed in 1838 — full fifty years ago — were all on an average fifteen years old, those vengeful ex-slaves of today will be all men of sixty-five years of age; and, allowing for the delay in getting the franchise, somewhat further advanced towards the human life-term of threescore and ten years. Again, in order to organise and carry out any scheme of legislative and social retaliation of the kind set forth in the *Bow of Ulysses*, there must be (which unquestionably there is not) a considerable, well-educated, and very influential number surviving of those who had actually been in bondage. Moreover, the vengeance of these people (also assuming the foregoing non-existent condition) would have, in case of opportunity, to wreak itself far more largely and vigorously upon members of their own race than upon Whites, seeing that the increase of the Blacks, as correctly represented in the *Bow of Ulysses*, is just as rapid as the diminution of the White population. And therefore, Mr Froude's 'Danger-to-the-Whites' cry in support of his anti-reform manifesto would not appear, after all, to be quite so justifiable as he possibly thinks.

Feeling keenly that something in the shape of the foregoing programme might be successfully worked up for a public defence of the maligned people, I disregarded the bodily and mental obstacles that have beset and clouded my career during the last twelve years, and cheerfully undertook the task, stimulated thereto by what I thought weighty considerations. I saw that no representative of Her Majesty's Ethiopic West Indian subjects cared to come forward to perform this work in the more permanent shape that I felt to be not only desirable but essential for our self-vindication. 1 also realised the fact that the *Bow of Ulysses* was not likely to have the same ephemeral existence and effect as the newspaper and other periodical discussions of its contents, which had poured from the press in Great Britain, the United States, and very notably, of course, in all the English Colonies of the Western Hemisphere. In the West Indian papers the best writers of our race had written masterly refutations, but it was clear how difficult the task would be in future to procure and refer to them whenever occasion should require. Such productions, however, fully satisfied those qualified men of our people, because they were legitimately convinced (even as I myself am convinced) that the political destinies of the people of colour could not run one tittle of risk from anything that it pleased Mr Froude to write or say on the subject. But, meditating further on the question, the reflection forced itself upon me that, beyond the mere political personages in the circle more directly addressed by Mr Froude's volume, there were individuals whose influence or possible sympathy we could not afford to disregard, or to esteem lightly. So I deemed it right and a patriotic duty to attempt the enterprise myself, in obedience to the above stated motives.

At this point I must pause to express on behalf of the entire coloured population of the West Indies our most heartfelt acknowledgements to Mr C. Salmon for the luminous and effective vindication of us, in his volume on *West Indian Confederation*, against Mr Froude's libels. The service thus rendered by Mr Salmon possesses a double significance and value in my estimation. In the first place, as being the work of a European of high position, quite independent of us (who testifies concerning Negroes, not through having gazed at them from balconies, decks of steamers, or the seats of moving carriages, but from actual and long personal intercourse with them, which the internal evidence of his book plainly proves to have been as sympathetic as it was familiar), and, secondly, as the work of an individual entirely outside of our race, it has been gratefully accepted by myself as an incentive to self-help, on the same more formal and permanent lines, in a matter so important to the status which we can justly claim as a progressive, law-abiding, and self-respecting section of Her Majesty's liege subjects.

It behoves me now to say a few words respecting this book as a mere literary production.

Alexander Pope, who, next to Shakespeare and perhaps Butler, was the most copious contributor to the current stock of English maxims, says:

> 'True ease in writing comes from Art, not Chance,
> As those move easiest who have learnt to dance.'

A whole dozen years of bodily sickness and mental tribulation have not been conducive to that regularity of practice in composition which alone can ensure the 'true ease' spoken of by the poet; and therefore is it that my style leaves so much to be desired, and exhibits, perhaps, still more to be pardoned. Happily, a quarrel such as ours with the author of *The English in the West Indies* cannot be finally or even approximately settled on the score of superior literary competency, whether of aggressor or defender. I feel free to ignore whatever verdict might be grounded on a consideration so purely artificial. There ought to be enough, if not in these pages, at any rate in whatever else I have heretofore published, that should prove me not so hopelessly stupid and wanting in self-respect, as would be implied by my undertaking a contest in artistic phrase-weaving with one who, even among the foremost of his literary countrymen, is confessedly a master in that craft. The judges to whom I do submit our case are those Englishmen and others whose conscience blends with their judgment, and who determine such questions as this on their essential rightness which has claim to the first and decisive consideration. For much that is irregular in the arrangement and sequence of the subject-matter, some blame fairly attaches to our assailant. The erratic manner in which he launches his injurious statements against the hapless Blacks, even in the course of passages which no more led up to them than to any other section of mankind, is a very notable feature of his anti-Negro production. As he frequently repeats, very often with cynical aggravations, his charges and sinister prophecies against the sable objects of his aversion, I could see no other course open to me than to take him up on the points whereto I demurred, exactly how, when, and where I found them.

My purpose could not be attained up without direct mention of, or reference to, certain public employees in the Colonies whose official conduct has often been the subject of criticism in the public press of the West Indies. Though fully aware that such criticism has on many occasions been much more severe than my own strictures, yet, it being possible that some special responsibility may attach to what I here reproduce in a more permanent shape, I most cheerfully accept, in the interests of public justice, any consequence which may result.

A remark or two concerning the publication of this rejoinder. It has been hinted to me that the issue of it has been too long delayed to secure for it any attention in England, owing to the fact that the West Indies are but little known, and of less interest, to the generality of English readers. Whilst admitting, as in duty bound, the possible correctness of this forecast, and regretting the oft-recurring hindrances which occasioned such frequent and, sometimes, long suspension of my labour; and noting, too, the additional delay caused through my unacquaintance with English publishing usages, I must, notwithstanding, plead guilty to a lurking hope that some small fraction of Mr Froude's readers will yet be found, whose interest in the West Indies will be temporarily revived on behalf of this essay, owing to its direct bearing on Mr Froude and his statements relative to these Islands, contained in his recent book of travels in them. This I am led to hope will be more particularly the case when it is borne in mind that the rejoinder has been attempted by a member of that very same race which he has, with such eloquent recklessness of all moral considerations, held up to public contempt and disfavour. In short, I can scarcely permit myself to believe it possible that concern regarding a popular author, on his being questioned by an adverse critic of however restricted powers, can be so utterly dead within a twelvemonth as to be incapable of rekindling. Mr Froude's *Oceana*, which had been published long before its author voyaged to the West Indies, in order to treat the Queen's subjects there in the same more than questionable fashion as that in which he had treated those of the Southern Hemisphere, had what was in the main a formal rejoinder to its misrepresentations published only three months ago in this city. I venture to believe that no serious work in defence of an important cause or community can lose much, if anything, of its intrinsic value through some delay in its issue; especially when written in the vindication of Truth, whose eternal principles are beyond and above the influence of time and its changes.

At any rate, this attempt to answer some of Mr Froude's main allegations against the people of the West Indies cannot fail to be of grave importance and lively interest to the inhabitants of those Colonies. In this opinion I am happy in being able to record the full concurrence of a numerous and influential body of my fellow-West Indians, men of various races, but united in detestation of falsehood and injustice.

J.J.T.

LONDON, *June*, 1889.

Socialism and the Negro, Race First versus Class First, The White War and the Colored Races; and Hands Across the Sea

Hubert Harrison

"Socialism and the Negro,"

International Socialist Review 13 (July 1912): 65–48.

Economic Status of the Negro

The ten million Negroes of America form a group that is more essentially proletarian than any other American group. In the first place the ancestors of this group were brought here with the very definite understanding that they were to be ruthlessly exploited. And they were not allowed any choice in the matter. Since they were brought here as chattels their social status was fixed by that fact. In every case that we know of where a group has lived by exploiting another group, it has despised that group which it has put under subjection. And the degree of contempt has always been in direct proportion to the degree of exploitation.

Inasmuch then, as the Negro was at one period the most thoroughly exploited of the American proletariat, he was the most thoroughly despised. That group which exploited and despised him, being the most powerful section of the ruling class, was able to diffuse its own necessary contempt of the Negro first among the other sections of the ruling class, and afterwards among all other classes of Americans. For the ruling class has always determined what the social ideals and moral ideas of society should be; and this explains how race prejudice was disseminated until all Americans are supposed to be saturated with it. Race prejudice, then, is the fruit of economic subjection and a fixed inferior economic status. It is the reflex of a social caste system. That caste system in America today is what we roughly refer to as the Race Problem, and it is thus seen that the Negro problem is essentially an economic problem with its roots in slavery past and present.

Notwithstanding the fact that it is usually kept out of public discussion, the bread-and-butter side of this problem is easily the most important. The Negro worker gets less for his work — thanks to exclusion from the craft unions — than any other worker; he works longer hours as a rule and under worse conditions than any other worker, and his rent in any large city is much higher than that which the white worker pays for the same tenement. In short, the exploitation of the Negro worker is keener than that of any group of white workers in America. Now the mission of the Socialist Party is to free the working class from exploitation, and since the Negro is the most ruthlessly exploited working class group in America, the duty of the party to champion his cause is as clear as day. This is the crucial test of Socialism's sincerity and therein lies the value of this point of view — Socialism and the Negro.

The Need of Socialist Propaganda

So far, no particular effort has been made to carry the message of Socialism to these people. All the rest of the poor have had the gospel preached to them, for the party has carried on special propaganda work among the Poles, Slovaks, Finns, Hungarians and Lithuanians. Here are ten million Americans, all proletarians, hanging on the ragged edge of the impending class conflict. Left to themselves they may become as great a menace to our advancing army as is the army of the unemployed, and for precisely the same reason: they can be used against us, as the craft unions have begun to find out. Surely we should make some effort to enlist them under our banner that they may swell our ranks and help to make us invincible. And we must do this for the same reason that is impelling organized labor to adopt an all-inclusive policy; because the other policy results in the artificial breeding of scabs. On grounds of common sense and enlightened self-interest it would be well for the Socialist party to begin to organize the Negroes of America in reference to the class struggle. You may depend on it, comrades, the capitalists of America are not waiting. Already they have subsidized Negro leaders, Negro editors, preachers and politicians to build up in the breasts of black people those sentiments which will make them subservient to their will. For they recognize the value (to them) of cheap labor power and they know that if they can succeed in keeping one section of the working class down they can use that section to keep the other sections down too.

The Negro's Attitude toward Socialism

If the Socialist propaganda among Negroes is to be effectively carried on, the members and leaders of the party must first understand the Negro's attitude toward Socialism. That attitude finds its first expression in ignorance. The mass of the Negro people in America are ignorant of what Socialism means. For this they are not much to blame. Behind the veil of the color line none of the great world-movements for social betterment have been able to penetrate. Since it is not yet the easiest task to get the white American worker — with all his superior intellect — to see Socialism, it is but natural to expect that these darker workers to whom America denies knowledge should still be in ignorance as to its aims and objects.

Besides, the Negroes of America — those of them who think — are suspicious of Socialism as of everything that comes from the white people of America. They have seen that every movement for the extension of democracy here has broken down as soon as it reached the color line. Political democracy declared that "all men are created equal," meant only all white men; the Christian church found that the brotherhood of man did not include God's bastard children; the public school system proclaimed that the school house was the backbone of democracy — "for white people only," and the civil service says that Negroes must keep their place — at the bottom. So that they can hardly be blamed for looking askance at any new gospel of freedom. Freedom to them has been like one of

> "those juggling fiends
> That palter with us in double sense;
> That keep the word of promise to our ear,
> And break it to our hope."

In this connection, some explanation of the former political solidarity of those Negroes who were voters may be of service. Up to six years ago the one great obstacle to the political progress of the colored people was their sheep-like allegiance to the Republican party. They were taught to believe that God had raised up a peculiar race of men called Republicans who had loved the slaves so tenderly that they had taken guns in their hands and rushed on the ranks of the southern slaveholders to free the slaves; that this race of men was still in existence, marching under the banner of the Republican party and showing their great love for Negroes by appointing from six to sixteen near-Negroes to soft political snaps. Today that great political superstition is falling to pieces before the advance of intelligence among Negroes. They begin to realize that they were sold out by the Republican party in 1876; that in the last twenty-five years lynchings have increased, disfranchisement has spread all over the south and "jim-crow" cars run even into the national capital — with the continuing consent of a Republican congress, a Republican Supreme Court and Republican presidents.

Ever since the Brownsville affair, but more clearly since [William Howard] Taft declared and put in force the policy of pushing out the few near-Negro officeholders, the rank and file have come to see that the Republican party is a great big sham. Many went over to the Democratic party because, as the *Amsterdam News* puts it, "they had nowhere else to go." Twenty years ago the colored men who joined that party were ostracized as scalawags and crooks — which they probably were. But today, the defection to the Democrats of such men as Bishop [Alexander] Walters, [Robert N.] Wood, [James D.] Carr and [Ralph E.] Langston — whose uncle was a colored Republican congressman from Virginia — has made the colored democracy respectable and given quite a tone to political heterodoxy.

All this loosens the bonds of their allegiance and breaks the bigotry of the last forty years. But of this change in their political view-point the white world knows nothing. The two leading Negro newspapers are subsidized by the same political pirates who hold the title-deeds to the handful of hirelings holding office in the name of the Negro race. One of these papers [the *New York Age*] is an organ of Mr. Washington, the other [the *Amsterdam News*] pretends to be independent — that is, it must be "bought" on the installment plan, and both of them are in New York. Despite this "conspiracy of silence" the Negroes are waking up; are beginning to think for themselves; to look with more favor on "new doctrines." And herein lies the open opportunity of the Socialist party. If the work of spreading Socialist propaganda is taken to them now, their ignorance of it can be enlightened and their suspicions removed.

The Duty of the Socialist Party

I think that we might embrace the opportunity of taking the matter up at the coming national convention. The time is ripe for taking a stand against the extensive disfranchisement of the Negro in violation of the plain provisions of the national constitution. In view of the fact that the last three amendments to the constitution contain the clause, "Congress shall have the power to enforce this article by appropriate legislation," the party will not be guilty of proposing anything worse than asking the government to enforce its own "law and order." If the Negroes, or any other section of the working class in America, is to be deprived of the ballot, how can they participate with us in the class struggle? How can we pretend to be a political party if we fail to see the significance of this fact?

Besides, the recent dirty diatribes against the Negro in a Texas paper [the *Rebel*], which is still on our national list of Socialist papers; the experiences of Mrs. Theresa Malkiel in Tennessee, where she was prevented by certain people from addressing a meeting of Negroes on the subject of Socialism, and certain other exhibitions of the thing called Southernism, constitute the challenge of caste. Can we ignore this challenge? I think not. We could hardly afford to have the taint of "trimming" on the garments of the Socialist party. It is dangerous — doubly dangerous now, when the temper of the times is against such "trimming." Besides it would be futile. If it is not met now it must be met later when it shall have grown stronger. Now, when we can cope with it, we have the issue squarely presented: Southernism or Socialism — which? Is it to be the white half of the working class against the black half, or all the working class? Can we hope to triumph over capitalism with one-half of the working class against us? Let us settle these questions now — for settled they must be.

The Negro and Political Socialism

The power of the voting proletariat can be made to express itself through the ballot. To do this they must have a political organization of their own to give form to their will. The direct object of such an organization is to help them to secure control of the powers of government by electing members of the working class to office and so secure legislation in the interests of the working class until such time as the workers may, by being in overwhelming control of the government, be able "to alter or abolish it, and to institute a new government, laying its foundation on such principles, and organizing its power in such form, as to them shall seem most likely to effect their safety and happiness" — in short, to work for the abolition of capitalism, by legislation — if that be permitted. And in all this, the Negro, who feels most fiercely the deep damnation of the capitalist system, can help.

The Negro and Industrial Socialism

But even the voteless proletarian can in a measure help toward the final abolition of the capitalist system. For they too have labor power — which they can be taught to withhold. They can do this by organizing themselves at the point of production. By means of such organization they can work to shorten the hours of labor, to raise wages, to secure an ever-increasing share of the product of their toil. They can enact and enforce laws for the protection of labor and they can do this at the point of production, as was done by the Western Federation of Miners in the matter of the eight-hour law, which they established without the aid of the legislatures or the courts. All of this involves a progressive control of the tools of production and a progressive expropriation of the capitalist class. And in all this the Negro can help. So far, they are unorganized on the industrial field, but industrial unionism beckons to them as to others, and the consequent program of the Socialist party for the Negro in the south can be based upon this fact.

"Race First versus Class First"

Negro World (March 27, 1920)

"In the old days white people derived their knowledge of what Negroes were doing from those Negroes who were nearest to them, largely their own selected exponents of Negro activity or of their white point of view ... Today the white world is vaguely, but disquietingly, aware that Negroes are awake; different, but perplexingly uncertain. Yet the white world by which they are surrounded retains its traditional method of interpreting the mass by the Negro nearest to themselves in affiliation or contact. The Socialist party still persists in thinking that the unrest now apparent in the Negro masses is due to their propaganda which its paid adherents support, and believes that the unrest will function largely along the lines of Socialist political thought."

It is necessary to insist on this point today when the Socialist party of America has secretly subsidized both a magazine and a newspaper to attempt to cut into the splendid solidarity which Negroes are achieving in response to the call of racial necessity. It is necessary to point out that "radical" young Negroes may betray the interests of the race into alien hands just as surely as "the old crowd." For, after all, the essence of both betrayals consists in making the racial requirements play second fiddle to the requirements dictated as best for it by other groups with other interests to serve. The fact that one group of alien interests is described as "radical" and the other as "reactionary" is of very slight value to us.

In the days when the Socialist Party of America was respectable, although it never drew lines of racial separation in the North, it permitted those lines to be drawn in the South. It had no word of official condemnation for the Socialists of Tennessee who prevented Theresa Malkiel in 1912 from lecturing to Negroes on Socialism either in the same hall with them or in meetings of their own. It was the national office of the party which in that same presidential year refused to route Eugene V. Debs in the South because the Grand Old Man let it be known that he would not remain silent on the race question while in the South. They wanted the votes of the white South then, and were willing to betray by silence the principles of inter-racial solidarity which they espoused on paper.

Now, when their party has shrunk considerably in popular support and sentiment, they are willing to take up our cause. Well, we thank honest white people everywhere who take up our cause, but we wish them to know that we have already taken it up ourselves. While they were refusing to diagnose our case we diagnosed it ourselves, and, now that we have prescribed the remedy — Race Solidarity — they came to us with their prescription — Class Solidarity. It is too late, gentlemen! This racial alignment is all our own product, and we have no desire to turn it over to you at this late day, when we are beginning to reap its benefits. And if you are simple enough to believe that those among us who serve your interests ahead of ours have any monopoly of intellect or information along the lines of modern learning, then you are the greater gulls indeed.

We can respect the Socialists of Scandinavia, France, Germany or England on their record. But your record so far does not entitle you to the respect of those who can see all around a subject. We say Race First, because you have all along insisted on Race First and class after when you didn't need our help. We reproduce below a brief portion of your record in those piping times of peace, and ask you to explain it. If you are unable to do so, set your lackeys to work; they may be able to do it in terms of their own "radical scientific" surface slush. The following is taken from the majority report of one of your national committees during one of your recent national conventions. It was signed by Ernest Untermann and J. Stitt Wilson, representing the West, and Joshua Wanhope, editor of the *Call*, and Robert Hunter, representing the East, and it was adopted as a portion of the party program. We learn from it that —

> Race feeling is not so much a result of social as of biological evolution. It does not change essentially with changes of economic systems. It is deeper than any class feeling and will outlast the capitalist system. It persists even after race prejudice has been outgrown. It exists not because the capitalists nurse it for economic reasons, but the capitalists rather have an opportunity to nurse it for economic reasons because it exists a product of biology. It is bound to play a role in the economics of the future society. If it should not assert itself in open warfare under a Socialist form of society, it will nevertheless lead to a rivalry of races for expansion over the globe as a result of the play of natural and sexual selection. We may temper this race feeling by education, but we can never hope to extinguish it altogether. Class-consciousness must be learned, but race consciousness is inborn and cannot be wholly unlearned. A few individuals may indulge in the luxury of ignoring race and posing as utterly raceless humanitarians, but whole races never.

> Where races struggle for the means of life, racial animosities cannot be avoided. When working people struggle for jobs, self-preservation enforces its decrees. Economic and political considerations lead to racial fights and to legislation restricting the invasion of the white man's domain by other races.

It is well that the New Negro should know this, since it justifies him in giving you a taste of your own medicine. The writer of these lines is also a Socialist; but he refuses in this crisis of the world's history to put either Socialism or your party above the call of his race. And he does this on the very grounds which you yourself have given in the document quoted above. Also because he is not a fool.

"The White War and the Colored Races"

(originally written in 1918) *New Negro* 4 (October 1919): 8–10.

The Nineteenth Christian Century saw the international expansion of capitalism — the economic system of the white peoples of Western Europe and America — and its establishment by force and fraud over the lands of the colored races, black and brown and yellow. The opening years of the Twentieth Century present us with the sorry spectacle of these same white nations cutting each other's throats to determine which of them shall enjoy the property which has been acquired. For this is the real sum and substance of the original "war aims" of the belligerents; although in conformity with Christian cunning, this is one which is never frankly avowed. Instead, we are fed with the information that they are fighting for "*Kultur*" and "on behalf of small nationalities." Let us look carefully at this camouflage.

"The Sham of Democracy"

In the first place, we in America need not leave our own land to seek reasons for suspecting the sincerity of democratic professions. While we are waging war to establish democracy three thousand miles away, millions of Negroes are disfranchised in our own land by the "cracker" democracies of the southern states which are more intent upon making slaves of their black fellow-citizens than upon rescuing the French and Belgians from the similar brutalities of the German Junkers. The horrible holocaust of East St. Louis was possible only in three modern states — Russia of the Romanoffs, Turkey and the United States — and it ill becomes any one of them to point a critical finger at the others.

But East St. Louis was simply the climax of a long series of butcheries perpetrated on defenseless Negroes which has made the murder rate of Christian America higher than that of heathen Africa and of every other civilized land. And, although our government can order the execution of thirteen Negro soldiers for resenting the wholesale insults to the uniform of the United States and defending their lives from civilian aggressors, not one of the murderers of black men, women and children has been executed or even ferreted out. Nor has our war Congress seen fit as yet to make lynching a federal crime. What wonder that the Negro masses are insisting that before they can be expected to enthuse over the vague formula of making the world "safe for democracy" they must

> "... the simple plan,
> That he shall take who hath the power,
> And he must keep who can."

THE ECONOMICS OF WAR

It is the same economic motive that has been back of every modern war since the merchant and trading classes secured control of the powers of the modern state from the battle of Plassy to the present world war. This is the natural and inevitable effect of the capitalist system, of what (for want of a worse name) we call "Christendom." For that system is based upon the wage relationship between those who own and those who operate the gigantic forces of land and machinery. Under this system no capitalist employs a worker for two dollars a day unless that worker creates more than two dollars worth of wealth for him. Only out of this surplus can profits come. If ten million workers should thus create one-hundred-million dollars' worth of wealth each day and get twenty five or fifty millions in wages, it is obvious that they can expend only what they have received, and that, therefore, every nation whose industrial system is organized on a capitalist basis must produce a mass of surplus products over and above, not the need, but the purchasing power of the nation's producers. Before these products can return to their owners as profits they must be sold somewhere. Hence the need for foreign markets, for fields of exploitation and "spheres of influence" in "undeveloped" countries whose virgin resources are exploited in their turn after the capitalist fashion. But, since every industrial nation is seeking the same outlet for its products, clashes are inevitable and in these clashes beaks and claws — armies and navies — must come into play. Hence beaks and claws must be provided beforehand against the day of conflict, and hence the exploitation of white men in Europe and America becomes the reason for the exploitation of black and brown and yellow men in Africa and Asia. And, therefore, it is hypocritical and absurd to pretend that the capitalist nations can ever intend to abolish wars. For, as long as black men are exploited by white men in Africa, so long must white men cut each other's throats over that exploitation. And thus, the selfish and ignorant white worker's destiny is determined by the hundreds of millions of those whom he calls "niggers." "The strong too often think that they have a mortgage upon the weak; but in the domain of morals it is the other way."

THE COLOR LINE

But economic motives have always their social side; and this exploitation of the lands and labor of colored folk expresses itself in the social theory of white domination; the theory that the worst human stocks of Montmarte, Seven Dials and the Bowery are superior to the best human stocks of Rajputana or Khartoum. And when these colored folk who make up the overwhelming majority of this world demand decent treatment for themselves, the proponents of this theory accuse them of seeking social equality. For white folk to insist upon the right to manage their own ancestral lands, free from the domination of tyrants, domestic and foreign, is variously described as "democracy" and "self-determination." For Negroes, Egyptians and Hindus to seek the same thing is impudence. What wonder, then, that the white man's rule is felt by them to rest upon a seething volcano whose slumbering fires are made up of the hundreds of millions of Chinese, Japanese, Hindus, and Africans! Truly has it been said that "the problem of the 20th Century is the problem of the Color Line." And wars are not likely to end; in fact, they are likely to be wider and more terrible — so long as this theory of white domination seeks to hold down the majority of the world's people under the iron heel of racial repression.

Of course, no sane person will deny that the white race is, at present, the superior race of the world. I use the word "superior" in no cloudy, metaphysical sense, but simply to mean that they are on top and their will goes — at present. Consider that fact as the pivotal fact of the war. Then, in the light of it, consider what is happening in Europe today. The white race is superior — its will goes — because it has invented and amassed greater means for the subjugation of nature and of man than any other race. It is the top dog by virtue of its soldiers, guns, ships, money, resources and brains. Yet there in Europe it is deliberately burning up, consuming and destroying these very soldiers, guns, ships, money, resources and brains, the very things upon which its supremacy rests. When the war is over, it will be less able to enforce its sovereign will upon the darker races of the world. Does any one believe that it will be as easy to hold down Egypt and India and Persia after the war as it was before? Hardly.

THE RACIAL RESULTS OF THE WAR

Not only will the white race be depleted in numbers, but its quality, physical and mental, will be considerably lowered for a time. War destroys first the strongest and the bravest, the best stocks, the young men who were to father the next generation. The next generation must, consequently, be fathered by the weaker stocks of the race. And thus, in physical stamina and in brain-power, they will be less equal to the task of holding down the darker millions of the world than their fathers were. This was the thought back of Mr. [William Randolph] Hearst's objection to our entering the war. He wanted the United States to stand as the white race's reserve of man-power when Europe had been bled white.

But what will be the effect of all this upon that colored majority whose preponderant existence our newspapers ignore? In the first place, it will feel the lifting of the pressure as the iron hand of "discipline" is relaxed. And it will expand, when that pressure is removed, to the point where it will first ask, then demand, and finally secure, the right of self-determination. It will insist that, not only the white world, but the whole world, be made "safe for democracy." This will mean a self-governing Egypt, a self-governing India, and independent African states as large as Germany and France —and larger. And, as a result, there will come a shifting of the basis of international politics and business and of international control. This is the living thought that comes to me from the newspapers and books that have been written and published by colored men in Africa and Asia during the past three years. It is what I have heard from their own lips as I have talked with them. And, yet, of this thought which is inflaming the international underworld, not a word appears in the parochial press of America, which seems to think that if it can keep its own Negroes down to servile lip-service, it need not face the worldwide problem of the "Conflict of Color," as Mr. Putnam-Weale [Bertram Lenox Simpson] calls it.

But that the more intelligent portions of the white world are becoming distressingly conscious of it, is evident from the first great manifesto of the Russian Bolsheviki last year when they asked about Britain's subject peoples.

And the British workingmen have evidently done some thinking in their turn. In their latest declarations they seem to see the ultimate necessity of compelling their own aristocrats to forego such imperial aspirations as that of Sir Harry Johnston, and of extending the principle of self-determination even to the black people of Central Africa. But eyes which for centuries have been behind the blinders of Race Prejudice cannot but blink and water when compelled to face the full sunlight. And Britain's workers insist that "No one will maintain that the Africans are fit for self-government." But no one has yet asked the Africans anything about it.

And on the same principle (of excluding the opinion of those who are most vitally concerned) Britain's ruling class may tell them that "No one maintains that the laboring classes of Britain are fit for self-government." But their half-hearted demand that an international committee shall take over the British, German, French and Portuguese possessions in Africa and manage them as independent nationalities (?) until they can "go it alone," would suggest that their eyesight is improving.

To sum it all up, the war in Europe is the result of the desire of the white governments of Europe to exploit for their own benefit the lands and labor of the darker races, and, as the war continues, it must decrease the white man's stock of ability to do this successfully against the wishes of the inhabitants of those lands. This will result in their freedom from thralldom and the extension of political, social and industrial democracy to the twelve-hundred-million black and brown and yellow peoples of the world. This, I take it, is what President Wilson had in mind when he wished to make the world "safe for democracy." But, whether I am mistaken or not, it is the idea which dominates today the thought of those darker millions.

"Hands across the Sea"

Negro World (September 10, 1921)

The most dangerous phase of developed capitalism is that of imperialism — when having subjugated its workers and exploited its natural resources at home, it turns with grim determination toward "undeveloped" races and areas to renew the same process there. This is the phase in which militarism and navalism develop with dizzying speed with their accumulating burden of taxation for "preparedness" against the day when the capitalist class of the nation must use the final argument of force against its foreign competitors for markets. These markets change their character under the impact of international trade, and are no longer simply markets for the absorption of finished products, but become fields for the investment of accumulated surplus profits, in which process they are transformed into original sources for the production of surplus profits by the opening up of mines, railroads and other large-scale capitalist enterprises. It becomes necessary to take over the government of the selected areas in order that the profits may be effectually guaranteed, and "spheres of influence," "protectorates," and "mandates" are set up.

Thus the lands of "backward" people are brought within the central influence of the capitalist economic system and the subjection of black, brown and other colored workers to the rigors of "the white man's burden" comes as a consequence of the successful exploitation of white workers at home, and binds them both in an international opposition to the continuance of the capitalist regime. Most Americans who are able to see this process more or less clearly in the case of other nations are unable to see the same process implicit and explicit in the career of their own.

The case of Hayti and the present plight of the Haytian people helps us to see the aims of our own American imperialists in the white light of pitiless publicity. A people of African descent, scarcely seven hundred miles from our own shores, with a government of their own, have had their government suppressed and their liberties destroyed by the Navy Department of the United States without even the slightest formality of a declaration of war by the United States Congress as required by the Constitution. In the presidential chair our "cracker" marines have installed a puppet in the person of Monsieur [President Phillipe Sudre] D'Artiguenave to carry out their will; the legislative bodies of the erstwhile republic have been either suppressed or degraded; unoffending black citizens have been wantonly butchered in cold blood, and thousands have been forced into slavery to labor on the military roads without pay. Here is American imperialism in its stark, repulsive nakedness. And what are we going to do about it?

The fight which will soon be waged in Congress for the restoration of Haytian rights is receiving no help from the millions of Negroes who are presumably interested in the international movement for the practical advancement of people of Negro blood. It is high time that it should. This is an opportunity that lies ready to our hands. And if we would use our votes here in an intelligent, purposeful way we could at least make our voices heard and heeded in Washington on behalf of our brothers in black who are suffering seven hundred miles away. Pending this, we could inaugurate gigantic propaganda meetings in such places as Faneuil Hall, Madison Square Garden and the Negro churches; we could in our newspapers and magazines agitate for the withdrawal of the forces of the American occupation, as the Irish did on behalf of Ireland; we could at least, get up a gigantic petition with a million signatures and carry it to congress. Even a "silent protest parade" would become us better than this slavish apathy and servile acquiescence in which we are now sunk.

Believe it or not as we will, the Negro American is now on trial before the eyes of the world and if he fails to act he may yet hear the God of opportunity utter those fateful words recorded in the third chapter of Revelations concerning the angel of the church of the Laodiceans. For we may be sure that French, British and Belgian imperialism is a limb of the same tree of white domination on which our home-made branch grows.

Africa for the Africans

Marcus Garvey

For five years the Universal Negro Improvement Association has been advocating the cause of Africa for the Africans—that is, that the Negro peoples of the world should concentrate upon the object of building up for themselves a great nation in Africa.

When we started our propaganda toward this end several of the so-called intellectual Negroes who have been bamboozling the race for over half a century said that we were crazy, that the Negro peoples of the western world were not interested in Africa and could not live in Africa. One editor and leader went so far as to say at his so-called Pan-African Congress that American Negroes could not live in Africa, because the climate was too hot. All kinds of arguments have been adduced by these Negro intellectuals against the colonization of Africa by the black race. Some said that the black man would ultimately work out his existence alongside of the white man in countries founded and established by the latter. Therefore, it was not necessary for Negroes to seek an independent nationality of their own. The old time stories of "African fever," "African bad climate," "African mosquitos," "African savages," have been repeated by these "brainless intellectuals" of ours as a scare against our people in America and the West Indies taking a kindly interest in the new program of building a racial empire of our own in our Motherland. Now that years have rolled by and the Universal Negro Improvement Association has made the circuit of the world with its propaganda, we find eminent statesmen and leaders of the white race coming out boldly advocating the cause of colonizing Africa with the Negroes of the western world. A year ago Senator MacCullum of the Mississippi Legislature introduced a resolution in the House for the purpose of petitioning the Congress of the United States of America and the President to use their good influence in securing from the Allies sufficient territory in Africa in liquidation of the war debt, which territory should be used for the establishing of an independent nation for American Negroes. About the same time Senator France of Maryland gave expression to a similar desire in the Senate of the United States. During a speech on the "Soldiers' Bonus." He said: "We owe a big debt to Africa and one which we have too long ignored. I need not enlarge upon our peculiar interest in the obligation to the people of Africa. Thousands of Americans have for years been contributing to the missionary work which has been carried out by the noble men and women who have been sent out in that field by the churches of America."

Germany To The Front

This reveals a real change on the part of prominent statesmen in their attitude on the African question. Then comes another suggestion from Germany, for which Dr. Heinrich Schnee, a former Governor of German East Africa, is author. This German statesman suggests in an interview given out in Berlin, and published in New York, that America takes over the mandatories of Great Britain and France in Africa for the colonization of American Negroes. Speaking on the matter, he says:

> "As regards the attempt to colonize Africa with the surplus American colored population, this would in a long way settle the vexed problem, and under the plan such as Senator France has outlined, might enable France and Great Britain to discharge their duties to the United States, and simultaneously ease the burden of German reparations which is paralyzing economic life."

With expressions as above quoted from prominent world statesmen, and from the demands made by such men as Senators France and McCullum, it is clear that the question of African nationality is not a far-fetched one, but is as reasonable and feasible as was the idea of an American nationality.

A "Program" At Last

I trust that the Negro peoples of the world are now convinced that the work of the Universal Negro Improvement Association is not a visionary one, but very practical, and that it is not so far fetched, but can be realized in a short while if the entire race will only co-operate and work toward the desired end. Now that the work of our organization has started to bear fruit we find that some of these "doubting Thomases" of three and four years ago are endeavoring to mix themselves up with the popular idea of rehabilitating Africa in the interest of the Negro. They are now advancing spurious "programs" and in a short while will endeavor to force themselves upon the public as advocates and leaders of the African idea.

It is felt that those who have followed the career of the Universal Negro Improvement Association will not allow themselves to be deceived by these Negro opportunists who have always sought to live off the ideas of other people.

The Dream Of A Negro Empire

It is only a question of a few more years when Africa will be completely colonized by Negroes, as Europe is by the white race. What we want is an independent African nationality, and if America is to help the Negro peoples of the world establish such a nationality, then we welcome the assistance.

It is hoped that when the time comes for American and West Indian Negroes to settle in Africa, they will realize their responsibility and their duty. It will not be to go to Africa for the purpose of exercising an over-lordship over the natives, but it shall be the purpose of the Universal Negro Improvement Association to have established in Africa that brotherly co-operation which will make the interests of the African native and the American and West Indian Negro one and the same, that is to say, we shall enter into a common partnership to build up Africa in the interests of our race.

Oneness Of Interest

Everybody knows that there is absolutely no difference between the native African and the American and West Indian Negroes, in that we are descendants from one common family stock. It is only a matter of accident that we have been divided and kept apart for over three hundred years, but it is felt that when the time has come for us to get back together, we shall do so in the spirit of brotherly love, and any Negro who expects that he will be assisted here, there or anywhere by the Universal Negro Improvement Association to exercise a haughty superiority over the fellows of his own race, makes a tremendous mistake. Such men had better remain where they are and not attempt to become in any way interested in the higher development of Africa.

The Negro has had enough of the vaunted practice of race superiority as inflicted upon him by others, therefore he is not prepared to tolerate a similar assumption on the part of his own people. In America and the West Indies, we have Negroes who believe themselves so much above their fellows as to cause them to think that any readjustment in the affairs of the race should be placed in their hands for them to exercise a kind of an autocratic and despotic control as others have done to us for centuries. Again I say, it would be advisable for such Negroes to take their hands and minds off the now popular idea of colonizing Africa in the interest of the Negro race, because their being identified with this new program will not in any way help us because of the existing feeling among Negroes everywhere not to tolerate the infliction of race or class superiority upon them, as is the desire of the self-appointed and self-created race leadership that we have been having for the last fifty years.

The Basis Of An African Aristocracy.

The masses of Negroes in America, the West Indies, South and Central America are in sympathetic accord with the aspirations of the native Africans. We desire to help them build up Africa as a Negro Empire, where every black man, whether he was born in Africa or in the Western world, will have the opportunity to develop on his own lines under the protection of the most favorable democratic institutions.

It will be useless, as before stated, for bombastic Negroes to leave America and the West Indies to go to Africa, thinking that they will have privileged positions to inflict upon the race that bastard aristocracy that they have tried to maintain in this Western world at the expense of the masses. Africa shall develop an aristocracy of its own, but it shall be based upon service and loyalty to race. Let all Negroes work toward that end. I feel that it is only a question of a few more years before our program will be accepted not only by the few statesmen of America who are now interested in it, but by the strong statesmen of the world, as the only solution to the great race problem. There is no other way to avoid the threatening war of the races that is bound to engulf all mankind, which has been prophesied by the world's greatest thinkers; there is no better method than by apportioning every race to its own habitat.

The time has really come for the Asiatics to govern themselves in Asia, as the Europeans are in Europe and the Western world, so also is it wise for the Africans to govern themselves at home, and thereby bring peace and satisfaction to the entire human family.

Feminism, Nationalism, and the Early Women's Movement in the English-Speaking Caribbean
(with Special Reference to Jamaica and Trinidad and Tobago)

Rhoda Reddock

That's the basic error of the so-called feminist movement, which is really a masculinist movement. The pervasity of this philosophy is the false assumption that men and women are the same kind of being, and that woman has been kept down by man and has lapsed into an inferior position. Hence it urges women to force themselves onto the same level as man, learning to do all the things men do and behaving as men behave. But this is trying to change nature itself.

—*Port of Spain Gazette*, September 27, 1927

According to one writer, the first recorded use of the term *feminism* in English was in 1894, close to fifty years after what we now know as the first feminist wave was supposed to have emerged. This term, according to the 1933 Supplement to the *Oxford English Dictionary*, was derived from the French *féminisme*, first coined by Utopian socialist Charles Fourier (Rendall, 1985: 1).

For those of us former colonials who write in the English language, the contradiction of defining our cultural autonomy in the language of the colonizers is a problem we face daily and in some ways surmount. But possibly no other word in modern times has been so vilified for its European origins as *feminism* and its derivative *feminist*.

For us Caribbean women, in recent times the struggle to define our womanness as well as our Caribbeanness has, especially in the 1960s and 1970s, been fraught with demands that we deny and reject any feminist consciousness or the need for a feminist struggle. Feminist consciousness and action preceded the actual coining of the word. This was so not only in Europe, but in all parts of the world where women (at rare times with the support of men) have sought to challenge the subordination and exploitation that have to varying degrees been the history of most women.

What is interesting about emergent feminism is its tendency to develop out of the wombs of other social movements. Contradictorily, it is often the attempts by males to reject this natural interrelationship between movements for women's emancipation and other movements for class, national, or ethnic emancipation that provides the impetus for the emergence of the feminist question.

This essay defines feminism very simply as the awareness of the subordination and exploitation of women in society and the conscious action to change that situation. Feminists differ in their understanding of the nature of the problem and therefore on the strategies for its solution. This paper aims to explore the manifestations of feminist consciousness during the first half of the twentieth century in Jamaica and Trinidad and Tobago. Characteristic of the early women's movement in the English-speaking Caribbean was its close association with the nationalist struggle in its peculiarly Caribbean form.

Little theoretical work has so far been done on the national question in the English-speaking Caribbean. In an area consisting primarily of the descendants of migrants, the search for a national identity goes beyond the boundaries of the individual island, or indeed of the Caribbean region as a whole. Within the English-speaking Caribbean, nationalism during the early twentieth century usually implied an identification with Africa or India for the majority of the people, at a time when these two continents were also under the yoke of colonial rule. In spite of this difference a clear link between the movement for women's emancipation and nationalist movements characteristic of many other parts of the colonial world could be discerned. In the words of Kumari Jayawardena:

> The movement for women's emancipation and the feminist struggles which emerged in Asia and Africa must be considered in the context of the resistance that developed in many countries to imperialism and various forms of foreign domination on the one hand, and to movements of opposition to feudal monarchies, exploitive local rulers and traditional patriarchal and religious structures on the other. (Jayawardena, 1982:8)

In common with other countries, two streams can be discerned. The first contained the dominant middle-class or bourgeois nationalists, many of whom were educated in the colonial country and imbibed colonial liberal values of progress and advancement. The second contained the working-class nationalists strongly influenced by socialist and particularly Marxist (Comintern) approaches to the "national question." By far the majority of the early feminists were associated with the first stream. Many of them were middle-class, educated, cultured ladies who sought to improve the lot of their sex and race. Not surprisingly, their demands reflected the strong influence of liberalism—the right to education, citizenship, and political participation.

For most of these middle-class nationalists, in spite of a reidentification with the ancestral culture, the adoption of "modern" (read "Western") values on family, economy, and society were paramount. Education in general, and for women in particular, was to be the key to enlightenment and modernization. In Asia this meant the rejection of "backward" practices against women such as suttee and foot-binding; in the Caribbean it often meant the rejection of the so-called matrifocal family and female economic autonomy (now known to be largely the result of African adaptations in the New World) and a stress on the Euro-Christian Western nuclear family.

Central to this process were the male reformers, men who went out of their way (sometimes paternistically, sometimes not) to champion the women's cause. Some of these men, the modern educated men, needed companions of equal stature who could converse with them and see to the education of their children. Others believed that basic rights for women in the colonies were only reasonable if these women were to be brought in line with those of the mother country. Still others reflected a genuine concern for the denial of humanity to one half of the human race.

I hope to make it clear that whatever the context, feminism has not been a 1960s import into the Caribbean. The modern women's movement in the English-speaking Caribbean is the continuation of a rich struggle for women's emancipation, a struggle fraught with contradictions but one nevertheless firmly based within the sociopolitical and historical context of the region.

The Women's Movement, 1900–1950: The Women's Self-Help Movement

One of the earliest manifestations of women organizing in their own interest was the Women's Self-Help Movement. The first such group, the Lady Musgrave Self-Help Society of Jamaica, founded in 1865, stated as its aim the development "of feminine industries such as embroideries, native jams, jellies and drawn thread work to provide employment for poor needlewomen" (French and Ford-Smith, 1984: 170). These self-help societies, although ostensibly to assist poor women, were a main means through which upper-class ladies, white and colored, attempted to gain some economic autonomy or even to survive economically in spite of the norms of society.

The Trinidad and Tobago equivalent, the Trinidad Home Industries and Women's Self-Help Society, was established in 1901 following the example of the Jamaica society. This organization, however, was much more explicit in stating its true aim of providing a means through which "all gentlewomen in reduced circumstances should be assisted to add to their incomes" (Trinidad Information Bureau, 1919:35–36).

A similar organization, the Barbados Women's Self-Help, still exists today. In general, all three organizations provided retail outlets for handicraft and preserves produced by women and sought to train young women in "housewifery skills." In 1899, black activist Robert Love criticized the Jamaica society for "pushing the work of poor women to one side to make way for the work of the upper crust" (*Advocate*, June 10, 1899, quoted in French and Ford-Smith, 1984: 171).

It is important to note the class of women involved in this "income-generating" activity. Lady Musgrave, founder of the Jamaica society, was the wife of the governor. In 1901, the Trinidad society was inaugurated by Mrs. Maloney, also a governor's wife, and the revitalized society in 1904 had as its first president another governor's wife, Mrs. Hugh Clifford.

Historically, these groups have usually been perceived as charities, largely because of the widely held view that social or religious work was the only acceptable public activity for women of that class. Apparently this was an issue of some debate in Trinidad society. According to one member, in the beginning many "ladies" refused to work in shops. They would surreptitiously have their products delivered but did not want to be seen to be "in reduced circumstances." Others felt that the work should be done "for sweet charity's sake" because for them working for money was beneath their station. Clearly, this latter view was a minority one. Most of the women saw themselves as making a statement for "honest work" and breaking away from "false pride." They even criticized the common practice of hiring "coolies" to carrying parcels and the shame felt by both women and men in carrying parcels. They defended their right to work when they were attacked for being vulgar (Aldric-Perez, 1920:11).

Clearly, even among the colonial elite of the Caribbean at this time, women could not depend economically on their male breadwinners. In addition, as with some women of their class in other countries, they defended their right to earn an income even in ways circumscribed by the bourgeois sexual division of labor.

The Middle-Strata Women's Movement

Although social work was not the primary concern of the early self-help movement, this would not be true of other early organizations of women. During the late nineteenth and early twentieth centuries, social work was a highly prestigious activity carried out primarily by the white women of the local and colonial ruling classes. Later in the century and up to the 1950s, women activists of the labor and feminist movements incorporated social work into their political activity as a significant component. For most of these groups, social work with women and girls was especially important.

In 1918, the Women's Social Service Club (WSSC) was formed in Jamaica. Like most middle-strata women's organizations of the time, its attempts to uplift womanhood seldom went outside the parameters of domesticity, morality, and class-boundness defined by the colonial ideology. One of the main foci of the group was women's employment—a recurrent theme in the Caribbean women's movement. Others included illegitimacy and political representation (French and Ford-Smith, 1984:177–86). Unlike the self-help movement, however, the middle-strata women's movement's emphasis was on employment for the working classes and not for themselves, employment in areas suitable to their sex and station in life. In 1919, for example, the WSSC established a Girls' Workroom, training unemployed women in handicraft and needlework and seeking markets for their products. This project expanded to other parts of Jamaica by 1921.

In its campaign against moral vice, the WSSC reflected many of the views of early twentieth-century feminists on women's moral responsibility. They collaborated with the Social Purity Association (SPA) of Jamaica, which was formed in 1917 for the purpose of eradicating immorality and venereal disease (French and Ford-Smith, 1984:180). The SPA and WSSC attacked prostitution and joined with the Jamaica Baptist Union to ensure the responsibility of fathers. Although sympathetic with the plight of unmarried mothers and their difficulties with the bureaucracy in getting support from fathers, the transition to the recognition of mothers as economic breadwinners was never made.

The main political struggle was for women's representation on the Legislative Council. In making their demands, women used their housewifery management experience to justify their potential contribution to government. Though seeking political equality for themselves, they accepted that such rights need not be extended to the working classes. A pattern of a complex division of labor based on sex, race, and class becomes apparent. Income-earning activity was necessary for the poor (black) working-class women but not for women of the upper class. These women, however, were due the same political rights as their menfolk, rights that could not be extended to working-class women.

For most of these early twentieth-century middle-strata women's organizations, charity and not solidarity characterized their relationships with women of other classes and ethnic groups.

In 1921, the first of the black middle-strata women's organizations was formed in Trinidad and Tobago. It was the Coterie of Social Workers (CSW) founded by Audrey Layne Jeffers, a member of the then small well-to-do black property-owning class. Although Jeffers could be described politically as a feminist and a black nationalist, like others throughout the world the class differential between herself and those she sought to serve was never in question. In addition, like other black nationalists, especially during the early years, the struggle for the dignity of non-European people took place within the context of the British Empire.

The Coterie membership consisted mainly of black and colored women of the educated middle classes. For these women, participation in social work, once the preserve of the European ladies, was a significant means of raising the status of people of African origin in general and of their class in particular. Participation in social work also became increasingly a form of social fulfillment as more and more women were excluded from the labor force during the post-World War I economic depression. In 1934–35, civil service legislation and the education code banned the employment of married women except when no alternative could be found.

The feminist component of the activities of the Coterie was evident in its social work as well as in its political work. In the 1920s, for example, it founded the St. Mary's Home for Blind Girls and the Maud Reeves Hostel for Working Girls. In 1935, the Bishop Anstey House for (Respectable) Women was founded.

A significant aspect of CSW activity lay in alleviating much of the childcare burden of working-class mothers. This was attempted through the establishment of a school meal program popularly known as Breakfast Sheds, which spread throughout the country, including Tobago. Children at primary schools received hot meals daily free of cost or for one Penny. In addition, the CSW established the first day-care centers for children initially in John John, a poor working-class urban area.

In addition to the Coterie's focus on women and girls, an emphasis on the plight of nonwhite women and girls was also evident. During her student years in Britain, Jeffers had been one of the founders of the Union of Students of African Descent, later the League of Colored Peoples. During World War I she had served among the West African troops and started a West African Soldiers Fund (Comma-Maynard, 1971:2).

In its nationalist and political activity the Coterie collaborated with the socialist-oriented Trinidad Workingmen's Association (TWA). Although the Coterie was clearly influenced by that association, there is less evidence of its collaboration with the Garvey movement—the United Negro Improvement Association (UNIA)—which was popular at this time. In 1936, four Coterie members attended the Negro Progress Convention held in British Guiana. They were Laura Beard, Mrs. Scott, Budosy Jeffers, and southern social worker Marcelline Archibald. At this convention, which marked the one hundredth year of freedom from slavery, Audrey Jeffers at a special women's section spoke on women and their responsibility to the race. She called on women to take a serious view of life and to come forward and help in the new epoch of reconstruction of the race (Comma-Maynard, 1971:92–93).

During the late 1920s and early 1930s, three significant events took place. These were the struggle of women to be eligible for seats on the Port of Spain City Council, the Divorce Bill

Agitation, and the West Indian and British Guiana Conference of Women Social Workers. Examination of these events is crucial to an understanding of the character of the feminist struggle during this period.

In Jamaica, the equivalent of the Coterie of Social Workers appears to have been the Jamaica Women's Liberal Club (LC), formed around 1937. This organization, consisting mainly of black middle-strata women, carried the women's struggle begun by the Women's Social Service Club in new directions. The core of this organization, according to French and Ford-Smith (1984), was a small group of women teachers who had begun to agitate within the Jamaica Union of Teachers for jobs for women in the administration of education and in the colonial civil service in general. Leading members of this group included Amy Bailey, Mary Morris Knibb, and Edith Dalton James. In a speech in 1938, Amy Bailey noted:

> The time has come for women teachers from all colleges to get together and demand improvements which are theirs by right. Why is it that there are no women assistant inspectors drawn from the ranks of the elementary school? If the principal is good enough for men, it is surely good enough for us women. (*Gleaner*, April 25, 1938, quoted in French and Ford-Smith, 1984)

As did the Coterie, LC members saw themselves as establishing a place for women within the developing national identity of their country. They saw women's place as clearly defined by their class, however, and accepted their natural superiority in relation to women of the laboring classes. The LC was also influenced by the ideas of Jamaican black nationalist leader Marcus Mosiah Garvey. The early aims and objectives of the club included the study of Negro history, native and foreign, and the advance of the status of Jamaican women socially and politically.

Leading member Amy Bailey defined herself as a feminist and took up a personal campaign against the refusal of commercial enterprises to hire black women. This issue had also been taken up by Audrey Jeffers in Trinidad in 1936 because black women were not yet accepted as suitable advertisement for commercial wares.

Acceptance of class differentiation by these early middle-strata feminists was a key factor in determining their social and political action. On the one hand, there was general acceptance of the colonial housewife ideology, which identified the dependent housewife and male breadwinner as the key actors of the bourgeois family. These feminists, however, accepted the right of women to earn an income even though they felt that this should be done in activities suitable to women's sex and station in life. The LC, in recognizing the contribution of women volunteers to the social services, therefore argued that they should be paid by the state for their work.

The emergence of the Domestic Science/Home Economics movement in North America as an influential section of the women's movement affected these Caribbean feminists. Bailey saw training in domestic science as one means through which women's work within the home could be given dignity. This could take place at two levels, first among middle-strata housewives, who could present certificates to their men showing their ability to "cook *his* food, spend *his* money wisely and train *his* children properly" (Bailey, 1938, quoted in French and Ford-Smith, 1984:255, emphasis added). At another level, domestic science could be the basis of vocational training to prepare underprivileged girls for jobs as waitresses, cooks, laundresses, upholsterers, domestics, and dressmakers.

As with feminists throughout the world at this time, little challenge was made to the existing sexual division of labor. Indeed, training in domestic work was a major means of bringing black women closer to European levels of housewifery and domesticity. This movement, unfortunately, was perceived as progress and upliftment.

Today, as Caribbean women contemplate the regional character of our struggle, it is important that we examine earlier efforts in this direction. In April of 1936, the Coterie celebrated its fifteenth anniversary with a little-remembered conference of West Indian and British Guianese women social workers in Port of Spain. The conference was attended by delegates from British Guiana, Barbados, Grenada, and St. Lucia, and it ended with the formation of the West Indies and British Guiana Women Social Workers Association. Throughout the conference a speaking ban was placed on all men who attended. It was temporarily lifted for one evening, when Jeffers announced that "men would be permitted to say a few words" but would not be allowed to ask questions. The highlight of the event was the speech by Audrey Jeffers, "The Urgent Needs of Women in Trinidad." She began by stating that:

> The needs of our women to my mind have been seriously neglected in the past. The men made it a transient concern and the women in high places socially and intellectually took a rather lukewarm interest in their own sex. (*Trinidad Guardian*, May 20, 1936, p. 8)

After an analysis of women's condition, especially that of black and colored women, she called for a scholarship for girls, the establishment of a high school for girls, and the establishment of a women's police force.

One of the most radical speeches of the event was given by Gertie Wood of British Guiana in "Political Aspirations and Achievements of women in British Guiana." This speech reflected many of the contradictions in consciousness inherent in the early women's movement. In the area of employment, Miss Wood noted:

> Women are engaged in the civil service, in commerce, in teaching, farming, in the professions, in trades, in fact in every branch of life or the Colony. I submit, and do so quite soberly, that woman has attained this position not because things were made easy for her by the powers that be. No! Oh no!—but because, ladies and gentlemen, she has proved without a shadow of a doubt that when she chooses her life job and trains for it she does it with her will, sparing not even herself in the execution of her duty. (*Trinidad Guardian*, May 8, 1936, p. 8)

She pointed out that the army of women engaged in domestic service and as homemakers "bear the brunt of their sex" silently without realizing it. In this way they put in far more self-sacrificing work than did men. She added that women had been taught to bow and smile to men for so long that now in the New Era, when conditions had changed, women were still too timid to do otherwise. In spite of the strident tone of most of her talk, she concluded in a conciliatory manner:

> I am an advocate of "Women's Rights," but am not an extremist and have no
> patience with extremists, for I know and believe that there is much that man alone can
> do, so we still have need for them ... But we aspire to a fair and square deal to be meted
> out to women workers. (*Trinidad Guardian*, May 8, 1936, p. 8)

Not surprisingly, the next conference was planned for British Guiana and did take place. It was the forerunner of subsequent regional organizations of women that developed over the course of this century.

The Struggle for Political Rights

The role of male reformers was extremely significant in the struggle for women's rights in many colonial countries. In many instances early feminists had to depend on these liberal or progressive men who held positions of power and influence to champion their legal and political causes. Although gains were made in this area at different periods during the century in both Jamaica and Trinidad and Tobago, the significant political battles took place at different times. In Jamaica, for example, the campaign for the extension of the franchise to women began in the aftermath of World War I, when women of the British middle classes had been granted the vote.

The campaign in Jamaica had the support of black members of the Kingston Council, as well as some sections of the emerging commercial bourgeoisie and its organ, the *Gleaner*. A leading champion was H. A. G. de Lisser, secretary of the Jamaica Imperial Association, which supported planter interests. The *Gleaner* argued that women had performed well during the war. They had done work which had previously been done only by men, and therefore deserved representation (*Gleaner*, July 4, 1918). It was clear, however, that the extension was to be limited to the "better class of women." De Lisser warned against "an army of women voters" swamping the votes of men, women who were not intellectually or academically their equals, and to ensure that this would not happen, he proposed a literacy test.

Black Council members such as Garveyite supporter H. A. Simpson proposed an extension of the franchise to include the black and colored middle strata. This, however, was not to be (French and Ford-Smith, 1984:187). In spite of this support, a more forceful campaign was needed to make even this limited gain. This campaign was eventually led by the Women's Social Service Club. Arguments against the franchise of women were similar to those in other countries, but some typically Caribbean ones also emerged. For example, one man feared that women would close down all rum shops and force the registration of fathers of illegitimate children (*Gleaner*, September 9, 1918). Another argument suggested that women's lack of political advancement was the result of their own lack of interest.

Women of the WSSC responded to these attacks through letters in the press, a women's petition, and demonstrations at Ward theater and public meetings. In July 1919, the franchise was extended to women over twenty-five years of age who earned an income of £50 or paid taxes of over £2 per year. Men could vote at the age of twenty-one if their annual income was £40 per year. Few men but even fewer women became eligible for the franchise, but no women could become candidates.

In Trinidad and Tobago, the struggle for women to become eligible for seats on the Port of Spain City Council was another milestone in the regional movement for women's political rights. Although initiated by women, it was eventually taken through the council by male reformer Captain Arthur Andrew Cipriani. On September 8, 1924, according to the *Mirror Almanack*, a delegation of women was received by the governor to discuss the issue of votes for women. This even took place within an atmosphere of legislative reform, which was being considered at the time.

In 1924, a new constitution was introduced. Although elected officials (members) were introduced into the Legislative Council, high property qualifications for voting and even higher ones for candidature were instituted. As a result, only six percent of the total population was eligible to vote (Brereton, 1981:166). To vote, men who qualified had to be over the age of twenty-one and women over thirty. Only men literate in English with large amounts of property or considerable income could become candidates.

Although the 1924 delegation may have called for further legislative reform, it was at the municipal level that the struggle was first manifested. In August 1927, Captain A. A. Cipriani, deputy mayor and president of the Trinidad Workingmen's Association (TWA), moved a motion in the Port of Spain Town Council calling for amendment of the Corporation Ordinance to make women eligible for seats on the council.

In supporting this motion, Cipriani noted that such action had already been taken in other parts of the British Empire and that since the war, women were holding their own in jobs in commerce, banks, and business firms, doing jobs previously carried out by men (*Trinidad Guardian*, September 26, 1927, p. 6). The motion was referred to a committee for consideration over one month, but during that period much debate occurred. It was the beginning of a long struggle, which did not end until 1935. The *Port of Spain Gazette* denounced the feminist movement, finding women chauffeurs, air pilots, professionals, and other "blue-stockinged women" to be "out of place" (*Port of Spain Gazette*, September 25, 1927). But numerous other articles in this and other newspapers reflect the various aspects of the debate.

Although the *Port of Spain Gazette* denounced the issue, the *Trinidad Guardian* bemoaned in an editorial that so far women of the city had given no public demonstration of their views:

> Certainly when their case was being put forward for the first time, one would have expected to see the leading feminists of Trinidad (if there are any) present to encourage and applaud their champion. But there were none. The development of political consciousness in the women of Trinidad does not therefore seem yet to have reached the articulate stage. (*Trinidad Guardian*, September 28, 1927, p. 10)

The *Labour Leader*, organ of the TWA, supported Cipriani's notion and pointed out that women had made no public demonstration because they knew they would win sooner or later and were content to wait. The paper threw out the challenge to find five women as qualified and suitable to sit on the council as any five men whom those opposing the motion could find (*Labour Leader*, September 3, 1927, p. 8).

It is interesting that although the leading feminists of the day were of the landowning or at least the upper middle classes, their support came from the socialist-oriented TWA. Cipriani, a Trinidadian of Caucasian origin, was a landowner who had taken over leadership of the

TWA in 1923. The TWA was oriented along Fabian socialist lines and followed the line of the British Labour party. Although worker-oriented, Cipriani sought a rapprochement between labor and capital and saw himself as the mediator between the two—the champion of the barefoot man. As mediator, Cipriani often sought to reduce direct confrontation between opposing forces. Diplomacy and discussion, usually by him on behalf of others, was often his solution.

One woman, however, made public her demands for women's political rights. She was Beatrice Greig, a Scotswoman and wife of a planter who supported feminist and worker-oriented causes. On March 13, 1928, Greig gave a public address, "The Position of Women in Public Life," at the Richmond Street Literary and Debating Association (*Mirror Almanack*, 1929). Throughout this struggle she was the main female protagonist in support of Cipriani's motion, arguing that women were ready to serve because they voted and paid taxes. This argument was strongly rejected by the *Port of Spain Gazette* (September 16, 1927) as not being representative of her sex.

On September 29, 1927, the committee of the town council considering the motion rejected any change in the ordinance. Many male radicals, including Dr. Tito Achong and Alfred Richards, voted against the motion. Again, the arguments against any change were similar to those heard in other countries. Achong argued that in this country women were not sufficiently educationally qualified to deal with the issues of taxation, sanitation, and engineering which were often raised in the council. But he went even further, stating that "at a certain stage of a woman's life she was not even fit to give evidence before a court of law" (*Trinidad Guardian*, September 30, 1927, p. 9). Again, the issue of women's apathy was raised. One councillor suggested they had not asked to serve, and another concluded that they preferred to leave such matters to their husbands, brothers, and other men.

The arguments in favor of the motion excelled in literary eloquence. Councillor Archibald accused the council of being like the mad hatter at the tea party in *Alice in Wonderland* who shouted "No! No!"—to which Alice replied, "There is plenty of room," and seated herself in a large armchair at the head of the table.

In the end, the motion was rejected by the mayor's deciding vote (*Port of Spain Gazette*, September 30, 1927, p. 12; October 7, 1927, p. 9). The motion was rejected again in April of 1929 but was eventually carried on May 29, 1930, with Cipriani's (as mayor) deciding vote. On this occasion fifty women attended the session. It was not until January 1935, however, that this amendment was actually accepted into the corporation ordinance.

One year later, in 1936, two women presented themselves as candidates for the town council. They were Audrey Layne Jeffers and Beatrice Greig, the country's two foremost social workers and feminists. This move was welcomed by the *Trinidad Guardian* which, in an editorial entitled "Challenge by Women," patronizingly noted:

> Should either of the two candidates be elected, an important stimulus would be given to the Women's Movement, which appears to be gathering force in the West Indies and which recently produced the first inter-colonial conference of women welfare workers ever convened in this part of the world … The appearance of these two women pioneers in the municipal election area is to be welcomed. They deserve

the sympathetic consideration of the burgesses of Port of Spain. And, should they win, the men candidates whom they are expected to oppose could feel that they had lost gloriously to women—albeit of the "weaker sex"—entirely worth their steel. (*Trinidad Guardian*, October 1, 1936, p. 6).

The atmosphere during the rest of the campaign was much less accommodating. One early casualty was Beatrice Greig, whose qualification papers were rejected. The qualifications of Audrey Jeffers were later also questioned, and the issue was eventually taken to court. Opposing Jeffers in the Woodbrook seat was A.P.T. Ambard of the *Port of Spain Gazette*, which had consistently campaigned against seats for women on the council. The election campaign for Audrey Jeffers served as a rallying point for middle-strata women. The court action unsuccessfully served against her only added controversy to the event and awakened greater interest. The *Trinidad Guardian* noted:

Municipal elections continue to provide many thrills, particularly in Wood-brook ... In this centre Trinidad women are very active and getting ready to give the lie to the statement that they do not wish to be interested in local politics, for they are determined to see Miss Jeffers win. (*Trinidad Guardian*, October 21, 1936, p. 1)

Opposing candidate Ambard was accused of being fascist because he had declared himself on the side of the Spanish fascists who supported Italy and Germany. In the aftermath of the 1935 Italian invasion of Ethiopia by Mussolini, antifascist, antiracist feeling ran high in Trinidad and Tobago. Responding to this issue, Cipriani declared, "Those who vote for Italy vote Ambard. Those who are voting Ethiopia are voting Miss Jeffers." Ironically, in spite of the class contradictions that continued to be reflected in Jeffers's life, the feminist struggle found its natural (although not always accepted) ally in the workers' and anti-fascist movement. On November 3, 1936, Audrey Jeffers won the Woodbrook seat in the municipal elections, defeating her two opponents and becoming the first woman to contest and win an election in Trinidad and Tobago.

In Jamaica, in the aftermath of the 1938 labor disturbances, women became eligible for seats on municipal councils. In 1939, the Jamaica Women's Liberal Club organized a campaign that resulted in the election of Mary Morris Knibb to the Kingston/St. Andrew Parish Council. As in Trinidad and Tobago, her election proved to be an important rallying point for middle-strata women.

Afro-Caribbean Nationalism and the Women's Movement

By the late nineteenth century, Afro-Caribbean nationalism and the struggle for women's emancipation had become linked. This was evident in one of the earliest organizations, the Pan African Association (PAA) founded by Trinidadian Henry Sylvester Williams, and its Jamaican counterpart, the People's Convention of Robert Love. According to his biographer Owen Mathurin, Williams emphasized women's participation in the political struggle. In his speeches Williams stressed the involvement of women in the PAA as well as the need for education for girls. Not surprisingly, Williams claims to have first been politically influenced by a woman, Mrs. Kinloch, who spoke in London on the situation in southern Africa. In his 1901 Caribbean tour, therefore, the mobilization of women was a key component of his work.

In Jamaica, a branch of the PAA was founded by radical black nationalist Robert Love after Williams's visit in 1901. Love had previously founded another organization, the People's Convention, in 1895 to assist in the election of blacks to the Legislative Council (French and Ford-Smith, 1984: 201–4). The PAA in Jamaica maintained Williams's position on the involvement of women, and the secretary of the Kingston branch, Cathryn McKenzie, can be identified as one of the earliest black feminists in the region (Ford-Smith, 1987:1–2).

In a paper entitled "The Rights of Women," published on August 10, 1901, in the *Advocate*, the organ of the People's Convention, Cathryn McKenzie put forward her view on women's emancipation. She argued that "the rights of women left much to be desired" and counseled that only by struggle could women ever win their rights. She referred to the struggles of American and British feminists and the efforts to achieve equality and education for women.

Little else is known of McKenzie because she died soon after in a fire. The work in women's emancipation was continued, however, through the PAA and the People's Convention and in the pages of the *Advocate*. Unlike with the middle-strata women's organizations that developed later, Robert Love challenged the existing sexual division of labor and the sexual division within the school curriculum. He opposed the limiting of girls' education to female teachers and the "domestic focus" in women's education.

The People's Convention was particularly concerned with the need for economic independence of poor black women, and championed their right to land as a means of achieving this independence. It supported one female teacher against the loss of her pension. In the words of French and Ford-Smith:

> The People's Convention supported unequivocally the admission of black women of the middle class to all professions and to administrative positions. It tentatively put forward the right of working class women to an independent income and sought to break the skewed sexual division of labour of the period. It was one of the few organizations which does not seem to have seen the solution to the problems of working-class women in their training to be domestic servants and handicraft experts. (French and Ford-Smith, 1984:213)

In spite of the PAA's relatively progressive position on women, its influence regionally and internationally was limited. A later organization, the United Negro Improvement Association (UNIA), was to be much more influential in scope both in this region and overseas. UNIA was founded in July of 1914 by Marcus Mosiah Garvey and Amy Ashwood, later Garvey. From an organization of two persons it grew to become one of the largest mass movements of all time. At its height in the 1920s, according to Garvey historian Tony Martin, there were over twelve hundred branches in more than forty countries, a large proportion of which were in the Caribbean, the United States, Canada, and Africa (Martin, 1987:11).

The involvement of Amy Ashwood in the early formation of UNIA may have contributed to the significance of the mobilization of women in the Garvey movement. Amy Ashwood was the first secretary of the Ladies Division of UNIA (Martin, 1987:33), which apparently developed into the Black Cross Nurses section of UNIA. Through its organizational structure, UNIA assured the participation of women in several ways. One of these was through the institution of specific leadership positions for women such as lady president and lady vice-president in branches, so that women were always represented at the executive level. There were also two divisions for women only, the Black Cross Nurses and the Universal African Motor Corps, a paramilitary organization that attracted large numbers of women.

In addition to its actual membership, the Garvey movement had a strong influence on middle-strata black and colored women. In addition to fostering racial pride, it provided a place for women in their quest for personal dignity and that of their oppressed race. In Trinidad and Tobago, for example, feminist Audrey Jeffers and women members of the Coterie of Social Workers stressed their aim of raising the status of black and colored women. Similarly, in Jamaica, middle-strata liberal feminists such as Una Marson, Amy Bailey, and others of the Women's Liberal Club challenged the leadership of white upper-class women's organizations (Ford-Smith, 1987:16–17).

From within the movement itself there emerged some of the most important women activists. The most well known was, of course, Amy Ashwood Garvey, Pan Africanist and feminist. Until recently very little had been written about the contribution of Amy Ashwood Garvey, first wife of Marcus Garvey, perhaps because unlike his also outstanding second wife Amy Jacques Garvey, she did not easily fit into the mold of loyal and faithful wife, mother, and supporter. In spite of a five-year courtship, the marriage of Amy Ashwood and Marcus Garvey lasted less than three months. The end of the marriage, however, did not mark the end of the political work Amy Ashwood would do until her death in 1969.

In London, Amy Ashwood, an associate of British socialist and feminist Sylvia Pankhurst, helped found the Nigerian Progress Union in 1924, and in 1926 in Harlem she collaborated with her companion Sam Manning of Trinidad in the production of three Afro-American musicals (Martin, 1987: 34). Two events of relevance here reflect clearly the intertwining of Amy Ashwood's nationalism and feminism. These were the Fifth Pan African Congress of 1945 and her Caribbean tour of 1953. As a leading member of the International African Service Bureau, Amy Ashwood Garvey worked with George Padmore, T. R. Makonnen, Kwame Nkrumah, and C. L. R. James in the organization of the important Fifth Pan African Congress. This congress, held October 13–21, 1945, attracted many of the future leaders of Africa and was to have far-reaching consequences. In the booklet commemorating this event, hers is one of the few names omitted from the cover. Her sterling contribution to the cause of Caribbean women, however, is documented within.

Not surprisingly, throughout most of the conference the issue of women was not mentioned. On October 19, however, in opening that day's first session, Amy Ashwood said:

Very much has been written and spoken of the Negro, but for some reason very little has been said about the black woman. She has been shunted into the social background to be a child-bearer. This has principally been her lot. (Padmore, 1963:52)

In this session Amy Ashwood, together with fellow Jamaican Alma la Badie (the only other woman participant), spoke on the problems of Jamaican women of various classes. In the final resolutions of the conference, those relating to the West Indies were the only ones to include clauses on women. These included demands for equal pay for equal work regardless of nationality, creed, or race; removal of all disabilities affecting the employment of women; modernization of bastardy laws with legal provisions for the registration of fathers; raising the age of consent to sixteen (or eighteen); and others (Padmore, 1963:61). Despite the consistent work of Afro-Caribbean women in the anticolonial and nationalist movement since the late nineteenth century, they remained marginal to that important congress.

In 1953 Amy Ashwood Garvey embarked on her second Caribbean tour. She visited Antigua, Aruba, Barbados, British Guiana, Dominica, Surinam, and Trinidad and Tobago with the aim of stimulating the women's movement. She hoped especially to reach middle-strata women, whom she felt were of the class best poised for enlightened political activity. In Barbados, she presided over the formation of the Barbados Women's Alliance (*Barbados Observer*, March 21, 1953) and lectured widely throughout the region. During her visit to Trinidad she hailed Audrey Jeffers as one of the region's leading feminists and social workers. In the lecture "Women as Leaders of World Thought" she concluded:

> I hope that when the history of the West Indies comes to be written, you will not only write it on West Indian pages in a heroic manner, but that you will join the great women of the world in writing your own history across the pages of world history. (*Port of Spain Gazette*, May 28, 1953, p. 3)

Garveyism undoubtedly provided a significant impetus for the organization of Afro-Caribbean women. In addition, most of the early feminists saw their struggle for women's emancipation as a component of the struggle for racial equality and human dignity. At the same time, the ideology of women and women's place in most cases reflected the colonial thinking on women and the family and its relation to the sexual division of labor and sexuality. The reality of Garveyite women's lives, however, often covered other issues, according to Ford-Smith: "It offered black women a concrete experience in organization and leadership which was unrivaled" (Ford-Smith, 1987:ii).

Indo-Caribbean Nationalism and the Woman Question

The early twentieth century was a period of heightening nationalist consciousness for Indo-Caribbean people. By 1917, the system of Indian immigration had been ended and an educated and propertied elite was emerging among Indians in Trinidad and Tobago. In addition, contact with the Indian nationalist movement was maintained through periodicals and newspapers as well as through visits of Indian emissaries. Within this movement two tendencies could be identified. The first involved a group of older propertied men who sought communal representation for Indians in the political system, and the second included younger men allied with the TWA who sought a more representative solution.

Throughout most of this period, however, no Indian women emerged as public proponents of their cause. The male writers in the *East Indian Weekly*, organ of the young Indian liberals, made frequent calls for Indian women to come forward to work for the upliftment of their sex. There is little evidence, however, that any did so. Beatrice Greig became the spokesperson on behalf of Indian womanhood in Trinidad and Tobago. Greig, the daughter of Scottish-Canadian missionaries, had lived in Trinidad since the age of sixteen. After a sojourn in India, she returned to Trinidad to marry William Greig, a large landowner. In India, Greig had been influenced by the theosophist movement and had befriended Catherine Mayo, author of the book *Mother India*, which had highlighted the subjugation of women in India.

In many ways Greig can be seen as one of that group of European women—feminists, socialists, and freethinkers—who participated in the anticolonial and women's movements of Third World countries early in this century. Among them were Annie Besant, an English socialist and feminist who became the first president of the Indian National Congress in 1917, and Margaret Cousins, an Irish feminist who was a founder of the All-India Women's Conference in 1927 (Jayawardena, 1986:20–21).

As a contributor to the *East Indian Weekly*, Beatrice Greig consistently raised issues related to Indian women. In January of 1929, for example, during the visit of Indian emissary Pundit Mehta Jaimini, Greig raised the issue of the subjugation of Indian women:

> Mahatmi Jaimini had come from a meeting which he had addressed to women only. …He had explained to them that in bygone years, women were free and equal with men, and not to educate them was considered a crime … In reply to my question, "how is it then that Indian women are kept in such darkness and subjugation today?"—he replied that it is due entirely to men's selfishness and ignorance and a desire to have all power in their own hands, and that these evils had gradually been introduced through the ages. (*East Indian Weekly*, February 2, 1929, p. 4)

On her suggestion, Pundit Jaimini gave a public lecture on October 31, 1929, chaired by Beatrice Greig. Using the title "The Ideals of Indian Womanhood," Jaimini put forward clearly the Indian nationalist position on the "upliftment of women." For him, *Sita* was the ideal of Indian womanhood, "with all patience and suffering she is ever chaste"—and he summarized five ideals of Indian womanhood: chastity, devotion to her husband, mistress of the house, production of children as good and useful citizens, and causing peace and happiness in the family and society (*East Indian Weekly*, November 9, 1929, p. 10).

It is not clear whether this talk achieved what Greig hoped it would, but it provides a clear example of the similarity between the Indian nationalist view of uplifted womanhood and the Victorian ideal.

In 1929, Gandhi's assistant C. J. Andrews visited Trinidad and in a meeting of Indian women at Debe denounced child marriage. On his departure, he left the book *Saroj Nalini: A Woman of India*, which was serialized by Greig in the *East Indian Weekly*. Saroj Nalini Dutt was the wife of an Indian nationalist. Her life combined the Indian nationalist ideals of support for Indian nationalism and loyal wifehood. In serializing this book Greig hoped that it would "inspire the Indian woman of Trinidad by her splendid example, enthusiasm and self-sacrifice to follow in her footsteps." This was not to be, and no Mahila Samitis or Ladies Associations were formed (*East Indian Weekly*, January 18, 1929, P. 5).

In addition to the *Weekly*, Greig also wrote the India section in the *Beacon*, literary journal of the 1930s. She founded the Trinidad Association of Girls' Clubs, was a close associate of the Trinidad Workingmen's Association and the early Teachers' Union, and was generally known as a bluestocking. Although the issue of the upliftment of Indian womanhood was a frequent subject in the pages of the *Weekly*, very few Indian women emerged as champions of this cause. The reasons for this cannot be explored here, but later generations of Indian women would make up for the lack. Nevertheless, early in this century women's emancipation and related issues were central to the nationalist debates of both Afro- and Indo-Caribbean people.

Conclusion

I have attempted to give a broad and general insight into the early women's movement in Jamaica and Trinidad and Tobago. One significant aspect I have omitted is the working-class and socialist women's movement, which will be discussed in another paper. I have tried here to begin the process of documenting the feminist struggles and movements of the women of our region. This history is important because it lays a basis from which we can analyze the processes that have shaped and continue to influence the situation of women today.

A key issue explored in this paper is the way in which the contradictions of race, sex, and class played themselves out in the lives and struggles of these middle-class women. It is interesting that in spite of their charity toward working-class women, both Amy Bailey and Audrey Jeffers voted against universal adult suffrage in the 1940s. In addition, like most middle-strata nationalists of the time, these women fought to attain colonial European standards rather than to challenge the extension of colonial values to our countries.

Maybe it is unfair to judge the past according to our understanding of the present, but the lesson is clear. The solution is not a greater piece of this exploitive, racist, and patriarchal system, but its fundamental transformation.

Bibliography

Aldric-Perez, J. *A Review of the Trinidad Home Industries Association, 1901–1920*. Port of Spain, 1920.

Brereton, Bridget. *A History of Modern Trinidad, 1783–1962*. London: Heinemann, 1981.

Comma-Maynard, Olga. *The Briarend Pattern: The Story of Audrey Jeffers O. B. E. and the Coterie of Social Workers*. Port of Spain, 1979.

French, Joan, and Ford-Smith, Honor. 'Women, Work and Organization in Jamaica, 1900–1944.' Kingston: ISS/DGIS Research Project, 1984.

Ford-Smith, Honor, 'Women and the Garvey Movement.' Mona: University of the West Indies, 1987. Paper presented at Marcus Garvey conference.

Garvey, Amy Ashwood. 'The Birth of the Universal Negro Improvement Association.' Introduction by Tony Martin. In Tony Martin, *The Pan-African Connection*. Cambridge, Mass.: Schenkman, 1983.

Jayawardena, Kumari. *Feminism and Nationalism in the Third World in the Nineteenth and Early Twentieth Centuries*. The Hague: ISS, 1982.

———. *Feminism and Nationalism in the Third World*. London: Zed Books, 1986.

Martin, Tony. 'Amy Ashwood Garvey: Wife.' *Jamaica Journal* 20, no. 3 (August–September 1987).

Padmore, George. *History of the Pan African Congress*. 2d ed. London, 1963.

Reddock, Rhoda. 'Women, Labour and Struggle in Twentieth Century Trinidad and Tobago, 1898–1900.' Ph.D dissertation, University of Amsterdam, 1984.

Rendall, Lane. *The Origins of Modern Feminism*. London: Macmillan, 1985.

Trinidad Information Bureau. *Trinidad: The Riviera of the Caribbean*. Port of Spain, 1919.

Puerto Rican Nationalism

Pedro Albizu Campos

Sixty-Eight years ago, our republic was formed. On September 23, 1868, we declared our independence from Spain. Puerto Rico was rich in name and in our soil. Our Christian foundation had created a family model that was to be a vanguard of modern civilization.

Influential, independent men have made a difference in our society. Men such as musician Morel Campos; intellectuals such as Eugenio María de Hostos; and poets like Gautier Benítez were among the great men who built and founded this nation.

The founders of our republic in 1868 held that our nation and its people would be sovereign – never belonging to another nation or people. This idea is not original, but is the basis of universal civilization, of international law. It is the basis of the family of free nations.

Our mother nation, Spain, founder of North and South American civilization, recognized this basic principle of sovereignty and, in 1868, paved the way for Puerto Rico to enter the family of free nations.

The United States (after the Spanish American War), on the other hand, saw Puerto Rico not as a nation, but as island property, and therefore took Puerto Rico through military intervention, and kept it.

Military intervention is the most brutal and abusive act that can be committed against a nation and a people. We demanded then, as we do today, the retreat of United States armed forces from Puerto Rico in order to embrace the liberty we held all too briefly in 1868.

We are not as fortunate as our forebears in 1868, who struggled to attain sovereignty. They never had a complaint against Spain, for Spain had every intention of granting Puerto Rico its liberty.

We stand today, docile and defenceless, because, since 1868, our political and economic power has been systematically stripped away by the United States for its own political and economic gain.

We stand as a nation forced not only to demand our liberty, but to demand reparations for having our political and economic liberty taken away.

We stand as a nation surrounded by industry, but with little of it belonging to our people. The business development in Puerto Rico since the United States intervention should have made the island one of the most prosperous islands in the world, but that is not the case.

The United States controls our economy, our commerce. Puerto Rico must determine a price for its products that is acceptable to the United States, while the United States issues their products to Puerto Rico at a rate that is comfortable to its own manufacturers and not the Puerto Rican consumer. The result is exploitation and abuses perpetrated at will, resulting in poverty for our people and wealth for the United States.

Seventy-six per cent of the wealth is in the hands of United States corporations, and their stability is ensured by the United States military. This economic exploitation will have a long-lasting impact. Our family structure will be weakened, and the intellectual, spiritual, and moral advancement of our race will be jeopardized as we are made to be more 'North American.'

Already United States government agencies, under the guise of Christian virtue and goodwill, are simply controlling our people, destroying its culture. By imposing its own culture and language, the United States destroys our own culture and language.

What will we have when we have nothing but dependency on those who destroyed us?

This is why I am dismayed by the effort among our own people to defeat the spirit of those who struggle for our liberation. Our own people see Puerto Rican nationalism as nothing but a path of terrorism and murder; but they defeat our spirit in denouncing themselves. They defeat our spirit by ignoring the historical terrorism and murder of the United States. In the end, they help only the United States, its industry, its imperialist objectives.

It stands to reason – it stands to common sense – that we must be a free nation in order to survive as a people. The future of those not yet born depends on respecting the independence of Puerto Rico. That respect alone – the respecting of Puerto Rico's independence – is what Puerto Rican nationalism is all about.

Fascism in the Colonies

George Padmore

New Sedition Law Proposed

DESPITE the appointment of a Royal Commission to inquire into labour conditions in Trinidad, the general political situation in that colony is going from bad to worse. Temporary economic concessions, such as increased wages and shorter hours, which many sections of the working class forced the employers to concede as a result of the general strike, are now being threatened. For the Government is inaugurating a policy which savours of Colonial Fascism, and which, if not challenged immediately, is bound to deprive the workers of their most elementary civil rights, such as freedom of the press, speech and assembly.

The authorities have proposed the enactment of a new Sedition Bill; public open-air meetings are being prohibited; newspaper editors are threatened with prosecution; British troops have been landed to garrison the industrial centres of the island; the sum of $51,000 has been voted for the purpose of arming a special middle-class volunteer force in order to protect vested interests; while several trade union leaders, including Uriah Butler, President of the British Empire Workers' and Citizens' Home Rule Party, were arraigned before the Criminal Assizes on charges of murder, sedition and incitement to riot. Butler has been sentenced to two years' imprisonment. A wave of terrorism and intimidation is sweeping over the country.

The Situation Reviewed

West Indian workers, Negroes as well as East Indians, are among the worst paid labourers in the world, and in consequence their standard of living is extremely low. In recent years their conditions have become almost intolerable, due to unemployment and the rising cost of living. Unorganised and without any political rights, they have been unable to obtain any form of social relief, despite the fact that for years Captain A.A. Cipriani, who, until recently, was looked upon as the undisputed leader of the toiling masses of the island, had been appealing to the Government to take measures to ameliorate the conditions of the workers.

Cipriani is a native-born white man of Corsican ancestry and a descendant of the Bonapartes. He is the President of the Trinidad Labour Party and one of the seven unofficial elected members of the Legislative Council.

Last May Cipriani was appointed by the Government as one of the two representatives of the colony to the Coronation. During his absence, the employers, especially those on the oilfields, started to rationalise industry, and the workers, goaded into desperation, declared a stay-in strike on June 19th. Immediately the strike was declared, the managers of the companies called upon the Government to assist them in crushing the strike. Police were despatched from Port of Spain to the south of the island, the centre of the oil industry. On arrival there they began to beat up the strikers and to drive them off the oilfields. In Trinidad most industrial and agricultural workers live in huts or barracks on the premises of the companies so that whenever they dare to strike the first thing the employers do is to declare them trespassers and evict them and their families. Although the workers protested against being thrown on the streets, they agreed to vacate peacefully the property of their masters.

It was while Butler, the strike leader, was addressing the workers on an open lot near the oilfields that the trouble started. The police, armed with pistols, attempted to break up the meeting and arrest Butler. This precipitated fighting in the course of which a police corporal was killed and several civilians wounded. On the following day the Governor ordered the commander of the local Forces to recruit a volunteer corps from among the European community. These men were armed and put in control of the oilfields at Point Fontin and Fyzabad. This was an incitement to further rioting, resulting in the death of ten workers and sixteen wounded. In the meantime the Governor cabled the Colonial Office for reinforcements. On the morning of June 22nd H.M.S. Ajax arrived in Port of Spain and landed hundreds of marines and bluejackets. Two days later the cruiser Apollo landed more troops, which were assigned to control the oil refineries and strategic points in the capital.

By this time the strike had already reached Port of Spain, where lightermen, stevedores, porters, carters and public works labourers declared solidarity with the oilfields workers. Processions were spontaneously organized and the workers marched through the busy section of the town with banners and slogans declaring: "We ask for bread and they give us hot lead." "Stop the murder of defenceless workers in the oilfields."

Despite all the military display which the Government mobilized to intimidate the people, the strikers refused to return to work until their grievances were redressed. By this time the strike was island-wide. Thousands of East Indian agricultural labourers on the great sugar plantations refused to work. Motor transport in many parts of the country had to stop for want of petrol; ships arriving in the harbour of Port of Spain were unable to discharge their cargoes. The entire economic life of the country was at a standstill.

Alarmed at the tremendous wastage of petroleum on the oilfields, the companies decided to negotiate with the strike leaders. The Government, however, obstructed negotiations by threatening to arrest Butler, who by this time had gone into hiding. The police, bent upon getting their man, went to the extent of offering £100 to any worker who would betray their leader. The strikers, however, spurned this offer and appointed a delegation to confer with the employers. After much haggling the companies agreed to certain of their demands and the men went back to work.

The Government Departments, especially the Public Works, also increased the pay of their workers and instituted an eight-hour day. Even the scavengers employed by the City Council of Port of Spain received an increase in wages.

Natives Lack Vitamins

Reviewing the situation before the members of the Legislative Council, the Governor, admitting the justice of the workers' case, declared that:

When I arrived in Trinidad, I was very painfully impressed by the effect of poverty here, more particularly by the physical appearance of the East Indian population. I have come from the South Seas where East Indians were introduced in exactly similar circumstances, brought in for the sugar estates, but the men there are of definitely finer physical figure. I think over my report written in 1935. It refers to a visit of a Dutch doctor. He was some weeks going through the country associated with one of our medical officers. He was always shocked by the evidence of malnutrition which he observed in these areas. He stated he had 20 years experience in these Dutch East Indies and, although he had personal knowledge of conditions resulting from vitamin deficiency, he had never seen such distressing conditions as existed here among the East Indian labouring population who were apparently – men and women – suffering from the absence of all the known vitamins. At the hospital the doctor took cases at random and showed me the ravages which are being caused by deficiency diseases among the East Indian labouring population.

This admission so aroused public opinion that the Governor, with the approval of the Secretary of State for the Colonies, appointed a Commission to investigate the cause of the unrest and the conditions of labour in the island.

Policy of Repression

Inspired by their success, the workers began to organise trade unions for the first time in the history of the island in order to safeguard their gains and to press for the right of collective bargaining. But as was to be expected, the employers, who are organised into a powerful Chamber of Commerce, bitterly opposed trade unionism, denouncing the unions as unlawful bodies, hot-beds of sedition and Bolshevism, and would have no dealings with them. On the other hand, the Government, while recognising the unions, has adopted a policy which, if continued, will reduce their effectiveness and usefulness in defending the economic interests of the workers.

In order to stifle all criticism, the first thing the Governor did was to impose a censorship upon the press during the strike and to threaten native editors with summary imprisonment if they dared to comment upon the military measures he had adopted, and especially the hunt which the police, aided by marines and volunteers had started for Butler and other strike leaders. Entire villages were rounded up and house-to-house searches carried out.

Since then a more direct move to curb the activities of the unions by denying them the possibility of public assembly has been made. It is significant that the Government made this move immediately after the United Kingdom members of the Commission departed from the colony. In a letter addressed to the Mayor, Aldermen and Councillors of the Municipality of Port of Spain, the Colonial Secretary, the Hon. A.W. Seymour, C.M.G , appealed to that body to co-operate with the Government to prohibit the workers from using public squares and open spaces in the city for meetings.

In Trinidad, like most other colonies, there are few halls suitable for workers' assembly, and those which exist are owned by employers who, naturally, would not rent them to unions, even if the workers were in a position to hire them. The only places, therefore, where workers can hold their meetings are on common lands; and since such places are under the direct control of the Municipal Corporation, the Government, in order to carry out its attack upon free speech and assembly, is importuning the Civic Council. The Government has even gone a step further in its determination to stifle all criticism and to put the fear of God into the hearts of the natives.

At a meeting of the Legislative Council on November 13th, a body whose majority are Government officials and nominees of the Governor representing vast interests such as oil, agriculture, commerce, etc., a new sedition ordinance received its first reading. The Bill provides that:

1. Whoever does or attempts to do, or makes any preparation to do, or conspires with any person to do any act with a seditious intention, and whoever utters any words having a seditious intention, shall be guilty of a misdemeanour.

2. Whoever publishes, sells, offers for sale, distributes, or, with a view to its being published, prints, writes, composes, makes, produces, imports, or has in his possession, power or control, any seditious publication, shall be guilty of a misdemeanour.

3. Every person guilty of a misdemeanour under this section shall on conviction on indictment, be liable to a fine not exceeding four thousand dollars or to imprisonment with or without hard labour for a term not exceeding too years or to both fine and imprisonment, or on summary conviction before a magistrate, to a fine not exceeding four hundred and eighty dollars or to imprisonment for a term not exceeding six months or to both such fine and imprisonment.

Three days later, to coincide with the opening of the trial of Butler and other trade union leaders before the Criminal Assizes, the Governor ordered H.M.S. York to Port of Spain and brought a company of Sherwood Foresters from Bermuda by Canadian Government steamer, as a salutary gesture to the populace. And to add insult to injury the maintenance of these troops will be borne by the taxpayers.

Intimidation has reached such a stage that even members of the Legislative Council cannot open their mouths without running the risk of being jailed. For example, at a recent meeting of the Legislative Council the Governor, in addition to charging the colony with the upkeep and maintenance of the British garrison, voted the suit of $51,000 for rearming the volunteer and local forces, on the excuse that it is necessary for the colony to prepare itself against foreign invasion. Captain Cipriani, however, objected to the expenditure of such a large sum upon military purposes at a time when the workers are suffering from economic depression. He described the measure as class legislation: arming the forces to quell labour unrest in the interests of the employers. The Governor took objection to Cipriani's statement and said he would refer the matter to the Attorney-General, adding the warning that there was no privilege to members of the Legislative Council.

Mr. Lloyd Smith, a native journalist and editor of the Sunday Chronicle, is being charged with sedition for publishing a letter signed by an ex-civil servant, alleged to be derogatory to the service. Mr. Smith will appear before the next Criminal Assizes.

Ten Years for Labour Leader

A similar wave of repression is sweeping over the island of Barbados, a neighbouring colony of Trinidad, also recently the scene of labour disturbances. A number of workers' leaders are now being charged before the Criminal Assizes with sedition and rebellion. The trial of all the accused has not been completed, but one man by the name of Ulric Grant has been sentenced to ten years' imprisonment for taking part in a demonstration of unemployed in Bridgetown, during which six workers were shot and several wounded. Marines were also landed on the island. Since then, the Governor of Barbados, Sir Mark Young, who is reputed to be less sympathetic to natives than Fletcher, has been sent to Trinidad, where the Duke of Montrose, the chairman of the oil companies, has demanded that the Colonial Office establish a naval base to protect vested interests.

On January 10th Mr. Ormsby-Gore announced that the King had accepted the resignation of Sir Murchison Fletcher. This should he an eye-opener to Socialists. The Governor was an Imperialist, but because he had the courage to criticise publicly the slave conditions in the island, the sugar kings and oil barons could not forgive him.

After 140 years of Crown Colony rule the people of Trinidad and other West Indian colonies are still smarting under a number of economic, political and social grievances which are becoming aggravated by the autocratic methods of administrators. It is high time for a fundamental change in the political constitutions of these colonies, along the road of self-determination. This is the task which history has placed on the toiling masses of the West Indies – Indians as well as Negroes; for the West Indian bourgeoisie is one of the most reactionary colonial ruling classes and will never make any concessions unless forced to.

It is the duty of British Socialists and trade unionists to help these colonial workers.

The Malaise of a Civilization

Suzanne Césaire

If in our legends and tales we see the appearance of a suffering, sensitive, sometimes mocking being that is our collective ego, we look in vain for an expression of that ego in Martinique's ordinary literary products.

Why is it that in the past we have been so unconcerned about telling our ancestral worries directly?

The urgency of this cultural problem escapes only those who have decided to put on blinders so as not to be disturbed from an artificial tranquillity—at any price, be it that of stupidity or death.

As for us, we feel that our troubling times will bud here a ripened fruit, irresistibly called by the ardor of the sun to disperse its creative forces to the wind; we feel in this tranquil, sun-drenched land the fearsome, inexorable pressure of destiny that will dip the whole world in blood in order, tomorrow, to give it its new face.

Let us inquire into the life of this island that is ours.

What do we see?

First the geographical position of this parcel of land: tropical. In this case here, the Tropics.

Whence the adaptation here of an African settlement. The Negroes imported here had to struggle against the intense mortality of slavery in its beginnings, against the harshest work conditions ever, against chronic malnutrition—a reality that is still alive. And nevertheless, it cannot be denied that on Martinican soil the colored race produces strong, tough, supple men and women of a natural elegance and great beauty.

But, then, is it not surprising that this people, who over the centuries has adapted to this soil, this people of authentic Martinicans is just now producing authentic works of art? How is it that over the centuries no viable survivors of the original styles have been revealed—for example, those styles that have flowered so magnificently on African soil? Sculptures, ornate fabrics, paintings, poetry? Let the imbeciles reproach the race and its so-called instinct for laziness, theft, wickedness.

Let's talk seriously:

If this lack of Negroes is not explained by the hardships of the tropical climate to which we have adapted, and still less by I know not what inferiority, it is explained, I believe, as follows, by:

(1) the horrific conditions of being brutally transplanted onto a foreign soil; we have too quickly forgotten the slave ships and the sufferings of our slave fathers. Here, forgetting equals cowardice.

(2) an obligatory submission, under pain of flogging and death, to a system of "civilization," a "style" even more foreign to the new arrivals than the tropical land.

(3) finally, after the liberation of people of color, through a collective error about our true nature, an error born of the following idea, anchored in the deepest recesses of popular consciousness by centuries of suffering: "Since the superiority of the colonizers arises from a certain style of life, we can access power only by mastering the techniques of this 'style' in our turn."

Let's stop and measure the importance of this gigantic mistake.

What is the Martinican fundamentally, intimately, and inalterably? And how does he live?

In answering these questions, we will see a surprising contradiction appear between his deep being, with his desires, his impulses, his unconscious forces—and how life is lived with its necessities, its urgencies, its weight. A phenomenon of decisive importance for the future of the country.

What is the Martinican?

—A human plant.

Like a plant, abandoned to the rhythm of universal life. No effort expended to dominate nature. Mediocre at farming. Perhaps. I'm not saying he makes the plant grow; I'm saying he grows, that he lives plantlike. His indolence? That of the vegetable kingdom. Don't say: "he's lazy," say: "he vegetates," and you will be doubly right. His favorite phrase: "let it flow." Meaning that he lets himself flow with, be carried by life, docile, light, not insistent, not a rebel—amicably, amorously. Obstinate besides, as only a plant knows how to be. Independent (the independence and autonomy of a plant). Surrender to self, to the seasons, to the moon, to the day whether shorter or longer. The picking season. And always and everywhere, in the least of his representations, primacy of the plant, the plant that is trod upon but alive, dead but reborn, the free, silent, and proud plant.

Open your eyes—a child is born. To which god should he be confided? To the Tree god. Coconut or Banana, in whose roots they bury the placenta.

Open your ears. One of the popular tales of Martinican folklore: the grass that grows on the tomb is the living hair of the dead person, in protest to death. Always the same symbol: the plant. The lively feeling of a life-death community. In short, *the Ethiopian feeling for life.*[1]

So, the Martinican is typically Ethiopian. In the depths of his consciousness, he is the human plant, and by identifying with the plant, his desire is to surrender to life's rhythm.

Does this attitude suffice to explain his failure in the world?

No—the Martinican has failed because, misrecognizing his true nature, he tries to live a life that is not suited to him. A gigantic phenomenon of collective lying, of "pseudomorphosis." And the current state of civilization in the Caribbean reveals to us the consequences of this error.

Repression, suffering, sterility.

How, why this fatal mistake among this people enslaved until yesterday? By the most natural of processes, by the play of the survival instinct.

Remember that what the regime of slavery above all forbade was the *assimilation of the Negro to the white.* Some choice ordinances: that of April 30, 1764, which forbids blacks and coloreds from practicing medicine; that of May 9, 1765, which forbids them from working as notary publics; and the famous ordinance of February 9, 1779, which formally forbids blacks from wearing the same clothes as whites, demands respect for and submission to "all whites in general," etc., etc.

Let's cite too the ordinance of January 3, 1788, which obliged free men of color "to request a permit if they wished to work *anywhere but in cultivation.*" It is understood henceforth that the essential goal for the colored man has become that of *assimilation.* And with a fearsome force, the disastrous conclusion forms in his head: *liberation equals assimilation.*

In the beginning, the movement was off to a good start: 1848; the masses of freed blacks, in a sudden explosion of primitive ego, incorrectly renounced all regular work, despite the danger of famine. But the Negroes, subdued by economics, no longer slaves but wage earners, submitted once more to the discipline of the hoe and the cutlass.

And this is the era that definitively establishes the repression of the ancestral desire for letting go.

That desire is replaced, especially in the colored bourgeoisie, by the foreign desire of struggle.

Whence the drama, evident to those who analyze in depth the collective ego of the Martinican people: their unconscious continues to be inhabited by the Ethiopian desire for letting go. But their consciousness, or rather their preconsciousness, accepts the Hamitic desire for struggle. The race to riches. To diplomas. Ambition. Struggle reduced to the level of the bourgeoisie. The race to monkey-like imitations. Vanity fair.

The most serious consequence is that the desire to imitate, which had formally been vaguely conscious—since it was a defense reaction against an oppressive society—now passed into the ranks of the fearsome, secret forces of the unconscious.

No "evolved" Martinican would accept that he is only imitating, so much does his current situation appear natural, spontaneous, born of his most legitimate aspirations. And, in so doing, he would be sincere. He truly does not KNOW that he is imitating. He is *unaware of* his true nature, which does not cease to exist for that matter.

Just as the *hysteric* is unaware that he is merely *imitating* an illness, but the doctor, who cares for him and delivers him from his morbid symptoms, knows it.

Likewise, analysis shows us that the effort to adapt to a foreign style that is demanded of the Martinican does not take place without creating a state of pseudocivilization that can be qualified as *abnormal, teratoid.*

The problem today is to determine if the Ethiopian attitude we discovered as the very essence of the Martinican's feeling for life can be the point of departure for a viable, hence imposing, cultural style.

It is exalting to imagine in these tropical lands, finally rendered to their internal truth, the long-lasting and fruitful accord between man and soil. Under the sign of the plant.

Here we are called upon finally to know ourselves, and here before us stand splendor and hope. Surrealism gave us back some of our possibilities. It is up to us to find the rest. By its guiding light.

Understand me well:

It is not a question of a return to the past, of resurrecting an African past that we have learned to appreciate and respect. On the contrary, it is a question of mobilizing every living force mingled together on this land where race is the result of the most continuous brazing; it is a question of becoming conscious of the tremendous heap of various energies we have until now locked up within ourselves. We must now put them to use in their fullness, without deviation and without falsification. Too bad for those who thought we were idle dreamers.

The most troubling reality is our own.

We shall act.

This land, our land, can only be what we want it to be.

Originally published as "Malaise d'une civilisation," *Tropiques* 5 (April 1942):43–49.
 Among other things, the title plays on the French translation of Sigmund Freud's *Civilization and Its Discontents* [Malaise de la civilisation].

Note
> Suzanne Césaire's italics, as are all others unless otherwise noted. She is here alluding to the theories of the ethnologist Leo Frobenius. See her essay 'Léo Frobenius et le Problème des Civilisations,' *Tropique* 1 (April 1941): 27–36.

Discourse on Colonialism (excerpt)

Aimé Césaire

A civilization that proves incapable of solving the problems it creates is a decadent civilization.

A civilization that chooses to close its eyes to its most crucial problems is a stricken civilization.

A civilization that uses its principles for trickery and deceit is a dying civilization.

The fact is that the so-called European civilization—"Western" civilization—as it has been shaped by two centuries of bourgeois rule, is incapable of solving the two major problems to which its existence has given rise: the problem of the proletariat and the colonial problem; that Europe is unable to justify itself either before the bar of "reason" or before the bar of "conscience"; and that, increasingly, it takes refuge in a hypocrisy which is all the more odious because it is less and less likely to deceive.

Europe is indefensible.

Apparently that is what the American strategists are whispering to each other.

That in itself is not serious.

What is serious is that "Europe" is morally, spiritually indefensible.

And today the indictment is brought against it not by the European masses alone, but on a world scale, by tens and tens of millions of men who, from the depths of slavery, set themselves up as judges.

The colonialists may kill in Indochina, torture in Madagascar, imprison in Black Africa, crack down in the West Indies. Henceforth the colonized know that they have an advantage over them. They know that their temporary "masters" are lying.

Therefore that their masters are weak.

And since I have been asked to speak about colonization and civilization, let us go straight to the principal lie that is the source of all the others.

Colonization and civilization?

In dealing with this subject, the commonest curse is to be the dupe in good faith of a collective hypocrisy that cleverly misrepresents problems, the better to legitimize the hateful solutions provided for them.

In other words, the essential thing here is to see clearly, to think clearly—that is, dangerously—and to answer clearly the innocent first question: what, fundamentally, is colonization? To agree on what it is not: neither evangelization, nor a philanthropic enterprise, nor a desire to push back the frontiers of ignorance, disease, and tyranny, nor a project undertaken for the greater glory of God, nor an attempt to extend the rule of law. To admit once and for all, without flinching at the consequences, that the decisive actors here are the adventurer and the pirate, the wholesale grocer and the ship owner, the gold digger and the merchant, appetite and force, and behind them, the baleful projected shadow of a form of civilization which, at a certain point in its history, finds itself obliged, for internal reasons, to extend to a world scale the competition of its antagonistic economies.

Pursuing my analysis, I find that hypocrisy is of recent date; that neither Cortéz discovering Mexico from the top of the great teocalli, nor Pizzaro before Cuzco (much less Marco Polo before Cambuluc), claims that he is the harbinger of a superior order; that they kill; that they plunder; that they have helmets, lances, cupidities; that the slavering apologists came later; that the chief culprit in this domain is Christian pedantry, which laid down the dishonest equations *Christianity* = *civilization*, *paganism* = *savagery*, from which there could not but ensue abominable colonialist and racist consequences, whose victims were to be the Indians, the Yellow peoples, and the Negroes.

That being settled, I admit that it is a good thing to place different civilizations in contact with each other; that it is an excellent thing to blend different worlds; that whatever its own particular genius may be, a civilization that withdraws into itself atrophies; that for civilizations, exchange is oxygen; that the great good fortune of Europe is to have been a crossroads, and that because it was the locus of all ideas, the receptacle of all philosophies, the meeting place of all sentiments, it was the best center for the redistribution of energy.

But then I ask the following question: has colonization really *placed civilizations in contact?* Or, if you prefer, of all the ways of *establishing contact*, was it the best?

I answer *no*.

And I say that between *colonization* and *civilization* there is an infinite distance; that out of all the colonial expeditions that have been undertaken, out of all the colonial statutes that have been drawn up, out of all the memoranda that have been dispatched by all the ministries, there could not come a single human value.

****

First we must study how colonization works to *decivilize* the colonizer, to *brutalize* him in the true sense of the word, to degrade him, to awaken him to buried instincts, to covetousness, violence, race hatred, and moral relativism; and we must show that each time a head is cut off or an eye put out in Vietnam and in France they accept the fact, each time a little girl is raped and in France they accept the fact, each time a Madagascan is tortured and in France they accept the fact, civilization acquires another dead weight, a universal regression takes place, a gangrene sets in, a center of infection begins to spread; and that at the end of all these treaties that have been violated, all these lies that have been propagated, all these punitive expeditions that have been tolerated, all these prisoners who have been tied up and "interrogated," all these patriots who have been tortured, at the end of all the racial pride that has been encouraged, all the boastfulness that has been displayed, a poison has been distilled into the veins of Europe and, slowly but surely, the continent proceeds toward *savagery*.

And then one fine day the bourgeoisie is awakened by a terrific boomerang effect: the gestapos are busy, the prisons fill up, the torturers standing around the racks invent, refine, discuss.

People are surprised, they become indignant. They say: "How strange! But never mind—it's Nazism, it will pass!" And they wait, and they hope; and they hide the truth from themselves, that it is barbarism, the supreme barbarism, the crowning barbarism that sums up all the daily barbarisms; that it is Nazism, yes, but that before they were its victims, they were its accomplices; that they tolerated that Nazism before it was inflicted on them, that they absolved it, shut their eyes to it, legitimized it, because, until then, it had been applied only to non-European peoples; that they have cultivated that Nazism, that they are responsible for it, and that before engulfing the whole edifice of Western, Christian civilization in its reddened waters, it oozes, seeps, and trickles from every crack.

Yes, it would be worthwhile to study clinically, in detail, the steps taken by Hitler and Hitlerism and to reveal to the very distinguished, very humanistic, very Christian bourgeois of the twentieth century that without his being aware of it, he has a Hitler inside him, that Hitler *inhabits* him, that Hitler is his *demon*, that if he rails against him, he is being inconsistent and that, at bottom, what he cannot forgive Hitler for is not *the crime* in itself, *the crime against man*, it is not *the humiliation of man as such*, it is the crime against the white man, the humiliation of the white man, and the fact that he applied to Europe colonialist procedures which until then had been reserved exclusively for the Arabs of Algeria, the "coolies" of India, and the "niggers" of Africa.

And that is the great thing I hold against pseudo-humanism: that for too long it has diminished the rights of man, that its concept of those rights has been—and still is—narrow and fragmentary, incomplete and biased and, all things considered, sordidly racist.

I have talked a good deal about Hitler. Because he deserves it: he makes it possible to see things on a large scale and to grasp the fact that capitalist society, at its present stage, is incapable of establishing a concept of the rights of all men, just as it has proved incapable of establishing a system of individual ethics. Whether one likes it or not, at the end of the blind alley that is Europe, I mean the Europe of Adenauer, Schuman, Bidault, and a few others, there is Hitler. At the end of capitalism, which is eager to outlive its day, there is Hitler. At the end of formal humanism and philosophic renunciation, there is Hitler.

And this being so, I cannot help thinking of one of his statements: "We aspire not to equality but to domination. The country of a foreign race must become once again a country of serfs, of agricultural laborers, or industrial workers. It is not a question of eliminating the inequalities among men but of widening them and making them into a law."

That rings clear, haughty, and brutal, and plants us squarely in the middle of howling savagery. But let us come down a step.

Who is speaking? I am ashamed to say it: it is the Western *humanist*, the "idealist" philosopher. That his name is Renan is an accident. That the passage is taken from a book entitled *La Réforme intellectuelle et morale*, that it was written in France just after a war which France had represented as a war of right against might, tells us a great deal about bourgeois morals.

> The regeneration of the inferior or degenerate races by the superior races is part
> of the providential order of things for humanity. With us, the common man is nearly
> always a déclassé nobleman, his heavy hand is better suited to handling the sword than

the menial tool. Rather than work, he chooses to fight, that is, he returns to his first estate. *Regere imperio populos*, that is our vocation. Pour forth this all-consuming activity onto countries which, like China, are crying aloud for foreign conquest. Turn the adventurers who disturb European society into a *ver sacrum*, a horde like those of the Franks, the Lombards, or the Normans, and every man will be in his right role. Nature has made a race of workers, the Chinese race, who have wonderful manual dexterity and almost no sense of honor; govern them with justice, levying from them, in return for the blessing of such a government, an ample allowance for the conquering race, and they will be satisfied; a race of tillers of the soil, the Negro; treat him with kindness and humanity, and all will be as it should; a race of masters and soldiers, the European race. Reduce this noble race to working in the *ergastulum* like Negroes and Chinese, and they rebel. In Europe, every rebel is, more or less, a soldier who has missed his calling, a creature made for the heroic life, before whom you are setting *a task that is contrary to his race*, a poor worker, too good a soldier. But the life at which our workers rebel would make a Chinese or a fellah happy, as they are not military creatures in the least. *Let each one do what he is made for, and all will be well.*

Hitler? Rosenberg? No, Renan.

But let us come down one step further. And it is the long-winded politician. Who protests? No one, so far as I know, when M. Albert Sarraut, the former governor-general of Indochina, holding forth to the students at the Ecole Coloniale, teaches them that it would be puerile to object to the European colonial enterprises in the name of "an alleged right to possess the land one occupies, and some sort of right to remain in fierce isolation, which would leave unutilized resources to lie forever idle in the hands of incompetents."

And who is roused to indignation when a certain Rev. Barde assures us that if the goods of this world "remained divided up indefinitely, as they would be without colonization, they would answer neither the purposes of God nor the just demands of the human collectivity"?

Since, as his fellow Christian, the Rev. Muller, declares: "Humanity must not, cannot allow the incompetence, negligence, and laziness of the uncivilized peoples to leave idle indefinitely the wealth which God has confided to them, charging them to make it serve the good of all."

No one.

I mean not one established writer, not one academic, not one preacher, not one crusader for the right and for religion, not one "defender of the human person."

And yet, through the mouths of the Sarrauts and the Bardes, the Mullers and the Renans, through the mouths of all those who considered—and consider—it lawful to apply to non-European peoples "a kind of expropriation for public purposes" for the benefit of nations that were stronger and better equipped, it was already Hitler speaking!

What am I driving at? At this idea: that no one colonizes innocently, that no one colonizes with impunity either; that a nation which colonizes, that a civilization which justifies colonization—and therefore force—is already a sick civilization, a civilization which is morally diseased, which irresistibly, progressing from one consequence to another, one denial to another, calls for its Hitler, I mean its punishment.

Colonization: bridgehead in a campaign to civilize barbarism, from which there may emerge at any moment the negation of civilization, pure and simple.

Elsewhere I have cited at length a few incidents culled from the history of colonial expeditions.

Unfortunately, this did not find favor with everyone. It seems that I was pulling old skeletons out of the closet. Indeed!

Was there no point in quoting Colonel de Montagnac, one of the conquerors of Algeria: "In order to banish the thoughts that sometimes besiege me, I have some heads cut off, not the heads of artichokes but the heads of men."

Would it have been more advisable to refuse the floor to Count d'Hérisson: "It is true that we are bringing back a whole barrelful of ears collected, pair by pair, from prisoners, friendly or enemy."

Should I have denied Saint-Arnaud the right to profess his barbarous faith: "We lay waste, we burn, we plunder, we destroy the houses and the trees."

Should I have prevented Marshal Bugeaud from systematizing all that in a daring theory and invoking the precedent of famous ancestors: "We must have a great invasion of Africa, like the invasions of the Franks and the Goths."

Lastly, should I have cast back into the shadows of oblivion the memorable feat of arms of General Gérard and kept silent about the capture of Ambike, a city which, to tell the truth, had never dreamed of defending itself. "The native riflemen had orders to kill only the men, but no one restrained them; intoxicated by the smell of blood, they spared not one woman, not one child. … At the end of the afternoon, the heat caused a light mist to arise: it was the blood of the five thousand victims, the ghost of the city, evaporating in the setting sun."

Yes or no, are these things true? And the sadistic pleasures, the nameless delights that send voluptuous shivers and quivers through Loti's carcass when he focuses his field glasses on a good massacre of the Annamese? True or not true? And if these things are true, as no one can deny, will it be said, in order to minimize them, that these corpses don't prove anything?

For my part, if I have recalled a few details of these hideous butcheries, it is by no means because I take a morbid delight in them, but because I think that these heads of men, these collections of ears, these burned houses, these Gothic invasions, this steaming blood, these cities that evaporate at the edge of the sword, are not to be so easily disposed of. They prove that colonization, I repeat, dehumanizes even the most civilized man; that colonial activity, colonial enterprise, colonial conquest, which is based on contempt for the native and justified by that contempt, inevitably tends to change him who undertakes it; that the colonizer, who in order to ease his conscience gets into the habit of seeing the other man as *an animal*, accustoms himself to treating him like an animal, and tends objectively to transform *himself into* an animal. It is this result, this boomerang effect of colonization that I wanted to point out.

Unfair? No. There was a time when these same facts were a source of pride, and when, sure of the morrow, people did not mince words. One last quotation; it is from a certain Carl Siger, author of an *Essai sur la colonisation* (Paris, 1907):

> The new countries offer a vast field for individual, violent activities which, in the
> metropolitan countries, would run up against certain prejudices, against a sober and
> orderly conception of life, and which, in the colonies, have greater freedom to develop
> and, consequently, to affirm their worth. Thus to a certain extent the colonies can

serve as a safety valve for modern society. Even if this were their only value, it would
be immense.

Truly, there are sins for which no one has the power to make amends and which can never
be fully expiated.

But let us speak about the colonized.

I see clearly what colonization has destroyed: the wonderful Indian civilizations—and
neither Deterding nor Royal Dutch nor Standard Oil will ever console me for the Aztecs and
the Incas.

I see clearly the civilizations, condemned to perish at a future date, into which it has
introduced a principle of ruin: the South Sea Islands, Nigeria, Nyasaland. I see less clearly
the contributions it has made.

Security? Culture? The rule of law? In the meantime, I look around and wherever there
are colonizers and colonized face to face, I see force, brutality, cruelty, sadism, conflict, and,
in a parody of education, the hasty manufacture of a few thousand subordinate functionaries,
"boys," artisans, office clerks, and interpreters necessary for the smooth operation of business.

I spoke of contact.

Between colonizer and colonized there is room only for forced labor, intimidation,
pressure, the police, taxation, theft, rape, compulsory crops, contempt, mistrust, arrogance,
self-complacency, swinishness, brainless elites, degraded masses.

No human contact, but relations of domination and submission which turn the colonizing
man into a classroom monitor, an army sergeant, a prison guard, a slave driver, and the
indigenous man into an instrument of production.

My turn to state an equation: colonization = "thingification."

I hear the storm. They talk to me about progress, about "achievements," diseases cured,
improved standards of living.

I am talking about societies drained of their essence, cultures trampled underfoot,
institutions undermined, lands confiscated, religions smashed, magnificent artistic creations
destroyed, extraordinary *possibilities* wiped out.

They throw facts at my head, statistics, mileages of roads, canals, and railroad tracks.

I am talking about thousands of men sacrificed to the Congo-Océan. I am talking about
those who, as I write this, are digging the harbor of Abidjan by hand. I am talking about
millions of men torn from their gods, their land, their habits, their life—from life, from the
dance, from wisdom.

I am talking about millions of men in whom fear has been cunningly instilled, who have
been taught to have an inferiority complex, to tremble, kneel, despair, and behave like flunkeys.

They dazzle me with the tonnage of cotton or cocoa that has been exported, the acreage
that has been planted with olive trees or grapevines.

I am talking about natural *economies* that have been disrupted—harmonious and viable
economies adapted to the indigenous population—about food crops destroyed, malnutrition
permanently introduced, agricultural development oriented solely toward the benefit of the
metropolitan countries; about the looting of products, the looting of raw materials.

They pride themselves on abuses eliminated.

I too talk about abuses, but what I say is that on the old ones—very real—they have superimposed others—very detestable. They talk to me about local tyrants brought to reason; but I note that in general the old tyrants get on very well with the new ones, and that there has been established between them, to the detriment of the people, a circuit of mutual services and complicity.

They talk to me about civilization, I talk about proletarianization and mystification.

For my part, I make a systematic defense of the non-European civilizations.

Every day that passes, every denial of justice, every beating by the police, every demand of the workers that is drowned in blood, every scandal that is hushed up, every punitive expedition, every police van, every gendarme and every militiaman, brings home to us the value of our old societies.

They were communal societies, never societies of the many for the few.

They were societies that were not only ante-capitalist, as has been said, but also *anti-capitalist*.

They were democratic societies, always.

They were cooperative societies, fraternal societies.

I make a systematic defense of the societies destroyed by imperialism.

They were the fact, they did not pretend to be the idea; despite their faults, they were neither to be hated nor condemned. They were content to be. In them, neither the word *failure* nor the word *avatar* had any meaning. They kept hope intact.

Whereas those are the only words that can, in all honesty, be applied to the European enterprises outside Europe. My only consolation is that periods of colonization pass, that nations sleep only for a time, and that peoples remain.

This being said, it seems that in certain circles they pretend to have discovered in me an "enemy of Europe" and a prophet of the return to the pre-European past.

For my part, I search in vain for the place where I could have expressed such views; where I ever underestimated the importance of Europe in the history of human thought; where I ever preached a *return* of any kind; where I ever claimed that there could be a *return*.

The truth is that I have said something very different: to wit, that the great historical tragedy of Africa has been not so much that it was too late in making contact with the rest of the world, as the manner in which that contact was brought about; that Europe began to "propagate" at a time when it had fallen into the hands of the most unscrupulous financiers and captains of industry; that it was our misfortune to encounter that particular Europe on our path, and that Europe is responsible before the human community for the highest heap of corpses in history.

In another connection, in judging colonization, I have added that Europe has gotten on very well indeed with all the local feudal lords who agreed to serve, woven a villainous complicity with them, rendered their tyranny more effective and more efficient, and that, it has actually tended to prolong artificially the survival of local pasts in their most pernicious aspects.

I have said—and this is something very different—that colonialist Europe has grafted modern abuse onto ancient injustice, hateful racism onto old inequality.

That if I am attacked on the grounds of intent, I maintain that colonialist Europe is dishonest in trying to justify its colonizing activity *a posteriori* by the obvious material progress that has been achieved in certain fields under the colonial regime—since *sudden change* is always possible, in history as elsewhere; since no one knows at what stage of material development these same countries would have been if Europe had not intervened; since the introduction of technology into Africa and Asia, their administrative reorganization, in a word, their "Europeanization," was (as is proved by the example of Japan) in no way tied to the European *occupation;* since the Europeanization of the non-European continents could have been accomplished otherwise than under the heel of Europe; since this movement of Europeanization was in progress; since it was even slowed down; since in any case it was distorted by the European takeover.

The proof is that at present it is the indigenous peoples of Africa and Asia who are demanding schools, and colonialist Europe which refuses them; that it is the African who is asking for ports and roads, and colonialist Europe which is niggardly on this score; that it is the colonized man who wants to move forward, and the colonizer who holds things back.

****

One of the values invented by the bourgeoisie in former times and launched throughout the world was *man*—and we have seen what has become of that. The other was the nation.

It is a fact: the *nation* is a bourgeois phenomenon.

Exactly; but if I turn my attention from *man* to *nations*, I note that here too there is great danger; that colonial enterprise is to the modern world what Roman imperialism was to the ancient world: the prelude to Disaster and the forerunner of Catastrophe. Come, now! The Indians massacred, the Moslem world drained of itself, the Chinese world defiled and perverted for a good century; the Negro world disqualified; mighty voices stilled forever; homes scattered to the wind; all this wreckage, all this waste, humanity reduced to a monologue, and you think all that does not have its price? The truth is that this policy *cannot but bring about the ruin of Europe itself*, and that Europe, if it is not careful, will perish from the void it has created around itself.

They thought they were only slaughtering Indians, or Hindus, or South Sea Islanders, or Africans. They have in fact overthrown, one after another, the ramparts behind which European civilization could have developed freely.

I know how fallacious historical parallels are, particularly the one I am about to draw. Nevertheless, permit me to quote a page from Edgar Quinet for the not inconsiderable element of truth which it contains and which is worth pondering.

Here it is:

> People ask why barbarism emerged all at once in ancient civilization. I believe I know the answer. It is surprising that so simple a cause is not obvious to everyone. The system of ancient civilization was composed of a certain number of nationalities, of countries which, although they seemed to be enemies, or were even ignorant of each other, protected, supported, and guarded one another. When the expanding Roman, Empire undertook to conquer and destroy these groups of nations, the dazzled sophists thought they saw at the end of this road humanity triumphant in Rome. They talked

about the unity of the human spirit; it was only a dream. It happened that these nationalities were so many bulwarks protecting Rome itself. ... Thus when Rome, in its alleged triumphal march toward a single civilization, had destroyed, one after the other, Carthage, Egypt, Greece, Judea, Persia, Dacia, and Cisalpine and Transalpine Gaul, it came to pass that it had itself swallowed up the dikes that protected it against the human ocean under which it was to perish. The magnanimous Caesar, by crushing the two Gauls, only paved the way for the Teutons. So many societies, so many languages extinguished, so many cities, rights, homes annihilated, created a void around Rome, and in those places which were not invaded by the barbarians, barbarism was born spontaneously. The vanquished Gauls changed into Bagaudes. Thus the violent downfall, the progressive extirpation of individual cities, caused the crumbling of ancient civilization. That social edifice was supported by the various nationalities as by so many different columns of marble or porphyry.

When, to the applause of the wise men of the time, each of these living columns had been demolished, the edifice came crashing down; and the wise men of our day are still trying to understand how such mighty ruins could have been made in a moment's time.

And now I ask: what else has bourgeois Europe done? It has undermined civilizations, destroyed countries, ruined nationalities, extirpated "the root of diversity." No more dikes, no more bulwarks. The hour of the barbarian is at hand. The modern barbarian. The American hour. Violence, excess, waste, mercantilism, bluff, conformism, stupidity, vulgarity, disorder.

In 1913, Ambassador Page wrote to Wilson:

"The future of the world belongs to us. ... Now what are we going to do with the leadership of the world presently when it clearly falls into our hands?"

And in 1914: "What are we going to do with this England and this Empire, presently, when economic forces unmistakably put the leadership of the race in our hands?"

This Empire ... And the others ...

And indeed, do you not see how ostentatiously these gentlemen have just unfurled the banner of anti-colonialism?

"*Aid to the disinherited countries*," says Truman. "The time of the old colonialism has passed." That's also Truman.

Which means that American high finance considers that the time has come to raid every colony in the world. So, dear friends, here you have to be careful!

I know that some of you, disgusted with Europe, with all that hideous mess which you did not witness by choice, are turning—oh! in no great numbers—toward America and getting used to looking upon that country as a possible liberator.

"What a godsend!" you think.

"The bulldozers! The massive investments of capital! The roads! The ports!"

"But American racism!"

"So what? European racism in the colonies has inured us to it!"

And there we are, ready to run the great Yankee risk.

So, once again, be careful!

American domination—the only domination from which one never recovers. I mean from which one never recovers unscarred.

And since you are talking about factories and industries, do you not see the tremendous factory hysterically spitting out its cinders in the heart of our forests or deep in the bush, the factory for the production of lackeys; do you not see the prodigious mechanization, the mechanization of man; the gigantic rape of everything intimate, undamaged, undefiled that, despoiled as we are, our human spirit has still managed to preserve; the machine, yes, have you never seen it, the machine for crushing, for grinding, for degrading peoples?

So that the danger is immense.

So that unless, in Africa, in the South Sea Islands, in Madagascar (that is, at the gates of South Africa), in the West Indies (that is, at the gates of America), Western Europe undertakes on its own initiative a policy of *nationalities*, a new policy founded on respect for peoples and cultures—nay, more—unless Europe galvanizes the dying cultures or raises up new ones, unless it becomes the awakener of countries and civilizations (this being said without taking into account the admirable resistance of the colonial peoples primarily symbolized at present by Vietnam, but also by the Africa of the Rassemblement Démocratique Africain), Europe will have deprived itself of its last *chance* and, with its own hands, drawn up over itself the pall of mortal darkness.

Which comes down to saying that the salvation of Europe is not a matter of a revolution in methods. It is a matter of the Revolution—the one which, until such time as there is a classless society, will substitute for the narrow tyranny of a dehumanized bourgeoisie the preponderance of the only class that still has a universal mission, because it suffers in its flesh from all the wrongs of history, from all the universal wrongs: the proletariat.

American Imperialism and the British West Indies

Claudia Jones

THE ELECTION on March 25th of the first Federal Assembly in the West Indies marks a new political stage in the history of the Caribbean.

This period will also witness the advancing role of American capital investment in the forthcoming West Indian Federation. Increasing United States economic penetration is not, of course, unrelated to the struggle of the West Indian people for full political and economic independence.

Bearing in mind only highlights: there is the Texaco Oil purchase of Trinidad oil, the growing U.S. investments in Jamaican bauxite, and in British Guiana's aluminum deposits. Clearly the West Indian Federation is already heavily mortgaged to U.S. export capital. Nor does it appear that this indebtedness to Uncle Sam worries John Bull unduly. Seemingly a sort of family arrangement has been worked out to prevent the burgeoning freedom struggle of the West Indian people from too rapid advancement or "getting out of hand." While the outward political responsibility remains with Britain, increasingly Washington controls the economic basis of the Federation.

This crucial interconnection was clearly shown when a *London Daily Express* staff reporter wrote that in talks he had had last October in Washington, a State Department official had pointed out that while American trade is less than half the West Indian trade with Britain, it is growing at a faster rate. And he added:

> The islands' 3,000,000 people offer a reservoir of cheap labor to attract more American capital. A mighty American naval base mushrooming in Trinidad is encouraging the whole dollar flow to the West Indies. The U.S. Defense Department makes no bones about it—the Trinidad base is now regarded as the Caribbean keystone to the Panama Canal. American forces are going to be there for a long time to come and businessmen look on the Trinidad base as a guarantee of military and political stability for the future.

This rather bald face analysis likewise underscores the scandal of Chaguaramus, the Federation's capital site chosen after examination of other locations by a West Indies Commission. The United States blandly refused to cede Chaguaramus—site of the U.S. Trinidad base—despite questions in Commons as to the original legality of the Churchill-Roosevelt 99-year lease (no legal authority exists for this and the other U.S. military bases in Antigua, St. Lucia and the Bahamas); despite special talks in London last summer between West Indian leaders and British and United States representatives; despite angry criticism of West Indian leaders that not even a by-your-leave request was ever made to the people of Trinidad as to the use of their land; despite an uproarious clamor of protest by important sections of the West Indian and British press criticizing the usual U.S. high-handedness.

The growth of American economic and political influence in the West Indies was facilitated by the establishment in 1942 of an Anglo-American Caribbean Commission, renamed the Caribbean Commission in 1946. Presumably its function was "to advise and consult" the governments concerned on matters pertaining to "labor, agriculture, health, education, social welfare, finance, economics, etc." But with the help of this Commission, American monopolists have been seizing possession of the natural resources of the West Indies. For example, in 1955, they received the right to exploit the resources of Jamaica. Dominion Oil, a subsidiary of Standard Oil of California, operates in Trinidad. In 1955, Reynolds Metals started mining bauxite in St. Ann's Bay, Jamaica. These projects are financed by the United States government which, in 1951, advanced $1,500,000 for this purpose through the Economic Cooperation Administration. Some idea of the inroads made by American monopolies into the British position may be gleaned from the fact that while British Union Oil spent one million pounds since 1950, prospecting for oil in Barbados, when oil was found, the concession was obtained by Gulf Oil of Pittsburgh.

For Britain, the West Indies is not only a source of cheap food and raw material, it is also a market for her manufactured products. Britain holds a predominant position in West Indian trade. Between 1948–51, she took 43.8 per cent of the total exports of the area and supplied 37.2 per cent of her imports. British trade superiority is facilitated by the imperial preference system. But despite all obstacles, American business has penetrated this market. The United States, as of 1955, was taking 7.1 per cent of the exports and supplying 17.5 per cent of the imports of the West Indies.

American capital has also penetrated West Indian agriculture. The notorious United Fruit Company owns extensive plantations—in Jamaica alone, 15,000 acres. Through the Royal Bank of Canada and the Canadian Bank of Commerce, which have branches on all the big West; Indian islands, American capital exercises its influence on the economic affairs of all the British colonies.

ANGLO-AMERICAN RIVALRY

Anglo-American antagonisms have particularly been reflected around the Federation issue—with Washington distinctly pooh-poohing it. Washington opposes any idea of strengthening Britain's position in the Caribbean. The U.S., moreover, has systematically encouraged opposition to the British Federation plan by neighbor states in the Latin and Central American Republics and by encouraging the opposition of certain sections of the West Indian bourgeoisie.

The danger of the new West Indies Federation falling into the pit of U.S. imperialist domination cannot be sounded too often. For, faced with the immense task of solving the economic problems of the West Indies (the problem aptly termed by Labor Minister Bradshaw as the "lame foot" of the Federation) many of the present national leaders in the West Indies look increasingly to the U.S. for salvation, based on a one-sided estimate of the relative progress of Puerto Rico and on the hope of a growth of tourism from Americans. A third factor explaining why the dangers of U.S. imperialism are not fully grasped is the leaning among the West Indian masses towards the more prosperous United States—masses in revolt against British imperialism which they see as their ever-present and age-old enemy.

Still a fourth factor is the view of many bourgeois-nationalist West Indian leaders that they can thus tactically bargain between the two imperialisms for greater benefits for the West Indies. Thus, as recently reported in the *London Times*, the Chief Minister of Jamaica, Norman Manley, publicly denounced the "parsimonious" handouts of the British Government to the Federation. He also criticized the saddling on the Federation of the military contribution of 325,000 West Indian dollars for the West Indian Regiment. Dr. Eric Williams, of Trinidad, has spoken in similar terms. A 200-million pound loan requested as a minimum for a 5-year period to launch the Federation, has not yet been agreed to or satisfactorily settled by the British Government. Yet a recent issue of *Trumpet*, official organ of the People's National Party, the government party in Jamaica, revealed that Jamaica received from the U.S.A. a loan of $34 millions—more than the total granted by the Colonial Development Corporation to all the West Indian islands.

MASS STRUGGLE

The struggle of the West Indian people for the right to live and work and for national independence has taken on greater intensity in recent years with the spread of the national liberation movement in the colonial world. It is also one of the evidences of the deepening crisis of the British Empire under the growing influence of the liberation movement in the colonies.

Six times since the end of the war the British found it necessary to send punitive expeditions to "restore law and order" in the West Indies. In 1951, when Negro strikers in Grenada (pop. 80,000) demanded that their wages be increased—from 36 to 54 cents a day!—two cruisers, a gunboat, marine and police units went into action. In 1955, following the victory of the Peoples Progressive Party in British Guiana, British Tommies and gunboats invaded British Guiana, deposing its legally elected legislators headed by Dr. Jagan, and revoking its progressive Constitution as a "Communist-inspired coup." But four years later the people of Guiana, in a victorious mandate despite a party split, re-elected Jagan, and the PPP now holds important elected ministerial posts.

Only a few weeks ago, as witnessed in Nassau, Bahamas, the same step was taken when a general strike exposed the shocking conditions under which the 90 per cent colored population live.

The West Indian people have not taken lightly the extensive exploitation of their resources and human labor. Record profits have been declared by domestic and foreign capital interests in the sugar, oil and bauxite industries.

But there have been many instances of working-class, resistance: strikes among port workers in Jamaica, the workers of St. Vincent have been heroically struggling to win concessions from arrogant landlords in sugar. Throughout the West Indies, teachers, match workers, waterfront workers were aroused to defend their interests. In Barbados printers and port workers were locked in struggle with the powerful Advocate Printers. In British Guiana the PPP victory forced revocation of reactionary laws which restricted the movement of their leaders. In Trinidad, store clerks, sugar, oil and educational workers have similarly displayed commendable class consciousness in defending their interests in the face of menacing threats from employers and government.

These and other examples make it necessary to be mindful of the astute observation of Mao Tse-tung—namely, that imperialism is not prepared to permit the independent development of any new capitalist state, is out to stultify it, make it impossible for the native capitalist to carry out the bourgeois-democratic revolution. We know, of course, that as its foundations totter, imperialism seeks more flexible methods of governing the colonies and seeks to devise new means to camouflage its rule. Central then to Britain's desire to revise the status of her West Indian possessions is the spread of the national colonial liberation movement and the deepening crisis she finds herself in.

THE NEW FEDERATION

Exactly what will the Federation mean to the West Indies? To begin with, except for British Guiana, British Honduras and the Bahamas, the remaining 10 British colonial units, composing approximately 3 million people will be federated into a new national structure. This national structure will be comprised of an appointed or nominated Council of State. A bi-cameral legislature will consist of a nominated Senate of 19 members, and a House of Representatives of 45 members. The House is to be elected based on population with Jamaica, representing one-half of the Federation's population, having 17 members; Trinidad 10; Barbados 6; and 2 each from Grenada, St. Lucia, St. Vincent, Antigua, St. Kitts, Dominica and one from Montserrat.

A Supreme Court of the Federation is to be established, having original jurisdiction in specified federal or inter-unit matters. It will also have jurisdiction to hear appeals from unit Courts of Appeal and recourse may be had to this court by British Caribbean territories not members of the Federation.

This new federal structure will in no wise substitute for self-government in each unit, where territorial constitutions, already hobbled and proscribed by colonial administrative restrictions, must constantly be improved by the increasing struggles of the people and their political representatives.

Indicative of the measure of this struggle are the constitutional changes in Barbados where since October 1957, a Cabinet Committee excluding the Governor is the main instrument of Government. Similar changes have taken place in Jamaica, where, since November 1957, the Peoples National Party has been successful in its fight to put power in the hands of its Chief Minister, and to exclude the Governor from the Council of Ministers. But responsibility for criminal affairs will still remain within the control of the appointed Attorney-General. Although the Governor will not normally appear in the Council of Ministers, he will still have the right to summon Special Meetings, to preside at them and he will still retain his wide Reserved Powers.

The impact of these advances on other islands was recently summed up when the Bahamas Federation of Labor in the recent general strike demanded: "We want to be governed like our brothers in Trinidad, Barbados and Jamaica."

Still another example of the fight for broader party representation was the sweeping election victory of the Peoples National Movement, headed by Dr. Eric Williams in Trinidad, when the PNM was allowed to name two of the nominated members, thus creating a constitutional precedent.

But these examples are the exceptions rather than the rule. At present in most of the units there exists Legislative Councils of both Nominated and Elected Members and Officials. All the Governor-Generals hold wide Reserved Powers, as will Lord Hailes, new Governor-General of the W. I. Federation, who took office January 3, 1958.

It is no accident in face of this undemocratic system that for years the chief demand of the West Indian political movement and particularly its advanced sectors has been for greater internal self-government for each unit based on wholly elected legislatures.

CONFLICTING VIEWS

So tenacious has been this key demand that it has now extended to the Federation itself. Some West Indian ideologists however, have counterposed self-government to Federation—as though the two concepts are mutually exclusive. Such, for example, is the view of W. A. Domingo, outstanding student of West Indian affairs. In his pamphlet, *British West Indian Federation—A Critique*, Domingo urges Jamaicans to reject Federation outright—primarily on the grounds that as the largest and most populous of the West Indian islands, she can easily achieve self-government without being hampered by the underdeveloped economies of the Leeward and Windward islands, dependent as they still are on grants-in-aid which are to be curtailed after the first five years of the Federal Government. He further holds that "to equate federation with self-government obscures the real issue—the right of every colonial people to seek and win control of their political life."

But no one who advocates a federated progressive West Indies *equates* these concepts. In fact, those who have consistently fought for a progressive federation structure have always accompanied this demand with one for autonomy of the island units as well. Besides, how can the unity of a people who have similar cultural and historical experiences be held to be violative of "a right" of self-determination if, in seeking to control their political life, they strengthen their ties with others similarly situated? We can assume that Domingo's arguments, like other pre-Federation critics, had as their aim that of modifying the present federation structure. But to base one's arguments largely on the pragmatic grounds that Britain considers the West Indian colonies as "financial liabilities" and that they are of "no strategic value to England today," that Britain will "grant self-government" to the West Indian colonies, because of the "proclaimed official British policy to grant independence to the colonies" flies in the face of a fundamental, scientific assessment of imperialism today.

Still other political ideologists, including some progressives and even some adherents of Marxism, have denounced the current Federation proposals as a "fraud" and appear to be resisting its arrival.

Such approaches appear to be utterly unrealistic politically. For while serious limitations hedge the new federal structure, can it be denied that it is a political advance over the previous colonial status of 300 years?

Basically, the struggle for the free West Indian market by both the foreign and local bourgeoisie is what has given the movement for Federation its urgency. John La Rose, leading Marxist of Trinidad's West Indian. Independence Party, in his Report to the Second Congress of that Party, in July, 1956, places it this way:

The basic economic law of West Indian life which gives this movement such urgency is the struggle for the free West Indian market by both the local and foreign bourgeoisie (interlocked and not interlocked) caused by the inability of the markets of the local territories to satisfy the capacity for expansion and exploitation engendered by capital accumulation in their hands.

Both the foreign and native commercial bourgeoisie have expanded their interests beyond the confines of territories. ...

Both local and foreign banking and insurance institutions of finance capital (like Bookers Trading concerns, Barbados Mutual, etc.) have expanded their interests beyond the confines of a single territory ... besides the activities of foreign banking and insurance institutions.

Both the local and foreign industrial bourgeoisie have expanded beyond the confines of a single territory, e.g., shirt manufacturers, biscuit manufacturers, gin and rum manufacturers, edible oil manufacturers, citrus juices, time clocks, cement manufacturers exporting to British Guiana, Barbados, Grenada, etc., and vice versa. Even at the level of small agricultural producers, e.g., Grenada, St. Vincent, this need is felt and exists as a powerful urge to Federation.

While not all political forces in the West Indies are prepared to formulate immediate demands they are nevertheless broadly united on the aim of Dominion Status. Thus it seems that here once again is reflected the inevitable process of development which cannot be halted—the quest for full national independence.

Consequently, the chief programmatic demand to overcome the limitations advanced by progressive and socialist minded forces in the West Indies include:

1. Internal self-government for the Federation entailing a wholly elected Parliament (a nominated Senate is a retrograde step), full cabinet status based on the Party principle with the elected Prime Minister wholly responsible, and restriction of the Governor-General's powers to representation of the Sovereign as is the case of Ghana, or a republican form of government, as in India, with the Crown as the head of the Commonwealth.

2. Civil liberties embracing the entire Federation including freedom to travel, freedom to organize and to discuss.

3. Protection of rights of minorities for cultural and other forms of development.

4. For full national independence for the West Indies.

* * * *

Despite the serious limitations it would be fundamentally wrong to assess the forthcoming Federation as being simply the brain-child of the Colonial Office. To understand the significance of this development it must be realized that what is taking place in the West Indies is the unfolding of the classical bourgeois-democratic revolution, with, of course, its own special features.

Leadership of the national political movement is today in the hands of middle class intellectuals who either come from the class of the national bourgeoisie, or are representative of their interests.

Because federation of the West Indies occurs at a time when the local capitalist class is developing, every nuance of the federal structure is, naturally, tempered by their influence. Motivated firstly by their own desire for improved status, and a desire to be free of their inferior colonial status, essentially this influence is anti-imperialist and anti-colonial.

What unites the *all-class* struggle of the West Indian peoples is opposition to foreign imperialism. This stage of political development in general coincides with the historic aim and dream of the West Indian working class, its militant industrial and agricultural workers, who in the 30's hoisted the banner of Federation, with Dominion status and self-government for the units, to their standard. These and other demands have today been incorporated into the political platforms of the present national political parties and movements in the islands.

It is important to stress that leadership of the national political movement has passed relatively recently into the hands of the national bourgeoisie.

Prior to World War II, leadership of the national movement was in the hands of the working class, arising from the upheavals during the mass strikes of 1937–38. The working class spearheaded the mass struggle; their leaders won their confidence through their selfless and courageous actions. This was the period in which trade unionism rapidly developed in the Caribbean and a new sense of power was felt by the workers.

There then emerged the Caribbean Labor Congress, a united West Indian people's anti-colonial movement for Federation with Dominion status and self-government for the units. It comprised an all-class coalition in which the working class shared leadership with other anti-imperialist classes including important sections of the national bourgeoisie.

But this movement was split and declined.

Basic to the answer as to how this decline and split arose was the "divide and rule" tactic of imperialism, which, fearful of this forward development, facilitated the separation of the Right-wing from the Left-wing in accommodation with some of the bourgeois national leaders.

True, imperialism, faced with the mounting pressure of the national liberation movement is seeking to develop the national bourgeoisie as a reliable bulwark to protect its interests for as long as possible even after national independence is won. But India's experience proves that that does not always work.

The working class was also handicapped in that it lacked a scientific approach to the national and class struggle, in many instances pursued sectarian policies, and consequently lost leadership to the developing middle class intellectuals.

It is this background, given briefly, which largely accounts for the hesitations which have marked sections of the working class and socialist-oriented groupings in the West Indies in definitely committing themselves to the present Federation.

Here, a distinction is made between the justified reservations shared by all sections of West Indian opinion and the imperative task of the working class and its advanced sector to play its indispensable role in carrying forward the movement for West Indian national independence.

To sit it out, instead of entering fully as leading partners in the national struggle for independence is to abdicate a contribution they alone can make. The working class and the Left in such a role can encourage the progressive tendencies of the national bourgeoisie. It can steady the middle class intellectuals towards firmer anti-imperialist stands (criticizing where necessary but not from outside this development).

TRADE-UNION ACTIVITY

A most imperative conclusion appears to be the need to coordinate and strengthen trade union activity. In recent months support for the idea of a united militant trade-union movement on a federal scale has been underway in the West Indies. Such a trade-union movement would not only help to facilitate independence and national unity but would be the instrument for achieving improved living standards, higher wages and in general defense of the workers' rights against pressure by U.S. and British capital. Such a united trade-union movement would have a decisive effect on the policies of the two main federal parties—the West Indian Federal Labor Party, and the Democratic Labor Party, who will contest seats for the Federal Assembly.

Together with improved living standards and economic advancement is the need for expanded educational development. Educational standards in the West Indies are today frightfully low—too low to fulfill the needs of a country aiming at nationhood.

A prime necessity is the development from the working class itself of a class-conscious cadre and leadership. This is especially important because of the mistaken conception current among West Indian intellectuals that political parties in the West Indies do not represent social classes. Buttressing this false theory is the fact that all mass parties in the West Indies have to rely on support of the working class.

Political pressure and leadership by the Left has already vitally affected the national political movement in the West Indies. One such contribution has been their pointing up the contrast between Soviet economic aid with no strings attached, and the historic significance of Bandung. Advocacy of such policies can help change the pace with which the national bourgeoisie and middle-class intellectuals press for full national independence in the West Indies.

While at this juncture the bourgeois national struggle is directed against foreign imperialism, without doubt as the development of the national bourgeoisie takes place the internal class struggle will grow in importance and scope.

All political observers would do well to follow the course of West Indian development; in Britain this course has been forced on all political forces anew with the presence of 80,000 West Indian immigrants now resident in Britain—the largest immigration of colonial people in recent years. Faced with impoverishment and unbearable conditions and barred by the infamous racially biased Walter-McCarran immigration laws which retards West Indian immigration to 100 persons a year from all the West Indies to the U.S.A., they have trekked in thousands to Britain, where they are confronted with an extension of their problems as colonials in a metropolitan country in the form of color prejudice, joblessness, housing shortages, etc.

Progressive and Communist forces in Britain, mindful of their own responsibilities and of the greed of the U.S. imperialist colossus, are advocating economic assistance to the West Indies; solidarity with their trade-union and other struggles and full national independence for the West Indian people.

Fascism or Freedom

Cheddi Jagan

> Today America is no longer the inspirer and leader of the world revolution ... by contrast America is today the leader of the worldwide anti-revolutionary movement in defence of vested interests. She now stands for what Rome stood for.
>
> *Arnold Toynbee*

The title of this book is perhaps somewhat dated. The West is no longer on trial; it is guilty. As Arthur M. Schlesinger revealed in *A Thousand Days, John F. Kennedy in the White House*: "Then in May 1962, Burnham came to Washington ... Burnham's visit left the feeling as I reported to the President, that 'an independent British Guiana under Burnham (if Burnham will commit himself to a multi-racial policy) would cause us many fewer problems than an independent British Guiana under Jagan.' And the way was open to bring it about, because Jagan's parliamentary strength was larger than his popular strength: he had won 57 percent of the seats on the basis of 42.7 percent of the vote. An obvious solution would be to establish a system of proportional representation. This, after prolonged discussion, the British government finally did in October 1963; and elections held finally at the end of 1964 produced a coalition government under Burnham."

"After prolonged discussion", should have read "CIA-financed and fomented strikes and riots", which had given as Drew Pearson stated, "London the excuse it wanted."

The final exposé came soon after *Ramparts* disclosed that the National Students Association was in the pay of the Central Intelligence Agency (CIA) with U.S. $1 million per year. Neil Sheehan, in a special article to the *New York Times* of February 22, 1967, "CIA Is Linked to Strikes That Helped Oust Jagan," documented the CIA operation in Guyana. Soon after on April 16, the Insight Team, in a story in the *Sunday Times*, "How the CIA got rid of Jagan," wrote: "As coups go, it was not expensive: over five years the CIA paid out something over £250,000. For the colony, British Guiana, the result was about 170 dead, untold hundreds wounded, roughly £10 million-worth of damage to the economy and a legacy of racial bitterness."

The CIA's agents, William Doherty Jr. and William McCabe worked through the American Federation of State, County and Municipal Employees, the Public Services International (PSI) and the Gotham Foundation, a conduit for the channelling of CIA money.

On April 23, the Insight Team in another story, "Macmillan, Sandys backed CIA's anti-Jagan plot," implicated Harold Macmillan, former Prime Minister; Duncan Sandys, former Commonwealth and Colonial Secretary; two top security men in Britain and a number of British officials in Guyana, no doubt the Governor, the Commissioner of Police and the Chief Security Officer.

It stated that "not all the British officials on the spot were happy with what the Americans were doing … (with) such massive manipulation of the local political scene. This feeling was strengthened by the fact that the CIA's efforts were worsening the colony's already severe racial difficulties: the Africans supported Burnham and the Indians supported Jagan, and tension between the two racial groups grew as the CIA levered the two sides further apart. (Eventually, this broke out in bloodshed.)"

The story also asserted that "the CIA were also operating under consular cover in Guyana."

British complicity explains why the police and armed forces did not give full and firm support to the PPP government; why the PNC terrorist organisation was not smashed; and why the security's "Research Paper on the PNC Terrorist Organisation" was withheld from us before the 1963 Independence Conference, and its possession was made a criminal offense just prior to the 1964 election.

The justification for the U.S. three-pronged attack — CIA subversion and riots inside Guyana, diplomatic pressure on the British government and diplomatic pressure on the Venezuelan government — on the PPP government was that we would have abandoned parliamentary democracy. According to Schlesinger, "the President went on to express doubt whether Jagan would be able to sustain his position as a parliamentary democrat. 'I have a feeling,' he said, 'that in a couple of years he will find ways to suspend his constitutional provisions and will cut his opposition off at the knees … Parliamentary democracy is going to be damn difficult in a country at this stage of development. With all the political jockeying and all the racial tensions, it's going to be almost impossible for Jagan to concentrate the energies of his country on development through a parliamentary system'."

U.S. aim, it would appear, is the attainment of economic development and social progress through a parliamentary democracy. But this is sheer hypocrisy. Neither the United States or any of its client-states is interested in democracy *per se*; instead, of paramount importance are the vested interests of the monopoly capitalists.

President Dwight Eisenhower warned about "the acquisition of unwarranted influence, whether sought or unsought, by the military-industrial complex", but cancelled elections planned for 1956 under the 1954 Geneva Agreement to unite North and South Vietnam, and installed the corrupt Ngo-dinh-Diem as head of South Vietnam.

Under the so-called liberal administration of President Kennedy, the same interests prevailed. On April 19, 1965, *Newsweek* disclosed that "American diplomats can be expected to intensify their help to U.S. businessmen overseas. Directives now awaiting Dean Rusk's signature will remind U.S. embassies that their efficiency will be rated not only by diplomatic and political prowess but by how well they foster American commercial interests abroad. Moreover, prominent businessmen will be recruited as inspectors of the Foreign Service."

As regards Guyana, Schlesinger disclosed that the State Department at first thought of trying to work with us, "then Rusk personally reversed this policy in a stiff letter to the British early in 1962". This was done in spite of the assurances of President Kennedy in December 1961 that the United States would not intervene in our domestic affairs; and further in spite of the fact that, as Schlesinger put it, "thus far, our policies had been based on the assumption that Forbes Burnham was, as the British described him, an opportunist, racist and demagogue, intent only on personal power."

Apparently the British ruling circles, having firstly failed by hook or crook to defeat us at 3 successive general elections and having secondly succeeded in taming some flaming leftist anti-colonial politicians like Jomo Kenyatta and Hastings Banda, were prepared to take a chance with us and to honour their pledges at the 1960 Constitutional Conference in London by transfering complete power to Guyana under our leadership. But the U.S. administration, obsessed by Communism, and hysterical about the socialist direction of the Cuban revolution, was determined not to let Britain honour its pledges.

What is the record of the U.S.-backed, Burnham-led coalition, and now the PNC government? Guyana is passing through a period of mounting social, political and economic crisis. It has been brought to near-bankruptcy. And step by step, a neo-fascist, Latin American type of dictatorship is being established.

Instead of progressing, the country is stagnating if not retrogressing. It is facing grave economic and social problems — rising debt charges, balance of payments deficit, a growing and costly bureaucracy, continued outflow of profits, inflation, unemployment, discrimination and corruption.

The United Force Manifesto in 1964, *Highways to Happiness*, promised "$900 million for the economic and social development of Guyana" for a 6-year plan. Not to be outdone, the PNC's *New Road* declared that its target of $130 million annually was feasible. But even the much publicised $300 million 7-year Development Plan (1966–72), formulated with imperialist rather than national objectives in mind, collapsed prematurely at the end of 1969. With its main emphasis on infrastructure — roads, sea walls, airports and airstrip, harbour and stellings, public buildings, etc. — rather than on industry and agriculture, it has hampered real development and the generation of wealth to cope with mounting debt charges to service a huge national debt, domestic and foreign.

Very little has been done to industrialise and diversify the economy. Industry, with the exception of the extractive bauxite industry, is virtually at a standstill. This is in keeping with the imperialist-designed plan for the Caribbean and Guyana – the Caribbean Free Trade Area (CARIFTA) has relegated to Guyana the role of an agricultural appendage to a foreign-dominated industrialised West Indies.

The PPP had the will but not the political power to industrialise and diversify; the PNC has the power, but lacks the will. Forgotten are the earlier PNC promises. On January 20, 1960, Burnham, attacking the PPP government in the Legislative Assembly, shouted: "Where is the plan for the towns, and where is the plan even for villages? ... No industry for villagers; no plan to get an industrial area and see whether it is possible for government to erect factories."

In a budget debate on January 11, 1963, Burnham observed : "The country is going to export more sugar, bauxite, manganese and so on, therefore, we should be happy. If exports are increased and the government is likely to get more revenue, we will be very happy. Is that what the people of Guyana are looking forward to? Must an improvement in conditions depend upon the export of sugar and bauxite and increased import duties? Shades of the old colonial budgets."

All that has been done is the expansion of government activities in the field of construction, the extraction of bauxite, the extension of some existing factories and the erection of factories which were contemplated during the PPP regime in the private sector; those in the public sector were dropped.

With the future of manufacturing industry bleak, the government has belatedly recognised the importance of agriculture, which, it claims, constitutes the backbone of the economy. This is in sharp contrast to the epithets hurled against the PPP regime, that it was a "coolie government", "a rice government", concentrating too much in the countryside, on agriculture, on drainage and irrigation.

But even so, there is a progressive decline in agriculture. Dependence on foreign-owned sugar grows, while imports of foods are increasing; they have jumped from $25 million in 1960 to $38 million in 1970. This is largely due to malice and vindictiveness against the farmers, the large majority of whom are PPP supporters. The government has conspired to penalise the farmers by sabotaging the PPP-planned programme of drainage and irrigation, dismantling the scheme of minimum guaranteed prices, withdrawing crop bonuses and duty-free petrol, reducing crop prices, credit facilities and expenditure on pest control, and discriminating against PPP supporters in the allocation of land, credit and other facilities.

There is a perpetual deficit in the balance of payments with respect to goods and services, which have to be met from standby credit from the International Monetary Fund and by running down the reserves of foreign exchange. Huge capital inflows in the form of grants and loans from the United Kingdom and United States have helped to offset the deficits, but have contributed to a huge national debt and high service charges. The public debt has trebled in the past decade from $107 million in 1961 to $319 million in 1971 ($202 million external and $117 million internal). Debt servicing together with the expanded bureaucratic machine (between 1965 and 1971, expenditure on general administration increased by 275 percent as compared with an increase of only 150 percent for social services) necessitated high current expenditures which "amount to about 25 percent of the gross domestic product at factor cost — an extremely high proportion for an underdeveloped country. This compares with under 10 percent in very low underdeveloped countries such as India and Nigeria, between 15 percent and 20 percent in Jamaica and Trinidad ..." These expenditures led to budgetary deficits which had to be offset by the imposition of further burdens on the people — more indirect taxation; cuts in social services; a wages freeze; reduction on prices to farmers; cuts in subsidies. Taxation, mostly indirect, increased by geometric progression — $2.79 million in 1966, $5.4 million in 1967, $7.95 million in 1968 and $15.1 million in 1969. In 4 years, cumulative taxation yielded $58 million as compared with the sum of $10 million previously contemplated for financing, by way of taxation, the G$300 million 7-year Development Plan.

In 1966, the Minister of Finance in a White Paper disclosed that the government incurred annual losses of $14 million and embarked on a programme of progressive reduction of what was actually subsidies to the workers, farmers and consumers.

While the PNC government's fiscal policies have resulted in a crushing burden on the poor, over-generous tax, mining and other concessions have been made to the foreign monopolies. An advertisement by the Guyana Development Corporation in "Focus on Guyana", *New Commonwealth*, Supplement Number 1, 1969, says: "We are here to make sure that your investments pay you bigger dividends." Devaluation of our currency following that of the pound sterling in 1967 brought an extra annual windfall of about $8 to $10 million to the big capitalists, mainly foreign, operating in Guyana.

Wages for government unskilled workers are frozen at $4 per day; forgotten are the electoral promises of $5 to $10 per day. Temporary allowances granted pending a job evaluation and salaries and wages revision did not cope adequately with the high cost of living. For many categories of non-governmental workers the minimum wage is much lower; sawmill and quarry workers who in our time received the same wage as government employees now get by government regulations only $3.52 per day.

Since 1966, rice farmers have suffered a reduction in prices of about 15 percent for rice sold to the government-controlled Rice Marketing Board. Prices are now lower than they were a decade ago even though costs of production have risen by nearly 50 percent. Other categories of farmers have met the same fate.

Unemployment and underemployment are soaring. Between 20 to 25 percent of the labour force is unemployed. In Georgetown, the capital, one-third of the youths is unemployed, and another one-third underemployed. New job opportunities are not being created to cope with the reservoir of unemployed and the large numbers of school-leavers. Instead, retrenchment is taking place in the sugar industry and elsewhere.

The contributory National Insurance Scheme (NIS) has imposed further hardships on the people. No provision has been made for unemployment relief; the pensionable age of 65 is unrealistic; and benefits for injuries at work are less than under the non-contributory Workmen's Compensation Act which it replaced.

Other social services have deteriorated. Current budget expenditure on health dropped from 13 percent in 1959 to 9.4 percent in 1971. Out of every dollar of development expenditure, only half a cent goes towards the expansion of the health services. Drugs at government institutions are in short supply; patients are invariably told by doctors to procure medicines outside if they want to save their lives.

The PNC government is spending a lower percentage of the budget on education than the PPP government did even though schools are overcrowded. And by raising the age of entry to primary schools, it discriminates against the poor; the children of the well-to-do, by affording private tuition and education, are able to win most of the scholarships which amount to about 85 percent, for free places in secondary schools.

Little wonder that Dr. Wilfred David, who had been asked to formulate a new 10-year Development Plan, commented that "we have had growth without development."

Apart from high taxation and cuts in social services, the Guyanese people have to bear the burdens of "squandermania", nepotism, corruption and discrimination. These have their roots in the corrupt practices introduced by the United States. In the 1964 general elections the CIA intervened with massive financial support. According to the *New York Times* of April 28, 1966, the CIA "has poured money into Latin American election campaigns in support of moderate candidates and against leftist leaders such as Cheddi Jagan of British Guiana."

The *Sunday Times* story of April 23, 1967, stated that the CIA resorted to corrupt means to split the PPP. It took out an insurance policy for "one ex-Jagan supporter for 30,000 dollars in 1964."

In 1967, the Minister of Finance disclosed in the National Assembly that $1.5 million was illegally spent on the East Coast highway and not properly accounted for. The Director of Audit in his report for 1967 disclosed that no vouchers were available for $19.5 million of government expenditure. The report claimed that during 1966, the year of independence some $4 million was spent, for which no vouchers had been submitted. This elicited from the then PNC Lord Mayor of Georgetown, Archibald Codrington, a caustic commentary: "The Director of Audit's report makes grim reading and shows that all is far from well in many departments of the government ... with the ever-increasing large sums of money being spent and the heavy taxes wrested from our people, we have the right to demand proper care in handling and expending our money, the proper keeping of accounts and that the light-fingered gentry in high-powered cars be put where they belong, behind bars. Some of those get-rich-quick Wallingfords should be made to explain where their new-found wealth came from."

Earlier in 1967, the then deputy Lord Mayor, Cleveland Hamilton, a government supporter, cried out against a new elite, creating "a new, larger area of snobbery", and against bribery and corruption which "is all over the place and is fast becoming a national industry". He observed that "the harm done in any situation in which bribery, corruption, nepotism and favouritism assume national proportions and is a way of life from top down, can never be calculated."

The Service Commissions, concerned with the employment, promotion and dismissal of civil servants, police and judicial officers have been subverted. Instead of being impartial they have become mere rubber-stamps.

In 1967, the Civil Service Association, which helped to bring the PNC to power, accused the government of causing a breach of industrial principle and a display of gross irresponsibility and arrogance. It expressed its grave dissatisfaction with several appointments made by the Public Service Commission, some of which were "most questionable and seriously disrupted the Association's confidence in the integrity of the PSC." In a letter, it appealed to the Trades Union Council to "intercede before it's too late."

The President of the Police Federation, giving evidence before the Collins Commission on July 27, 1968, charged that favouritism was rampant in the promotion system in the police force. He declared: "The merit principle is seldom applied. Many men have belittled and degraded themselves in order to find favour with an officer in the hope that they would be recommended for promotion ... There have even been cases where men who have been before the court on charges touching on their integrity and honesty, have been favoured when neither characteristic could recommend them."

Writing about nepotism and the sharp criticisms levelled by L.R.D. Ainsworth, president of the Guyana Teachers Association (GTA), "Lucian", a strong government supporter, in the *Guyana Graphic* of April 25, 1968 declared: "In effect and by inference, this warning could mean that the GTA's group is meeting with successful competition. So the war in the doghouse rattles on. The picture sickens me and will alarm other parents to know that the writing of books for use in Guyana's schools is not determined by competence, truth and values, but by what Mr. Ainsworth terms privilege. I long suspected that. But privilege theoretically ended with the colonial legislature and the colonial government. Has it been resurrected? The faster it is kicked into the dustbin of colonialism, the better for everybody."

The Archbishop of the West Indies and Guyana, Dr. Alan John Knight, in the Diocesan magazine of December 1969 called for a real and drastic cleanup of the society. "For example," he charged, "bribery and corruption in all forms are prevalent. Money in the hands of the unscrupulous can outbid social justice at every level. It is amazing to see what $5,000 can do! And much more modest sums can secure appointment for the less qualified, make files and records conveniently disappear, miraculously reduce amounts due in tax, secure contracts, evade penalties and secure privileges."

So alarming had corruption become that by the end of 1970 the government was forced to dismiss many persons in high places, and to include the investigation of corrupt practices within the scope of the Ombudsman's functions.

Corruption, nepotism and discrimination have led to moral degeneracy and inefficiency; high taxation to deterioration in living standards. During the first 4 years of PNC rule, the cost of living index figure jumped 16 points as compared with only 9 points during the 7 years of the PPP regime. And as debt charges mount and the bureaucracy, particularly the military, grows, there will be further deterioration.

The end result has been disillusionment and grave dissatisfaction. Commenting on the latter, columnist "Lucian" wrote in the *Sunday Graphic* of July 16, 1967: "Many people — Guyanese and non-Guyanese — are disgusted with the present state of affairs in this country. Some are packing up to leave out of sheer frustration, while others are dejected from unbearable disgust."

Frustration and disgust are leading on the one hand to heightened political consciousness, and on the other to anti-social and anti-national tendencies. The exodus of Guyanese, especially of the young and skilled, continues unabated. Large queues for passports to emigrate is a common daily sight. Violence, crime and juvenile delinquency are on the increase even though "choke-and-robbers" have been threatened by judges with life imprisonment. And there has been a record-breaking number of strikes, mostly wildcat.

The government's response to discontent has been characteristic of puppet, client states — coercion and force with military and police intimidation and harassment on the political and industrial fronts; and fraud on the electoral front.

In 1966, the coalition enacted the National Security Act, a measure far more vicious than its U.S. counterpart of 1950, which spawned McCarthyism. It gave the government powers to suspend the right of *Habeas Corpus*, and to restrict and detain any Guyanese without trial for an indefinite period. Many persons have since been arbitrarily locked up and intimidated. And police harassment has been widespread. In a search, an occupant was told that if he knew what was good for him, he would not be in possession of books like Lenin's *State And Revolution* found in his home.

Other restrictive practices deny basic human rights. There is no equality of opportunity. Discrimination on political, racial and other grounds is widely practised. Many public officers have been hounded out of their posts. Many others have been bypassed.

In mid-1968, the government refused permission to the PPP to have a countrywide demonstration in protest against the rigged registration system for the compilation of the voters' list for the December 16, 1968 general election. Since then it has become routine practice for the government to deny the opposition the right of peaceful demonstration.

And the right to vote has been virtually denied. The 1968 general election and the local government elections were fraudulent from beginning to end.

The official returns for the December 1968 general election gave the People's National Congress 55.6 percent, the People's Progressive Party 36 percent and the United Force 7 percent of the votes. The results of the 1964 election were PNC, 40 percent; PPP, 46 percent; and UF, 12 percent.

In the 53-member National Assembly the number of seats now held by the PNC, PPP and UF are 30, 19 and 4 respectively; in 1964, the corresponding numbers were 22, 24 and 7.

It has been clearly established that extensive fraud helped the PNC to "win" and to form the government alone. Without fabricated, padded voters' lists, extensive proxy voting and ballot-box tampering, the PNC could not have secured 50.4 percent of the votes inside Guyana, equivalent to a majority of 1 seat; without overseas votes the PNC would not have had a working majority of 7 seats.

Through manipulation, the PNC secured 94 percent of the overseas votes, absentee balloting being permitted for the first time in Guyana's history.

The rigging of the election was thoroughly exposed by the Granada Television Company (U.K.) in its two "World in Action" films, and by Alexander Mitchell in the London *Sunday Times* of December 15, 1968, with "Jagan v. Burnham … It's polling day tomorrow. Has Guyana election already been decided in Britain?"

The first film, "The Trail of the Vanishing Voters" shown December 9, 1968, disclosed that most of the U.K. voters' lists were fakes. It found only 117 genuine names in a sample of 551 registered in London, and only 19 in another sample of 346 registered in Manchester.

Joe Hughes, a PNC activist turned registration officer, who registered only 41 voters in Wolverhampton (U.K.) is shown doubting that over 200 persons could have been on the voters' list.

So devastating was the effect that the Guyana High Commission in London claimed that Granada TV was mischievous. And the publisher and editor of the Guyana *Evening Post* were charged with public mischief for publishing an *Associated Press* dispatch which had reported that "two horses were grazing where a Lily and Olga Barton should have been. Where Gladys Porter should live, there had been a railway since 1874." Accordingly, Granada's request for re-entry to, and free movement in Guyana, was met by a terse cabled reply: "All Requests Negative."

The transcript of the second film, appropriately called "The Making of a Prime Minister," declared that "a hanged man voted in the Guyana General Election. So did children." It went on to say that "the newly re-elected Prime Minister of Guyana, Forbes Burnham, arrives in London today (January 6, 1969) for the Prime Minister's Conference. He should not be attending."

According to the second programme, only 4,700 of the 11,750 registered "voters" in the United States, and 13,050 of the 44,301 registered in the United Kingdom, were genuine. If all the 12,550 voters registered in the rest of the world were genuine and had voted, the most generous estimate of Guyanese voters abroad should be 30,300, but 36,745 voted. "Inescapably," said the commentator, "at least 6,445 voters were faked, and that's being excessively cautious."

Humphrey Taylor, director of Opinion Research Centre, which conducted an independent survey, said in the second Granada programme: "Obviously I don't know what happened in Guyana, but so far as Britain is concerned, the compilation of the register was a totally dishonest and corrupt operation. And, as we have clearly established, the great majority of people listed do not exist. This I would think is unprecedented for a Commonwealth country, as far as I know; and it's, you know, a pretty awful and disgraceful episode."

Peter d'Aguiar bitterly stated: "To call it an election is to give it a name it does not deserve; it was a seizure of power by fraud, not election."

Inside Guyana the voters' list was also padded. It increased by 21 percent in the 4-year period, 1964–68, as compared with 19 percent in the 11-year period, 1953–64. Within this overall increase, there were many discrepancies — an increase of only 10 percent in 6 districts in the PPP area of strength, the Corentyne, as compared with huge increases in PNC areas of strength — 189 percent, 58 percent and 49 percent for the Mackenzie, Mazaruni-Potaro, and Abary districts respectively. For the Abary district, sub-districts with strong PPP support increased by only 5 to 6 percent compared with 50 to 100 percent increases in PNC-supported sub-districts.

At 53 Russell Street, Georgetown, where less than 15 adults could be housed, 58 "voters" were listed and allowed to vote by proxy.

Over 19,000 proxies, equivalent to 3 seats, were issued to facilitate the casting of ballots for the PNC by dead, underage and "phantom" voters. Also, large numbers of PPP supporters were unable to exercise their votes because others had "voted" for them.

This was the reason for the secrecy shrouding the issue of proxy lists. Many Returning Officers refused to make them available to PPP agents and subagents, although by law the lists should have been made available 4 days before polling day. Efforts to see them even after the election failed.

There was also tampering with ballot boxes. In one box for the Pomeroon District, *4 parcels of ballot papers bound with rubber bands were found!* In several other boxes, the number of ballots did not tally with the number recorded at the end of polling.

This tampering was facilitated by changing the 1964 method of counting the ballots in each of the 35 electoral districts (now 38) to 3 centres only. Ballot boxes were transported over long distances and PPP agents were prevented from observing their movement.

These factors, coupled with the involvement of the U.S. company, Shoup Registration Systems International, and the bypassing of the Elections Commission in the registration of voters, were responsible for the PNC "victory".

The voters' lists were extracted from the National Register of all Guyanese 14 years and over. In the compilation of the Register, the constitutionally provided Elections Commission, made up of a Chairman appointed by the Prime Minister and 1 nominee of each of the 3 political parties, was completely bypassed. The operational headquarters was under tight security and police guard. And the whole machinery of hand-picked appointees was under the control of the Minister of Home Affairs. Supervising the registration was Shoup Registration System International, which, according to Paul L. Montgomery in the *New York Times* of December 17, 1967 "has previously performed national registration tabulations in Trinidad, Jamaica and Venezuela. D. E. McFeely, the concern's resident manager, said in an interview that he also understood that the company had helped with registration last year in South Vietnam."

Was Shoup a CIA front? The *New York Times* of December 17, 1967, wrote: "The CIA had no comment on the assertion that the Shoup concern is a front." After the election, when investigations were mounted, the Shoup company had conveniently disappeared!

Because the Elections Commission merely served as an instrument to rubber-stamp the government's decisions and to condone the many irregularities, Janet Jagan, the PPP nominee in the Commission, tendered her resignation before the election.

Thus Forbes Burnham's claim of victory and boast that the PNC had "breached the PPP strongholds in the Corentyne and elsewhere", a reference to its gain by 144 percent of the votes in Suddie and 143 percent in 3 Corentyne districts, is hollow and without merit. These are predominantly rice-growing areas with disgruntled rice farmers who received about $3 less per bag for rice sold to the government-controlled Rice Marketing Board; and a minimum of $ 3.14 per bag for padi, as compared with $5.19 under the PPP regime, from the government-owned Rice Development Corporation.

The international scandal of the 1968 general election was repeated at the 1970 local government elections. The already heavily padded 1968 general election voters' lists were further padded through supplementary lists, which showed unduly large increases in the number of voters ranging from 17 to 27 percent. Many of the persons named, being non-existent, could not be found.

The government surpassed itself in the use of proxy voting. For the June 1970 local government election, out of 65,000 votes cast in 5 areas, over 10,800 were cast by proxy. Bartica recorded a 37 percent proxy vote! At Sheet-Anchor-Cumberland, proxy voting reached 30 percent of the votes cast. Proxy forms were issued by PNC activists quite indiscriminately. Many PPP supporters on presenting themselves to vote found that other unauthorised persons had already "voted" for them; this included a PPP candidate for Georgetown.

There was also evidence of ballot-box tampering. Invariably PPP agents were not allowed to accompany the vehicles in which ballot boxes were transported. At Leguan, ballot boxes were taken not to the counting centre, but to a guest house where PNC activists were resident and kept there for nearly two hours; PPP activists were debarred entry.

There were other discrepancies. From a district in Georgetown (Kitty), a ballot box when counted disclosed only 310 votes as compared with 410 which had been cast; in another box, there were 157 excess ballot papers; in still another, 437 voted but only 407 ballot papers were found in the box.

Leguan and Sheet-Anchor-Cumberland are PPP areas of strength, yet the PNC claimed landslide victories. In the latter area, the PNC "got" 2,045 votes; the PPP 525. But in the 1964 and 1968 elections for a much larger area, the PNC received 1,405 and 1,590 respectively; the PPP 5,331 and 5,806 respectively.

In 1968, for the Essequibo Islands, of which Leguan forms a part, the PNC secured 1,623 votes and the PPP 4,221 out of a total electorate of 6,690. But in the June 1970 election for Leguan alone with a voters' list of 2,583, the PNC "polled" 1,814 votes! The United Force "polled" 31 votes even though 50 voters sponsored its list of candidates!

Because of the blatant rigging, we decided to boycott the remainder of the local government elections held in December 1970. Now the PNC, with no more than 30 percent support of the population, rules roughshod not only in the central government but also in all local authorities.

Soon after the 1968 general election, the unrepresentative PNC regime ruthlessly crushed the rebellion by small ranchers and Amerindians in the Rupununi Savannahs, near the Brazilian border and moved to militarise our politics. Making incessant calls for greater sacrifices to build a bigger army and police so that "our nation can be protected", it railroaded a "Defense Levy" of 3 percent on all imports in 1969.

The revolt had its origin in a combination of factors — resentment by the people of the Rupununi against the PNC government for the electoral fraud and the eviction of the United Force from the coalition; dissatisfaction with the government's high-handed action in connection with their leased lands; subversion by Venezuela in its quest for a Guyanese "fifth column".

Venezuela's claim to nearly three-fifths of our territory was part of the Anglo-American conspiracy. It was resurrected in 1962 to be used as an aggressive weapon against the PPP and any future progressive regime in an independent Guyana. In 1965, the British, Venezuelan and the PNC-UF coalition governments signed the 5-year Geneva Agreement and set up a Mixed Commission (Guyana-Venezuela). Recognition was thus given to the spurious Venezuelan territorial claim, and what was a closed case since 1899 was re-opened. With the Port-of-Spain Protocol, the Agreement was extended in 1970 for another 12 years.

From 1965 to 1968, the claim was used for jingoistic and diversionary purposes in support of U.S.-puppet regimes in both Guyana and Venezuela. In the 1968 election, it served as an intimidatory weapon; the PNC with its main electoral slogan, "Peace not conflict", openly suggested the threat of Venezuelan aggression in case of a PPP victory.

These were the reasons for the failure of the PNC-UF coalition to take to the UN Security Council Venezuela's aggression (occupation of the whole of Ankoko Island), threat of aggression (Venezuela's edict authorising its Navy to patrol Guyana's offshore waters), and subversion. The U.S.A., while not wishing to be placed in a position of deciding between Guyana's "right" and Venezuela's "might", wants at the same time the Venezuelan "claim" to remain open indefinitely.

With growing expenditure for the police and army, the PNC government will rely more and more on the U.S. government for military support. From time to time, U.S. jeeps and trucks have been given to the police and army; in May 1971, a naval vessel was handed over.

As part of the militarisation process and control, Brazil, which has agreed with the U.S. concept of a Latin-American "peace" force, is now posing as Guyana's big brother and protector, and has posted an ex-general as her Ambassador to Guyana. It was Brazil's U.S.-supported dictator, Costa e Silva, who as Defence Minister, said that "any candidate in the 1969 gubernatorial or presidential election will be officially recognised only with the approval of the armed forces."

The militarisation of Guyana's politics has become necessary not because of Venezuelan aggression and subversion, but internal dissension. The use of armed police and troops, and police dogs against workers on strike has become common practice.

The government has also eroded further the rights of the people. It assumed powers to censor and ban films — progressive films dealing with revolts of students and black people, and struggles against colonialism and imperialism, which we had been screening outdoors; and more particularly, the two Granada films on our election. The second Granada film, 'The Making of a Prime Minister", was seized from me at the airport in July 1969 and never returned on the spurious ground that I had brought it into the country illegally.

On February 24, 1969, the government railroaded a bill through the National Assembly empowering it to prevent any person from leaving the country if the Minister of Home Affairs considers that "it is necessary in the interests of defence, public safety or public order or for the purpose of preventing the subversion of democratic institutions in the country." Guyanese who were awarded scholarships in socialist countries were either refused passports or prevented from leaving. The Act also empowers the government to create "protected areas" and to prevent the movement of persons in these areas.

The Labour Disputes Bill providing for compulsory arbitration and the banning of strikes was introduced in the National Assembly.

To counter discontent, resort is being made increasingly not only to electoral fraud, force and the denial of rights, but also to ideological and psychological warfare. On every front — academic, cultural, religious, social and political — the people are constantly bombarded with half-truths and lies.

The intention is to perpetuate the *status quo* by confusion, and to transfer blame for failure from the PNC government to others.

The people were dubbed lazy. Hence Burnham's slogan: "Eat less, sleep less, and work harder" — quite a sharp contrast from a previous electioneering slogan that promised that, with the PNC in power, no one would go to bed hungry, and everyone would receive free milk and cassava.

The people were told that they lacked skills, that they were inefficient and unproductive. Hence, Burnham's dubbing of 1968 as "Efficiency Year".

Sir Arthur Lewis, Chancellor of the University of Guyana, declared in his inaugural address in January 1967, that the underdeveloped countries were poor because they did not have as many skilled people as the developed countries! According to Sir Arthur, who "sold" the Puerto Rican economic model to the Commonwealth Caribbean territories, foreign ownership and control of the economy and country had nothing to do with backwardness and poverty!

A University of Guyana circular nearly went out stating that if the University was to attract money from foundations abroad, its image must be changed. The circular was withdrawn, but the same objective was achieved by administrative action. Leftist Stuart Bowes was relieved of his post in the Sociology Department. And Professor Horace Davis, with a doctorate degree (Ph.D.) from Harvard University, was removed as dean of the Social Sciences faculty, and eventually "smoked out" of his job as head of the Department of Economics.

The University of Guyana, our high schools and government ministries are all infiltrated today by CIA spies, who pose as advisers and experts, and by Peace Corps personnel. And hundreds of thousands of U.S. books and magazines swamp our schools and libraries. The purpose is to "sell" the American way of life and the American free-enterprise or capitalist system, to gather intelligence, and to smear the PPP and socialism.

Meanwhile, Guyana is having an ever-increasing stream of American evangelist crusaders, no doubt also financed by the CIA, like Billy Graham's Latin-American Crusade. The main enemy, these Christian crusaders declare, is Communism. Now and then, for good measure, they attack some of the ills of capitalism — not the system itself. All systems are bad, they add; politics and politicians cannot help the people — all the politicians have failed the people; only the return of Christ can save them. Religion in the hand of these "Sunday Christians" is made into an opiate to withdraw the people from the path of struggle for a better life.

Other half-truths peddled refer to the lack of capital, an excessive birth rate, and a small population as factors militating against economic development. Thus the call for greater incentives to foreign investors, family planning and birth control, and integration and unity with the Commonwealth Caribbean.

The objectives of the U.S. imperialists and their puppets are to cast blame on the working class for the failures of the ruling capitalist class; to dangle fresh "carrots" and create new hopes so as to extend U.S. hegemony — political, economic and military— over territories where British and other European competitors once held sway.

The means by which these objectives are to be attained are close association with the Organization of American States (OAS), partnership and Caribbean unity — a Caribbean Free Trade Area (CARIFTA). Caribbean unity is held out as the greatest hope for viability and progress.

Unity and integration are essential if the purpose is to break with imperialism and neocolonialism. But this is not the kind of unity contemplated. What is projected is the strengthening of the position of foreign capital, particularly U.S. capital.

That no fundamental change is intended in the Caribbean was clearly pointed out by the Incorporated Commonwealth Caribbean Chambers of Industry and Commerce after their delegation met the Trinidad Prime Minister and other experts and advisers. Throwing in the red herring of Communism, the delegation wrote: "Communist infiltration: It was felt that the danger of communist infiltration in the area should not be regarded lightly and the earlier situation in Guyana was referred to. The delegation was asked to bear the problem in mind and to emphasize in their talks the importance of preserving the traditional system of free enterprise."

George Ball, former Under-Secretary of State and one-time chairman of the big investment banking firm of Lehman Bros., made this clear to the New York Chamber of

Commerce when he said: "The multi-national U.S. corporation is ahead of, and in conflict with, existing world political organizations represented by the nation-state. Major obstacles to the multi-national corporation are evident in Western Europe, Canada and a good part of the developing world."

CARIFTA has facilitated the foreign branch-plants of the multi-national corporations in the area to the detriment of Guyana and the smaller Commonwealth Caribbean territories. Goods produced particularly in Trinidad and Jamaica, in many cases high-priced and inferior in quality, now move freely within the region with the result that on the second anniversary of CARIFTA, Jamaica increased her trade by over 60 percent, Trinidad by over 30 percent, and Guyana by a mere 5 percent. St. Lucia, Dominica and other territories are now seriously questioning the usefulness of CARIFTA

With revolution as the main trend in the world today, the imperialists and their puppets are demagogically resorting to new slogans and gimmicks. President Nixon talks about "revolution"; so did Eduardo Frei in Chile. In Guyana, Minister of Agriculture, Dr. P. Reid talks about the green revolution; Eusi Kwayana, formerly Sydney King, calls for cultural revolution, and L.F.S. Burnham advocates socialist revolution. At the same time, they are taking certain *ad hoc* measures in the economic field to create the impression that they are taking an anti-imperialist course, and slowly but surely confronting imperialism.

These moves have become necessary because of increasing pressures, internal and external, for change — firstly, revolutionary upheavals in each country; and secondly, the growing strength and influence of the world socialist system.

From one socialist state (U.S.S.R.) after World War I, the world socialist system which came into being after World War II now includes several socialist states in Europe, Asia and Latin America. The CMEA (Council for Mutual Economic Assistance) socialist countries of Europe alone with only 10 percent of the world's population produce one-third of the world's industrial output. In the past 10 years, their national income increased by 93 percent as compared with only 63 percent for the developed capitalist states. Consequently, as was stated by the Preparatory Meeting of the World Communist Parties in its report *Indictment of Imperialism*, June 5–17, 1969: "The economic and social challenge of the socialist world terrifies the ruling circles of imperialism. They are employing every method to prevent the growing influence of socialist ideas and practice on the peoples of the capitalist and former colonial countries, realising that time is working for socialism."

Earlier Gunnar Myrdal, the famous Swedish economist, in his book, *The Challenge of Affluence*, wrote: 'It is enough to take as established that the present rate of economic growth is considerably higher in the Soviet Union than in the United States — at least double or perhaps more... the magic of compound interest is such that if the United States should fail to overcome its relative stagnation very soon, the Soviet Union would within a not too distant future, approach, reach and eventually surpass the United States in important fields."

Apart from the serious competition from the socialist world, imperialism has been beset during the past decade by many failures.

The UN Development Decade (1960–70) failed to narrow the wide gap in living standards between the peoples in the imperialist states and those of the imperialist-dominated states.

The Puerto Rico model of economic planning and development based on the creation of an investment climate and incentives to foreign capital is rejected in all progressive circles. Young academics in the universities of the West Indies and Guyana are now openly voicing the same sharp criticisms which the PPP made during the past twenty years.

The reformist Alliance for Progress did not reach its objectives. Dante D. Fascell, chairman of the U.S. House of Representatives Sub-Committee on Inter-American Affairs, in mid-February 1969 declared: "I would be less than frank if I would not admit that the initial record of the Alliance for Progress inspires more gloom than satisfaction."

Pointing out that the per capita gross national product increase of 1.5 percent was a little more than one-half of the expected Alliance goal of 2.5 percent, he said: "I have serious doubt that this increase has had any significant impact on the masses of the people. At this rate of progress Latin Americans who live at the edge of subsistence — whose annual income is estimated at about $200 — will have to wait half a century to double the level of their standard of living. Furthermore, Latin America may have actually lost ground in such fields as education, housing, and food production when the growth in its population is taken into account."

In this new situation, the imperialists have been forced to devise new, ever more crafty, methods as had been done a little over a decade ago. Then the British and French moved swiftly to hand over independence particularly to their African colonies. "If reform doesn't come in time," John Gunther warned, "Africa, the greatest prize on earth, may be lost to the West, as much as Asia was lost."

Fresh in Gunther's mind no doubt were the revolutionary upheavals in the post-World War II period, which shook the foundations of the Old Order. Mutiny of the British Navy in Bombay Harbour in 1946 and uprisings throughout India compelled the British government to concede independence to India in 1947 despite the fact that Winston Churchill, the great wartime hero, had adamantly refused to grant independence during the war. The Dutch were expelled from Indonesia. In 1949, the Chinese Communist Party had kicked out the imperialist puppet Chiang Kai-shek; the Americans were pushed out of North Korea in 1953 and General MacArthur, Far-East World War II hero, sacked; the French were disastrously defeated in Indochina in 1954 and were facing defeat in Algeria in the late 1950's; in Egypt, the corrupt King Farouk was overthrown in 1952, the British forced out of their military base in the Canal Zone, and the Anglo-French-Israeli attack in 1956 repulsed. The 1958 revolution in Iraq destroyed the regime of U.S. puppet, Nuri es-Said, and broke up the Baghdad Pact; Sekou Touré opted for independence for Guinea in 1958 and turned for help to the Soviet Union. The Cuban revolution in 1959 established the first free territory in the Americas.

These developments shattered the "containment of Communism" cold-war policy of the imperialists; U.S.S.R. presence was felt not only in the Far East, but also in Africa, the Middle East, and Latin America.

Imperialism's cold-war strategy was in disarray; at the United Nations, the U.S.S.R. was also pressing for the ending of colonialism. It was in this context that Harold Macmillan talked about the "wind of change" and the necessity to win men's minds, and called on the

South African government to ease up in its racist (apartheid) policy, and the colonial powers to concede independence as quickly as possible.

The imperialists had learnt that their military might was not enough to stem the rising tide of socialism and national liberation. Experience in India had also shown that political independence meant neither the end of British "influence" nor the "expropriation of the expropriators". For the British imperialists, neocolonialism was better than violent revolution. And there was "big brother", the U.S.A., on whom they were keeping a watchful eye.

The United States was advocating political independence for European possessions in Africa, the better to penetrate them economically as it had done in Latin America by muscling out Britain and West Germany, which had themselves muscled out Spain and Portugal.

The African colonies were tied to the metropolitan "mother" countries by economic agreements and preferential tariff systems. The U.S. had been blocked immediately after the war when it demanded of other European powers the abolition of preferential tariff systems and the adoption of world free trade. These devastated countries were forced to make some concessions such as the devaluation of the pound (sterling) in Britain and ejection of Communism and left-wingers from united-front governments in Europe; they could have adopted world free trade only at the price of their ruin. As a consequence, the United States played what appeared to be a Jekyll-Hyde role. In its confrontation with the socialist bloc, it joined with the other Western partners; at the same time it supported a limited type of struggle for independence, and worked through the younger nationalist leaders, particularly in the trade union field. The U.S. was aiming to achieve in the 20th century what the British had succeeded in doing in the 19th century; as for examples the economic penetration of Latin America after they had aided Simon Bolivar to oust the Spanish from their possessions in South America.

Now, with 5 to 10 years of experience, the peoples have realised that mere formal independence is not enough, that neocolonialism has brought not liberation but even greater burdens. Consciousness of the need for change through an anti-imperialist programme embracing nationalisation of the commanding heights of the economy as advocated by the PPP and other revolutionary parties and movements, has also been developing.

In the face of these developments, the imperialists have embarked firstly on their "Vietnamisation" policy — getting Asians to fight Asians, Africans to fight Africans and Latin Americans to fight Latin Americans; and secondly, on their policy of so-called "partnership" — joint ownership as enunciated by leading spokesmen and pro-imperialist organs.

Joseph Reidy's book, *Strategy for the Americas* gave advice to U.S. business to form as close links as possible with the national economy of the countries in which it operates.

Time magazine praised the joint undertaking in 1965 between Hanna Mining Co. (U.S.) and the local Brazilian industrialist Augusto Antunes as a means of respecting national sentiments and offering protection against "the attacks that Brazilian nationalists have made on other foreign interests." According to *Business Week* foreign monopolies are now "setting up new companies with Mexican partners, or reorganising existing subsidiaries to take in Mexican capital on a majority basis."

Frei's government in Chile had clearance with the U.S. State Department. According to Richard Bourne in his *Political Leaders of Latin America:* 'The Chileanisation of copper was an electoral gimmick designed to trump the FRAP proposal for full nationalisation in 1964. There is some evidence that it was produced in haste and cleared by the prospective Christian Democrat foreign minister, Gabriel Valdes, with the State Department and New York banking leaders rather than with the Braden and other companies concerned. The agreement, passed in 1965, provided for the Chilean state to own 51 percent of the shares in the biggest mine, Braden's El Teniente."

William Rogers, U.S. Secretary of State, during his African tour in early 1970 said: 'There has been a steady growth in U.S. private investment in Africa since most of the African nations achieved their independence. By the end of 1968 the value of U.S. private investment in OAU member states was almost $2,000 million. Between 1963 and 1968, U.S. private investment in Africa grew at an average annual rate of about 14 percent. We believe that private investment can and should play a growing role, above and beyond public assistance, in African development. Africans themselves desire to participate in such investment. In many countries, in the face of limited capital resources, it is the government rather than the private sector which has the financial wherewithal to join with foreign private investors. Thus, 'joint ventures' frequently involve a combination of foreign private and African governmental capital. We are prepared to encourage American investors to cooperate in such endeavours under adequate investment protection."

Responding to the call for Caribbean national control of natural resources, the *Financial Times* (U.K.) in early 1971 said that there were as many opportunities and needs for investment as there ever were, but investments would have to be in partnership with the people of the territories and not unilaterally.

"Joint ventures" are thus seen not only as a safeguard against "attacks by nationalists", and a way to counteract "nationalisation", but also as a means of providing stability and earning greater profits. The imperialists have learnt that nationals who buy shares or become directors in joint ventures generally also become "denationalised" and imbibe the ideology and mores of the foreign investors. And local participation, especially by government, leads in the name of patriotism to restrictions like anti-strike laws.

Within this imperialist framework, the PNC puppet government, while mouthing revolutionary slogans, has embarked on a reformist course. With the failure of its 7-year Development Plan, it now lays emphasis on community development, self-help and cooperatives, instead of on a planned proportional development of the economy. The Cooperative Republic, the official designation of Guyana since its assumption of republican status in 1969, "will make the small man into a real man", and cooperatives "will be the means to bring about socialism in Guyana", and not the reverse as the PPP holds.

In late 1970, the call was put for "meaningful participation" in the Demerara Bauxite Company (Demba). This was reluctantly changed in early 1971 to nationalisation due to firstly, the charge by the People's Progressive Party and the Ratoon Group (academics and students mainly associated with the University of Guyana) of collaboration with imperialism; and secondly, the inflexible position of Alcan, the owners of Demba.

The move against Demba was taken not only in response to the pressures of the PPP and the Ratoon Group. ASCRIA, the cultural arm of the PNC, had long been concerned about "jim-crow" practices and attitudes at Mackenzie (now Linden) where mostly PNC supporters live and work. It is also becoming increasingly apparent that the Burnham government has acted in collusion with U.S. imperialism against Canadian imperialism.

U.S. pressure on the PNC government no doubt stems from the fear that if the present trend continues, and Alcan, set up in Canada by Alcoa in 1928 to hold all (except Surinam) its foreign properties becomes Canadian-owned and controlled, U.S. imperialism not only will be deprived of the strategic raw material, bauxite, but also will be unable to compete with Canada, which even now with her abundant hydroelectric power is the cheapest world producer of aluminium ingots.

It might be that the United States has remained strangely silent on the Demba nationalisation out of fear that its opposition would force the PNC into an anti-imperialist unity with the PPP. It is also likely that the U.S. military-industrial complex calculated it would be easier to control a client, financially weak Guyana, than an industrially strong Canada which sees itself playing an independent role in the Americas similar to that of France under De Gaulle; that nationalised Demba could serve U.S. short and long-term interests not only by maintaining supplies of high-grade bauxite, but also facilitating the U.S.-owned Reynolds Metals Company.

Reynolds has long complained about the high costs of operation at two points, Kwakwani and Everton, because of the sand-banked, shallow Berbice River. It would prefer in the absence of the government dredging and maintaining the Berbice River to close Everton, connect by a 15-mile rail Kwakwani to Ituni, take its ore to Linden for cleaning and drying and ship via the Demerara River; it could also get alumina from the Guyana Bauxite Company (Guybau), the nationalised Demba, for its aluminium smelter in Venezuela.

Aid and control! An $8 million, government-guaranteed loan was made to Guybau even before July 15, 1971, the date of the takeover of Demba, by the Chase Manhattan Bank, controlled by the Rockefeller interests, and headed by David Rockefeller. The PNC government justified this loan on the ground that it was good business. It's good business also to trade with Cuba, but the U.S. military-industrial complex does not.

Soon after the Chase Manhattan loan, the World Bank granted a $10 million loan, and the U.S. government renewed the sugar quota for Guyana!

Clearly, what we are witnessing is not yet a real confrontation with imperialism, but what is more likely a confrontation between imperialisms, between the "shark" U.S.A. and the "sardine" Canada. Thus the rebuke from the Canadian government expressed in mild diplomatic language that while it was not opposed to nationalisation, it wanted non-discriminatory treatment, a clear reference to the exclusion of Reynolds Metals Company from the bauxite nationalisation.

It must not be assumed from what I have related that there is 100 percent unanimity or accord in the imperialist camp. Just as there are contradictions between big and small capitalists, and big and small imperialist states, just so there are contradictions between the imperialists and their puppets.

Even though the PNC government got clearance from the U.S. State Department on the bauxite deal, this does not mean that U.S. imperialism is happy about everything happening in Guyana. For instance, it did not like the expulsion from the government of the United

Force, its ideological base in Guyana. Nor is it too happy about the degree of corruption in high ruling quarters.

At the same time, because of internal and external pressures, the puppets sometimes overstep the tight limits set upon them by their masters. For instance, although Colombia, Venezuela, Ecuador and Chile (under Eduardo Frei), with Christian and Social-democratic reformist rule, side with imperialism in any confrontation with socialism, they nevertheless are forced by popular pressure to carry out certain reforms and to oppose certain imperialist moves, such as the formation of the so-called Latin American Peace Force.

In Guyana, the American government has to tolerate certain PNC aberrations and to continue to support the PNC since there is no alternative except the PPP. The one condition that the U.S.A. exacts for its continued support is that the PNC must hold the line against the PPP with intimidation and harassment, and have only nominal relations with the socialist world.

Nationalisation and some aspects of state trading (External Trade Bureau) are permitted so long as radical transformation with socialist help and cooperation is not contemplated; very generous compensation is paid ($107 million to be paid for Demba over 20 years at 6 percent interest), and Guyana continues to be a primary producer of bauxite and restricts its trade to the capitalist world.

While the "hawks" of imperialism resort to the "club", the liberals prefer to combine the "club" with the "carrot". More crafty, they see the need for change — change in partnership with imperialism. I have already related that President Kennedy and his aides had told me that they were not opposed to nationalisation. But to these liberals, nationalisation must be seen as change of the *status quo* internally not externally; within *capitalism*, but not *towards socialism.*

To maintain the international *status quo*, the balance of forces between capitalism and socialism, the United States, although pledged to support non-alignment, helped to destroy the non-aligned regimes of Nkrumah in Ghana, Sukarno in Indonesia, Goulart in Brazil and Obete in Uganda. It refused to go along with the British for a neutral Laos, and with France for a neutral Vietnam. And the rightist military Suharto regime is now a member of the non-aligned bloc!

Little wonder that the Burnham government, despite its claims to non-alignment, voted against the seating of People's China at the United Nations in 1968 and 1969 and abstained in 1970; broke off trade with Cuba; placed quantitative restrictions and a 10 percent discriminatory tax on imports from the socialist countries, and entered into nominal, non-residential diplomatic relations with the Soviet Union. (The latter decision was taken while the Prime Minister was on his way to the Lusaka Non-Aligned Conference.)

The PNC government's non-resident ambassador to the U.S.S.R. is Sir John Carter, who as leader of the UDP attacked Burnham and me in 1954 as "agents of the Kremlin" and had seen the necessity "to strangle and root out for all time the traitors in our midst". Then Burnham attacked Carter as a "loyal Kikuyu". On October 23, 1954, he wrote: "So far as we are aware, the Soviet Union is a socialist country and as such cannot be imperialist at the same time … . Mr. Carter is deliberately confusing the issues of Guyanese independence and deliberately distorting the peaceful international policy of the Soviet Union." Now, they both make anti-Sovietism their special brand of anti-Communism, and propagate the theory of self-interest of the two super-powers, equating Western imperialism with so-called "Soviet imperialism".

The PNC regime thus justifies its refusal to develop relations with, and to accept aid from, the socialist world by criticising aid generally as raid, while remaining in the imperialist bloc and taking handouts from time to time.

This is the explanation for the fact that on a division in the National Assembly on a debate on foreign affairs in mid-1971, the United Force voted with the PNC government.

At the Lusaka Non-Aligned Conference, the Prime Minister projected a radical anti-imperialist image. He offered aid to the African freedom fighters, but nothing to the Vietnamese freedom fighters; he offered sanctuary to the African freedom fighters, but not to the Brazilian freedom fighters; he condemned racism in Southern Africa, but remained silent about racism and the harassment and murder of black leaders in the U.S.A. Indeed, some manoeuvreability is permitted by imperialism to the puppet regime!

Resort is also made to psychological warfare. The impression is being fostered that the PNC regime, backed by the United States, is invincible; that the PPP could never again win; and should it win there would be more disturbances and violence.

The intention is to make our supporters develop a mood of despair and hopelessness, which could lead either to rightist opportunism, compromise and retreat or to ultra-left adventurism. Both of these tendencies are dangerous and must be combatted.

Right opportunism is rooted in the proposition that racial feelings are too deep, that the Africans will always support the PNC and that the PPP will never be able to get political power by winning or neutralising them. Therefore, it is argued, the PPP must change its image (a variation on this theme is that I must step down from the leadership because of my avowed Marxism until the PPP gets power) and make a compromise with the U.S.A.

What kind of compromise? Would the U.S.A. agree to a non-aligned, anti-imperialist Guyana? Would a U.S.-backed PPP regime be allowed to go any further than the PNC-UF coalition or the PNC regime or any Latin-American puppet state?

The answer is clear. The United States wants subservience, not independence. Under its tutelage and dictation, Guyana will fare no better than Latin America, where there is chronic underdevelopment, backwardness and poverty.

To those pessimists who say that the Indian and African workers cannot be united, I say, look back to the situation before the 1950's. Then too it appeared that the two ethnic groups could not be united. John Carter then, as Burnham now, ruled in Georgetown. But by 1953 Carter and his friends were unable to win a single seat in the capital. In the same way that the workers then marched united behind the PPP, they will march again.

Who could have predicted a few years ago the overwhelming welcome I received at Linden in May 1971 during the strike of bauxite workers?

In Trinidad, "black power" rebellion in February–April 1970 with about two-thirds of the army revolting nearly toppled the Eric Williams' PNM regime in Trinidad. And in Surinam, black teachers precipitated the resignation of Minister-President Pengel.

If the right deviationists overestimate the role of race in politics, the left adventurists underestimate it. They call us revisionists and attack us for participating in the parliamentary struggle. They fail to realise that this is only one aspect of the PPP's many-sided anti-imperialist struggle and that any premature violent (armed) struggle can degenerate into racial conflict, as in 1964, and give the PNC regime the excuse for ruthless suppression and assumption of more dictatorial powers, even for the creation of a one-party, fascist state, as was proposed in 1971 by the women's section of the PNC. It must not be forgotten that both race and religion have been used somewhat successfully by the ruling class in its divide-exploit-and rule politics.

The UF, using religion and anti-Communism, succeeded in subjugating and winning over a large section of the Amerindians in the Interior and some of the workers in the capital. And the PNC has maintained the allegiance of the majority of the Africans, who constitute the main segment of the working class in the urban, mining and Interior areas and in the strategic services — army, police, civil service, electricity, telephone, airport, etc. — by fear and demagogy — fear that their future is imperilled not by foreign economic and cultural domination, but by "coolie" (Indian) domination.

I do not see any need for despair. Imperialism is today beleaguered in the face of a worldwide revolutionary upsurge. Superficially, it appears strong in its aggressiveness; but internally, it is weak. The correlation of world forces has changed and the positions of the U.S.A. and its allies weakened.

The recurrent monetary crises of international capitalism are a manifestation not only of the fatal contradiction of the system itself but also of the growing contradictions that are developing between the major imperialist powers. Efforts to prevent the collapse of the key currencies, and therefore, of international capitalism, such as the proposal to create Special Drawing Rights on "paper gold" in the IMF, will merely buy time — at the expense of the weak and the third-world countries. Anyway, time is no cure for this chronic malaise; it cannot forestall the impending doom.

In the imperialist states, the democratic and popular forces are becoming more and more assertive. Rank and file pressures have forced the U.S. Congress to call for the withdrawal of troops from Cambodia and to repeal the Bay of Tonkin resolution which, based on a lie that North Korean PT boats had attacked U.S. naval ships, was used by the Johnson administration as the basis for the bombing of North Vietnam.

With the publication by the *New York Times* and other newspapers of the secret Pentagon papers in June 1971, the whole basis of U.S. aggression in Vietnam was exposed and undermined. The U.S. Senate by voting for the withdrawal of all troops from Vietnam by the end of 1971 has put on record the stand of the American people against the crafty Nixon doctrine of "Vietnamisation" of the war.

The Nixon administration suffered a major setback when the Congress overrode the President's veto on two bills aimed at increasing funds for education and social welfare.

In Europe, the treaty between U.S.S.R. and the Federal Republic of Germany, renouncing the use of force, is a severe setback to the hawks in Washington and the fascist, revanchist elements inside West Germany. France and Italy are rocked by mass action of the progressive and democratic forces led by the Communists. And Britain, recognising the military debacle of her allies (the Dutch, the French and the Americans) in the Far East, has abandoned her "East of Suez" military role.

In the Middle East, the U.S.A., recognising the growing influence of the U.S.S.R. in particular, and socialism in general, and fearing a confrontation as in the Far East, has been forced to apply pressure on her puppet, Israel, to give up her territorial gains of aggression and to come to terms with the Arab World.

In Turkey, a pivot of the Western alliance linking NATO and CENTO, U.S. warships were forced in 1969 by mass demonstrations to terminate prematurely their one-week goodwill visit. The Japanese people's clamour for ending the U.S. military occupation of Okinawa will not end.

In the U.S. client-state, Pakistan, the "house of cards" has come tumbling down. For 10 years, the publicity agents made the dictator Ayub Khan into a great father-figure. In the same way that the London *Daily Telegraph* once advocated, on the basis of false PNC/UF statistics, that Guyana should be the economic model for Africa, so too was Pakistan touted as the model for Southeast Asia. But after two months of mass action, the "bubble" burst; General Ayub was forced to resign. And military force used by his successor against the liberation movement will in the end suffer the same fate as in Vietnam.

Mass action in Northern Ireland, Trinidad, and Surinam also brought about marked changes in the political situation. In the May 1971 general election in Trinidad, which was boycotted by the main democratic forces, the ruling puppet People's National Movement led by Dr. Eric Williams, demonstrated its utter bankruptcy by winning all the 36 seats with only 28 percent of the total votes!

Many countries in Asia, Africa and Latin America, including Sudan, South Yemen, Congo Brazaville, Somalia, Libya, Equatorial Guinea, the Central African Republic, Ceylon, Peru and Chile and Bolivia have achieved anti-imperialist successes.

Bogged down in Vietnam and plagued by internal dissension, the United States has neither the moral authority nor the resources to intervene as it did with over half a million troops in Vietnam and with 65,000 troops in the Dominican Republic in 1965. In the Far East, it was paralysed in the face of the seizure by North Korea of the spy ship, *Pueblo*. In Peru, it could neither intervene nor impose economic sanctions even after the new military regime had attacked U.S. fishing trawlers in Peruvian waters and nationalised U.S. oil, sugar and telephone companies. In Chile, the plotting of the CIA and the right-wing General Robert Viaux, could not prevent the inauguration of Salvador Allende as President in November 1970.

The United States and their puppets will fail in Guyana also. This country is caught up in the deepening crisis of world capitalism. A vicious circle of taxation-poverty-discontent-force is resulting in sharpening contradictions and a widening gulf between the PNC elitist leadership and the people, even the PNC rank and file.

The largely middle-class, bureaucratic, capitalist leadership is neither psychologically nor ideologically opposed to U.S. political, economic, cultural and military domination of Guyana. It is prepared to play the role of a governing élite, to carry out limited reforms while foreign vested interests control the commanding heights of the economy — factories, mines, plantations, banks, insurance, shipping, and foreign trade — and to use the state apparatus to crush the workers.

The Trades Union Congress, which helped to bring the PNC to power, has come under increasing pressure from the workers. Consequently, it has attacked the government for its anti-strike proposals, and its use of police dogs and armed police and troops against workers on strike. Caught in this predicament, the government has not pressed on with its Trades Disputes Bill.

Meanwhile, working class unity, and thus racial unity, and militancy in the sugar industry under the banner of the Guyana Agricultural Workers Union (GAWU), which is closely associated with the PPP, have precipitated a near crisis. Unable to push through its anti-strike measure, and having a vested interest in industrial peace for purposes of maintaining international sugar quotas and enhancing capitalist profits and governmental revenues, the government through the Minister of Labour moved towards the recognition of the GAWU. But the ruling party, fearful that Indian-African industrial support for the GAWU will blossom into political support for the PPP, introduced a new union in the sugar industry. For this, the government has been condemned by the TUC and a section of the pro-imperialist press which normally backs it.

Like the United States, Guyana is today a sick society. Discrimination, nepotism and corruption have developed deep scars. Side by side with a "crisis of confidence" is a "crisis of authority."

Norman Semple, President of the Berbice Branch of the Guyana Public (formerly Civil) Service Association, in May 1971, warned of "a crisis of authority", due to "a blurring of the line of authority between political and administrative decision-making", which "has taken a toll of the efficiency of the administrative machinery of the State . . ." As regards complaints from the public, he pointed out: "These reports have been identified with the lethargy of public servants when dealing with complaints from members of the public, with the wastage of valuable materials and time in doing everything but that for which we are paid; the lack of a sense of urgency when dealing with matters vital to the proper administration of the State, or lack of integrity, and last but by no means least, the flouting of authority which has assumed alarming proportions within recent times."

Inefficiency and indiscipline have been brewing for some time. In April 1968, a British Council representative, Stephen Alexander, just prior to his departure from Guyana told the *Daily Chronicle:* "We see a lot of money coming into the country and plans are made for the spending of this money. But when we look at the final result, there isn't much to show, is there?" Referring to a British radiographer who had been seconded for two years to help establish a new X-ray unit at Mabaruma, he went on: "Sometimes, experts come to help but are given little encouragement so they become frustrated and leave... The equipment was donated by OXFAM and it remained in Georgetown for more than a year. All the while, the radiographer was doing nothing—and she started out on the job 18 months late! Already her two years are almost up and there is no one to replace her."

That there was a "crisis of confidence" was visibly demonstrated in April 1971 when bauxite workers at Linden, traditionally PNC supporters, went on strike for the speedy conclusion and release of the Tyndal Arbitration Tribunal's findings, the payment of the award before the date of the takeover of Demba by government, and against the attempt of the government to convert their Canadian-based insurance pension plan (RILA) to a local, government-run scheme.

This "crisis of confidence" is the result of growing consciousness among the people that the PNC ruling elite, not having a principled position, moves and adopts *ad hoc* measures which are bankrupting the country; that the PNC's reformist nationalisation carried out within the framework of imperialism, like those of the British Labour governments and the regimes of the Nationalist Revolutionary Movement in Bolivia (1952–64) and the Nationalist Party led by Dr. Mossadegh of Iran (1951–53), cannot and will not bring an end to exploitation and oppression and will fail.

The Guyanese people like the Chilean people, are learning from their own experience. In 1958, Salvador Allende, whose Popular Front won the election in September 1970, lost to Jorge Alessandri, the representative of the conservative, capitalist interests. At the next election in November 1964, the people, dissatisfied and discontented, turned to Eduardo Frei, the leader of the Christian Democratic Party, an alliance of capitalists and Catholics. Frei, who defeated Allende at his second attempt to win the presidency, resorted to sloganeering, demagogy and reformism. Using Juanita Castro's theme in his successful election campaign, he attacked the Castro regime for "revolution in dictatorship"; his method, he said, would be "revolution in liberty". His reform measures, "Chileanisation of copper", embraced the new strategy of imperialism — participation in imperialist enterprises. His land reform law did not get to the root of the problem. Landlords were allowed to retain as much as 380 hectares, and any small farmer who wanted land had to lodge 10 percent of the price as a cash down payment!

This programme did not alleviate the suffering of the masses. It merely allowed the big mining sector to become wealthier — before Frei's 51 percent partnership with U.S. copper monopolies, foreign mining interests made only $44 million in profits; in 1968, they pocketed $126 million. It caused dissatisfaction, not only among the people, but also within Frei's party; a splinter breakaway group joined with Allende's Popular Front.

Midway in the 6-year term of Eduardo Frei as President, the Chilean people were thoroughly disillusioned. By the end of his term of office in 1970, they recognised that only the revolutionary anti-imperialist programme of Allende's alliance would save them and they elected him President. As Allende put it: "This is a clear victory with a well-defined, very clear programme, with a great national sense, and with a clean anti-imperialist direction."

In Guyana also, there has been development of the people's consciousness. At the 1961 and 1964 general elections, it was propagated that Peter d'Aguiar, the UF leader and counterpart of Jorge Alessandri, would bring to the government the same kind of financial wizardry that made him from a vendor of Pepsi Cola and beer into a successful business tycoon and a millionaire. But he was soon forced out; in 1967, he resigned as Minister of Finance and in 1969 quit active politics — his economic and fiscal policies helped not the small man but the local and foreign capitalist class.

L.F.S. Burnham, Frei's counterpart, has substituted "consultative democracy" for "revolution in liberty". But between 1964 and 1968, there was neither consultation nor democracy. Now "consultative democracy" has given way to "Cooperative Republic".

Demagogy and sloganeering will fail in Guyana as they have failed in Chile, where the people step by step learnt that neither capitalism nor reformism can solve their basic problems.

As the small man becomes smaller, and as the ideological struggle shifts from whether or not to nationalise to what kind of nationalisation, more and more people are becoming aware that any policy of confrontation with imperialism must involve an overall strategy, not just the takeover of a few capitalist positions, that state capitalism, what Frederick Engels called "collective capitalism" under Bismarck in Germany and later under Hitler, is not the same as anti-imperialism and socialism. An all-embracing anti-imperialist pro-socialist strategy would involve:

Nationalisation of the economy — foreign and local "comprador" capitalist-owned and controlled factories, mines, plantations, banks, insurance companies, and foreign trade;

Full democracy and workers' participation and control;

Genuine diplomatic, economic and cultural relations with the socialist world;

Training of administrative, diplomatic, technical and professional personnel in socialist states; ending the policy of refusing employment to students who have graduated in socialist countries;

Imbuing the people with the revolutionary scientific socialist (Marxist-Leninist) ideology and involving them meaningfully in the process of socio-economic reconstruction;

Planned proportional development of the economy with emphasis on industry and agriculture;

Land reform;

Strict system of foreign-exchange control;

Effective rent and price controls;

Continuation and strengthening of the class struggle;

Settlement of the border issues so that they cannot be used for launching attacks against Guyana;

Ending corruption, nepotism and favouritism; fighting and taking strict measures against all forms of racial discrimination; providing special opportunities to all depressed groups, particularly the Amerindians, for development.

Unlike the PNC which merely carries out certain reform measures to improve its image, the PPP sees the need for public (state) ownership to go hand in hand with workers' control and the closest cultural, political and economic links with the socialist world. In any confrontation with imperialism, only the socialist world can help to counter imperialist economic and military aggression by providing firstly, the markets for sugar, bauxite etc., and the means to industrialise and transform; secondly, the military equipment for defense as in Cuba and the United Arab Republic; and thirdly, the scientific-socialist (Marxist-Leninist) ideological development of civil servants, teachers, army and police officers and the people generally, which is so necessary for combatting imperialist subversion and intervention.

As regards bauxite, the question at issue today is not just getting "some more" of the profits now draining away, or getting other Western (U.S. and its allies) buyers of bauxite. What is needed is a structural economic change which will involve the generation of power, smelting of bauxite into aluminium, and fabricating industries; in other words, laying the basis for a heavy industry in Guyana based on bauxite-aluminium. It is mainly the socialist world which can help in such transformation as has been done in Cuba and elsewhere.

Emphasis on industry and agriculture and not infrastructure will help to generate wealth more rapidly to cope with growing debt payments and for self-sustaining growth.

Foreign exchange control will husband our financial resources. Effective rent and price controls will protect consumers, and house and land occupiers. Land reform will aid agriculture, which will provide not only cheap foods, but also the raw materials for industry, and the economic base in the countryside for manufactured goods.

In addition to the overall programme listed above, there must be progressive policies for agriculture including incentives and guaranteed markets, education, health, housing, etc., for which adequate financial allocations must be made.

In the framework of this anti-imperialist programme, the cooperative sector will complement the public sector and not be submerged, as now, by the private sector. There will also be a place for the national, patriotic capitalist sector.

And all Guyanese, skilled and unskilled, without political and racial discrimination, will be embraced in the exciting process of nation building.

With the sharpening of the national liberation and class struggle, political polarisation is becoming intensified. The United Force is in the process of disintegration. While the more reactionary and anti-Communist elements have moved towards the PNC government, the rest of the leadership and the rank and file have been forced into a position of hostility. Many of the latter, particularly the Amerindians, now support us. And more and more Guyanese, once hostile to the PPP, are looking to us for the solution to their problems and the fulfilment of their aspirations.

Other protest groups — the Patriots, Anti-Discrimination Movement, Committee For Human Rights, Ratoon Group, Movement Against Oppression — mainly led by middle-class professionals and academics have become increasingly critical of the government, particularly as regards corruption, discrimination and the denial of civil liberties. Generally they take the same stand on these issues as the PPP, but because of ideological aberrations and opportunistic considerations, they shy away from forging an alliance and taking joint action with us. Such groups must be warned that division in the face of a ruthless and cunning enemy at home and abroad is not only dangerous but also suicidal.

What is not so apparent is the danger of Burnham's pseudo-reformism, which is dangerous not because it does not confer certain benefits, but because it sows illusions about the failure. Marxists support reforms as a step towards socialism, not as an end in itself. V.I. Lenin in his *Marxism and Reformism* warned: "Reformism, even when quite sincere, in practice becomes a weapon by means of which the bourgeoisie corrupt and weaken the workers. The experience of all countries shows that the workers who put their trust in the reformists are always fooled."

The crossroad has now been reached in our country's history. The people now realise that with the PNC in full control of the electoral machinery, there are severe limitations to the electoral road to power. The lesson has dawned that through unity, mass confrontation and day-to-day struggles, the PNC must be forced to respect the constitution and to take an anti-imperialist course. If it fails to do so and sets up an outright dictatorship, Guyana will be brought to a new stage of struggle.

The need is also seen by us for forging a new weapon, a better disciplined and ideologically sound party to wage a relentless many-sided battle on all fronts — political, ideological, economic, cultural —for genuine independence.

Whatever the obstacles, cost and sacrifice, we will continue to work for racial and working class unity and the creation of a broad-based, anti-imperialist alliance under the banner of "unity and struggle" — struggle against those who vacillate and support imperialism, and unity with those who fight for democracy, freedom and socialism.

Such unity has made significant headway in Ceylon and Chile. There imperialism has been defeated. So will it be in Guyana: of this, I am certain.

Those who say that we are irrelevant, that we are finished, should be reminded that the same tune was sung after the dark days following the rape of our constitution in 1953 and the breakaway by the right and left opportunists in 1955 and 1956. But we won in 1957 and 1961. Today, though defrauded and cheated, we remain the strongest force in the country. Difficulties there will be; the battle will be long and hard. But win again we will.

Independent Thought and Caribbean Freedom

Lloyd Best

I — THOUGHT AND FREEDOM

The Caribbean Condition

When we think of the Caribbean we have in mind a canvas larger than that usually found in the gallery of the colonial mind. Certainly it includes the Antilles — Greater and Lesser — and the Guyanas. These together form the heartland of the system which it is our expressed purpose to change. But many times the Caribbean also includes the littoral that surrounds our sea. Admittedly, it is an extensive shore. And the contours which may be taken to mark it off, are still — to an uncomfortable degree — a matter of personal taste. Yet our choice of boundaries is not, for that fact, baseless. For what we are trying to encompass within our scheme is the cultural, social, political and economic foundations of the "sugar plantation" variant of the colonial mind. Hence we sometimes include Carolina, and Caracas with Kingston and Chacachacave, Corentyne and Camaguey; Recife with Paramaribo, Port-of-Spain and Pointe-a-Pitre; and British Honduras with Blanchisseuse and Barranquitas.

Let us look. Choose any point of vantage. Most everywhere there is disorder: fragmentation, segmentation and disarray. What is more, it is mounting disorder: growing populations, lagging incomes, increasing unemployment; widening disequality, lengthening dependence and rising discontent.

This confusion — apparently — does not much respect differences in political history, or in current political affiliation and current political status. Puerto Rico is Estado Libre Asociado — with the United States of America. The Little Eight are, or are soon to be, asociado in their own peculiar way with the United Kingdom, while Surinam and the Dutch Antilles are equal partners in the Kingdom of the Netherlands.

Trinidad, Jamaica and Barbados have all moved smoothly to become independent kingdoms of an English monarch. Guyana has laboured to the same status — but with the help of the State Department. Louisiana achieved her incorporation into God's own country by purchase. Bolivar threw Iberian royalty out and Venezuela became an independent Republic; Brazil brought Iberian royalty in, but became in the end an Independent Republic just the same.

Toussaint defeated the French, the Spanish and the English and then shilly-shallied, but Dessalines claimed the freedom for Haiti willy-nilly. Cuba was forced twice over to exchange imperial masters. First she had to exchange the Papal Donation of 1493 for the Platt Amendment of 1902. And then, bidding for independence a second time in 1960, was forced into voluntary association with the Marxist-Leninist Church. Les Antilles francaises sont, bien entendu, une partie de la metropole. Look at the picture Les trois capitaines l'auraient appelee vilainel

Traditional Political Economy

The economy which underlines this disorder is literally a pappy-show. To elicit any considerable response from it there first has to be prompting by metropolitan demand and metropolitan investment. The Governments are busy, it is true. Busy, busy. They are engaged in modernising the public utilities and in expanding the infrastructure. Indeed, this they have to do. It is a necessary condition of welcome to metropolitan business. And it is their fundamental — if false — assumption that economic development is to be equated with the growth of manufacturing industry and the rapid rise of income per head of population; that it can best be achieved with continued, indeed, with extended metropolitan participation; and that it is a goal so separate and distinct from both political independence and social equalization, that each is pursuable more or less on its own.

It may be interesting here to make a brief exploration of some of the consequences of this view of change in the Caribbean context. To this end, let us consider the case of Governments which, admittedly as a mere strategic device, deliberately assume the role of house-slave, as it were, to metropolitan business.

Their strategy is in the short-run to rely on metropolitan initiatives in investment, technology and marketing, on continued metropolitan ownership and control of the main means of production and therefore on a (temporary) reinforcement of the traditional economic relationships. They reason that this will secure them more time and in the end create more auspicious material conditions for an ultimate exercise of political independence and for the promotion of social equality and social justice.

It is here largely immaterial whether or not the political leaders of the national movement adopt this strategy before gaining formal independence as with the People's National Congress in Guyana and the People's National Party in Jamaica; or after it has been virtually won, as in the case of the Barbados Democratic Labour Party and the People's National Movement in Trinidad and Tobago. All that is important is that the leaders accept the possibility of separating objectives and of trying for economic development by acting as if they were politically not independent and not interested in promoting social equality.

Playing possum, so to speak, they start by creating — for a while — they reason — permissive conditions for metropolitan investors. Here, in the nature of the case, the major requirement is next to restrict the political activity of those most inclined and best placed to challenge the traditional basis of power. Hence, the first groups to come under close scrutiny by the national political leadership are precisely those on which it had counted most in the struggle against the old colonial regime: the articulate professional classes, the organized workers, and the group of emerging national entrepeneurs and industrialists.

The Problem of Political Stabilization

This need to stabilise politics does not however, present itself in the beginning as a problem at all. The minimum concession which the old regime must make to the national movement for social, economic and political change must in any case hold a promise rich enough for the first generation of national aspirants to office. An initial stability is therefore achieved by the immediate incorporation of professional, business, and labour leaders into positions of responsibility. This is entirely feasible in a situation where the public sector is only just taking its place with metropolitan business as one of the two major avenues for gainful employment and for entry into public life.

It is largely a matter of establishing and manning public corporations, of instituting national machinery for planning and consultation, and of opening to the talents in the public service careers that had previously been denied them. The effect, though probably not the intention, is to "buy off" those best placed to provide political opposition in the short run. But it is not simply — perhaps not at all — a question of mere jobs for the boys. The renovation, expansion and overhauling of public institutions is in any case a necessary, legitimate, and forward step. The entrants into office could justly feel a sense of public duty in going forward to serve.

Indeed, these holders of new positions in the public sector take their places with great zeal and with a heightened sense of political participation. They soon discover however, that the compromise between the national political leadership and metropolitan business in effect restricts them to playing roles largely in public relations or in a sterile technocracy. Most of the creative roles within the establishment are assigned to outsiders.

Nor can they beat an easy retreat. There are hardly any alternatives to the public service and metropolitan business. Local industrial business, never significant, and perhaps only just emerging will all but a few have been snuffed out by the pressure of subsidized metropolitan "entrepreneurship" in the colonial economy. As for locally-owned commerce, that is merely another frying pan.

The professionals find themselves therefore, in a position where in, order to be allowed to do creative work and to deal in real power as a class, they would have to create an entirely new movement and undo the compromise with metropolitan business. Alternatively, they could choose to trade their interest in power for a bureaucratic influence on the political leadership and for what are, by national standards, high material rewards and along with that high status.

It is when this choice dawns upon them that a second phase begins and the question of political stabilisation becomes a real problem for the political leadership. To contain those determined and therefore highly dangerous few who have the energy, the courage, and the will to withdraw from their commitments to the movement and to start afresh, the political leaders are easily persuaded to brand them as subversive and unpatriotic. This initiates a steady erosion of the right to dissent.

On the other hand, to secure the continued support of the many who seek to play the system because it is less painful and less costly than to re-align themselves, the political leaders try to buy them off in earnest. Within the party, this soon brings a virtual field day for corruption. There soon appears a fresh new brand of second-line political operators, with no interest in national politics save as trouble-shooters for a few political high-priests — more likely for a single political Pope. This is a class of *condottieri*, so to speak, each a tough and ruthless boss-man with some small area of the national life as his personal preserve.

Within the public service (including the government-financed universities) there emerges a set of tight-lipped bureaucrats, technocrats and unctuous public-relations cadres, all demanding a high price in perquisites for doing limited service tasks well and for staying out of "politics".

But both within the party and in the public service, the price of this kind of political commitment escalates automatically as the participants become more and more cynical and therefore increasingly not so really trustworthy. The unholy scramble for rewards among its main servants soon forces the political movement to abandon, along with the right of dissent, any policy commitment it might have had to social equality. Inequality will have become the second part of the price of political control of one of the two well-placed groupings.

Stabilisation of Organised Labour

The other grouping is organised labour. Where the Unions had from the start been organised by professionals of the national political movement, political control is simply exercised through the joint party-Union leadership. Where not, it is necessary to influence the Unions by incorporating the Union leaders into the leadership at the level of Government "planning" machinery. In either case, collaboration in the first phase is comparatively easy to achieve. At least, until the political promise has been jeopardised by the compromise with traditionalist metropolitan economic interests, conflicts are not sharp even if the non-party unions might tend to waver or to remain aloof.

As the need for depoliticisation arises following the compromise, here too, as with the professional classes, there is a split. Some of the Unions and Unionists dissent from the development strategy more from an intuitive understanding of its significance than from any articulate analysis of its consequences. Whatever the reason, there is opportunity for new Unions and for new leaders of old ones (or splinterings from them).

By and large the dissidents among the Unions tend to be proportionally more significant than among the professionals partly because labour is a more seasoned political grouping than professionals; partly because, in an important sense, labour is more independent of the national government, and perhaps even because the rewards for playing the game are not so universally high. Be that as it may, the resolution of the choice is marked by sharper conflict. This takes the form of a multiplication of "irrational" strikes focussing attention on the survival of the traditional structure of economic power.

At this point the political leadership is forced to take positive steps to stabilise the situation. Whatever form the stabilisation takes, its main purpose must be to keep organised labour too, out of politics. The aim is to stop strikes and the formation of new unions — not so much to restrict the rise of wages. So far from restricting material rewards, the aim must be the opposite — to buy labour effectively off. While this is not as easy as with the professional classes, it is facilitated, for one thing, by the kind of unemployment situation which results from a strategy of industrialisation by metropolitan participation.

For another thing, the same conditions which are tailored to suit metropolitan capital also favour a wholesale adoption by the Trades Unions of the practices of metropolitan labour.

To promote these narrow practices of simply bargaining for better terms for those lucky to be employed, there is a well-oiled international machine. It has all sorts of rewards of its own to offer to local union leaders for abandoning the political militancy which first gained them their place in the Establishment. This is one of the ways in which the new mercantilism maintains its hold — by helping to depoliticise the workers. And this, incidentally, to anticipate a little, is just one reason why, perhaps, the Marxist analysis is not quite so relevant to an understanding of the processes at work.

For yet another thing, control of wages by the governments would hardly bring any clear gain to the rest of the economy. In the externally-run sectors — mining, sugar, manufacturing and tourism — the vertical integration of the local companies with metropolitan parent firms admits such manipulation with export pricing, with costing, and with profit and loss accounting, that a restriction of wages does not necessarily show up in larger local profits and larger government revenue. But even if it did, the additional powers of manoeuvre granted to the firms by the range of "pioneer" concessions which even the highly profitable international mining concerns seem able to secure, serve to frustrate attempts by the government to gain any marked increase in the yield of company-tax.

In the sectors which either produce for local consumption or provide ancillary services for export business — the civil service, the public corporations, some of manufacturing and agriculture — the rise in wages and salaries is also assisted by the prevailing arrangements.

This time the reasons are different. In the public sector, the peculiar service-relation of the Senior Officials in the Central Banks, the Planning Boards, the Development Corporations, the Embassies and the Ministries to business men and experts from international and metropolitan agencies sets a high floor to the level of living. And this automatically puts an upward pressure on all emoluments.

Political Economy of Inequality

There remain two other reasons why in the interest of their compromise with metropolitan business, the governments have to be very circumspect about incomes policy. The first is that the technological path followed by the economies is an imitative one. Indeed, the typical enterprise being a metropolitan subsidiary, affiliate or branch plant, the techniques of production are actually programmed abroad. So that, there tends always to be technical obstacles to the automatic substitution of national labour for imported machinery even where wage costs permit.

Imitative technology and branchplant organization also provide the second reason for *not* controlling incomes. The pattern of supply and the character of the goods available are, in an important sense, beyond local regulation. Therefore, for the programme of "industrialisation by invitation" to proceed at all, not only has there to be demand, but *taste* has first to be shaped by the importation of commodities from the source of the technology. The level of wages and the distribution of income have therefore to permit these comparatively high-price purchases of taste-forming imports by relatively well-to-do groups. This is the dynamic of "development" by import- *replacement* rather than by import *displacement.*

The Present Caribbean Economy therefore needs inequality in much the same way as current Caribbean Politics.

From this it can be seen that it is the lack of local initiative in production and supply which is at the heart of the economic disorder. To put it another way, any attempt to control incomes and to regulate demand implies that the burden of the effort in investment and production must simultaneously be shifted away from foreign business towards local entrepreneurship — public or private. In any event, it must be switched to a class of operators whose survival depends not upon matching local demand with a foreign designed supply, but on matching locally programmed supply with locally determined demand. It is in that context alone that the politics of social inequality can be abandoned.

There are many other aspects of the current situation with which we cannot here deal. For example the cultural anarchy created by an economy where men — among them the most capable — are forced, by the needs of living, to show excellence in purveying metropolitan propaganda — political and academic; where other men, standing always on the wings of power, have no choice but to preoccupy themselves with public relations; where the working people are confined to technological mimicry and the assembly of parts; where the population seeks dignity in a scramble for consumer durables; and where the political leadership survives by submissiveness to imperial power.

In a society imported from all corners of the world and integrated over three centuries by a common subordination to imperial power, it may also have been fruitful to explore the damage done in the way of political segmentation, social fragmentation and racial antagonism; by the fact that Caribbean men cannot together share the task of mastering their own environment, of creating their own world, of forming their own standards of judgment of situations, of other men, of their own value!

If it has been necessary here to deal at some length with the roles of Government and labour and the new professional classes in the current economic and political confusion in the Caribbean, it is because we are concerned with change; and among the main changes which differentiate this period from what went before, is that these agencies of the popular will have come to office. In the years before say, 1940, labour had had no legitimate place in the order of things; and Government, if claiming to be responsible for all interests, had nevertheless been the unabashed representative of sectional or alien ones. The hope then has been that popular participation in the Government and Union influence on economic policy would bring a real independence and a real sense of equality as well as better times — a change in the system, in other words. Moyne, reporting on the British Antilles perceived this quite clearly in 1938.

> "...the discontent that underlies the disturbances of recent years", he reported in characteristic imperial understatement, "is a phenomenon of a different character, representing no longer a mere blind protest, against a worsening of conditions, but a positive demand for the creation of new conditions."

The Enterprise of the Indies

James, it was, I think, in *Black Jacobins*, who reminded us that, having landed in the New World, Columbus praised God and enquired urgently after gold. Nowadays the industrialists arrive by jet clipper, thank the Minister of Pioneer industry and enquire after bauxite. "The Enterprise of the Indies" is still good business.

Yet for things to have stayed as they were, they have had to change. The traditional and continuing process of underdevelopment in the Caribbean has been serviced by a whole new range of institutions and activities: Colonial Development and Welfare, the Anglo-American Commission, the Caribbean Commission, the Caribbean Organization; Economic Planning Boards, Units and Divisions; Industrial Development Corporations, Development Finance Corporation, Agricultural Marketing Corporations. There have been World Bank Missions, Monetary Fund Missions and World Food Programme Missions; Indian Missions and German Missions. There have been first Development Programmes and second Development Programmes; first Development Plans and second Development Plans. In Jamaica there has even been *the man with the plan*. There have been projects for Land Reform and for Civil Service Reform.

While Moyne, Simey, and Prest were sent from the metropolis, Lewis and Kaldor, Balogh and Dumont were *brought* from the metropolis. The Caribbean has been placed on the international *tennis* circuit, on the International *golf* circuit, on the international *casino* circuit. We have had the Pan American Games and the Commonwealth Games; a Meeting of the Commonwealth Ministers of Finance and a Meeting of the Commonwealth Parliamentary Association. In other words, Havana has been put on the map. Kingston and San Juan, Georgetown and Port of Spain in their turn have been put.

So there has been a veritable round-robin of changes. *But plus ca change.*

Why then, is it the same? What is all the bureaucratic chinksing in the name of development? From London to Washington, Geneva and New York; from Ottawa to Santiago de Chile. Consultation, conferences, des colloques. Brer Anancy in the councils of the world! Up and down the oceans looking for obeah?

Why then does the initiative still lie outside? Not a prospect on the horizon of solving the unemployment problem, of equalizing benefits, of assuming full and popular responsibility for economic development? Why does Goliath still preside? In Guatemala when it suits him, in the Dominican Republic when it suits him. Withdrawing missiles when it suits him! Manipulating the terms of trade and the flow of capital, the price of petroleum and the quota for sugar.

Is it because we are too small? Then where is the sling shot?

Means of Change

Much of the thinking in the Caribbean assumes that the marines will always be in Guantanamo. It is therefore useful to consider the view that one of these days it is Caribbean troops which will, fut-il, be occupying the imperial capitals. It is a view which may shock some. The aim however is not merely to shock.

The aim is to force the Caribbean colonial mind to face the question: how? For it is certain that the same mind which is prepared to submit to imperial power is covertly obsessed with the possibilities of turning the tables. They are two aspects of the same view of the world.

How, then? Two means suggest themselves. The first is a technological one. Clearly if we developed superior military technology we would be able to confront imperial power and crush it. *We* would then be in the position to dominate international business. This way, however, surely would not change the *system*. It would change the *masters*. And in any event, it leaves unanswered the question as to how to develop superior military techniques. Which brings us to the alternative road.

This we may call the moral road. As Brother Malcolm X so clearly appreciated, it involves changing the view which men have of themselves in relation to other men and in relation to the universe. This is one of the main lessons of Christianity, of Islam, *and* of Marxism. It is the further lesson of these systems of thought, that the attitude of the new morality must be sceptical rather than credulous. On this ground, Marxist doctrine, still so popular among the promoters of social change in the new states, may have to be substantially revised. By the same token, Christianity and other systems of moral and political philosophy must be subjected to considerable re-appraisal.

Certainly in our part of the world, there is growing evidence of a healthy scepticism among Christian political theorists. From all reports, the Christian Democrats in Latin America seem to be adopting a Christ-like irreverence towards the contemporary Scribes and Pharisees and seem at long last willing to abandon modes of thought which clearly do not fit the demands of the current human condition. A few Jesuits everywhere, we are told, are among the leaders of revolt against restrictive doctrine and are making direct contact with the facts. If this is true, it becomes a fact which we in turn, cannot ignore. But the evidence is still too scanty and the task too large for us here to make more than a mental note for future reference.

Marxist Thought and Change

Marxism here can stand a longer treatment. This body of political thought places "class-war" at the centre of the dynamic of change. This it does by focussing attention on the sociology of ideology, as it were. Crudely put, group solidarity and group interest as determined by the structure and functioning of the economy are taken to be decisive in the formation of principles of political action.

The undoubted power of this model derives from the fact that it integrates into a single if merely plausible scheme, the working of the economic system, the social order and the polity. But within the trinity, there is a relationship of dependence between the ideological superstructure and the ultimate governor, the economic base. Here lies one major deficiency of the model. For the space it leaves for men and movements to formulate ideas independent of the categories to which the established economic and social order directs them is uncomfortably close. The concession that it makes to the social imagination in the way of freedom to re-shape the social matrix by precepts not deriving from the existing intellectual order is too tiny. And, in being definitive, it postulates a social mind too constricted by the established order to perceive the wide and constantly changing range of possible social objectives and of feasible social action. In this sense, the model encompasses too narrow a part of reality to be scientific and constitutes too restrictive a frame for movements of radical social change.

The evidence of Western Europe indicates that the model has been imperfectly applicable even within the culture-sphere where it was evolved. There, race, nationality and individuality seem to have modified the anticipated patterns of ideology-formation and with that have multiplied the possibilities of political action. Hence World War I witnessed political ideas and political alignments by the Western European working classes which, if not unprecedented, were nevertheless unforeseen by the Marxist theorists. It was national rather than workers' solidarity which prevailed under stress.

In areas far beyond the precincts of the model, international, interracial and inter-cultural contact have indicated the need for even more extensive modifications so much so that even the Marxists acknowledge the inadequacy of what they describe as their theory of imperialism.

In Eastern Europe and China there is interesting paradox in the experience of Marxism here to be explored to advantage. In the first place, two major successes in these areas which are claimed to have been inspired by Marxism, did, in fact, involve substantial innovation in the established theory of political change. In the second place, the innovations, so far from having been acknowledged as such, have, on the contrary, been legitimated only in terms of an alleged conformity to the doctrine. We are faced therefore with a double paradox on which it is important here to elaborate and reflect.

To begin with, we may note that both in Russia and China, the Marxist movements were offshoots of a larger movement based elsewhere. From the simple fact of being "fragment" movements these Trojan Horses, as they were, derived certain clear benefits. On the military and political planes, comrades could rely — or so they thought — on the international apparatus of the movement to mobilise the help and support of other comrades abroad. Besides, by their subscription to a doctrine — regardless of its content — which had been born in the homeland of the culture which then dominated the world, they could make an easy communication in the external field. Besides, they did not have to face afresh the problem which Marxism had once had in Western Europe, of winning incorporation into the longer philosophical and intellectual tradition. Neither the Bolshevik nor Mao, after him has had to proceed from scratch.

Next, the actual content of the doctrine — as distinct from the fact of being part of the larger movement which adhered to it — endowed the fragments with additional assets. For one thing, Marxism's claim to be scientific helped to satisfy the desire for intellectual respectability. For another, by placing the revolution in the logic of history it made sure the victory which international solidarity could only make probable. What is more, by harnessing the political transformation to the majority, and to the underprivileged majority at that, the doctrine made it difficult for even its opponents to withhold a certain moral approval. Finally, by being catholic, the doctrine permitted the comrades to share, at best with other men — at worst, with other *workers* — the vision of the good society that was to come. This in turn, may well have shifted the balance of advantage away from traditional religion and towards political commitment to the socialist movement.

But both the fact of being a fragment and the adherence to a ready-made doctrine involved heavy costs. Evolved in altogether different conditions the political directives of the doctrine were neither susceptible of an easy translation into practice nor of easy acceptance by the popular consciousness. In other words, success in the field, in so far as it depended upon local operation, necessarily introduced a conflict. The fragment leadership had therefore to choose. On the one hand, any major revision of operational principle would be near-heretical. On the other, the maintenance of external support and doctrinal legitimacy would hamper progress.

The Russian Case

In the case of Russia, the conflict over strategy and within the party became at times quite sharp in the years before the October victory. For barring only Mao perhaps, Lenin faces posterity as the revisionist supreme But success counted for him. In the series of unorthodox decisions which took him first to the Finland Station and then into the Kremlin, inhered Stalin's later dictum of socialism in a single state. But who then, in the flush of victory and with all power to the soviets could have stopped to reckon the consequences?—though one imagines that Trotsky, for all his expectations of revolutionary developments in the West, would surely have hazarded a few mental calculations!

If victory counted, when, in the early days of the Revolution, it obscured the path of revision, it counted even more when later, universalism was all but overtly abandoned by Stalin. For revision in bringing success had also brought with it the power to define heresy. State power for the socialists had made the Soviet Union the Worker's Fatherland, Moscow the locus of authority, and ultimately, Stalin the Pope. The tail had come to wag the dog, as it were, the fragment the whole. This the Comrades in the International were soon to discover — and to their cost.

The Chinese Case

In the case of China, Mao was not to be so lucky. His very decision to get on with the revolution was open heresy. It was therefore natural that he should have continued freely to revise and to revise comprehensively. He could hardly have avoided it if he was to complete the long march forward. In the end, he did, following nearly a quarter a century of struggle. And here again, as always, victory was welcome. But in the nature of the case, there could this time be few rosy illusions about the lasting solidarity of an international movement which now had to operate simultaneously from both Byzantium *and* Rome, so to speak.

This time, the child did not find the parent powerless. Mao had innovated and devised his own political theories and principles of action. He may even have proved them more convincingly than Lenin. But in spite of all this he became merely *another* Pope and therefore not wholly infallible. On this ground alone — let alone the vastly different operational needs of two great countries — the common myths and the common rhetoric, the sharing of radical intention and the joint source of legitimacy, were the surest pledge of impending trouble.

Independent Socialism

The current conflict between China and the Soviet Union appears then, as a consequence of the Church being one foundation, and of its development later into two, with the emergence of two Popes each striking out, his Cardinals behind, on an independent road to socialism. Ironically, the model is being systematically and relentlessly revised. Doubtless there will be other Pontiffs yet. It is just this which inevitably leads to a breakdown in contact and erects obstacles in the way of communication. For it was mutual understanding more than anything else that the doctrinal community had facilitated in the first place.

Equally inevitable, the path of revisionism must involve a continual re-orientation and a periodic defrocking of the established high priests. Hence we have had Stalin's quarrels with Trotsky and the other Bolshevik leaders and his ruthless control of the International.

Now it is Mao's turn to set the Red Guards on the heels, of the old party cadres. In some ways it is a repetition of the Russian experience: In both instances, the process of re-orientation has taken a special character first, from the religious aspect of the doctrine — from the faith which all comrades must profess in the creed; and secondly, from the fact that revision is undertaken from the top — by the Pope himself.

The high priests must declare solidarity with His Holiness in terms which have at once to be general enough to respect the right of the ultimate authority to revise at will; and yet specific enough in their disavowal of any connection with the parent heresy. But in history the same is always different.

If the development of China's revision has been different in some ways, it is on no account surprising. Much more than the Bolshevik Revolution had reformed Lenin's, Mao's initial revisions had re-shaped his precepts to fit a local consciousness infinitely different from the European — Western and even Eastern. It is precisely the extent of this pre-revolutionary adaptation which is now being reflected — at least, on the mythological plane — in a complete dissociation from Western values. Besides, it is in this logic that, being the *second* in a line of heretics, Chinese Communism needs in its struggle for authority with its predecessor, Soviet Communism, to implicate the latter not merely in revisionism but in bourgeois revision of the creed.

The point for us here is that the fragment parties are in fact wriggling out of their Marxist prison. Science is asserting itself in a curious way and however much allegiance to the doctrine is announced, it is the facts which are dictating the path of politics. The difference in situation is imposing its own revisions.

The Marxists have been learning that we cannot approach the building of a better society with prepared positions — or at least, with positions so fully prepared that they lead us to suspend our discrimination as to context. But the cost of the lesson is already high — for individuals, for nations and for the world. The evangelistic character of the doctrine has helped to promote quasi-religious confrontations both within societies and between them. This crusading has, in turn, provided an excuse — if not a cause — for rival political systems to restrict freedom and to resort far more to coercion than to political persuasion. One result of this has been to place an inordinately high premium on military technology as an agent of contemporary social change. So for us to reject scientific socialism is twice over to reject the solution to change in the Caribbean by way of the development and application of military technology.

The Western Scientific Tradition

If we are to adopt the alternative religion of science the question arises as to where this places us in relation to what is alleged to be the scientific tradition of the West? Here we may want to begin by arguing a little with those who claim that the scientific attitude has in some way been a contribution by the Western intellectual tradition. I fear that here we must first insist on pointing out that the scientific attitude cannot but have been part of the human tradition from the start; and that successive cultures have strengthened it and may possibly continue to do so. The suggestion that it belongs to any one cultural sphere is, like the Marxist pretension to universality, merely another manifestation of arrogance. In this case, it is the arrogance of a temporarily dominant civilization though perhaps we would want quickly to concede that the distortion is probably inevitable in a contemporary and therefore short perspective.

It does take a long view of human history to make us humble. Consider how we happened to reach where we were in say, 650 B.C. I wonder too, what the chauvinists of the modern West imagine that say, Vercingetorix or some such chieftain of Angle-land used to do around the fireside before Cesar had made the crossing — if not mull over and order the fresh experience of the tribe and revise the laws of action. These theorists may wish to pause and reflect on what pre-occupied the Kings of Dahomey before the Portugese dropped in on their way to India (and stayed, unfortunately).

I suspect that if we really attempted to be scientific and to look squarely at the whole span of human experience we might be a little more inclined to regard the modern Western contribution not so much as a change in the *attitude* to experience as a change in the *techniques* of transmitting it. Far more than is generally admitted in fact — though it is often announced in theory — Western thought and attitudes too, carry a fund of lore and a set of sacred myths which impede the process of enquiry and delay the progress of the international community. This is true not only in the social and moral sciences but also in the fields of technology and natural science where the character of the subject matter sometimes makes it more rewarding to be curious and less uncomfortable to be sceptical.

Certainly Western improvements in the techniques and methods of recording and transmission of information have modified attitudes too, and we are not to dismiss the point that we all have, in consequence, made a very real advance. But one advantage of revising the formulation of the point is that we may then be less likely to overlook one of the most frightening aspects of Western intellectual culture today: its tendency — abroad, in particular — to sacrifice exact observation on the altar of elegant theorizing. Here paradoxically, we have the danger that the improvement in the means of science may serve to frustrate its ends.

Sadly, one has to report that to both the Eastern and Western sections of the West, the world seems to have become a remarkably simple set of two-sector models: of Cowboys and Indians as it were; of developed and under-developed countries, of traditional and modern societies and so on. One appreciates that to some extent, the very dominance of the culture and the political responsibilities which necessarily go with it, compel some provisional theorizing. To act, it *is* necessary to have categories and hypotheses which give some view of how the system under treatment works as a whole. But in science too, as in politics, we often have to be informed by the philosophy of second-best and to admit that none of the explanations fit. When on the contrary, we attempt smugly to impose an easy order onto fresh and complex experience we tend to convert science into scienticism, to make slogans out of analytical categories and to transform information into propaganda. Perhaps, in the case of the West, this tendency reflects in part, an attempt by the culture to protect itself. This is understandable if unfortunate.

Intellectual Legitimacy in the New States

But what is, for us, more unfortunate — and still more relevant — is that owing to the facts of power, the easiest way for the intellectual elites of the so-called new states to acquire legitimacy abroad (they have not yet acquired it at home) is for them at best, to show technical competence in the methods and procedures of what is in their own habitat, western scientism and western propaganda. At worst, if they cannot acquire the competence, they must have the paquotille, the trinketry of western science.

From this further consequences are derived. For one thing, the institutions of learning at home become tied up in the most absurd ways with sponsoring institutions abroad in much the same ways as the firms in the economy are tied up with metropolitan corporations — and with very similar results. For another thing, the intellectual work at home often lacks relevant (or even just local empirical) content. In the West Indies for example, we have elegant national accounts and on one assessment, some of the best statistical services on this side of the Atlantic. But we cannot easily find estimates of the effective price of sugar though so much of the politics turns on it. Nor do we attempt to measure say, the volume of sou-sou transactions though so much of the population deals in them. Professionalism demands something else. And for precisely that reason the prescriptions which follow from this work cannot readily be translated into action — which is one reason why we have so many unimplemented Development Plans.

Yet another outcome of the way in which the intellectual classes derive their legitimacy is that professional work — for being largely abstract — tends to lack practical political content. The field is therefore abandoned to political theory developed in other conditions — and particularly to the more militant systems of thought. This leaves those who by inclination or by occupation are forced to utilise some set of political ideas either to create new schemes themselves or to muddle through with old and inadequate ones. Thus we are most everywhere able to find politicians who, too busy to adopt the first course, are trapped with a rhetoric which carries no operability. It may be to Nkrumah's credit that he seems to have appreciated this difficulty though his preoccupation with African *socialism* indicated to what extent he might have been prisoner of the situation.

We may pass now to acknowledge that the degeneration of science and information into scientism and propaganda is not a phenomenon to be witnessed in the relationships *between* cultures and nations alone. It may be more satisfying to our sense of self-righteousness to believe that what we are dealing with is "intellectual imperialism". But it is not true, or at least, not wholly true. We can see the same phenomenon *within* cultures too, and within nations. It may express itself in a number of ways: sometimes as a conflict of generation as the Latin Americans in particular, have tended to see it; sometimes as a conflict between national and regional policy, as say, the French Canadians may put it.

In the strictly intellectual field, there have certainly been periods in the history of Western culture when prior improvements in the methods of science have engendered an excessive concern with pre-conceived if elegant modes of theorizing about new evidence. The post-Newtonian preoccupation of physics with formalistic mathematics is one excellent case in point. One has the uncomfortable feeling that the current obsession of the social sciences with a set of categories drawn from Marxist political sociology and crudely aggregative Keynesian economics is another.

Happily, the 18th century did, in the end, witness a swing back to greater scientific effort on the part of men who, on one interpretation, rejected the view of the world as a dying classical tragedy and founded little scientific societies up and down the country. It was out of such dissenting academies as the Lunar Society that came much of the drive towards the Industrial Revolution.

That was after Newton. There may well be a parallel following Keynes. We must of course be properly sceptical about facile analogies. But one does see on the horizon a new group of men — principally in Latin America. They have been described as the structuralists. In fact, they are simply calling for a return to the facts of each case. It is true that Boulton and Wedgwood, Faraday, Darwin and Priestly dealt in the natural sciences while Furtado and Pinto, Demas and Sunkel have been treating with the social sciences. But the approach is the same. It has been known to men long before the sun rose in the West. The simple rule is to face the reality of what is — of the *particular* situation. The West has improved the methods of facing its own reality. One wonders what the "new" states will do.

The Structuralist Approach

Facing their own situation, the structuralists advocate, first, a typology of structures, a demarcation of the field into its constituent matrices of social relations. Secondly, they seek to make an exact observation of the institutions, mechanisms and patterns of behaviour that make the matrix a functioning whole. And then, and *only* then, the inferences are to be drawn about what prohibits and what promotes development and change. In due course, theory so derived, they insist, will acquire its own elegant formulation, its own establishment. In the first flush, it cannot but be produced in dissenting academies and expressed in terms of rough hypotheses — in journalese, to use the term of abuse by which the current intellectual establishment is forced (in its own defence) to describe it.

Does this approach not postulate that every society is an entity unto itself? — it is legitimate to pose the question? Are we not here advocating a different kind of chauvinism? Are we not arguing for a closed society? Will it not divide men? Those — of all persuasions — who in one way or another, support the idea behind the International, are quite in order to show some concern here.

I think that their suspicions would be allayed if they appreciated what happens when men address their intellectual and other resources to the particular habitat in which they find themselves. When men do this, they soon discover a whole kingdom of opportunities and of limitations. The opportunities they begin to exploit; the limitations they are forced in the first place to respect only to subsequently remove in successive stages of fresh initiative. In this process of conquering the environment, they develop a sense of pride in what has been accomplished tempered by a humility in the face of what remains still to be achieved; they accumulate a knowledge of what has been done and they develop a sure judgment of what cannot — at least, not yet — be done. They formulate laws of man and laws of nature; they form the habit of at once exploiting as well as respecting the environment and of all the time devising and revising rules of procedures which makes of the human community a single indivisible one. For it provides the basis for discussion, for exchange of goods, as of ideas.

Thus, the problem with the new states today is that they have forgotten the basis on which they may discuss and seek therefore to gain a vicarious legitimacy by opting slavishly to follow the cultural initiatives of the North Atlantic. In technology as in politics their characteristic form of behaving is a response to metropolitan stimuli. And it is to change the character of this behaviour pattern that the new religion is needed. To say this, incidentally, is to acknowledge that the troops which we, in our turn, will have in the imperial capitals are already there. It is merely that they are now treating in metropolitan propaganda. The task of social change is to arm them with science.

The New Caribbean Mind

By now it may have been possible to define that what I am arguing is that social change in the Caribbean has to and can only begin in the minds of Caribbean men. If we are to act for change, our philosophers and our theorists have first to understand how we relate to ourselves and to the wider world in which we live. Since we have been the footstool of mercantilism — old and new — with the economy enjoying an unusual dominance over our consciousness we may have here a case in which Marx may yet be left standing with his head the right way up. On the other hand, since ours has been a stage on which international, interracial and inter-cultural mixing has played a leading part among the dramatis personae of the social process, we may have some important modifications and amendments to make.

II. – THOUGHT AND ACTION

I have argued that we need independent thought. One of the most blatant manifestations of the colonial condition in the Caribbean — of the plantation mind — is the refuge which our intellectual classes take in a sterile scientism on the one hand, or in a cheap populism on the other.

One half of our intellectual classes is a-political. They are engrossed in technical exercises or they are busy dissipating their energies in administration and public relations — running the public service, running the Universities, running this, running that, running in effect, away from the issues.

The other half is clamouring to lead the people. Like so many brave Bustamantes, their burning ambition is to march before the masses. Confronted with the questions as to how, where, and when, their answer is a stony silence. They too, one fears are merely idling their resources away in impractical rhetoric.

It is being proposed here, that being who we are, what we are and where, the kind of action to which we must be committed is determinate. Action in the field, if it is not to be blind, presupposes theory. To acknowledge this is to set ourselves three tasks. The first is to fashion theory on which may be based the clear intellectual leadership for which the nation calls and which it has never had. The second is to conduct the enquiry on which theory can be soundly based. This is what may be called, in the jargon of my original trade, the creation of intellectual capital goods. Thirdly, we are to establish media by which these goods may be transmitted to the rest of us who are otherwise engaged. As one of our statements in the **New World** has put it: we may wish to create a media of direct democratic expression suitable to the native Caribbean imagination.

It seems to me that with these three tasks, our plate is full enough. If we devoted our attention to the production of books, pamphlets and journals, and if we did it well, that would be plenty. The political organisers might then arise with something to say — at least with something that they did not simply fudge from **Monthly Review** or borrow from (the late) Jules Dubois.

It is a fashion among us to think of this as quietism and that politics is activity in the streets. Which it is. But it is more. It is also and decisively this — a consciousness of the possibilities among the population and a commitment to specific kinds of action. It is on the absence of these that much of current Caribbean politics now founders. In this context, perhaps the biggest political contribution that we can now make is to heighten political consciousness and build political commitment. This we are in the best position to do being, in virtue of our trade, concerned with articulation and communication.

The case which is here being made is not, then, against action, but for action of a specific and realistic kind. Thought is the action for us. This leads us next to acknowledge that there is action of other types. But we cannot be so presumptuous as to assume that there are not elsewhere other men who will accept them as their responsibility and address their attention to them with a dedication and a competence equal to our own. Do we dare to show such utter lack of confidence in the people for whom we wish to do so much? Are we not aware that there are everywhere to be found journalists, Trade Unionists and politicians; farmers, preachers and poets, all able and willing to change the system every bit as much as we are?

We are the People, too

At any rate, there is one other fundamental truth which we cannot overlook. It is that we are the people too. So that, to work among us is also to work among them. I have argued that we tend uncritically to take over political doctrine from others. Are we not now adopting one which glorifies the masses, the workers and the farmers? With nothing to lose but their chains, having no stake in the existing system of property, as it were, they have become for us the class which will necessarily promote the reorganization of society for the better. This is a consideration but not one which history allows us to affirm with any confidence.

We are therefore back to the need for our own evaluation of Caribbean experience. How much of our existence is passing by without the slightest public appraisal, with little or no addition to the fund of consciousness! There is much that is private experience, much that people know, much that is real to **the people**. But the society is not moved only by what is real to individuals and groups. In an important sense, what is collectively real is what is politically significant. To arrive at that, and then to make it common public property is our task. To abstract and distil from the anarchy that is the sum of individual reality, the wisdom that informs successful social action. To do this is to opt for the view of the people not as an abstraction, the masses, but as a community of **persons.**

We have remarked how many well-intentioned movements have foundered on the magic of their own rhetoric. There have been Peoples Movements, Peoples Parties and Peoples Congresses — national, democratic and progressive; Labour parties and Farmers parties; Liberals and Socialists. They have come and they have gone; flowered and then withered away to be trampled upon by the very people for and by whom they had been once so assiduously cultivated.

Why? I suggest that the fit, the linkage of consciousness has, in most cases, only tenuously been forged. Not a single Caribbean movement has dared to stand firm against Goliath. Not even Castro has succeeded in slaying the giant — though he has certainly wounded him.

This failure has had its consequences and we have had to live with them. The more angry among us are therefore disposed to conclude that the current political leaders are mere bucaneers — plundering the society for their own gain in power if not always in wealth. No; this interpretation is as wrong as it is unprofitable. For one thing, these men have advanced our cause not inconsiderably. They have at least won some formal independence and for many they have bettered material conditions. It is simply untrue to say that they are mere thieves in the night.

It is doubly wrong for men who are in a position to pass judgment largely because of the changes which these leaders have wrought. And for the new intellectual elites, so-called, which, precisely because of current policies, are able to win fine jobs and good living, it is downright immoral.

Moreover, it is politically unprofitable. The population, in whose goodness we claim to have such faith, have judged these men to be dedicated, competent leaders of goodwill. They see in them investments which they are not going to abandon to jump up in steel-band in exchange for the promises of mere pretenders to office who dare so blandly to attack the popular judgment. So here is another reason why we may have more work to do yet, work to demonstrate why, through quite ordinary human error and circumstances other than diabolic motive, programmes of social change have gone wrong. The present generation of leaders have made mistakes — as we in our turn, I might add, will do — but that is only part of the story.

The whole story reaches a long way back. For leaders, there have been such as Marti, Bolivar and Betances; Garvey, Cipriani and Critchlow; Payne and Edun, Toussaint, Quamaina and

Damon; Adoe and Araby, Cuffy, Accabreh and Accra. To learn from them we have to know about them. How much do we now know. How many of us know even who they were — let alone why they have left us the legacy of plantation society only slightly modified?

There is a whole history still to be appraised. Sugar, slavery and emancipation; war and plunder; mercantilism and neo-mercantilism; the foundation period, the nineteenth century, the two Wars and the critical period in between; the trauma of the thirties with the rise of labour; and the determined struggle to break the imperial chains that has ended in the moral defeat of **estado libre asoclado**, formal or informal.

Our ignorance about our own historical experience is a most damaging thing and needs to be corrected at once. Further delay may cost very dear. With the possible exception of Cuba, the Governments of the Caribbean are bankrupt almost beyond redemption. But they have power and it is a power they are already beginning to use destructively.

We may displace these Governments, of course. But what good would it serve the succeeding regimes unless we also eroded the intellectual, philosophical and psychological foundations of current politics? — unless the next generation were served with some coherent statement of Caribbean historical process?

Taking the Power

There is of course, a sense in which we cannot escape taking the power. It is simply a matter of generation. We do not know who the political leaders will be or who will hold what offices. This may disappoint some. But what we do know is that by virtue of normal succession, the youngish men of today will, as a class, be holding responsibility tomorrow.

From all accounts, it is already well known what we intend to do with the power when we get it: reorganize the economy, integrate the region, open the way to popular participation, call a new world into existence, and so on. This is an exciting vision and the prospect of this better world should lighten the load of the work that is to go into its making.

But there are some things that we cannot afford to ignore. First, it is that the course of events will not evolve in anything like the way we now imagine, The lesson of the past is that no theory of social and political process — of historical process, one might say — is so definitive that we can predict with any great exactness what will come to pass and how. This of course, is the most powerful argument for and not against some theory of change. It would be an abdication of our responsibility if we did not try to limit the margin of indeterminancy to the minimum and restrict ourselves only to such error as is necessary.

Secondly, to use power effectively and wisely, we must, before we have gotten it, largely have agreed with other men (or persuaded them) about what the issues are in social change. In other words, it is the terms on which we have gotten power which will determine our ultimate use of it. So that the politics of the Trojan Horse, of the Vanguard Party, of the high priests who will seize power and then liberate the people, might well be the politics of conservation. In this respect it is of the same genre as that of the men who now join the going regime in order to beat it, who accept procedures they claim to oppose in order to gain positions from which later, they hope, they will be able to change the rules.

A Mode of Living

We are well advised to abandon these dubious strategies. To change the world it is not enough to announce our intention to do so when we get the power. We have also, it seems to me, to demonstrate the sorts of changes we are aiming at by starting to live them now ... so far as that is possible. Which admittedly, may not be very far.

If we are dissatisfied with the body of doctrine we have inherited, let us begin to work afresh. If we think the existent media frustrate dialogue let us found new ones that are not. If we think economic development requires the restriction of consumption let us restrict our own and get on with it. Whatever it is we say we believe, let us live it now.

To be sure, it is not as easy a matter as I think I am making it sound. We do not run the world. The problems of personal reorganisation are not always manageable. The transition will be difficult. There are situations in which every solution is no solution and the best only the second best. But none of this is an excuse for doing nothing and letting things ride. It does not exempt us from the moral concern with facing up now. If this concern does not show itself among us we will succeed only in convincing others that we are just looking for office. And this is what we will in effect be doing.

To shift the focus into our mode of living as an instrument of social change is to imply that real change is a comparatively slow process. It results from the patient and purposeful building which each of us undertakes in the personal sphere. It takes time and many rounds of fresh initiative to transform an individual breakaway into a social movement.

I hasten to add though that I am not arguing for the Finland Station, neither am I advocating the inevitability of gradualness. Change is not at all inevitable. And besides, there are occasions in history when a quite radical break from the past is feasible.

Chaguaramas

Take for example, the case of Chaguaramas 1960 which I have elsewhere discussed (NEW WORLD QUARTERLY, Dead Season 1965). I find that there has been much misunderstanding about the significance of that issue. It is worth re-stating the appraisal here in brief.

The issue was important not because the site of the Federal capital had been withheld from the West Indian nation; nor because valuable resources had been withdrawn from the people of Trinidad and Tobago. It was important because of the moral conjuncture to which it became central. So past mistakes cannot be corrected by getting the base back a few years later.

Here was a small nation struggling to raise its head out of the mud of modern colonialism. At the other end of the Caribbean — for four hundred and fifty years the centre-court of North Atlantic abuse of power — Cuba was also stirring. Against them both: the biggest bully ever known to nations. In Trinidad and Tobago therefore, for all the half-heartedness and the reliance for legitimacy on an earlier stand taken by an Imperial Governor, the stand taken against the base raised a moral issue of universal import.

In question was the right of might, of large nations to dictate to small; by extension of strong to bully weak. Though the issue was never properly spelt out, it was sufficiently well articulated to evoke a response from people throughout the Eastern and Southern Caribbean in general, and from the people in the University of Woodford Square in particular. What is more, the issue could only have been resolved by moral means, by the application of intellect and wit, by dedication and sacrifice. To have attempted to resolve it by the exercise of force would have been a contradiction for it was the use and abuse of power which was itself under scrutiny. And in any event, the imbalance of power being, in the nature of the case, what it was, the issue, fought on the plane of violence, would have been decided without ever being joined.

For a political leadership and a social movement which had had any notion of what commits men, it was the chance of a lifetime. Men do not have to be persuaded to support David against Goliath. But even if they did, the issues of Independence and Federation which were so much in the air in 1959-60, and the fall of the old regime in Cuba could have been persuasion enough. What was needed was a linkage of the issues and an integration of the regional consciousness. Consider what might have happened if the Government of Trinidad and Tobago had declared the base nationalised, proclaimed independence and joined Cuba in taking over the sugar industry.

The colonial answer is to say that the marines would have come and that the other Caribbean governments would have sold out as they did in 1953 when the PPP ran into trouble in Guyana. But 1960 was not 1953 and neither Castro's movement nor the PNM a mere Marxist Trojan Horse! They had struck their roots in a Caribbean consciousness and it would not have been easy to cut them down. Manley might have equivocated following the endorsement he had just recently had for the Puerto Rican policies he had adopted in his first term. But the tilt of opinion in the region as a whole would have made that a very uncomfortable stance – especially if the stakes included sugar and the land, and if the hand had been played in the way that both Castro and Williams then had the moral resources with which to play it. Could either Jagan or Burnham for example, have failed to respond if they had been summoned to attend a Havana Conference on the reorganisation of the Caribbean sugar industry?

And even if the marines had come. Would we not have fought them as the Cubans were in any case to do against their agents at the Bay of Pigs and the Constitutionalists, in Santo Domingo in 1965? How much territory could they have held if they had had the whole Caribbean roused against them? And even if they did hold territory — for a while — they would never have enjoyed any moral conquest and the satisfaction of seeing Cuba turn to another imperialism for support. And the Caribbean would have emerged from the struggle as morally and politically integrated as it has always been culturally ... thanks to sugar, mercantilism and imperial domination. It certainly could not have emerged more fragmented and cowed, and politically more degraded than it is now.

If the opportunity was missed then, it was largely for lack of political experience. But the time will come again. And if we have in the meantime evaluated the reasons why we muffed the last chance, we will make good of the next. That is the only value of history and social theory — to inform the present and to instruct the future. "Chaguaramas to Slavery" then was neither romantic speculation as to what might have been nor a lament about the God that failed, but largely hard-headed preparation for the next round. It is taking the long-view. But that only, underlines the points being made here: that change is a slow process; and that it is the consciousness built by work and life today which will tell in the politics of tomorrow.

Note: The original version of this paper was presented to the Second Conference on W.I. Affairs held in Montreal in October 1966. Since then, the paper has been revised and expanded and has been read to a number of New World Groups throughout the region.

The Pitfalls of National Consciousness

Frantz Fanon

HISTORY teaches us clearly that the battle against colonialism does not run straight away along the lines of nationalism. For a very long time the native devotes his energies to ending certain definite abuses: forced labour, corporal punishment, inequality of salaries, limitation of political rights, etc. This fight for democracy against the oppression of mankind will slowly leave the confusion of neo-liberal universalism to emerge, sometimes laboriously, as a claim to nationhood. It so happens that the unpreparedness of the educated classes, the lack of practical links between them and the mass of the people, their laziness, and, let it be said, their cowardice at the decisive moment of the struggle will give rise to tragic mishaps.

National consciousness, instead of being the all-embracing crystallization of the innermost hopes of the whole people, instead of being the immediate and most obvious result of the mobilization of the people, will be in any case only an empty shell, a crude and fragile travesty of what it might have been. The faults that we find in it are quite sufficient explanation of the facility with which, when dealing with young and independent nations, the nation is passed over for the race, and the tribe is preferred to the state. These are the cracks in the edifice which show the process of retrogression that is so harmful and prejudicial to national effort and national unity. We shall see that such retrograde steps with all the weaknesses and serious dangers that they entail are the historical result of the incapacity of the national middle class to rationalize popular action, that is to say their incapacity to see into the reasons for that action.

This traditional weakness, which is almost congenital to the national consciousness of under-developed countries, is not solely the result of the mutilation of the colonized people by the colonial regime. It is also the result of the intellectual laziness of the national middle class, of its spiritual penury, and of the profoundly cosmopolitan mould that its mind is set in.

The national middle class which takes over power at the end of the colonial regime is an under-developed middle class. It has practically no economic power, and in any case it is in no way commensurate with the bourgeoisie of the mother country which it hopes to replace. In its wilful narcissism, the national middle class is easily convinced that it can advantageously replace the middle class of the mother country. But that same independence which literally drives it into a corner will give rise within its ranks to catastrophic reactions, and will oblige it to send out frenzied appeals for help to the former mother country. The university and merchant classes which make up the most enlightened section of the new state are in fact characterized by the smallness of their number and their being concentrated in the capital, and the type of activities in which they are engaged: business, agriculture and the liberal professions. Neither financiers nor industrial magnates are to be found within this national middle class. The national bourgeoisie of under-developed countries is not engaged in production, nor in invention, nor building, nor labour; it is completely canalized into activities of the intermediary type. Its innermost vocation seems to be to keep in the running and to be part of the racket. The psychology of the national bourgeoisie is that of the businessman, not that of a captain of industry; and it is only too true that the greed of the settlers and the system of embargoes set up by colonialism has hardly left them any other choice.

Under the colonial system, a middle class which accumulates capital is an impossible phenomenon. Now, precisely, it would seem that the historical vocation of an authentic national middle class in an under-developed country is to repudiate its own nature in so far as it is bourgeois, that is to say in so far as it is the tool of capitalism, and to make itself the willing slave of that revolutionary capital which is the people.

In an under-developed country an authentic national middle class ought to consider as its bounden duty to betray the calling fate has marked out for it, and to put itself to school with the people: in other words to put at the people's disposal the intellectual and technical capital that it has snatched when going through the colonial universities. But unhappily we shall see that very often the national middle class does not follow this heroic, positive, fruitful and just path; rather, it disappears with its soul set at peace into the shocking ways – shocking because anti-national – of a traditional bourgeoisie, of a bourgeoisie which is stupidly, contemptibly, cynically bourgeois.

The objective of nationalist parties as from a certain given period is, we have seen, strictly national. They mobilize the people with slogans of independence, and for the rest leave it to future events. When such parties are questioned on the economic programme of the state that they are clamouring for, or on the nature of the regime which they propose to install, they are incapable of replying, because, precisely, they are completely ignorant of the economy of their own country.

This economy has always developed outside the limits of their knowledge. They have nothing more than an approximate, bookish acquaintance with the actual and potential resources of their country's soil and mineral deposits; and therefore they can only speak of these resources on a general and abstract plane. After independence this under-developed middle class, reduced in numbers and without capital, which refuses to follow the path of revolution, will fall into deplorable stagnation. It is unable to give free rein to its genius, which formerly it was wont to lament, though rather too glibly, was held in check by colonial domination. The precariousness of its resources and the paucity of its managerial class forces it back for years into an artisan economy. From its point of view, which is inevitably a very limited one, a national economy is an economy based on what may be called local products. Long speeches will be made about the artisan class. Since the middle classes find it impossible to set up factories that would be more profit-earning both for themselves and for the country as a whole, they will surround the artisan class with a chauvinistic tenderness in keeping with the new awareness of national dignity, and which moreover will bring them in quite a lot of money. This cult of local products and this incapability to seek out new systems of management will be equally manifested by the bogging down of the national middle class in the methods of agricultural production which were characteristic of the colonial period.

The national economy of the period of independence is not set on a new footing. It is still concerned with the ground-nut harvest, with the cocoa crop and the olive yield. In the same way there is no change in the marketing of basic products, and not a single industry is set up in the country. We go on sending out raw materials; we go on being Europe's small farmers who specialize in unfinished products.

Yet the national middle class constantly demands the nationalization of the economy and of the trading sectors. This is because, from their point of view, nationalization does not mean placing the whole economy at the service of the nation and deciding to satisfy the needs of the nation. For them, nationalization does not mean governing the state with regard to the new social relations whose growth it has been decided to encourage. To them, nationalization quite simply means the transfer into native hands of those unfair advantages which are a legacy of the colonial period.

Since the middle class has neither sufficient material nor intellectual resources (by intellectual resources we mean engineers and technicians) it limits its claims to the taking over of business offices and commercial houses formerly occupied by the settlers. The national bourgeoisie steps into the shoes of the former European settlement: doctors, barristers, traders, commercial travellers, general agents and transport agents. It considers that the dignity of the country and its own welfare require that it should occupy all these posts. From now on it will insist that all the big foreign companies should pass through its hands, whether these companies wish to keep on their connexions with the country, or to open it up. The national middle class discovers its historic mission: that of intermediary.

Seen through its eyes, its mission has nothing to do with transforming the nation; it consists, prosaically, of being the transmission line between the nation and a capitalism, rampant though camouflaged, which today puts on the masque of neocolonialism. The national bourgeoisie will be quite content with the role of the Western bourgeoisie's business agent, and it will play its part without any complexes in a most dignified manner. But this same lucrative role, this cheap-jack's function, this meanness of outlook and this absence of all ambition symbolize the incapability of the national middle class to fulfil its historic role of bourgeoisie. Here, the dynamic, pioneer aspect, the characteristics of the inventor and of the discoverer of new worlds which are found in all national bourgeoisies are lamentably absent. In the colonial countries, the spirit of indulgence is dominant at the core of the bourgeoisie; and this is because the national bourgeoisie identifies itself with the Western bourgeoisie, from whom it has learnt its lessons. It follows the Western bourgeoisie along its path of negation and decadence without ever having emulated it in its first stages of exploration and invention, stages which are an acquisition of that Western bourgeoisie whatever the circumstances. In its beginnings, the national bourgeoisie of the colonial countries identifies itself with the decadence of the bourgeoisie of the West. We need not think that it is jumping ahead; it is in fact beginning at the end. It is already senile before it has come to know the petulance, the fearlessness or the will to succeed of youth.

The national bourgeoisie will be greatly helped on its way towards decadence by the Western bourgeoisies, who come to it as tourists avid for the exotic, for big-game hunting and for casinos. The national bourgeoisie organizes centres of rest and relaxation and pleasure resorts to meet the wishes of the Western bourgeoisie. Such activity is given the name of tourism, and for the occasion will be built up as a national industry. If proof is needed of the eventual transformation of certain elements of the ex-native bourgeoisie into the organizers of parties for their Western opposite numbers, it is worth while having a look at what has happened in Latin America. The casinos of Havana and of Mexico, the beaches of Rio, the little Brazilian and Mexican girls, the half-breed thirteen-year-olds, the ports of Acapulco and Copacabana – all these are the stigma of this depravation of the national middle class. Because it is bereft of ideas, because it lives to itself and cuts itself off from the people, undermined by its hereditary incapacity to think in terms of all the problems of the nation as seen from the point of view of the whole of that nation, the national middle class will have nothing better to do than to take on the role of manager for Western enterprise, and it will in practice set up its country as the brothel of Europe.

Once again we must keep before us the unfortunate example of certain Latin American republics. The banking magnates, the technocrats and the big businessmen of the United States have only to step on to a plane and they are wafted into sub-tropical climes, there for a space of a week or ten days to luxuriate in the delicious depravities which their 'reserves' hold for them.

The behaviour of the national landed proprietors is practically identical with that of the middle classes of the towns. The big farmers have, as soon as independence was proclaimed, demanded the nationalization of agricultural production. Through manifold scheming practices they manage to make a clean sweep of the farms formerly owned by settlers, thus reinforcing their hold on the district. But they do not try to introduce new agricultural methods, nor to farm more intensively, nor to integrate their farming systems into a genuinely national economy.

In fact, the landed proprietors will insist that the state should give them a hundred times more facilities and privileges than were enjoyed by the foreign settlers in former times. The exploitation of agricultural workers will be intensified and made legitimate. Using two or three slogans, these new colonists will demand an enormous amount of work from the agricultural labourers, in the name of the national effort of course. There will be no modernization of agriculture, no planning for development, and no initiative; for initiative throws these people into a panic since it implies a minimum of risk, and completely upsets the hesitant, prudent, landed bourgeoisie, which gradually slips more and more into the lines laid down by colonialism. In the districts where this is the case, the only efforts made to better things are due to the government; it orders them, encourages them and finances them. The landed bourgeoisie refuses to take the slightest risk, and remains opposed to any venture and to any hazard. It has no intention of building upon sand; it demands solid investments and quick returns. The enormous profits which it pockets, enormous if we take into account the national revenue, are never reinvested. The money-in-the-stocking mentality is dominant in the psychology of these landed proprietors. Sometimes, especially in the years immediately following independence, the bourgeoisie does not hesitate to invest in foreign banks the profits that it makes out of its native soil. On the other hand large sums are spent on display: on cars, country houses, and on all those things which have been justly described by economists as characterizing an under-developed bourgeoisie.

We have said that the native bourgeoisie which comes to power uses its class aggressiveness to corner the positions formerly kept for foreigners. On the morrow of independence, in fact, it violently attacks colonial personalities: barristers, traders, landed proprietors, doctors and higher civil servants. It will fight to the bitter end against these people 'who insult our dignity as a nation'. It waves aloft the notion of the nationalization and Africanization of the ruling classes. The fact is that such action will become more and more tinged by racism, until the bourgeoisie bluntly puts the problem to the government by saying 'We must have these posts'. They will not stop their snarling until they have taken over every one.

The working class of the towns, the masses of unemployed, the small artisans and craftsmen for their part line up behind this nationalist attitude; but in all justice let it be said, they only follow in the steps of their bourgeoisie. If the national bourgeoisie goes into competition with the Europeans, the artisans and craftsmen start a fight against non-national Africans. In the Ivory Coast, the anti-Dahoman and anti-Voltaic troubles are in fact racial riots. The Dahoman and Voltaic peoples, who control the greater part of the petty trade, are, once independence is declared, the object of hostile manifestations on the part of the people of the Ivory Coast. From nationalism we have passed to ultra-nationalism, to chauvinism, and finally to racism. These foreigners are called on to leave; their shops are burned, their street stalls are wrecked, and in fact the government of the Ivory Coast commands them to go, thus giving their nationals satisfaction. In Senegal it is the anti-Sudanese demonstrations which called forth these words from Mr Mamadou Dia:

> The truth is that the Senegalese people have only adopted the Mali mystique through attachment to its leaders. Their adhesion to the Mali has no other significance than that of a fresh act of faith in the political policy of the latter. The Senegalese territory was no less real, in fact it was all the more so in that the presence of the Sudanese in Dakar was too obviously manifested for it to be forgotten. It is this fact which explains that, far from being regretted, the break-up of the Federation has been greeted with relief by the mass of the people and nowhere was a hand raised to maintain it.[1]

While certain sections of the Senegalese people jump at the chance which is afforded them by their own leaders to get rid of the Sudanese, who hamper them in commercial matters or in administrative posts, the Congolese, who stood by hardly daring to believe in the mass exodus of the Belgians, decide to bring pressure to bear on the Senegalese who have settled in Leopoldville and Elizabethville and to get them to leave.

As we see it, the mechanism is identical in the two sets of circumstances. If the Europeans get in the way of the intellectuals and business bourgeoisie of the young nation, for the mass of the people in the towns competition is represented principally by Africans of another nation. On the Ivory Coast these competitors are the Dahomans; in Ghana they are the Nigerians; in Senegal, they are the Sudanese.

When the bougeoisie's demands for a ruling class made up exclusively of Negroes or Arabs do not spring from an authentic movement of nationalization but merely correspond to an anxiety to place in the bourgeoisie's hands the power held hitherto by the foreigner, the masses on their level present the same demands, confining, however, the notion of Negro or Arab within certain territorial limits. Between resounding assertions of the unity of the continent and this behaviour of the masses which has its inspiration in their leaders, many different attitudes may be traced. We observe a permanent see-saw between African unity, which fades quicker and quicker into the mists of oblivion, and a heart-breaking return to chauvinism in its most bitter and detestable form.

> On the Senegalese side, the leaders who have been the main theoreticians of African unity, and who several times over have sacrificed their local political organizations and their personal positions to this idea, are, though in all good faith, undeniably responsible. Their mistake—our mistake—has been, under pretext of fighting 'Balkanization', not to have taken into consideration the pre-colonial fact of territorialism. Our mistake has been not to have paid enough attention in our analyses to this phenomenon, which is the fruit of colonialism if you like, but also a sociological fact which no theory of unity, be it ever so laudable or attractive, can abolish. We have allowed ourselves to be seduced by a mirage; that of the structure which is the most pleasing to our minds; and, mistaking our ideal for reality, we have believed it enough to condemn territorialism, and its natural sequel, micro-nationalism, for us to get the better of them, and to assure the success of our chimerical undertaking.[2]

From the chauvinism of the Senegalese to the tribalism of the Yolofs is not a big step. For, in fact, everywhere that the national bourgeoisie has failed to break through to the people as a whole, to enlighten them, and to consider all problems in the first place with regard to them – a failure due to the bourgeoisie's attitude of mistrust and to the haziness of its political tenets – everywhere where that national bourgeoisie has shown itself incapable of extending its vision of the world sufficiently, we observe a falling back towards old tribal attitudes, and, furious and sick at heart, we perceive that race feeling in its most exacerbated form is triumphing. Since the sole motto of the bourgeoisie is 'Replace the foreigner', and because it hastens in every walk of life to secure justice for itself and to take over the posts that the foreigner has vacated, the 'small people' of the nation – taxi-drivers, cake-sellers and shoeblacks – will be equally quick to insist that the Dahomans go home to their own country, or will even go further and demand that the Foulbis and the Peuhls return to their jungle or their mountains.

It is from this view-point that we must interpret the fact that in young, independent countries, here and there federalism triumphs. We know that colonial domination has marked certain regions out for privilege. The colony's economy is not integrated into that of the nation as a whole. It is still organized in order to complete the economy of the different mother countries. Colonialism hardly ever exploits the whole of a country. It contents itself with bringing to light the natural resources, which it extracts, and exports to meet the needs of the mother country's industries, thereby allowing certain sectors of the colony to become relatively rich. But the rest of the colony follows its path of under-development and poverty, or at all events sinks into it more deeply.

Immediately after independence, the nationals who live in the more prosperous regions realize their good luck, and show a primary and profound reaction in refusing to feed the other nationals. The districts which are rich in ground-nuts, in cocoa and in diamonds come to the forefront, and dominate the empty panorama which the rest of the nation presents. The nationals of these rich regions look upon the others with hatred, and find in them envy and covetousness, and homicidal impulses. Old rivalries which were there before colonialism, old inter-racial hatred come to the surface. The Balubas refuse to feed the Luluas; Katanga forms itself into a state, and Albert Kalondji gets himself crowned king of South Kasai.

African unity, that vague formula, yet one to which the men and women of Africa were passionately attached, and whose operative value served to bring immense pressure to bear on colonialism, African unity takes off the mask, and crumbles into regionalism inside the hollow shell of nationality itself. The national bourgeoisie, since it is strung up to defend its immediate interests, and sees no farther than the end of its nose, reveals itself incapable of simply bringing national unity into being, or of building up the nation on a stable and productive basis. The national front which has forced colonialism to withdraw cracks up, and wastes the victory it has gained.

This merciless fight engaged upon by races and tribes, and this aggressive anxiety to occupy the posts left vacant by the departure of the foreigner, will equally give rise to religious rivalries. In the country districts and the bush, minor confraternities, local religions and maraboutic cults will show a new vitality and will once more take up their round of excommunications. In the big towns, on the level of the administrative classes, we will observe the coming to grips of the two great revealed religions, Islam and Catholicism.

Colonialism, which had been shaken to its very foundations by the birth of African unity, recovers its balance and tries now to break that will to unity by using all the movement's weaknesses. Colonialism will set the African peoples moving by revealing to them the existence of 'spiritual' rivalries. In Senegal, it is the newspaper *New Africa* which week by week distils hatred of Islam and of the Arabs. The Lebanese, in whose hands is the greater part of the small trading enterprises on the western seaboard, are marked out for national obloquy. The missionaries find it opportune to remind the masses that long before the advent of European colonialism the great African empires were disrupted by the Arab invasion. There is no hesitation in saying that it was the Arab occupation which paved the way for European colonialism; Arab imperialism is commonly spoken of, and the cultural imperialism of Islam is condemned. Moslems are usually kept out of the more important posts. In other regions the reverse is the case, and it is the native Christians who are considered as conscious, objective enemies of national independence.

Colonialism pulls every string shamelessly, and is only too content to set at loggerheads those Africans who only yesterday were leagued against the settlers. The idea of a Saint Bartholomew takes shape in certain minds, and the advocates of colonialism laugh to themselves derisively when they hear magnificent declarations about African unity. Inside a single nation, religion splits up the people into different spiritual communities, all of them kept up and stiffened by colonialism and its instruments. Totally unexpected events break out here and there. In regions where Catholicism or Protestantism predominates, we see the Moslem minorities flinging themselves with unaccustomed ardour into their devotions. The Islamic feastdays are revived, and the Moslem religion defends itself inch by inch against the violent absolutism of the Catholic faith. Ministers of state are heard to say for the benefit of certain individuals that if they are not content they have only to go to Cairo. Sometimes American Protestantism transplants its anti-Catholic prejudices into African soil, and keeps up tribal rivalries through religion.

Taking the continent as a whole, this religious tension may be responsible for the revival of the commonest racial feeling. Africa is divided into Black and White, and the names that are substituted – Africa south of the Sahara, Africa north of the Sahara – do not manage to hide this latent racism. Here, it is affirmed that White Africa has a thousand-year-old tradition of culture; that she is Mediterranean, that she is a continuation of Europe and that she shares in Graeco-Latin civilization. Black Africa is looked on as a region that is inert, brutal, uncivilized – in a word, savage. There, all day long you may hear unpleasant remarks about veiled women, polygamy and the supposed disdain the Arabs have for the feminine sex. All such remarks are reminiscent in their aggressiveness of those that are so often heard coming from the settler's lips. The national bourgeoisie of each of these two great religions, which has totally assimilated colonialist thought in its most corrupt form, takes over from the Europeans and establishes in the continent a racial philosophy which is extremely harmful for the future of Africa. By its laziness and will to imitation, it promotes the ingrafting and stiffening of racism which was characteristic of the colonial era. Thus it is by no means astonishing to hear in a country that calls itself African remarks which are neither more nor less than racist, and to observe the existence of paternalist behaviour which gives you the bitter impression that you are in Paris, Brussels or London.

In certain regions of Africa, drivelling paternalism with regard to the blacks and the loathsome idea derived from Western culture that the black man is impervious to logic and the sciences reign in all their nakedness. Sometimes it may be ascertained that the black minorities are hemmed in by a kind of semi-slavery which renders legitimate that species of wariness, or in other words mistrust, which the countries of Black Africa feel with regard to the countries of White Africa. It is all too common that a citizen of Black Africa hears himself called a 'Negro' by the children when walking in the streets of a big town in White Africa, or finds that civil servants address him in pidgin English.

Yes, unfortunately it is not unknown that students from Black Africa who attend secondary schools north of the Sahara hear their schoolfellows asking if in their country there are houses, if they know what electricity is, or if they practise cannibalism in their families. Yes, unfortunately it is not unknown that in certain regions north of the Sahara Africans coming from countries south of the Sahara meet nationals who implore them to take them 'anywhere at all on condition we meet Negroes'. In parallel fashion, in certain young states of Black Africa members of parliament, or even ministers, maintain without a trace of humour that the danger is not at all of a reoccupation of their country by colonialism but of an eventual invasion by 'those vandals of Arabs coming from the North'.

As we see it, the bankruptcy of the bourgeoisie is not apparent in the economic field only. They have come to power in the name of a narrow nationalism and representing a race; they will prove themselves incapable of triumphantly putting into practice a programme with even a minimum humanist content, in spite of fine-sounding declarations which are devoid of meaning since the speakers bandy about in irresponsible fashion phrases that come straight out of European treatises on morals and political philosophy. When the bourgeoisie is strong, when it can arrange everything and everybody to serve its power, it does not hesitate to affirm positively certain democratic ideas which claim to be universally applicable. There must be very exceptional circumstances if such a bourgeoisie, solidly based economically, is forced into denying its own humanist ideology. The Western bourgeoisie, though fundamentally racist, most often manages to mask this racism by a multiplicity of nuances which allow it to preserve intact its proclamation of mankind's outstanding dignity.

The Western bourgeoisie has prepared enough fences and railings to have no real fear of the competition of those whom it exploits and holds in contempt. Western bourgeois racial prejudice as regards the nigger and the Arab is a racism of contempt; it is a racism which minimizes what it hates. Bourgeois ideology, however, which is the proclamation of an essential equality between men, manages to appear logical in its own eyes by inviting the sub-men to become human, and to take as their prototype Western humanity as incarnated in the Western bourgeoisie.

The racial prejudice of the young national bourgeoisie is a racism of defence, based on fear. Essentially it is no different from vulgar tribalism, or the rivalries between septs or confraternities. We may understand why keen-witted international observers have hardly taken seriously the great flights of oratory about African unity, for it is true that there are so many cracks in that unity visible to the naked eye that it is only reasonable to insist that all these contradictions ought to be resolved before the day of unity can come.

The people of Africa have only recently come to know themselves. They have decided, in the name of the whole continent, to weigh in strongly against the colonial regime. Now the nationalist bourgeoisies, who in region after region hasten to make their own fortunes and to set up a national system of exploitation, do their utmost to put obstacles in the path of this 'Utopia'. The national bourgeoisies, who are quite clear as to what their objectives are, have decided to bar the way to that unity, to that coordinated effort on the part of two hundred and fifty million men to triumph over stupidity, hunger and inhumanity at one and the same time. This is why we must understand that African unity can only be achieved through the upward thrust of the people, and under the leadership of the people, that is to say, in defiance of the interests of the bourgeoisie.

As regards internal affairs and in the sphere of institutions, the national bourgeoisie will give equal proof of its incapacity. In a certain number of under-developed countries the parliamentary game is faked from the beginning. Powerless economically, unable to bring about the existence of coherent social relations, and standing on the principle of its domination as a class, the bourgeoisie chooses the solution that seems to it the easiest, that of the single party. It does not yet have the quiet conscience and the calm that economic power and the control of the state machine alone can give. It does not create a state that reassures the ordinary citizen, but rather one that rouses his anxiety.

The state, which by its strength and discretion ought to inspire confidence and disarm and lull everybody to sleep, on the contrary seeks to impose itself in spectacular fashion. It makes a display, it jostles people and bullies them, thus intimating to the citizen that he is in continual danger. The single party is the modern form of the dictatorship of the bourgeoisie, unmasked, unpainted, unscrupulous and cynical.

It is true that such a dictatorship does not go very far. It cannot halt the processes of its own contradictions. Since the bourgeoisie has not the economic means to ensure its domination and to throw a few crumbs to the rest of the country; since, moreover, it is preoccupied with filling its pockets as rapidly as possible but also as prosaically as possible, the country sinks all the more deeply into stagnation. And in order to hide this stagnation and to mask this regression, to reassure itself and to give itself something to boast about, the bourgeoisie can find nothing better to do than to erect grandiose buildings in the capital and to lay out money on what are called prestige expenses.

The national bourgeoisie turns its back more and more on the interior and on the real facts of its undeveloped country, and tends to look towards the former mother country and the foreign capitalists who count on its obliging compliance. As it does not share its profits with the people, and in no way allows them to enjoy any of the dues that are paid to it by the big foreign companies, it will discover the need for a popular leader to whom will fall the dual role of stabilizing the regime and of perpetuating the domination of the bourgeoisie. The bourgeois dictatorship of under-developed countries draws its strength from the existence of a leader. We know that in the well-developed countries the bourgeois dictatorship is the result of the economic power of the bourgeoisie. In the under-developed countries on the contrary the leader stands for moral power, in whose shelter the thin and poverty-stricken bourgeoisie of the young nation decides to get rich.

The people who for years on end have seen this leader and heard him speak, who from a distance in a kind of dream have followed his contests with the colonial power, spontaneously put their trust in this patriot. Before independence, the leader generally embodies the aspirations of the people for independence, political liberty and national dignity. But as soon as independence is declared, far from embodying in concrete form the needs of the people in what touches bread, land and the restoration of the country to the sacred hands of the people, the leader will reveal his inner purpose: to become the general president of that company of profiteers impatient for their returns which constitutes the national bourgeoisie.

In spite of his frequently honest conduct and his sincere declarations, the leader as seen objectively is the fierce defender of these interests, today combined, of the national bourgeoisie and the ex-colonial companies. His honesty, which is his soul's true bent, crumbles away little by little. His contact with the masses is so unreal that he comes to believe that his authority is hated and that the services that he has rendered his country are being called in question. The leader judges the ingratitude of the masses harshly, and every day that passes ranges himself a little more resolutely on the side of the exploiters. He therefore knowingly becomes the aider and abettor of the young bourgeoisie which is plunging into the mire of corruption and pleasure.

The economic channels of the young state sink back inevitably into neo-colonialist lines. The national economy, formerly protected, is today literally controlled. The budget is balanced through loans and gifts, while every three or four months the chief ministers themselves or else their governmental delegations come to the erstwhile mother countries or elsewhere, fishing for capital.

The former colonial power increases its demands, accumulates concessions and guarantees and takes fewer and fewer pains to mask the hold it has over the national government. The people stagnate deplorably in unbearable poverty; slowly they awaken to the unutterable treason of their leaders. This awakening is all the more acute in that the bourgeoisie is incapable of learning its lesson. The distribution of wealth that it effects is not spread out between a great many sectors; it is not ranged among different levels, nor does it set up a hierarchy of half-tones. The new caste is an affront all the more disgusting in that the immense majority, nine-tenths of the population, continue to die of starvation. The scandalous enrichment, speedy and pitiless, of this caste is accompanied by a decisive awakening on the part of the people, and a growing awareness that promises stormy days to come. The bourgeois caste, that section of the nation which annexes for its own profit all the wealth of the country, by a kind of unexpected logic will pass disparaging judgements upon the other Negroes and the other Arabs that more often than not are reminiscent of the racist doctrines of the former representatives of the colonial power. At one and the same time the poverty of the people, the immoderate money-making of the bourgeois caste, and its widespread scorn for the rest of the nation will harden thought and action.

But such threats will lead to the re-affirmation of authority and the appearance of dictatorship. The leader, who has behind him a lifetime of political action and devoted patriotism, constitutes a screen between the people and the rapacious bourgeoisie since he stands surety for the ventures of that caste and closes his eyes to their insolence, their mediocrity and their fundamental immorality. He acts as a braking-power on the awakening consciousness of the people. He comes to the aid of the bourgeois caste and hides his manoeuvres from the people, thus becoming the most eager worker in the task of mystifying and bewildering the masses. Every time he speaks to the people he calls to mind his often heroic life, the struggles he has led in the name of the people and the victories in their name he has achieved, thereby intimating clearly to the masses that they ought to go on putting their confidence in him. There are plenty of examples of African patriots who have introduced into the cautious political advance of their elders a decisive style characterized by its nationalist outlook. These men came from the backwoods, and they proclaimed, to the scandal of the dominating power and the shame of the nationals of the capital, that they came from the backwoods and that they spoke in the name of the Negroes. These men, who have sung the praises of their race, who have taken upon themselves the whole burden of the past, complete with cannibalism and degeneracy, find themselves today, alas, at the head of a team of administrators who turn their back on the jungle and who proclaim that the vocation of their people is to obey, to go on obeying and to be obedient till the end of time.

The leader pacifies the people. For years on end after independence has been won, we see him, incapable of urging on the people to a concrete task, unable really to open the future to them or of flinging them into the path of national reconstruction, that is to say, of their own reconstruction; we see him reassessing the history of independence and recalling the sacred unity of the struggle for liberation. The leader, because he refuses to break up the national bourgeoisie, asks the people to fall back into the past and to become drunk on the remembrance of the epoch which led up to independence. The leader, seen objectively, brings the people to a halt and persists in either expelling them from history or preventing them from taking root in it. During the struggle for liberation the leader awakened the people and promised them a forward march, heroic and unmitigated. Today, he uses every means to put them to sleep, and three or four times a year asks them to remember the colonial period and to look back on the long way they have come since then.

Now it must be said that the masses show themselves totally incapable of appreciating the long way they have come. The peasant who goes on scratching out a living from the soil, and the unemployed man who never finds employment do not manage, in spite of public holidays and flags, new and brightly-coloured though they may be, to convince themselves that anything has really changed in their lives. The bourgeoisie who are in power vainly increase the number of processions; the masses have no illusions. They are hungry; and the police officers, though now they are Africans, do not serve to reassure them particularly. The masses begin to sulk; they turn away from this nation in which they have been given no place and begin to lose interest in it.

From time to time, however, the leader makes an effort; he speaks on the radio or makes a tour of the country to pacify the people, to calm them and bemuse them. The leader is all the more necessary in that there is no party. During the period of the struggle for independence there was one right enough, a party led by the present leader. But since then this party has sadly disintegrated; nothing is left but the shell of a party, the name, the emblem and the motto. The living party, which ought to make possible the free exchange of ideas which have been elaborated according to the real needs of the mass of the people, has been transformed into a trade union of individual interests. Since the proclamation of independence the party no longer helps the people to set out its demands, to become more aware of its needs and better able to establish its power. Today, the party's mission is to deliver to the people the instructions which issue from the summit. There no longer exists the fruitful give-and-take from the bottom to the top and from the top to the bottom which creates and guarantees democracy in a party. Quite on the contrary, the party has made itself into a screen between the masses and the leaders. There is no longer any party life, for the branches which were set up during the colonial period are today completely demobilized.

The militant champs on his bit. Now it is that the attitude taken up by certain militants during the struggle for liberation is seen to be justified, for the fact is that in the thick of the fight more than a few militants asked the leaders to formulate a dogma, to set out their objectives and to draw up a programme. But under the pretext of safeguarding national unity, the leaders categorically refused to attempt such a task. The only worthwhile dogma, it was repeatedly stated, is the union of the nation against colonialism. And on they went, armed with an impetuous slogan which stood for principles, while their only ideological activity took the form of a series of variants on the theme of the right of peoples to self-determination, borne on the wind of history which would inevitably sweep away colonialism. When the militants asked whether the wind of history couldn't be a little more clearly analysed, the leaders gave them instead hope and trust, the necessity of decolonialization and its inevitability, and more to that effect.

After independence, the party sinks into an extraordinary lethargy. The militants are only called upon when so-called popular manifestations are afoot, or international conferences, or independence celebrations. The local party leaders are given administrative posts, the party becomes an administration, and the militants disappear into the crowd and take the empty title of citizen. Now that they have fulfilled their historical mission of leading the bourgeoisie to power, they are firmly invited to retire so that the bourgeoisie may carry out *its* mission in peace and quiet. But we have seen that the national bourgeoisie of under-developed countries is incapable of carrying out any mission whatever. After a few years, the break-up of the party becomes obvious, and any observer, even the most superficial, can notice that the party, today the skeleton of its former self, only serves to immobilize the people. The party, which during the battle had drawn to itself the whole nation, is falling to pieces. The intellectuals who on the eve of independence rallied to the party, now make it clear by their attitude that they gave their support with no other end in view than to secure their slices of the cake of independence. The party is becoming a means of private advancement.

There exists inside the new regime, however, an inequality in the acquisition of wealth and in monopolization. Some have a double source of income and demonstrate that they are specialized in opportunism. Privileges multiply and corruption triumphs, while morality declines. Today the vultures are too numerous and too voracious in proportion to the lean spoils of the national wealth. The party, a true instrument of power in the hands of the bourgeoisie, reinforces the machine, and ensures that the people are hemmed in and immobilized. The party helps the government to hold the people down. It becomes more and more clearly anti-democratic, an implement of coercion. The party is objectively, sometimes subjectively, the accomplice of the merchant bourgeoisie. In the same way that the national bourgeoisie conjures away its phase of construction in order to throw itself into the enjoyment of its wealth, in parallel fashion in the institutional sphere it jumps the parliamentary phase and chooses a dictatorship of the national-socialist type. We know today that this fascism at high interest which has triumphed for half a century in Latin America is the dialectic result of states which were semi-colonial during the period of independence.

In these poor, under-developed countries, where the rule is that the greatest wealth is surrounded by the greatest poverty, the army and the police constitute the pillars of the regime; an army and a police force (another rule which must not be forgotten) which are advised by foreign experts. The strength of the police force and the power of the army are proportionate to the stagnation in which the rest of the nation is sunk. By dint of yearly loans, concessions are snatched up by foreigners; scandals are numerous, ministers grow rich, their wives doll themselves up, the members of parliament feather their nests and there is not a soul down to the simple policeman or the customs officer who does not join in the great procession of corruption.

The opposition becomes more aggressive and the people at once catch on to its propaganda. From now on their hostility to the bourgeoisie is plainly visible. This young bourgeoisie which appears to be afflicted with precocious senility takes no heed of the advice showered upon it, and reveals itself incapable of understanding that it would be in its interest to draw a veil, even if only the flimsiest kind, over its exploitation. It is the most Christian newspaper *The African Weekly*, published in Brazzaville, which addresses the princes of the regime thus:

> You who are in good positions, you and your wives, today you enjoy many comforts; perhaps a good education, a fine house, good contacts and many missions on which you are delegated which open new horizons to you. But all your wealth forms a hard shell which prevents your seeing the poverty that surrounds you. Take care.

This warning coming from *The African Weekly* and, addressed to the henchmen of Monsieur Youlou has, we may imagine, nothing revolutionary about it. What *The African Weekly* wants to point out to the starvers of the Congolese people is that God will punish their conduct. It continues: 'If there is no room in your heart for consideration towards those who are beneath you, there will be no room for you in God's house.'

It is clear that the national bourgeoisie hardly worries at all about such an indictment. With its wave-lengths tuned in to Europe, it continues firmly and resolutely to make the most of the situation. The enormous profits which it derives from the exploitation of the people are exported to foreign countries. The young national bourgeoisie is often more suspicious of the regime that it has set up than are the foreign companies. The national bourgeoisie refuses to invest in its own country and behaves towards the state that protects and nurtures it with, it must be remarked, astonishing ingratitude. It acquires foreign securities in the European markets, and goes off to spend the week-end in Paris or Hamburg. The behaviour of the national bourgeoisie of certain under-developed countries is reminiscent of the members of a gang, who after every hold-up hide their share in the swag from the other members who are their accomplices and prudently start thinking about their retirement. Such behaviour shows that more or less consciously the national bourgeoisie is playing to lose if the game goes on too long. They guess that the present situation will not last indefinitely but they intend to make the most of it. Such exploitation and such contempt for the state, however, inevitably gives rise to discontent among the mass of the people. It is in these conditions that the regime becomes harsher. In the absence of a parliament it is the army that becomes the arbiter: but sooner or later it will realize its power and will hold over the government's head the threat of a manifesto.

As we see it, the national bourgeoisie of certain under-developed countries has learned nothing from books. If they had looked closer at the Latin American countries they doubtless would have recognized the dangers which threaten them. We may thus conclude that this bourgeoisie in miniature that thrusts itself into the forefront is condemned to mark time, accomplishing nothing. In under-developed countries the bourgeois phase is impossibly arid. Certainly, there is a police dictatorship and a profiteering caste, but the construction of an elaborate bourgeois society seems to be condemned to failure. The ranks of decked-out profiteers whose grasping hands scrape up the bank-notes from a poverty-stricken country will sooner or later be men of straw in the hands of the army, cleverly handled by foreign experts. In this way the former mother country practises indirect government, both by the bourgeoisie that it upholds and also by the national army led by its experts, an army that pins the people down, immobilizing and terrorizing them.

The observations that we have been able to make about the national bourgeoisie bring us to a conclusion which should cause no surprise. In under-developed countries, the bourgeoisie should not be allowed to find the conditions necessary for its existence and its growth. In other words, the combined effort of the masses led by a party and of intellectuals who are highly conscious and armed with revolutionary principles ought to bar the way to this useless and harmful middle class.

The theoretical question that for the last fifty years has been raised whenever the history of under-developed countries is under discussion – whether or not the bourgeois phase can be skipped – ought to be answered in the field of revolutionary action, and not by logic. The bourgeois phase in under-developed countries can only justify itself in so far as the national bourgeoisie has sufficient economic and technical strength to build up a bourgeois society, to create the conditions necessary for the development of a large-scale proletariat, to mechanize agriculture and finally to make possible the existence of an authentic national culture.

A bourgeoisie similar to that which developed in Europe is able to elaborate an ideology and at the same time strengthen its own power. Such a bourgeoisie, dynamic, educated and secular, has fully succeeded in its undertaking of the accumulation of capital and has given to the nation a minimum of prosperity. In under-developed countries, we have seen that no true bourgeoisie exists; there is only a sort of little greedy caste, avid and voracious, with the mind of a huckster, only too glad to accept the dividends that the former colonial power hands out to it. This get-rich-quick middle class shows itself incapable of great ideas or of inventiveness. It remembers what it has read in European textbooks and imperceptibly it becomes not even the replica of Europe, but its caricature.

The struggle against the bourgeoisie of under-developed countries is far from being a theoretical one. It is not concerned with making out its condemnation as laid down by the judgement of history. The national bourgeoisie of under-developed countries must not be opposed because it threatens to slow down the total, harmonious development of the nation. It must simply be stoutly opposed because, literally, it is good for nothing. This bourgeoisie, expressing its mediocrity in its profits, its achievements and in its thought, tries to hide this mediocrity by buildings which have prestige value at the individual level, by chromium plating on big American cars, by holidays on the Riviera and week-ends in neon-lit night-clubs.

This bourgeoisie which turns its back more and more on the people as a whole does not even succeed in extracting spectacular concessions from the West, such as investments which would be of value for the country's economy or the setting up of certain industries. On the contrary, assembly plants spring up and consecrate the type of neo-colonialist industrialization in which the country's economy flounders. Thus it must not be said that the national bourgeoisie retards the country's evolution, that it makes it lose time or that it threatens to lead the nation up blind alleys. In fact, the bourgeois phase in the history of under-developed countries is a completely useless phase. When this caste has vanished, devoured by its own contradictions, it will be seen that nothing new has happened since independence was proclaimed, and that everything must be started again from scratch. The change-over will not take place at the level of the structures set up by the bourgeoisie during its reign, since that caste has done nothing more than take over unchanged the legacy of the economy, the thought and the institutions left by the colonialists.

It is all the easier to neutralize this bourgeois class in that, as we have seen, it is numerically, intellectually and economically weak. In the colonized territories, the bourgeois caste draws its strength after independence chiefly from agreements reached with the former colonial power. The national bourgeoisie has all the more opportunity to take over from the oppressor since it has been given time for a leisurely *tête-à-tête* with the ex-colonial power. But deep-rooted contradictions undermine the ranks of that bourgeoisie; it is this that gives the observer an impression of instability. There is not as yet a homogeneity of caste. Many intellectuals, for example, condemn this regime based on the domination of the few. In under-developed countries, there are certain members of the *élite*, intellectuals and civil servants, who are sincere, who feel the necessity for a planned economy, the outlawing of profiteers and the strict prohibition of attempts at mystification. In addition, such men fight in a certain measure for the mass participation of the people in the ordering of public affairs.

In those under-developed countries which accede to independence, there almost always exists a small number of honest intellectuals, who have no very precise ideas about politics, but who instinctively distrust the race for positions and pensions which is symptomatic of the early days of independence in colonized countries. The personal situation of these men (breadwinners of large families) or their background (hard struggles and a strictly moral upbringing) explain their manifest contempt for profiteers and schemers. We must know how to use these men in the decisive battle that we mean to engage upon which will lead to a healthier outlook for the nation. Closing the road to the national bourgeoisie is, certainly, the means whereby the vicissitudes of new-found independence may be avoided, and with them the decline of morals, the installing of corruption within the country, economic regression, and the immediate disaster of an anti-democratic regime depending on force and intimidation. But it is also the only means towards progress.

What holds up the taking of a decision by the profoundly democratic elements of the young nation and adds to their timidity is the apparent strength of the bourgeoisie. In newly independent under-developed countries, the whole of the ruling class swarms into the towns built by colonialism. The absence of any analysis of the total population induces onlookers to think that there exists a powerful and perfectly organized bourgeoisie. In fact, we know today that the bourgeoisie in under-developed countries is non-existent. What creates a bourgeoisie is not the bourgeois spirit, nor its taste or manners, nor even its aspirations. The bourgeoisie is above all the direct product of precise economic conditions.

Now, in the colonies, the economic conditions are conditions of a foreign bourgeoisie. Through its agents, it is the bourgeoisie of the mother country that we find present in the colonial towns. The bourgeoisie in the colonies is, before independence, a Western bourgeoisie, a true branch of the bourgeoisie of the mother country, that derives its legitimacy, its force and its stability from the bourgeoisie of the homeland. During the period of unrest that precedes independence, certain native elements, intellectuals and traders, who live in the midst of that imported bourgeoisie, try to identify themselves with it. A permanent wish for identification with the bourgeois representatives of the mother country is to be found among the native intellectuals and merchants.

This native bourgeoisie, which has adopted unreservedly and with enthusiasm the ways of thinking characteristic of the mother country, which has become wonderfully detached from its own thought and has based its consciousness upon foundations which are typically foreign, will realize, with its mouth watering, that it lacks something essential to a bourgeoisie: money. The bourgeoisie of an under-developed country is a bourgeoisie in spirit only. It is not its economic strength, nor the dynamism of its leaders, nor the breadth of its ideas that ensures its peculiar quality of bourgeoisie. Consequently it remains at the beginning and for a long time afterwards a bourgeoisie of the civil service. It is the positions that it holds in the new national administration which will give it strength and serenity. If the government gives it enough time and opportunity, this bourgeoisie will manage to put away enough money to stiffen its domination. But it will always reveal itself as incapable of giving birth to an authentic bourgeois society with all the economic and industrial consequences which this entails.

From the beginning the national bourgeoisie directs its efforts towards activities of the intermediary type. The basis of its strength is found in its aptitude for trade and small business enterprises, and in securing commissions. It is not its money that works, but its business acumen. It does not go in for investments and it cannot achieve that accumulation of capital necessary to the birth and blossoming of an authentic bourgeoisie. At that rate it would take centuries to set on foot an embryonic industrial revolution, and in any case it would find the way barred by the relentless opposition of the former mother country, which will have taken all precautions when setting up neo-colonialist trade conventions.

If the government wants to bring the country out of its stagnation and set it well on the road towards development and progress, it must first and foremost nationalize the middleman's trading sector. The bourgeoisie, who wish to see both the triumph of the spirit of money-making and the enjoyment of consumer goods, and at the same time the triumph of their contemptuous attitude towards the mass of the people and the scandalous aspect of profit-making (should we not rather call it robbery?), in fact invest largely in this sector. The intermediary market which formerly was dominated by the settlers will be invaded by the young national bourgeoisie. In a colonial economy the intermediary sector is by far the most important. If you want to progress, you must decide in the first few hours to nationalize this sector. But it is clear that such a nationalization ought not to take on a rigidly state-controlled aspect. It is not a question of placing at the head of these services citizens who have had no political education. Every time such a procedure has been adopted it has been seen that the government has in fact contributed to the triumph of a dictatorship of civil servants who had been set in the mould of the former mother country, and who quickly showed themselves incapable of thinking in terms of the nation as a whole. These civil servants very soon began to sabotage the national economy and to throw its structure out of joint; under them, corruption, prevarication, the diversion of stocks and the black market came to stay. Nationalizing the intermediary sector means organizing wholesale and retail cooperatives on a democratic basis; it also means decentralizing these cooperatives by getting the mass of the people interested in the ordering of public affairs. You will not be able to do all this unless you give the people some political education. Previously, it was realized that this key problem should be clarified once and for all. Today, it is true that the principle of the political education of the masses is generally subscribed to in under-developed countries. But it does not seem that this primordial task is really taken to heart. When people stress the need to educate the people politically, they decide to point out at the same time that they want to be supported by the people in the action that they are taking. A government which declares that it wishes to educate the people politically thus expresses its desire to govern with the people and for the people. It ought not to speak a language destined to camouflage a bourgeois administration. In the capitalist countries, the bourgeois governments have long since left this infantile stage of authority behind. To put it bluntly, they govern with the help of their laws, their economic strength and their police. Now that their power is firmly established they no longer need to lose time in striking demagogic attitudes. They govern in their own interests, and they have the courage of their own strength. They have created legitimacy, and they are strong in their own right.

The bourgeois caste in newly independent countries have not yet the cynicism nor the unruffled calm which are founded on the strength of long-established bourgeoisies. From this springs the fact that they show a certain anxiety to hide their real convictions, to side-track, and in short to set themselves up as a popular force. But the inclusion of the masses in politics does not consist in mobilizing three or four times a year ten thousand or a hundred thousand men and women. These mass meetings and spectacular gatherings are akin to the old tactics that date from before independence, whereby you exhibited your forces in order to prove to yourself and to others that you had the people behind you. The political education of the masses proposes not to treat the masses as children but to make adults of them.

This brings us to consider the role of the political party in an under-developed country. We have seen in the preceding pages that very often simple souls, who moreover belong to the newly born bourgeoisie, never stop repeating that in an under-developed country the direction of affairs by a strong authority, in other words a dictatorship, is a necessity. With this in view the party is given the task of supervising the masses. The party plays understudy to the administration and the police, and controls the masses, not in order to make sure that they really participate in the business of governing the nation, but in order to remind them constantly that the government expects from them obedience and discipline. That famous dictatorship, whose supporters believe that it is called for by the historical process and consider it an indispensable prelude to the dawn of independence, in fact symbolizes the decision of the bourgeois caste to govern the under-developed country first with the help of the people, but soon against them. The progressive transformation of the party into an information service is the indication that the government holds itself more and more on the defensive. The incoherent mass of the people is seen as a blind force that must be continually held in check either by mystification or by the fear inspired by the police force. The party acts as a barometer and as an information service. The militant is turned into an informer. He is entrusted with punitive expeditions against the villages. The embryo opposition parties are liquidated by beatings and stonings. The opposition candidates see their houses set on fire. The police increase their provocations. In these conditions, you may be sure, the party is unchallenged and 99·99 per cent of the votes are cast for the governmental candidate. We should add that in Africa a certain number of governments actually behave in this way. All the opposition parties, which moreover are usually progressive and would therefore tend to work for the greater influence of the masses in the conduct of public matters, and who desire that the proud, money-making bourgeoisie should be brought to heel, have been by dint of baton charges and prisons condemned first to silence and then to a clandestine existence.

The political party in many parts of Africa which are today independent is puffed up in a most dangerous way. In the presence of a member of the party, the people are silent, behave like a flock of sheep and publish panegyrics in praise of the government of the leader. But in the street when evening comes, away from the village, in the cafés or by the river, the bitter disappointment of the people, their despair but also their unceasing anger makes itself heard. The party, instead of welcoming the expression of popular discontentment, instead of taking for its fundamental purpose the free flow of ideas from the people up to the government, forms a screen, and forbids such ideas. The party leaders behave like common sergeant-majors, frequently reminding the people of the need for 'silence in the ranks'. This party which used to call itself the servant of the people, which used to claim that it worked for the full expression of the people's will, as soon as the colonial power puts the country into its control hastens to send the people back to their caves. As far as national unity is concerned the party will also make many mistakes, as for example when the so-called national party behaves as a party based on ethnical differences. It becomes, in fact, the tribe which makes itself into a party. This party which of its own will proclaims that it is a national party, and which claims to speak in the name of the totality of the people, secretly, sometimes even openly organizes an authentic ethnical dictatorship. We no longer see the rise of a bourgeois dictatorship, but a tribal dictatorship. The ministers, the members of the cabinet, the ambassadors and local commissioners are chosen from the same ethnological group as the leader, sometimes directly from his own family. Such regimes of the family sort seem to go back to the old laws of inbreeding, and not anger but shame is felt when we are faced with such stupidity, such an imposture, such intellectual and spiritual poverty. These heads of the government are the true traitors in Africa, for they sell their country to the most terrifying of all its enemies: stupidity. This tribalizing of the central authority, it is certain, encourages regionalist ideas and separatism. All the decentralizing tendencies spring up again and triumph, and the nation falls to pieces, broken in bits. The leader, who once used to call for 'African unity' and who thought of his own little family wakes up one day to find himself saddled with five tribes, who also want to have their own ambassadors and ministers; and irresponsible as ever, still unaware and still despicable, he denounces their 'treason'.

We have more than once drawn attention to the baleful influence frequently wielded by the leader. This is due to the fact that the party in certain districts is organized like a gang, with the toughest person in it as its head. The ascendancy of such a leader and his power over others is often mentioned, and people have no hesitation in declaring, in a tone of slightly admiring complicity that he strikes terror into his nearest collaborators. In order to avoid these many pitfalls an unceasing battle must be waged, a battle to prevent the party ever becoming a willing tool in the hands of a leader. 'Leader': the word comes from the English verb 'to lead', but a frequent French translation is 'to drive'. The driver, the shepherd of the people no longer exists today. The people are no longer a herd; they do not need to be driven. If the leader drives me on, I want him to realize that at the same time I show him the way; the nation ought not to be something bossed by a Grand Panjandrum. We may understand the panic caused in governmental circles each time one of these leaders falls ill; they are obsessed by the question of who is to succeed him. What will happen to the country if the leader disappears? The ruling classes who have abdicated in favour of the leader, irresponsible, oblivious of everything and essentially preoccupied with the pleasures of their everyday life, their cocktail parties, their journeys paid for by government money, the profits they can make out of various schemes – from time to time these people discover the spiritual waste land at the heart of the nation.

A country that really wishes to answer the questions that history puts to it, that wants to develop not only its towns but also the brains of its inhabitants, such a country must possess a trustworthy political party. The party is not a tool in the hands of the government. Quite on the contrary, the party is a tool in the hands of the people; it is they who decide on the policy that the government carries out. The party is not, and ought never to be, the only political bureau where all the members of the government and the chief dignitaries of the regime may meet freely together. Only too frequently the political bureau, unfortunately, consists of all the party and its members who reside permanently in the capital. In an underdeveloped country, the leading members of the party ought to avoid the capital as if it had the plague. They ought, with some few exceptions, to live in the country districts. The centralization of all activity in the city ought to be avoided. No excuse of administrative discipline should be taken as legitimizing that excrescence of a capital which is already over-populated and over-developed with regard to nine-tenths of the country. The party should be decentralized in the extreme. It is the only way to bring life to regions which are dead, those regions which are not yet awakened to life.

In practice, there will be at least one member of the political bureau in each area and he will deliberately not be appointed as head of that area. He will have no administrative powers. The regional member of the political bureau is not expected to hold the highest rank in the regional administrative organization. He ought not automatically to belong to the regional administrative body. For the people, the party is not an authority, but an organism through which they as the people exercise their authority and express their will. The less there is of confusion and duality of powers, the more the party will play its part of guide and the more surely it will constitute for the people a decisive guarantee. If the party is mingled with the government, the fact of being a party militant means that you take the short cut to gain private ends, to hold a post in the government, step up the ladder, get promotion and make a career for yourself.

In an under-developed country, the setting up of dynamic district officials stops the progress whereby the towns become top-heavy, and the incoherent rush towards the cities of the mass of country people. The setting up early in the days of independence of regional organizations and officials who have full authority to do everything in their power to awaken such a region, to bring life to it and to hasten the growth of consciousness in it is a necessity from which there is no escape for a country that wishes to progress. Otherwise, the government bigwigs and the party officials group themselves around the leader. The government services swell to huge proportions, not because they are developing and specializing, but because new-found cousins and fresh militants are looking for jobs and hope to edge themselves into the government machine. And the dream of every citizen is to get up to the capital, and to have his share of the cake. The local districts are deserted; the mass of the country people with no one to lead them, uneducated and unsupported, turn their backs on their poorly-laboured fields and flock towards the outer ring of suburbs, thus swelling out of all proportion the ranks of the *lumpen-proletariat*.

The moment for a fresh national crisis is not far off. To avoid it, we think that a quite different policy should be followed: that the interior, the back-country ought to be the most privileged part of the country. Moreover, in the last resort, there is nothing inconvenient in the government choosing its seat elsewhere than in the capital. The capital must be deconsecrated; the outcast masses must be shown that we have decided to work for them. It is with this idea in mind that the government of Brazil tried to found Brazilia. The dead city of Rio de Janeiro was an insult to the Brazilian people. But, unfortunately, Brazilia is just another new capital, as monstrous as the first. The only advantage of this achievement is that, today, there exists a road through the bush to it.

No, there is no serious reason which can be opposed to the choice of another capital, or to the moving of the government as a whole towards one of the most under-populated regions. The capital of under-developed countries is a commercial notion inherited from the colonial period. But we who are citizens of the under-developed countries, we ought to seek every occasion for contacts with the rural masses. We must create a national policy, in other words a policy for the masses. We ought never to lose contact with the people which has battled for its independence and for the concrete betterment of its existence.

The native civil servants and technicians ought not to bury themselves in diagrams and statistics, but rather in the heart of the people. They ought not to bristle up every time there is question of a move to be made to the 'interior'. We should no longer see the young women of the country threaten their husbands with divorce if they do not manage to avoid being appointed to a rural post. For these reasons, the political bureau of the party ought to treat these forgotten districts in a very privileged manner; and the life of the capital, an altogether artificial life which is stuck on to the real, national life like a foreign body ought to take up the least space possible in the life of the nation, which is sacred and fundamental.

In an under-developed country the party ought to be organized in such fashion that it is not simply content with having contacts with the masses. The party should be the direct expression of the masses. The party is not an administration responsible for transmitting government orders; it is the energetic spokesman and the incorruptible defender of the masses. In order to arrive at this conception of the party, we must above all rid ourselves of the very Western, very bourgeois and therefore contemptuous attitude that the masses are incapable of governing themselves. In fact, experience proves that the masses understand perfectly the most complicated problems. One of the greatest services that the Algerian revolution will have rendered to the intellectuals of Algeria will be to have placed them in contact with the people, to have allowed them to see the extreme, ineffable poverty of the people, at the same time allowing them to watch the awakening of the people's intelligence and the onward progress of their consciousness. The Algerian people, that mass of starving illiterates, those men and women plunged for centuries in the most appalling obscurity have held out against tanks and aeroplanes, against napalm and 'psychological services', but above all against corruption and brain-washing, against traitors and against the 'national' armies of General Bellounis. This people has held out in spite of hesitant or feeble individuals, and in spite of would-be dictators. This people has held out because for seven years its struggle has opened up for it vistas that it never dreamed existed. Today, arms factories are working in the midst of the mountains several yards underground; today, the people's tribunals are functioning at every level, and local planning commissions are organizing the division of large-scale holdings, and working out the Algeria of tomorrow. An isolated individual may obstinately refuse to understand a problem, but the group or the village understands with disconcerting rapidity. It is true that if care is taken to use only a language that is understood by graduates in law and economics, you can easily prove that the masses have to be managed from above. But if you speak the language of every day; if you are not obsessed by the perverse desire to spread confusion and to rid yourself of the people, then you will realize that the masses are quick to seize every shade of meaning and to learn all the tricks of the trade. If recourse is had to technical language, this signifies that it has been decided to consider the masses as uninitiated. Such a language is hard put to it to hide the lecturers' wish to cheat the people and to leave them out of things. The business of obscuring language is a mask behind which stands out the much greater business of plunder. The people's property and the people's sovereignty are to be stripped from them at one and the same time. Everything can be explained to the people, on the single condition that you really want them to understand. And if you think that you don't need them, and that on the contrary they may hinder the smooth running of the many limited liability companies whose aim it is to make the people even poorer, then the problem is quite clear.

For if you think that you can manage a country without letting the people interfere, if you think that the people upset the game by their mere presence, whether they slow it down or whether by their natural ignorance they sabotage it, then you must have no hesitation: you must keep the people out. Now, it so happens that when the people are invited to partake in the management of the country, they do not slow the movement down but on the contrary they speed it up. We Algerians have had occasion and the good fortune during the course of this war to handle a fair number of questions. In certain country districts, the politico-military leaders of the revolution found themselves in fact confronted with situations which called for radical solutions. We shall look at some of these situations.

During the years 1956–7, French colonialism had marked off certain zones as forbidden, and within these zones people's movements were strictly controlled. Thus the peasants could no longer go freely to the towns and buy provisions. During this period, the grocers made huge profits. The prices of tea, coffee, sugar, tobacco and salt soared. The black market flourished blatantly. The peasants who could not pay in money mortgaged their crops, in other words their land, or else lopped off field after field of their fathers' farms and during the second phase worked them for the grocer. As soon as the political commissioners realized the danger of the situation they reacted immediately. Thus a rational system of provisioning was instituted: the grocer who went to the town was obliged to buy from nationalist wholesalers who handed him an invoice which clearly showed the prices of the goods. When the retailer got back to the village, before doing anything else he had to go to the political commissioner who checked the invoice, decided on the margin of profit and fixed the price at which the various goods should be sold. However, the retailer soon discovered a new trick, and after three or four days declared that his stocks had run out. In fact, he went on with his business of selling on the black market on the sly. The reaction of the politico-military authorities was thorough-going. Heavy penalizations were decided on, and the fines collected were put into the village funds and used for social purposes or to pay for public works in the general interest. Sometimes it was decided to shut down the shop for a while. Then if there was a repetition of black marketeering, the business was at once confiscated and a managing committee elected to carry it on, which paid a monthly allowance to the former owner.

Taking these experiences as a starting-point, the functioning of the main laws of economics were explained to the people, with concrete examples. The accumulation of capital ceased to be a theory and became a very real and immediate mode of behaviour. The people understood how that once a man was in trade, he could become rich and increase his turnover. Then and then only did the peasants tell the tale of how the grocer gave them loans at exorbitant interest, and others recalled how he evicted them from their land and how from owners they became labourers. The more the people understand, the more watchful they become, and the more they come to realize that finally everything depends on them and their salvation lies in their own cohesion, in the true understanding of their interests and in knowing who are their enemies. The people come to understand that wealth is not the fruit of labour but the result of organized, protected robbery. Rich people are no longer respectable people; they are nothing more than flesh-eating animals, jackals and vultures which wallow in the people's blood. With another end in view the political commissioners have had to decide that nobody will work for anyone else any longer. The land belongs to those that till it. This is a principle which has through explanation become a fundamental law of the Algerian revolution. The peasants who used to employ agricultural labourers have been obliged to give a share of the land to their former employees.

So it may be seen that production per acre trebled, in spite of the many raids by the French, in spite of bombardments from the air, and the difficulty of getting manures. The *fellahs* who at harvest-time were able to judge and weigh the crops thus obtained wanted to know whence came such a phenomenon; and they were quick to understand that the idea of work is not as simple as all that, that slavery is opposed to work, and that work presupposes liberty, responsibility and consciousness.

In those districts where we have been able to carry out successfully these interesting experiments, where we have watched man being created by revolutionary beginnings, the peasants have very clearly caught hold of the idea that the more intelligence you bring to your work, the more pleasure you will have in it. We have been able to make the masses understand that work is not simply the output of energy, nor the functioning of certain muscles, but that people work more by using their brains and their hearts than with only their muscles and their sweat. In the same way in these liberated districts which are at the same time excluded from the old trade routes we have had to modify production, which formerly looked only towards the towns and towards export. We have organized production to meet consumers' needs for the people and for the units of the national army of liberation. We have quadrupled the production of lentils and organized the manufacture of charcoal. Green vegetables and charcoal have been sent through the mountains from the north to the south, whereas the southern districts send meat to the north. This coordination was decided upon by the F.L.N. and they it was who set up the system of communications. We did not have any technicians or planners coming from big Western universities; but in these liberated regions the daily ration went up to the hitherto unheard-of figure of 3,200 calories. The people were not content with coming triumphant out of this test. They started asking themselves theoretical questions: for example, why did certain districts never see an orange before the war of liberation, while thousands of tons are exported every year abroad? Why were grapes unknown to a great many Algerians whereas the European peoples enjoyed them by the million? Today, the people have a very clear notion of what belongs to them. The Algerian people today know that they are the sole owners of the soil and mineral wealth of their country. And if some individuals do not understand the unrelenting refusal of the F.L.N. to tolerate any encroachment on this right of ownership, and its fierce refusal to allow any compromise on principles, they must one and all remember that the Algerian people is today an adult people, responsible and fully conscious of its responsibilities. In short, the Algerians are men of property.

If we have taken the example of Algeria to illustrate our subject, it is not at all with the intention of glorifying our own people, but simply to show the important part played by the war in leading them towards consciousness of themselves. It is clear that other peoples have come to the same conclusion in different ways. We know for sure today that in Algeria the test of force was inevitable; but other countries through political action and through the work of clarification undertaken by a party have led their people to the same results. In Algeria, we have realized that the masses are equal to the problems which confront them. In an under-developed country, experience proves that the important thing is not that three hundred people form a plan and decide upon carrying it out, but that the whole people plan and decide even if it takes them twice or three times as long. The fact is that the time taken up by explaining, the time 'lost' in treating the worker as a human being, will be caught up in the execution of the plan. People must know where they are going, and why. The politician should not ignore the fact that the future remains a closed book so long as the consciousness of the people remains imperfect, elementary and cloudy. We African politicians must have very clear ideas on the situation of our people. But this clarity of ideas must be profoundly dialectical. The awakening of the whole people will not come about at once; the people's work in the building of the nation will not immediately take on its full dimensions: first because the means of communication and transmission are only beginning to be developed; secondly because the yardstick of time must no longer be that of the moment or up till the next harvest, but must become that of the rest of the world, and lastly because the spirit of discouragement which has been deeply rooted in people's minds by colonial domination is still very near the surface. But we must not overlook the fact that victory over those weaknesses which are the heritage of the material and spiritual domination of the country by another is a necessity from which no government will be able to escape. Let us take the example of work under the colonial regime. The settler never stopped complaining that the native is slow. Today, in certain countries which have become independent, we hear the ruling classes taking up the same cry. The fact is that the settler wanted the native to be enthusiastic. By a sort of process of mystification which constitutes the most sublime type of separation from reality, he wanted to persuade the slave that the land that he worked belonged to him, that the mines where he lost his health were owned by him. The settler was singularly forgetful of the fact that he was growing rich through the death-throes of the slave. In fact what the settler was saying to the native was 'Kill yourself that I may become rich'. Today, we must behave in a different fashion. We ought not to say to the people: 'Kill yourselves that the country may become rich.' If we want to increase the national revenue, and decrease the importing of certain products which are useless, or even harmful, if we want to increase agricultural production and overcome illiteracy, we must explain what we are about. The people must understand what is at stake. Public business ought to be the business of the public. So the necessity of creating a large number of well-informed nuclei at the bottom crops up again. Too often, in fact, we are content to establish national organizations at the top and always in the capital: the Women's Union, the Young People's Federation, Trade Unions, etc. But if one takes the trouble to investigate what is behind the office in the capital, if you go into the inner room where the reports ought to be, you will be shocked by the emptiness, the blank spaces, and the bluff. There must be a basis; there must be cells that supply content and life. The masses should be able to meet together, discuss, propose and receive directions. The citizens should be able to speak, to express themselves and to put forward new ideas. The branch meeting and the committee meeting are liturgical acts. They are privileged occasions given to a human being to listen and to speak. At each meeting, the brain increases its means of participation and the eye discovers a landscape more and more in keeping with human dignity.

The large proportion of young people in the under-developed countries raises specific problems for the government, which must be tackled with lucidity. The young people of the towns, idle and often illiterate, are a prey to all sorts of disintegrating influences. It is to the youth of an under-developed country that the industrialized countries most often offer their pastimes. Normally, there is a certain homogeneity between the mental and material level of the members of any given society and the pleasures which that society creates for itself. But in underdeveloped countries, young people have at their disposal leisure occupations designed for the youth of capitalist countries: detective novels, penny-in-the slot machines, sexy photographs, pornographic literature, films banned to those under sixteen, and above all alcohol. In the West, the family circle, the effects of education and the relatively high standard of living of the working classes provide a more or less efficient protection against the harmful action of these pastimes. But in an African country, where mental development is uneven, where the violent collision of two worlds has considerably shaken old traditions and thrown the universe of the perceptions out of focus, the impressionability and sensibility of the young African are at the mercy of the various assaults made upon them by the very nature of Western culture. His family very often proves itself incapable of showing stability and homogeneity when faced with such attacks.

In this domain, the government's duty is to act as a filter and a stabilizer. But the Youth Commissioners in underdeveloped countries often make the mistake of imagining their role to be that of Youth Commissioners in fully developed countries. They speak of strengthening the soul, of developing the body, and of facilitating the growth of sportsmanlike qualities. It is our opinion that they should beware of these conceptions. The young people of an under-developed country are above all idle: occupations must be found for them. For this reason the Youth Commissioners ought for practical purposes to be attached to the Ministry for Labour. The Ministry for Labour, which is a prime necessity in an under-developed country, functions in collaboration with the Ministry for Planning, which is another necessary institution in under-developed countries. The youth of Africa ought not to be sent to sports stadiums but into the fields and into the schools. The stadium ought not to be a show place erected in the towns, but a bit of open ground in the midst of the fields that the young people must reclaim, cultivate and give to the nation. The capitalist conception of sport is fundamentally different from that which should exist in an under-developed country. The African politician should not be preoccupied with turning out sportsmen, but with turning out fully conscious men, who play games as well. If games are not integrated into the national life, that is to say in the building of the nation, and if you turn out national sportsmen and not fully conscious men, you will very quickly see sport rotted by professionalism and commercialism. Sport should not be a pastime or a distraction for the bourgeoisie of the towns. The greatest task before us is to understand at each moment what is happening in our country. We ought not to cultivate the exceptional or to seek for a hero, who is another form of leader. We ought to uplift the people; we must develop their brains, fill them with ideas, change them and make them into human beings.

We once more come up against that obsession of ours – which we would like to see shared by all African politicians – about the need for effort to be well-informed, for work which is enlightened and free from its historic intellectual darkness. To hold a responsible position in an under-developed country is to know that in the end everything depends on the education of the masses, on the raising of the level of thought, and on what we are too quick to call 'political teaching'.

In fact, we often believe with criminal superficiality that to educate the masses politically is to deliver a long political harangue from time to time. We think that it is enough that the leader or one of his lieutenants should speak in a pompous tone about the principle events of the day for them to have fulfilled this bounden duty to educate the masses politically. Now, political education means opening their minds, awakening them, and allowing the birth of their intelligence; as Césaire said, it is 'to invent souls'. To educate the masses politically does not mean, cannot mean making a political speech. What it means is to try, relentlessly and passionately, to teach the masses that everything depends on them; that if we stagnate it is their responsibility, and that if we go forward it is due to them too, that there is no such thing as a demiurge, that there is no famous man who will take the responsibility for everything, but that the demiurge is the people themselves and the magic hands are finally only the hands of the people. In order to put all this into practice, in order really to incarnate the people, we repeat that there must be decentralization in the extreme. The movement from the top to the bottom and from the bottom to the top should be a fixed principle, not through concern for formalism but because simply to respect this principle is the guarantee of salvation. It is from the base that forces mount up which supply the summit with its dynamic, and make it possible dialectically for it to leap ahead. Once again we Algerians have been quick to understand these facts, for no member of the government at the head of any recognized state has had the chance of availing himself of such a mission of salvation. For it is the rank-and-file who are fighting in Algeria, and the rank-and-file know well that without their daily struggle, hard and heroic as it is, the summit would collapse; and in the same way those at the bottom know that without a head and without leadership the base would split apart in incoherence and anarchy. The summit only draws its worth and its strength from the existence of the people at war. Literally, it is the people who freely create a summit for themselves, and not the summit that tolerates the people.

The masses should know that the government and the party are at their service. A deserving people, in other words a people conscious of its dignity, is a people that never forgets these facts. During the colonial occupation the people were told that they must give their lives so that dignity might triumph. But the African peoples quickly came to understand that it was not only the occupying power that threatened their dignity. The African peoples were quick to realize that dignity and sovereignty were exact equivalents, and, in fact, a free people living in dignity is a sovereign people. It is no use demonstrating that the African peoples are childish or weak. A government or a party gets the people it deserves and sooner or later a people gets the government it deserves.

Practical experience in certain regions confirms this point of view. It sometimes happens at meetings that militants use sweeping, dogmatic formulae. The preference for this shortcut, in which spontaneity and over-simple sinking of differences dangerously combine to defeat intellectual elaboration, frequently triumphs. When we meet this shirking of responsibility in a militant it is not enough to tell him he is wrong. We must make him ready for responsibility, encourage him to follow up his chain of reasoning and make him realize the true nature, often shocking, inhuman and in the long run sterile, of such oversimplification.

Nobody, neither leader nor rank-and-file, can hold back the truth. The search for truth in local attitudes is a collective affair. Some are richer in experience, and elaborate their thought more rapidly, and in the past have been able to establish a greater number of mental links. But they ought to avoid riding roughshod over the people, for the success of the decision which is adopted depends upon the coordinated, conscious effort of the whole of the people. No one can get out of the situation scot free. Everyone will be butchered or tortured; and in the framework of the independent nation everyone will go hungry and everyone will suffer in the slump. The collective struggle presupposes collective responsibility at the base and collegiate responsibility at the top. Yes; everybody will have to be compromised in the fight for the common good. No one has clean hands; there are no innocents and no onlookers. We all have dirty hands; we are all soiling them in the swamps of our country and in the terrifying emptiness of our brains. Every onlooker is either a coward or a traitor.

The duty of those at the head of the movement is to have the masses behind them. Allegiance presupposes awareness and understanding of the mission which has to be fulfilled; in short, an intellectual position, however embryonic. We must not voodoo the people, nor dissolve them in emotion and confusion. Only those under-developed countries led by revolutionary *élites* who have come up from the people can today allow the entry of the masses upon the scene of history. But, we must repeat, it is absolutely necessary to oppose vigorously and definitively the birth of a national bourgeoisie and a privileged caste. To educate the masses politically is to make the totality of the nation a reality to each citizen. It is to make the history of the nation part of the personal experience of each of its citizens. As President Sékou Touré aptly remarked in his message to the second congress of African writers:

> In the realm of thought, man may claim to be the brain of the world; but in real life where every action affects spiritual and physical existence, the world is always the brain of mankind; for it is at this level that you will find the sum total of the powers and units of thought, and the dynamic forces of development and improvement; and it is there that energies are merged and the sum of man's intellectual values is finally added together.

Individual experience, because it is national and because it is a link in the chain of national existence, ceases to be individual, limited and shrunken and is enabled to open out into the truth of the nation and of the world. In the same way that during the period of armed struggle each fighter held the fortune of the nation in his hand, so during the period of national construction each citizen ought to continue in his real, everyday activity to associate himself with the whole of the nation, to incarnate the continuous dialectical truth of the nation and to will the triumph of man in his completeness here and now. If the building of a bridge does not enrich the awareness of those who work on it, then that bridge ought not to be built and the citizens can go on swimming across the river or going by boat. The bridge should not be 'parachuted down' from above; it should not be imposed by a *deus ex machina* upon the social scene; on the contrary it should come from the muscles and the brains of the citizens. Certainly, there may well be need of engineers and architects, sometimes completely foreign engineers and architects; but the local party leaders should be always present, so that the new techniques can make their way into the cerebral desert of the citizen, so that the bridge in whole and in part can be taken up and conceived, and the responsibility for it assumed by the citizen. In this way, and in this way only, everything is possible.

A government which calls itself a national government ought to take responsibility for the totality of the nation; and in an under-developed country the young people represent one of the most important sectors. The level of consciousness of young people must be raised; they need enlightenment. If the work of explanation had been carried on among the youth of the nation, and if the Young People's National Union had carried out its task of integrating them into the nation, those mistakes would have been avoided which have threatened or already undermined the future of the Latin American Republics. The army is not always a school of war; more often, it is a school of civic and political education. The soldier of an adult nation is not a simple mercenary but a citizen who by means of arms defends the nation. That is why it is of fundamental importance that the soldier should know that he is in the service of his country and not in the service of his commanding officer, however great that officer's prestige may be. We must take advantage of the national military and civil service in order to raise the level of the national consciousness, and to detribalize and unite the nation. In an under-developed country every effort is made to mobilize men and women as quickly as possible; it must guard against the danger of perpetuating the feudal tradition which holds sacred the superiority of the masculine element over the feminine. Women will have exactly the same place as men, not in the clauses of the constitution but in the life of every day: in the factory, at school and in the parliament. If in the Western countries men are shut up in barracks, that is not to say that this is always the best procedure. Recruits need not necessarily be militarized. The national service may be civil or military, and in any case it is advisable that every able-bodied citizen can at any moment take his place in a fighting unit for the defence of national and social liberties.

It should be possible to carry out large-scale undertakings in the public interest by using recruited labour. This is a marvellous way of stirring up inert districts and of making known to a greater number of citizens the needs of their country. Care must be taken to avoid turning the army into an autonomous body which sooner or later, finding itself idle and without any definite mission, will 'go into politics' and threaten the government. Drawing-room generals, by dint of haunting the corridors of government departments, come to dream of manifestoes. The only way to avoid this menace is to educate the army politically, in other words to nationalize it. In the same way another urgent task is to increase the militia. In case of war, it is the whole nation which fights and works. It should not include any professional soldiers, and the number of permanent officers should be reduced to a minimum. This is in the first place because officers are very often chosen from the university class, who could be much more useful elsewhere; an engineer is a thousand times more indispensable to his country than an officer; and secondly, because the crystallization of the caste spirit must be avoided. We have seen in the preceding pages that nationalism, that magnificent song that made the people rise against their oppressors, stops short, falters and dies away on the day that independence is proclaimed. Nationalism is not a political doctrine, nor a programme. If you really wish your country to avoid regression, or at best halts and uncertainties, a rapid step must be taken from national consciousness to political and social consciousness. The nation does not exist except in a programme which has been worked out by revolutionary leaders and taken up with full understanding and enthusiasm by the masses. The nation's effort must constantly be adjusted into the general background of underdeveloped countries. The battle-line against hunger, against ignorance, against poverty and against unawareness ought to be ever present in the muscles and the intelligences of men and women. The work of the masses and their will to overcome the evils which have for centuries excluded them from the mental achievements of the past ought to be grafted on to the work and will of all under-developed peoples. On the level of underdeveloped humanity there is a kind of collective effort, a sort of common destiny. The news which interests the Third World does not deal with King Baudouin's marriage nor the scandals of the Italian ruling class. What we want to hear about are the experiments carried out by the Argentinians or the Burmese in their efforts to overcome illiteracy or the dictatorial tendencies of their leaders. It is these things which strengthen us, teach us and increase our efficiency ten times over. As we see it, a programme is necessary for a government which really wants to free the people politically and socially. There must be an economic programme; there must also be a doctrine concerning the division of wealth and social relations. In fact, there must be an idea of man and of the future of humanity; that is to say that no demagogic formula and no collusion with the former occupying power can take the place of a programme. The new peoples, unawakened at first but soon becoming more and more clear-minded, will make strong demands for this programme. The African people and indeed all under-developed peoples, contrary to common belief, very quickly build up a social and political consciousness. What can be dangerous is when they reach the stage of social consciousness before the stage of nationalism. If this happens, we find in under-developed countries fierce demands for social justice which paradoxically are allied with often primitive tribalism. The under-developed peoples behave like starving creatures; this means that the end is very near for those who are having a good time in Africa. Their government will not be able to prolong its own existence indefinitely. A bourgeoisie that provides nationalism alone as food for the masses fails in its mission and gets caught up in a whole series of mishaps. But if nationalism is not made explicit, if it is not enriched and deepened by a very rapid transformation into a consciousness of social and political needs, in other words into humanism, it leads up a blind alley. The bourgeois leaders of under-developed countries imprison national consciousness in sterile formalism. It is only when men and women are included on a vast scale in enlightened and fruitful work that form and body are given to that consciousness. Then the flag and the palace where sits the government cease to be the symbols of the nation. The nation deserts these brightly lit, empty shells and takes shelter in the country, where it is given life and dynamic power. The living expression of the nation is the moving consciousness of the whole of the people; it is the coherent, enlightened action of men and women. The collective building up of a destiny is the assumption of responsibility on the historical scale. Otherwise there is anarchy, repression and the resurgence of tribal parties and federalism. The national government, if it wants to be national, ought to govern by the people and for the people, for the outcasts and by the outcasts. No leader, however valuable he may be, can substitute himself for the popular will; and the national government, before concerning itself about international prestige, ought first to give back their dignity to all citizens, fill their minds and feast their eyes with human things, and create a prospect that is human because conscious and sovereign men dwell therein.

Notes
1. Mamadou Dia, *Nations Africaines et Solidarité Mondial* (Paris: Presses Universitaires de France, 1960), 140.
2. Ibid.

CARIBBEAN INTERNATIONALISMS

Dialectical Materialism and the Fate of Humanity

C.L.R. James

Mankind has obviously reached the end of something. The crisis is absolute. Bourgeois civilisation is falling apart, and even while it collapses, devotes its main energies to the preparation of further holocausts. Not remote states on the periphery but regimes contending for world power achieve the most advanced stages of barbarism known to history. What civilised states have ever approached Nazi Germany and Stalinist Russia in official lies, official murder and the systematic brutalisation and corruption of their population? Only a shallow empiricism can fail to see that such monstrous societies are not the product of a national peculiarity (the German character) or a system of government ("communism") but are part and parcel of our civilisation. Everything that has appeared in these monstrous societies is endemic in every contemporary nation. Millions in the United States know that Nazi Germany and Stalinist Russia will have nothing to teach the American bourgeoisie when it finds itself threatened by the revolutionary American workers seeking the complete expression of democracy which is socialism. The dream of progress has become the fear of progress. Men shrink with terror at the hint of scientific discoveries. If it were known tomorrow that the crown of human technical achievement, the processes of manufacturing atomic energy, had been lost beyond recovery, this scientific disaster would be hailed as the greatest good fortune of decades.

But the seal of the bankruptcy of bourgeois civilisation is the bankruptcy of its thought. Its intellectuals run to and fro squealing like hens in a barnyard when a plane passes overhead. Not a single philosopher or publicist has any light to throw on a crisis in which the fate not of a civilisation but of civilisation itself is involved. The Keynesian theories are now part of the history of economics. The ridiculous "four freedoms" of the late President Roosevelt take their place with the Three Principles of Sun Yat-Sen (the father-in-law of Chiang Kai-shek), the thousand years of Hitler's Reich and the "socialism in a single country" of Stalin. The chattering of Sidney Hook and Harold Laski is stunned into silence by the immensity of their own inadequacies. Thought has abdicated. The world is rudderless. All illusions have been destroyed. "Man is at last compelled to face with sober sense his real conditions of life, and his relations with his kind." And in face of this the bourgeoisie has nothing to say.

The method of thinking is rooted in society. Bourgeois thought has collapsed because bourgeois society has collapsed. We have learnt by hard necessity the truth of the following dictum of Trotsky: "Hegel in his *Logic* established a series of laws: change of quantity into quality, development through contradictions, conflict of content and form, interruption of continuity, change of possibility into inevitability, etc., which are just as important for theoretical thought as is the simple syllogism for more elementary tasks." (Trotsky, *In Defence of Marxism.*)

Hegel defines the principle of Contradiction as follows: "Contradiction is the root of all movement and life, and it is only in so far as it contains a contradiction that anything moves and has impulse and activity." (*Science of Logic*, translated by Johnson and Struthers, volume 2, page 67.) The first thing to note is that Hegel makes little attempt to prove this. A few lines later he says: "With regard to the assertion that contradiction does not exist, that it is non-existent, we may disregard this statement."

We here meet one of the most important principles of the dialectical logic, and one that has been consistently misunderstood, vilified or lied about. Dialectic for Hegel was a strictly scientific method. He might speak of inevitable laws, but he insists from the beginning that the proof of dialectic as scientific method is that the laws prove their correspondence with reality. Marx's dialectic is of the same character. Thus he excluded what later became *The Critique of Political Economy* from *Capital* because it took for granted what only the detailed argument and logical development of *Capital* could prove. Still more specifically, in his famous letter to Kugelmann on the theory of value, he ridiculed the idea of having to "prove" the labour theory of value. If the labour theory of value proved to be the means whereby the real relations of bourgeois society could be demonstrated in their movement, where they came from, what they were, and where they were going, that was the proof of the theory. Neither Hegel nor Marx understood any other scientific proof. To ask for some proof of the laws, as Burnham implied, or to prove them "wrong" as Sidney Hook tried to do, this is to misconceive dialectical logic entirely. Hegel complicated the question by his search for a completely closed system embracing all aspects of the universe; this no Marxist ever did. The frantic shrieks that Marx's dialectic is some sort of religion or teleological construction, proving inevitably the victory of socialism, spring usually from men who are frantically defending the inevitability of bourgeois democracy against the proletarian revolution.

So convinced a Marxist as Trotsky reminded the revolutionaries in 1939 that Marxists were not fatalists. "If'", said he, "the international proletariat, as a result of the experience of our entire epoch and the current new war, proves incapable of becoming the master of society, this would signify the foundering of all hope for a socialist revolution, for it is impossible to expect any other more favourable condition for it." The Marxian expectation of socialism arising from the contradictions of capitalism would have proved itself to be utopia.

The law of contradiction is what for the moment we can call a "hypothesis" for the grouping of empirical facts. All men use hypotheses for the grouping of facts. That is what logic consists of. The bourgeois hypotheses are for the most part unconscious. They are the inevitability of bourgeois society, natural division of labour, more particularly of men into capitalists and workers, constantly expanding technical progress, constantly expanding production, constantly expanding democracy, constantly rising culture. But during the last thirty years, these have crumbled to dust in their hands. They have no hypotheses they can believe in and that is why they cannot think. Historical facts, large and small, continuously deliver shattering blows at the foundation of their logical system. Nothing remains for them but the logic of the machine gun, and the crude empiricism of police violence.

Quite different is the mode of thought of Marxism. It understands its own logical laws. For Marxists, the fundamental logical law is the contradictory nature of all phenomena and first of all human society. The dialectic teaches that in all forms of society we have known, the increasing development of material wealth brings with it the increasing degradation of the large mass of humanity. Capitalism, being the greatest wealth-producing system so far known, has carried its contradictions to a pitch never known before. Thus it is that the moment when the world system of capitalism has demonstrated the greatest productive powers in history is exactly the period when barbarism threatens to engulf the whole of society. The anti-dialecticians stand absolutely dumbfounded before the spectacle of the mastery of nature for human advancement and the degradation of human nature by this very mastery. The greater the means of transport, the less men are allowed to travel. The greater the means of communication, the less men freely interchange ideas. The greater the possibilities of living, the more men live in terror of mass annihilation. The bourgeoisie cannot admit this, for to admit it is themselves to sanction the end of the bourgeois civilisation. Hence the complete paralysis of bourgeois thought. Yet never was thought of a fundamental character so necessary to mankind. As our political tendency has recently written:

> It is precisely the character of our age and the maturity of humanity that obliterates the opposition between theory and practice, between the intellectual preoccupations of the "educated" and of the masses. All the great philosophical concepts, from the nature of the physical universe (atomic energy) through the structure and function of productive systems (free enterprise, "socialism", or "communism"), the nature of government (the state versus the individual), to the destiny of man (can mankind survive?), these are no longer "theory", but are in the market-place, tied together so that they cannot be separated, matters on which the daily lives of millions upon millions depend (*The Invading Socialist Society*).

Never were such universal questions asked by the whole of the civilised world. Never have such inadequate answers been given. All that the bourgeoisie can answer is the purely technical question of the manufacture of atomic energy, and it wishes that it could not.

Now it is precisely because this contradiction of society has reached its farthest point in Stalinist Russia that the dialectical materialist analysis of Russia is the most important key to the perspective of world civilisation.

The second law of dialectical materialism is the change of quantity into quality. At a certain stage a developing contradiction, so to speak, explodes, and both the elements of contradiction are thereby altered. In the history of society these explosions are known as revolution. All the economic, social and political tendencies of the age find a point of completion which becomes the starting-point of new tendencies. The Russian revolution is one such explosion. But the examination of the Russian revolution involves both the laws of development through contradictions and the change of quantity into quality.

Let us examine the Russian revolution in some of its most important features, such as would be agreed upon by most observers, excepting the diehard reactionaries.

The revolution was the greatest outburst of social energy and creativity that we have yet seen. Previously the French revolution had astonished mankind by the rapidity and grandeur of its achievements. So much so that to this day 14 July 1789 is the date in all probability most widely known among the great majority of mankind. But the Russian revolution exceeded the

French. A combination of workers and peasants, the lowest classes of mankind, tore up an established government by the roots and accomplished the greatest social overturn in history. Starting from nothing, they created a new state, created an army of millions, defended the new regime against famine, blockade and wars of intervention on all fronts. They reorganised the economy. They made Russia a modern state. They passed and tried honestly to carry out a series of laws on popular education, equality of women, repudiation of religious superstition, sexual sanity, workers' control of production, all of which constituted the greatest potential democracy and enlightenment that the world had ever seen. They organised a world-wide Communist International devoted to the achievement of the same ideals in the entire world. The gradual decline and final failure are treated in the text. But the accomplishments are history, imperishable and of permanent significance for mankind. Taken in its entirety the heroic period of the Russian revolution is the most glorious episode in human history.

Lenin, the leader of the revolution, claimed always that one of the greatest achievements was the establishment of a new type of democracy, the Soviets of Workers', Soldiers' and Peasants' Deputies, which was able to unloose the creative energies of the great masses of the people. Their mere administration of the state in his opinion would make the further existence of capitalism impossible. This administration by the masses is "not yet" socialism, but it is no longer capitalism. "It is a tremendous step towards socialism, a step from which, if complete democracy is retained, no backward step towards capitalism would be possible without the most atrocious violence perpetrated upon the masses" (*The Threatening Catastrophe*).

Capital, in the form of state capital, once more rules in Russia. Democracy has not been retained. But this has been done only at the cost of the condition foreseen by Lenin. The most atrocious violence has been perpetrated upon the masses of the people. Thus, the Russian revolution, as it has developed and declined, shows us the two most violent extremes that we have known in history. It is only dialectical materialism that can unite these extremes in logical and intelligible connection. It is the creative power, the democratic desires, the expansion of human personality, the record of achievement that was the Russian revolution. It is these which have called forth the violence, the atrocities, the state organised as Murder Incorporated. Only such violence could have repressed such democracy.

One can see the glint in the eye of the enemy of the proletarian revolution. Without perspective, himself, intellectually helpless before the contemporary barbarism, indulging in nonsensical opposites like Yogis and Commissars, or searching diligently in his own writhing insides for the solution to the problems of the world, he hastens to use the fact of the Russian degeneration as an unanswerable argument against the ideas of Bolshevism. Patience, my friend, patience. "Bolshevism", says Trotsky, "is above all a philosophy of history and a political conception." Without the philosophy, the political conception falls to the ground. We have to get to the philosophy step by step. We have arrived at this much. The atrocious violence and crimes which now distinguish the state of Stalin are the necessary and inevitable response to the revolutionary fervour and democratic organisation and expression of the Russian people. Not the Russian people in general, however, but the Russian people as they had developed and expressed themselves in the socialist revolution of 1917. This is not merely a Russian phenomenon. The Russian revolution is a climax to a series of revolutions which have moved according to certain laws. Briefly: The British revolution in the seventeenth century embraced only small sections of the population—some revolutionary bourgeois, petty-bourgeois farmers and yeomen and a small number of artisans, and others in the few and small towns. They could not create the new but they could destroy the old. The work of the revolution having been accomplished the counter-revolution, heir to the new social order, established itself by a mere invitation to Charles II to return. A handful of people only were punished. With the development of economy and its socialisation, i.e. the increasing inter-relation of all classes in production, the French revolution embraces the great mass of the nation. The revolution destroys feudalism and establishes the modern state. Its basic work accomplished, "order" must be restored to society by the counter-revolution, the heirs to the new regime, but this time there are millions of aroused people. It is the great body of the nation which is to be disciplined. No mild return of royalty, no forgiveness, no mutual amnesty. Only the military police-dictatorship of Napoleon can hold this country down. The contradiction between the revolution and the counter-revolution has sharpened.

Society established itself on new foundations. Bur the contradiction between the classes grows. If the revolution in Russia was the broadest and deepest development of the revolution of the seventeenth century, the Stalinist regime is the similar development of the counter-revolution. The German revolution of 1918 did not overthrow bourgeois property. But the German proletariat, infinitely larger and more highly developed than the Russian, had a long history of democratic achievement and organisation behind it. After the revolution, its organisation continued and expanded. That is why the Nazi counter-revolution was as brutal as it was. But if the German proletariat in 1918 had established a Soviet state embracing workers, agricultural proletarians and semi-proletarians, the lower ranks of the petty-bourgeoisie and the sympathetic intelligentsia, then logically speaking one of two things would have happened. Either the new democratic formation would have gone on from strength to strength awakening the deepest reserves of social power and aspirations of the already highly-developed German people and spreading throughout Europe; either this or something else. The atrocities and the violence which would have been needed to suppress a successful German proletarian revolution and the response it would have awakened in the German and other European peoples would have exceeded the crimes of Hitler as much as Hitler exceeded the crimes of Napoleon.

The pervading barbarism of the Stalinist regime, therefore, is not to be attributed to this or that weakness in the theory of "communism", or some partial aspect of the Stalinist state. Stage by stage, we have seen the revolution and the counter-revolution develop in Europe over the centuries. At each new stage of development, both the revolution and the counter-revolution assume a new quality with the new quality of the social development. Precisely because the Russian revolution assumed a new quality in attempting to establish a universal democracy, the Russian counter-revolution assumes a new quality of universal barbarism in the sense that it embraces all aspects of the Russian state.

At this stage, to try to separate progressive aspects from so comprehensive and all-pervading an enemy of human development as is the Stalinist state, is to strike down the dialectical method at the root. Hegel understood the limits within which one could designate a corruption as partial:

> The Reformation resulted from the *corruption of the Church*. That corruption was not an accidental phenomenon; it is not the mere *abuse* of power and domination. A corrupt state of things is very frequently represented as an "abuse"; it is taken for granted that the foundation was good—the system, the institution itself faultless—but that the passion, the subjective interest, in short the arbitrary volition of men has made use of that which in itself was good to further its own selfish ends, and that all that is required to be done is to remove these adventitious elements. On this showing the institute in question escapes obloquy, and the evil that disfigures it appears something foreign to it. But when accidental abuse of a good thing really occurs it is limited to particularity. A great and general corruption affecting a body of such large and comprehensive scope as a Church is quite another thing. ... The corruption of the Church was a native growth (*Philosophy of History*).

The Russian revolution is the completion of a historical process, the development of class society. Its relation to past revolution can be illuminated by the laws of changes of quantity into quality. The British revolution, although it pointed the road for the rest of Europe, was only to a subordinate degree of international significance. The French revolution shook the whole of Europe to its foundations and established the logical lines along which revolution and counter-revolution would struggle in Europe for the succeeding century. It is in the very nature of modern society and the Russian revolution that Russia today is symbolical of the whole fate of modern civilisation. There is no further stage. Either the revolution succeeds in encompassing the whole of the world or the whole of the world collapses in counter-revolution and barbarism. The whole path of Western civilisation for two thousand years has reached an ultimate stage in Russia. There is no by-pass. There is no third alternative.

Therefore, as dialectical materialists, we do not bewail nor do we underestimate or in any way attempt to minimise the monstrous character of the Stalinist regime. We repudiate utterly any idea that what is there has any socialist character whatever. But we draw from it for Russia itself and for the whole world an ultimate, a universal conclusion. The barbarism is not to come. It is there.

In our previously quoted pamphlet, we have written:

> The unending murders, the destruction of peoples, the bestial passions, the sadism, the cruelties and the lusts, all the manifestations of barbarism of the last thirty years are unparalleled in history. But this barbarism exists only because nothing else can suppress the readiness for sacrifice, the democratic instincts and creative power of the great masses of the people.

Those are the two forces in conflict. The philosophy of history which is Bolshevism bases itself upon the destruction of the barbarism by the inevitable triumph of the socialist revolution. There are even revolutionaries who deny this. For them it is not scientific to believe in inevitability. Such a belief implies that dialectic is a religion or mysticism. For them the correct scientific attitude is to reserve judgement. Yet these very ones turn out to be the mystics and the practitioners of an ill-concealed religiosity. If they recognise the bankruptcy of bourgeois democracy, if they accept the need for universality in the masses, if they recognise that barbarism is the only force that can suppress this need, then to refuse to accept the inevitability of socialism leaves only one of two choices. Either the inevitability of barbarism, that is to say, the acceptance of the principle of inevitability which they have just rejected or the hope, the faith, the belief that history will offer some way out of the impasse. This is the denial of a philosophy of history, that is to say, the denial of a method of thought, for which the only name is irrationalism or mysticism.

The deniers of the inevitability of socialism can be routed both historically and logically.

Marx developed his philosophical doctrines in the years which preceded the 1848 revolutions. The revolution was obviously on the way. Yet society was dominated by the experience of the great French revolution which had achieved such miracles but had failed to achieve universality (liberty, equality and fraternity), and despite all its sacrifices and bloodshed, had ended in the triumph of the counter-revolution. The experience of 1830 had only multiplied both the fears and the hopes which had been engendered by the colossal experience of the French revolution. In this period, so similar to ours, philosophy came out of the study, particularly in Germany, and attempted to give some answers to the problems that were shaking society.

The utopian socialists of all stripes were distinguished precisely by this, that they argued interminably about the possibility as opposed to the inevitability of the socialist revolution. They were tortured by these doubts because, after the experience of the French revolution and its obvious failure to relieve the conditions of the great masses of the people, they themselves had lost faith in the inevitability of socialism. Which is only another way of saying the inevitability of the achievement by the people of complete self-expression, complete democracy, socialism. In so far as their beliefs were the result of theoretical speculation, they had, in the words of Marx, lost the capacity to draw from the experience of man's past in order to establish perspectives for man's future.

The result was a complete chaos, disorder, confusion in their own thoughts with an absolute inability to meet the challenge of the approaching revolution. It was into this ulcer that Marx drove the knife of scientific socialism. Bolshevism is a philosophy of history. Marx first clarified himself philosophically. As he wrote to Ruge in 1843:

> Almost greater than the outer obstacles appear in the inner difficulties. For although there is no doubt about the "whence", there prevails the more confusion about the "whither". Not only has a general anarchy broken out among the reformers; each of them also must himself confess that he has no exact conception of what ought to be. Precisely in this is the advantage of the new movement, that we do not anticipate the new world dogmatically but intend to find the new in the criticism of the old world. Up to now the philosophers have had the solution of all riddles lying in their desks and the dumb exoteric world had only to gape in order for the ready-baked pies of wisdom to fly into their mouths. Philosophy has become worldly, and the most decisive proof of this is that philosophic consciousness has been drawn into the anguish of the struggle not only superficially but thoroughly.

If the construction of the future and the preparation for all time is not our affair, it is all the more certain what we have to complete at present, i.e., the most relentless criticism of all existing things, relentless both in the sense that the criticism fears no results and even less fears conflicts with the existing powers.

We face the same situation today in the radical and revolutionary movement. In 1947, however, not only is philosophy worldly. In the face of the universal character of the crisis the world is driven to become philosophical. It is compelled to examine in their nature and in the totality of their relations (that is to say, philosophically), economics, politics, science and even the very nature of the universe and society. All agitation about the possibility of barbarism, third alternatives, the mysticism of the inevitability of socialism, these are no more than what they were in Marx's day, only infinitely more so: terror before the destructive contradictions of modern society, doubts of the capacity of the proletariat to resolve them. This amounts to no more than a defence of bourgeois society in so far as bourgeois society still can provide thinkers with freedom enough to substitute the analysis of their own thoughts for a positive intervention in the chaos of society.

So far historically. Logically, the inevitability of socialism is the absolute reverse of religion or mysticism. It is a consciously constructed necessity of thought. As we have quoted in the article on *Historical Retrogression*, Hegel recognised that without holding fast in thought to your ultimate goal, it is impossible to think properly.

> To hold fast the positive in its negative, and the content of the presupposition in the result, is the most important part of rational cognition: also only the simplest reflection is needed to furnish conviction of the absolute truth and necessity of this requirement, while with regard to the examples of proofs, the whole of Logic consists of these. (*Logic*, vol. II, p. 476).

Precisely because they held fast to the presupposition of the inevitability of bourgeois society, the bourgeois thinkers in the early days of capitalism made their tremendous contributions to the science of human thought. Even without philosophical perspective, the bourgeoisie at least has one reality, maintenance of power against the workers and rival bourgeoisies. But without presupposing the inevitability of socialism, that is to say, without thinking always in terms of the victory of the masses, thinking among those hostile to bourgeois society must become a form of scholasticism and gnosticism, self-agitation and caprice.

Over a hundred years ago, Hegel said that the simplest reflection will show the necessity of holding fast the positive in the negative, the presupposition in the result, the affirmation that is contained in every negation, the future that is in the present. It is one of the signs of the advanced stage of human development that this is not longer a mere philosophical but a concrete question. To anyone that does not accept bourgeois society, the simplest reflection shows that it is impossible not only to think but to take any kind of sustained positive action in the world today unless one postulates the complete victory of the great masses of the people. What is this but the exemplification in life of the logical theory, the inevitability of socialism?

The Stalinist state, the Nazi state, and in their varying degrees all states today, based upon property and privilege, are the negation of the complete democracy of the people. It is this state which is to be destroyed, that is to say, it is this state which is to be negated by the proletarian revolution. Thus, the inevitability of socialism is the inevitability of the negation of the negation, the third and most important law of the dialectic.

I have said earlier that the laws of the dialectic are "hypotheses". Any Deweyite pragmatist who is rubbing his hands with joy at this "reasonable" Marxism is in for rude disillusionment.

"Dialectics", said Lenin, "is the theory of knowledge of (Hegel and) Marxism." So far I have been dealing with it as a theory of knowledge, as a mode of thought, examining more or less empirically contemporary society and the Russian revolution, and showing how by means of the dialectical approach, some order, some perspective, some understanding come out of them, showing equally why the bourgeoisie can make no sense of anything except to hold on to power.

But Marx's hypotheses were not hypotheses in general. They were not empirically arrived at, tentatively used, discarded if not satisfactory, experimental or instrumentalist. They were logical abstractions organised according to the *method* of Hegel and reflecting *the movement of human society*. This is no simple matter. But it has remained obscured and neglected too long.

The dialectic is a theory of knowledge, but precisely for that reason, it is a theory of the nature of man. Hegel and Marxism did not first arrive at a theory of knowledge which they applied to nature and society. They arrived at a theory of knowledge from their examination of men in society. Their first question was: What is man? What is the *truth* about him? Where has he come from and where is he going? They answered that question first because they knew that without any answer to that general question, they could not think about particular questions.

Both Hegel and Marx in their different ways believed that man is destined for freedom and happiness. *They* did not wish this (or they did, that does not matter). They came to this conclusion by examining man's history as a totality. Man for Marx was not Christian man nor the man of the French revolution (nor Stalin's bloodstained secret police). The concept of man was a constantly developing idea which was headed for some sort of completeness. When Marx said that with the achievement of the socialist revolution the "real" history of humanity will begin, he was not being rhetorical or inspiring (or optimistic). He was being strictly and soberly scientific.

> The truth is the whole. The whole, however, is merely the essential nature reaching its completeness through the process of its own development. Of the Absolute it must be said that it is essentially a result, that only at the end is it what it is in very truth.

Thus Hegel in the *Phenomenology of Mind;* Marx worked on the sample principles. The essential nature of man was becoming clear only as it approached its completeness in bourgeois society. It is in bourgeois society that we could see what man really is. And it is "only at the end" of bourgeois society that we can see what man is in very truth. Thus it is in the contemporary barbarism that can be seen most clearly what is the "real" nature of humanity. The need and desire for socialism, for complete democracy, for complete freedom, that is the "real" nature of man. It is this which explains his past. But it could be expressed within the concrete circumstances of past ages only to the degree that objective circumstances allowed. Did man, therefore, suffer through all those centuries to produce completed man? The defenders of bourgeois society are ready to defend and rage over all these unjustified sufferings of past mankind in their die-hard opposition to the proletarian revolution which will relieve present mankind. They will get nothing to comfort themselves with. "The truth is the whole." All the various stages constitute the nature of man. Continues Hegel: "And just in that consists its nature, which is to be actual, subject or self-becoming, self-development."

Man is the subject, that which is developing itself. The subject becomes more and more real, and therefore the truth about man becomes deeper and wider, more universal, more complex, more concrete. Complete universality, complete democracy in the sense that every man is able to do what every other man does, this is the ultimate stage. The Russian revolution was an imperfect, limited, handicapped but nevertheless decisive step in this direction. The nature of man, therefore, becomes the search for this completeness and the overcoming of the obstacles which stood and stand in its way. Past history therefore becomes intelligible and what is more important, the road to the solution of the overwhelming problems to the present day becomes open.

If today we say that now we know what is the "real" man, it is because we see him as a totality, as the result of his whole past. But from there we make another step. The terrible crisis of civilisation is the result of the fact that man is at last real, he has become himself, completely developed. But the old type of world which developed him cannot contain him. He must burst through it. That world was a world in which he was subjected to nature. It was in the subjection of nature that he fully realised himself, a continuous negation of the obstacles which impeded his development. That being accomplished, his real history will begin. He negates all that has previously impeded him, i.e. negated him, in the full realisation of his inherent nature. Socialism is the negation of all previous negations. It is obvious that these are large conceptions. But the death of a world civilisation is not a small thing.

The conception being stated, it is now necessary not to prove it (only life can do that) but to show where it came from.

Western civilisation, and therefore, the Hegelian dialectic begins with Christianity.[1] It was Christianity which established universality in its most abstract form, that very universality which we are now seeing concretely striving for expression in the proletariat all over the contemporary world. The very early or "primitive" Christians attempted a universality that was extremely concrete, commonalty of goods and absolute equality. But it soon collapsed. The abstract universality was established by that historical Christianity which superseded the Roman Empire. Christianity united all men, before birth, in the universality of original sin, and after death, in the possibility of universal redemption in heaven. Thus it carefully avoided a concrete universality. It was the religion of the millions who had been released from slavery by the collapse of the Roman Empire. The narrow straitened circumstances of their material lives were compensated for by the subjective conception of an after-life in which all their material needs would be satisfied or, better still, there would be no need for material satisfactions at all. But, extreme abstraction though it was, man is for the first time established as universal man. Hegel expresses the idea in all its fullness in the *Philosophy of History*:

> Man, finite when regarded *for himself*, is yet at the same time the Image of God and a fountain of infinity *in himself*. He is the object of his own existence—has in himself an infinite value, an external destiny. Consequently, he has his true home in a supersensuous world—an infinite subjectivity, gained only by a rupture with mere natural existence and violation, and by his labour to break their power from within. ...

These conditions are not yet a concrete order, but simply the first abstract principles, which are won by the instrumentality of the Christian religion for the secular state. First, under Christianity slavery is impossible; for man as man—in the abstract essence of his nature—is contemplated in God; each unit of mankind is an object of the grace of God and of the Divine purpose; "God will have all men to be saved." Utterly excluding all speciality, therefore, man, in and for himself—in his simple quality of man—has infinite value; and this infinite value abolishes, *ipso facto*, all particularity attaching to birth or country.

This is what Hegel calls an abstract universal. The history of humanity is no more than this abstract universal becoming concrete. International socialism is the concrete embodiment of the abstract principle of Christianity. And Christianity appeared and international socialism is now appearing because they are of the very nature of man. To call the recognition of this teleology and religion is a sign of the greatest ignorance, or, is not ignorance, but a determination at all costs to defend bourgeois society against the philosophy of Bolshevism today so as not to have to defend it against the revolutionary masses tomorrow. To have been Christian and to be socialist is an expression of the need for concrete universality which is not so much in as of the very nature of man. And dialectic bases itself upon this precisely because it is not religious and not teleological. If this, scientifically speaking, is not the nature of man, then what do the opponents of dialectic offer instead? Either man has expressed these desires and these aims by accident, i.e. they have no significance whatever, for he might have expressed entirely different aims and had entirely different needs, and may do so tomorrow. Or these needs and aims are not the nature of man but came from some outside agency or God.

It is only in the sense described above that dialectic speaks of freedom and happiness being the purpose of man's existence. Purpose, not in the religious sense, but in the sense that if we examine man's history through the centuries he has sought these aims. It is difficult therefore to say what other purpose his existence has, and the anti-dialectician is left with the alternative that man's life has no purpose at all, which is only another way of accommodating one's self to the existing society, bourgeois society.

The logical principle of universality contains within it a logical contradiction, the contradiction of abstract and concrete. This logical contradiction is a direct reflection of the objective circumstances in which the men of early Christianity lived. Their physical and material circumstances were on the lowest possible level. And therefore, to make their existence a totality, they had to fill it out with this tremendous abstraction. Thus is established the basic logical contradiction in the universal between concrete and abstract, between objective and subjective, between real and ideal, between content and form. But both together form a whole and have no meaning apart from each other. They are opposites but interpenetrated. To Christian man, the conception of heaven was *real* and *necessary* an integral part of his existence in the objective world. Those who accuse dialectics of being a religion understand neither dialectics nor religion.

The history of man is his effort to make the abstract universal concrete. He constantly seeks to destroy, to move aside, that is to say, to negate what impedes his movement towards freedom and happiness. Man is the subject of history. "(The) subject, (man) is pure and simple negativity." This is a cardinal principle of the dialectical movement. The process is molecular, day by day never resting, continuous. But at a certain stage, the continuity is interrupted. The molecular changes achieve a universality and explode into a new quality, a revolutionary change.

Previous to the revolutionary explosion, the aims of the struggle can be posed in partial terms, possibility. It is the impossibility of continuing to do this that interrupts the continuity.

The revolution, precisely because it is a revolution, demands all things for all men. It is an attempt to leap from the realm of objective necessity to the realm of objective freedom.

But in the limited objective circumstances to which the low level of productivity has confined society, what is demanded by, of and for all men, only some men can have. The concrete universality, therefore, becomes the property of some men, a class. They are therefore compelled to use objective violence against those excluded and to substitute an abstract universality for the concrete universality of which the mass has been deprived. But the absence of concrete universality from the whole also limits the universality of the few. Their own concrete universality therefore begins to be limited and its limitations substituted for by abstractions. This is the Hegelian process of "mediation". The new state established after the revolution, the ideology which accompanies it, are a form of mediation between abstract and concrete, ideal and real, etc.

The mediation usually assumes the form of the state power, and the specific ideological combinations of abstract and concrete to bind the new relations are developed by the philosophy of the age. A new equilibrium in the process of the development of man has been established. At a later stage, the same developing process will be repeated in the attempt to negate the actual stage of man previously established There will be the mass revolution for undifferentiated universality, the class differentiation in its realisation, the splitting of the nation into opposing factors, and the attempt to realise in ideology the reconciliation of the opposing factors. Man is not only what he does but what he thinks and what he aims at. But this can only be judged by the concrete, what actually takes place. The truth is always concrete. But it is the concrete viewed in the light of the whole. In the decisive page of the preface to the *Phenomenology*, Hegel writes:

> As subject it is pure and simple negativity, and just on that account a process of splitting up what is simple and undifferentiated, a process of duplicating and setting factors in opposition, which (process) in turn is the negation of this indifferent diversity and of the opposition of factors it entails. ... It is the process of its own becoming, the circle which presupposes its end as its purpose, and has its end for its beginning, it becomes concrete and actual only by being carried out, and by the end it involves.

Marx is expressing concretely just this concentrated Hegelian generalisation when he says:

> For each new class which puts itself in the place of one ruling before it is compelled, merely in order to carry through its aim, to represent its interest as the common interest of all the members of society, put in an ideal form, it will give its ideas the form of universality and represent them as the only rational, universally valid ones. The class making a revolution appears from the very start, merely because it is opposed to a *class*, not as a class but as the representative of the whole society; it appears as the whole mass of society confronting the one ruling class. It can do this because, to start with, its interest really is more connected with the common interest of all other non-ruling classes, because under the pressure of conditions its interest has not yet been able to develop as the particular interest of a particular class. Its victory, therefore, benefits

also many individuals of other classes which are not winning a dominant position, but only in so far as it now puts these individuals in a position to raise themselves into the ruling class. … Every new class, therefore, achieves its hegemony only on a broader basis than that of the class ruling previously, in return for which the opposition of the non-ruling class against the new ruling class later develops all the more sharply and profoundly. Both these things determine the fact that the struggle to be waged against this new ruling class, in its turn, aims at a more decided and radical negation of the previous conditions of society than could all previous classes which sought to rule.

This organisation of historical development did not fall from the sky. It is the result of the concept of the dialectic worked out by Hegel and without the dialectic it could not be done at all. It is this Hegel that Burnham calls the "arch-muddler" of human thought. It is from the examination of this process, the developing conflicts between abstract and concrete, subjective and objective, the abstract universal assuming a certain content which becomes concentrated in a special form, the form gradually becoming infused with a new content until it can contain it no longer and explodes, it is from the examination of all this in society and nature but particularly in its ideological reflection in philosophy that Hegel works out the significance of categories and the movement of his *Logic.* Just as Marx's economic categories were in reality social categories, just in the same way the logical categories, contradictions, etc., of Hegel were a reflection of social categories and social movement. Hegel, and for very good reasons of his time, led his *Logic* into an impossible and fantastic idealism about world-spirit, etc, But the basis of his work was solidly materialistic. He himself explains that:

> The community of principle which, *really* links together individuals of the same class and in virtue of which they are similarly related to other existences, assumes a *form* in human consciousness; and that form is the thought or idea which summarily comprehends the constituents of generic character. Every universal in thought has a corresponding generic principle in Reality, to which it gives intellectual expression or *form.* (*The Philosophy of History*)

Marx and Engels knew this. They could carry over the Hegelian dialectic into a materialistic form because it had been derived originally not from religion but from a study of the stages of man in nature and society and the reflection of these stages in human thought. The dialectic of negativity, the negation of the negation, the inevitability of socialism are a culmination in logical thought of social processes that have now culminated in contemporary society. You look in vain in writings of Hook, Professor of Philosophy at New York University and Burnham, a member of the same faculty, for the slightest understanding of this.

The beginning of this process for the modern world is Christianity and the beginning "presupposes its end as its purpose". For Hegel, these stages are the work of the universal spirit. Marx here is his diametrical opposite. Marx is a dialectical *materialist.* For him, and right from the very start, *these concrete revolutionary stages are the work of the great masses of the people forever seeking the concretion of universality as the development of the productive forces creates the objective circumstances and the subjective desires which move them.*

Hegel could see the abstract universal, the relation between abstract and concrete in historical Christianity and the developing relation in human history. Marx saw that, but because he was closer to the end, he could see more of the "real" man. Because he had seen the revolutionary *proletariat*, he was able to complete the dialectical analysis of previous stages by the recognition of the role of the revolutionary *masses*. These appear at the very beginning of history.

In his introduction to *Class Struggles in France*, Engels writes:

> This party of revolt, of those known by the name of Christian, was also strongly represented in the army; whole legions were Christian. When they were ordered to attend the sacrificial ceremonies of the pagan established church, in order to do the honours there, the rebel soldiers had the audacity to stick peculiar emblems—across on their helmets in protest. Even the wonted barrack cruelties of their superior officers were fruitless. The Emperor Diocletian could no longer quietly look on while order, obedience and discipline in his army were being undermined. He intervened energetically, while there was still time. He passed an anti-Socialist, I should say anti-Christian, law. The meetings of the rebels were forbidden, their meeting halls were closed or even pulled down, the Christian badges, crosses, etc., were like the red handkerchiefs in Saxony, prohibited. Christians were declared incapable of holding offices in the state, they were not to be allowed even to become corporals. Since there were not available at that time judges so well trained in "respect of persons" as Herr von Koller's anti-revolt bill assumes, the Christians were forbidden out of hand to seek justice before court. This exceptional law was also without effect. The Christians tore it down from the walls with scorn; they are even supposed to have burnt the Emperor's palace in Nicomedia over his head. Then the latter revenged himself by the great persecution of Christians in the year 303, according to our chronology. It was the last of its kind. And it was so effective that seventeen years later the army consisted overwhelmingly of Christians, and the succeeding autocrat of the whole Roman Empire, Constantine, called the Great by the priests, proclaimed Christianity as the state religion.

The Christian revolutionaries, however, were not struggling to establish the medieval papacy. The medieval papacy was a mediation to which the ruling forces of society rallied in order to strangle the quest for universality of the Christian masses. In one sense the papacy merely continued the Roman Imperium, and, in Hobbes's phrase, was indeed "no other than the ghost of the deceased Roman Empire sitting crowned upon the grave thereof".

But it was much more than that. Primitive Christianity had begun as a mass revolt that had sought to establish the community of men upon earth. By the time of Gregory the Great, when the papacy began to take over the functions of the declined and fallen Roman Empire, the papacy was beginning its career as a combination of the Empire *and the tremendous impact of the mass revolution*. It was the ghost of the Roman empire and living symbol of Christ on Earth. Heaven was too abstract to satisfy completely the masses of the people. The Church guaranteed them, in return for obedience, the happy future life. But it also took care of the life on earth, and performed the functions of teacher, protector and provider for the poor and sick and needy. It mediated between society and heaven and between the secular rulers of society and the masses. It succoured the poor and was a centre of learning and the improvement of agriculture. In the method by which it was established, in its mediation, of contending classes and its manipulation of concrete abstract, the medieval papacy, as the culmination of the Christian revolution, contains in embryo all the development to the modern age. The dialectical materialist method, the product of a stage nearer to the end, is infinitely superior to Hegel's dialectic. Constantly, contemporary events throw a penetrating light into the past and thereby illuminate the future. It is, for example, the concrete history of the last thirty years of proletarian revolutions that for the first time makes it possible to grasp fully the meaning of Renaissance. But the dialectical materialist study of the Renaissance drives the last nail in the coffin of those who hesitate before the conception of the negation of the negation, the inevitability of socialism and the dictatorship of the proletariat.

The leading ideological characteristic of the early Renaissance can be usefully designated by the popular term "humanism". The medieval towns produced a brilliant civilisation. With the growth of wealth, chiefly a result of commercial capitalism, there arise classes of men whom the early Christian contradiction between objective and subjective, abstract and concrete, is no longer tenable. It is not merely a question of objective wealth. The idea of universality becomes more concrete because of the "energetic position which man is sensible of occupying in his subjective power over outward and material things in the natural world, in which he feels himself free and so gains for himself an absolute right." (Hegel, *Philosophy of History*)

The papacy is itself mediated. It became humanised, i.e. more completely secular, and thus took the road to its own ruin. St. Thomas Aquinas had already begun the rationalisaton of faith, making it reasonable by a brilliant and profound misuse of the writings of Aristotle. Dante, whom Engels calls one of the first modern men, though profoundly religious, wished to substitute Emperor for Pope. The national monarchy begins to substitute for the papal authority.

So far so good. But, and here the Marxist dialectic sharply departs from the Hegelian, the new universal was established and took its form by such violent revolutions of the European proletariat as Europe did not see again until the period which opened in 1917. It is only recently that bourgeois historians have begun to recognise these. The historians of the socialist society will in time make of this one of the great chapters of human history.

As always in critical periods, there were a series of peasant revolutions in Europe throughout the fourteenth century. They were of tremendous range and power, some of them semi-socialistic. But they were not decisive. The decisive revolutions were revolutions of the workers and the petty bourgeoisie of the towns. If the phrase had not already been appropriated by Marxists for the revolution of the socialist proletariat, it would be perfectly correct to say that within the various municipalities the workers aimed at, consciously, and in some few cases actually achieved, the dictatorship of the proletariat.

In the last half of the fourteenth century, these revolutions swept from one end of Europe to another. In Salonika, the sailors and the artisans ruled the rich, the landowners, the commercial magnates and the clergy for ten years. In Italy, the struggle between the "fat" and the "thin". In Bologna, in Genoa, in Sienna, the masses sought to obtain absolute mastery of municipal power. In Florence, under the leadership of Michel Lando, they organised the celebrated revolt of the Ciompi and established the dictatorship of the proletariat whom they called "God's people". Rome and other towns saw similar battles. But it was in the Lowlands, in towns of Ghent, Ypres, and Bruges that the workers made the most desperate efforts to establish their own dictatorship. Revolutionary history badly needs a study of the incidents which centre around the van Artevelde family. Over and over again during a period of decades, the workers rose. More than once they established their dictatorship, they proclaimed an equality of fortunes and the suppression of all authority except the authority of people who live by manual labour. They repeatedly defeated the flower of feudal chivalry. It is reported that in Ghent, the workers went so far as to plan the complete extermination of the bourgeoisie and the nobles with the exception of children of six years of age. In the German towns of Cologne, Strasbourg, Aix-la-Chapelle, Lubeck, Stettin, and many others, in Barcelona, Valencia, and the other towns in Spain, the same desperate battles took place. The working class and its allies closest to it fought for fifty years all over Europe to establish proletarian democracy. Why they failed to achieve substantial successes was due not only to the low level of production but the fact that they fought only as members of isolated municipalities. Some of them indeed aimed boldly at an international proletarian revolution. But their time was not yet.

Let Boissonade, a bourgeois historian, speak in the concluding paragraph of his *Life and Work in Medieval Europe*. The reader should read carefully and note particularly the words we have underlined:

> For the first time the masses, ceasing to be mere herds without rights or thoughts of their own, became associations of freemen, proud of their independence, conscious of the value and dignity of their labour, *fitted by their intelligent activity* to collaborate in all spheres, political, economic, and social, in the *tasks which the aristocrats believed themselves alone able to fulfil*. Not only was the *power of production multiplied a hundredfold by their efforts*, but society was regenerated by the incessant influx of new and vigorous blood. Social selection was henceforth better assured. It was thanks to *the devotion and spirit of these medieval masses that the nations became conscious of themselves, for it was they who brought about the triumph of national patriotism*, just as their local patriotism had burned for town or village in the past. The martyrdom of a peasant girl from the marshes of Lorraine saved the first of the great nations, France, which had become the most brilliant home of civilisation in the Middle Ages. *They gave to the modern states their first armies*, which were superior to those of feudal chivalry. *Above all, it was they who prepared the advent of democracy and bequeathed to the labouring masses the instruments of their power, the principles of freedom and of association*. Labour, of old despised and depreciated, became a *power of incomparable force in the world*, and its social value became increasingly recognised. It is from the Middle Ages that this capital evolution takes its date, and it is this which makes this period, so often misunderstood, and so full of a confused but singularly powerful activity, the *most important in the universal history of the labour before the great changes witnessed by the eighteenth and nineteenth centuries*.

This was the working class five hundred years ago. They were not proletarians in the modern sense. They were, for the most part, free workers in the guilds. They did not function within the socialised organisation of modern labour. But note, Messrs. anti-dialecticians and anti-Marxists, that these workers, five hundred years ago, all over Europe, believed that they were "fitted by their intelligent activity to collaborate in all spheres, political, economic and social in the tasks which the aristocrats believed themselves alone able to fulfil". That is what the millions of proletarians all over the world today believe. They will fight for it.

We believe they will succeed. You believe what? Their ancestors of five hundred years ego were not as developed as are the workers of today. But they fought for complete equality, for complete democracy, for universality. They failed, but they established the foundations of what we know as liberalism. Some of you still live on it, thin fare though it has become. The bourgeoisie had the feudal lords, in terror of these workers, rallied behind the absolute monarchy and the national state. Both humanism and the national state of the absolute monarchy were mediations of the mass proletarian desire for universality no longer in heaven but on earth. Humanism was the substitution of a liberal culture for the rich in place of the complete self-expression desired by the workers; the national state, disciplining the church, supplemented the concrete objective protection of wealth by abstract subjective claims of being the arbiter of justice, the guardian of law and order, and the protector of all the people. The contradictions, the antagonisms in the quest for universality had grown sharper then ever.

So, Messrs. doubters and sceptics and sneerers at dialectic, you will begin to see perhaps that what dialecticians believe in is not the result of religion. We have a certain conception of the nature of man based on history. When Marx and Engels wrote about the proletarian revolution in connection with the negation of the negation, when they wrote that in the present stage of society, man would either achieve this revolution or society would tear itself to pieces, they were being guided not by the dislocations of Marx's "psyche" as Edmund Wilson thinks or by any Hegelian triads or historical religiosity, as is the opinion of Burnham and Hook. It was a logical deduction from the experience of history. The struggle of the masses for universality did not begin yesterday. An intellectual like Dewey believes that men's quest is the quest for certainty. The intellectual believes that all men are intellectuals. That is wrong. Men seek not intellectual certainty. The quest is the mass quest for universality in action and in life. It is the moving force of history. And history has reached a climax because this quest has reached a climax.

Space compels rapid compression of the next great stages in the process of social development—the Protestant reformation and the French revolution. Rising capitalism expropriated the agricultural labourer and in the creation of wage-labour threw the masses further back from universality than they had ever been. Humanism had dragged universality from heaven down to earth and had by that made the contradiction between real and ideal an intolerable antagonism. The new proletariat could not play any great part in the struggles of the Protestant reformation, as the mature workers of the medieval towns had done. Hence the classes which took the lead were the bourgeoisie, the petty bourgeoisie and the peasants. Let us concentrate on one outstanding and familiar example, the English revolution.

The Puritans give us the key to the understanding of the whole period in the light of the struggle for democracy. The revolution of Dewey had shattered forever the claims of the Pope as mediator between God and man. It placed the responsibility for the individual's moral salvation squarely on the individual man. As Hegel put it: "This is the essence of the Reformation: Man is in his very nature destined to be free", and in his own peculiar but profound manner he sums up modern history. "Time, since that epoch, has had no other work to do than the formal imbuing of the world with this principle, in bringing the Reconciliation implicit (in Christianity) into objective and explicit realisation." If you stand it on its head, and say that the objective development of man in society has been the various stages through which various classes have sought to realise the freedom implicit in Christianity, a great truth will have been grasped.

But the mass of men do not think, and certainly do not act according to those terms. The Puritans of town and country, petty-bourgeois, and semi-proletarian, shut off from freedom by the state, attempted to establish democracy in religion. The sects each attempted to form a social community in which the individual would exercise the new freedom, unlimited except by the equal freedom of other men. James I of England did not misunderstand them one bit. He knew what their anti-Ecclesiasticism meant. To all their arguments for religious freedom he invariably croaked in reply, "No Bishop, no King." Their weakness was a social weakness, the lack of organisation which reflected the scattered character of their labour. But when the big bourgeoisie and some liberal aristocrats started the revolution, and the small farmers and small masters of the towns organised in the army, the Puritans showed what social passions were hidden behind their psalm-singing. In 1646, tired of the vacillations of their bourgeois and aristocratic leaders, they seized the person of the King and held him as a hostage. They then began negotiations with Cromwell and in the twin documents, the agreement of the People and the Heads of the Proposals, they put forward a programme for such a parliamentary democracy as was not even put forward in England until the Chartist movement two hundred years later. They put it forward to Cromwell; and in the discussion with Cromwell and his brother-in-law, Ireton, they raised the property question as a barrier to democracy in the most plain-spoken manner. These were not the Levellers, and the Diggers, who were the extreme left. These were the main body of the army. They were suppressed by a combination of fraud and force, but Cromwell, striking to the left, was compelled to strike at the right also. Charles I was executed and the monarchy was destroyed. In the familiar phrase, it was not monarchy but royalty which returned at the restoration. Monarchy in Britain was gone forever, destroyed by the religious democrats. They held power for eleven years, but as always, and particularly in this case, they were too few to represent the nation and the old process of mediation once more took place. They had cleared the way for capitalism, and nowhere was the antagonism sharper between developing capitalism and the masses of the nation than in England.

The history of the French revolution is familiar to all Marxists and the conclusions for our main argument are therefore easy to draw.

The intervention of the masses, its range and power, the social desires, the capacity for achievement and sacrifice, revealed itself to an educated Europe which had not dreamt that the shabby exterior of workers and peasants and the common people hid such colossal energies and such social needs. The quest for universality was no longer a secret. Liberty, equality and fraternity were the slogans of the revolution. If the Reformation had sought to establish a "democratic" freedom of religion, the French revolution attempted to establish a social freedom of political democracy. If out of the individual's responsibility for his own salvation, there had leapt democracy, out of his political freedom, there leapt communism. Robespierre's dictatorship was an attempt to establish the reign of virtue. But the French masses, not only Babeuf, saw and were ready for what was needed, drastic regulation and even confiscation of the property of the rich. The modern problem was posed. But it was the old problem in a new and more aggravated, a more contradictory form.

When the French revolution was over and men had time to think, it was seen that the revolution of reason and the mighty struggle for liberty, equality and fraternity had left men farther apart than ever before. Behind the formal equality before the law, capitalist production was accumulating wealth at one pole and misery, subordination and degradation at the other on a scale hitherto unknown. The universality of men, honour, loyalty, humanism, liberty, equality, fraternity, democracy, these were as abstract to the mass of men as the heaven of the early Popes. These ideals had a certain existence among the ruling classes, but thinking man could see that the needs and deprivations of the excluded mass reached with devastating effect upon the humanity of the rulers. The masses had tried to make a state a popular state. The result had been the creation of a monster such as had never been seen before and far surpassed in range and power the state of absolute monarchy. It was in the throes of this contradiction which was shaking all Europe that Hegel, the culmination of the German classical philosophers, set himself to study the problem of human destiny and elaborated a theory of knowledge. Hegel recognised what men were striving for and he recognised that the French revolution was a climax in this struggle.

Hegel understood Adam Smith and Ricardo. He understood the fragmentation and dehumanisation of man in the process of capitalist production. Many of Marx's most famous pages in *Capital* have as their direct origins some of Hegel's descriptions of the workers in capitalist industry. This was, for Hegel, the final insuperable barrier to any community of association among men. Hence universality for the mass of men was impossible. By means of his dialectical method he drew the necessary conclusions. We who live toward the end in the epoch of Hitler and Stalin can understand Hegel's conclusions better than most men of previous generations, with the exception of Marx.

Universality for the mass of men was impossible. Only the state, said Hegel, could embody universality for the community. But, in particular, the state was a defence against the revolutionary masses. Hegel had seen them and their activities in European history and now the French Revolution had shown that nothing could ever come of it. So it had been and it would ever be. At each stage, a few chosen individuals represented the abstract spirit of mankind. Universality had to be restricted to these. This was the basis of Hegel's idealism. But with the clear insight of a great scholar of both past and contemporary history, and by his mastery of his method, he analysed and drew his analysis to its conclusion. The state would have to organise production. The chaos of capitalist production would have to be disciplined by organising the separate industries into corporations. The state would be the state of the corporations. Universality being impossible to all men, the state bureaucracy would embody universality and represent the community. Hegel did not know the modern proletariat. He operated therefore on the basis of the inevitability of proletarian subordination. But grant him that premise and his dialectical method shows that he made an astonishing anticipation in thought of the inevitable end of bourgeois society—the totalitarian state. Hegel must not be misjudged. He wrote and propounded in the name of freedom and Reason. But those who today sneer at him and his dialectics are not fit even to wipe the dust off his books. To this day, except for the writings of the great Marxists, no single writer since the French revolution has so much to say that is indispensable to modern thought and particularly modern politics.

This is where Marx began. It was as impossible to go any farther along the road of Hegel as it is impossible to go farther than the totalitarian state of contemporary history. Beyond both lies only decay. Marx had to abandon the quest for universality or find a new basis for it.

A long line of European thinkers, Ricardo, Fourier, Saint-Simon, Feuerbach, and the classical economists, the ferment in Europe which preceded the revolutionary outburst in 1848, and, what Hegel had never seen, the emergence of the proletariat as an organised social force—these gave to Marx, already a master of Hegel's system, the impetus to the new system. Men had sought universality in heaven, in the freedom of religion, in the freedom of politics. Politics had failed. Neither Hegel nor Marx ever had any illusions about bourgeois democracy as a solution to the unquenchable desires and aspirations of men.

Nothing is more indicative of the philosophical character of Marxism and its organic continuity of the tradition of the great philosophers of Europe than the method by which Marx dismissed democratic politics. For Marx bourgeois democratic politics was a fraud, but like all the great panaceas from Christianity on, it was an expression of the perennial need historically conditioned. The productive process of capitalism denied any real community to men. And democratic politics, like religion, was a form of mediation by which men gained the illusion that they were all members of one social community, an illusion of universality. How not to remember Hitler's insistence that his tyrannical regime represented the folk community. The more the Nazi regime deprived the masses of all human rights, the more imperative it was to substitute an abstraction of abstractions to create the totality of existence, a sense of universality, without which men cannot live.

Marx reversed Hegel at all points. It was not an intellectual construction. Men were doing it and had been doing it all around him for years.

Hegel saw objective history as the successive manifestation of a world spirit. Marx placed the objective movement in the process of production. Hegel had been driven to see the perpetual quest for universality as necessarily confined to the process of knowledge. Marx reversed this and rooted the quest for universality in the need for the free and full development of all the inherent and acquired characteristics of the individual in productive and intellectual labour. Hegel had made the motive force of history the work of a few gifted individuals in whom was concentrated the social movement. Marx propounded the view that it was only when the ideas seized hold of the masses that the process of history moved. Hegel dreaded the revolt of the modern mass. Marx made the modern proletarian revolution the motive force of modern history. Hegel placed the future guardianship of society in the hands of the bureaucracy. Marx saw future society as headed for ruin except under the rulership of the proletariat and the vanishing distinction between intellectual and manual labour.

That was the conflict. That is the conflict today. The proletariat, said Marx, is revolutionary or it is nothing. The proletariat, he said, will conquer or society will destroy itself. The bureaucracy as conceived by Hegel he subjected to a merciless analysis. Let the reader think of Hitlerite Germany and Stalinist Russia and see how profound, how realistic, how anticipatory of the absolute crisis was the battle between the last of the great bourgeois philosophers and the first philosopher of the proletarian revolution. The smug anti-dialecticians have not yet caught up with this conflict between the masters of dialectic over a hundred years ago.

> Hegel's conception of history is nothing other than the speculative expression of the Christian-German dogma of the opposition of spirit and manner, God and the world. This opposition expresses itself within history, within the human world itself, as a few chosen individuals, active spirits, confronting the rest of humanity, the spiritless mass matter. Hegel's conception of history presupposes an abstract or absolute spirit which develops itself so that humanity is only a mass bearing this spirit unconsciously or consciously. Within the empirical exoteric history, he sees a speculative esoteric history. The history of mankind is transformed into the history of the abstract spirit of mankind, beyond actual men.

> Parallel with this Hegelian doctrine, there was developed in France the theory of the doctrinaires proclaiming the sovereignty of reason in opposition to the sovereignty of the people, in order to exclude the masses and rule alone. The result is that if the activity of the actual masses is nothing more than the activity of a mass of human individuals, the abstract universality, reason, spirit, possesses abstract expression exhausted in a few individuals. It depends upon the position and the strength of imagination of each individual whether he will pass as representative of "spirit". (Marx, *The Holy Family*)

Hegel had observed the unconscious development of the process of mediation. The bureaucracy of his corporate state was a conscious final mediation. Marx, in the *Critique* of Hegel's *Philosophy of Right* took up the challenge. The passage which follows might have been strange or difficult twenty years ago, not today. The reader must remember that both Hegel and Marx had common pre-suppositions—the recognition of the quest for universality, the recognition that the French revolution had brought the perpetual mediation of the growing contradictions to some final stage. The essence of the passage is that while Hegel believed that the bureaucracy can and must be a mediation for universality, Marx shows that the contradiction between objective and subjective, between ideal and real, concrete and abstract, has now reached such a stage, that the universality of the bureaucracy can have no reality. The quest for universality, embodied in the masses, constituting the great mass of the nation, forbids any mediation. The bureaucracy is compelled to become objectively the embodiment of the crassest materialism and subjectively, in its words, the embodiment of the crassest hypocrisy.

Here is the passage with certain words emphasised:

> The "state formalism" which the bureaucracy is, is the "state as formalism" and as such formalism Hegel has described it. Since this "state formalism" is constituted as actual power and its own material content becomes itself, *it is self-understood that the "bureaucracy" is a network of practical illusions or the "illusion of the state". The bureaucratic spirit is a thoroughly Jesuitical theological spirit. The bureaucrats are the Jesuits and theologians of the state. The bureaucracy is the "republique pretre".*

Since the bureaucracy is essentially the "state as formalism", it is this also in its purpose. Thus the actual purpose of the state appears to the bureaucracy as a purpose against the state. The spirit of the bureaucracy is the "formal spirit of the state". *It makes therefore the "formal spirit of the state" or the actual emptiness of spirit of the state into a categorical imperative.* The bureaucracy thus is driven to the final end and purpose of the state. Since *the bureaucracy makes its "formal" purpose into its content, it gets into conflicts everywhere with the "real" purposes. It is therefore necessary to substitute the form for the content, the content for the form. The purposes of the state are transformed into administrative ones or the administrative purpose into state purposes. The bureaucracy is a circle out of which no one can get.* Its hierarchy is a hierarchy of knowledge. The apex entrusts to the lower circles insight into particular things, and the lower circles entrust to the apex insights into the universal and thus they mutually interchange.

The bureaucracy is the imaginary state besides the real state, the spiritualism of the state. *Everything therefore has a double meaning, a real one and a bureaucratic one*, as knowledge is double, real knowledge and bureaucratic (also the will). The real essence is handled according to its bureaucratic essence, according to its other worldly spiritual essence. *The bureaucracy has* the essence of the state, the *spiritual essence of society in its possession, it is its private property*. The general spirit of the bureaucracy is the secret, the mystery, guarded internally through the hierarchy, externally as the closed corporation. The apparent spirit of the state, the opinion of the state, appear therefore to the bureaucracy as a treason to its mysteries. *Authority is therefore the principle of its knowledge, and deifying of authority is its principle. Within itself, however, spiritualism becomes a crass materialism, the materialism of passive obedience, of belief in authority, the mechanism of fixed formal behaviour, fixed principles, observations, traditions.* As for the individual bureaucrat, the purpose of the state becomes a private purpose, a hunt for higher posts, for careers. First, he regards real life as material, for the spirit of this life has its exclusive existence in the bureaucracy. The bureaucracy must therefore proceed to make living as material as possible. Secondly, it is material for itself, i.e. so far as it becomes an object of bureaucratic handling, for its spirit is prescribed to it, its purpose lies outside of it, its existence is the existence of administration. The state exists henceforth only as fixed spirits of various offices, whose connection is subordination and passive obedience. *Actual science appears as without content, actual life is as dead, for the imaginary knowing and imaginary living pass as the essence.* The bureaucrat must therefore believe Jesuitically with the actual state, be this Jesuitism now conscious, or unconscious. It is, however, necessary that as soon as his opposite is knowing, he also achieve self-consciousness and purposeful Jesuitism.

That is the political anatomy of the Stalinist bureaucracy. In the review *After Ten Years*, I could touch only briefly (such are the trials of political minorities) upon the dehumanisation of the Russian bureaucracy itself. The Russian bureaucracy, as the Nazi bureaucracy in its time, represents essentially the opposition to the universality of the people in every single sphere of life.

As the same article says:

> In socialist society or in a society transitional to socialism, politics, science, art, literature, education all become truly social. The *individual* is able to exercise his gifts to the highest capacity, to become truly universal, because of the essentially *collective* life of the society in which he lives. Look at Stalinist society. No individual is more "political" than the individual in Stalinist society. Nowhere are art, literature, education, science, so integrated with "society". This is the appearance. In reality, never before has there been such a prostitution of all these things for the corruption and suppression of the direct producer, with the resulting degradation of the producers and managers alike.

Hitler called his state the truest democracy, his community was the folk community of the whole nation. His regime was "socialism". The Stalinist regime goes farther. The state possesses all the virtues. The internationalist conception of the human welfare is maintained through the connection with the corrupt and depraved communist parties and the constant appeal to the masses of the world. The state guarantees a "genuine" democracy, a *"genuine"* freedom of speech. Science, art and literature, like production, exist only to serve all the people. The state only administers the property which is the possession of all the people. Liberty, equality (within reason) and fraternity, honour, loyalty, chivalry, geniality, are the possession of all the people (except the Trotskyists). The leader is the leader because he possesses all these qualities to a superlative degree. Any oppositionist to the slightest of these claims becomes immediately an enemy devoid of all these virtues and fit only for extermination. The totality of the abstraction is to be explained only by the totality of the deprivation. Today this state is not only confined to Russia as an isolated phenomenon. It is spreading. Trotsky taught that the growth of the Stalinist state was due to the struggle over consumption. We cannot accept this at all. The Stalinist state is the completest expression of the class state—not the distorted beginning of something new but the culmination, the final form of the old. To believe that this state has roots only in consumption and not in the whole productive system is to saddle the concepts of Marxian socialism with a burden which they cannot indefinitely carry. The Stalinist state is a class state, a culmination of the old, not in any shape or form the beginning, however distorted, of the new.

Of precisely the same genre are the abstractions of the bourgeois democracies, different not in quality but only in the degree. Phrases like the "century of the common man" and the "four freedoms" are abstractions to satisfy the suppression of objective needs. The League of Nations of 1919 becomes the United Nations of 1947. The more concrete the negation of the need, the more abstract, empty and flamboyant becomes the subjective mediation.

There is a school of Marxists today who preach the ridiculous doctrine that in Russia today politics governs production. In reality, production governs politics. In appearance, the state takes hold of capital. In reality, capital takes hold of the state, and upon the mediation of the antagonisms of social and political life is superimposed and the antagonisms of capitalist production itself. In its most developed form, it is state capital.

It is this modern state, the negation of universality for so many millions, which is to be negated. The negation of this is the negation of the negation. The agent of this negation is the revolutionary proletariat. When the modern millions take hold of this state, they negate the root of their degradation, production itself, for to control the state of state capitalism is to control production itself. At this moment, the state begins to wither away.

I can sum up best by a quotation from an article I wrote in *New International* of June 1944:

> But the outstanding feature of the contemporary world is that the *principles* for which Christianity stood in its best days are now regarded as matters of life and death by the average worker. This is no accident at all though we can only state the facts here. European civilisation must become a unity? Hundreds of millions of European workers know that this must be achieved or the continent will perish. Equality of nations? That, too, the great masses of Europe passionately desire, not as an ideal but to be able to live in peace. A central government to represent the interests of all? As late as 1935,

Lord Cecil could get eleven million votes in a plebiscite in Britain supporting the idea of a League of Nations. And when workers say a League of Nations and collective security they mean it. And that early attempt to succour the poor, to help the afflicted, to teach the ignorant? The great mass of the workers in European countries conceive of Labour Parties as doing just that, within the conditions of the modern world.

Our anti-dialecticians believe the negation of negation and the inevitability of socialism are religion. But when one attempts to penetrate into *their* philosophy of history, one increasingly meets a vacuum or the most arbitrary combinations of historical phenomena, tied together by bits of string, by subjective analysis and a crude determinism which even sometimes has the presumption to call itself Marxism. For us there is no philosophy of history without Marxism, and there can be no Marxism without the dialectic. In the article quoted above, I continued:

> He who would exhibit the Marxist method must grasp the full significance of that early uprising of the masses when Christianity proclaimed its message. We must watch not only the primitiveness and simplicity of its aims but their comprehensive scope. Then by slow degrees, through the centuries, we see one part of the aim becoming concrete for one section of the population, and then another part for another section. Ideas arise from concrete conditions to become partially embodied in social classes and give rise to further interrelations between the spiral of real and ideal, content and form. This is the dialectic to which Marx gave a firm materialistic basis in the developing process of production. As society develops, the possibilities for individual development of man become greater and greater, but the conflict of classes becomes sharper and sharper. We stand today at an extreme state of these interrelated phenomena of social development. When a modern worker demands the right of free speech, the right of free press, of free assembly, continuous employment, social insurance, the best medical attention, the best education, he demands in reality the "social republic". Spinoza and Kant would stand aghast at what the average worker takes for granted today. But he does not demand them as an individual or in the primitive manner the early Christian did. In America, for instance, there are some thirteen million workers organised for nothing else but the preservation and extension of these values. These are the values of modern civilisation. They are embodied in the very web and texture of the lives of the masses of the people. Never were such precious values so resolutely *held* as necessary to complete living by so substantial and so powerful a section of society. Socialism means simply the complete expansion and fulfillment of these values in the life of the individual. This can only be attained by the most merciless struggle of the whole class against its capitalist masters. The realisation of this necessity is the final prelude to full self-consciousness.

You still believe, gentlemen, that these ideas and conclusions are the result of a dialectical religion? Go your way. God be with you. Amen.

Bolshevism is above all a philosophy of life and a political conception. The political conception is the organised preparation for the proletarian revolution. Lenin was the originator of Bolshevism, the Marxism of our time. The world was to be saved by reason, but reason lay not in the heads of philosophers and intellectuals but in the actions of the masses. The world as we know it, under the control of its present masters, is unreasonable, chaotic, lacking in energy and creative force, gangrenous, barbarism. For Lenin, reason, order, historical creativeness, lay precisely in the forces which would destroy the old world. This is how he saw the councils of the workers, the soviets, and the revolutionary actions of the masses in 1905:

> The old power, as a dictatorship of the minority, could maintain itself only by the aid of police stratagems, only by preventing and diverting the masses from participating in the government, from controlling the government. The old power persistently distrusted the masses, feared the light, maintained itself by means of deception. The new power, as a dictatorship of the overwhelming majority, could and did maintain itself only by winning the confidence of the great masses, only by drawing, in the freest, broadest, and most energetic manner, all the masses into the work of government. Nothing hidden, nothing secret, no regulations, no formalities. You are a working man? You wish to fight to liberate Russia from a handful of police thugs? Then you are our comrade. Choose your delegate at once, immediately. Choose as you think best. We shall willingly and gladly accept him as a full member of our Soviet of Workers' Deputies, of our Peasants' Committee, of our Soviet of Soldiers' Deputies, etc., etc. It is a power that is open to all, that does everything in sight of the masses, that is accessible to the masses, that springs directly from the masses; it is the direct organ of the masses and their will. Such was the new power, or rather its embryo, for the victory of the old power very soon trampled upon the tender shoots of this new plant. (*Selected Works*, vol. VII, pp. 252–3)

There are innumerable people opposed to bourgeois society, as they think, but who fear the uprising of the proletarian masses from that passive obedience, which is precisely the basis of bourgeois society. They want socialism but want to be sure of order, system, reason. Lenin had a different conception of where order was to be sought:

> When the history of humanity moves forward at the speed of a locomotive (the petty-bourgeois intellectual) calls it a "whirlwind", a "deluge", the "disappearance" of all "principles and ideas". When history moves at the speed of a horse and cart he calls it reason, system. Then the masses themselves, with all their virgin primitiveness, their simple, rough determination, begin to make history to apply "principles and theories" directly and immediately, the bourgeoisie takes fright and wails that "reason is thrust into the background". (Is not the very opposite the case, you philistine heroes? Is it not precisely in such moments of history that the reason of the masses is displayed rather than the reason of single individuals? Is it not precisely at such times that reason of the masses becomes a living, active force, and not an armchair force?) When direct action by the masses is crushed by shootings, executions, floggings, unemployment and famine, when the bugs of professorial science, subsidised by Dubasov, crawl out of the cracks and begin to speak on behalf of the people, *in the name of the masses*, and sell and betray the interests of the latter to a privileged few—the knights of philistinism imagine that an epoch of peace and calm progress has set in, that "the turn of sense and reason has now come again. (*Selected Works*, vol. VII, pp. 260–1)

The bourgeois world is rejected completely. Only what destroys it is reasonable. But the reason of the masses was not merely destructive. It was destructive of the *bourgeois world*. But it was itself a "mighty creative force".

The point is that it is precisely the revolutionary periods that are distinguished for their greater breadth, greater wealth, greater intelligence, greater and more systematic activity, greater audacity and vividness of historical creativeness compared with periods of philistine, Cadet, reformist progress. But Mr Blank and Co. picture it the other way about. They pass off poverty as historical-creative wealth. They regard the inactivity of the suppressed, downtrodden masses as the triumph of the systematic activity of the bureaucrats and the bourgeoisie. They shout about the disappearance of sense and reason, when the picking to pieces of parliamentary bills by all sorts of bureaucrats and liberal "penny-a-liners" gives way to a period of direct political activity by the "common people", who in their simple way directly and immediately destroy the organs of oppression of the people, seize power, appropriate for themselves what was considered to be the property of all sorts of plunderers of the people in a word, precisely when the sense and reason of millions of downtrodden people is awakening, not only for reading books, but for action, for living human action, for historical creativeness. (*Selected Works*, vol. VII, pp. 261–2)

This is creative reason during the revolution and this is creative reason after the revolution. Readers of the following articles in this pamphlet and of the documents of our tendency will know that for us the economic planning of the new society must be the result of the same creativeness and energy of the masses expressed through their soviets, their councils, their party or parties. As we have shown in our pamphlet this was Lenin's conception. For us therefore, once the masses in Russia were totally subordinated to the bureaucracy, then capital as an economic force resumed sway, and objective economic law reasserted itself. The proletarians of the fourteenth century failed, but the masses today begin from a society in which the socialisation of the labour process is the dominant feature of the economy. The education, the training, the discipline, the social awareness, the material and spiritual needs of the great millions have reached astonishing proportions. These are the new economic forces. They are worldwide. If the earlier revolutions were outstanding peaks in a world in which the periphery was large, backward and stagnant, it is not so today. Disparate as are the economic levels of the United States and China, the world is today one system and a social unit. The need for universality of the individual man is only part of the need for universality in the world at large; "only with this universal development of productive forces is a *universal* intercourse between men established which produces in all nations simultaneously the phenomenon of the 'propertyless' mass (universal competition), makes each nation dependent on the revolutions of the others, and finally has put world-historical, empirically universal individuals in place of local ones." Thus Marx in *The German Ideology*, in 1846. Today we are at the end.

It would be a grave mistake not to attempt to show, however briefly, the theoretical link between these concepts and the practical activity of building a revolutionary organisation. The dialectician is often seriously thrown back by the fact that the great masses of the workers do not seem to think in a way that corresponds to these ideas. He should remember that the number who thought of socialist revolution in Russia in February 1917 was pitifully few. There was not one single republican in France on 14 July 1789. How many of the Founding

Fathers advocated independence in 1776? The anticipations of these ideas accumulate and then under suitable conditions explode into a new quality.

But with the masses the matter goes even deeper. *They do not think as intellectuals do and this intellectuals must understand.* In one of his most remarkable pages Lenin confesses that at a critical moment of the Russian revolution he was performing the most critical of all tasks, evaluating the events of July in order to change the policy and organisation of the Bolshevik Party. He was living with a working-class family. The hostess placed bread on the table. "Look," says the host, "what fine bread. 'They' dare not give us bad bread now. And we had almost forgotten that good bread could be had in Petrograd." Let Lenin himself continue:

> I was amazed at this class evaluation of the July days. My mind had been revolving around the political significance of the event, weighing is importance in relation to the general course of events, analysing the situation that had given rise to this zigzag of history and the situation it would create. And debating how we must alter our slogans and party apparatus in order to adapt them to the changed situation. As for bread, I, who had never experienced want, never gave it a thought. Bread to me seemed a matter of course, a by-product, as it were, of the work of a writer. Fundamentally, the mind approaches the class struggle for bread by a political analysis and an extraordinarily complicated and involved path.

> But this representative of the oppressed class, although one of the better-paid and well-educated workers, took the bull by the horns with that astonishing simplicity and bluntness, with that firm resolution and amazingly clear insight, which is as remote from your intellectual as the stars in the sky. (*Selected Works*, vol. VI, pp. 280–81)

The key phrase in this passage is "although one of the better-paid and well-educated workers". Better paid and well-educated workers are very often corrupted by bourgeois education. It is the great millions, very often unorganised in unions but "disciplined, and united and organised by the very mechanism of capitalist production" itself that constitute the most heroic, the most self-sacrificing battalions of the new social order. They do not approach great questions by a complicated and involved path as intellectuals do. Their most effective method of expression is action, corresponding to the astonishing simplicity, bluntness … firm resolution and amazingly clear insight" of their speech when they do speak. For long years they appear entirely subordinated to bourgeois ideas and the place bourgeois society has reserved for them. But they have their own ideas and in the continuous crisis and catastrophic decline of society, they have in recent decades repeatedly entered upon the field of history with world-shaking effects. Since 1917, no lasting victory has been theirs but the future is with them or there is no future.

Revolutionary politics consists of a conscious relating of the needs of the objective situation to the state of development of the masses. But decisive always is the objective situation, the world of today, and a superficial conception of the stage of development of the masses can be a terrible trap for the unwary. The objective conditions of our world demand universal solutions. It is absolutely impossible to propose a proletarian programme to counter the imperialism of the "Marshall Plan" without counterposing an international plan of socialist economic construction. That is the world in which we live.

In Europe, adequate wages, stable prices, food, housing and heating are no longer partial questions. Any reasonable satisfaction of the needs of the people demands a total reorganisation of the economy, a plan for continental rehabilitation, and close association with the economic power of the United States. Peace is indivisible. The need for universality stretches out from the hearth to the whole world.

But the same need exists intensively. It is the crime of capitalism that it uses men only partially. Labour bureaucracies which call on men only for votes or sending telegrams, are only partially mobilising vast stores of creative energy which are crying for release. Bankrupt economies which cannot mobilise the universal contained in modern man are doomed to remain bankrupt. That and nothing else but that can rebuild the vast wreck which is the modern world. Objectively and subjectively the solution of the crisis demands a total mobilisation of all forces in society. Partial solutions only create further disorders in the economy; partial demands, as such, because they are abstractions from the reality, lead only to disappointment; partial demands by leaders on the workers fail to mobilise their energies and leave them with a sense of frustration and hopelessness. Thus not only the concept but the need for universality reigns throughout all phases of society.

This was the constant theme of Trotsky before he was murdered in 1940. In previous periods the socialists fought for partial demands and held before the masses the social revolution as a distant goal. Today those days are over. The revolutionaries hold always before the masses the concept of the proletarian revolution but do not neglect to snatch this and that partial demand to better the position of the toilers and mobilise them for the final struggle.

This only is reason. The modern intellectual, once he breaks with bourgeois conceptions, finds a vast new world of ideas open before him. But he can pursue and present these ideas in their inner essence only with the inevitable universality of the revolutionary proletariat in mind. Without this there is no dialectic, and without dialectic, thought soon bogs down in the chaotic disintegration of the modern world. Quite different is it with the dialectical materialist. In his boldest flights, he is conscious that he will not exceed the real history of humanity which is being prepared by the revolutionary masses.

Note

1. Dialectic as a mode of thought had its origin among the Greek philosophers. In fact, the more one penetrates into dialectics, the more one is astonished at the colossal impudence and ignorance which passes for exposure of it. Lenin was very conscious of its historic significance. As he wrote in 1915: 'The division of the one and the cognition of its contradictory parts (see the quotation from Philo on Heraclitus at the beginning of Part III, "Knowledge," in Lassalle's book on Heraclitus) is the *essence* (one of the 'essentials', one of the principal, if not the principal, characteristics or features) of dialectics. This is precisely how Hegel also puts the matter (Aristotle in his *Metaphysics* continually grapples with it and combats Heraclitus and Heraclitan ideas).' But although Hegel learnt more about dialectic from Aristotle than from any other single philosopher, he himself accepts Christianity as the starting-point of our civilisation.

Notes on Man and Socialism in Cuba

Ernesto Che Guevera

A common argument from the mouths of capitalist spokesmen, in the ideological struggle against socialism, is that socialism, or the period of building socialism into which we have entered, is characterized by the subordination of the individual to the state. I will not try to refute this argument solely on theoretical grounds, but I will try to establish the facts as they exist in Cuba and then add comments of a general nature. Let me begin by sketching the history of our revolutionary struggle before and after the taking of power:

> As is well known, the exact date on which the revolutionary struggle began — which would culminate January 1st, 1959 — was the 26th of July, 1953. A group of men commanded by Fidel Castro attacked the Moncada barracks in Oriente Province on the morning of that day. The attack was a failure; the failure became a disaster; and the survivors ended up in prison, beginning the revolutionary struggle again after they were freed by an amnesty.

In this stage, in which there was only the germ of socialism, man was the basic factor. We put our trust in him — individual, specific, with a first and last name — and the triumph or failure of the mission entrusted to him depended on his capacity for action.

Then came the stage of guerrilla struggle. It developed in two distinct elements: the people, the still sleeping mass which it was necessary to mobilize; and its vanguard, the guerrillas, the motor force of the movement, the generator of revolutionary consciousness and militant enthusiasm. It was this vanguard, this catalyzing agent, which created the subjective conditions necessary for victory.

Here again, in the course of the process of proletarianizing our thinking, in this revolution which took place in our habits and our minds, the individual was the basic factor. Every one of the fighters of the Sierra Maestra who reached an upper rank in the revolutionary forces has a record of outstanding deeds to his credit. They attained their rank on this basis. It was the first heroic period and in it they contended for the heaviest responsibilities, for the greatest dangers, with no other satisfaction than fulfilling a duty.

In our work of revolutionary education we frequently return to this instructive theme. In the attitude of our fighters could be glimpsed the man of the future.

On other occasions in our history the act of total dedication to the revolutionary cause was repeated. During the October crisis and in the days of Hurricane Flora we saw exceptional deeds of valor and sacrifice performed by an entire people. Finding the formula to perpetuate this heroic attitude in daily life is, from the ideological standpoint, one of our fundamental tasks.

In January, 1959, the Revolutionary Government was established with the participation of various members of the treacherous bourgeoisie. The existence of the Rebel Army as the basic factor of force constituted the guarantee of power.

Serious contradictions developed subsequently. In the first instance, in February, 1959, these were resolved when Fidel Castro assumed leadership of the government with the post of Prime Minister. This stage culminated in July of the same year with the resignation under mass pressure of President Urrutia.

There now appeared in the history of the Cuban Revolution a force with well-defined characteristics which would systematically reappear — the mass.

This many-faceted agency is not, as is claimed, the sum of units of the self-same type, behaving like a tame flock of sheep, and reduced, moreover, to that type by the system imposed from above. It is true that it follows its leaders, basically Fidel Castro, without hesitation; but the degree to which he won this trust corresponds precisely to the degree that he interpreted the people's desires and aspirations correctly, and to the degree that he made a sincere effort to fulfill the promises he made.

The mass participated in the agrarian reform and in the difficult task of the administration of state enterprises; it went through the heroic experience of Playa Girón; it was hardened in the battles against various bands of bandits armed by the CIA; it lived through one of the most important decisions of modern times during the October crisis; and today it continues to work for the building of socialism.

Viewed superficially, it might appear that those who speak of the subordination of the individual to the state are right. The mass carries out with matchless enthusiasm and discipline the tasks set by the government, whether economic in character, cultural, defensive, athletic, or whatever.

The initiative generally comes from Fidel or from the Revolutionary High Command, and is explained to the people who adopt it as theirs. In some cases the party and government utilize a local experience which may be of general value to the people, and follow the same procedure.

Nevertheless, the state sometimes makes mistakes. When one of these mistakes occurs, a decline in collective enthusiasm is reflected by a resulting quantitative decrease of the contribution of each individual, each of the elements forming the whole of the masses. Work is so paralyzed that insignificant quantities are produced. It is time to make a correction. That is what happened in March, 1962, as a result of the sectarian policy imposed on the party by Aníbal Escalante.

Clearly this mechanism is not adequate for insuring a succession of judicious measures. A more structured connection with the masses is needed and we must improve it in the course of the next years. But as far as initiatives originating in the upper strata of the government are concerned, we are presently utilizing the almost intuitive method of sounding out general reactions to the great problems we confront.

In this Fidel is a master, whose own special way of fusing himself with the people can be appreciated only by seeing him in action. At the great public mass meetings one can observe something like a counterpoint between two musical melodies whose vibrations provoke still newer notes. Fidel and the mass begin to vibrate together in a dialogue of growing intensity until they reach the climax in an abrupt conclusion culminating in our cry of struggle and victory.

The difficult thing for someone not living the experience of the revolution to understand is this close dialectical unity between the individual and the mass, in which the mass, as an aggregate of individuals, is interconnected with its leaders.

Some phenomena of this kind can be seen under capitalism, when politicians capable of mobilizing popular opinion appear, but these phenomena are not really genuine social movements. (If they were, it would not be entirely correct to call them capitalist.) These movements only live as long as the persons who inspire them, or until the harshness of capitalist society puts an end to the popular illusions which made them possible.

Under capitalism man is controlled by a pitiless code of laws which is usually beyond his comprehension. The alienated human individual is tied to society in its aggregate by an invisible umbilical cord — the law of value. It is operative in all aspects of his life, shaping its course and destiny.

The laws of capitalism, blind and invisible to the majority, act upon the individual without his thinking about it. He sees only the vastness of a seemingly infinite horizon before him. That is how it is painted by capitalist propagandists who purport to draw a lesson from the example of Rockefeller — whether or not it is true — about the possibilities of success.

The amount of poverty and suffering required for the emergence of a Rockefeller, and the amount of depravity that the accumulation of a fortune of such magnitude entails, are left out of the picture, and it is not always possible to make the people in general see this.

(A discussion of how the workers in the imperialist countries are losing the spirit of working-class internationalism due to a certain degree of complicity in the exploitation of the dependent countries, and how this weakens the combativity of the masses in the imperialist countries, would be appropriate here; but that is a theme which goes beyond the aim of these notes.)

In any case the road to success is pictured as one beset with perils but which, it would seem, an individual with the proper qualities can overcome to attain the goal. The reward is seen in the distance; the way is lonely. Further on it is a route for wolves; one can succeed only at the cost of the failure of others.

I would now like to try to define the individual, the actor in this strange and moving drama of the building of socialism, in his dual existence as a unique being and as a member of society.

I think it makes the most sense to recognize his quality of incompleteness, of being an unfinished product. The sermons of the past have been transposed to the present in the individual consciousness, and a continual labor is necessary to eradicate them. The process is two-sided: On the one side, society acts through direct and indirect education; on the other, the individual subjects himself to a process of conscious self-education.

The new society being formed has to compete fiercely with the past. The latter makes itself felt in the consciousness in which the residue of an education systematically oriented towards isolating the individual still weighs heavily, and also through the very character of the transitional period in which the market relationships of the past still persist. The commodity is the economic cell of capitalist society; so long as it exists its effects will make themselves felt in the organization of production and, consequently, in consciousness.

Marx outlined the period of transition as a period which results from the explosive transformation of the capitalist system of a country destroyed by its own contradictions. However in historical reality we have seen that some countries, which were weak limbs of the tree of imperialism, were torn off first — a phenomenon foreseen by Lenin.

In these countries capitalism had developed to a degree sufficient to make its effects felt by the people in one way or another; but, having exhausted all its possibilities, it was not its internal contradictions which caused these systems to explode. The struggle for liberation from a foreign oppressor, the misery caused by external events like war whose consequences make the privileged classes bear down more heavily on the oppressed, liberation movements aimed at the overthrow of neo-colonial regimes — these are the usual factors in this kind of explosion. Conscious action does the rest.

In these countries a complete education for social labor has not yet taken place, and wealth is far from being within the reach of the masses simply through the process of appropriation. Underdevelopment on the one hand, and the inevitable flight of capital on the other, make a rapid transition impossible without sacrifices. There remains a long way to go in constructing the economic base, and the temptation to follow the beaten track of material interest as the moving lever of accelerated development is very great.

There is the danger that the forest won't be seen for the trees. Following the will-o'-the-wisp method of achieving socialism with the help of the dull instruments which link us to capitalism (the commodity as the economic cell, profitability, individual material interest as a lever, etc.) can lead into a blind alley.

Further, you get there after having traveled a long distance in which there were many crossroads and it is hard to figure out just where it was that you took the wrong turn. The economic foundation which has been formed has already done its work of undermining the development of consciousness. To build communism, you must build new men as well as the new economic base.

Hence it is very important to choose correctly the instrument for mobilizing the masses. Basically, this instrument must be moral in character, without neglecting, however, a correct utilization of the material stimulus — especially of a social character.

As I have already said, in moments of great peril it is easy to muster a powerful response to moral stimuli; but for them to retain their effect requires the development of a consciousness in which there is a new priority of values. Society as a whole must be converted into a gigantic school.

In rough outline this phenomenon is similar to the process by which capitalist consciousness was formed in its initial epoch. Capitalism uses force but it also educates the people to its system. Direct propaganda is carried out by those entrusted with explaining the inevitability of class society, either through some theory of divine origin or through a mechanical theory of natural selection.

This lulls the masses since they see themselves as being oppressed by an evil against which it is impossible to struggle. Immediately following comes hope of improvement — and in this, capitalism differed from the preceding caste systems which offered no possibilities for advancement.

For some people, the ideology of the caste system will remain in effect: The reward for the obedient after death is to be transported to some fabulous other-world where, in accordance with the old belief, good people are rewarded. For other people there is this innovation: The division of society is predestined, but through work, initiative, etc., individuals can rise out of the class to which they belong.

These two ideologies and the myth of the self-made man have to be profoundly hypocritical: They consist in self-interested demonstrations that the lie of the permanence of class divisions is a truth.

In our case direct education acquires a much greater importance. The explanation is convincing because it is true; no subterfuge is needed. It is carried on by the state's educational apparatus as a function of general, technical and ideological culture through such agencies as the Ministry of Education and the party's informational apparatus.

Education takes hold of the masses and the new attitude tends to become a habit; the masses continue to absorb it and to influence those who have not yet educated themselves. This is the indirect form of educating the masses, as powerful as the other.

But the process is a conscious one; the individual continually feels the impact of the new social power and perceives that he does not entirely measure up to its standards. Under the pressure of indirect education, he tries to adjust himself to a norm which he feels is just and which his own lack of development had prevented him from reaching theretofore. He educates himself.

In this period of the building of socialism we can see the new man being born. His image is not yet completely finished — it never could be — since the process goes forward hand in hand with the development of new economic forms.

Leaving out of consideration those whose lack of education makes them take the solitary road toward satisfying their own personal ambitions, there are those, even within this new panorama of a unified march forward, who have a tendency to remain isolated from the masses accompanying them. But what is important is that everyday men are continuing to acquire more consciousness of the need for their incorporation into society and, at the same time, of their importance as the movers of society.

They no longer travel completely alone over trackless routes toward distant desires. They follow their vanguard, consisting of the party, the advanced workers, the advanced men who walk in unity with the masses and in close communion with them. The vanguard has its eyes fixed on the future and its rewards, but this is not seen as something personal. The reward is the new society in which men will have attained new features: the society of communist man.

The road is long and full of difficulties. At times we wander from the path and must turn back; at other times we go too fast and separate ourselves from the masses; on occasions we go too slow and feel the hot breath of those treading on our heels. In our zeal as revolutionists we try to move ahead as fast as possible, clearing the way, but knowing we must draw our sustenance from the mass and that it can advance more rapidly only if we inspire it by our example.

The fact that there remains a division into two main groups (excluding, of course, that minority not participating for one reason or another in the building of socialism), despite the importance given to moral stimuli, indicates the relative lack of development of social consciousness.

The vanguard group is ideologically more advanced than the mass; the latter understands the new values, but not sufficiently. While among the former there has been a qualitative change which enables them to make sacrifices to carry out their function as an advance guard, the latter go only half way and must be subjected to stimuli and pressures of a certain intensity. That is the dictatorship of the proletariat operating not only on the defeated class but also on individuals of the victorious class.

All of this means that for total success a series of mechanisms, of revolutionary institutions, is needed. Fitted into the pattern of the multitudes marching towards the future is the concept of a harmonious aggregate of channels, steps, restraints, and smoothly working mechanisms which would facilitate that advance by ensuring the efficient selection of those destined to march in the vanguard which, itself, bestows rewards on those who fulfill their duties, and punishments on those who attempt to obstruct the development of the new society.

This institutionalization of the revolution has not yet been achieved. We are looking for something which will permit a perfect identification between the government and the community in its entirety, something appropriate to the special conditions of the building of socialism, while avoiding to the maximum degree a mere transplanting of the commonplaces of bourgeois democracy — like legislative chambers — into the society in formation.

Some experiments aimed at the gradual development of institutionalized forms of the revolution have been made, but without undue haste. The greatest obstacle has been our fear lest any appearance of formality might separate us from the masses and from the individual, might make us lose sight of the ultimate and most important revolutionary aspiration, which is to see man liberated from his alienation.

Despite the lack of institutions, which must be corrected gradually, the masses are now making history as a conscious aggregate of individuals fighting for the same cause. Man under socialism, despite his apparent standardization, is more complete; despite the lack of perfect machinery for it, his opportunities for expressing himself and making himself felt in the social organism are infinitely greater.

It is still necessary to strengthen his conscious participation, individual and collective, in all the mechanisms of management and production, and to link it to the idea of the need for technical and ideological education, so that he sees how closely interdependent these processes are and how their advancement is parallel. In this way he will reach total consciousness of his social function, which is equivalent to his full realization as a human being, once the chains of alienation are broken.

This will be translated concretely into the regaining of his true nature through liberated labor, and the expression of his proper human condition through culture and art.

In order for him to develop in the first of the above categories, labor must acquire a new status. Man dominated by commodity relationships will cease to exist, and a system will be created which establishes a quota for the fulfillment of his social duty. The means of production belong to society, and the machine will merely be the trench where duty is fulfilled.

Man will begin to see himself mirrored in his work and to realize his full stature as a human being through the object created, through the work accomplished. Work will no longer entail surrendering a part of his being in the form of labor-power sold, which no longer belongs to him, but will represent an emanation of himself reflecting his contribution to the common life, the fulfillment of his social duty.

We are doing everything possible to give labor this new status of social duty and to link it on the one side with the development of a technology which will create the conditions for greater freedom, and on the other side with voluntary work based on a Marxist appreciation of the fact that man truly reaches a full human condition when he produces without being driven by the physical need to sell his labor as a commodity.

Of course there are other factors involved even when labor is voluntary: Man has not transformed all the coercive factors around him into conditioned reflexes of a social character, and he still produces under the pressures of his society. (Fidel calls this moral compulsion.)

Man still needs to undergo a complete spiritual rebirth in his attitude towards his work, freed from the direct pressure of his social environment, though linked to it by his new habits. That will be communism.

The change in consciousness will not take place automatically, just as it doesn't take place automatically in the economy. The alterations are slow and are not harmonious; there are periods of acceleration, pauses and even retrogressions.

Furthermore we must take into account, as I pointed out before, that we are not dealing with a period of pure transition, as Marx envisaged it in his *Critique of the Gotha Program*, but rather with a new phase unforeseen by him: an initial period of the transition to communism, or the construction of socialism. It is taking place in the midst of violent class struggles and with elements of capitalism within it which obscure a complete understanding of its essence.

If we add to this the scholasticism which has hindered the development of Marxist philosophy and impeded the systematic development of the theory of the transition period, we must agree that we are still in diapers and that it is necessary to devote ourselves to investigating all the principal characteristics of this period before elaborating an economic and political theory of greater scope.

The resulting theory will, no doubt, put great stress on the two pillars of the construction of socialism: the education of the new man and the development of technology. There is much for us to do in regard to both, but delay is least excusable in regard to the concepts of technology, since here it is not a question of going forward blindly but of following over a long stretch of road already opened up by the world's more advanced countries. This is why Fidel pounds away with such insistence on the need for the technological training of our people and especially of its vanguard.

In the field of ideas not involving productive activities it is easier to distinguish the division between material and spiritual necessity. For a long time man has been trying to free himself from alienation through culture and art. While he dies every day during the eight or more hours that he sells his labor, he comes to life afterwards in his spiritual activities.

But this remedy bears the germs of the same sickness; it is as a solitary individual that he seeks communion with his environment. He defends his oppressed individuality through the artistic medium and reacts to esthetic ideas as a unique being whose aspiration is to remain untarnished.

All that he is doing, however, is attempting to escape. The law of value is not simply a naked reflection of productive relations: The monopoly capitalists — even while employing purely empirical methods — weave around art a complicated web which converts it into a willing tool. The superstructure of society ordains the type of art in which the artist has to be educated. Rebels are subdued by its machinery and only rare talents may create their own work. The rest become shameless hacks or are crushed.

A school of artistic "freedom" is created, but its values also have limits even if they are imperceptible until we come into conflict with them — that is to say, until the real problem of man and his alienation arises. Meaningless anguish and vulgar amusement thus become convenient safety valves for human anxiety. The idea of using art as a weapon of protest is combated.

If one plays by the rules, he gets all the honors — such honors as a monkey might get for performing pirouettes. The condition that has been imposed is that one cannot try to escape from the invisible cage.

When the revolution took power there was an exodus of those who had been completely housebroken; the rest — whether they were revolutionaries or not — saw a new road open to them. Artistic inquiry experienced a new impulse. The paths, however, had already been more or less laid out and the escapist concept hid itself behind the word "freedom." This attitude was often found even among the revolutionaries themselves, reflecting the bourgeois idealism still in their consciousness.

In those countries which had gone through a similar process they tried to combat such tendencies by an exaggerated dogmatism. General culture was virtually tabooed, and it was declared that the acme of cultural aspiration was the formally exact representation of nature. This was later transformed into a mechanical representation of the social reality they wanted to show: the ideal society almost without conflicts or contradictions which they sought to create.

Socialism is young and has made errors. Many times revolutionaries lack the knowledge and intellectual courage needed to meet the task of developing the new man with methods different from the conventional ones — and the conventional methods suffer from the influences of the society which created them.

(Again we raise the theme of the relationship between form and content.)

Disorientation is widespread, and the problems of material construction preoccupy us. There are no artists of great authority who at the same time have great revolutionary authority. The men of the party must take this task to hand and seek attainment of the main goal, the education of the people.

But then they sought simplification. They sought an art that would be understood by everyone — the kind of "art" *functionaries* understand. True artistic values were disregarded, and the problem of general culture was reduced to taking some things from the socialist present and some from the dead past (since dead, not dangerous). Thus Socialist Realism arose upon the foundations of the art of the last century.

But the realistic art of the nineteenth century is also a class art, more purely capitalist perhaps than this decadent art of the twentieth century which reveals the anguish of alienated man. In the field of culture capitalism has given all that it had to give, and nothing of it remains but the offensive stench of a decaying corpse, today's decadence in art.

Why then should we try to find the only valid prescription for art in the frozen forms of Socialist Realism? We cannot counterpose the concept of Socialist Realism to that of freedom because the latter does not yet exist and will not exist until the complete development of the new society. Let us not attempt, from the pontifical throne of realism-at-any-cost, to condemn all the art forms which have evolved since the first half of the nineteenth century for we would then fall into the Proudhonian mistake of returning to the past, of putting a straitjacket on the artistic expression of the man who is being born and is in the process of making himself.

What is needed is the development of an ideological-cultural mechanism which permits both free inquiry and the uprooting of the weeds which multiply so easily in the fertile soil of state subsidies.

In our country we don't find the error of mechanical realism, but rather its opposite, and that is so because the need for the creation of a new man has not been understood, a new man who would represent neither the ideas of the nineteenth century nor those of our own decadent and morbid century.

What we must create is the man of the twenty-first century, although this is still a subjective and not a realized aspiration. It is precisely this man of the next century who is one of the fundamental objectives of our work; and to the extent that we achieve concrete successes on a theoretical plane — or, vice versa, to the extent we draw theoretical conclusions of a broad character on the basis of our concrete research — we shall have made an important contribution to Marxism-Leninism, to the cause of humanity.

Reaction against the man of the nineteenth century has brought us a relapse into the decadence of the twentieth century; it is not a fatal error, but we must overcome it lest we open a breach for revisionism.

The great multitudes continue to develop; the new ideas continue to attain their proper force within society; the material possibilities for the full development of all members of society make the task much more fruitful. The present is a time for struggle; the future is ours.

To sum up, the fault of our artists and intellectuals lies in their original sin: They are not truly revolutionary. We can try to graft the elm tree so that it will bear pears, but at the same time we must plant pear trees. New generations will come who will be free of the original sin. The probabilities that great artists will appear will be greater to the degree that the field of culture and the possibilities for expression are broadened.

Our task is to prevent the present generation, torn asunder by its conflicts, from becoming perverted and from perverting new generations. We must not bring into being either docile servants of official thought, or scholarship students who live at the expense of the state — practicing "freedom." Already there are revolutionaries coming who will sing the song of the new man in the true voice of the people. This is a process which takes time.

In our society the youth and the party play an important role.

The former is especially important because it is the malleable clay from which the new man can be shaped without any of the old faults. The youth is treated in accordance with our aspirations. Its education steadily grows more full, and we are not forgetting about its integration into the labor force from the beginning. Our scholarship students do physical work during their vacations or along with their studying. Work is a reward in some cases, a means of education in others, but it is never a punishment. A new generation is being born.

The party is a vanguard organization. The best workers are proposed by their fellow workers for admission into it. It is a minority, but it has great authority because of the quality of its cadres. Our aspiration is that the party will become a mass party, but only when the masses have reached the level of the vanguard, that is, when they are educated for communism.

Our work constantly aims at this education. The party is the living example; its cadres should be teachers of hard work and sacrifice. They should lead the masses by their deeds to the completion of the revolutionary task which involves years of hard struggle against the difficulties of construction, class enemies, the sicknesses of the past, imperialism. . .

Now, I would like to explain the role played by personality, by man as the individual leader of the masses which make history. This has been our experience; it is not a prescription.

Fidel gave the revolution its impulse in the first years, and also its leadership. He always strengthened it; but there is a good group who are developing in the same way as the outstanding leader, and there is a great mass which follows its leaders because it has faith in them, and it has faith in them because they have been able to interpret its desires.

This is not a matter of how many pounds of meat one might be able to eat, nor of how many times a year someone can go to the beach, nor how many ornaments from abroad you might be able to buy with present salaries. What is really involved is that the individual feels more complete, with much more internal richness and much more responsibility.

The individual in our country knows that the illustrious epoch in which it was determined that he live is one of sacrifice; he is familiar with sacrifice. The first came to know it in the Sierra Maestra and wherever else they fought; afterwards all of Cuba came to know it. Cuba is the vanguard of the Americas and must make sacrifices because it occupies the post of advance guard, because it shows the road to full freedom to the masses of Latin America.

Within the country the leadership has to carry out its vanguard role, and it must be said with all sincerity that in a real revolution, to which one gives himself entirely and from which he expects no material remuneration, the task of the revolutionary vanguard is at one and the same time glorious and agonizing.

At the risk of seeming ridiculous, let me say that the true revolutionary is guided by a great feeling of love. It is impossible to think of a genuine revolutionary lacking this quality. Perhaps it is one of the great dramas of the leader that he must combine a passionate spirit with a cold intelligence and make painful decisions, without contracting a muscle. Our vanguard revolutionaries must idealize this love of the people, the most sacred cause, and make it one and indivisible. They cannot descend, with small doses of daily affection, to the level where ordinary men put their love into practice.

The leaders of the revolution have children just beginning to talk, who are not learning to call their fathers by name; wives, from whom they have to be separated as part of the general sacrifice of their lives to bring the revolution to its fulfillment; the circle of their friends is limited strictly to the number of fellow revolutionists. There is no life outside of the revolution.

In these circumstances one must have a great deal of humanity and a strong sense of justice and truth in order not to fall into extreme dogmatism and cold scholasticism, into an isolation from the masses. We must strive every day so that this love of living humanity will be transformed into actual deeds, into acts that serve as examples, as a moving force.

The revolutionary, the ideological motor force of the revolution, is consumed by his uninterrupted activity which can come to an end only with death until the building of socialism on a world scale has been accomplished. If his revolutionary zeal is blunted when the most urgent tasks are being accomplished on a local scale and he forgets his proletarian internationalism, the revolution which he leads will cease to be an inspiring force, and he will sink into a comfortable lethargy which imperialism, our irreconcilable enemy, will utilize well. Proletarian internationalism is a duty, but it is also a revolutionary necessity. So we educate our people.

Of course there are dangers in the present situation, and not only that of dogmatism, not only that of weakening the ties with the masses midway in the great task. There is also the danger of weaknesses. If a man thinks that dedicating his entire life to the revolution means that in return he should not have such worries as that his son lacks certain things, or that his children's shoes are worn out, or that his family lacks some necessity, then he is entering into rationalizations which open his mind to infection by the seeds of future corruption.

In our case we have maintained that our children should have or should go without those things that the children of the average man have or go without, and that our families should understand this and strive to uphold this standard. The revolution is made through man, but man must forge his revolutionary spirit day by day.

Thus we march on. At the head of the immense column — we are neither afraid nor ashamed to say it — is Fidel. After him come the best cadres of the party, and immediately behind them, so close that we feel its tremendous force, comes the people in its entirety, a solid mass of individualities moving toward a common goal, individuals who have attained consciousness of what must be done, men who fight to escape from the realm of necessity and to enter that of freedom.

This great throng becomes organized; its clarity of program corresponds to its consciousness of the necessity of organization. It is no longer a dispersed force, divisible into thousands of fragments thrown into space like splinters from a hand grenade, trying by any means to achieve some protection against an uncertain future, in desperate struggle with their fellows.

We know that sacrifices lie before us and that we must pay a price for the heroic act of being a vanguard nation. We leaders know that we must pay a price for the right to say that we are at the head of a people which is at the head of the Americas. Each and every one of us must pay his exact quota of sacrifice, conscious that he will get his reward in the satisfaction of fulfilling a duty, conscious that he will advance with all toward the image of the new man dimly visible on the horizon.

Let me attempt some conclusions:

We socialists are freer because we are more complete; we are more complete because we are freer.

The skeleton of our complete freedom is already formed. The flesh and the clothing are lacking. We will create them.

Our freedom and its daily maintenance are paid for in blood and sacrifice.

Our sacrifice is conscious: an installment payment on the freedom that we are building.

The road is long and in part unknown. We understand our limitations. We will create the man of the twenty-first century — we, ourselves.

We will forge ourselves in daily action, creating a new man with a new technology.

Individual personality plays a role in mobilizing and leading the masses insofar as it embodies the highest virtues and aspirations of the people and does not wander from the path.

It is the vanguard group which clears the way, the best among the good, the party.

The basic clay of our work is the youth. We place our hope in them and prepare them to take the banner from our hands.

*   *   *

If this inarticulate letter clarifies anything it has accomplished the objective which motivated it. I close with our greeting – which is as much of a ritual as a handshake or an "Ave Maria Purissima"– Our Country or Death!

Pan-Africanism or Communism (excerpt)

George Padmore

AUTHOR'S NOTE

Since the end of the Second World War it has become notorious, both in the press and in certain political circles of the Western world, to ascribe every manifestation of political awakening in Africa to Communist inspiration. This is gross hypocrisy, part of the cold war propaganda designed to discredit African nationalists and to alienate from their movements the sympathy and support of anti-colonial elements within Labour and progressive organizations, which, while friendly towards the political aspiration of the colonial peoples, are hostile to Communism.

The facts revealed in this book will prove the falsity of this smear campaign and pinpoint the danger to the Western peoples of allowing the policies of their Governments to destroy the latent friendship and goodwill of the Africans; policies which may well force Africans to seek allies among the Communists in their efforts to gain their independence.

At the moment none of the African independence movements is influenced by Communism. Indeed, this book will show that the struggles of Africans and peoples of African descent began with their endeavours to establish a 'National Home' on the West African coast nearly a century before Communist Russia emerged as a power in world politics. As a matter of fact, much of the first Back to Africa efforts belongs to the period of the Abolitionist movements in Britain and America. At that time, the Russian peoples themselves were living very close to slavery under the yoke of Czarist serfdom.

In order to place this phase of African nationalism in its true historical perspective, I have found it necessary to survey in broad outline the progress of the colonization of Sierra Leone and Liberia and to trace their constitutional and political development.

The main purpose of the book, however, is to record the rise and growth of the contemporary Negro political movements: 'Pan-Africanism' and 'Garveyism' or 'Black Zionism'. The latter was, primarily, an attempt to revive the nineteenth-century Back to Africa movements which inspired the foundation of Sierra Leone and Liberia.

During the nineteen-twenties, Black Zionism as expounded by its founder, Marcus Aurelius Garvey, was the most militant expression of African nationalism. As affirmed by C. L. R. James, the West Indian historian, the name of Garvey 'rolled through Africa. The King of Swaziland told a friend some years after that he knew the names of only two black men in the Western world, Jack Johnson and Marcus Garvey.'[1] Though Black Zionism did not sustain itself as an organized movement, 'one thing Garvey did do. He made the American Negro conscious of his African origin and created for the first time a feeling of international solidarity among Africans and people of African descent.'

Both Garveyism and Pan-Africanism, which originated about the same time, have much influenced the present generation of nationalists, but neither movement has drawn inspiration or support from Communism. On the contrary, the philosophies and programmes of both movements have been bitterly assailed by the Communists. For instance, the Sixth Congress of the now defunct Communist International declared open war upon the Garvey movement when the leaders refused to allow white Communists to exploit their organization in the service of Soviet foreign policy. In its directive to American Communists the International declared that 'Garveyism, which was formerly the ideology of the masses, like Gandhism, has become a hindrance to the revolutionization of the Negro masses. Originally advocating social equality for Negroes, Garveyism subsequently developed into a peculiar form of Negro "Zionism", which, instead of fighting American imperialism, advanced the slogan "Back to Africa". This dangerous ideology, which bears not a single democratic trait, and which toys with the aristocratic attributes of a non-existent "Negro Kingdom", must be strongly resisted, for it is not a help but a hindrance to the mass Negro struggle for liberation against American imperialism'. Pan-Africanism, too, was branded as 'reactionary petit-bourgeois nationalism', and its founder, the distinguished Afro-American scholar, Dr W.E.B. DuBois, was denounced as 'a betrayer of the Negro people'.

When, therefore, Western imperialists and their apologists in the Labour movement credit the Communists with inspiring emerging African nationalism, they are either being deliberately misleading or self-deceiving. The dynamic forces of post-war anti-colonialist movements which are challenging the political and economic domination of the West are the spontaneous expression of the hopes and desires of the Africans, looking forward to a place as free men in a free world. Africans do not have to wait for Communists to 'incite' them. The realities of their status have infused their determination to be free. And they prefer to attain freedom under the standard of Pan-Africanism, a banner of their own choosing.

For if there is one thing which events in Africa, no less than in Asia, have demonstrated in the post-war years, it is that colonial peoples are resentful of the attitude of Europeans, of both Communist and anti-Communist persuasion, that they alone possess the knowledge and experience necessary to guide the advancement of dependent peoples. Africans feel that they are quite capable of leading themselves, and of developing a philosophy and ideology suited to their own special circumstances and needs, and have come to regard the arrogance of white 'loftiness' in this respect as unwarranted interference and unpardonable assumption of superiority. Africans are quite willing to accept advice and support which is offered in a spirit of true equality, and would prefer to remain on terms of friendship with the West. But they want to make their way under their own steam. If, however, they are obstructed they may in their frustration turn to Communism as the only alternative means of achieving their aims. The future pattern of Africa, therefore, will, in this context, be in large measure determined by the attitudes of the Western nations.

Recognizing the oneness of the struggles of the Coloured World for freedom from alien domination, Pan-Africanism endorses the conception of an Asian-African front against that racial arrogance which has reached its apogee in the *Herrenvolk* philosophy of *Apartheid*. Pan-Africanism, moreover, draws considerable inspiration from the struggles of the national freedom movements of the Asian countries, and subscribes to the Gandhian doctrine of non-violence as a means of attaining self-determination and racial equality. It rejects the unbridled system of monopoly capitalism of the West no less than the political and cultural totalitarianism of the East. It identifies itself with the neutral camp, opposed to all forms of oppression and racial chauvinism—white or black—and associates itself with all forces of progress and goodwill, regardless of nationality, race, colour, or creed, working for universal brotherhood, social justice, and peace *for all peoples everywhere*.

Africans, like Asians, have a vested interest in *Peace*, since only in a world, ordered and free from violence and war can they hope to create a new life for themselves and make their positive contribution to modern civilization.

Pan-Africanism recognizes much that is true in the Marxist interpretation of history, since it provides a rational explanation for a good deal that would otherwise be unintelligible. But it nevertheless refuses to accept the pretentious claims of doctrinaire Communism, that it alone has the solution to all the complex racial, tribal, and socio-economic problems facing Africa. It also rejects the Communist intolerance of those who do not subscribe to its ever-changing party line even to the point of liquidating them as 'enemies of the people'. Democracy and brotherhood cannot be built upon intolerance and violence.

In their struggles to attain self-government and self-determination, the younger leaders of Pan-Africanism have the task of building upon the ideological foundations laid by Dr DuBois, the 'father' of Pan-Africanism. The problems facing these men are very much more varied and complex than those which beset the founders of the Sierra Leone and Liberian settlements. They are under the necessity to evolve new political means and organizational techniques adapted to African traditions and circumstances. They also have to work out a social philosophy which will integrate and uplift peoples making the transition from primitive tribal forms of society to modern industrialized states with the speed demanded by present-day pressures.

So that the reader may appreciate some of the difficulties facing emerging African nationalism, I have given a brief review of political evolution in the Gold Coast and Nigeria since the end of the Second World War. In these West African colonies political advance has been along constitutional lines, in contrast to Kenya, where the tensions in multi-racial society have erupted in Mau Mau conflict and bloody violence. A comparison of British colonial policies in West and East Africa will enable the reader to appreciate better the explosive effects which the denial of racial equality in a plural society can have. The problem of European settlements in East, Central and Southern Africa can be solved only by the creation of *a common citizenship for all the races—indigenous and immigrant—on the basis of absolute equality for Africans in Church and State*. There is no other solution, since Africans are not going to tolerate being treated as inferiors in their own lands.

In the hope of throwing some light on to the conflicting and bewildering medley of colonial systems in Africa, I have attempted to define and interpret the political and social status of Africans living under the rule of the different European powers which exercise dominion over the continent. Africa is, without doubt, the continent, *par excellence*, of administrative anarchy. Each of the ruling powers pursues its own particular form of government; some even pursue two or three conflicting policies at one and the same time.

For instance, while British policy in East, Central, and Southern Africa is to support white colonization and European domination, in West Africa, Colonial Office policy is based upon the principle of national self-determination for Africans by process of gradual constitutional reform. If this policy were only honestly and vigorously pursued by the British Government, irrespective of the party in office, it would be the most effective bulwark against Communism, the spectre haunting the white settlers and British colonial officials. For African nationalists will only turn to Communism when they feel frustrated in their aspirations and become resentful of what they consider to be a betrayal of the professions enunciated by the Western democracies in the Atlantic Charter.

Our criticism of British colonial policy is not in what it professes to stand for—'self government within the Commonwealth'—but the failure to make good this promise unless actually forced to do so by the colonial peoples. It has always been a case of 'too little and too late'. The result is that the dependent peoples, who would otherwise be Britain's friends and allies, become her implacable enemies. What British colonial policy needs to do today is to make open recognition of awakening African self-awareness, and instil its own acts with boldness and imagination. Deeds and not vague promises are what is wanted.

For their part, the African nationalist leaders must resolve their own internal communal conflicts and tribal differences, so that, having established a democratically elected government, the imperial power will find less danger in passing power to the popularly elected leaders than in withholding it. Once a colonial people have achieved freedom, as the history of the recently emerged Asian nations has so well illustrated, they will know how to defend it against those subversive elements within their midst who seek to make them pawns in the power politics of the cold war belligerents.

In the coming struggle for Africa, the issue, as I have already inferred, will be between Pan-Africanism and Communism. Imperialism is a discredited system, completely rejected by Africans. As for white colonization, it can maintain itself only with outside military support. The white man in East and Central Africa has forfeited the loyalty and goodwill of the Africans, who no longer have illusions about professions of 'trusteeship' and 'partnership'. These British settlers, to say nothing of the fanatical racialists and rabid defenders of *Apartheid* in South Africa, have made it abundantly clear to the Africans that they regard them merely as hewers of wood and drawers of water in their own countries.

As to Communism, Africans have no reason to be scared of the red bogey as long as their political leaders remain true to the ideals and principles of Pan-Africanism. For politically, Pan-Africanism seeks the attainment of the government of Africans by Africans for Africans, with respect for racial and religious minorities who desire to live in Africa on a basis of equality with the black majority. Economically and socially, Pan-Africanism, subscribes to the fundamental objectives of Democratic Socialism, with state control of the basic means of production and distribution. It stands for the liberty of the subject within the law and endorses the Fundamental Declaration of Human Rights, with emphasis upon the Four Freedoms.

The post-war happenings in Asia have shown that forms of government are not of paramount importance to the masses of the people. Their interest is in the satisfaction of their elemental needs. Communism exploits misery, poverty, ignorance and want. The only effective answer to Communism, therefore, is to remove these conditions by satisfying the wants and material needs of the common people, which revolve primarily round food, clothing, and shelter. Any honest, incorruptible government seeking to do this will provide the best guarantee against Communism. Hence, Pan-Africanism sets out to fulfil the socio-economic mission of Communism under a libertarian political system.

Finally, for Pan-Africanism, the self-determination of the dependent territories is the prerequisite to the federation of self-governing states on a regional basis, leading ultimately to the creation of a United States of Africa. For there is a growing feeling among politically conscious Africans throughout the continent that their destiny is one, that what happens in one part of Africa to Africans must affect Africans living in other parts. As far back as forty years ago, Dr DuBois, in his book, *The Negro*, pointed out a truth which, if anything, is even more pregnant today. '*There is slowly arising not only a curiously strong brotherhood of Negro blood throughout the world, but the common cause of the darker races against the intolerable assumption and insults of Europeans has already found expression. Most men in the world are coloured. A belief in humanity means a belief in coloured men. The future world will, in all reasonable possibility, be what coloured men make it.*'

This is the inescapable challenge of the second part of the twentieth century.

George Padmore.

London
July, 1955

Note
1.   C. L. R. James, *A History of Negro Revolt*, 68.

An End to the Neglect of the Problems of Negro Women!

Claudia Jones

An outstanding feature of the present stage of the Negro liberation movement is the growth in the militant participation of Negro women in all aspects of the struggle for peace, civil rights, and economic security. Symptomatic of this new militancy is the fact that Negro women have become symbols of many present-day struggles of the Negro people. This growth of militancy among Negro women has profound meaning, both for the Negro liberation movement and for the emerging anti-fascist, anti-imperialist coalition.

To understand this militancy correctly, to deepen and extend the role of Negro women in the struggle for peace and for all interests of the working class and the Negro people, means primarily to overcome the gross neglect of the special problems of Negro women. This neglect has too long permeated the ranks of the labor movement generally, of Left-progressives, and also of the Communist Party. The most serious assessment of these shortcomings by progressives, especially by Marxist-Leninists, is vitally necessary if we are to help accelerate this development and integrate Negro women in the progressive and labor movement in our own Party.

The bourgeoisie is fearful of the militancy of the Negro woman, and for good reason. The capitalists know, far better than many progressives seem to know, that once Negro women undertake action, the militancy of the whole Negro people, and thus of the anti-imperialist coalition, is greatly enhanced.

Historically, the Negro woman has been the guardian, the protector, of the Negro family. From the days of the slave traders down to the present, the Negro woman has had the responsibility of caring for the needs of the family, of militancy shielding it from the blows of Jim Crow insults, of rearing children in an atmosphere of lynch terror, segregation, and policy brutality, and of fighting for an education for the children. The intensified oppression of the Negro people, which has been the hallmark of the postwar reactionary offensive, cannot therefore but lead to an acceleration of the militancy of the Negro woman. As mother, as Negro, and as worker, the Negro woman fights against the wiping out of the Negro family, against the Jim Crow ghetto existence which destroys the health, morale and the very life of millions of her sisters, brothers, and children.

Viewed in this light, it is not accidental that the American bourgeoisie has intensified its oppression, not only of the Negro people in general, but of Negro women in particular. Nothing so exposes the drive to fascization in the nation as the callous attitude which the bourgeoisie displays and cultivates toward Negro women. The vaunted boast of the ideologists of Big Business — that American women possess 'the greatest equality' in the world is exposed in all its hypocrisy in the Soviet Union, the New Democracies and the formerly oppressed land of China, women are attaining new heights of equality. But above all else, Wall Street's boast stops at the water's edge where Negro and working-class women are concerned. Not equality, but degradation and super-exploitation: this is the actual lot of Negro women!

Consider the hypocrisy of the Truman Administration, which boasts about 'exporting democracy throughout the world' while the state of Georgia keeps a widowed Negro mother of twelve children under lock and key. Her crime? She defended her life and dignity — aided by her two sons — from the attacks of a 'white supremacist'. Or ponder the mute silence with which the Department of Justice has greeted Mrs. Amy Mallard, widowed Negro school teacher, since her husband was lynched in Georgia because he had bought a new Cadillac and become, in the opinion of the 'white supremacists', 'too uppity'. Contrast this with the crocodile tears shed by the US delegation to the United Nations for Cardinal Mindszenty, who collaborated with the enemies of the Hungarian People's Republic and sought to hinder the forward march to fuller democracy by the formerly oppressed workers and peasants of Hungary. Only recently, President Truman spoke solicitously in a Mother's Day Proclamation about the manifestation of 'our love and reverence' for all mothers of the land. The so-called 'love and reverence' for the mothers of the land by no means includes Negro mothers who, like Rosa Lee Ingram, Amy Mallard, the wives and mothers of the Trenton Six, or the other countless victims, dare to fight back against lynch law and 'white supremacy' violence.

Economic Hardships

Very much to the contrary, Negro women — as workers, as Negroes, and as women — are the most oppressed stratum of the whole population.

In 1940, two out of every five Negro women, in contrast to two out of every eight white women, worked for a living. By virtue of their majority status among the Negro people, Negro women not only constitute the largest percentage of women heads of families, but are the main breadwinners of the Negro family. The large proportion of Negro women in the labor market is primarily a result of the low-scale earnings of Negro men. This disproportion also has its roots in the treatment and position of Negro women over the centuries.

Following the emancipation, and persisting to the present day, a large percentage of Negro women — married as well as single — were forced to work for a living. But despite the shift in employment of Negro women from rural to urban areas, Negro women are still generally confined to the lowest-paying jobs. The Women's Bureau, US Department of Labor, *Handbook of Facts for Women Workers* (1948, Bulletin 225), shows white women workers as having median earnings more than twice as high as those of non-white women, and non-white women workers (mainly Negro women) as earning less than $500 a year! In the rural South, the earnings of women are even less. In three large Northern industrial communities, the median income of white families ($1,720) is also 60 percent higher than that of Negro families ($1,095). The super-exploitation of the Negro woman worker is thus revealed not only in that she receives, as woman, less than equal pay for equal work with men, but in that the majority of Negro women get less than half the pay of white women. Little wonder, then, that in Negro communities the conditions of ghetto-living — low salaries, high rents, high prices, etc. — virtually become an iron curtain hemming in the lives of Negro children and undermining their health and spirit! Little wonder that the maternity death rate for Negro women is triple that of white women! Little wonder that one out of every ten Negro children born in the United States does not grow to manhood or womanhood!

The low scale of earnings of Negro woman is directly related to her almost complete exclusion from virtually all fields of work except the most menial and underpaid, namely, domestic service. Revealing are the following data given in the report of 1945, *Negro Women War Workers* (Women's Bureau, US Department of Labor, Bulletin 205): Of a total 7½ million Negro women, over a million are in domestic and personal service. The overwhelming bulk — about 918,000 — of these women workers are employed in private families, and some 98,000 are employed as cooks, waitresses, and in like services in other than private homes. The remaining 60,000 workers in service trades are in miscellaneous personal service occupations (beauticians, boarding house and lodging-house keepers, charwomen, janitors, practical nurses, housekeepers, hostesses, and elevator operators).

The next largest number of Negro women workers are engaged in agricultural work. In 1940, about 245,000 were agricultural workers. Of them, some 128,000 were unpaid family workers.

Industrial and other workers numbered more than 96,000 of the Negro women reported. Thirty-six thousand of these women were in manufacturing, the chief groups being 11,300 in apparel and other fabricated textile products, 1,000 in tobacco manufacturers, and 5,600 in food and related products.

Clerical and kindred workers in general numbered only 13,000. There were only 8,300 Negro women workers in civil service.

The rest of the Negro women who work for a living were distributed along the following lines: teachers, 50,000; nurses and student nurses, 6,700; social and welfare workers, 1,700; dentists, pharmacists, and veterinarians, 120; physicians and surgeons, 129; actresses, 200; authors, editors and reporters, 100; lawyers and judges, 39; librarians, 400; and other categories likewise illustrating the large-scale exclusion of Negro women from the professions.

During the anti-Axis war, Negro women for the first time in history had an opportunity to utilize their skills and talents in occupations other than domestic and personal service. They became trail blazers in many fields. Since the end of the war, however, this has given way to growing unemployment, to the wholesale firing of Negro women, particularly in basic industry.

This process has been intensified with the development of the economic crisis. Today, Negro women are being forced back into domestic work in great numbers. In New York State, for example, this trend was officially confirmed recently when Edward Corsi, Commissioner of the State Labor Department, revealed that for the first time since the war, domestic help is readily obtainable. Corsi in effect admitted that Negro women are not voluntarily giving up jobs, but rather are being systematically pushed out of industry. Unemployment, which has always hit the Negro woman first and hardest, plus the high cost of living, is what compels Negro women to re-enter domestic service today. Accompanying this trend is an ideological campaign to make domestic work palatable. Daily newspaper advertisements which base their arguments on the claim that most domestic workers who apply for jobs through USES 'prefer this type of work to work in industry', are propagandizing the 'virtues' of domestic work, especially of 'sleep-in positions'.

Inherently connected with the question of job opportunities where the Negro woman is concerned, is the special oppression she faces as Negro, as woman and as worker. She is the victim of the white chauvinist stereotype as to where her place should be. In the film, radio and press, the Negro woman is not pictured in her real role as breadwinner, mother, and protector of the family, but as a traditional 'mammy' who puts the care of children and families of others above her own. This traditional stereotype of the Negro slave mother, which to this day appears in commercial advertisements, must be combatted and rejected as a device of the imperialists to perpetuate the white chauvinist ideology that Negro women are 'backward', 'inferior', and the 'natural slaves' of others.

Historical Aspects

Actually, the history of the Negro woman shows that the Negro mother under slavery held a key position and played a dominant role in her own family grouping. This was due primarily to two factors: the conditions of slavery, under which marriage, as such, was non-existent, and the Negro's social status was derived from the mother and not the father; and the fact that most of the Negro people brought to these shores by the slave traders came from West Africa where the position of women, based on active participation in property control, was relatively higher in the family than that of European women.

Early historians of the slave trade recall the testimony of travelers indicating that the love of the African mother for her child was unsurpassed in any part of the world. There are numerous stories attesting to the self-sacrificial way in which East African mothers offered themselves to the slave traders in order to save their sons and Hottentot women refused food during famines until after their children were fed.

It is impossible within the confines of this article to relate the terrible sufferings and degradation undergone by Negro mothers and Negro women generally under slavery. Subject to legalized rape by the slaveowners, confined to slave pens, forced to march for eight to fourteen hours with loads on their backs and to perform back-breaking work even during pregnancy, Negro women bore a burning hatred for slavery, and undertook a large share of the responsibility for defending and nurturing the Negro family.

The Negro mother was mistress in the slave cabin, and despite the interference of master or overseer, her wishes in regard to mating and in family matters were paramount. During and after slavery, Negro women had to support themselves and the children, necessarily playing an important role in the economic and social life of her people.

The Negro Woman Worker

The negligible participation of Negro women in progressive and trade union circles is thus all the more startling. In union after union, even in those unions where a large concentration of workers are Negro women, few Negro women are to be found as leaders or active workers. The outstanding exceptions to this are the Food and Tobacco Workers' Union and the United Office and Professional Workers' Union.

But why should these be exceptions? Negro women are among the most militant trade unionists. The sharecroppers' strike of the '30's were sparkplugged by Negro women. Subject to the terror of the landlord and white supremacist, they waged magnificent battles together with Negro men and white progressives in that struggle of great tradition led by the Communist Party. Negro women played a magnificent part in the pre-CIO days in strikes and other struggles, both as workers and as wives of workers, to win recognition of the principle of industrial unionism, in such industries as auto, packing, steel, etc. More recently, the militancy of Negro women unionists is shown in the strike of the packing-house workers, and even more so, in the tobacco workers' strike — in which such leaders as Moranda Smith and Velma Hopkins emerged as outstanding trade unionists. The struggle of the tobacco workers led by Negro women later merged with the political action of Negro and white which led to the election of the first Negro in the South (in Winston-Salem, North Carolina) since Reconstruction days.

It is incumbent on progressive unionists to realize that in the fight for equal rights for Negro workers, it is necessary to have a special approach to Negro women workers, who, far out of proportion to other women workers, are the main breadwinners in their families. The fight to retain the Negro woman in industry and to upgrade her on the job, is a major way of struggling for the basic and special interests of the Negro woman worker. Not to recognize this feature is to miss the special aspects of the effects of the growing economic crisis, which is penalizing Negro workers, particularly Negro women workers, with special severity.

The Domestic Worker

One of the crassest manifestations of trade union neglect of the problems of the Negro woman worker has been the failure, not only to fight against relegation of the Negro woman to domestic and similar menial work, but to *organize* the domestic worker. It is merely lip-service for progressive unionists to speak of organizing the un-organized without turning their eyes to the serious plight of the domestic worker, who, unprotected by union standards, is also the victim of exclusion from all social and labor legislation. Only about one in ten of all Negro women workers are to be found in states having minimum-wage laws. All of the arguments heretofore projected with regard to the real difficulties of organizing the domestic workers — such as the 'casual' nature of their employment, the difficulties of organizing day workers, the problem of organizing people who work in individual households, etc., — must be overcome forthwith. There is a danger that Social-Democratic forces may enter this field to do their work of spreading disunity and demagogy, unless progressives act quickly.

The lot of the domestic worker is one of unbearable misery. Usually, she has no definition of tasks in the household where she works. Domestic workers may have 'thrown in', in addition to cleaning and scrubbing, such tasks as washing windows, caring for the children, laundering, cooking etc., and all at the lowest pay. The Negro domestic worker must suffer the additional indignity, in some areas, of having to seek work in virtual 'slave markets' on the streets where bids are made, as from a slave block, for the hardiest workers. Many a domestic worker, on returning to her own household, must begin housework anew to keep her own family together.

Who was not enraged when it was revealed in California, in the heinous case of Dora Jones, that a Negro woman domestic was enslaved for more than 40 years in 'civilized' America? Her 'employer' was given a minimum sentence of a few years and complained that the sentence was for 'such a long period of time'. But could Dora Jones, Negro domestic worker, be repaid for more than 40 years of her life under such conditions of exploitation and degradation? And how many cases, partaking in varying degrees of the condition of Dora Jones, are still tolerated by progressives themselves!

Only recently, in the New York State Legislature, legislative proposals were made to 'fingerprint' domestic workers. The Martinez Bill did not see the light of day, because the reactionaries were concentrating on other repressive legislative measures; but here we see clearly the imprint of the African 'pass' system of British imperialism (and of the German Reich in relation to the Jewish people!) being attempted in relation to women domestic workers.

It is incumbent on the trade unions to assist the Domestic Workers' Union in every possible way to accomplish the task of organizing the exploited domestic workers, the majority of whom are Negro women. Simultaneously, a legislative fight for the inclusion of domestic workers under the benefits of the Social Security Law is vitally urgent and necessary. Here, too, recurrent questions regarding 'administrative problems' of applying the law to domestic workers should be challenged and solutions found.

The continued relegation of Negro women to domestic work has helped to perpetuate and intensify chauvinism directed against all Negro women. Despite the fact that Negro women may be grandmothers or mothers, the use of the chauvinist term 'girl' for adult Negro women is a common expression. The very economic relationship of Negro women to white women, which perpetuates 'madam-maid' relationships, feeds chauvinist attitudes and makes it incumbent on white women progressives, and particularly Communists, to fight consciously against all manifestations of white chauvinism, open and subtle.

Chauvinism on the part of progressive white women is often expressed in their failure to have close ties of friendship with Negro women and to realize that this fight for equality of Negro women is in their own self-interest, inasmuch as the super-exploitation and oppression of Negro women tends to depress the standards of all women. Too many progressives, and even some Communists, are still guilty of exploiting Negro domestic workers, of refusing to hire them through the Domestic Workers' Union (or of refusing to help in its expansion into those areas where it does not yet exist), and generally of participating in the vilification of 'maids' when speaking to their bourgeois neighbours and their own families. Then, there is the expressed 'concern' that the exploited Negro domestic worker does not 'talk' to, or is not 'friendly' with, her employer, or the habit of assuming that the duty of the white progressive employer is to 'inform' the Negro woman of her exploitation and her oppression which she undoubtedly knows quite intimately. Persistent challenge to every chauvinist remark as concerns the Negro woman is vitally necessary, if we are to break down the understandable distress on the part of the Negro women who are repelled by the white chauvinism they often find expressed in progressive circles.

Manifestations of White Chauvinism

Some of the crassest expressions of chauvinism are to be found at social affairs, where, all too often, white men and women and Negro men participate in dancing, but Negro women are neglected the acceptance of white ruling-class standards of 'desirability' for women (such as light skin), the failure to extend courtesy to Negro women and to integrate Negro women into organizational leadership, are other forms of chauvinism.

Another rabid aspect of the Jim Crow oppression of the Negro woman is expressed in the numerous laws which are directed against her as regards property rights, inter-marriage (originally designed to prevent white men in the South from marrying Negro women), and laws which hinder and deny the right of choice, not only to Negro women, but Negro and white men and women.

For white progressive women and men, and especially for Communists, the question of social relations with Negro men and women is above all a question of strictly adhering to social equality. This means ridding ourselves of the position which sometimes finds certain progressives and Communists fighting on the economic and political issues facing the Negro people, but 'drawing the line' when it comes to social intercourse or inter-marriage. To place the question as a 'personal' and not a political matter, when such questions arise, is to be guilty of the worst kind of Social-Democratic bourgeois-liberal thinking as regards the Negro question in American life; it is to be guilty of imbibing the poisonous white-chauvinist 'theories' of a Bilbo or a Rankin. Similarly, too, with regard to guaranteeing the 'security' of children. This security will be enhanced only through the struggle for the liberation and equality of all nations and peoples, and not by shielding children from the knowledge of this struggle. This means ridding ourselves of the bourgeois-liberal attitudes which 'permit' Negro and white children of progressives to play together at camps when young, but draw the line when the children reach teenage and establish boy-girl relationships.

The bourgeois ideologists have not failed, of course, to develop a special ideological offensive aimed at degrading Negro women, as part and parcel of the general reactionary ideological offensive against women of 'kitchen, church and children'. They cannot, however, with equanimity or credibility, speak of the Negro woman's 'place' as in the home; for Negro women are in other people's kitchens. Hence, their task has been to intensify their theories of male 'superiority' as regards the Negro woman by developing introspective attitudes which coincide with the 'new school' of 'psychological inferiority' of women. The whole intent of a host of articles, books, etc., has been to obscure the main responsibility for the oppression of Negro women by spreading the rotten bourgeois notion about a 'battle of the sexes' and 'ignoring' the fight of both Negro men and women — the whole Negro people — against their common oppressors, the white ruling class.

Chauvinist expressions also include paternalistic surprise when it is learned that Negroes are professional people. Negro professional women workers are often confronted with such remarks as 'Isn't your family proud of you?' Then, there is the reverse practice of inquiring of Negro women professionals whether 'someone in the family' would like to take a job as a domestic worker.

The responsibility for overcoming these special forms of white chauvinism rests, not with the 'subjectivity' of Negro women, as it is often put, but squarely on the shoulders of white men and white women. Negro men have a special responsibility particularly in relation to rooting out attitudes of male superiority as regards women in general. There is need to root out all 'humanitarian' and patronizing attitudes toward Negro women. In one community, a leading Negro trade unionist, the treasurer of her Party section, would be told by a white progressive woman after every social function: 'Let me have the money; something may happen to you". In another instance, a Negro domestic worker who wanted to join the Party was told by her employer, a Communist, that she was 'too backward' and 'wasn't ready' to join the Party. In yet another community, which since the war has been populated in the proportion of sixty percent Negro to forty percent white, white progressive mothers maneuvered to get their children out of the school in this community. To the credit of the initiative of the Party section organizer, a Negro woman, a struggle was begun which forced a change in arrangements which the school principal, yielding to the mothers' and his own prejudices, had established. These arrangements involved a special class in which a few white children were isolated with 'selected Negro kids' in what was termed an 'experimental class in race relations'.

These chauvinist attitudes, particularly as expressed toward the Negro woman, are undoubtedly an important reason for the grossly insufficient participation of Negro women in progressive organizations and in our Party as members and leaders.

The American bourgeoisie, we must remember, is aware of the present and even greater potential role of the masses of Negro women, and is therefore not loathe to throw plums to Negroes who betray their people and do the bidding of imperialism.

Faced with the exposure of their callous attitude to Negro women, faced with the growing protests against unpunished lynchings and the legal lynchings 'Northern style', Wall Street is giving a few token positions to Negro women. Thus, Anna Arnold Hergeman, who played a key role in the Democratic National Negro Committee to Elect Truman, was rewarded with the appointment as Assistant to Federal Security Administrator Ewing. Thus, too, Governor Dewey appointed Irene Diggs to a high post in the New York State Administration.

Another straw in the wind showing attempts to whittle down the militancy of Negro women was the State Department's invitation to a representative of the National Council of Negro Women — the only Negro organization so designated — to witness the signing of the Atlantic Pact.

Key Issues of Struggle

There are many key issues facing Negro women around which struggle can and must be waged.

But none so dramatizes the oppressed status of Negro womanhood as does the case of Rosa Lee Ingram, widowed Negro mother of fourteen children — two of them dead — who faces life imprisonment in a Georgia jail for defending herself from the indecent advances of a 'white supremacist'. The Ingram case illustrates the landless, Jim Crow oppressed status of the Negro family in America. It illumines particularly the degradation of Negro women today under American bourgeois democracy moving to fascism and war. It reflects the daily insults to which Negro women are subjected in public places, no matter what their class, status, or position. It exposes the hypocritical alibi of the lynchers of Negro manhood who have historically hidden behind the skirts of white women when they try to cover up their foul crimes with the 'chivalry' of 'protecting white womenhood'. But white women, today, no less than their sisters in the abolitionist and suffrage movements, must rise to challenge this lie and the whole system of Negro oppression.

American history is rich in examples of the cost — to the democratic rights of both women and men — of failure to wage this fight. The suffragists, during their first failings, were purposely placed on cots next to Negro prostitutes to 'humiliate' them. They had the wisdom to understand that the intent was to make it so painful, that no women would dare to fight for her rights if she had to face such consequences. But it was the historic shortcoming of the women's suffrage leaders, predominantly drawn as they were from the bourgeoisie and the petty-bourgeoisie, that they failed to link their own struggles to the struggles for the full democratic rights of the Negro people following emancipation.

A developing consciousness on the woman question today, therefore, must not fail to recognize that the Negro question in the United States is *prior* to, and not equal to, the woman question; that only to the extent that we fight all chauvinist expressions and actions as regards the Negro people and fight for the full equality of the Negro people, can women as a whole advance their struggle for equal rights. For the progressive women's movement, the Negro woman, who combines in her status the worker, the Negro, and the woman, is the vital link to this heightened political consciousness. To the extent, further, that the cause of the Negro woman worker is promoted, she will be enabled to take her rightful place in the Negro-proletarian leadership of the national liberation movement, and by her active participation contribute to the entire American working class, whose historic mission is the achievement of a Socialist America — the final and full guarantee of woman's emancipation.

The fight for Rosa Lee Ingram's freedom is a challenge to all white women and to all progressive forces, who must begin to ask themselves: How long shall we allow this dastardly crime against all womenhood, against the Negro people, to go unchallenged? Rosa Lee Ingram's plight and that of her sisters also carries with it a challenge to progressive cultural workers to write and sing of the Negro woman in her full courage and dignity.

The recent establishment of the National Committee to Free the Ingram Family fulfills a need long felt since the early movement which forced commutation to life imprisonment of Mrs. Ingram's original sentence of execution. This National Committee, headed by Mary Church Terrell, a founder of the National Association of Colored Women, includes among its leaders such prominent women, Negro and white, as Therese Robinson, National Grand Directoress of the Civil Liberties Committee of the Elks, Ada B. Jackson, and Dr. Gene Weltfish.

One of the first steps of the Committee was the visit of a delegation of Negro and white citizens to this courageous, militant Negro mother imprisoned in a Georgia cell. The measure of support was so great that the Georgia authorities allowed the delegation to see her unimpeded. Since that time, however, in retaliation against the developing mass movement, the Georgia officials have moved Mrs. Ingram, who is suffering from a severe heart condition, to a worse penitentiary, at Reedsville.

Support to the work of this committee becomes a prime necessity for all progressives, particularly women. President Truman must be stripped of his pretense of 'know-nothing' about the Ingram case. To free the Ingrams, support must be rallied for the success of the million-signatures campaign, and for UN action on the Ingram brief soon to be filed.

The struggle for jobs for Negro women is a prime issue. The growing economic crisis, with its mounting unemployment and wage-cuts and increasing evictions, is making its impact felt most heavily on the Negro masses. In one Negro community after another, Negro women, the last to be hired and the first to be fired, are the greatest sufferers from unemployment. Struggles must be developed to win jobs for Negro women in basic industry, in the white-collar occupations, in the communities, and in private utilities.

The successful campaign of the Communist Party in New York's East Side to win jobs for Negro women in the five-and-dime stores has led to the hiring of Negro women throughout the city, even in predominantly white communities. This campaign has extended to New England and must be waged elsewhere.

Close to 15 government agencies do not hire Negroes at all. This policy gives official sanction to, and at the same time further encourages, the pervasive Jim Crow policies of the capitalist exploiters. A campaign to win jobs for Negro women here would thus greatly advance the whole struggle for jobs for Negro men and women. In addition, it would have a telling effect in exposing the hypocrisy of the Truman Administration's 'Civil Rights' program.

A strong fight will also have to be made against the growing practice of the United States Employment Service to shunt Negro women, despite their qualifications for other jobs, only into domestic and personal service work.

Where consciousness of the special role of Negro women exists, successful struggle can be initiated which will win the support of white workers. A recent example was the initiative taken by white Communist garment workers in a shop employing 25 Negro women where three machines were idle. The issue of upgrading Negro women workers became a vital one. A boycott movement has been initiated and the machines stand unused as of this writing, the white workers refusing to adhere to strict seniority at the expense of Negro workers. Meanwhile, negotiations are continuing on this issue. Similarly, in a Packard UAW local in Detroit, a fight for the maintenance of women in industry and for the upgrading of 750 women, the large majority of whom were Negro, was recently won.

The Struggle for Peace

Winning the Negro women for the struggle for peace is decisive for all other struggles. Even during the anti-Axis war, Negro women had to weep for their soldier-sons, lynched while serving in a Jim Crow army. Are they, therefore, not interested in the struggle for peace?

The efforts of the bipartisan war-makers to gain the support of the women's organizations in general, have influenced many Negro women's organizations, which, at their last annual conventions, adopted foreign-policy stands favouring the Marshall Plan and Truman Doctrine. Many of these organizations have worked with groups having outspoken anti-imperialist positions.

That there is profound peace sentiment among Negro women which can be mobilized for effective action is shown, not only in the magnificent response to the meetings of Eslande Goode Robeson, but also in the position announced last year by the oldest Negro women's organization, under the leadership of Mrs. Christine C. Smith, in urging a national mobilization of American Negro women in support of the United Nations. In this connection, it will be very fruitful to bring to our country a consciousness of the magnificent struggles of women in North Africa, who, though lacking in the most elementary material needs, have organized a strong movement for peace and thus stand united against a Third World War, with 81 million women in 57 nations, in the Women's International Democratic Federation.

Our Party, based on its Marxist-Leninist principles, stands four-square on a program of full economic, political and social equality for the Negro people and of equal rights for women. Who, more than the Negro woman, the most exploited and oppressed, belongs in our Party? Negro women can and must make an enormous contribution to the daily life and work of the Party. Concretely, this means prime responsibility lies with white men and women comrades. Negro men comrades, however, must participate on this task. Negro Communist women must everywhere now take their rightful place in Party leadership on all levels.

The strong capacities, militancy and organizational talents of Negro women, can, if well utilized by our Party, be a powerful lever for bringing forward Negro workers — men and women — as the leading forces of the Negro people's liberation movement, for cementing Negro and white unity in the struggle against Wall Street imperialism, and for rooting the Party among the most exploited and oppressed sections of the working class and its allies.

In our Party clubs, we must conduct an intense discussion of the role of the Negro women, so as to equip our Party membership with clear understanding for undertaking the necessary struggles in the shops and communities. We must end the practice, in which many Negro women who join our Party, and who, in their churches, communities and fraternal groups are leaders of masses, with an invaluable mass experience to give to our Party, suddenly find themselves involved in our clubs, not as leaders, but as people who have 'to get their feet wet' organizationally. We must end this failure to create an atmosphere in our clubs in which new recruits — in this case Negro women — are confronted with the 'silent treatment' or with attempts to 'blueprint' them into a pattern. In addition to the white chauvinist implications in such approaches, these practices confuse the basic need for Marxist-Leninist understanding which our Party gives to all workers, and which enhances their political understanding, with chauvinist disdain for the organizational talents of new Negro members, or for the necessity to promote them into leadership.

To win the Negro women for full participation in the anti-fascist, anti-imperialist coalition, to bring her militancy and participation to even greater heights in the current and future struggles against Wall Street imperialism, progressives must acquire political consciousness as regards her special oppressed status.

It is this consciousness, accelerated by struggles, that will convince increasing thousands that only the Communist Party, as the vanguard of the working class, with its ultimate perspective of Socialism, can achieve for the Negro women — for the entire Negro people — the full equality and dignity of their stature in a Socialist society in which contributions to society are measured, not by national origin, or by color, but a society in which men and women contribute according to ability, and ultimately under Communism receive according to their needs.

Problematic People and Epistemic Decolonization: Toward the Postcolonial in Africana Political Thought

Lewis R. Gordon

Introduction

The relationship between the West and the rest in political thought has been one of the constructions of the world in which the latter have been located outside and thus, literally, without a place on which to stand. Hidden parenthetical adjectives of "European," "western," and "white" have been the hallmarks of such reflection on political reality and the anthropology that informs it. For the outsiders, explicit adjectival techniques of appearance thus became the rule of the day, as witnessed by, for instance, "African," "Asian," or "Native," among others, as markers of their subaltern status in the supposedly wider disciplines. The role of these subcategories is, however, not a static one, and as historical circumstances shift, there have been ironic reversals in their various roles. In the case of (western and white) liberal political theory, for instance, the commitment to objectivity by way of the advancement of a supposedly value-neutral moral and political agent stood as the universal in an age in which such a formulation did not face its own cultural specificity. Where the parenthetical adjective is made explicit by critics of liberal political theory, such a philosophy finds itself in the face of its own cultural particularity, and worse: It finds itself so without having done its homework on that world that transcends its particularity. On the one hand, liberal and other forms of western political theory could engage that other world for the sake of its own rigor or, more generously, rigor in general. But such an approach carries the danger of simply systemic adjustment and application; it would, in other words, simply be a case of re-centering the west by showing how the non-west offers ways of strengthening western thought, much like the argument used in elite universities, that the presence of children of color will enhance the education of white children. On the other hand, there could be the realization of the ongoing presence of the non-western in the very advancement of the western. Just as the assertion of "white" requires the dialectical opposition of black (as the absence of white), the coherent formulation of western *qua* itself requires its suppressed or repressed terms. Modern western discussions of freedom require meditations on slavery that become more apparent in their displacements: Think of how slavery in the ancient Greek world has received more attention from western political thinkers, with few exceptions such as Marx and Sartre, than the forms of enslavement that have marked the modern world.[1]

Yet even here there is a misrepresentation in terms of the very structure of exclusion itself. The "outsider" is, after all, paradoxically also an "insider." For alongside white western political thinkers have always been their Africana counterparts, hybrids of the western and other worlds, who, in their criticisms and innovations, expanded the meaning and scope of the west. Anton Wilhelm Amo, the Asante-born philosopher who was educated in the

Dutch and German systems and eventually taught at the University of Halle, offered not only his readings of international law and questions of political equality in the eighteenth century, but he also challenged the mind-body dichotomy that informed its insider-outsider political anthropology. The Fanti-born Ottobah Cugoano, in similar kind and in the same century, brought this question of insider-outsider to the fore in his discussion of the theodicy that dominated Christian rationalizations of slavery and racism. Theodicy, which explains the goodness of an omnipotent God in the face of evil and injustice, is often identified by Africana (African Diaspora) thinkers as a hallmark of (white) western political thought.[2] Even where the (white) thinker is admitting the injustice of the system and showing how it could be made good, the logic of ultimate goodness is inscribed in the avowed range of the all-enveloping alternative system. Such a new system's rigor requires, in effect, the elimination of all outsiders by virtue of their assimilation. This is a paradox of the question of systemic self-criticism: In such an effort stands the potential completeness of a system through its incompleteness, its ongoing susceptibility to inconsistency, error, and, at times, injustice. What this means is that making a system more rigorous is not necessarily a good thing. The result could be a complete injustice avowed as the culmination of justice. The "role" of the Africana political thinker, then, requires doing more.

In one sense, the role of the Africana political thinker is no different from the traditional western thinker, which is the articulation of thought with which one struggles in the political world. But in another sense, the Africana role involves bringing to the fore those dimensions of thought rendered invisible by virtue of the questioned legitimacy of those who formulate them. Such thought faces a twofold path. The first is the question of recognition. If it is a matter of recognition by those who have traditionally excluded them, then the logic of that group as the center is affirmed, which would make such contribution, albeit of great interest, conservative.[3] The second is an appeal to reality beyond questions of centered recognition. Here, the project is to articulate political reality itself, which entails a criticism of the centered standpoint and its own particularity: The centered standpoint is a false representation of reality. The task then faced by the Africana western political thinker becomes manifold: (1) since the modern political world has formulated non-western humanity, particularly indigenous Africa and the indigenous peoples of the New Worlds, as sub- or even non-human, a philosophical anthropology as the grounding of social and political change freed of dehumanizing forces is necessary; (2) since thought does not float willy-nilly but requires an infrastructure on which to appear and become consequential, creative work on building such infrastructures, which includes the kinds of political institutions necessary for their flourishing, is necessary; and (3) meta-reflection on the process of such inquiry is needed if ideas themselves are to meet the test of scrutiny.[4]

In my own work on Africana philosophy, such as *Existentia Africana* and *An Introduction to Africana Philosophy*, I have explored how contemporary Africana philosophy, as a hybrid of thought from the African Diaspora in the modern world, offers a set of challenging questions and innovative responses with which humanity should grapple. These efforts involve showing the importance of phenomenology in political theory and, in effect, the importance of Africana philosophy in phenomenology. In this chapter, I offer an outline of the argument that undergirds this work through an exploration of how the modern construction of problem people and the epistemic structure that supports such a category are theorized by W.E.B. Du Bois and Frantz Fanon. After outlining their positions, I will offer a discussion of how their innovative understanding of epistemological colonialism—at the semantic and syntactic levels (i.e., even at the level of method and methodology)—addresses the tasks of philosophical anthropology, infrastructural conditions, and metareflective critique raised here.

What Does It Mean to be a Problem?

Du Bois, in *The Souls of Black Folk*, posed this insight into the condition of black folk at first through the subjectivist formulation of how does it *feel* to be a problem. His own meditations on problematization had begun a few years earlier when he composed "The Study of the Negro Problems," namely, that groups of people are studied as problems instead of as people with problems. The result is the emergence of "problem people," and since the logical course of action toward problems is their resolution, their elimination, then the fate of problem people is unfortunately grim.

It is significant that Du Bois formulated this problem experientially and eventually hermeneutically, from how does it feel to be a problem to, in *Darkwater*, the *meaning* of suffering wrought by it. Donald Matthews has argued that the roots of this reflection are located in the thought of Wilhelm Dilthey, who, along with Husserl, offered a phenomenological approach to the study of modern humanity. Phenomenology examines the constitution of meaning from conscious reality. Dilthey and his European intellectual descendants, who include Karl Jaspers, were keen on the understanding of the human sciences as fundamentally more interpretive than exact. It was a concern that was rife in nineteenth-century European thought, which included Max Weber's efforts at creating rigorous social science and Bergson's concerns with the relations of mind to matter and the articulation of awareness and durationality, much of which converged in the thought of Alfred Schutz in Vienna in the 1920s. In the United States, these concerns were advanced in the thought of Du Bois, but we should bear in mind that the questions that brought Du Bois to such social theoretical reflection preceded his doctoral Teutonic encounters in Germany. He was, after all, animated by a realization that although he shared the social world of the white Other, his reaching out was weighted down with an air of transgression. Ordinary activities in that social world were displaced when he attempted to occupy the anonymous roles that made them possible. For he was not simply a student and then a professor; he was not simply a man and then a citizen. Being black, he found himself as an adjectival problematic in each instance. That his *lived* understanding of self as this problematic would have been a contradiction of his understanding of himself as a human being, the question of interpretation offered the hope of explanation. His situation was not, in other words, ontological; it was not about what he "is." The situation was about how he is interpreted, about what other people *think* he is. The relation between meaning and being beckons him, then, in an ironic way, for in the human world, meaning collapses into being, but the latter need not have meaning.

Although he did not make it explicit, Du Bois's analysis of the situation of problem people involves an indictment of theodicean dimensions of the modern world. Theodicy, as we have seen, involves proving the compatibility between the goodness of God and the presence of evil and injustice. Maleficence, in this view, is external to God. In the modern world, where rationalizations have been secularized, the role of God is replaced by systems that are asserted as deontological or absolute. The goodness of the system means that evil and injustice are extrasystemic. Problem people, then, are extrasystemic; they belong outside of the system. In effect, they belong nowhere, and their problems, being they themselves, mean that they cannot gain the legitimating force of recognition. It is the notion of a complete, perfect system that enables members of the system to deny the existence of problems within the system.

A system that denies its incompleteness faces the constant denial of its contradictions. In the modern world, this required avowing freedom while maintaining slavery; humanism while maintaining racism; free trade through colonialism.[5] Du Bois, in raising the question of the meaning of living such contradictions, of reminding modern triumphs of their dialectical underside of slavery, racism, and colonialism, brought forth a logic of reversals. On one level, there were the contradictions. The "universal" was, and continues to be, an over-asserted particularity. The disciplines by which knowledge is produced often hid, by way of being presumed, a Eurocentric and racial prefix in which European and white self-reflection became the supposed story of the world. Since studying the particularized black involves understanding the relation of whiteness by which it is constituted, the scope of black particularity proved broader than the denial of white particularity. In short, the universal, should it exist, would most certainly be colored. But the logic of universal and particular is already flawed by virtue of the anxiety that should occur at the moment each human boundary appears complete. Here, Du Bois thus moves the question of problem people into their lived reality: "What does it mean to be a problem?" returns to "How does it feel to be a problem?" and becomes also "How does one live as a problem?" and in those movements, the question of the inner-life of problem people—a problem in itself since it should be self-contradictory—emerges. What can be said of the inner life of those who should lack an inner life?

Du Bois, as is well known, formulated these problems as those of double consciousness. In its first stage, it involves being yoked to views from others; one literally cannot see oneself through one's own eyes. The dialectics of recognition that follow all collapse into subordination, into living and seeing the self only through the standards and points of view of others. Without their recognition, one simply does not exist. To exist means to appear with a point of view in the intersubjective world of others. But to do so requires addressing the contradictions that militate against one's existence in the first place. Paget Henry (2005) has described this next move as "potentiated double consciousness." It requires that "second sight" in which the contradictions of one's society and system of values are made bare. Double consciousness, in this sense, unmasks the theodicean dimensions of the system. Where the political system presents itself as all-just, as complete, the result is the abrogation of responsibility for social problems. But how could social problems exist without people who are responsible for them by virtue of being the basis of the social world itself?

Who Is Responsible for the Social World?

"[Society,] unlike biochemical processes," wrote Fanon in *Black Skin, White Masks*, "cannot escape human influence. Man is what brings society into being" (p. 11). Human beings are responsible for the social world, from which and through which meaning is constructed and, consequently, new forms of life. Fanon recognized that the process of creating such forms of life also held and generated its own problems; the battle, in other words, against the colonization of knowledge and colonizing knowledge required addressing its source at the level of method itself. Colonialism, in other words, has its methodology, and its goal requires the colonization of method itself. The battle against epistemological colonialism requires, then, a radical, reflective critique (as well as a radically reflective one), and so were Fanon's efforts in *Black Skin, White Masks*, where every effort to assert an understanding of human behavior under a system of accommodations, a system of promised membership, resulted in failures. Announcing that he preferred to examine these failures, Fanon raised a paradoxical methodology of suspending method. To make the human being actional, his avowed aim, required showing the failures of a world in whose palms rested an ugly seed: The happy slave.

That the happy slave is a project of modern freedom led Fanon to considering the contradictory implications of freedom struggles. Colonialism, for instance, raised a peculiar problem of ethics. To act "ethically" required a commitment not to harming others. But if inaction meant the continuation of a colonial situation, then the notion that harm is absent only where certain groups of people are harmed becomes the order of the day. Harm would be maintained in the interest of avoiding harm. Fanon's insight was that this contradictory situation could not be resolved *ethically*, since ethics, as with method, was here under scrutiny. Colonialism, in other words, introduced a fundamental inequality that outlawed the basis of ethics in the first place. When Fanon argues that we need to set humanity into its proper place, he means by this that this ethical problem has a political cause. In other words, unlike the modern liberal paradigm, which seeks an ethics on which to build its politics, Fanon argues that colonialism has created a situation in which a politics is needed on which to build an ethics. I have called this, in my book *Fanon and the Crisis of European Man*, the tragedy of the colonial condition.

When ethics is suspended, almost all is permitted. And where all is permitted, consent will become irrelevant and violence one, inevitable result. Fanon's meditations on violence have been notorious precisely because they have been so misunderstood in this regard. As long as the ethics of colonialism—in effect, colonial ethics—dominates *as ethics*, then decolonization would be its enemy; it would be unethical to fight against it. This was the basis, Fanon observed, of the rationalization of colonialism as an ethical enterprise through the interpretation of the colonized as enemies of values:

> Native society is not simply described as a society lacking in values. It is not enough for the colonist to affirm that those values have disappeared from, or still better never existed in, the colonial world. The native is declared insensible to ethics; he represents not only the absence of values, but also the negation of values. He is, let us dare to admit, the enemy of values, and in this sense he is the absolute evil (p. 41).

The "Graeco-Latin pedestal," as Fanon calls this, would be an impediment to action by placing upon decolonization a neurotic situation: A condition of membership that it could not fulfill since its admission would by definition disqualify the club. Fanon, the psychiatrist as well as theorist of decolonization, understood that the demand of decolonization without innocent suffering fails to account for the innocence of those who suffer colonization; in effect, since innocence suffers on both accounts, it stands as an irrelevant criterion.

It is perhaps this insight on the suspension of ethics that made Fanon's concern about the inheritors of decolonization, those entrusted to forge a *post*colonial reality, more than a dialectical reflection. For, just as Moses could only lead the people but not enter the Promised Land, so, too, do the generations that fight the decolonizing struggle face their illegitimacy in the postcolonial world. The type of people who could do what needs to be done in an environment of suspended ethical commitments is not the kind who may be the best suited for the governing of mundane life. Fanon's analysis of the national so-called postcolonial bourgeoisie is a case in point. Locked in the trap of political mediations with former colonizers, the effect of which is their becoming new colonizers, the task of building the infrastructure of their nations lay in wait, unfulfilled and often abandoned. This seizure of the post-decolonization process leads to a yoking of national consciousness by nationalism, of making the interest of the nation collapse into the interest of groups within the nation *as* the nation, and a return of the political condition that precedes an ethics. Part of the liberation struggle, then, is the emancipation of ethical life.

Who Rules the World?

This question, raised by Ortega Y Gasset in *The Revolt of the Masses*, gets to the point of coloniality and the question of postcoloniality and its relation to political theory. Rule, after all, is not identical with politics. It involves, by definition, setting standards, and the ancient relationship of priestly leaders and kings to their subjects was free of politics the extent to which fundamental inequalities had divine and cosmic foundations. Affairs between priests and each other, kings and their kind, or even priests and kings were another matter. There arose a sufficient level of equality between powers to call upon resources of rhetoric and persuasion, and it is from such a discursive transformation of conflicts that politics was born. Such activity, as its etymology suggests, is rooted in the city, a space and place that was often enclosed, if not encircled, in a way that demanded a different set of norms "inside" than "without." Within, there is the tacit agreement that conflicts need not collapse into war, which means, in effect, the maintenance of opposition without violence, of, as the proverb goes, "war by other means." In this case, the internal opposition afforded a relationship to the world that differed from what awaited beyond city walls. Out there was the space of violence par excellence, the abyss in which all is proverbially permitted. Ruling the polis, then, demanded a set of norms unique to such a precious place, and where rule is distributed nearly to all, the conflicts over standards require discursive safeguards.

The modern world has, however, been marked by the rise of rule over politics in relation to certain populations.[6] Colonialism, its, in Foucauldian language, *episteme* and, in Mudimbe's, *gnosis*, renders whole populations receiving their orders, their commands, as the syntactical mode of existence itself. Standards are set, but they are done so through a logic that both denies and affirms the spirits that modernity was to hold at bay. Our analysis of Du Bois and Fanon reveal that a problem with colonialism is that it creates a structure of rule over politics in relation to the colonized. Since, as we just saw in our discussion of the roots of politics versus mere rulership, the discursive dimensions of politics properly require a sufficient level of equality between disputants, then the call for political solutions requires, as well, the construction of egalitarian institutions or places for the emergence of such relations for a political sphere. We find, then, another dimension of the ethical in relation to the political, for the political construction of egalitarian orders entails, as well, the basis for new ethical relations. In other words, the construction of a standard that enables ethical life requires a transformation of political life as well from the violence on which it was born to the suspension of violence itself. Such a suspension would be no less than the introduction of a public realm, a place in which, and through which, opposition could occur without the structure of the command. But here we find paradox, for how could such a space exist without peripheral structures held together by force?

A Postcolonial Phenomenology

The examination of consciousness and the realities born from it has spawned a variety of phenomenologies in the modern world. I am, however, here interested in examinations of consciousness that emerge from a suspension of what is sometimes called the natural standpoint but which I prefer to call an act of ontological suspension. By suspending our ontological commitments, it is not that we have eradicated them but that we have shifted and honed our foci. Such an act of suspension affects, as well, our presumptions, which means, as in Fanon's reflections on epistemological colonization, that even our method cannot be presumed. One may ask about the initial moment of ontological suspension. To reintroduce an ontological commitment to a stage of our reflection would mean to presume its validity, which means that the objection requires the necessity of the suspension that it is advanced against. Such a realization is an epistemic move forward.

In many ways, the term "postcolonial phenomenology" is redundant in this context, for the act of ontological suspension means that no moment of inquiry is epistemologically closed. As a rejection of epistemic closure, this form of phenomenology is pitted against colonialism precisely because such a phenomenon requires such closure, which, in more than a metaphorical sense, is the construction of epistemological "settlements." Such settlements lead to forms of crises.

There are crises everywhere in the modern world, and their increase is near exponential. An odd feature of crises, however, is that they are sociogenic. Their solutions should, then, also be a function of the social world. Yet crises are lived as though they have emerged either from the heavens or out of the mechanisms of nature. Crises seem "to happen" to us. The word itself emerges from the Greek term *krinein*, which means "to decide." We paradoxically decide or choose our crises by choosing no to choose, by hiding from ourselves as choosing agents. We lead ourselves into believing what we do not believe, into bad faith. Social crises are just this: Institutional forms of bad faith. They are instances in which the social world is saturated with a closure on its own agency. How is this possible?

On one account, it is that the social world itself is a generative concept, by which is meant that it is part of a complex web of knowledge claims or meanings on which certain forms of subjectivity are produced. The historical imposition of such an order of things makes it nearly impossible to live outside of such an organization of reality while, ironically, enacting and maintaining it. From this point of view, which we shall call the archaeological, poststructural one, the phenomenological account is wanting because its foundation, namely, consciousness, is also an effect of such an order which could very well change as new, future constellation of things emerge. Yet this claim faces its own contradiction at the level of lived reality: Its completeness is presupposed when, as posited as an object of investigation, its limits are transcended. It is, in other words, a particular advanced as a universal while presuming its own changeability. The error, then, in dismissing consciousness at simply the conceptual level is that the question of positing a concept is presupposed in the very grammar and semantics of its rejection. The phenomenological insight, in this sense of suspending ontological commitments, is that the concept emerges as an object of investigation without having a presumed method for its positing. In other words, the very posing of investigation presupposes the validity of consciousness' *form*. And since even that form transcends its own domestication or subordination, it cannot function as a subcategory of an order of things. In other words, the archaeological, poststructural critique only pertains to a particular *form* of consciousness, namely, one that is already yoked to a particular order of things.

What, however, about a genealogical critique? What are the power interests in the assertion of a phenomenological approach? The response is that it is no more so than a genealogical one. Genealogical accounts regard disciplines and methodological approaches as "tools," as Foucault (2003: 6) avows, as useful but not absolute resources in processes of reflection. Since a postcolonial phenomenology begins with an act of ontological suspension, then each stage of reflection, including its own metacritical assessments, cannot be asserted as ontological without contradiction.

The continued impact of identifying contradictions at moments of ontological assertion suggests that there are limits to what can be permitted even in acts of ontological suspension. Take, for instance, the problem of evidence. A criticism that could be made of these reflections is how self-centered they are, as if an individual consciousness could simply suspend and construct thought itself. That would be a fair criticism so long as the process was *psychological*. This is the point about a particular form of consciousness itself. But the kind of consciousness is not here classified nor presumed within the framework of natural phenomena; it is not, in other words, consciousness subordinated by the relativism of naturalistic frameworks or, to make it plain, modern science. It cannot be presumed, then, to be an act of a single individual. Instead, it is the articulation of a process through which even the individual who is reflecting upon the process is not located as its subject but an anonymous participant in an effort of understanding; it is not the fish in the water but the realization by a fish that it is in water and potentially many other layers or frames of and through which it is located as somewhere. The problem of evidence emerges, however, precisely because it is a concept that requires more than one standpoint. For something to be evident, it must potentially appear to others. Thus even when one sees something as evident, it is from the standpoint of oneself as an Other. There is, in other words, an inherent sociality to evidence. And since an intellectual reflection makes no sense without making its claims evident, the importance of this insight for *thought* itself is also evident.

So the question of sociality emerges, and it does so in the form of making itself evident. The task is made difficult, however, by having to continue these reflections without an act of ontological commitment. The social world will have to be *understood* through being made evident. In many ways, as I have argued in *Existentia Africana* (pp. 74–80), we already have a transcendental argument at work here since sociality is a precondition of evidentiality, and we have already established the necessity of evidence in our reflections. What makes the project more complicated is that it is one thing to presuppose others, it is another thing to articulate the reality presumed by a world of others. After all, genuine others often do what they wish, and when it comes to our shared world of things and meanings, there is the complicated question of whether they are willing to admit what they see, feel, hear, smell, or taste. But we have already revealed much in this admission, for how else could others and their independent variations of senses be meaningful without the individuating addition of their being embodied?

That others are embodied raises the question of how the social world emerges. For, given the metaphysics that dominate most discussions of living bodies, there is the Cartesian problem of how one consciousness could reach another beyond the mere appearance of her or his body. There is something wrong with the Cartesian model could be our response, but that would involve explaining in exactly which way is it misguided. The first is the notion of "mind and body." In her introduction and first chapter of *The Invention of Women*, Oyèrónké Oyewùmí offers an Africana postcolonial, poststructural critique of this problem by challenging knowledge claims and the subsequent biological science that centers the physical body over social relations in the first place. The Africana postcolonial dimension of this critique is that Cartesianism offered an epistemological model of the self that demanded the colonization of body by mind through having to create a problem of the body. The history of colonialism as one in which colonizing groups constructed themselves as minds that control the colonized and the enslaved, beings whose sole mode of being is the body itself brings the colonial dimension of this dichotomy to the fore. Yet this critique, powerful though it may be, does not account for the reality of how we live as extended beings in the world. In other words, it really is a criticism of an *over-emphasis* on the body or on the mind, especially as separate, but not on how we live them as creatures that move through the world. Even social activities such as trading or enjoying the company of others require an interplay of what it means to be "here" versus "there," and of communicating welcome or rejection through shaking hands, hugging, or simply standing back, all activities expressed not "through" the body but, literally, in that sense as singular—that is, *embodied*. Further, drawing upon similar premises that render colonizers mind and the colonized body, Fanon noted in the 1950s in his discussion of negrophobia, phobogenesis, and the black athlete in *Black Skin, White Masks* in his chapter, "The Negro and Psychopathology," that such reductionism leads, ultimately, to a fear of the biological in which the black male, for example, is eclipsed by his penis in the eyes of the negrophobe. This argument suggests that rejecting engagement with the biological may not be the right direction for a postcolonial critique to take. To capture this dimension of social embodiment, which we might wish to call its "lived" reality, while addressing the limits of Cartesianism would require some additional considerations.

Cartesianism advances the human being as a meeting of two substances, but in truth, many of the problems we face emerge from the first substance, so we needn't even go to the second one. How, in other words, does mind reach mind? But now we see the difficulty where body is denied; mind cannot "reach" mind, in other words, where neither mind exists anywhere. To be somewhere means to occupy a space in a particular time, which means to be embodied.[7] A similar argument could be made about brain-body distinctions; but the difference here is that the borders are successions of physical bodies. Consider, however, the following thought experiment. What would be required for a consciousness or a mind to be embodied? It will have to be extended in the world, which means that it will have to be able to stand on or be oriented by something. As well, it could not be active without being able to extend beyond its initial grounding, which means it would require limbs, and as it reaches out to its environment in ways that involve detecting electromagnetic radiation to discerning the chemicals and gases with which it has contact, we will see the unfolding of a body that has a front and a back and sides as well as an up and a down. In short, "the body" is another way of saying "an extended brain" or "a living, conscious thing." And though the Cartesian might point out that limbs can be cut off without the self being destroyed, a surgeon could point out that bits of brain can be taken away without the same effect. The contingency of parts of an organism does not mean that those parts are not extended expressions of that organism. Mind, in other words, is from toe to finger tip to forehead. What all this amounts to is that consciousness/mind *appears* in the world, is evident to other minds, and is read and interacted with precisely because it is evident, it appears.

The social world is, then, a complex one of intersubjectivity, but that does not mean a mysterious spiritual world behind physical reality. It is in and through that reality and is evident in the multitude of signifiers that constitute the expression of reality from the social world, which is what Fanon, in his introduction to *Black Skin, White Masks*, means by *sociogeny*.[8] That is why it would be correct to say that we learn to read our world and inscribe and constitute our relationship to it. And more, we can also see that this relationship is one in which we play the active role of making meanings while encountering a world of meanings already available to us. It is in this sense that the social world and its plethora of meanings are an achievement. Among these meanings is the subject that is the focus of decolonizing struggles to begin with, namely, the human being.[9]

The act of ontological suspension and the necessity of embodied consciousness raise the question of philosophical anthropology. Unlike empirical anthropology, which focuses on empirical phenomena and the application of methods designed for such study, philosophical anthropology explores the concepts by and through which any understanding of the human being is both possible and makes sense.[10] It also involves the implications of these ideas *as ideas*, as they are, that is, when freed as much as possible from the grip of colonizing epistemic forces. In one sense, the postcolonial phenomenological move requires understanding the human being as a subject over whom laws find their limits. In effect, the human question, from this point of view, becomes one of studying a being that lacks a nature and yet is a consequence of natural phenomena—although these reasons have already been outlined in phenomenological terms, which is that another human being relates to one as part of a world that transcends the self. What this means is that the other's contingency entails the other's freedom, and given that freedom, the philosophical anthropology that follows is one of an open instead of a closed subject. In another sense, the openness of human subjectivity is already presupposed in the project of liberation and social change. A human being must, in other words, be able to live otherwise for his or her liberation to make sense. And at the level of groups, the sociogenic argument here returns: What is created by human beings can be changed by human beings. The human being is, in other words, the introduction of the artificial into the world. Thus, to impose the maxim of nature on the human being is to set the human element on a path toward its own destruction. And third, the argument recognizes the relationship between knowledge and being, that new forms of life are also a consequence of the production of knowledge. This outcome, too, is another natural development of an unnatural reality.

The openness of philosophical anthropology also emerges from the contingency of human subjectivity. Human beings bring new concepts into the world and, in doing so, face the anxiety of unpredictability. In the human world, things do not often work out, and part of the intellectual struggle has been about facing that dimension of living in a human world, a world of others. Theoretical models that appeal to human necessity often face the danger of requiring a neatness of human behavior and human institutions that collapses them into clear-cut notions as, for example, the distinction between black and white. Yet, as most human adults know, the world is not simple, and the consequences of life are not always fair. They face, then, the problem of living in a world that is without neat, theodicean dictates in which evil and injustice stand outside. Such phenomena are aspects of life through which we must live, and they do not always emerge in grandiose forms but, instead, at the level of everyday life. What such reflection brings to discourses on social change is the rather awkward question: Will such efforts create a world in which human beings could actually live? To live requires, from the complex set of interrelations that constitute the social world, mundane life, and the challenge posed by decolonization of such a life is a function of what is involved in each group of people achieving what could be called "the ordinary."[11]

The options available for an everyday existence are not the same across groups in a colonial world. In such a world, an absence of spectacular efforts facilitates the everyday life of the dominating group. We could call this simply ordinary existence. For the dominated group, the achievement of the ordinary requires extraordinary efforts. Here we see another one of those subverted categories through the lens of Du Boisian double consciousness, for the averageness of everyday life for the dominant group conceals the institutions that support such ordinariness. This reality reveals, for instance, a major problem in recent appeals to "cosmopolitanism" in Africana liberal thought as found in the work of K. Anthony Appiah or the feminist, cosmopolitan position of Martha Nussbaum.[12] While it is laudable that they defend the inter-connectedness of the human species and, in Appiah's case, stand critical of "strong universalism," they pose a value system premised upon an individual who, as in the elites of F. Scott Fitzgerald's *The Great Gatsby*, can afford it.[13] One can believe that one is a citizen of the world when most global institutions are already designed for one's benefit (as opposed to others). The folly of this position comes to the fore when one imagines how ridiculous it would be to deride a poor person for failing to be cosmopolitan. It is as ridiculous as applauding a rich person or a person of fair means for globetrotting. What is cosmopolitanism, then, in its concrete practice but the assertion of the values of the affluent as the standards for everyone—including the poor? After all, cosmopolitanism is advanced by cosmopolitanists as their claim to a universal logic, or at least a near-universal one. How could such a value-system be consistent without simply erasing those who contradict it or simply rendering them irrelevant?[14] Such forms of political theorizing treat individuals and their values as though they do not stand on social infrastuctures. Where institutions are against a particular group, that group faces a constant problem of insufficiency. How can a group ever be good enough when its members' actions cannot qualify their membership by virtue of never serving as the standard of membership?

A radical philosophical anthropology would point out the contradiction of a system governed by such a logic of membership since such a system would require presenting some groups of people as epistemologically closed while making other groups of people the standard by which humanity is forged, which, ironically, would also be a form of epistemic closure, but it would be so at the level of an ideal. In effect, it would eliminate some human beings from the human community through the creation of a nonhuman standard of being human. The question of lived-reality would then disintegrate since each set of human beings would "be" a surface existent instead of the complex dynamic of an expressed inner life *in the world*. Lacking such a dimension, the human world would simply become an ossification of values, and the avowed goal of setting humanity free would collapse into its opposite.

Why such a focus on the human in a postcolonial phenomenology? On one hand, the answer is historical. Colonialism, slavery, and racism have degraded humankind. The reassertion of humankind requires the assertion of the humanity of the degraded. But such an assertion is, as we have been seeing, not as simple as it appears, for there was not, and continues not to be, a coherent notion of the human subject on which emancipation can be supported. It is much easier to assert a humanity that supports oppression than it is to construct one that carries, paradoxically, the burden of freedom. On the other hand, the answer is "purely" theoretical. A radically critical examination of epistemic colonizing practices must be metacritical, which means, as we have seen through Fanon, being radically self reflective. It would be bad faith to deny that this means questioning our own humanity.

A Geopolitical Conclusion

Our explorations thus far have moved back and forth through two conceptions of theory that have not been made explicit. The word theory has its origins in theological notions. From the ancient Greek word *theoria*, which means "view," or, in the infinitive, "to view" or "to see," a further etymological break down reveals the word *theo*, from which was *theus* or *Zdeus* (*Zeus*) or, in contemporary terms, "God." To do theoretical work meant, then, to attempt to see what God sees. And since God has the power of omniscience, it meant to see all, and what would such an achievement be other than truth itself? Yet implicit in such an effort is the reality that human beings could only make such an attempt *as an attempt*, because human beings are not gods, and although the gods do sometimes smile on an individual human being and thereby stimulate a glimpse of clarity, for the most part, most of us are kept in the proverbial dark, or at least twilight. In a godless world, the theory is in some ways like the continued grammar that supports a rationalization without the God that animated it. The "theorist" thus becomes an embarrassing figure, a searcher seeking an outcome that would be ashamed of its origins. What, in other words, does it mean to do theory in a godless universe?

One response would be to give up theory and focus simply on criticism, on showing where the continued effort to do theory leads to embarrassing and fruitless outcomes. Another response would be to approach ideas as objects in a dark room. Theoretical work then becomes at first the lighting of a match with which to light a candle with which to find one's way to a light switch. At each stage, the contents of the room, including its walls, become clearer and offer a more coherent context in which to make decisions about how to live in the room. The process of increasing clarity continues well after the light switch in the form of thought itself, often captured by the term "illumination." And then there is another model, where thought itself creates new relationships and things much like the Big Bang view of an expanding universe; as there is an expansion of matter, there is, as well, an expansion of thought. How these views of thought unfold in postcolonial thought can be seen through a very influential recent metaphor. In the 1980s, Audre Lorde, in her collection *Sister Outsider*, argued that the master's tools will never dismantle the master's house. The result of this insight has, however, been both positive and negative. On the one hand, it has been a rallying cry against Eurocentrism and colonizing concepts, against the dialectics of recognition in which dominating ideals reign. But on the other hand, it has also served the interest of the "criticisms only" groups, those who regard theory as ultimately imperial and, historically, western. This response emerges from the negative aspect of the metaphor, namely, tearing down the master's house. It is odd that a metaphor that builds upon the struggles of slaves did not consider other aspects of the lived reality of slaves. Why, for instance, would people who are linked to production regard themselves in solely destructive terms? Yes, they want to end slavery. But they also want *to build freedom*. To do that, what they may wish to do with the master's tools is to use them, *along with the tools they had brought with them and which facilitated their survival*, to build their own homes. How could the master's house function as such in a world of so many houses not premised upon mastery? Would not that render such a house, in the end, irrelevant and in effect drain its foundations of mastery?

Such a shift would be one both of space and place. Postcolonial thought cannot afford to be locked in the role of negative critique. An inauguration of a shift in the geography of reason needs to be effected wherein the productive dimensions of thought can flourish. In other words, thought needs a place in which to live. Ideas dwell across the ages in the concepts and institutions human beings have built, and the more livable those institutions are for human beings, the healthier, no doubt, this symbiotic relationship will be as it takes on the legacy of that resounding echo from which symbolic life was born so long ago.

Notes

1. For discussion of these themes of recognition and their limitations, see Lewis Gordon, *Disciplinary Decadence* (2006, especially the final chapter) and Gordon and Gordon (eds.), *Not Only the Master's Tools* (2006).

2. This is not to say that theodicean problems are not raised in African and Africana thought. See, e.g., Kwame Gyekye's discussion of theodicy in the Akan in *An Essay on African Philosophical Thought* (1995: 123–128).

3. This is one of the themes of Frantz Fanon's *Black Skin, White Masks* (1967), where the black petit-bourgeoisie seek recognition in a world in which they are not, and in its very systems of values *could not be*, the standard. They, in effect, affirm their inferiority.

4. I also provide an exploration of how these themes have unfolded in Africana philosophy in Lewis Gordon, *An Introduction to Africana Philosophy* (forthcoming).

5. On this theme, particularly on how it unfolded in debates over the Black Republic of Haiti, see Sibylle Fischer, *Modernity Disavowed* (2004).

6. On this theme, there are many studies, but for Africa, see Fanon's classic *The Wretched of the Earth* (1963) and for the Americas, Tzevan Todorov's *The Conquest of America* (1984). See also Mahmood Mamdani, *Citizen and Subject* (1996) for a more recent discussion of politics and rule in a colonial context.

7. For a longer discussion of this argument, see my chapter "The Body in Bad Faith," in *Bad Faith and Antiblack Racism* (1995).

8. For discussion, see Sylvia Wynter's "Towards the Sociogenic Principle" (2001) and Lewis Gordon, "Through the Zone of Nonbeing" (2005) and "Is the Human a Teleological Suspension of Man?" (2006).

9. Africana philosophy, and by implication Africana postcolonial thought, brings this question of the human being to the fore for the obvious reason, at least in its modern instantiation, of its being theory advanced through the world of subjects whose humanity has been denigrated or denied. See Lewis Gordon, *Existentia Africana* (2000, *passim*) and see, also, Bogues (ed.), *After Man, Towards the Human* (2006).

10. There are many roads to philosophical anthropology in the modern age and in postcolonial thought. The situating of the question is infamously raised in Immanuel Kant's practical philosophy, although it has been a leitmotif of modern thought as early as Hobbes's atomistic natural philosophy, which attempts a theory of human nature as the basis of his argument for legitimate political order. The Haitian humanist Anténor Firmin has shown, in *Equality of the Human Races* (2002; originally published in 1885), however, that Kant's, and also Hegel's claims to philosophical anthropology, were not properly anthropological at all but, in fact, *geographical*. The legacy of that geological political construction continues in contemporary constructions of intelligent, civilized people of the Nordic regions versus supposedly doltish, savage ones from tropical zones. In more recent times, the question took a marked turn in Sartrean existential Marxism, as found in Sartre's *Critique of Dialectical Reason*, which placed him in conflict with structuralist anthropology, and one could see how the question of the human being as a limit to imposed structures took its return in Foucault's archaeology and genealogy, where the production of the human being as a subject of inquiry came about in the face of the subject's role as both producer and product. See Bogues (2006) for a variety of Africana postcolonial writers on this subject. See also Paget Henry's essay on potentiated double consciousness (2005) and his essay in the Bogues volume for a discussion of the limits of poststructural moves and questions of agency addressed by the phenomenological turn, and Lewis Gordon, *Fanon and the Crisis of European Man* (1995b) and *Existentia Africana* (2000) for a similar argument.

11. For elaboration of the value of the ordinary, see Maurice Natanson, *Anonymity* (1986), and see chapter 3 of Lewis Gordon, *Fanon and the Crisis of European Man* (1995b).

12. Appiah's argument would require his work not being identified as "Africana" liberal thought. That he advances anecdotes on Ghana and has built his ideas out of his work on race theory in Africana

philosophy, however, brings out the question of what it means for an Africana philosopher to write as though the African world plays any serious role in forging the conditions of global access available to its members. That the degree to which that African can be materially dissociated from blackness plays a significant role, as compared to the access available to a European who strongly identifies with whiteness, renders the notion of Africana cosmopolitanism in the terrain of self-deception. We may pose the same point to Nussbaum on the distinction between the women who are part of the communities of women who share governance of the world versus, basically, the rest.

13. F. Scott Fitzgerald was, however, a lot less naive on these matters as evidenced by his portrayal of the callous attitude of these ruling cosmopolitans, whose globetrotting depends on constantly meeting each other everywhere. Contemporary cosmopolitans continue to work under the assumption that ruling elites actually give a damn about the suffering of people in the rest of the world and the social systems that support the inequalities on which such suffering is built. How do we judge such recognition and kindness to "strangers" when the subject in question controls all the conditions of the exchange?

14. This is not to say that globalism and cosmopolitanism are identical. Buying access to the world is global in consequence, but since only few people can afford that, it becomes a clear case of confusing their global access with universal access. Such individuals could only become universal if, and only if, they are the only individuals under consideration. In effect, although unintentionally so, we find ourselves here on theodicean terrain. Those who cannot afford global access are simply rendered outside of the system of cosmopolitan values or simply presumed to be so, if they could afford it, which means that the whole point is not really about the values at all but the access. In effect, Fanon's critique of modern colonial values returns, where the political economy of social transformation trumps the ethics that was presumed independent of social infrastructures.

References

Abraham, William E. 2004. Anton Wilhelm Amo. In *A Companion to African Philosophy*, ed. Kwasi Wiredu. Malden, MA: Blackwell's, 191–99.

Appiah, K. Anthony. 2005. *Cosmopolitanism: Ethics in a World of Strangers*. New York: W.W. Norton.

Bogues, B. Anthony (ed.). 2006. *After Man, Towards the Human: Critical Essays on the Thought of Sylvia Wynter*. Kingston, JA: Ian Randle Publishers.

Descartes, René. 1952. *Descartes' Philosophical Writings*, trans. and ed. Norman Kemp Smith. London: Macmillan.

Du Bois, W.E.B. 1898. The Study of the Negro Problems. *Annals of the American Academy of Political and Social Science* XI (January): 1–23.

———. 1920. *Darkwater: Voices from Within the Veil*. New York: Harcourt, Brace, and Howe.

———. 1982. *The Souls of Black Folk*. Intro. Dr. Nathan Hare and Alvin Poussaint, M.D. Revised and updated bibliography. New York: New American Library.

Dussel, Enrique. 1996. *The Underside of Modernity*. Ithaca, NY: Humanity Books.

———. 2003. *Beyond Philosophy: Ethics, History, Marxism, and Liberation Theology*, trans. and ed. Eduardo Mendieta. Lanham, MD: Rowman & Littlefield.

Fanon, Frantz. 1952. *Peau Noire, Masques Blancs*. Paris: Éditions du Seuil.

———. 1961/1991. *Les Damnés de la Terre*. Préface de Jean-Paul Sartre. Paris: François Maspero éditeur S.A.R.L./Paris: Éditions Gallimard.

———. 1963. *The Wretched of the Earth*. Translated by Constance Farrington with an introduction by Jean-Paul Sartre. New York: Grove Press.

————. 1967a. A *Dying Colonialism*. Translated by Haakon Chevalier with an introduction by Adolfo Gilly. New York: Grove Weidenfeld.

————. 1967b. *Black Skin, White Masks*. Translated by Charles Lamm Markman. New York: Grove Press.

————. 1967c. *Toward the African Revolution*. Translated by Haakon Chevalier. New York: Grove Press.

————. 1975 /1968 [1959]. *Sociologie d'une Révolution: L'an V de la Révolution Algérienne*, 2me ed. Paris: François Maspero.

Firmin, Anténor. 1999. *Equality of Human Races: A Nineteenth Century Haitian Scholar's Response to European Racialism*. New York: Taylor and Francis.

Fischer, Sibylle. 2004. *Modernity Disavowed*. Durham: Duke University Press.

Fitzgerald, F. Scott. 1995. *The Great Gatsby*. New York: Scribners.

Foucault, Michel Foucault. 1973. *The Order of Things: An Archaeology of the Human Sciences*. New York: Vintage.

————. 1979. *Discipline and Punish: The Birth of the Prison*, trans. Alan Sheridan. New York: Vintage.

————. 2003. *'Society Must Be Defended': Lectures at the Collège de France (1975–1976)*, trans. David Macey. New York: St Picador.

Gordon, Jane Anna. 2005. The General Will as Political Legitimacy: Disenchantment and Double Consciousness in Modern Democratic Theory. Philadelphia: University of Pennsylvania Political Science Doctoral Dissertation.

Gordon, Lewis R. 1995a. *Bad Faith and Antiblack Racism*. Amherst, NY: Humanity Books.

————. 1995b. *Fanon and the Crisis of European Man: An Essay on Philosophy and the Human Sciences*. New York: Routledge.

————. 1997. *Her Majesty's Other Children: Sketches of Racism from a Neocolonial Age*. Lanham, MD: Rowman & Littlefield.

————. 2000. *Existentia Africana: Understanding Africana Existential Thought*. New York: Routledge.

————. 2005. Through the Zone of Nonbeing: A Reading of *Black Skin, White Masks* in Celebration of Fanon's Eightieth Birthday. *The C.L.R. James Journal* 11, no. 1 (Summer 2005): 1–43.

————. 2006a. *Disciplinary Decadence: Living Thought in Trying Times*. Boulder, CO: Paradigm Publishers.

————. 2006b. Is the Human a Teleological Suspension of Man?: A Phenomenological Exploration of Sylvia Wynter's Fanonian and Biodicean Reflections. In *After Man, Towards the Human: Critical Essays on the Thought of Sylvia Wynter*, ed. Anthony Bogues. Kingston, JA: Ian Randle Publishers, 237–57.

Gordon, Lewis R. and Jane Anna Gordon, eds. 2006. *Not Only the Master's Tools: African-American Studies in Theory and Practice*. Boulder, CO: Paradigm Publishers.

————. 2006. *A Companion to African-American Studies*. Malden, MA: Blackwell Publishers.

Gordon, Lewis R., T. Denean Sharpley-Whiting, Renée T. White, eds. 1996. *Fanon: A Critical Reader*. Oxford: Blackwell Publishers.

Grosfoguel, Ramón, Nelson Maldonado Torres, and José David Saldívar, eds. 2005. *Latin@s in the World-System: Towards the Decolonization of the US Empire in the 21st Century*. Boulder, CO: Paradigm Publishers.

Henry, Paget. 2000a. *Caliban's Reason: Introducing Afro-Caribbean Philosophy*. New York: Routledge.

————. 2005. Africana Phenomenology: A Philosophical Look. *The C.L.R. James Journal* 11, no. 1 (Summer): 79–112.

Husserl, Edmund. 1965. Philosophy as Rigorous Science. In *Phenomenology and the Crisis of Philosophy*, trans. and ed. Quentin Lauer. New York: Harper & Row, 71–147.

Lorde, Audre. 1984. *Sister Outsider: Essays and Speeches*. New York: Crossing Press.

Mamdani, Mahmood. 1996. *Citizen and Subject: Contemporary Africa and the Legacy of Late Colonialism*. Princeton NJ: Princeton University Press.

Matthews, Donald H. Unpublished. Du Bois, the Black Dilthey: W.E.B. Du Bois, Wilhelm Dilthey and the Study of African American Culture. Presentation at the American Academy of Religion. Philadelphia, PA. 2005.

Mudimbe, V.Y. 1988. *The Invention of Africa*. Bloomington, IN: Indiana University Press.

Natanson, Maurice. 1986. *Anonymity: A Study in the Philosophy of Alfred Schutz*. Bloomington: Indiana University Press.

Nussbaum, Martha C. 1996. *For Love of Country: Debating the Limits of Patriotism*, ed. Joshua Cohen. Boston: Beacon Press.

Oliver, Kelly. 2004. *The Colonization of Psychic Space*. Minneapolis, MN: University of Minnesota Press.

Oyewùmí, Oyèrónké. 1997. *The Invention of Women: Making an African Sense of Western Gender Discourses*. Minneapolis: University of Minnesota Press.

Ricoeur, Paul. 1991. *From Text to Action: Essays in Hermeneutics, II*, trans. Kathleen Blamey and John B. Thompson. Evanston, IL: Northwestern University Press.

Ray, Sangeeta and Henry Schwarz, eds. 2000. *A Companion to Postcolonial Studies*. Malden, MA: Blackwell Publishers.

Sartre, Jean-Paul. 2004. *Critique of Dialectical Reason*, Volume One, Foreword by Fredric Jameson. Jonathan Ree (ed.), trans. Alan Sheridan-Smith. London: Verso.

Schutz, Alfred. 1962. *Collected Papers*, vol. 1, *The Problem of Social Reality*. Ed. with an intro. by Maurice Natanson and a preface by H. L. Van Breda. The Hague: Martinus Nijhoff.

————. 1970. *The Phenomenology of the Social World*. Translated by George Walsh and Frederick Lehnhert, with an intro. by George Walsh. Evanston: Northwestern University Press.

Williams, Patrick and Laura Chrisman, eds. 1994. *Colonial Discourse and Post-Colonial Theory: A Reader*. New York: Columbia University Press.

Afterword: Contours of Political Thought in the Pre-Independence Caribbean

Paget Henry

This volume, *Caribbean Political Thought: The Colonial State to Caribbean Internationalisms*, together with its companion, *Caribbean Political Thought: Theories of the Post-Colonial State*, definitely provides its readers with an excellent introduction to the field of Caribbean political thought. Jointly, they make available some of the classic speeches, manifestos and theories of Caribbean states that have defined this tradition of political thought – a tradition that was born of our resistance to European colonialism. As such, it is a welcomed contribution that will make more visible this important area of political and academic endeavour. These volumes are particularly important as for most of its existence this tradition of political thought has remained hidden by the shadow cast over it by the hegemonic political tradition of the West. Thus for the most part, we have framed our politics in relation to the state formations and the legitimating arguments of the Western tradition, such as its absolute monarchy, its liberal, socialist, conservative, and other political formations. Consequently, a comprehensive collection of this type will certainly help to bring our political tradition out of this shadow, further define its unique contours and make more visible its distinct contents.

In collections of this type, the issue of what to include and exclude is indeed a most difficult one to successfully resolve. Editor, Aaron Kamugisha, has certainly provided us with a very unusual and unique sampling of this literature. His selection definitely reflects the themes and issues that he considers important, and also the broader trends and concerns that mark the present period in the post-colonial politics of our region. As some one from an older political economy generation, I am indeed fascinated by Kamugisha's approach and the strong emphasis it places on the cultural aspects of politics, including the themes of identity and gender that reflect strong tendencies in our current conjuncture.

My strategy in this Afterword will be a complementary one as I fully appreciate the difficulties of making selections for volumes such as these. Consequently, I will flesh out the contextual background in a way that after or while reading these essays their place in the Caribbean political tradition will be easier to see and grasp. This easier grasp should help to make the reading of these essays a more enlightening experience.

The opening section of *Caribbean Political Thought: The Colonial State to Caribbean Internationalisms* contains some of the classic constitutions, laws, manifestos and speeches that have shaped the Caribbean political tradition. This first section of the volume opens with the text of the Haitian Constitution of 1805. This is a document that expresses and summarizes the ideals, goals, values and principles of the Haitian Revolution of 1791. Behind this event and the constitutions that it produced, there is so much that is vital to our understanding of the origins of Caribbean political thought. First, it speaks to us of African slaves in revolutionary revolt against French colonialism, and before that resisting colonialism and slavery in the form of marronage, and still earlier this revolution speaks to us of West and Central Africans engaging in the political practices required by their chiefdoms and kingdoms. It is important to note here that this revolution and its constitution also speak to us about processes of mixing or creolization between the African and European political traditions. These processes of mixing were taking place in the early eighteenth century in contexts such as lodges and friendly societies.

At the start of the colonial period, the European political tradition was in the process of moving out of its monarchist phase and into liberal and republican forms of government. The major theorists of this tradition included thinkers such as Thomas Hobbes, John Locke, Jeremy Bentham, David Hume and Denis Diderot. These political theorists became crucial models and guides for the Euro-Caribbean thinkers, such as Francisco de Vitoria, Gonzalo Oviedo, Bartolomé de Las Casas, Edward Long, Bryan Edwards, and Pere Labat, who defined and shaped the Euro-Caribbean political tradition. At the core of this tradition, was a philosophy of right – the right of Europeans to rule over the Caribbean and its people. The thinking that legitimated the claim to this right to rule over the region included detailed arguments that were based on grounds such as the fact of conquest, the Christian/heathen dichotomy, the racial superiority of Europeans, and the immaturity of Native Caribbeans, Africans and Indians. This philosophy of right and the tradition that it supported developed in phases as it became necessary to justify ruling over these various groups, who arrive in the region at widely differing points in time. We cannot understand the mixed or creole nature of the Haitian Constitution of 1805 without references to the presence of this Euro-Caribbean tradition of political thought.

Similarly, we cannot understand this historic document without references to the African political tradition. At the start of the colonial period the African political tradition was in the process of moving between systems of chiefdoms and systems of monarchical kingdoms. Chiefdoms were the elementary form of political life in pre-colonial Africa, and thus they provided the basic political socialization of the millions of Africans who were forcibly transported to the Caribbean and the Americas. The five primary features of Chiefdoms were: 1) the queen mother who symbolized the birth of the state; 2) the chief, who was the highest authority figure and executive centre of this political system; 3) the council of elders with which the chief was expected to govern; 4) the royal families from which the council would select and enstool a new chief; and 5) the members of the political community. The council was responsible for bringing the voice of the people to the chief and to act as a check on his power. In cases of extreme misrule, the council was empowered to destool the chief. Thus the power of the chief was not absolute.

From as early as Ancient Egypt and Nubia, these chiefdoms have experienced dramatic periods of expansion that resulted in the formation and rise of monarchical kingdoms such as Ancient Ghana, Mali and Songhay. These political formations were much larger and more militarized than the chiefdoms. However, they retained many of the features of these smaller chiefdoms such as the governing council of elders and the queen mother. The political and military strategies practiced by Afro-Caribbean maroon leaders such as Cudjoe and Boni, or revolutionary leaders such as Toussaint L'Ouverture had their roots in these traditions of chiefdoms and kingdoms. In the case of the Haitian Revolution and the constitutions that it produced we can observe processes of hybridization as African political traditions began to mix with European ones. The Haitian constitutions are among the earliest documents that provide us with clear evidence of the processes of hybridization that resulted in the creolization of our political culture. The constitution of 1805 is a hybrid mixture; African monarchism and French republicanism as the democratic preamble and the giving of the title of 'His Majesty' to the head of state makes it very clear. In short, the Haitian constitutions point us to the African political heritage that preceded them and also to the speeches, theories and newer constitutions that would follow them.

Similarly, the other great documents that fill the opening section of this first of two volumes reveal their full significance only when viewed against this backdrop of resisting European colonialism and racial slavery. For example, the 1909 Program of the Independent Party of Color in Cuba introduces us to the experiences of the Cuban people with colonialism, neo-colonialism, and racism and also to the larger world of the Spanish-speaking Caribbean. In particular, this party document makes clear the problems that Afro-Cubans had with the mestizo and mulatto constructions of race that came to dominate Cuba and the Dominican Republic after gaining their independence. Similar constructions of race also developed in Puerto Rico even though that territory became an American colony rather than an independent state after the collapse of the Spanish empire in the Caribbean region. These issues of neo-colonialism and the persistence of racism in the post-independence period will later be problems in the Dutch-, English-, and French-speaking territories of the region.

Another good example of an anti-colonial document is the 'Appeal to the United Nations' by Richard Moore on behalf of Caribbean people. This appeal takes us to the English-speaking Caribbean and thus to territories that were still in the grip of colonialism and a long way from independence. Unlike the case of the Spanish empire, the strength of the British in the region only continued to grow until the rise of the American empire to a position of hegemonic dominance. Hence we get the anti-colonial tone and content of Moore's appeal, and his very specific suggestion that all changes without self-determination be opposed. Moore's appeal also echoes many of the themes in Marcus Garvey's 'Declaration of the Rights of the Negro Peoples of the World'. Finally, in spite of being separated by several decades Maurice Bishop's, 'In Nobody Backyard', shares this commitment to resisting European colonialism neo-colonialism and racism, which links it to the documents of the Haitian Revolution, those of the Independent Party of Color, Garvey's 'Declaration', and Moore's 'Appeal'.

The second section of this volume on Caribbean political theory consists of more systematic writings on the colonial state. These writings are consistently critical as they give voice and discursive representation to the African urge to resist European colonialism. These critiques of the colonial state developed the scholarly texts of the Caribbean political tradition in a more systematic fashion. Thus following the initial attempts at marronage and open slave revolts, eighteenth century writers like Prince Hall (1738–1807), John Marrant (1755–91), Albert Gronniosaw, Ottobah Cugoano (1757–?) and Lemuel Haynes (1753–1833) were members of the first group of Africana political theorists, who began the writing of systematic critiques of the racial and economic workings of colonial state. In addition, they went on to make strong cases for the freedom of Africans from being enslaved by Europeans, and to outline the kinds of political orders that should be established in the post-slavery period. Cugoano was born in Ghana, kidnapped, sold into slavery and shipped to Grenada at the tender age of 13. For just nine months he lived the horrors and torments of plantation slavery in the region. But it was enough to create in him a great desire for freedom. On a trip to London with his master, Cugoano made the break that gave him his freedom. Further, his short experience in the Caribbean was enough to radically transform his self-consciousness, and made him into the Africana author of the classic work, *Thoughts and Sentiments on the Evil of Slavery*. In this work, Cugoano also outlined a political order based on the natural rights of individuals that was at the same time governed by the Providence of God. In other words, he combined an original approach to natural rights theory with an even more original formulation of an Africana providential historicism. The combination of these two produced the outlines of a political vision that we could call an Africana providential liberalism.

As Cugoano stands at the beginning of the Afro-Caribbean tradition of political thought, Lemuel Haynes looms large as one of the founding figures of the African American tradition of political thought and was influenced by the work of Cugoano. Like the latter, Haynes at an early age converted to Calvinism and thus shared with Cugoano a providential view of history. Because he was a mulatto (his mother was white), Haynes grew up as an indentured servant rather than a slave. At age 22, after his period of indenture was over, he joined the army of George Washington in support of America's fight for freedom from British colonialism. Equally important for Haynes were the republican ideas that Washington and Thomas Jefferson were making the foundation of the new American nation. However, on realizing that both men had no intentions of freeing African Americans from slavery or stopping the African slave trade, he turned a critical eye on their republican philosophies that embraced the practice of slavery. In his first major essay, 'Liberty Further Extended: Or Free Thoughts on the Illegality of Slave-keeping' (1990), Haynes would go on to argue that slavery and republicanism were incompatible and to make the case for full citizenship rights for African Americans. These were some of the ideas produced by our first political theorists as they undertook their critiques of the colonial state and its practices of slavery and racism.

Further, this section on the colonial state introduces the anti-colonial voice of the Indo-Caribbean community. This community developed in the period after the end of African slavery as indentured servants from India were brought in to fill the shortages of labour that arose from Africans leaving the plantations and becoming independent farmers. Between 1848 and 1917 approximately half a million labourers from India were brought to the Caribbean as indentured servants. Most went to Trinidad and Tobago, Guyana and Suriname, with smaller portions going to Jamaica, Martinique and Guadeloupe. The 'Memorandum by Bechu to the West India Royal Commission, 1897' is one of the earliest statements that we have of Indo-Caribbean political thought. As in the case of the Haitian Constitution, this early document points back to the Indian political heritage of these new forced migrants as well as forward to a rich creolized collection of anti-racist and anti-colonial documents. This heritage is overwhelmingly Hindu, although a small portion of it is Islamic. Similar to the case of Africans, Indians came out of a political tradition of Hindu and Islamic kingdoms, which they were forced by Caribbean colonial states to abandon on their arrival in the region. This political disenfranchisement was the beginning of their political re-socialization and creolization, which also contributed the emergence of a distinct Indo-Caribbean identity and to hybrid traditions of liberalism and socialism.

The source of the parallels between the Indo- and the Afro-Caribbean political traditions was the deeply felt need on the part of both groups to resist their racialization as 'coolies' and 'negroes', and their economic exploitation on the basis of these dehumanized, stereotypical and racialized identities. Bechu's memorandum expresses very strongly the resistance of Indo-Caribbeans to their dehumanization and exploitation as 'coolies'. In addition to critics like Bechu, there were also figures like Joseph Ruhomon, Krishna Deonarine (Adrian Rienzi), who worked closely with Afro-Caribbean political leader, Uriah Butler, and organizations like the East Indian National Congress in Trinidad and Tobago, and the British Guiana East Indian Association. At the same time that the Afro- and Indo-Caribbean political traditions shared this anti-colonial outlook, there were also significant racial tensions between the two of them. Thus the Caribbean political tradition, in both its anti-colonial and post-colonial phases, is one that includes a strong Indo-Caribbean component.

The texts of Cugoano and Haynes established a dialogical pattern with particular writers in European imperial tradition that would become one of the classic markers of the Caribbean and the larger Africana tradition of political thought. For example, Cugoano engaged directly the racial discourses of David Hume and the Euro-Caribbean planter James Tobin, while Haynes challenged those of George Washington and Thomas Jefferson. Further, as Anthony Bogues's article makes clear, Cugoano political thought was very much that of an Africana natural rights theorist. Continuing this tradition of critical dialogical engagement with the discourses of the European colonial tradition are later authors such as José Martí, Antenor Firmin, JJ Thomas, Hubert Harrison, Claudia Jones, CLR James, and Franz Fanon, who fill the third section of this book on Caribbean anti-colonial thought. In these authors, the patterns of critique and creolization that informed their works incorporated and expanded the earlier patterns and strategies that marked the discourses of Cugoano and his generation. However, separating these two generations of Afro-Caribbean political thinkers was the ending of the practice of enslaving Africans on the plantations of the Caribbean and the Americas. Further, in this latter group of theorists, we can feel the goal of political independence becoming a progressively more graspable reality even though it is still a good distance away. Consequently, these late nineteenth and early twentieth century thinkers were the primary ideological voices that would set the stage for the next generation of post-colonial theorists.

Although the members of this late nineteenth and early twentieth century group of Caribbean political theorists were united in their opposition to European colonialism, they differed significantly in regard to what form of the post-colonial state should replace European rule. In the case of thinkers like James, Fanon, Jones, Padmore and Harrison, the envisioned post-colonial state was a socialist one. In other words, this was a group of Caribbean political theorists who were profoundly influenced by the European political tradition of Marxism.

They combined this Marxism in different ways with Africana discourses of race inherited from the earlier writers to inaugurate a tradition of black or Africana Marxism. In the cases of scholars like José Martí, Antenor Firmin and JJ Thomas, they were much more influenced by the liberal and republican discourses of European political thought. These Caribbean figures combined republican and liberal discourses with black and mestizo discourses of race to produce creolized discursive formations that were the counterparts of black Marxism. In these explicit engagements with European Marxism, liberalism and republicanism, we can see a further deepening of the patterns of creolization that continue to mark the tradition of Caribbean political thought.

Further, in the works of this generation of Caribbean political theorists, we can see some of the problems that have arisen within the hybrid or creole framework of our tradition of political theory and practice. For example, the presence and awareness of the African heritage of chiefdoms and kingdoms were much less visible in the texts of this group of political theorist than in the works of Cugoano and his generation. The formative influences of these political institutions had clearly begun to decline. Their creative codes, governing structures, legitimating arguments, and practices of statecraft all declined in visibility and relevance while those of European traditions of liberalism, republicanism and socialism increased in visibility and relevance. However, this decline in the visibility of the African political heritage did not entail a corresponding decline in the presence or importance of the race issue. Indeed, it was primarily through this issue that the African heritage continued to make its presence felt on the Afro-Caribbean political scene. In other words, it was as Africans who had been racialized as 'blacks' in relation to Europeans who had racialized themselves as 'whites' that the African heritage continued to be a vital force in Afro-Caribbean politics. However, this retention of a strong engagement with the race question did not reverse the declining fortunes of the African political heritage in what Rex Nettleford has called its 'battle for space' (1993) with its European counterpart. In short, these selections from the literature on the critique of the colonial state allow us to see how Caribbean political thinking had changed in the post-slavery period but prior to the regaining of political independence.

This first volume of essays and readings on Caribbean political theory concludes with a section on 'Caribbean Internationalisms'. One is immediately struck by the number of theorists in this final section who were also in the previous section on anti-colonial thought. This is not an accident. Rather it points to the reality and importance of the diaspora to Caribbean political theory during this particular period of time. Indeed, Cugoano and the first generation of political theorists had already demonstrated how much easier it was to get books published in the imperial centres than in the colonies. Equally important was the fact that, although social and political conditions were quite restrictive in these metropolitan centres for blacks, it was also easier for them to organize protests, publish newspapers and journals, and to engage in other types of oppositional activity. These were just some of the factors that made Caribbean diasporic communities vitally important for the production and development of Caribbean political theory. In taking this section in this diasporic direction, I am aware that I am departing from the editor's position somewhat, whose intent here was to sample texts by Caribbean writers that were not about the Caribbean.

It was in the more open spaces of the diasporic communities of London, Paris and New York that many of these theorists of the late nineteenth and early twentieth centuries were able to develop their ideas and get them published. Thus it was in New York that Hubert Harrison developed the critiques that informed his New Negro Movement and later his socialism. It was also in New York that Garvey's Pan African Movement was really able to flourish. It was in the diasporic spaces of London that Padmore and James were able to launch the African Services Bureau and its journal. Finally, it was in Paris that Antenor Firmin was able to produce and publish his classic work, *The Equality of the Human Races*. With exceptions of writers like Firmin and Che Guevara, most of these political thinkers were individuals who remained far from state power or the possibility of gaining control of it. Thus in the cases of Jones, Padmore and James, although they were members of communist and socialist parties, they were also at the head of smaller mobilizing and consciousness-raising groups. Their organizations did a wide variety of things – organized protests, published journals and newspapers, and undertook a number of community activities. Because these smaller organizations were not political parties, or the parties that these writers did join were not likely to win state power, their political thinking tended to be of a normative and anticipatory nature – anticipatory in the sense of gesturing toward or imagining a time in the future when Afro-Caribbean or Afro-American people would be in power.

Consequently, these expressions of Caribbean internationalism contained critiques of the colonial state, its practices of racism and sexism, and proposals for ways in which power should be organized and administered in the post-colonial period. In other words, the political thought of these diasporic writers moved largely between critique and normative constructions of alternative political orders for a still distant post-colonial future. For example, in the case of James, his political writing focused primarily on what a proletarian socialist state should look like, the distribution of power within it, how it should be administered, and the possible intermediary stages that might precede the establishing of such a state. For a brief period (1965–66) in Trinidad and Tobago, James helped to form the Workers and Farmers Party and did enter the competition for state power. However, he did not succeed in this electoral bid for power, as his party was defeated at the polls. But this occurred well into the early phases of the post-colonial period – the period that will be the focus of the companion to this volume of documents, speeches and essays.

In sum, the selection of readings in this first volume on Caribbean political thought need to be read against a socio-historical background that begins with the West and Central African traditions of state-making and statecraft, which became the bases for the political structures and African nationalist outlooks of maroon communities in the early colonial period. This African nationalist resistance to the colonial experience – which included slavery, racism and sexism – became the basis on which our first political theorists of the eighteenth century would develop their anti-slavery, anti-racist, and anti-colonial ideas and also go on to propose new political orders from which slavery was absent. This tradition of political theorizing continued throughout the nineteenth century and on into the early decades of the twentieth century, producing even more trenchant critiques of European colonialism and more fully elaborated visions of a post-colonial future. The works of this phase in the development of our tradition of political thought were vital for the preparation of the next generation of political leaders and theorists who would have to grapple with the struggle for political independence and all the difficulties that have come with being in control of state power and also the process of economic development. It is against this complex trajectory of the colonization, racialization, and enslaving of Africans in the Caribbean, the bold and multiple forms of African resistance to these types of domination, without in most cases the possibility of re-gaining control of state power, that the texts in this first volume on Caribbean political theory must be read. Together, they constitute a very important preface to those writings on the post-colonial state that are collected in the second volume that is a companion to this one. This second volume is entitled, *Caribbean Political Thought: Theories of the Post-Colonial State.*

References

Haynes, Lemuel. 1990. *Lemuel Haynes: Black Preacher to White America,* ed. Richard Newman. New York: Carlson.

Nettleford, Rex. 1993. *Inward Stretch, Outward Reach.* London: Macmillan Press.